ÖSTERREICH
- ✪ Hauptstadt
- ◉ Landeshauptstadt
- • Stadt
- ▲ Berg
-)(Tunnel/Pass

TSCHECH...

DEUTSCHLAND

Passau

der Inn

Linz

NIEDERÖSTERREICH

die Donau

die SLOWAKEI

Melk

WIEN

Pressburg

OBERÖSTERREICH

St.Pölten

Wien

Steyr

Salzburg

Wiener Neustadt

Eisenstadt

der Bodensee

Bregenz

VORARLBERG

die ZUGSPITZE 2.963 m

Kitzbühel

die Salzach

BURGENLAND

der Neusiedler See

Vaduz

ALPEN

der Inn

Innsbruck

SALZBURG

▲*der DACHSTEIN 2.995m*

Leoben

STEIERMARK

LIECHTENSTEIN

TIROL

der BRENNER PASS

der GROSSGLOCKNER 3.798 m (Zu Tirol)

)(*der TAUERN TUNNEL*

Graz

die Mur

die SCHWEIZ

KÄRNTEN

der Wörther See

UNGARN

Lienz

Villach

Klagenfurt

die Drau

Meilen

0   50

Kilometer

0   50

ITALIEN

SLOWENIEN

die Schweiz
- ✪ Hauptstadt
- ◉ Landeshauptstadt
- • Stadt
- ▲ Berg
-)(Tunnel/Pass

der Rhein

DEUTSCHLAND

SCHAFFHAUSEN

Schaffhausen

der Bodensee

BASEL-STADT

Frauenfeld

THURGAU

Basel

Liestal

AARGAU

ZÜRICH

Winterthur

St Gallen

Delémont

BASEL-LAND

die Aare

Aarau

Zürich

Herisau

APPENZELL AUSSERRHODEN

Appenzell

JURA

der Zürichsee

APPENZELL INNERRHODEN

FRANKREICH

SOLOTHURN

der Bieler See

Biel

Solothurn

Zug

ZUG

SCHWYZ

SANKT GALLEN

LIECHTENSTEIN

NEUENBURG

Neuenburg

BERN

LUZERN

Schwyz

Glarus

Vaduz

der Neuenburger See

Bern

Luzern

GLARUS

ÖSTERREICH

Freiburg

Sarnen

Stans

der Vierwaldstätter See

Chur

Davos

die Aare

Thun

UNTERWALDEN OBW.

NIDW.

Altdorf

der Rhein

GRAUBÜNDEN

WAADT

FREIBURG

der Thuner See

Interlaken

URI

der Inn

Lausanne

Grindelwald

ALPEN

St. Moritz

die JUNGFRAU 4.158 m

der ST. GOTTHARD-TUNNEL

der Genfer See

Montreux

die Rhône

TESSIN

ITALIEN

GENF

WALLIS

der SIMPLON-TUNNEL

Locarno

Bellinzona

Genf

Sion

Saas-Fee

das MATTERHORN 4.478 m

Zermatt

der Lago Maggiore

Meilen

0   40

FRANKREICH

der MONT BLANC 4.807 m

ITALIEN

Lugano

Kilometer

0   40

Instructor's Annotated Edition

Wie geht's?

An Introductory German Course

Seventh Edition

Dieter Sevin

Vanderbilt University

Ingrid Sevin

THOMSON

HEINLE

Australia Canada Mexico Singapore Spain United Kingdom United States

Wie geht's? Instructor's Annotated Edition
Seventh Edition
Dieter Sevin, Ingrid Sevin

Senior Editor: *Sean Ketchem*
Production Editor: *Lianne Ames*
Director of HED Marketing: *Lisa Kimball*
Marketing Manager: *Jill Garrett*
Manufacturing Coordinator: *Marcia Locke*
Compositor: *Progressive Publishing Alternatives*
Project Manager: *Donna King*

Photo Researcher: *Sheri Blaney*
Illustrator: *Progressive Publishing Alternatives*
Cover Designer: *Diane Levy*
Text Designer: *Studio Montage*
Cover Image: © *Hans Wolf/The Image Bank/Getty Images*
Printer: *Transcontinental*

Printed in Canada.
1 2 3 4 5 6 7 8 9 10   06 05 04 03 02

For more information contact Heinle, 25 Thomson Place, Boston, Massachusetts 02210 USA, or you can visit our Internet site at http://www.heinle.com

For permission to use material from this text or product contact us:
Tel   1-800-730-2214
Fax   1-800-730-2215
Web   www.thomsonrights.com

0-03-035231-2 (Instructor's Annotated Edition)

To the Instructor

About the Program

Welcome to the Seventh Edition of *Wie geht's?*, an introductory German program that has proven itself to be one of the leading German programs in the country! Over 250,000 students have learned German with *Wie geht's?*, and it's no surprise why teachers adopt this program, plainly put by its users: "It works!" The goal of *Wie geht's?* is simple: the program presents a well-integrated package of material that focuses on speaking, listening, reading, writing, and comprehension, combined with an introduction to life and culture in the German-speaking countries today. The approach is student-oriented, manageable, and up-to-date. Students will communicate in meaningful ways after only one year, and also be provided with significant cultural insights.

About the Authors

Dieter Sevin, a native of Germany, is Professor of German at Vanderbilt University. He has gone back to Europe regularly to travel, do research, and take part in an exchange program with the University in Regensburg. He has received grants from organizations such as the American Philosophical Association, American Council of Learned Societies, German Academic Exchange Service, and the Vanderbilt Research Council. He is the author of several academic books on exile literature and East German literature; he also has written numerous articles in professional journals and is a frequent speaker at professional meetings.

Ingrid Sevin, a native of Germany, has been teaching German and French at the high school and college level in the United States and in Germany for over ten years. From 1987 to 2002, she has been the editor of the German audio-magazine *Schau ins Land*. She has also co-authored a German conversation text.

General Course Objectives

Listening. The students should be able to understand German spoken at a moderate conversational speed as long as the conversation deals with everyday occurrences. The audio program, video program, and the pronunciation guide of the Workbook complement the text well in enhancing a student's listening skills.

Speaking. The students should be able to engage in simple conversation with other speakers of German. Each pre-unit and chapter provides ample opportunity for oral practice in meaningful contexts.

Reading. The students should be able to read nontechnical German of moderate difficulty. These skills are developed through the study of dialogues, reading text, exercises in the Workbook, and Web activities.

Writing. The students should be able to write simple sentences correctly on the topics presented in the text. Written exercises extend and reinforce oral exercises. The book and the Workbook provide suggestions for writing dialogues and compositions on the chapter theme.

Highlights of the Program

All aspects of the program have been reevaluated, updated, and revised as necessary. The sections most extensively revised are the introductory cultural notes in all chapters, the dialogue and reading selections in many of the chapters, and the *Hören Sie zu!* listening sections in some of the chapters. This seventh edition has retained and enhanced the following core features:

Schritte. The purpose of these pre-units is to acquaint the student with the German language and the language learning process by focusing on listening and speaking before any grammar is officially introduced.

Vorschau. This element previews the culture for each chapter and supplies the necessary background information.

Gespräche + Wortschatz.   The *Gespräche* are dialogue sections that focus on the chapter theme and function as models for conversation. The *Wortschatz* supplies the student with the necessary active vocabulary; *Zum Erkennen* is meant to be passive vocabulary.

Hören Sie zu!   This element, located at the end of the dialogue section and the main reading section *(Einblicke),* should improve listening comprehension skills.

Struktur.   This section teaches the basics of German grammar. After every 3–4 chapters, it is followed by a review section *(Rückblick)* with accompanying exercises in the Workbook.

Einblicke.   This section, introduced by pre-reading and post-reading activities, is a reading passage that features one or more cultural aspects related to the chapter topic.

Fokus.   These are cultural notes interspersed throughout each chapter that point out or explain differences between life in North America and in the German-speaking countries.

Gedichte + Kurzgeschichten.   In the later chapters, the main reading passage is followed by a poem or short story for the students' enrichment and enjoyment.

Video-Ecke.   This section points to the video that accompanies each chapter and gives a brief summary of its content.

Web-Ecke.   This section points to the **Wie geht's?** Web site at **http://wiegehts.heinle.com** that gives students access to a variety of online activities which it summarizes briefly.

Rückblicke.   These are periodic summaries of what has been introduced in the chapters. They are intended for reference and as preparation and review for quizzes, tests, and finals, summing up points of structure.

New to this Edition

The following features are new to this edition:

- Extensive updating of all materials.
- All prices in marks are now listed as prices in **euro.**
- The **spelling reform** has been fully implemented and updated.
- New communicative **realia-based activities** were added throughout.
- All grammar sections now progress **from guided to more open-ended communicative exercises.**
- The idiomatic expressions of the *Sprechsituationen* **have been integrated** in the chapters.
- The pre-reading section of the *Einblicke* was enhanced with new *Lesestrategien* to prepare students for the upcoming reading text.
- Some of the poems in the later chapters were replaced by **short stories,** adding some literary variety to the reading. Pertinent **questions** were added to both poems and short stories to enhance comprehension.

- **New video segments** *(Blickpunkte)* were filmed in Berlin especially for this new edition, adding authentic cultural footage to the previous content *(Minidramas).* Both videos are now integrated into one.
- The book has a **new homepage,** and the specific Web sites and corresponding activities *(Web-Ecke)* have been updated.
- The book has been enhanced with many new **photos** and **color illustrations.** All **maps** have been updated and revised.
- The audio program has been updated, the written exercises revised extensively, and the video activities redone completely.
- The audio program, written activities, video activities, as well as a complete Pronunciation Guide have been integrated into **one Workbook** *(Arbeitsbuch);* in fact, the first three components are now consolidated in each chapter.
- The **testing program** has been updated and placed in ExamView® Pro format, allowing teachers to easily customize the tests to meet their needs.

A Visual Guide to *Wie Geht's?*

In order to give users of *Wie geht's?* a better understanding of the structure of the text, here is a visual guide to the main features of the book:

Vorschau

This element previews the culture for each chapter by supplying the necessary background information.

Lernziele

A quick summary of each chapter's learning goals.

> "I have used Wie geht's? for many years, it has always worked! With the changes in this new edition, I am convinced it will be the best textbook on the market for this level."
>
> Jutta Arend
> Holy Cross College

Gespräche + Wortschatz

The *Gespräche* are dialogues that focus on the chapter topic. They function as models for conversation; they are **not** intended to demonstrate new grammar, but rather recycle previous materials and introduce new vocabulary. The CD and track number of the Audio Program appear beside each dialog. The *Wortschatz* supplies the student with a list of new vocabulary that must be mastered. It is followed by *Zum Erkennen*, a brief listing of words and phrases intended for recognition only.

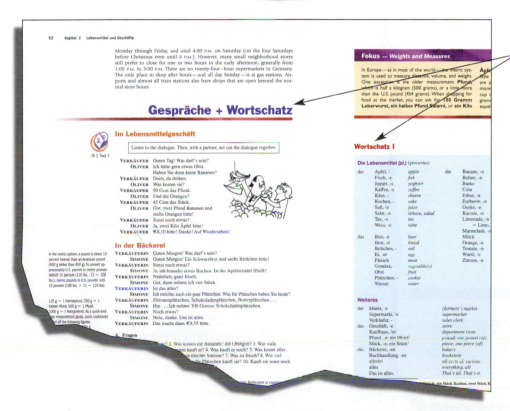

Struktur

All major grammar explanations and practice activities appear in this section. Grammar topics are double-numbered for easier reference.

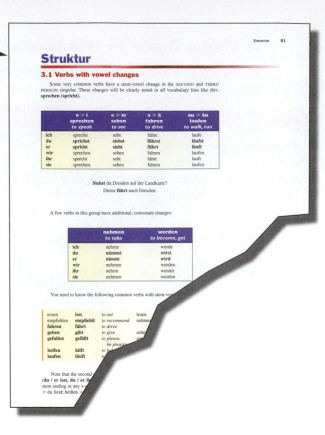

Struktur

3.1 Verbs with vowel changes

Some very common verbs have a stem-vowel change in the SECOND and THIRD PERSON singular. These changes will be clearly noted in all vocabulary lists like this: **sprechen (spricht)**.

	e > i **sprechen** *to speak*	e > ie **sehen** *to see*	a > ä **fahren** *to drive*	au > äu **laufen** *to walk, run*
ich	spreche	sehe	fahre	laufe
du	sprichst	siehst	fährst	läufst
er	spricht	sieht	fährt	läuft
wir	sprechen	sehen	fahren	laufen
ihr	sprecht	seht	fahrt	lauft
sie	sprechen	sehen	fahren	laufen

Siehst du Dresden auf der Landkarte?
Dieter **fährt** nach Dresden.

A few verbs in this group have additional, consonant changes:

	nehmen *to take*	**werden** *to become, get*
ich	nehme	werde
du	nimmst	wirst
er	nimmt	wird
wir	nehmen	werden
ihr	nehmt	werdet
sie	nehmen	werden

You need to know the following common verbs with stem-vo...

essen	isst	*to eat*	lesen
empfehlen	empfiehlt	*to recommend*	nehm...
fahren	fährt	*to drive*	
geben	gibt	*to give*	sehe...
gefallen	gefällt	*to please,* *be pleasi...*	sp...
helfen	hilft	*to h...*	
laufen	läuft	*to...*	

Note that the second
(du / er isst, du / er li...
stem ending in any s-...
> du liest; heißen >...

N. Mein Alltag *(my daily life)*. Schreiben Sie 8–10 Sätze über *(about)* Ihren Alltag, zum Beispiel wann Sie aufstehen, wann Sie essen, wann Sie zur Schule / Uni gehen, welche Klassen Sie wann haben, was Sie abends und am Wochenende tun usw.! Benutzen Sie so viele Zeitausdrücke wie möglich *(as possible)*!

BEISPIEL: Ich bin fast jeden Tag an der Uni. Morgens stehe ich um sechs auf . . .

Einblicke

Lesestrategie: Ein Land, drei Meinungen *(opinions)*

Drei Touristen in der Schweiz (Felix, Frau Weber und Frau Lorenz) beschreiben ihre Reiseerlebnisse. Lesen Sie den Text und vergleichen Sie *(compare)* die drei Reisen! Was hat den drei Leuten am besten gefallen? Gibt es etwas, was ihnen nicht so gut gefallen hat?

Wortschatz 2

das Dorf, ̈er	village
Schnäppchen, -	bargain
die Gegend, -en	area, region
Geschichte, -n	history; story
herrlich	wonderful, great
hinauf-fahren (fährt hinauf),	to go or drive up (to)
ist hinaufgefahren	
weiter-fahren (fährt weiter),	to drive on, keep on driving
ist weitergefahren	

Jeder Preis ein tolles Schnäppchen!

Vor dem Lesen

A. Etwas Geographie. Sehen Sie auf die Landkarte der Schweiz und beantworten Sie die Fragen!
1. Wie heißen die Nachbarländer der Schweiz? Wo liegen sie?
2. Wie heißt die Hauptstadt der Schweiz?

Einblicke

This section provides a reading passage that features one or more cultural aspects related to the chapter theme. It also includes a second list of active vocabulary (*Wortschatz 2*), reading strategies, as well as pre-reading and post-reading activities.

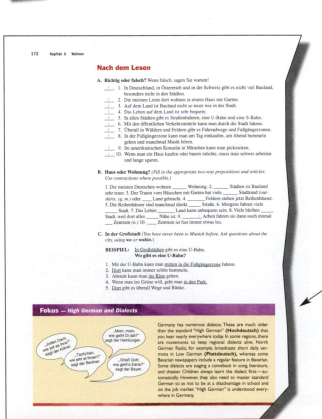

Nach dem Lesen

A. Richtig oder falsch? Wenn falsch, sagen Sie warum!
___ 1. In Deutschland, in Österreich und in der Schweiz gibt es nicht viel Bauland, besonders nicht in den Städten.
___ 2. Die meisten Leute dort wohnen in einem Haus mit Garten.
___ 3. Auf dem Land ist Bauland nicht so teuer wie in der Stadt.
___ 4. Das Leben auf dem Land ist sehr bequem.
___ 5. In allen Städten gibt es Straßenbahnen, eine U-Bahn und eine S-Bahn.
___ 6. Mit den öffentlichen Verkehrsmitteln kann man durch die Stadt fahren.
___ 7. Überall in Wäldern und Feldern gibt es Fahrradwege und Fußgängerzonen.
___ 8. In der Fußgängerzone kann man am Tag einkaufen, am Abend bummeln gehen und manchmal Musik hören.
___ 9. Im amerikanischen Konsulat in München kann man picknicken.
___ 10. Wenn man ein Haus kaufen oder bauen möchte, muss man schwer arbeiten und lange sparen.

B. Haus oder Wohnung? *(Fill in the appropriate two-way prepositions and articles. Use contractions where possible.)*

1. Die meisten Deutschen wohnen _____ Wohnung. 2. _____ Städten ist Bauland sehr teuer. 3. Der Traum vom Häuschen mit Garten hat viele _____ Stadtrand *(outskirts, sg. m.)* oder _____ Land gebracht. 4. _____ Feldern stehen jetzt Reihenhäuser. 5. Die Reihenhäuser sind manchmal direkt _____ Straße. 6. Morgens fahren viele _____ Stadt, weil dort alles _____ Nähe ist. 9. _____ Arbeit fahren sie dann noch einmal ___ Zentrum *(n.)* 10. _____ Zentrum ist fast immer etwas los.

C. In der Großstadt *(You have never been to Munich before. Ask questions about the city, using wo or wohin.)*

BEISPIEL: In Großstädten gibt es eine U-Bahn.
Wo gibt es eine U-Bahn?

1. Mit der U-Bahn kann man mitten in die Fußgängerzone fahren.
2. Dort kann man immer schön bummeln.
3. Abends kann man ins Kino gehen.
4. Wenn man ins Grüne will, geht man in den Park.
5. Dort gibt es überall Wege und Bänke.

Fokus — High German and Dialects

„Joten Dach, wia jeit et Ihne?" sagt der Kölner.
„Tachchen, wie jeht et Ihnen?" sagt der Berliner.
„Moin, moin, wie geiht Di dat?" sagt der Hamburger.
„Grüß Gott, wia geht's Eana?" sagt der Bayer.

Germany has numerous dialects. These are much older than the standard "High German" **(Hochdeutsch)** that you hear nearly everywhere today. In some regions, there are movements to keep regional dialects alive. North German Radio, for example, broadcasts short daily sermons in Low German **(Plattdeutsch)**, whereas some Bavarian newspapers include a regular feature in Bavarian. Some dialects are staging a comeback in song, literature, and theater. Children always learn the standard first—automatically. However, they also need to master standard German so as not to be at a disadvantage in school and on the job market. "High German" is understood everywhere in Germany.

Fokus

These sections appear throughout the chapters and present additional cultural information on the chapter topic. In the second half of the book, the last *Fokus* note in each chapter spotlights one or several literary figures with one of their poems or short stories, followed by pertinent questions.

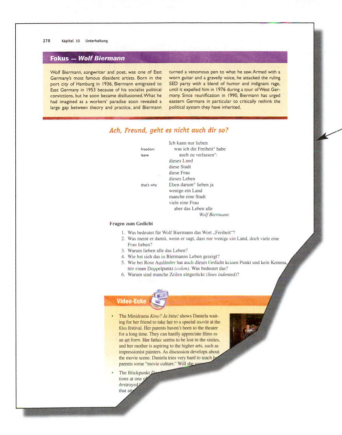

Gedichte + Kurzgeschichten

As a gradual introduction to literary texts, the second half of the book has a poem or an authentic narrative text in each chapter, followed by pertinent questions to enhance understanding and stimulate discussion.

"Great addition! Moving into the 21st century."

Katherine Tosa
Muskegon Community College

Video- + Web-Ecke

Each chapter closes with a "video corner" that gives a brief summary of the accompanying video as well as an "Internet corner" that features specific Web sites and online activities corresponding to the chapter topics.

The Complete Package

The following is a list of the program components that accompany the seventh edition of *Wie geht's?*

Student Edition with Text Audio CD

The student text and text audio CD for the *Hören Sie zu!* sections are available for purchase by the student. The printed version of the audioscript is in your teachers' preface, starting on p. IAE-13. This way, if you like, you can easily familiarize yourself with the story on the CD when going over the corresponding questions in the main text with your students.

Workbook/Lab Manual

This component is available for purchase by the student. The Workbook *(Arbeitsbuch)* provides students with the opportunity to practice listening, speaking, and writing skills. Each chapter combines materials for use with the lab audio CDs *(Zum Hören)* and for review and practice at home *(Zum Schreiben),* as well as supplementary questions and activities to accompany the video *(Video-aktiv)*. A complete Pronunciation Guide *(Aussprache)* is given at the beginning of the Workbook.

Instructor's Annotated Edition with Text Audio CD

This Instructor's Annotated Edition includes instructor teaching suggestions, the script for the *Hören Sie zu!* sections, an active vocabulary list for the whole book, and the entire student text.

QUIA Online Activities

The Workbook is now available online! The *QUIA* Online Activities offer students the benefit of instant feedback, and the convenience of online learning. The *QUIA* passcard allows students to access the Workbook activity content through the Web.

Lab Audio CDs

This component is available for purchase by the student, but can also be used in a listening laboratory by a lab instructor. The CDs should be used in conjunction with the language lab activities *(Zum Hören)* in the Workbook.

Lab Audioscript and Answer Key

This printed component contains the lab audioscript as well as the Workbook answer key.

Multimedia CD-ROM

This text-specific interactive component is available for purchase by the student. It is interesting and challenging, and should enable students to develop their listening comprehension skills and cultural awareness and provide engaging material for review.

Video Program

The videos, available for purchase in both DVD and VHS formats, are specifically correlated to the various chapters. They consist of authentic cultural footage, and model language used in realistic situations. The Workbook has extensive previewing and post-viewing activities *(Video-aktiv)* for classroom conversation.

ExamView® Pro Testbank on CD-ROM

With this easy-to-use assessment and tutorial system, you can create, customize, and print out tests in minutes. You can use the tests provided or easily create your own activities. With ExamView®, your students can even take their test online.

WebTutor for WebCT™ and Blackboard™

Self-study review and practice activities for students, and classroom management tools for instructors, allow *Wie geht's?* adopters to take advantage of the most popular formats for online learning.

Wie geht's? World Wide Web Site

Wie geht's? has its own Web site: **http://wiegehts.heinle.com**. Each chapter includes a *Web-Ecke* section that features specific Web sites and online activities that correspond with the chapter topics.

Planning the Course

Wie geht's? is designed for a one-year college-level course. In planning the schedule, take into consideration the number of class hours available per week as well as student background and motivation. In most situations, there will be enough time not only to complete the book, but also see the accompanying videos, and use the *Arbeitsbuch* materials. On the other hand, those who have only three hours of instruction time per week, or who feel that some grammar topics are better left for the second year, may prefer to spread the work over three semesters.

It is important not to regard a schedule as unchangeable, but to remain flexible and respond to the special needs of a class. Overly strict adherence to a schedule can be detrimental to the success of the course. Below are scheduling suggestions for the semester and quarter system. Normally, 1 1/2 days per pre-unit and 1 1/2 weeks per chapter should be appropriate.

The Semester System

(NOTE: S = *Schritt;* 1, 2, 3 etc. = *Kapitel;* R = Rückblick)

Week	1st Semester	Week	2nd Semester
1	S1–S5, R	1	
2		2	8 + 9
3		3	
4	1 + 2	4	
5		5	10 + 11
6	3, R, Test	6	
7		7	R, Test
8		8	
9	4 + 5	9	12 + 13
10		10	
11		11	
12	6 + 7	12	14 + 15
13		13	
14	R, Test	14	R, Test

The Quarter System

Week	1st Qtr.	Week	2nd Qtr.	Week	3rd Qtr.
1	S1–S5, R	1	6	1	11, R
2		2		2	
3		3	7, R	3	12
4	1 + 2	4		4	
5		5	Test, 8	5	13, Test
6		6		6	
7	3, R, Test	7	9	7	14
8		8		8	
9	4 + 5, Test	9	10, Test	9	15, R, Test
10		10		10	

Resources

If you plan well in advance, it might be feasible for you or your Learning Resources Center to make slides and transparencies of charts, maps, menus, ads, TV or radio programs, pictures from books and magazines, and so on for you. Sources of supplementary materials are, among others, the German Consulate in your area, the German Information Center, the various Offices of Tourism (www.city name.de [for Germany]/at [for Austria]/ch [for Switzerland]), and the International Film Bureau. The AATG Web site (see below) has many links to other interesting sites. You can write to:

AATG
American Assoc. of Teachers of German, Inc.
112 Haddontowne Court #104
Cherry Hill, N.J. 08034-3668
Tel.: 865-795-5553; Fax: 865-795-9398
e-mail: headquarters@aatg.org
Web site: http://www.aatg.org

Goethe-Institut
Helene-Weber-Allee 1
80637 München
Tel.: (0)89-15921-248; Fax: (0)89-15921-414
e-mail: muenchen@goethe.de
Web site: http://www.goethe.de

Presse- und Informationsamt der Bundesregierung
Dorotheenstr. 84
11044 Berlin
Tel.: (0)30-22440; Fax (0)30-2244-1365
e-mail: postmaster@bpa.bund.de
Web site: http://www.bundesregierung.de

Deutscher Akademischer Austauschdienst
Kennedyallee 50
53175 Bonn
Tel.: (0)228-882-0; Fax: (0)228-882-444
e-mail: postmaster@daad.de
Web site: http://www.daad.de

Deutsche Zentrale für Tourismus e.V.
Beethovenstr. 69
60325 Frankfurt am Main
Tel.: (0)69-974640-287/Fax: (0)69-974640-233
Web site: http://www.germany-tourism.de
or http://www.visits-to-germany.com

Suggested Syllabi

The authors of the seventh edition of **Wie geht's?** understand that every classroom is different and that you and your students vary considerably in the amount of time you devote to language learning. Therefore, the following syllabi present only suggested methods for teaching the course.

Teaching the Pre-units

The pacing of the *Schritte* will depend on the number of class hours, student motivation, aptitude, and background. The following guidelines can be followed:

    Day 1—Introduction to the course: Dialogue of *Schritt 1*
    Day 2—*Schritt 1;* Dialogue of *Schritt 2*
    Day 3—*Schritt 2;* Dialogue of *Schritt 3*
    Day 4—*Schritt 3*
    Day 5—Review; Dialogue of *Schritt 4*
    Day 6—*Schritt 4;* Dialogue of *Schritt 5*
    Day 7—*Schritt 5*
    Day 8—*Rückblick;* Quiz

Teaching the Chapters

As with the pre-units, the pacing of the chapters will depend on various factors: hours per week, quarter or semester system, the students' background, and so on. For an average class, here is how a schedule for teaching Chapter 1 might look.

	Class	Assignment
Day 1	• Review of *Rückblick* • Quiz on pre-units • Introduce *Gespräche,* Ch. 1 + *Wortschatz 1*	• Prepare to read fluently and understand meaning of *Gespräche* • Start *Wortschatz 1: Familie* • Read *Struktur 1.1;* learn endings
Day 2	• Warm-up: personal questions • Review *Gespräche:* in chorus, groups of 2, "perform" • *Zum Thema* A • *Übungen* A–C	• *Wortschatz 1: Länder und Sprachen* • Fill in *Übung* D, write out E • Study *Struktur 1.2*
Day 3	• Warm up: *Zum Thema* B • Ask content questions on *Gespräche* • *Zum Thema* C • *Übungen* F–H • Check vocabulary	• Complete *Wortschatz 1: Weiteres* • Prepare *Zum Thema* D • Study *Struktur 1.3* • Listen to *Hören Sie zu!* A
Day 4	• Warm-up: *Zum Thema* D • Check *Hören Sie zu!* A • *Übungen* I, J • *Zum Thema* E • Start *Einblicke: Wortschatz 2, Vor dem Lesen*	• Read *Struktur 1.4* • Write out *Strukturübung* L • Learn *Wortschatz 2*
Day 5	• Warm-up: *Etwas Geographie* (base questions on *Zum Text* C) • *Aussprache* • *Übung* K, M • Collect *Übung* L • Text of *Einblicke*	• Review *Einblicke* • Prepare *Zum Text* A • Listen to *Hören Sie zu!* B
Day 6	• Warm-up: questions on text • *Zum Text* A, B (C, if not done before text), D • Return *Übung L,* discuss • Check *Hören Sie zu!* B	• Workbook • Prepare for quiz
Day 7	• Collect Workbook assignment • Quiz • Introduce *Gespräche,* Ch. 2	• Read fluently and understand meaning of *Gespräche,* Ch. 2 • Learn *Wortschatz 1: Lebensmittel* • Read *Struktur 2.1*

Some Dos and Don'ts of Language Learning

• Make maximum use of German.

• Speak distinctly and accurately.

• Use words and constructions that are within the students' comprehension.

• Organize each class meeting into a variety of activities.

• Make it clear when one activity ends and another begins.

• Maintain a fairly lively pace, especially in choral responses.

• Don't constantly lapse back into English.

• Don't speak too slowly, since the students need to get used to German spoken at a normal conversational speed.

• Don't use German that is beyond their current level.

• Don't stretch any activity beyond the students' attention span.

• Don't confuse students by suddenly asking them to do something else without clear instructions.

• Don't let one student hold up the class too long. Special discussions that don't benefit the entire class should be saved until after class.

- Be flexible, imaginative, and attentive. Take advantage of special situations and student interests.
- Be well prepared.
- Be honest.

- Encourage all students to participate actively.
- Praise good performances and originality. Positive feedback makes all the difference!
- Ignore minor mistakes if the answer is original. Repeat a correct version of the answer to the rest of the class.
- Be tactful in correcting mistakes; some students are very sensitive. Gently remind them that they are all in the same boat, that only "practice makes perfect" (Es ist noch kein Meister vom Himmel gefallen). They are all there to learn and to help one another learn.
- Address questions to the entire class before asking individual students. This will get everyone thinking.
- Stop an exercise when all students understand and know the material.
- Be clear and strict with assignments. Spot-check frequently.

- Don't give the impression that it is impossible to deviate from your plan and that there is no time for anything else.
- Don't be caught without things to do.
- Don't make mistakes by improvising. Sometimes students will have to wait a whole day for an answer; that's better than telling them something incorrect.
- Don't monopolize class time yourself.
- Don't take special efforts for granted.
- Don't discuss every little mistake. That only inhibits the students.
- Don't put students on the spot, unless they habitually don't pay attention.

- Don't bore students.
- Don't accept sloppy work.

The Spelling Reform

The German spelling reform (Rechtschreibreform) has been implemented throughout the book. A Fokus section in Chapter 15 summarizes the changes. Below is a list of words and phrases used in this book that are affected by it:

OLD	NEW
ß (after short vowel)	ss
Club	Klub
Da hast du recht / unrecht.	Da hast du Recht / Unrecht.
Dein, Euer, Euch (in letters)	dein, euer, euch
auf deutsch, englisch, etc.	auf Deutsch, Englisch, usw.
Donnerstag morgens	donnerstagmorgens
heute morgen / vormittag / mittag / nachmittag / abend / nacht	heute Morgen / Vormittag / Mittag / Nachmittag /Abend / Nacht
fertigmachen	fertig machen
gutaussehend	gut aussehend
im großen und ganzen	im Großen und Ganzen
Joghurt	Jogurt
Parties	Partys
phantastisch, Phantasie	fantastisch, Fantasie
photographieren, Photo	fotografieren, Foto
radfahren, radgefahren	Rad fahren, Rad gefahren
selbständig	selbstständig

OLD	NEW
spazieren**g**ehen, kenne**n**lernen	spazieren **g**ehen, kennen **l**ernen
Skilaufen gehen	Ski laufen gehen
Ti**p**, Sto**p**	Ti**pp**, Sto**pp**
Tschüß	**t**schüss (if used within a sentence)
tut mir **l**eid	tut mir **L**eid
wiede**ra**ufbauen	wiede**r a**ufbauen
wi**e**viel	wi**e v**iel

Script for the *Hören Sie zu!* Sections

Schritte

Das Klassenzimmer

p. 24

Das Klassenzimmer ist sehr groß. Es hat zwei Türen und fünf Fenster. Die Wände sind grau, die Türen sind braun und die Stühle sind rot. Die Tafel ist nicht schwarz; sie ist weiß. Der Professor heißt Oskar Thieme. Er hat drei Bleistifte. Sie sind blau, grün und rot. Er schreibt an die Tafel. Wir haben sieben Bilder von Deutschland. Sie sind sehr schön. Der Professor fragt und wir antworten. Wir lernen Deutsch. Bitte sprechen Sie laut und langsam, Professor Thieme! Wir verstehen Sie nicht.

Kapitel I

A. Guten Morgen!

p. 35

PROFESSOR	Guten Morgen! Ich bin Professor Hugo Schmidt.
STUDENTIN	Guten Morgen, Herr Professor! Ich heiße Monika Müller.
PROFESSOR	Ach ja, Frau Müller. Sie sind Studentin hier, nicht wahr? Wie geht's?
STUDENTIN	Sehr gut, danke.
PROFESSOR	Sie sprechen Spanisch, nicht?
STUDENTIN	Ja. Ich spreche Deutsch, Englisch und Spanisch.
PROFESSOR	Prima! Woher kommen Sie?
STUDENTIN	Ich bin aus Venezuela. Mein Vater ist aus Deutschland und meine Mutter ist Amerikanerin.
PROFESSOR	Und wie alt sind Sie?
STUDENTIN	Ich bin 22.
PROFESSOR	Gut. Hören Sie! Ich brauche eine Assistentin: Montag, Mittwoch und Freitag von zwei Uhr bis sechs Uhr.
STUDENTIN	Oh, wunderbar! Ich brauche Arbeit.
PROFESSOR	Wie lange sind Sie denn hier?
STUDENTIN	Zwei Jahre.

B. Europäer in Deutschland

p. 48

1. Guten Tag! Mein Name ist Vittorio. Ich bin 21 Jahre alt und Student hier in Kiel. Meine Eltern sind Italiener; sie sind aus Florenz. Meine Eltern wohnen schon 24 Jahre in Deutschland. Wir sprechen Deutsch, aber meine Großeltern und ich sprechen Italienisch. Ich studiere Physik. Wir finden es prima hier in Kiel, aber Italien ist auch sehr schön. In Italien ist es warm und die Sonne scheint.

2. Ich heiße Manuel. Meine Frau und ich sind aus Spanien. Wir wohnen schon 33 Jahre in Hamburg. Ich bin zuerst Hamburger, dann Europäer und dann Spanier.

3. Mein Name ist Maria. Ich bin 20. Meine Familie wohnt schon 16 Jahre hier in Düsseldorf. Ich habe zwei Brüder. Meine Eltern sind aus Griechenland. Es ist komisch, in Griechenland sind wir Deutsche und in Deutschland sind wir Griechen.

4. Ich heiße José und komme aus Portugal. Ich bin schon 24 Jahre hier. Ich bin Professor hier in Bonn. Meine Frau ist Berlinerin. Wir haben drei Kinder. Die Kinder sprechen hier Deutsch, aber die Kinder und meine Eltern sprechen Portugiesisch. Wir finden es hier alle sehr schön.

Kapitel 2

A. Essen und Trinken p. 57

1. Tag! Ich heiße Hanjo Schulz. Was ich gern esse und trinke? Also, ich esse sehr gern Obst: Äpfel, Orangen, Bananen, Erdbeeren usw. Ich esse auch gern Fisch. Und was trinke ich gern? Ach, Cola oder Saft, manchmal auch ein Bier.
2. Guten Tag! Ich bin Martina Schneider. Ich esse gern Fleisch, Kartoffeln und Gemüse—und natürlich Kuchen: Käsekuchen, Erdbeerkuchen, Apfelkuchen. Ich trinke gern Tee, aber ich finde Kaffee furchtbar.
3. Mein Name ist Dirk Taeger. Was esse und trinke ich nicht gern? Ich esse nicht gern Gemüse—Karotten, Erbsen, Gurken. Und ich trinke nicht gern Milch oder Cola.

B. Neu in Regensburg p. 72

CLAUDIA	Guten Morgen! Bist du Ursula?
URSULA	Ja, und wie heißt du?
CLAUDIA	Ich bin Claudia.
URSULA	Freut mich.
CLAUDIA	Wie lange wohnst du schon hier in Regensburg?
URSULA	Schon zwei Jahre. Bist du neu hier?
CLAUDIA	Ja, ich bin aus Passau. Sag mal, wo gibt es hier billig Jeans und Sweatshirts?
URSULA	Ich gehe heute Nachmittag einkaufen. Ich brauche auch Jeans und einen Rock. Gehen wir zusammen?
CLAUDIA	Ach, gern. Wann gehst du?
URSULA	So um drei. Und nachher *(afterwards)* gehen wir in ein Café und essen ein Stück Kuchen.
CLAUDIA	Prima! Bis später dann!

Kapitel 3

A. Im Gasthaus p. 80

Jürgen, Helga und Michael, drei Studenten, sind zum Abendessen im Restaurant. Sie essen hier gern, denn das Essen ist sehr gut und nicht teuer. Sie kommen früh und finden einen Tisch. Eine Kellnerin bringt die Speisekarten. Jürgen bestellt eine Cola, Helga Apfelsaft und Michael Mineralwasser. Die Kellnerin bringt die Getränke und fragt, was sie essen möchten. Helga bestellt Schnitzel mit Pommes frites, Jürgen Pizza und Michael Würstchen mit Sauerkraut. Zehn Minuten später bringt die Kellnerin das Essen. Die Studenten haben wirklich Hunger und alles schmeckt prima. Zum Nachtisch bestellt Michael Vanilleeis. Jürgen möchte Schokoladenpudding und Helga Käsekuchen. Die Kellnerin kommt wieder und Jürgen sagt: „Wir möchten zahlen bitte!" Die Kellnerin schreibt die Rechnung: eine Cola €1,75, ein Apfelsaft €1,50, ein Mineralwasser €1,20, einmal Schnitzel €7,50, Pizza €5,–, Würstchen €6,25, ein Eis €2,50, Schokoladenpudding €1,40 und Käsekuchen €2,00. Die Kellnerin sagt: „Das macht zusammen €29,92." Ist das richtig?

B. Gäste zum Wochenende p. 97

KAI	Du, wann kommen Ruth und Uwe?
GERDA	Am Samstag um vier.
KAI	Also zum Kaffee sind sie schon hier. Kaufen wir Kuchen, oder machst du etwas?
GERDA	Ich glaube, ich mache einen Erdbeerkuchen. Der schmeckt Ruth so gut.
KAI	Prima! Haben wir Kaffee?
GERDA	Oh ja!—Zum Abendessen gibt's Käsefondue, Weißbrot und Wein.
KAI	Zum Frühstück machen wir Eier. Wir haben genug Wurst, Käse und Marmelade.
GERDA	Richtig. Aber wir brauchen Schwarzbrot und Joghurt. Uwe isst gern Jogurt.
KAI	Und was gibt's zum Mittagessen?
GERDA	Vielleicht Fisch? Bei Tengelmann gibt's Forelle, ganz frisch.
KAI	Mit Kartoffelsalat und Bohnen?
GERDA	Warum nicht? Zum Nachtisch gibt's Eis, oder machen wir Obstsalat?
KAI	Obstsalat. Ich kaufe Orangen, Äpfel und Bananen.
GERDA	Ich glaube, wir brauchen auch Mineralwasser.

KAI	Richtig. Wann gehen wir einkaufen?
GERDA	Morgen früh. Fährst du zum Supermarkt? Ich gehe zum Markt und kaufe Eier, Obst, Gemüse und Blumen.
KAI	Gut.

Kapitel 4

A. Die Geburtstagsparty

ANKE	Hallo, hier Anke Müller.
PAUL	Tag, Anke! Hier Paul.
ANKE	Tag, Paul! Wie geht's denn?
PAUL	Gut, danke. Du, am zehnten Oktober hat Claire Geburtstag und Peter am zwölften. Geben wir eine Party?
ANKE	Ja, gute Idee! Aber wann?
PAUL	Am Wochenende? Samstag ist der 9.
ANKE	Ich glaube, Claire arbeitet samstags bis um drei. Aber Samstagabend geht's sicher. Wir haben ja noch zwei Wochen Zeit.
PAUL	Richtig. Und wo geben wir die Party?
ANKE	Bei mir, mein Zimmer ist schön groß.
PAUL	Super! Ich bringe meine CDs und etwas zu essen und Klaus bringt etwas zu trinken.
ANKE	Toll! Und ich telefoniere mit Peter und Claire.
PAUL	Um wie viel Uhr beginnen wir mit der Party?
ANKE	Vielleicht um acht, oder ist das zu spät?
PAUL	Nein, das ist gut. Also am 9. um 8 Uhr.
ANKE	Schön. Mach's gut!
PAUL	Du auch. Tschüss! Bis später!

B. Das Straßenfest

MATTHIAS	Tag, Bibi! Was gibt's?
BIBI	Eigentlich nichts Besonderes. Warum?
MATTHIAS	Ich bin am Samstag bei euch gewesen, aber niemand hat die Tür geöffnet.
BIBI	Wir haben Straßenfest gehabt und da haben wir etwas geholfen.
MATTHIAS	Ach so.
BIBI	Vater hat mit den Tischen und Stühlen geholfen und Mutter hat Würstchen und Cola verkauft.
MATTHIAS	Was haben sie noch verkauft?
BIBI	Ach, Bücher, Bilder, Kleidung und Krimskrams.
MATTHIAS	Und du, was hast du getan?
BIBI	Ich habe mit den Kindern Spiele gespielt.
MATTHIAS	Hat's Spaß gemacht?
BIBI	Ja, das ist eigentlich immer sehr schön. Alle Nachbarn sind da gewesen, Jung und Alt. Und abends haben wir dann noch ein bisschen getanzt.
MATTHIAS	Toll! Du, ich habe nicht viel Zeit. Mach's gut!
BIBI	Ich auch nicht. Tschüss, Matthias!

Kapitel 5

A. Touristen in Innsbruck

TOURIST	Entschuldigung! Können Sie uns sagen, wo das Goldene Dachl ist?
INNSBRUCKERIN	Ja, natürlich. Möchten Sie mit dem Bus fahren oder zu Fuß gehen?
TOURISTIN	Ist es weit?
INNSBRUCKERIN	Nein, nein. Sie können leicht zu Fuß gehen. Sehen Sie die Brücke da drüben? Dort beginnt die Fußgängerzone. Gehen Sie immer geradeaus, und dann ist links das Dachl.
TOURIST	Können Sie uns auch sagen, wo der Dom ist? Da ist später ein Konzert. Das möchten wir hören.

INNSBRUCKERIN	Der Dom ist ganz in der Nähe vom Dachl. Fragen Sie dort noch einmal. Wann beginnt denn das Konzert?
TOURISTIN	Um fünf.
INNSBRUCKERIN	O, da haben Sie noch viel Zeit. Es ist ja erst halb vier.
TOURIST	Hm, was machen wir bis fünf?
TOURISTIN	Wo können wir eine Tasse Kaffee und ein Stück Kuchen bekommen?
INNSBRUCKERIN	In der Nähe vom Dachl ist ein Café.
TOURIST	Und dann können wir noch etwas die Maria-Theresia-Straße entlanglaufen.
INNSBRUCKERIN	Ja, von dort sehen Sie die Berge wunderbar. Aber gehen Sie nicht zu spät zum Dom! Da sind heute sicher furchtbar viele Leute.
TOURIST	Vielen Dank für die Information!
TOURISTIN	Ja, danke!
INNSBRUCKERIN	Bitte, bitte. Viel Spaß!

B. Schon lange nicht mehr gesehen!

p. 150

UWE	Tag, Erika!
ERIKA	Tag, Uwe! Ich habe dich ja schon lange nicht mehr gesehen. Wo bist du denn immer?
UWE	Jürgen und ich sind eine Woche in Österreich gewesen.
ERIKA	In Österreich? Super! Wie ist es denn gewesen?
UWE	Einfach wunderbar! Mit dem Wetter haben wir auch Glück gehabt. Es hat nur einmal geregnet.
ERIKA	Wo seid ihr denn gewesen?
UWE	Wir sind nach Maria Alm gefahren. Von dort haben wir ein paar tolle Bergwanderungen gemacht.
ERIKA	Maria Alm? Wo ist denn das?
UWE	In der Nähe von Salzburg.
ERIKA	Prima! Was habt ihr denn noch gemacht?
UWE	Wir sind natürlich auch in Salzburg gewesen.
ERIKA	Salzburg finde ich wunderschön. Habt ihr die Burg besichtigt?
UWE	Natürlich. Wir haben den Dom besichtigt und sind zu Fuß zur Burg gelaufen. Von dort kann man Salzburg ganz toll sehen.
ERIKA	Ja, ich weiß. Seid ihr auch in Wien gewesen?
UWE	Nein, wir wollen im Oktober nach Wien, wenn meine Eltern kommen.
ERIKA	Ja, Wien musst du wirklich sehen. Du, mach's gut! Ich muss in meine Vorlesung. Sie beginnt in fünf Minuten.
UWE	Tschüss, Erika! Bis später!

Kapitel 6

A. Hier Müller!

p. 158

FRAU MÜLLER	Hier Müller!
INGE	Hallo, Mutti!
FRAU MÜLLER	Tag, Inge! Wie geht's?
INGE	Oh, mir geht's gut. Ich will dir nur sagen, dass ich ein Zimmer gefunden habe.
FRAU MÜLLER	Das ist ja prima. Wo denn?
INGE	In der Schillerstraße, Schillerstraße 23. Die Telefonnummer ist 68 91.
FRAU MÜLLER	Und wie hast du das Zimmer gefunden?
INGE	Du weißt ja, wie lange ich schon gesucht habe. Aber die Wohnungen sind viel zu teuer. Vor ein paar Tagen habe ich Horst in einer Vorlesung gesehen und er hat mir gesagt, dass in seiner Wohngemeinschaft ein Platz frei geworden ist.
FRAU MÜLLER	In einer Wohngemeinschaft?
INGE	Ja. Er und ein paar Freunde haben ein Haus gemietet. Jens, Gisela und Renate sind auch Studenten. Sie sind wirklich nett. Wir haben vier Schlafzimmer. Ein Zimmer ist sehr groß und Gisela und ich teilen es.
FRAU MÜLLER	Was bezahlst du denn?
INGE	Weil wir ein Zimmer teilen, bezahle ich nur €175,– im Monat.
FRAU MÜLLER	Ist es weit zur Uni?
INGE	Nein, nein. Wir gehen zu Fuß oder fahren mit dem Fahrrad.
FRAU MÜLLER	Na gut. Das freut mich sehr. Wann kommst du mal nach Hause?

INGE	Ich weiß noch nicht, in zwei oder drei Wochen.
FRAU MÜLLER	Prima! Tschüss dann!
INGE	Tschüss, Mutti! Bis bald!

B. Die Großeltern kommen   p.174

Kinder, ich muss heute bis um sechs arbeiten und kann nicht einkaufen oder kochen. Ihr wisst, dass die Großeltern heute Abend kommen. Ihr müsst mir helfen.

Sebastian, fahr bitte zum Supermarkt und kauf zwei Pfund Bratwurst und etwas Käse zum Abendessen! Nimm €20,–, Geld ist im Schreibtisch! Bring die Mineralwasserflaschen zum Supermarkt! Stell auch zwei Flaschen Wein in den Kühlschrank!

Mareike, bitte mach einen Schokoladenpudding zum Nachtisch und koch Kartoffeln für den Kartoffelsalat!

Julia, fahr mit dem Fahrrad zum Blumengeschäft und kauf ein paar Blumen! Stell sie auf den Tisch im Esszimmer! Wenn die Großeltern kommen, zeig ihnen, wo sie schlafen, und häng ihre Kleidung in den Schrank!

Sagt Vati, das ich um halb sieben nach Hause komme. Spielt das Radio bitte nicht zu laut! Und esst den Apfelkuchen nicht—er ist nämlich für morgen! Also tschüss, bis bald!

Kapitel 7

A. Eine Busfahrt   p. 182

PROFESSOR	So, passen Sie auf! Wir wollen am Montag um 7 Uhr abfahren. Montag bis Mittwoch sind wir in der Schweiz und Donnerstag bis Samstag in Österreich. Wenn Sie Franken mitnehmen wollen, müssen Sie noch vor dem Wochenende auf die Bank gehen. Haben Sie Fragen?
STUDENT 1	Ja. Auf welcher Bank können wir Geld umtauschen?
PROFESSOR	Gehen Sie zu der Bank, wo Sie Ihr Konto haben!
STUDENT 2	Wie viel Geld sollen wir umtauschen?
PROFESSOR	Nicht viel. Die Jungendherbergen und das Essen sind schon bezahlt.
STUDENT 3	Wir brauchen Franken also nur, wenn wir etwas kaufen wollen?
PROFESSOR	Ja, für Cola, Eis, Postkarten oder Briefmarken zum Beispiel.
STUDENT 1	Und wenn wir ins Museum gehen wollen?
PROFESSOR	Museen, Schlösser und so weiter sind auch schon bezahlt.
STUDENT 2	Sollen wir bargeld bringen oder Reiseschecks?
PROFESSOR	Bargeld. Sie brauchen ja nicht viel.
STUDENT 3	Brauchen wir Kleingeld?
PROFESSOR	Kleingeld ist immer gut. Manchmal muss man Kleingeld für Toiletten haben.
STUDENT 1	Wie lange sind die Banken offen?
PROFESSOR	Nur bis 4 Uhr. Also, gehen Sie bald!

B. Hotel Lindenhof   p. 197

REZEPTION	Hier Hotel Lindenhof.
BAUMANN	Guten Morgen! Hier Baumann. Meine Familie und ich kommen im Sommer an den Bodensee und wir suchen ein Hotel.
REZEPTION	Von wann bis wann?
BAUMANN	Wir wollen am 10. Juli ankommen und eine Woche bleiben.
REZEPTION	Und für wie viele Personen brauchen Sie Zimmer?
BAUMANN	Für vier. Wir möchten ein Doppelzimmer für meine Frau und mich, und eins für unsere Töchter.
REZEPTION	Einen Moment! Lassen Sie mich bitte sehen, ob wir dann noch etwas frei haben.
BAUMANN	Danke! . . . *[Mr. Baumann is waiting.]*
REZEPTION	Hallo, Herr Baumann!
BAUMANN	Ja.
REZEPTION	Sie haben Glück. Wir haben noch zwei Doppelzimmer für die sieben Tage im Juli, beide mit Bad.
BAUMANN	Die Kinder können doch bei Ihnen schwimmen?
REZEPTION	Aber natürlich. Wir haben ein Schwimmbad. Ganz in der Nähe kann man auch Minigolf und Tennis spielen und zum See ist's auch nicht weit.

BAUMANN	Das klingt gut. Sagen Sie, wo liegen die Zimmer?
REZEPTION	Im 2. Stock. Vom Balkon haben sie einen Blick auf den See und die Alpen. Wir sind sehr ruhig gelegen.
BAUMANN	Haben sie ein Restaurant?
REZEPTION	Ja, wir haben ein Restaurant im Haus. Montags ist Ruhetag, aber es gibt genug Gasthöfe in der Nähe.
BAUMANN	Sehr schön.
REZEPTION	Darf ich die Zimmer dann reservieren?
BAUMANN	Ja, bitte.

Kapitel 8

A. Weg zur Post
p. 211

BILL	Guten Morgen, Claudia!
CLAUDIA	Grüß dich, Bill! Was gibt's?
BILL	Ich habe ein paar Fragen. Hast du einen Moment Zeit?
CLAUDIA	Na klar! Was willst du denn wissen?
BILL	Ich muss endlich mal meinen Eltern und Freunden schreiben. Wo kann ich Briefpapier, Ansichtskarten und Briefmarken bekommen?
CLAUDIA	Briefmarken gibt's bei Schlegel in der Beethovenstraße. Das ist ein Papierwarengeschäft; dort gibt's auch Luftpostpapier. Oder geh zum Kaufhaus Pollinger in der Fußgängerzone!
BILL	Und wo bekomme ich Ansichtskarten?
CLAUDIA	Ach, die findest du überall in der Fußgängerzone, in Buchhandlungen und auch am Bahnhof.
BILL	Und Briefmarken?
CLAUDIA	Die Post ist in der Lindenstraße, gegenüber vom Stadttheater. Schreib aber deine Briefe zuerst und lass Sie auf der Post wiegen! Auf der Post bekommst du auch Luftpostleicht-briefe mit Briefmarken.
BILL	Gut. Dann kaufe ich jetzt Briefpapier und Ansichtskarten und gehe morgen zur Post. Vielen Dank! Kann ich dir etwas mitbringen?
CLAUDIA	Kannst du vielleicht am Bahnhof vorbeigehen?
BILL	Natürlich.
CLAUDIA	Dann bring doch bitte einen Fahrplan mit! Ich kann meinen nicht finden.
BILL	Gern. Bis später dann!
CLAUDIA	Tschüss!

B. Im Reisebüro
p. 227

ULRIKE	Guten Morgen!
DAME	Guten Morgen! Was kann ich für Sie tun?
ULRIKE	Meine Freundin und ich möchten im März ein paar Tage zum Skilaufen in die Schweiz fahren.
DAME	Wissen Sie schon, wohin?
ULRIKE	Ja, ins Berner Oberland oder in die Gegend von Interlaken.
DAME	Und wann möchten Sie reisen?
ULRIKE	Vom 8. bis zum 15. März.
DAME	Schön. Lassen Sie mich mal sehen! . . . Ja, hier ist etwas: eine Woche in Grindelwald im Hotel Alpina, inklusive Frühstück, pro Person 900 Franken. Oder . . . Hotel Alpenrose in Wengen, 1 170 Franken die Woche, inklusive Halbpension, Skipass, Benützung der Eisbahn und des Solebads.
ULRIKE	Wie viel Euro sind 1 170 Franken?
DAME	€754,85. Hier sind die Broschüren.
ULRIKE	Hotel Alpenrose in Wengen klingt gut.
DAME	Brauchen Sie auch Zugfahrkarten?
ULRIKE	Ja, bitte.
DAME	Einen Moment . . . Sie fahren von hier über Zürich nach Bern; in Bern müssen Sie in den Zug nach Interlaken umsteigen. Abfahrt von hier um 8.25 Uhr, Abfahrt von Zürich um 10.30 Uhr, Ankunft in Bern um 11.10 Uhr und in Interlaken um 12.16 Uhr. Der Bus nach Wengen fährt um 12.30 Uhr ab und ist um ein Uhr dort.

ULRIKE	Ja, das ist gut. Und wie ist es mit der Rückfahrt?
DAME	Am 15. März um 14.00 Uhr; Ankunft hier um 18.44 Uhr.
ULRIKE	Gut.
DAME	Soll ich Zugplätze reservieren?
ULRIKE	Ja, bitte.
DAME	O.K., ich reserviere dann also das Hotel Alpenrose in Wengen und Fahrkarten für zwei Personen. Soll ich Ihnen die Karten mit der Post schicken oder wollen Sie sie abholen?
ULRIKE	Ich komme nächste Woche wieder hier vorbei.
DAME	Gut. Vielen Dank! Auf Wiedersehen!
ULRIKE	Auf Wiedersehen!

Kapitel 9

A. Beim Arzt   p. 237

ARZT	Guten Morgen, Frau Heller!
KIM	Guten Morgen, Herr Doktor!
ARZT	Was bringt Sie zu mir?
KIM	Mein rechtes Knie tut mir so weh.
ARZT	Lassen Sie mich mal sehen. Na, das Knie ist ganz schön dick. Wie ist denn das passiert?
KIM	Ich bin mit meiner Freundin zum Skilaufen im Harz gewesen. Alles war wunderschön, aber am letzten Tag bin ich gefallen und nun tut mir das ganze Bein weh. Mein Ellbogen ist auch ganz blau.
ARZT	Das tut mir Leid. Ich glaube Ihnen gern, dass das wehtut. Sie dürfen ein paar Tage nicht laufen. Legen Sie das Bein hoch! Wenn Sie wollen, können Sie auch Eis auf Ihr Knie tun— aber nicht zu lange, nur zwanzig Minuten. Zeigen Sie mir auch mal Ihren Ellbogen! . . . Ja, der ist wirklich blau. Tut das weh?
KIM	Au! Ja, das tut sehr weh. Können Sie mir Schmerztabletten geben?
ARZT	Ja, ich gebe Ihnen ein paar Tabletten mit.
KIM	Ich kann doch wieder Skilaufen gehen?
ARZT	Natürlich, aber nicht vorm Herbst. Aber Sie können bald wieder schwimmen oder spazieren gehen.
KIM	Na gut.
ARZT	Wenn Ihnen das Bein in einer Woche immer noch wehtut, kommen Sie bitte zurück!
KIM	Mach' ich. Vielen Dank! Auf Wiedersehen!
ARZT	Auf Wiedersehen!

B. Eine tolle Radtour   p. 252

Ich sitze jeden Tag lange genug im Büro. Da habe ich während der Ferien keine Lust, auch noch stundenlang im Auto zu sitzen. Da muss ich einfach etwas ganz anderes tun. Im Frühling habe ich mit ein paar Freunden eine fantastische Radtour gemacht. Wir sind mit der Bahn nach Romanshorn am Bodensee gefahren, wo wir unsere Mietfahrräder abgeholt haben. Wir sind auf Fahrradwegen am See entlang nach Rorschach gefahren und dann mit der Zahnradbahn bis nach Heiden im Appenzeller Land. Ein tolles Panorama! In Heiden haben wir auch übernachtet. Am zweiten Tag hat uns eine schnelle Talfahrt durch Weindörfer zurück an den See gebracht und dann sind wir durchs Rheindelta über Bregenz bis zur Insel Lindau gefahren. Dort sind wir gemütlich durch die Straßen gebummelt und haben abends in einem kleinen Restaurant schön gegessen. Am dritten Tag sind wir bis nach Friedrichshafen gekommen, wo uns eine Fähre dann zurück nach Romanshorn gebracht hat. In drei Tagen durch drei Länder, und das alles für nur 322 Franken. Nicht schlecht, was? Nur das Mittagessen hat extra gekostet. Meistens haben wir gepicknickt. So eine Radtour macht wirklich Spaß und man hält sich fit.

Kapitel 10

A. *Biedermann und die Brandstifter*   p. 261

FRAU WEISS	Hier Weiß.
CHRISTIAN	Guten Tag, Frau Weiß! Hier ist Christian Kolb. Kann ich mal eben mit Daniel sprechen?
FRAU WEISS	Natürlich. Einen Moment, bitte!

DANIEL	Christian? Was gibt's?
CHRISTIAN	Hör zu! Mein Vetter hat mir gerade zwei Theaterkarten für heute Abend gegeben. Hast du Lust mitzukommen?
DANIEL	Was steht denn auf dem Programm?
CHRISTIAN	Max Frisch, *Biedermann und die Brandstifter.* Die Inszenierung soll ausgezeichnet sein. Die Plätze sind auch gut, dritte Reihe im Parkett.
DANIEL	Na klar, das sehen wir uns an. Wer sind die Schauspieler?
CHRISTIAN	Ulrich Hoening und Dirk Meinhart spielen die Hauptrollen.
DANIEL	Toll! Wann fängt die Vorstellung an?
CHRISTIAN	Um 20.30 Uhr.
DANIEL	Jetzt ist es schon halb sieben. Du, Christian, ich muss mich noch rasieren und duschen; und essen möchte ich auch was.
CHRISTIAN	Wenn du dich beeilst, können wir schnell zusammen was essen.
DANIEL	Wo wollen wir uns treffen?
CHRISTIAN	Beim U-Bahnausgang in der Breslauer Straße.
DANIEL	Gut. Ich bin um Viertel nach sieben dort. Vielen Dank für die Einladung!
CHRISTIAN	Bitte, bitte. Bis gleich! Tschüss!

B. Pläne für den Abend
p. 277

STEFAN	Na, Kinder, was machen wir heute Abend?
MONIKA	Habt ihr Lust, ins Theater zu gehen?
FELIX	Woran denkst du denn?
MONIKA	Die Komödie *Jahre später, gleiche Zeit,* von Bernhard Slate, soll ganz gut sein.
STEFAN	Das habe ich auch gehört.
FELIX	Ja, die möchte ich schon lange mal sehen.
FELIX	Ich auch.
MONIKA	Soll ich mal schnell anrufen und fragen, ob es noch Karten für heute Abend gibt?
FELIX	Ja, tu das!
MONIKA	*(Sound of the telephone dialing)* . . . Hallo? Sagen Sie, hätten Sie noch Karten für heute Abend? . . . Gar nichts mehr? . . . Vielen Dank! . . . Schade, alles ausverkauft!
STEFAN	Wie wär's mit einem Kabarett?
FELIX	Klingt gut. Hier sind zwei Anzeigen. Gehen wir zur DISTEL oder zum KARTOON?
STEFAN	Beim KARTOON können wir dann auch gleich essen.
MONIKA	Wann beginnt denn die Vorstellung?
FELIX	Um 21 Uhr.
STEFAN	Ich rufe mal an. Vielleicht können wir einen Tisch bestellen. Wann wollen wir denn essen?
MONIKA	Um halb acht?
FELIX	Schön. Wisst ihr, wie wir dorthin kommen?
MONIKA	Keine Ahnung!
STEFAN	Ich kann ja gleich mal fragen, wenn ich anrufe.
FELIX	Gut.

Kapitel 11

A. Leute sind verschieden
p. 288

1. Kennst du Kirsten, das Mädchen da drüben mit den langen schwarzen Haaren? Obwohl sie nicht viel Geld hat, hat sie immer Pläne. Letzten Sommer war sie in Afrika, wo sie in einem Krankenhaus geholfen hat. Nächsten Sommer ist sie wieder bei so einem Programm in Südamerika. Sie arbeitet, während sie studiert, und abends ist sie bis spät in der Bibliothek.

2. Martin kenne ich schon lange. Wir sind zusammen in die Schule gegangen. In der Schule war er faul und hat seine Hausaufgaben oft nicht gemacht. Im Sport war er eine Katastrophe. Er konnte weder laufen noch Ball spielen; er konnte nicht einmal Rad fahren. Aber er hat schon immer toll Klavier gespielt. Jetzt komponiert er Musik für Fernsehfilme und ist damit reich und erfolgreich geworden.

3. Oliver ist mein Cousin, ein netter Mann, blond, groß und schlank. Er studiert Medizin in Tübingen. Das Studium findet er nicht schwer. Schon in der Schule war er immer sehr gut. Er sagt nicht viel, wenn er mit seinen Freunden zusammen ist. Er hat aber viele Freunde und Freundinnen.

4. Sabine ist eine gute Freundin. Ich finde sie prima. Sie studiert Psychologie in Hamburg. Im Winter besucht sie mich und wir gehen zusammen Ski laufen. Sie treibt viel Sport: Sabine schwimmt fast jeden Tag und spielt viel Tennis. Wir verstehen uns sehr gut—was mir natürlich wichtig ist. Sie kann gut zuhören, wenn man ihr etwas erzählt. Sie zieht sich schick an und lacht viel.

B. Vier berühmte Märchen
p. 303

MÄRCHEN 1: Sie gingen durch den Wald, bis sie ein kleines Häuschen fanden. Das Häuschen war aus Kuchen und Brot und die Fenster aus Zucker. Da brachen sie ein Stück Kuchen ab und fingen an zu essen.

MÄRCHEN 2: Da musste nun das Mädchen von morgens bis abends schwer arbeiten, früh aufstehen, Wasser tragen, Feuer machen, kochen und waschen. Die Schwestern lachten nur über sie und schütteten ihr Erbsen und Linsen in die Asche. Die musste sie dann wieder auslesen. Abends, wenn sie müde war, hatte sie kein Bett, sondern musste sich in die Asche legen und war darum immer schmutzig.

MÄRCHEN 3: Es geschah, dass an dem Tag, als das Mädchen 15 Jahre alt wurde, der König und die Königin nicht zu Hause waren. Da wanderte das Mädchen im Schloss herum, sah in alle Kammern und kam dann auch zu einem alten Turm. Sie ging die Treppe hinauf, kam zu einer kleinen Tür und machte sie auf. Da saß eine alte Frau an einem Spinnrad. „Guten Tag, du altes Mütterchen", sagte die Königstochter. „Was machst du da?" „Ich spinne", sagte die Alte. „Was ist das?" sprach das Mädchen und nahm die Spindel und wollte auch spinnen. Kaum aber hatte sie die Spindel in der Hand, so erfüllte sich der Zauberspruch. Das Mädchen stach sich in den Finger, fiel auf ein Bett und schlief sofort ein.

MÄRCHEN 4: Das Mädchen lief durch den Wald, solange die Füße es tragen wollten, bis es fast Abend war. Da sah es ein kleines Häuschen und ging hinein, um sich auszuruhen. In dem Häuschen war alles klein, aber sehr schön und sauber. Da stand ein Tischchen mit sieben kleinen Tellern, jedes Tellerchen mit seinem Löffelchen, sieben Messerchen, Gäbelchen und sieben Gläschen. An der Wand standen sieben Bettchen. Das Mädchen war so hungrig und durstig. Also aß es von jedem Tellerchen ein bisschen und trank aus jedem Gläschen ein bisschen Wein. Danach, weil sie so müde war, wollte sie sich hinlegen, aber kein Bettchen war lang genug. So legte sie sich quer über alle Betten und schlief ein.

Kapitel 12

A. Was bin ich?
p. 318

1. Ich bin Mädchen für alles: Putzfrau, Köchin, Lehrerin, Beraterin, Sekretärin und Chauffeur. Meine Arbeit hat kein Ende, sie fängt immer wieder neu an. Dabei verdiene ich nichts, nur ab und zu ein Dankeschön. Was bin ich?
2. In meinem Beruf habe ich mit vielen jungen Menschen zu tun. Viele meinen, dass mein Beruf leicht ist, weil ich so viele Ferien habe. Aber mein Beruf ist manchmal sehr anstrengend. Meine Arbeit geht zu Hause weiter, weil ich viel lesen und korrigieren muss. Was bin ich?
3. Ich bin viel unterwegs. Wenn es eine Katastrophe oder etwas Besonderes gibt, bin ich da. Ich spreche mit Politikern, Wissenschaftlern, Rechtsanwälten, Polizisten, Menschen aus allen Berufen, mit den Leuten auf der Straße. Ich hoffe, dass Sie dann meine Artikel in der Zeitung lesen. Was bin ich?
4. Viele Leute kommen zu mir nur, wenn ihnen etwas wehtut. Meistens kommen sie nicht gern, weil sie denken, dass ich ihnen noch mehr wehtue. Aber da haben sie Unrecht. Sie kommen mit Schmerzen, setzen sich in meinen gemütlichen Stuhl, öffnen ihren Mund und bald sind die Schmerzen weg. Was bin ich?
5. Ich habe fünf Jahre an der Universität Hamburg studiert und arbeite jetzt in einer kleinen Firma. Wir haben viel zu tun und ich arbeite manchmal bis spät abends. Oft sitze ich stundenlang in unserer Bibliothek, um Anworten auf komplizierte Fragen zu finden. Aber ich habe auch viele Klienten. Sie kommen zu mir, weil sie mit ihren Nachbarn Probleme haben oder weil sie ein Testament machen wollen. Was bin ich?

B. Drei Lebensläufe

p. 334

1. LEBENSLAUF: Ich heiße Claudia Schmidt und bin am 4. Mai 1988 als älteste Tochter von Alfred und Ulrike Schmidt in Freiburg geboren. Mein Vater ist Ingenieur, meine Mutter arbeitet halbtags als Sekretärin. Ich habe eine zwei Jahre jüngere Schwester. Im September 1994 kam ich in die Grundschule. Nach vier Jahren wechselte ich auf die Freiburger Realschule. Im Juli 2004 werde ich sie mit der Mittleren Reife verlassen. Vor zwei Monaten habe ich einen Computerkurs in der Abendschule besucht. In meiner Freizeit lese ich gern und treibe viel Sport, vor allem Schwimmen.

2. LEBENSLAUF: Ich heiße Wolf Wicke und bin am 23. November 1987 in Bremen als jüngstes Kind von Norbert und Ursula Wicke geboren. Mein Vater ist Vorarbeiter bei der Firma Eggebrecht, meine Mutter ist Lebensmittelverkäuferin. Meine Eltern sind geschieden. Ich lebe bei meiner Mutter und habe zwei ältere Schwestern. Vom September 1993 bis Juli 1997 habe ich die Grundschule besucht. Danach ging ich bis Juli 2002 zur Hauptschule. Seit 1. September 2002 mache ich eine Lehre als Automechaniker bei der Firma Behrens. Außerdem gehe ich zweimal die Woche zur Berufsschule. Nächstes Jahr muss ich zum Militär. In meiner Freizeit spiele ich gern Fußball.

3. LEBENSLAUF: Mein Name ist Christina Bayer. Ich bin am 31. Januar 1983 als zweites Kind von Richard und Susanne Bayer in Bayreuth geboren. Mein Vater war Journalist; er ist 1988 bei einem Autounfall gestorben. Meine Mutter ist Architektin. Ich habe einen fünf Jahre älteren Bruder. Nach vier Jahren Grundschule besuchte ich das Gymnasium in Bayreuth. Im Juni 2002 habe ich mein Abitur gemacht, mit der Note „sehr gut". Seit Oktober 2002 studiere ich Medizin an der Universität Heidelberg. In meiner Freizeit höre ich gern Musik. Außerdem spiele ich Tennis und Golf.

Kapitel 13

A. Ein guter Start

p. 343

Der MBA, kurz für Master of Business Administration, ist nicht nur ein Privileg amerikanischer Universitäten. Man kann ihn auch in Deutschland—zum Beispiel am Europa-Institut in Saarbrücken, an der Fachhochschule in Berlin oder an der privaten Wissenschaftlichen Hochschule in Koblenz—bekommen. Die Studenten kommen nicht nur aus Deutschland, sondern aus anderen europäischen Nachbarländern, aus Asien und den USA. Die 26-jährige Terry Furman hat in Deutschland ihr Abitur gemacht und dann in England Jura studiert. Jetzt möchte sie ihre wirtschaftswissenschaftlichen Kenntnisse verbessern. Der 24-jährige Franzose Dominique Laurent hofft, mit dem MBA bessere Berufschancen als Ingenieur zu haben.

An der Fachhochschule für Wirtschaft in Berlin können Vollzeitstudenten das 1. Semester in Spanien, Finnland, Frankreich oder Berlin studieren. Im 2. Semester nehmen sie dann MBA-Vorlesungen an der South Bank University in London. Danach beginnt das „Company Project", ein Praktikum mit Abschlussarbeit. Billig ist so ein MBA natürlich nicht. Die Studenten am Europa-Institut in Saarbrücken zum Beispiel müssen pro Semester €1 200,— bezahlen. An der privaten Wissenschaftlichen Hochschule für Management in Koblenz kostet das Studium ungefähr €42,000,—. Trotzdem ist der Titel populär, denn er verspricht einen guten Start für eine internationale Karriere.

B. Zwei Briefe

p. 359

1. An das Reisebüro Eckhardt in Würzburg
   Sehr geehrter Herr Eckhardt, in Ihrem Stellenangebot suchen Sie eine Reiseleiterin mit Auslandserfahrung, Fremdsprachenkenntnissen und Organisationstalent. Diese Wünsche kann ich erfüllen. Ich habe einen guten Mittelschulabschluss, drei Jahre Auslandserfahrung—ein Jahr in den USA, ein Jahr in Frankreich und ein Jahr in Italien. Meine Muttersprache ist Deutsch, aber ich spreche auch Englisch, Französisch und Italienisch. Mein Mann ist Italiener. Ich kann gut selbstständig arbeiten, habe Computerkenntnisse und arbeite sehr gern mit Menschen. Seit drei Jahren arbeite ich beim ADAC in Wiesbaden. Meinen Lebenslauf habe ich dem Brief beigelegt. Dürfte ich mich bei Ihnen vorstellen? Mit freundlichem Gruß, Dagmar Schröder.

2. An die Carl-Duisburg Gesellschaft in Köln

Sehr geehrte Damen und Herren, nach meinem Studium in Betriebswirtschaft und Deutsch an der University of California in Santa Barbara würde ich gern ein Praktikum in Deutschland absolvieren. Von Freunden habe ich gehört, dass es möglich ist, bei Ihnen Geschäftsdeutsch zu belegen und dass Sie danach auch Praktika in Deutschland vermitteln. Ich wäre Ihnen sehr dankbar, wenn Sie mir weitere Informationen und Formulare dazu schicken könnten. Mit freundlichen Grüßen, Joe Jackson.

Kapitel 14

A. Die Info-Box
p. 368

MARTIN	Also Heike, wenn man hier so durch die Straßen und Geschäfte bummelt, kann man sich kaum vorstellen, das hier noch vor nicht allzu langer Zeit Niemandsland war. Von der Mauer ist kaum noch was zu sehen.
HEIKE	Ja, Wahnsinn!
MARTIN	Meine Freunde, die 1998 Berlin besucht haben, schwärmten alle von der Info-Box.
HEIKE	Ja, super. Damals war ganz Berlin noch eine Baustelle, aber am Potsdamer Platz war's extrem. Rund sechzig Kräne und 4 000 Arbeiter bauten zur gleichen Zeit an dem Projekt mit 19 Gebäuden.
MARTIN	Und das rote Informationshäuschen, die Info-Box, war mittendrin.
HEIKE	Na klar, mit einem einmaligen Blick auf alles.
MARTIN	Ich wünschte, ich wäre hier gewesen. Das hätte mich schon interessiert.
HEIKE	Ich bin immer wieder hingegangen, um zu sehen, wie aus dem Nichts etwas wird. Auch die Ausstellungen, Filme und Computeranimationen in der Info-Box hätten dich interessiert.
MARTIN	Ich weiß.
HEIKE	Es hätte dir einen Einblick in den Städtebau von morgen gegeben, mit aller Technologie und Planung.
MARTIN	Das dürfte interessant gewesen sein. Aber was ich jetzt hier sehe, ist auch nicht schlecht.
HEIKE	Wolltest du nicht Ingenieur werden?
MARTIN	Ja, Tiefbauingenieur.
HEIKE	Na komm, da kann ich dir einiges zeigen!

B. Ein paar Gedanken von so genannten Ossis
p. 386

Die Wiedervereinigung Deutschlands war sehr viel schwieriger und komplizierter, als die Menschen in Westdeutschland und Ostdeutschland erwartet hatten. Es ist interessant, dass die Menschen im Osten drei Jahre nach der Wiedervereinigung optimistischer waren als die Menschen im Westen. Im Osten glaubten 28 Prozent, dass es ihnen bald besser gehen würde; im Westen glaubten nur 7 Prozent, dass es ihnen besser gehen würde. Nach den drei Jahren hatten mehr als 75 Prozent aller Familien im Osten ein Auto und 95 Prozent hatten einen Farbfernseher. Obwohl die Arbeiter im Osten weniger verdienten als die Arbeiter im Westen, verdiente ein Arbeiter im Osten so viel wie dreißig Arbeiter in Russland.

In Döbeln, einer kleinen Stadt nicht weit von Dresden, hatte man in drei Jahren 164 neue Geschäfte und Firmen eröffnet. Eine der Geschäftsfrauen dort ist Jutta Laubach. Sie hat ein Textilgeschäft aufgemacht. Sie sieht die Situation so: „Wir haben seit der Wende wirklich viel geschafft. Fahren Sie mal durch die neuen Bundesländer und da sehen Sie, dass sich viel geändert hat! Natürlich haben nicht alle Leute hier profitiert. Viele saßen anfangs nur da und warteten. Sie wussten nicht, was sie tun sollten. Früher war alles garantiert: die Wohnung, die Arbeit, selbst der Kindergarten. Viele haben sich geärgert, weil sie zu viel erwartet hatten. Ich finde trotzdem, dass das neue System viel besser ist als das alte. Jetzt können wir wenigstens wieder sagen, was wir wollen. Nur braucht man Eigeninitiative. Von nichts kommt nichts."

Helga Müller war Lehrerin in der Schule von Döbeln. Sie war ihr ganzes Leben lang Kommunistin. Als die Berliner Mauer sich öffnete, hat sie nicht mitgefeiert, sondern nur geweint. Das System, an das sie ihr ganzes Leben glaubte, existierte plötzlich nicht mehr. Nach der Wende verlor sie ihre Stelle an der Schule und seitdem ist sie arbeitslos.

Monika Bernhart ist Direktorin in dieser Schule. Unter dem Kommunismus wäre sie nie Direktorin geworden. Sie sagt heute: „Ich bin sehr froh. Wir können jetzt wieder reisen, wohin wir wollen. Ich war sogar schon in Amerika. Leider sind aber heute auch viele arbeitslos und es ist nicht alles so, wie man sich's vorgestellt hatte. Es läuft alles noch nicht so richtig. Trotzdem gefällt es mir nicht, dass manche Leute immer nur über alles klagen. Das bringt nichts. Alles dauert seine Zeit."

Kapitel 15

A. Habitat Wattenmeer
p. 394

Das flache Vorland der Nordseeküste heißt Watt oder Wattenmeer. Es grenzt an mehrere Länder und ist die größte Wattlandschaft der Erde. Alle sechs Stunden wechselt es von Ebbe zu Flut. Bei Ebbe kann man weit ins Meer hinaus wandern und Muscheln suchen. So eine Wanderung ist unheimlich interessant, denn überall gibt es Leben. Es ist ein wahres Paradies für Vögel und Fische. Beim Wandern durchs Watt kann es natürlich auch passieren, dass mal eine Krabbe am Fuß knabbert; aber da muss man einfach ein bisschen aufpassen. Wer eine längere Wanderung machen möchte, muss das gut planen, denn man möchte nicht von der Flut überrascht werden. Die Wanderung von Cuxhaven nach Neuwerk zum Beispiel ist 12 Kilometer lang. Wer zu faul ist zu laufen, kann mit dem Pferdewagen fahren. Zurück geht es mit dem Schiff. Auf diese Weise erlebt man Ebbe und Flut und kann sicherlich auch Seehunde beobachten, was Spaß macht.

Das Wattenmeer hat ein sehr empfindliches Ökosystem. Die größten Gefahren sind die Verschmutzung des Meeres durch Öl und Giftstoffe von Schiffen, aber auch durch Düngemittel in der Landwirtschaft entlang der Küste. Deshalb haben Deutschland, Dänemark und die Niederlande sich zum gemeinsamen Schutz dieser Landschaft entschieden. Deutschlands Watt ist heute Naturschutzgebiet, wo man die Natur allein lässt und einfach nichts tut. Menschen, die dort an der Küste zu Hause sind, sehen dieses Nichtstun aber oft mit anderen Augen. Seit Generationen leben sie vom Meer und seinem Vorland und sind darum weniger interessiert, es nur als schöne Landschaft zu sehen. Als Kompromiss hat man für sie in den 90er Jahren einige Stellen als besonderes Reservat erklärt, wo Fischfang erlaubt ist, aber nur sehr begrenzt. Man ist auch hier viel umweltbewusster geworden.

B. Europa-Schulen
p. 410

Wie kann man Kinder zu Europäern statt zu Deutschen, Luxemburgern, Belgiern oder Italienern erziehen? Nun, man kann sie in eine internationale Schule schicken. Die Europäische Union oder EU hat internationale Schulen in den verschiedensten europäischen Ländern. Die größte dieser Schulen ist in Brüssel, mit 3.300 Kindern vom Kindergarten bis zur 12. Klasse. Andere Schulen sind zum Beispiel in München, Karlsruhe und in Luxemburg.

Juan, ein Junge aus Spanien, ist 15 und Schüler an der Brüsseler Schule. Er lernt Literatur, Mathematik, Naturwissenchaften und Religion auf Spanisch und Geschichte und Geographie auf Englisch. Dreimal pro Woche hat er Französisch. Mit seinem Sportlehrer spricht er nur Französisch. Seine Klassenkameradin Greta ist aus Dänemark. Sie lernt Geschichte und Geographie auf Französisch und spricht in der Musikstunde Englisch. Mit ihrem Freund Carlo spricht sie Italienisch.

Alle Schüler lernen wenigstens drei Sprachen. Sie lernen auch, ihr eigenes Land objektiver zu sehen. Geschichte zum Beispiel haben sie immer in einer Fremdsprache. Leider gibt es keine internationalen Lehrbücher in Geschichte; darum haben sie Geschichtsbücher aus dem Land, in dessen Sprache sie Geschichte lernen. So lernen zum Beispiel Schüler aus England aus einem französischen Buch, dass ihre Kultur lange nicht so hoch steht wie die französische Kultur. Schüler aus Belgien, den Niederlanden oder Luxemburg lernen, dass ihre Länder in deutschen, französischen oder englischen Lehrbüchern kaum zu finden sind. Nicht nur die Schüler, sondern auch die Lehrer lernen dadurch und werden weniger chauvinistisch. Ein Lehrer aus England zum Beispiel findet es unmöglich, seinen spanischen Schülern stolz zu sagen, dass Nelson bei Trafalgar die spanische Flotte zerstört hat. So konzentriert er sich in seinen Klassen weniger auf die Kriege und mehr auf den Frieden. 1990 wurde die erste Europa-Universität in Frankfurt an der Oder eröffnet. Der erste Rektor—in Deutschland geboren—kam von der Stanford Universität in Kalifornien. Die fast 4 000 Studenten kommen aus rund 50 Ländern, ein Drittel davon aus dem Nachbarland Polen. Fächer wie Management für Mittel- und Osteuropa spielen hier eine besondere Rolle. Wer Sprachen studiert, geht über die Oderbrücke ins polnische Slubice. Inzwischen sind mehrere solche Europa-Universitäten eröffnet worden. Auf diese Weise wird es der jüngeren Generation leichter gemacht, wirklich Europäer zu werden.

Active Vocabulary List

This section will help you prepare tests and supplementary practice. Nouns are grouped by gender and alphabetically within that group. Words preceded by G are introduced in the grammar section. The symbol (—) is used to mark the beginning of *Wortschatz 2*.

Ch.	Nouns		Verbs	Adjectives	Other
S1	Herr	Frau	heißen	gut/schlecht	auch
				müde	Auf Wiedersehen!
				wunderbar	Bis später!
					danke/bitte
					Es geht mir . . .
					Freut mich.
					Guten Abend/Morgen/Tag!
					Ich bin . . .
					Ich heiße/Sie heißen
					ja/nein
					Mach's gut!
					Mein Name ist . . .
					nicht
					Tschüss!
					und
					wie?
					Wie geht's?
					Wie geht es Ihnen?
					Wie heißen Sie?
S2	Bleistift	Farbe	antworten	richtig/falsch	auf Deutsch/Englisch
	Kuli	Kreide	fragen	rot . . .	Das ist (nicht) . . .
	Stuhl	Tafel	hören		für morgen
	Tisch	Tür	lernen		hier/da
		Wand	lesen		noch einmal
	Bild		sagen		Was bedeutet . . . ?
	Buch		sein		Was ist das?
	Fenster		wiederholen		Weiteres
	Heft				Welche Farbe hat . . . ?
	Papier				Wie sagt man . . . ?
	Zimmer				Wo ist . . . ?
S3	Cent	Bluse	brauchen	dick/dünn	aber
	Euro	Hose	kosten	groß/klein	Das kostet . . .
	Mantel	Jacke	nehmen	lang/kurz	oder
	Pulli	Jeans (pl.)	zählen	langsam/schnell	Was kostet/kosten . . . ?
	Pullover	Kleidung		neu/alt	wie viel(e)?
	Rock	Zahl . . .		sauber/schmutzig	zu
				teuer/billig	
	Gegenteil				
	Hemd				
	Kleid				
	T-Shirt				
	Sweatshirt				
S4	Frühling . . .	Uhrzeit	finden	furchtbar	Das finde ich auch.
	Januar . . .	Woche		heiß/kalt	Die Sonne scheint.
	Monat			prima	Die Woche hat . . .
	Montag . . .			schön	Es ist . . .
	Tag			super	Es regnet.
				toll	Es schneit.
	Jahr			warm/kühl	heute/morgen
	Wetter			windig	Ich bin im . . . geboren.
					Ich finde es . . .
					nicht wahr?
					nur
					schade
					schon wieder
					sehr
					Wann sind Sie geboren?
					wirklich

Ch.	Nouns		Verbs	Adjectives	Other
S5	Kurs Student	Minute Sekunde Stunde Studentin Uhr Vorlesung Zeit	beginnen essen gehen haben Tennis spielen	fertig	Bitte! Das verstehe ich nicht. Es ist ein (. . .) Uhr. Es ist eins (. . .). Ich habe eine Frage. Ich habe keine Zeit. Ich weiß nicht. jetzt morgens . . . Öffnen Sie das Buch auf Seite . . . ! Schreiben Sie das bitte! (Sprechen Sie) bitte langsam! (um) Viertel nach . . . (um) halb . . . (um) Viertel vor . . . Wie bitte? Wie spät ist es? Wie viel Uhr ist es?
1	Ausländer Berg Bruder Cousin Deutsche . . . Fluss Großvater Junge Onkel Mann Satz See Sohn Vater Deutsch . . . Deutschland . . . Kind Land Mädchen — Mensch Nachbar Teil	Deutsche . . . Eltern (pl.) Familie Frage Frau Geschwister (pl.) Großeltern (pl.) Großmutter Hauptstadt Kusine Landkarte Leute (pl.) Mutter Prüfung Schwester Sprache Stadt Tante Tochter — Nachbarin	kommen liegen wohnen — arbeiten	amerikanisch kanadisch — wichtig	Ich bin/komme aus . . . im Norden . . . mein/dein/Ihr nördlich . . . von woher? — so . . . wie ungefähr
2	Apfel Fisch Jogurt Kaffee Käse Kuchen Saft Salat (Super)markt Tee Verkäufer Wein Bier Brot Brötchen Ei Fleisch Gemüse Geschäft Kaufhaus Obst Pfund Plätzchen	Bäckerei Banane Bohne Buchhandlung Butter Cola Erbse Erdbeere Gurke Karotte Lebensmittel (pl.) Limo(nade) Marmelade Milch Orange Tomate Wurst Zitrone G: Franzose, Herr, Junge, Mensch, Nachbar, Student — Apotheke	glauben machen suchen (ver)kaufen G: sein, haben	frisch — offen/zu	allerlei (Das ist) alles. dann doch es gibt etwas . . . ich esse/trinke gern . . . ich hätte/möchte gern . . . natürlich was für (ein) . . . ? zusammen G: durch, für, gegen, ohne, um G: kein/nicht G: aber, denn, oder, und — Ach du liebes bisschen! Bitte, bitte! ein paar Ich gehe . . . einkaufen Ich habe Durst/Hunger. montags . . . warum?

Ch.	Nouns		Verbs	Adjectives	Other
	Stück	Blume			
	Wasser	Drogerie			
	—	Tasse			
	Durst/Hunger				
	Glas				
	Würstchen				
3	Kellner	Bedienung	bestellen		Danke. gleichfalls!
	Ober	Gabel	(be)zahlen		Das schmeckt (gut/mir)
	Löffel	Kartoffel	bleiben		etwas (zu essen)
	Nachtisch	Mensa	bringen		Guten Appetit!
	Pfeffer	Nudel	empfehlen		Herr Ober!
	Pudding	Pizza	frühstücken		Ich mag kein(e/en) . . .
	Reis	Pommes (frites)	schmecken		Ich möchte/hätte gern . . .
	Teller	Rechnung			(Ich möchte) zahlen bitte!
	Zucker	Serviette	G: essen,		nichts (zu trinken)
		Speisekarte	empfehlen,		noch ein(e)
	Café	Suppe	fahren, geben,		viel(e)
	Eis	—	gefallen, helfen,		Was gibt's zum . . . ?
	Essen	Freundin	laufen, lesen,		wie viel(e)?
	Abendessen	Flasche	nehmen, sehen,		zu/nach Hause
	Mittagessen	Hand	sprechen, tragen,		
	Frühstück		werden		G: aus, außer, bei, mit, nach
	Messer		G: antworten,		seit, von, zu
	Restaurant		danken,		—
	Salz		gefallen,		besonders
	—		gehören,		gewöhnlich
	Freund		glauben, helfen		man
					manchmal
			dick machen		nicht nur . . . , sondern auch
			schlafen		überall
					vielleicht
4	Feiertag	Feier	bekommen	—	Alles Gute (. . .)!
	Geburtstag	Ferien (pl.)	dauern	laut	am Wochenende
	Sekt	(Ordinal)zahl . . .	denken	lustig	Bitte/danke schön!
		Party	feiern	verrückt	Das gibt's doch nicht!
	Datum	Überraschung	gratulieren		Die Ferien sind vom . . . bis zum . . .
	Fest	—	schenken		Ein gutes neues Jahr!
	Geschenk	Kerze	singen		(Ein) schönes Wochenende!
	—		tanzen		Frohe/fröhliche Weihnachten!
	Lied		tun		gerade
			überraschen		gestern/vorgestern
					morgen/übermorgen
			G: danken,		Gute Besserung!
			gefallen,		Herzlichen Glückwunsch!
			gehören,		Heute ist . . .
			scheinen . . .		Ich bin 1960 geboren.
			—		Ich bin am . . . geboren.
			fallen		Ich gratuliere dir . . . !
			Glück/Pech haben		Ich habe am . . . Geburtstag.
			Spaß machen		Ich wünsche dir . . . !
			studieren		Nichts zu danken!
					noch
					sicher
					So eine Überraschung!
					übermorgen/vorgestern
					Vielen/herzlichen Dank!
					Viel Glück!
					vom . . . bis
					vor einer Woche
					Wann haben Sie Geburtstag?
					Wann sind Sie geboren?
					Welches Datum ist . . . ?
					Wie lange?
					zu (Weihnachten . . .)
					G: bevor, dass, ob,

Ch.	Nouns		Verbs	Adjectives	Other
					obwohl, weil, wenn
					—
					Das macht mir Spaß.
					dort
					eigentlich
					ein bisschen
					Glück/Pech gehabt!
					immer
					(noch) nie
5	Bahnhof	Bank	besichtigen	nah/weit	an/am . . . vorbei
	Bus	Bibliothek	halten	—	bis Sie . . . sehen
	Dom	Brücke	zeigen	bekannt	da drüben
	Park	Dame	zu Fuß gehen	gemütlich	dorthin
	Platz	Haltestelle	—	interessant	die erste Straße links/rechts
	Stadtplan	Kirche	bummeln	lieb	(den Fluss) entlang
	Tourist	Post			Entschuldigen Sie/Entschuldigung/
	Weg	Schule			Verzeihung!
		Straße			Es tut mir Leid.
	Auto	Straßenbahn			Fahren Sie mit dem Bus!
	Fahrrad	Touristin			gegenüber von
	Hotel	U-Bahn			Gibt es hier in der Nähe . . . ?
	Kino	Uni(versität)			Ich möchte zum/zur . . .
	Museum				(immer) geradeaus
	Rathaus				in der Nähe von
	Schloss				Können Sie mir sagen, wo . . . ist?
	Taxi				Sie können zu Fuß gehen.
	Theater				sondern
					Wie kommt man von hier zum/zur . . . ?
					G: aber, sondern
					—
					Das macht nichts.
					einmal
					genug
					hoffentlich
					leider
					stundenlang . . .
6	Balkon	Ecke	baden	hell/dunkel	Auf Wiederhören!
	Baum	Garage	duschen	praktisch	(Das ist) kein Problem.
	Fernseher	Kommode	hängen	(un)bequem	(Das) klingt gut.
	Flur	Küche	kochen	—	(Das) stimmt.
	Garten	Lampe	legen	ausgezeichnet	im Parterre
	Keller	Möbel	liegen	leicht/schwer	im ersten Stock
	Kühlschrank	Toilette	setzen		im Monat
	Schrank	Wohnung	sitzen		im Wohnzimmer
	Sessel	—	stehen		in der Küche
	Stuhl	das Reihenhaus	stellen		oben/unten
	Teppich		(ver)mieten		sogar
	Tisch	Arbeit	waschen		ziemlich
	Vorhang	Eigentumswohnung			
			G: (imperative)		G: an, auf, hinter, in,
	Bad		G: wissen,		neben, über, unter, vor, zwischen
	Bett		kennen		G: wo? wohin?
	Dach		—		—
	Haus		bauen		am Abend/Tag
	Problem		leben		aufs Land/auf dem Land(e)
	Radio		lieben		außerdem
	Regal		sparen		fast
	Sofa				mitten in
	Studentenheim				noch nicht
	Telefon				trotzdem
	(. . .)zimmer				
	—				
	Reihenhaus				
7	Aus-/Eingang	Bank	einlösen	frei	auf/zu
	Ausweis	Kasse	lassen	geöffnet	bald
	Dollar	Nacht	umtauschen	geschlossen	Das glaube ich nicht.

Ch.	Nouns		Verbs	Adjectives	Other
	Gast	Nummer	unterschreiben	laut/ruhig	Das ist doch nicht möglich!
	Koffer	Tasche	wechseln	möglich	Das kann doch nicht wahr sein!
	Pass	Uhrzeit		—	einen Moment
	(Reise)scheck	—		einfach	Halt!
	Schalter	Jugendherberge	G: anrufen,		Pass auf! . . .
	Schlüssel	Pension	aufmachen,		Quatsch!
		Reise	aufpassen,		Vorsicht!
	Bargeld		aufschreiben,		Wann machen Sie auf/zu?
	Kleingeld		aufstehen,		Warte! . . .
	Doppelzimmer		ausgehen,		
	Einzelzimmer		einkaufen,		G: der, dieser, jeder, mancher,
	Gepäck		einlösen,		solcher, welche; mein . . .
	Hotel		mitbringen,		G: prefixes
	—		mitgehen,		G: ab er, denn, doch, ja
	Gasthof		mitkommen,		—
	Wald		mitnehmen,		Das kommt darauf an.
			umtauschen,		meistens
			vorbeigehen,		
			zuhören,		
			zumachen,		
			zurückkommen		
			—		
			ankommen		
			annehmen		
			kennen lernen		
			packen		
			reisen		
			reservieren		
			übernachten		
8	Absender	Abfahrt	abfahren	—	Ach du meine Güte!
	Aufenthalt	Adresse	abfliegen	herrlich	Das freut mich (für dich).
	Bahnsteig	Ankunft	aussteigen		Das ist doch egal.
	Brief	(Ansichts)karte	einsteigen		Das sieht dir (. . .) ähnlich.
	Briefkasten	Bahn	umsteigen		Gott sei Dank!
	Fahrplan	Briefmarke	besuchen		in einer (Drei)viertelstunde
	Flug	E-Mail	erzählen		in einer halben Stunde
	Flughafen	(Hin- und	fliegen		Na und?
	Wagen	Rück)fahrkarte	landen		
	Zug	Fahrt	schicken		G: (an)statt, trotz, während,
		Post	telefonieren		wegen
	Fax	Postleitzahl	mit . . . fahren		G: morgen früh, heute Morgen,
	Flugzeug	Reise	—		Montagmorgen; täglich . . . ;
	Gleis	Telefonkarte	hinauffahren		montags, montagmorgens;
	Handy	Telefonnummer	weiterfahren		Anfang/Ende der Woche, Mitte
	Paket	Vorwahl			des Monats; jeden Tag; diese
	Postfach				Woche; einen Monat; eines
	—	G: Franzose, Herr,			Tages
	Dorf	Junge, Mensch,			
	Schnäppchen	Nachbar, Student,			
		Tourist, Name			
		Gegend			
		Geschichte			
9	Arm	CD	angeln, backen	gesund/krank	Ach so.
	Bauch	Freizeit	faulenzen,	fantastisch	andere/die anderen
	Finger	Gitarre	fernsehen,	—	Bis bald/gleich!
	Fußball	Hand	fotografieren	ander-	Ja, sicher.
	Hals	Idee	kochen, malen	beliebt	Lust haben, zu . . . /Ich habe (keine)
	Kopf	Karte	Rad fahren,	ganz	Lust, . . . zu spielen
	Körper	Kassette	sammeln,		Nein, das geht (heute) nicht.
	Mund	Nase	schwimmen		nichts Besonderes
	Rücken	—	(gehen), Ski		Schmerzen haben/Ich habe (Kopf)schmerzen
	Sport		laufen (gehen),		Was gibt's (Neues)?
	Zahn	Musik	spazieren gehen,		Was ist los?
			(Schach . . .)		wehtun/Mir tut der Hals weh.
	Auge		spielen,		zuerst/danach
	Bein		(Freunde)		—

Ch.	Nouns		Verbs	Adjectives	Other
	Gesicht		treffen,		anders
	Haar		Sport treiben,		etwas (ganz) anderes
	Hobby		wandern		(genauso) wie . . .
	Klavier				
	Knie		G: s. fragen,		
	Ohr		treffen; s.		
	Spiel		wünschen . . .		
	—		G: s. anhören,		
	Urlaub		ansehen,		
			ausziehen,		
	Leben		umziehen,		
			baden, beeilen,		
			duschen,		
			erkälten, (wohl)		
			fühlen,		
			(hin)legen,		
			kämmen,		
			konzentrieren,		
			(die Zähne/		
			Nase) putzen,		
			rasieren,		
			(hin)setzen,		
			waschen		
			—		
			ausgeben		
			s. entspannen		
			s. erholen		
			erleben		
			s. fit halten		
			s. langweilen		
			vorziehen		
10	Anfang	Kunst	anfangen	dumm	am Anfang/Ende
	Autor	Oper	anmachen	komisch	Das ärgert mich.
	Chor	Pause	ausmachen	langweilig	Das hängt mir zum Hals heraus.
	Film	Vorstellung	s. entscheiden	nächst-/letzt-	Das ist zu . . .
	Komponist	Unterhaltung	klatschen	spannend	(Das ist doch) unglaublich!
	Krimi	Werbung	lachen/weinen	traurig	(Das ist ja) Wahnsinn!
	Maler	Zeitschrift	malen	monatlich . . .	diesmal
	Roman	Zeitung	vergessen	—	ein Blick (in/auf)
	Schauspieler	—		folgend	Ich habe die Nase voll.
		Art (von)	G: denken an,	öffentlich/privat	Keine Ahnung!
	Ballett	Auswahl (an)	schreiben an,	verschieden	Jetzt habe ich aber genug.
	Ende	Nachricht	s. freuen auf,		vor kurzem
	Gemälde	Sendung	s. vorbereiten		Was gibt's im Fernsehen?
	Konzert		auf, warten auf,		G: dafür . . . ; wofür . . .
	Orchester		s. ärgern über,		—
	Programm		s. informieren		also
	Stück		über, lächeln		etwa
	—		über, s.		vor allem
			interessieren für,		weder . . . noch
	Bürger		erzählen von,		
	Einfluss		halten von,		
	Zuschauer		sprechen von/über		
	—		—		
	Fernsehen		s. anschauen		
11	Hund	Anzeige	ein.laden	anhänglich	Ach, wie süß!
	Partner	Beziehung	heiraten	attraktiv	beide
	Vogel	Ehe	meinen	charmant	damals
	Wunsch	Eigenschaft	passieren	dynamisch	Das gefällt mir aber!
		Freundschaft	träumen von	eigen-	jemand
	Pferd	Hochzeit	vergleichen	ernst/lustig	So ein süßes Kätzchen!
	Tier	Katze	s. verlieben in	fleißig/faul	Was für ein hübscher Hund!
	Vertrauen	Liebe	verlieren	gemeinsam	Wenn du meinst.
	—	Scheidung	s. verloben mit	geschieden	
	König	—	versuchen	gut aussehend	G: als, wann, wenn
		Königin	—	hübsch/hässlich	G: nachdem

Ch.	Nouns		Verbs	Adjectives	Other
	Gold	Welt	geschehen	intelligent/dumm	—
			hereinkommen	jung	das 1. Mal
			nennen	ledig	zum 1. Mal
			spinnen	lieb(evoll)	niemand
			springen	nett	nun
			sterben	reich/arm	plötzlich
			versprechen	schick	sofort
				schlank	
				schrecklich	
				selbstbewusst	
				seltsam	
				süß	
				verliebt in	
				verlobt mit	
				vielseitig	
				(un)ehrlich	
				(un)freundlich	
				(un)gebildet	
				(un)geduldig	
				(un)glücklich	
				(un)kompliziert	
				(un)musikalisch	
				(un)selbstständig	
				(un)sportlich	
				(un)sympathisch	
				(un)talentiert	
				(un)verheiratet	
				(un)zuverlässig	
				zärtlich	
				—	
				allein	
				froh	
				voll	
12	Architekt	Ausbildung	anbieten	anstrengend	Ach was!
	Arzt	Erfahrung	s. bewerben um	früher	Das ist doch lächerlich.
	Beruf	Firma	erklären	gleich	einerseits/andererseits
	Betriebswirt	Geschäftsfrau	s. gewöhnen an	hoch/hoh-	Genau!
	Geschäftsmann	Hausfrau	glauben an	(un)sicher	Ich will . . . werden.
	Hausmann	Klasse	Recht haben	—	Im Gegenteil!
	Ingenieur	Krankenschwester	verdienen	(gut) ausgebildet	Nun/also/na ja/tja, . . .
	Journalist	Schule	werden	unbedingt	Unsinn!
	Krankenpfleger	Sicherheit	—		Was willst du (mal) werden?
	Künstler	Stelle	aussehen (wie)		
	Kurs	Stunde	bitten		G: gern, groß, gut, hoch, nah, viel (mehr,
	Lehrer	Verantwortung	erwarten		meist-) . . . ; genauso . . . wie;
	Plan	Zukunft	genießen		nicht so . . . wie; . . . als; immer . . . ;
	Polizist		hoffen		je . . . desto . . .
	Rechtsanwalt	G: Angestellte,	s. Sorgen machen um		—
	Reiseleiter	Bekannte,	s. vorstellen		darum
	Sekretär	Deutsche, Kranke,			Ich stelle mir vor, dass . . .
	Wissenschaftler	Verlobte, Beamte			im/ins Ausland
	Zahnarzt	—			jedoch
		Arbeitslosigkeit			unter (among)
	Büro	Berufswahl			
	Einkommen	Entscheidung			
	Geschäft	(Fach)kenntnis			
	—				
	Arbeiter				
	Bereich				
	Handel				
	Ort				
	Rat				
	Praktikum				
	Unternehmen				

Ch.	Nouns		Verbs	Adjectives	Other
13	Hörsaal	Fachrichtung	ausfüllen	schwierig	Hast du etwas dagegen, wenn . . . ?
	Mitbewohner	Note	belegen	—	Mal sehen
	Professor	(Natur)wissenschaft	etwas dagegen haben	ausländisch	Na klar.
	Schein	(Seminar)arbeit	holen		wieso?
	Student		lehren		—
	Zimmerkollege		eine Prüfung machen		an deiner Stelle
			eine Prüfung		auf diese Weise
	Fach		bestehen		bestimmt
	Haupt/Nebenfach		(bei einer Prüfung)		Das geht (nicht).
	Labor		durchfallen		deshalb
	Referat		ein Referat halten		jedenfalls
	Quartal		(an)		so dass
	Semester		teilnehmen (an)		sowieso
	Seminar		—		wahrscheinlich
	Stipendium		Angst haben vor		wenigstens
	Studium		annehmen		
	System		aufhören		
			teilen		
14	Augenblick	Grenze	berichten	einmalig	einst
	Frieden/Krieg	Mauer	erinnern an	historisch	kaum
	Spitzname	Umgebung	s. erinnern an	underwartet	oder?
	Turm	—	führen	unheimlich	Und ob!
		Heimat	klagen über	wunderschön	
	Erlebnis	Insel	s. lustig machen über	—	
	Gebäude	Jugend	rechnen mit	berühmt	
	Volk	Luft	(s.) verändern	leer	
	—	Macht	verschwinden		
	Gedanke	(Wieder)vereinigung	vorbeiführen an		
	Tor		austauschen		
			erkennen		
			verlassen		
15	Abfall	Erhaltung	abreißen	umweltbewusst	allerdings
	Bau	Küste	(wieder) aufbauen	—	echt schön
	Müll	Landschaft	finanzieren	einzeln	schließlich
	Schutz	Mülltonne	garantieren	gefährlich	übrigens
		Natur	planen	stolz auf	—
	Denkmal	Rede	reden mit/über	typisch	endlich
	(Naturschutz)-gebiet	Sammelstelle	renovieren	vereint	inzwischen
	—	Umwelt	restaurieren		
	(Geld)schein	Verschmutzung	retten		
	Staat	—	schaden		
		Bevölkerung	schonen		
	Jahrtausend	Münze	schützen		
			trennen		
			verbieten		
			wegwerfen		
			verwenden		
			zerstören		
			—		
			verbinden		
			wachsen		

Wie geht's?

An Introductory German Course

Seventh Edition

Dieter Sevin

Vanderbilt University

Ingrid Sevin

THOMSON

™

HEINLE

Australia   Canada   Mexico   Singapore   Spain   United Kingdom   United States

Wie geht's? An Introductory German Course
Seventh Edition
Dieter Sevin, Ingrid Sevin

Senior Editor: *Sean Ketchem*
Production Editor: *Lianne Ames*
Director of HED Marketing: *Lisa Kimball*
Marketing Manager: *Jill Garrett*
Manufacturing Coordinator: *Marcia Locke*
Compositor: *Progressive Publishing Alternatives*
Project Manager: *Donna King*

Photo Researcher: *Sheri Blaney*
Illustrator: *Progressive Publishing Alternatives*
Cover Designer: *Diane Levy*
Text Designer: *Studio Montage*
Cover Image: © *Hans Wolf/The Image Bank/Getty Images*
Printer: *Transcontinental*

For permission to use material from this text or product contact us:
Tel   1-800-730-2214
Fax   1-800-730-2215
Web   www.thomsonrights.com

0-03-035162-6 (Student Edition)
0-03-035253-3 (Student Edition with Text Audio CD)

Library of Congress Cataloging-in-Publication Data
Sevin, Dieter,
   Wie geht's? : an introductory German course/ Dieter Sevin,
     Ingrid Sevin.—7th ed.
        p. cm.
   Includes index.
   ISBN 0-03-035162-6
   1. German language—Grammar.   2. German language—
   Textbooks for foreign speakers—English.   I. Sevin, Ingrid.
   II. Title.

PF3112 .S4 2002
438.2'421—dc21

                                                        2002032888

Wie geht's?

Contents

To the Student

Welcome to *Wie geht's?*, a program for Introductory German that focuses on all four skills—listening, speaking, reading, and writing—and promotes cultural proficiency.

Organization of *Wie geht's?*

The main text is divided into five pre-units *(Schritte)*, fifteen chapters *(Kapitel)*, five review sections *(Rückblicke)* and an appendix *(Anhang)*.

The Pre-Units

The purpose of the pre-units is to acquaint you with the German language and the language learning process by focusing on listening and speaking. When you have completed the last pre-unit, you should be able to greet each other, describe your classroom and your clothes, use numbers, discuss the weather, and tell time, all in German.

The Fifteen Chapters

Each chapter opens with a summary of the learning objectives *(Lernziele)* for that chapter. This is followed by a cultural preview in English **(Vorschau)** that provides you with background information on the chapter topic. The first section of the learning material itself is called **Gespräche + Wortschatz.** It includes one or two dialogues that focus on the chapter topic and function as models for conversation. For your reference, English translations for these dialogues can be found in the Appendix.

Next comes **Wortschatz 1,** which contains most of the new chapter vocabulary; it is arranged thematically, with nouns listed in alphabetical order according to gender. That list of active vocabulary is followed by a brief list of vocabulary intended for recognition only *(Zum Erkennen)* containing words and phrases from the dialogue and some exercises that might make it easier to keep classroom conversation in German. The vocabulary list is followed by exercises and activities on the chapter theme *(Zum Thema)* that foster communication and help you learn the new words and expressions. A pronunciation section *(Aussprache),* recorded in your lab program, is included as well and is coordinated with more extensive practice in the supplementary *Aussprache* section of your Workbook *(Arbeitsbuch).* At the end of *Zum Thema,* and again after the reading text, you will find an activity **(Hören Sie zu!)** that will help improve your listening comprehension. To complete it, you will need to listen to the CD that accompanies the book.

The following **Struktur** section introduces two or three major points of grammar. A variety of exercises *(Übungen)* provides practice of the principles presented.

The grammar explanations and activities are followed by a reading section **(Einblicke).** It is introduced by a brief proposal for how to approach the reading text *(Lesestrategie),* followed by a second active vocabulary list **(Wortschatz 2),** and a pre-reading section *(Vor dem Lesen)* with a variety of activities. The reading passage itself features one or more cultural aspects related to the chapter topic. It offers additional examples of the new grammar and a review of the chapter vocabulary. The reading text is followed by post-reading exercises and activities *(Nach dem Lesen)* that check comprehension and provide additional grammar, speaking, and writing practice. They are followed by a second listening activity **(Hören Sie zu!).** In later chapters, some literary readings are added for your enrichment and enjoyment, such as poems (starting with chapter 8) and short stories (starting with chapter 12).

Cultural notes **(Fokus)** are interspersed throughout every chapter, as well as the pre-units; they point out or explain differences between life in North America and in countries where German is spoken.

Each chapter also includes a **Video-Ecke** ("video corner") that tells about the accompanying video and a **Web-Ecke** referring to the Web site at **http://wiegehts.heinle.com,** where you will find online activities related to the chapter theme. Using the videos and the Web site will enrich your language learning, add to cultural insights, and open new vistas of direct contact to the German-speaking countries.

Review Sections

After the pre-units and Chapters 3, 7, 11, and 15, you will find review sections (**Rückblicke**) that summarize the grammatical structures you have learned. Correlating review exercises can be found in the Workbook *(Arbeitsbuch).*

The Appendix

The Appendix includes information on predicting the gender of some nouns, a grammar summary in chart form, tables of all basic verb forms, lists of irregular verbs, translations of dialogues, supplementary charts for the information-gap activities *(Hoppla, hier fehlt was!),* answers to the optional English-to-German activities in the margins, a German-English and English-German vocabulary, and a grammar index.

Visual Icons for *Wie geht's?*

 This icon designates an activity where you'll be working with a partner.

 Activities marked with this icon are designed for work in small groups of perhaps 3–5

 This icon will also appear from time to time in a **Struktur** section; it identifies a grammar point where you should watch out that your knowledge of English doesn't interfere with the point under discussion.

 This denotes the listening activity (**Hören Sie zu!**) that appears twice in each chapter. To complete the activity, listen to the CD that accompanies the book.

 This icon references the Lab Audio CDs. The number on the sleeve indicates the CD, followed by the track number.

 This icon indicates a writing activity.

 This symbol marks the **Video-Ecke.**

 This symbol marks the **Web-Ecke.**

Student Program Components

- *Wie geht's?* comes packaged with a **Text Audio CD** that contains thirty-one listening texts (**Hören Sie zu!**): one for the pre-units and two for each regular chapter.

- The **Lab Audio CD program** provides additional practice in listening and speaking. On the CDs, you will find the dialogues, active vocabulary, supplementary grammar activities, pronunciation practice, listening-comprehension exercises, dictations, and the reading texts. The program is accompanied by a lab section printed in each chapter of the Workbook.

- The **videos** consist of a *Minidrama* that presents authentic dialogues and a *Blickpunkt* that gives cultural insights into the various aspects of life in the German-speaking countries. The latter, newly filmed for this edition, is more spontaneous and challenging; it appears only in every other chapter. The videos are accompanied by extensive pre-viewing and post-viewing activities *(Video-aktiv)* printed in the Workbook.

- The **Workbook** *(Arbeitsbuch)* has several components: the lab activities *(Zum Hören)*, written exercises *(Zum Schreiben)*, video activities *(Video-aktiv)*, as well as a complete Pronunciation Guide *(Zur Aussprache)*.

    The *Zum Hören* activities are correlated to the text audio CD program; it contains instructions and examples of the recorded activities.
    The *Zum Schreiben* activities focus on vocabulary building, structure, and cultural enrichment, with extensive review exercises that correlate with the review chapters *(Rückblicke)* of the main text.
    The *Video-aktiv* section provides exercises that are correlated to the *Wie geht's?* Video.
    The Pronunciation Guide *(Zur Aussprache)* shows brief explanations of correct sound production; corresponding exercises are available on the first lab audio CD.

- The Workbook activities are also available online. Use the *QUIA* Passcard to access the Workbook content (including the lab program) through the Web.

- A text-specific **Multimedia CD-ROM for Macintosh® and Windows®** offers interactive activities that will help to improve your listening comprehension skills, and provide further exposure to the culture of German-speaking countries.

- Taking advantage of the new possibilities of the Internet, the **Web-Ecke** refers you to the Web site of *Wie geht's?*, where you'll find **online activities** specifically tailored to the book. Go to **http://wiegehts.heinle.com**.

- The online Web Tutor™ activities for Web CT™ and Blackboard™ let you practice and review the topics in the book on your own; error analysis will guide you to correct answers.

We hope that you will find the *Wie geht's?* program enjoyable. You will be surprised at the rapid progress you will make in just one year. Many students have been able to study abroad after their first year of studying German!

Acknowledgments

We would like to thank the following colleagues who reviewed the seventh edition manuscript during its various stages of development:

Zsuzsanna Abrams
University of Texas at Austin

Gabriela Appel
Pennsylvania State University

Prisca Augustyn
Florida Atlantic University

Shana Bell
Arizona State University at Tempe

Elise Brayton
California State University, San Diego

Francis Brévart
University of Pennsylvania

Johannes Bruestle
Grossmont College

Bettina F Cothram
Georgia Technical University

Karl-Georg Federhofer
University of Michigan

Ingrid Fry
Texas Tech University

Christine M. Goulding
California State University, Chico

Yvonne Ivory
Duke University

Julia Karolle
Purdue University

Peter Meister
University of Alabama, Huntsville

George Mower
Allegheny County Community College

Lisa Parkes
University of California, Los Angeles

Hartmut Rastalsky
University of Michigan

Christine Staininger
San Diego University

Cordelia Stroinigg
University of Cincinnati

We are grateful to the following members of the Heinle editorial staff: Wendy Nelson, for shepherding the project through its early stages; Sean Ketchem, Senior Editor for World Languages, who helped carry **Wie geht's?** through to publication, Lianne Ames, Senior Production Editor, whose skill and expertise touched on all aspects of the bookmaking process, Ulrike Rapp for providing the native read of the text, Jill Garrett, Marketing Manager, and Dennis Hogan, President of Heinle, for their support of the **Wie geht's?** program.

Last but not least, we would like to express our appreciation to our co-author of previous editions, Katrin T. Bean, whose valuable contribution continues to be an integral part of this text.

Schritte

Wie geht's?

Wie geht's?—Danke, gut.

Lernziele (Learning objectives)

Vorschau (Preview)
The German language

Gespräche + Wortschatz (Dialogues and vocabulary)

The pre-units will help you take your first steps in German.
You will learn to . . .

- introduce yourself and say hello and good-bye
- say the alphabet and spell in German
- describe your classroom and name various colors
- talk about articles of clothing and use adjectives to describe them
- use numbers
- discuss the calendar and the weather
- tell time

- understand some basic classroom expressions.

Fokus (Cultural notes)
Coming and going
Trendsetters of the fashion world
The German climate
The benefits of learning German

Video-Ecke
Minidrama: *Was darf's sein?*

Web-Ecke

Vorschau

The German Language

More than 100 million people speak German as their native tongue. It is the official language in Germany, Austria, Liechtenstein, and large areas of Switzerland. It is also spoken in parts of Luxembourg, Belgium, France (Alsace), and Italy (South Tyrol), and by some of the German minorities in Poland, Romania, and a few of the republics of the former Soviet Union. Canada, the United States, and some South American countries have significant German-speaking populations.

German belongs to the Germanic branch of the Indo-European language family and is closely related to Dutch, English, the Scandinavian languages, Flemish, Frisian, Yiddish, and Afrikaans. For various political, literary, and linguistic reasons, we speak of Germans and the German language as dating from around the year 800. At that time, at least six major dialects with numerous variations were spoken. During the twelfth and thirteenth centuries, efforts were made to write a standardized form of German; thus, the period from 1170 to around 1250 became one of great literary achievements. Afterwards, however, this literary language declined and, with few exceptions, Latin was used in writing; it remained the sole language of instruction at German universities until the 1700s. Luther's translation of the Bible, coupled with the invention of the Gutenberg printing press in the fifteenth century, was a major influence on the development of a common written German language. Because of political fragmentation, a standard language was slow to develop in Germany. As late as the early 1900s, most people spoke only their regional dialects. First, newspapers and magazines, then radio and television, fostered the use of standard German; but regional accents are still common.

Because German and English are members of the same branch of the Indo-European language family, they share a considerable amount of vocabulary. Some of these related words, called cognates, are identical in spelling (e.g., **der Arm, die Hand, der Finger**), and others are similar (e.g., **der Vater, die Mutter, das Haus**). As the two languages developed, certain cognates acquired different meanings, such as **die Hose** *(pair of pants)* versus "hose" *(stockings)*. Differences between English and German cognates developed quite systematically; here are a few examples:

Assign as homework the reading of the *Vorschau, Fokus,* and *Lerntipp* sections in each chapter. At the end of the pre-units, you could show the video *Was darf's sein?*

	English	German
t > z	*ten*	zehn
	salt	Salz
p > pf	*pound*	Pfund
	apple	Apfel
t > ss	*water*	Wasser
	white	weiß
p > f	*ship*	Schiff
	help	helfen
k > ch	*book*	Buch
	make	machen
d > t	*bed*	Bett
	dance	tanzen
th > d	*bath*	Bad
	thank	danken

Ask students to give the English equivalent to these cognates. What other cognates do they know in English that are derived from German? For additional practice, see the *Zum Schreiben* section of the Workbook.

Schritt 1
Step 1

Gespräche + Wortschatz

Guten Tag!

CD 1, Track 9

Draw two faces or stick figures on the board; label one **Herr Sanders** and one **Frau Lehmann.** Point to each figure while introducing the first dialogue and have students repeat after you. Then walk around the room and greet several students, using the patterns they have just heard.

Begin by saying in German who you are (**Ich heiße . . .**), then write your name on the board. Repeat **Ich heiße . . .** and ask a student **Wie heißen Sie?** Repeat until students understand and can respond.

Read the following dialogues aloud until you can do so fluently, and be prepared to answer questions about them. If necessary, you may consult the translations in the Appendix.

HERR SANDERS	Guten Tag!
FRAU LEHMANN	Guten Tag!
HERR SANDERS	Ich heiße Sanders, Willi Sanders. Und Sie, wie heißen Sie?
FRAU LEHMANN	Mein Name ist Erika Lehmann.
HERR SANDERS	Freut mich.
HERR MEIER	Guten Morgen, Frau Fiedler! Wie geht es Ihnen?
FRAU FIEDLER	Danke, gut. Und Ihnen?
HERR MEIER	Danke, es geht mir auch gut.
HEIDI	Hallo, Ute! Wie geht's?
UTE	Tag, Heidi! Ach, ich bin müde.
HEIDI	Ich auch. Zu viel Stress. Bis später!
UTE	Tschüss! Mach's gut!

Was sagen Sie? *(What do you say? Read the cue lines and prepare appropriate responses. Then enact the scene with a partner.)*

S1 Guten Tag!
S2 . . .
S1 Ich heiße . . .   Und Sie, wie heißen Sie?
S2 Ich heiße . . .
S1 Freut mich.
S2 Wie geht es Ihnen?
S1 . . .   Und Ihnen?
S2 . . .
S1 Auf Wiedersehen!

For suggestions on how to deal with various points of this section, as well as other helpful teaching suggestions, read the *Lehrtipps* on the Web site at http://wiegehts.heinle.com.

Preferably, you would do this exercise after the students are more familiar with the new vocabulary. However, having the original dialogue close by might help. You could also have students create their own dialogue.

Wortschatz *(Vocabulary)*

You are responsible for knowing all the vocabulary of the *Wortschatz* (literally, "treasure of words"), including the headings. Be sure to learn the gender and plural forms of nouns! Words and phrases listed under *Zum Erkennen* are intended for comprehension only; you will not be asked to produce them actively.

Ideally, the *Schritte* should be done without much or any explanation of grammar rules; but if too many questions arise, refer students to the *Rückblick* that follows the *Schritte.*

- In German, all nouns are capitalized.
- The pronoun **ich** *(I)* is not capitalized unless it occurs at the beginning of a sentence. The pronoun **Sie** *(you)* is always capitalized.

If students ask, tell them that gender and the plural will be explained in *Schritt 2.*

Ask students if they have heard any other German greetings. Write them on the board.

der Herr, die Herren *(pl.)*	*Mr.; gentleman*
die Frau, die Frauen *(pl.)*[1]	*Mrs., Ms.; woman; wife*
Guten Morgen![2]	*Good morning.*
Guten Tag![2]	*Hello.*
Tag![3]	*Hi! (casual)*
Guten Abend![2]	*Good evening.*

Wie heißen Sie?	*What's your name? (formal)*
Mein Name ist . . .	*My name is . . .*
heißen	*to be called*
ich heiße . . .	*my name is . . .*
Sie heißen . . .	*your name is . . . (formal)*
Freut mich.	*Pleased to meet you.*
Wie geht es Ihnen?	*How are you? (formal)*
Wie geht's?	*How are you? (casual)*
wie?	*how?*
Es geht mir gut.[4]	*I'm fine.*
gut / schlecht	*good, fine / bad(ly)*
wunderbar	*wonderful(ly), great*
Ich bin müde.[4]	*I'm tired.*
ja / nein	*yes / no*
danke / bitte	*thank you / please*
auch	*also, too*
nicht	*not*
und	*and*
Auf Wiedersehen!	*Good-bye.*
Tschüss!	*Good-bye. Bye. (colloquial)*
Mach's gut!	*Take care! (colloquial)*
Bis später!	*See you later! (colloquial)*

Ich bin müde!

Draw students' attention to the verb endings in **ich heiße** and **Sie heißen**.

If students ask: *all right* **sehr gut, ganz gut**; *so so* **nicht so gut, so lala**; *I am exhausted* **ich bin k.o.**; *I am sick* **ich bin krank**

Point out the difference between **Es geht mir wunderbar** (*I feel great*) and **Ich bin wunderbar** (*I'm a wonderful person*). Point out that **Es geht mir gut** is an idiom, and as such it has a meaning that is different from its literal translation.

Note the spelling of **tschüss** and **auf Deutsch** (formerly **tschüß** and **auf deutsch**), which is in line with the spelling reform. For details of the changes, see "Instructor's Preface"

[1] In modern German, the title **Frau** is generally used for all adult women regardless of a woman's age or marital status. The title **Fräulein** (*Miss*) has more or less disappeared, although some people, especially in southern Germany, still use it to address young women under age 18.

[2] **Guten Morgen!** is generally used until about 10:00 A.M., **(Guten) Tag!** between then and early evening, and **Guten Abend!** from about 5:00 P.M. on. **Gute Nacht!** (*Good night!*) is normally used to wish someone who lives in the same house a good night's sleep.

[3] Other casual ways of saying *Hi!* are: **Hallo!** and **Grüß dich!**; **Grüß Gott!** (*lit.: Greetings in the name of God!*) and **Servus!** in southern Germany or Austria; and **Grüezi!** in Switzerland and Liechtenstein.

[4] **Es geht mir** gut (schlecht, wunderbar). BUT **Ich bin** müde.

Zum Erkennen *(Passive vocabulary, for comprehension only):* Hallo! (*Hi! Hello!*); ach *(oh)*; ich auch *(me too)*; zu viel Stress *(too much stress)*; AUCH: Lesen Sie laut! *(Read aloud!)*; Wie schreibt man das? *(How do you write that?)*; Buchstabieren Sie auf Deutsch! *(Spell in German!)*; Schreiben Sie, was ich buchstabiere! *(Write down what I spell!)*; Was sagen sie? *(What do they say?)*

The words in **Zum Erkennen** are for recognition only, i.e., passive vocabulary. They are listed in the order of their appearance in the dialogue(s). Following *"AUCH"* are a few other words or expressions from the chapter that might help keep classroom instructions in German.

Fokus — *Coming and Going*

When you ask **Wie geht's?** or **Wie geht es Ihnen?**, expect a detailed answer about the other person's well-being. In this sense, the question is different from the casual English expression *How are you?* and should be directed only to people you already know. The parting expression **Tschüss!** is more informal than **Auf Wiedersehen!**

Mündliche Übungen *(Oral exercises)*

A. Mustersätze *(Patterns and cues)*

These patterns give you a chance to practice phrases from the dialogues and the vocabulary of each *Schritt*. Listen carefully and repeat the sentences until you can say them fluently.

CD 1, Track 9
A: You can also use these patterns for role-playing activities, e.g., **Ich heiße . . . Und Sie, wie heißen Sie?**

1. Willi Sanders: **Ich heiße** Willi Sanders.
   Hugo Schmidt, Gudrun Kleese, Anna Peters
2. Erika Lehmann: **Heißen Sie** Erika Lehmann?
   Monika Schulz, Wolfgang Friedrich, Hermann Lorenz
3. Hugo Schmidt: **Ja, ich heiße** Hugo Schmidt.
   Hans Holbein, Brigitte Fischer, Simone Holtkamp
4. Oskar Meier: **Nein, ich heiße nicht** Oskar Meier.
   Gustav Mahler, Clara Schumann, Wolfgang Amadeus Mozart
5. Frau Fiedler: **Wie geht es Ihnen,** Frau Fiedler?
   Frau Lehmann, Herr Sanders, Herr und Frau Bauer

A.6: Act out the meanings of these adjectives.

6. gut: **Es geht mir** gut.
   auch gut, nicht schlecht, wunderbar

B. Das Alphabet

CD 1, Track 9

1. **Lesen Sie laut!** *(Read aloud.)*

a	ah	g	geh	m	emm	s	ess	y	üppsilon
b	beh	h	hah	n	enn	t	teh	z	tsett
c	tseh	i	ih	o	oh	u	uh	ä	äh (a-umlaut)
d	deh	j	yot	p	peh	v	fau	ö	öh (o-umlaut)
e	eh	k	kah	q	kuh	w	weh	ü	üh (u-umlaut)
f	eff	l	ell	r	err	x	iks	ß	ess-tsett

For explanations on the German spelling reform, see "Instructor's Preface" and the *Fokus*-note in Chapter 15.

You could introduce the alphabet song to your students.

Germans would say **äh, öh, üh** rather than **a-umlaut, o-umlaut,** or **u-umlaut.** The [ts] in the pronunciation of **c** and **z** is like that in *rats*.

Urge students to pay attention to the *Lerntipps*.

For capital letters, say **großes A (B, C . . .)**, for lower-case letters, **kleines D (E, F . . .)**. For further explanation of the ß-sound, see III A.6 in the pronunciation section of the Workbook. Note that there is also a specific pronunciation section (**Aussprache**) for each pre-unit in your lab program, each focusing on particular vowels and consonants. Make it a point to listen to it and to repeat.

Lerntipp

What's It Like to Learn a Language?

Learning another language is much like learning a musical instrument or a sport. Just as you can't learn to play the piano or swim by reading about it, you can't learn a foreign language by thinking or reading about it. You must practice. Listen to your instructor, to tapes, to the answers of your fellow students. Use every chance you get to speak German. Whenever possible, read the language aloud and write it.

Remember also that you are still improving your English; therefore, don't expect perfection in another language. You made mistakes while learning English; when you are learning a foreign language, mistakes are also inevitable. With daily practice, however, your fluency in German will rapidly increase.

2. **Ihr Name bitte!** *(Your name please. Ask classmates for their name and then to spell it.)*

BEISPIEL: Wie heißen Sie?   **Ich heiße Stefan Nentwig.**
             Wie schreibt man das?   *(Spell Nentwig in German.)*

3. **Wie schreibt man das?** *(How do you write that? Ask your partner to spell the following words in German.)*

BMW, VW, AUDI, UPS, USA; Autobahn, Kindergarten, Gesundheit, Zwieback, Strudel

4. **Schreiben Sie, was ich buchstabiere!** *(Write down what I spell. Pick one of the new words from your new vocabulary. Then ask a partner to write down what you spell. Take turns.)*

Aussprache *(Pronunciation):* a, e, er, i, o, u

(Read also Part II. 1–21 in the Pronunciation Guide of the Workbook.)

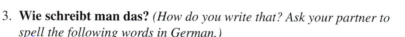

CD 1, Track 9

The words listed below are either familiar words, cognates (words related to English), or proper names (**Erika, Amerika**). A simplified phonetic spelling for each sound is given in brackets. The colon (:) following a vowel means that the vowel is long. Pay particular attention to word stress as you hear it from your instructor or the tape. For a while, you may want to mark words for stress.

Hören Sie gut zu und wiederholen Sie! *(Listen carefully and repeat.)*

[a:]	**A**bend, T**a**g, B**a**n**a**ne, N**a**me, j**a**
[a]	**A**nna, **A**lbert, w**a**s, H**a**nd, d**a**nke
[e:]	**E**rika, P**e**ter, Am**e**rika, g**e**ht, T**ee**
[e]	**E**llen, H**e**rmann, **e**s, schl**e**cht
[ə]	*(unstressed e)* Ut**e**, dank**e**, heiß**e**, Ihn**e**n, Gut**e**n Morg**e**n!
[ʌ]	*(final -er)* Diet**er** Fiedl**er**, Rain**er** Mei**er**, Wern**er** Schneid**er**
[i:]	**Ih**nen, Mar**i**a, Sab**i**ne, w**ie**, S**ie**
[i]	**i**ch b**i**n, b**i**tte, n**i**cht, Schr**i**tt
[o:]	M**o**nika, H**o**se, s**o**, w**o**, Z**oo**
[o]	**O**skar, **o**ft, M**o**rgen, S**o**mmer, k**o**sten
[u:]	**U**te, G**u**drun, g**u**t, N**u**del, Sch**uh**
[u]	**u**nd, w**u**nderbar, Ges**u**ndheit, H**u**nger, B**u**tter

- As you may have noticed, double vowels (**Tee, Boot**), vowels followed by **h** (**geht, Schuh**), and the combination **ie** (**wie, Sie**) are long. Vowels followed by double consonants (two identical consonants as in **Anna, Sommer**) are short.

For pronunciation practice, have students do the pronunciation exercises on the Lab Audio CDs. The exercises are printed in the Workbook.

Schritt 2
Step 2

Gespräche + Wortschatz

Was und wie ist das?

DEUTSCHPROFESSORIN	Hören Sie jetzt gut zu und antworten Sie auf Deutsch! Was ist das?
JIM MILLER	Das ist der Bleistift.
DEUTSCHPROFESSORIN	Welche Farbe hat der Bleistift?
SUSAN SMITH	Gelb.
DEUTSCHPROFESSORIN	Bilden Sie bitte einen Satz!
SUSAN SMITH	Der Bleistift ist gelb.
DEUTSCHPROFESSORIN	Ist das Heft auch gelb?
DAVID JENKINS	Nein, das Heft ist nicht gelb. Das Heft ist hellblau.
DEUTSCHPROFESSORIN	Gut!
SUSAN SMITH	Was bedeutet *hellblau*?
DEUTSCHPROFESSORIN	*Hellblau* bedeutet *light blue* auf Englisch.
SUSAN SMITH	Und wie sagt man *dark blue*?
DEUTSCHPROFESSORIN	*Dunkelblau.*
SUSAN SMITH	Ah, der Kuli ist dunkelblau.
DEUTSCHPROFESSORIN	Richtig! Das ist alles für heute. Für morgen lesen Sie bitte das Gespräch noch einmal und lernen Sie auch die Wörter!

Warm-ups: 1. **Guten Tag! Ich heiße . . . Wie heißen Sie? Heißen Sie . . . ? Ja/nein . . . 2. Wie geht's? Geht es Ihnen gut? Ja/nein . . . 3. Ich sage „Guten Tag!" Was sagen Sie?**

CD 1, Track 10

Act out the dialogue as you introduce it, so that students understand most of it without reference to the English translation in the Appendix. Bring a yellow pencil, a light-blue notebook, and a blue ballpoint pen.

Jetzt sind Sie dran! *(Now it's your turn. Once you have familiarized yourself with the new vocabulary, create your own dialogue with a partner talking about items in the classroom and their colors.)*

Wortschatz

- In English, the DEFINITE ARTICLE has just one form: *the*. The German singular definite article has three forms: **der, das, die.** Some nouns take **der** and are called MASCULINE; some take **das** and are called NEUTER; and some take **die** and are called FEMININE. This is a grammatical distinction and has little to do with biological sex, although it is true that most nouns referring to females are feminine and most referring to males are masculine.

  der Herr, **die** Frau, BUT **das** Kind *(child)*

  Inanimate objects such as *table, book,* and *blackboard* can be of any gender.

  der Tisch, **das** Buch, **die** Tafel

Because the gender of many nouns is unpredictable, you must always learn the article with the noun.

- In German the plural of nouns is formed in various ways that are often unpredictable. You must therefore learn the plural together with the article and the noun. Plurals are given in an abbreviated form in vocabulary lists and in dictionaries. These are the most common plural forms and their abbreviations.

Abbreviation	Listing	Plural Form
-	das Fenster, **-**	die Fenster
¨	der Mantel, **¨**	die Mäntel
-e	der Tisch, **-e**	die Tische
¨e	der Stuhl, **¨e**	die Stühle
-er	das Bild, **-er**	die Bilder
¨er	das Buch, **¨er**	die Bücher
-en	die Frau, **-en**	die Frauen
-n	die Farbe, **-n**	die Farben
-nen	die Professorin, **-nen**	die Professorinnen
-s	der Kuli, **-s**	die Kulis

NOTE: The plural article for all nouns is **die.** In this book, when the noun is not followed by one of the plural endings, it either does not have a plural or the plural is rarely used.

Die Farbe, -n *(color)*

blau   rot   orange   gelb

grün

braun   grau   rosa   schwarz   weiß

Das Zimmer, - *(room)*

der Bleistift, -e	*pencil*	das Heft, -e	*notebook*
Kuli, -s	*pen*	Papier, -e	*paper*
Stuhl, ¨e	*chair*	die Kreide	*chalk*
Tisch, -e	*table*	Tafel, -n	*blackboard*
das Bild, -er	*picture*	Tür, -en	*door*
Buch, ¨er	*book*	Wand, ¨e	*wall*
Fenster, -	*window*		

Weiteres *(Additional words and phrases)*

auf Deutsch / auf Englisch	*in German / in English*
für morgen	*for tomorrow*
hier / da	*here / there*
noch einmal	*again, once more*
richtig / falsch	*correct, right / wrong, false*
Was ist das?	*What is that?*
Das ist (nicht) . . .	*That is (not) . . .*
Welche Farbe hat . . .?	*What color is . . .?*
Was bedeutet . . .?	*What does . . . mean?*
Wie sagt man . . .?	*How does one say . . .?*
Wo ist . . .?	*Where is . . .?*
antworten	*to answer*
fragen	*to ask*
hören	*to hear*
lernen	*to learn; to study*
lesen	*to read*
sagen	*to say*
wiederholen	*to repeat*
sein	*to be*
ich bin	*I am*
es ist	*it is*
sie sind	*they are*
Sie sind	*you (formal) are*

Zum Erkennen: Hören Sie gut zu! *(Listen carefully!);* Bilden Sie einen Satz! *(Make a sentence.);* hell(grün) / dunkel(blau) *(light[green] / dark[blue]);* Das ist alles für heute. *(That's all for today.);* das Gespräch, -e *(dialogue, conversation);* das Wort, ⁻er *(word);* AUCH: der Artikel, - *(von) (article [of]);* der Plural, -e *(von) (plural [of]);* Alle zusammen! *(All together!);* Jetzt sind Sie dran! *(Now it's your turn.)*

Mündliche Übungen

A. Mustersätze

1. der Tisch: **Das ist** der Tisch.
   das Zimmer, die Tür, der Stuhl
2. das Papier: **Wo ist** das Papier? **Da ist** das Papier.
   der Kuli, die Kreide, das Bild
3. das Buch: **Ist das** das Buch? **Ja, das ist** das Buch.
   der Bleistift, das Fenster, die Tür
4. die Tafel: **Ist das** die Tafel? **Nein, das ist nicht** die Tafel.
   der Tisch, das Papier, der Stuhl
5. schwarz: **Das ist** schwarz.
   rot, gelb, weiß
6. der Bleistift: **Welche Farbe hat** der Bleistift?
   der Kuli, das Buch, die Tafel
7. lesen: Lesen **Sie bitte!**
   antworten, hören, fragen, lernen, wiederholen

B. Fragen und Antworten *(Questions and answers)*

1. Ist das Papier weiß? **Ja, das Papier ist weiß.**
   Ist das Buch gelb? die Tafel grün? die Kreide weiß? der Kuli rot?
2. Ist die Kreide grün? **Nein, die Kreide ist nicht grün.**
   Ist die Tafel rot? der Bleistift weiß? das Buch rosa? das Papier braun?

CD 1, Track 10

A: Bring with you a pencil, a ball-point pen, some paper, a picture, and items with the colors mentioned.

B: Modify the sentences to fit your particular surroundings.

3. Die Kreide ist weiß. Ist das richtig? **Ja, das ist richtig.**
Das Heft ist schwarz. Ist das richtig? **Nein, das ist nicht richtig.**
Das Papier ist weiß. Die Tür ist orange. Der Kuli ist blau. Das Buch ist rosa. Der Tisch ist braun.

4. Ist das richtig? *(Is that correct? Ask a partner whether certain items are indeed the color you say they are. Take turns.)*

C.1: a. **Guten Abend!** b. **Ich bin müde.** c. **Auf Wiedersehen! / Tschüss!**

Play the "Alphabet Game," by assigning each student a letter, including those with an umlaut. As you say a particular word (e.g., **Farbe**), one "letter" after the other will stand up and "identify itself" **(F, A, R, B, E).** Then the whole class repeats the word.

C. **Wiederholung** *(Review)*
1. **Was sagen sie?** *(What are they saying?)*

a.   b.   c.

2. **Wie schreibt man das?** *(How does one write that? Ask a partner to spell the following animals in German.)*

Elefant, Maus, Tiger, Löwe, Katze, Hund, Giraffe, Hamster, Ratte, Goldfisch, Dinosaurier, Känguru

3. **Was buchstabiere ich?** *(What am I spelling? Think of any German word or name and spell it in German without saying the word. Let your partner write it down and read it back to you.)*

D. **Artikel, Plurale und Farben** *(Determine the articles and plurals of the nouns listed below and ask questions about the colors of your German textbook.)*
1. Was ist der Artikel? **Tür → die Tür**
Zimmer, Bleistift, Bild, Kreide, Kuli, Stuhl, Tafel, Buch, Tisch, Fenster, Farbe, Papier, Wand, Heft, Wort, Herr, Frau
2. Was ist der Plural? **Kuli → die Kulis**
Tür, Bild, Bleistift, Buch, Heft, Tisch, Fenster, Tafel, Stuhl, Wort, Farbe
3. Welche Farben hat das Deutschbuch?

Aussprache: ä, ö, ü, eu, äu, ei, ie

(Read also Part II. 22–41 in the Pronunciation Guide of the Workbook.)

CD 1, Track 10

[e.] For most speakers, **Erika** and **Käthe** have the same long vowel. For [ö:] and [ü:] you may need the additional examples in the Workbook. The easiest way to learn to say [ö:] and [ü:] is to start from the tongue position for [e:] and [i:] and then round the lips. [ü:] and [ö:] need to be reviewed regularly, as students find it hard to hear and make these sounds.

Hören Sie gut zu und wiederholen Sie!

[e:]	Erika, Käthe, geht, lesen, Gespräch
[e]	Ellen Keller, Wände, Hände, hängen
[ö:]	Öl, hören, Löwenbräu, Goethe, Österreich
[ö]	Ötker, Pöppel, Wörter
[ü:]	Tür, für, Stühle, Bücher, müde, grün, typisch
[ü]	Jürgen Müller, Günter, müssen, tschüss
[oi]	Deutsch, freut, Europa, Löwenbräu
[au]	Frau Paula Bauer, auf, auch, blaugrau
[ai]	Rainer, Kreide, weiß, heißen, nein

• Pay special attention to the pronunciation of **ei** and **ie** (as in *Einstein's niece*):

[ai]	heißen, Heidi Meier, Heinz Beyer
[i:]	Sie, wie, Dieter Fiedler, Wiedersehen
[ai / i:]	Beispiel, Heinz Fiedler, Heidi Thielemann

Gespräche + Wortschatz

Im Kaufhaus

VERKÄUFERIN	Na, wie ist die Hose?
CHRISTIAN	Zu groß und zu lang.
VERKÄUFERIN	Und der Pulli?
MAIKE	Zu teuer.
CHRISTIAN	Aber die Farben sind toll. Schade!
VERKÄUFERIN	Guten Tag! Was darf's sein?
SILVIA	Ich brauche ein paar Bleistifte und Papier. Was kosten die Bleistifte?
VERKÄUFERIN	Fünfundfünfzig Cent (€ 0,55).
SILVIA	Und das Papier hier?
VERKÄUFERIN	Zwei Euro vierzig (€ 2,40).
SILVIA	Gut. Ich nehme sechs Bleistifte und das Papier.
VERKÄUFERIN	Ist das alles?
SILVIA	Ja, danke.
VERKÄUFERIN	Fünf Euro siebzig (€ 5,70) bitte!

CD 1, Track 11

Jetzt sind Sie dran! *(Now it's your turn. Once you have familiarized yourself with the new vocabulary, create your own dialogue. Ask a partner about certain items or going shopping in a store.)*

Warm-ups: 1. **Guten Tag! Wie geht es Ihnen?** 2. **Was ist das?** Point to various items in the classroom. 3. **Welche Farbe hat . . . ?** Ask for colors. 4. **Was sind Wörter mit B (F, H, T . . .)?**

Wortschatz

Die Zahl, -en *(number)*

1 eins	11 elf	21 einundzwanzig	0 null
2 zwei[1]	12 zwölf	22 zweiundzwanzig	10 zehn
3 drei	13 dreizehn	30 dreißig	100 hundert
4 vier	14 vierzehn	40 vierzig	101 hunderteins
5 fünf	15 fünfzehn	50 fünfzig	200 zweihundert
6 sechs	16 se**ch**zehn	60 se**ch**zig	1 000 tausend
7 sieben	17 sie**b**zehn	70 sie**b**zig	1 001 tausendeins
8 acht	18 achtzehn	80 achtzig	10 000 zehntausend
9 neun	19 neunzehn	90 neunzig	100 000 hunderttausend
10 zehn	20 zwanzig	100 hundert	1 000 000 eine Million

As a memory aid, note these similarities between English and German:

-**zehn** = -*teen*	vier**zehn** = *fourteen*	
-**zig** = -*ty*	vier**zig** = *forty*	

- 21–29, 31–39, and so on to 91–99 follow the pattern of "four-and-twenty (**vierundzwanzig**) blackbirds baked in a pie."
- German numbers above twelve are seldom written out, except on checks. When they are written out, however, they are written as one word, no matter how long:

  234 567

  zweihundertvierunddreißigtausendfünfhundertsiebenundsechzig

- German uses a period or a space, where English uses a comma, and vice versa:

  € 2,75   BUT $2.75

  € 1 600,00 (or € 1.600,00)   BUT $1,600.00.

- The numbers 1 and 7 are written differently. See illustration.

1
EINS

7
SIEBEN

Lerntipp
How does **Wie geht's?** *work?*

Take a few minutes to get acquainted with **Wie geht's?**. Read the table of contents, and see how each chapter is organized. See how the audio activities in your book correspond to your Text CD and the Lab Audio CDs. You can also watch the *Minidramas* and the *Blickpunkt* segments on the Video, or explore the chapter themes online through the Web site, where you can also find self-assessment tests to help you review what you've learned. The Web address is **http://wiegehts.heinle.com**.

[1] Occasionally, to reduce confusion with **drei,** speakers will use the term **zwo** as a substitute for **zwei,** especially on the phone.

Die Kleidung *(clothing)*

If students ask: *blazer* **der Blazer, -;** *boot* **der Stiefel, -;** *cap* **das Käppi, -s;** *cardigan* **die Strickjacke, -n;** *Jeans skirt* **der Jeansrock, ̈-e;** *miniskirt* **der Minirock, ̈-e;** *overall* **die Latzhose, -n;** *sandal* **die Sandale, -n;** *sneaker* **der Tennisschuh, -e;** *lady's suit* **das Kostüm, -e;** *pant suit* **der Hosenanzug, ̈-e;** *sportsshoe* **der Sportschuh, -e;** *turtleneck sweater* **der Rollkragenpullover, -;** *vest* **die Weste, -n**

das T-Shirt, -s   der Mantel, ̈   das Hemd, -en   die Jeans, -(pl)² die Hose, -n¹   die Bluse, -n

der Schuh, -e

das Sweatshirt, -s   die Jacke, -n   das Kleid, -er   der Pullover, der Pulli, -s   der Rock, ̈-e

---

² Note that **die Hose** is singular in German; **die Jeans,** however, is plural.

Das Gegenteil, -e *(opposite)*

dick / dünn	*thick, fat / thin, skinny*
groß / klein	*tall, big, large / short, small, little*
lang / kurz	*long / short*
langsam / schnell	*slow(ly) / fast, quick(ly)*
neu / alt	*new / old*
sauber / schmutzig	*clean, neat / dirty*
teuer / billig	*expensive / inexpensive, cheap*

The vocabulary of *Schritt 3* is rather large. Help students learn it by reviewing for several days the numbers and articles of clothing around you. Don't expect students to master all of it overnight.

Weiteres

aber	*but, however*
oder	*or*
zu	*too (+ adjective or adverb)*
wie viel? / wie viele?	*how much / how many?*
kosten	*to cost, come to (a certain amount)*
Was kostet / kosten . . . ?	*How much is / are . . .?*
Das kostet . . .	*That comes to . . .*
brauchen	*to need*
nehmen	*to take*
zählen	*to count*
ich zähl**e**	*I count*
wir	*we count*
sie } zähl**en**	*they count*
Sie	*you (formal) count*
der Cent, -s	*cent*
der Euro, -s	*euro*
ein Cent (zehn Euro)	*one cent (ten euros)*

Zum Erkennen: im Kaufhaus *(in the department store);* der Verkäufer, - / die Verkäuferin, -nen *(sales clerk);* na *(well);* toll *(super);* Schade! *(Too bad!);* Was darf's sein? *(May I help you?);* ein paar *(a couple of);* Ist das alles? *(Is that all?);* AUCH: von . . . bis *(from . . . to);* die Seite, -n *(page);* auf Seite . . . *(on page . . .);* der Preis, -e *(price);* Wie ist die Telefonnummer / Adresse (von) . . . ? *(What's the phone number / address of . . . ?);* das Beispiel, -e *(example);* Wie geht's weiter? *(What comes next?)*

Fokus — *Trendsetters of the Fashion World*

German fashion has always been known for outstanding quality and workmanship, but it is also beginning to have more of an impact on international fashion trends. Today, Jil Sander, Joop, and Hugo Boss are well-known names in every major city. Fresh ideas are also coming from the German "eco-fashion" scene: Britta Steilmann, for example, has explored new and interesting directions with her collections made of environmentally friendly materials. Twice a year, fashion takes center stage in the trade fair metropolises of Berlin, Düsseldorf, Cologne, and Munich. There, international designers and manufacturers meet with retail buyers to set the latest styles for the coming season.

Mündliche Übungen

A. Mustersätze

1. der Schuh: **Das ist** der Schuh.
   die Jacke, das Hemd, der Mantel, der Pulli
2. die Jacke / grau: **Ist** die Jacke grau? **Ja,** die Jacke **ist** grau.
   die Hose / braun; der Rock / blau; die Bluse / rosa; der Pullover / rot
3. der Mantel / lang: **Ist** der Mantel lang? **Nein,** der Mantel **ist nicht** lang.
   das Hemd / schmutzig; das Kleid / neu; der Pulli / dick; das Sweatshirt / teuer
4. Schuhe / groß: **Sind** die Schuhe groß? **Nein,** die Schuhe **sind nicht** groß.
   die Röcke / kurz; Mäntel / dünn; T-Shirts / blau; Jeans / schwarz
5. das Papier: **Was kostet** das Papier?
   das Heft, der Mantel, die Jacke, der Pulli
6. Bleistifte: **Was kosten** die Bleistifte?
   Kulis, Bücher, Bilder, Schuhe, Jeans

CD I, Track II

A.1: Make use of gestures and point to the various objects. Vary the cues and add to them, especially when books are closed. Make use of actual objects carried or worn by your students.

B. Hören Sie gut zu und wiederholen Sie!

1. Wir zählen von eins bis zehn: eins, zwei, drei, vier, fünf, sechs, sieben, acht, neun, zehn.
2. Wir zählen von zehn bis zwanzig: zehn, elf, zwölf, dreizehn, vierzehn, fünfzehn, sechzehn, siebzehn, achtzehn, neunzehn, zwanzig.
3. Wir zählen von zwanzig bis dreißig: zwanzig, einundzwanzig, zweiundzwanzig, dreiundzwanzig, vierundzwanzig, fünfundzwanzig, sechsundzwanzig, siebenundzwanzig, achtundzwanzig, neunundzwanzig, dreißig.
4. Wir zählen von zehn bis hundert: zehn, zwanzig, dreißig, vierzig, fünfzig, sechzig, siebzig, achtzig, neunzig, hundert.
5. Wir zählen von hundert bis tausend: hundert, zweihundert, dreihundert, vierhundert, fünfhundert, sechshundert, siebenhundert, achthundert, neunhundert, tausend.

You could introduce Exercise B on the first day by repeating several times in chorus the numbers from 1 to 12, 13 to 20, 21 to 30, 31 to 100, and do Exercise C the next day. Keep reviewing numbers. To sharpen listening skills, say a few every day and let students write them as numerals.

C. Zahlen

1. **Seitenzahlen** *(page numbers).* Lesen Sie laut auf Deutsch!

   Seite 1, 7, 8, 9, 11, 12, 17, 21, 25, 32, 43, 54, 66, 89, 92, 101

When counting, Germans use the thumb (not the index finger) to indicate number 1. Have students count students, women, men, fingers, feet, windows, chairs, etc.

2. **Inventar** *(With an employee, played by a partner, take inventory of the items you have in stock in your store.)*

   BEISPIEL: Jacke / 32
   Wie viele Jacken? — Zweiunddreißig Jacken.

a. Pullover / 42	d. Kleid / 19	g. Sweatshirt / 89
b. Rock / 14	e. Hose / 21	h. T-Shirt / 37
c. Hemd / 66	f. Jeans / 102	i. Schuh / 58

3. **Preise**
   a. **Lesen Sie laut!**

   € 0,25 / € 0,75 / € 1,10 / € 2,50 / € 8,90 / € 30,00 / € 45,54 / € 80,88

Show some euros and explain their value in relation to the dollar. As this book went to press, one euro = approx. 90 US cents.

   b. **Sonderangebote** *(Specials. Ask your partner about prices and colors of the clothes shown below. How much would these cost here in your country?)*

Shirt € 25,53
Hose € 35,73
Stiefel € 65,30
Pullover € 25,51
kurzer Rock € 30,62
langer Rock € 40,87

Hemd € 18,38
Jeans € 23,01
Schuh € 40,87

Note: When asking various Germans, we found out that the phrase **Wie ist** (or **Wie lautet**) **die Adresse / Telefonnummer?** seems to be just as common as **Was ist die Telefonnummer / Adresse?** Officially, however, **Was ist . . . ?** is an Anglicism.

4. **Telefonnummern und Adressen**
   a. **Wie ist die Telefonnummer und die Adresse?** *(Ask each other for the phone number and address of persons listed below. Note that, in German telephone books, the hyphen following a name usually indicates "street", e.g.,* **Bach-** = **Bachstraße.)**

   BEISPIEL: Wie ist die Telefonnummer von *(of)* Jutta Scheurer und was ist ihre Adresse?
   Die Nummer ist 4 27 18 12 (vier zwei sieben eins acht eins zwei *or* **vier siebenundzwanzig achtzehn zwölf) und die Adresse ist Wolfszugstraße 33.**

You could also have students circulate around the room, asking others for their phone numbers. They write down each number, then check by asking. **Ist das richtig? Ja, das ist richtig. Nein, das ist falsch.** When students are done, they could compile a class directory.

Scheufler Heike, Schiller-2	8 02 25 75	**Schiebel Renate**, Haydn-20	8 30 64 63
-Gisela, Dresdner-51	8 41 26 74	**Schiebold Heinz**, Hofmann-16	8 80 19 77
-Gustav, Schumann-8	4 11 65 75	-Katja, Busch-30	2 81 53 22
Scheumann Ulf, Zwingli-7	4 27 29 69	-Joachim, Lange-5	2 59 83 55
Scheurer Ingo, Schul-20b	2 84 48 43	**Schiebschick Kai**, Berliner-3	2 51 49 51
-Jutta, Wolfszug-33	4 27 18 12	**Schiedmeier Ina**, Torgauer 11	4 95 63 56
-Werner, Meißner- 8	4 41 46 40	**Schiedewitz Elke**, Schlüter-2	3 11 83 85
Scheurich Sven, Neue-5b	4 16 04 71	**Schiefer Birgit**, Ring-1	2 02 07 43
Scheuring Jan, Scheriner-9	2 59 15 91	-Christel, Park-17	2 84 13 08
-Jochen, Böttger-4	8 03 12 63	-Wolfgang, Werft-2	2 70 58 19
Schewe Cornelia, Tannen-3	8 80 82 35	**Schiefner Jobst**, Bahnhof-5	3 11 77 71
-Uwe, Blumen-1	2 81 34 51	-Manfred, Dom-3	3 13 93 62
Schibalski Paul, Bach-2a	4 21 94 83	**Schiffer Arndt**, Hohe-19	4 41 92 91
Schicht Carsten, Haupt-27	4 40 16 69	-Cornelia, Dürer-9	4 71 26 22
-Eberhard, Azaleenweg-3	8 38 72 78	-Dorothea, Niederauer-28	2 52 30 50
Schick Bettina, Görlitzer-12	8 36 33 78	-Torsten, Platanen-13	4 76 10 28
Schicke Detlef, Kant-16	2 01 24 71	**Schiffke Jens**, Oschatzer-33	4 96 79 83
-Oliver, Schäfer-10	2 61 01 96	**Schlachter Karl**, Leipziger-2	3 11 77 16
Schickedanz Ute, Bach-17	4 12 48 75	**Schlampi Mario**, Hofwiesen-7	3 10 49 18
Schickmann Udo, Park-31	4 11 26 61	**Schlaumann Hans**, Suttner-9	2 54 25 14

   b. **Wie ist Ihre Telefonnummer?** *(What's your phone number? Ask other students.)*

   BEISPIEL: Wie ist Ihre Telefonnummer?
   Meine Telefonnummer ist 2 46 01 95.

D. Wiederholung

1. **Fragen und Antworten** *(Ask each other the following questions.)*
   a. Wie geht es Ihnen? Sind Sie müde?
   b. Wie heißen Sie? Heißen Sie . . . ?
   c. Was ist das? Ist das . . . ? *(Point to items in the classroom.)*
   d. Welche Farbe hat der Tisch? die Tafel? . . .
   e. Was ist auch grün? blau? . . .

2. **Wie schreibt man das?** *(Ask your partner how to spell the following names. You can also add names to the list.)*

   Mozart, Beethoven, Strauß, Schönberg, Dürer, Barlach, Kandinsky, Goethe, Nietzsche, Aichinger, Wohmann, Einstein, Röntgen, Zeppelin, Schwarzenegger

E. Artikel, Plurale und Adjektive *(Ask your partner about the articles, plurals, and adjectives below.)*
1. Was ist der Artikel von Mantel? Kleidung? Pulli? Bluse? Hemd? Rock? Hose? Kleid? Jacke? Schuh? T-Shirt? . . .
2. Was ist der Plural von Schuh? Jacke? Rock? Kleid? Hemd? Bluse? Pullover? Mantel?
3. Sprechen Sie langsam oder schnell? Hören Sie gut oder schlecht? Sind Sie groß oder klein? Sind die Schuhe sauber oder schmutzig? . . .
4. Was ist das Gegenteil von richtig? alt? schlecht? schnell? billig? dick? da? nein? danke? . . .

F. Beschreiben Sie bitte! *(Describe some of your clothing or one or two items you have with you.)*

   BEISPIEL: Die Hose ist blau. Die Schuhe sind . . .

G. Kettenreaktion. Rechnen wir! *(Chain reaction. Let's do some counting!)*

1. **Wie viel ist das?** Lesen Sie laut!

   BEISPIEL: $4 + 4 = 8$ Vier plus vier ist acht.
                  $8 - 4 = 4$ **Acht minus vier ist vier.**

$3 + 2 = 5$	$8 + 1 = 9$	$8 - 2 = 6$
$7 + 3 = 10$	$10 - 2 = 8$	$7 - 6 = 1$
$1 + 1 = 2$	$9 - 4 = 5$	$5 - 5 = 0$

Explain to students that the pun is based on the word *Zehen*, "toes".

2. **Wie geht's weiter?** *(What comes next?)*

   a. $100 - 10 = 90$ b. $70 - 7 = 63$
       $90 - 10 = ?$ . . . $63 - 7 = ?$ . . .

H. Was sagen Sie? *(Read the dialogue in the left-hand column below. Then be prepared to enact a similar one with a partner, based on objects in the classroom.)*

S1	Ist das die Tafel?	**S1**	Ist das . . . ?
S2	Nein, das ist nicht die Tafel.	**S2**	Nein, das ist nicht . . .
	Das ist die Wand.		Das ist . . .
S1	Wo ist die Tafel?	**S1**	Wo ist . . . ?
S2	Da ist die Tafel.	**S2**	. . .
S1	Welche Farbe hat die Tafel?	**S1**	Welche Farbe hat . . . ?
S2	Die Tafel ist grün.	**S2**	. . . ist . . .
S1	Was ist auch grün?	**S1**	Was ist auch . . . ?
S2	Das Buch ist auch grün.	**S2**	. . . ist auch . . .
S1	Wie ist das Buch? Ist das Buch alt?	**S1**	Wie ist . . . ?
S2	Nein, das Buch ist neu.	**S2**	. . .

CD I, Track II

Aussprache: l, s, st, sp, sch, f, v, z

(Read also Part III. 1, 4, 6–9, 11–12 in the Pronunciation Guide of the Workbook.)

Hören Sie gut zu und wiederholen Sie!

[l]	lernen, lesen, Pullover, toll, Mantel, Tafel
[z]	sie sind, sieben, sauber, langsam, Bluse, Hose
[s]	Professorin, heißen, Preis, weiß, groß, alles
[st]	Fenster, kosten, ist
[št]	Stefan, Stuhl, Stein, Bleistift
[šp]	Sport, Beispiel, Gespräch, Aussprache
[š]	schnell, schlecht, schwarz, schade, falsch
[f]	fünf, fünfzehn, fünfzig, fünfhundertfünfundfünfzig
[f]	vier, vierzehn, vierzig, vierhundertvierundvierzig
[ts]	Zimmer, Zahl, zählen, zwei, zehn, zwölf, zwanzig, zweiundzwanzig, schmutzig, Satz
[z / ts]	sieben, siebzig, siebenundsiebzig, siebenhundertsiebenundsiebzig

Initial **z** [ts] is difficult. Point out to students that they have no trouble with [ts] in *rats* or *pizza* and that initial **z** is the same sound.

Schritt 4
Step 4

Gespräche + Wortschatz

Das Wetter im April

CD I, Track I2

NORBERT	Es ist schön heute, nicht wahr?
JULIA	Ja, wirklich. Die Sonne scheint wieder!
RUDI	Nur der Wind ist kühl.
JULIA	Ach, das macht nichts.
NORBERT	Ich finde es toll.
HANNES	Mensch, so ein Sauwetter! Es schneit schon wieder.
MARTIN	Na und?
HANNES	In Mallorca ist es schön warm.
MARTIN	Wir sind aber hier und nicht in Mallorca.
HANNES	Schade!
DOROTHEA	Das Wetter ist furchtbar, nicht wahr?
MATTHIAS	Das finde ich auch. Es regnet und regnet!
SONJA	Und es ist wieder so kalt. Nur 7 Grad!
MATTHIAS	Ja, typisch April.

Warm-ups: 1. **Was ist das?** Point to various articles of clothing. 2. **Welche Farbe hat . . . ?** Let students tell you something about their clothes. 3. **Was sage ich?** Have students write down numerals, prices, or telephone numbers that they hear you say. 4. **Wie viel ist . . . ?** Give simple arithmetic problems. 4. **Was ist das Gegenteil von . . . ?**

Inverted word order will be presented in Chapter 1.

Jetzt sind Sie dran! *(Based on the new vocabulary, create your own dialogue with a partner talking about the weather and how you like it.)*

Note: **der Frühling,** BUT **das Frühjahr.** The latter is not mentioned in this book.

Wortschatz

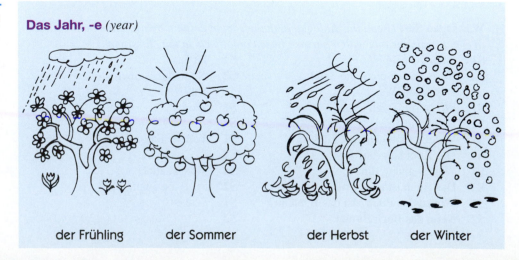

Das Jahr, -e *(year)*

der Frühling	der Sommer	der Herbst	der Winter

Der Monat, -e *(month)*[1]

Die Woche, -n *(week)*

Der Tag, -e *(day)*

der	Montag[1]	*Monday*	der	Januar	*January*
	Dienstag	*Tuesday*		Februar	*February*
	Mittwoch	*Wednesday*		März	*March*
	Donnerstag	*Thursday*		April	*April*
	Freitag	*Friday*		Mai	*May*
	Samstag[2]	*Saturday*		Juni	*June*
	Sonntag	*Sunday*		Juli	*July*
				August	*August*
				September	*September*
				Oktober	*October*
				November	*November*
				Dezember	*December*

Das Wetter *(weather)*

Es ist . . .	*It's . . .*	heiß / kalt	*hot / cold*
Es regnet.	*It's raining.*	warm / kühl	*warm / cool*
Es schneit.	*It's snowing.*	furchtbar	*awful, terrible*
Die Sonne scheint.	*The sun is shining.*	prima	*great, wonderful*
		schön	*nice, beautiful*
		super	*superb, super*
		toll	*great, terrific*
		windig	*windy*

Weiteres

Die Woche hat sieben Tage.	*The week has seven days.*
heute / morgen	*today / tomorrow*
nur	*only*
sehr	*very*
(schon) wieder	*(already) again*
wirklich	*really, indeed*
Schade!	*Too bad!*
nicht wahr?	*isn't it? isn't this true?*
Wann sind Sie geboren?	*When were you born?*
Ich bin im Mai[3] geboren.	*I was born in May.*
finden	*to find*
Ich finde es . . .	*I think it's . . .*
Das finde ich auch.	*I think so, too.*

---

[1] Note that the days, months, and seasons are all masculine!

[2] People in northern and central Germany prefer **Sonnabend,** those in southern Germany **Samstag** (derived from the Hebrew word *Sabbat*).

[3] **Im** is used with the names of the months and seasons: **im Mai, im Winter.**

Zum Erkennen: der Wind *(wind);* Das macht nichts. *(It doesn't matter. That's okay.);* Mensch, so ein Sauwetter! *(Man, what lousy weather!);* Na und? *(So what?);* wir sind *(we are);* Grad *(degrees);* typisch *(typically);* AUCH: Hören Sie gut zu! *(Listen carefully!);* die Jahreszeit, -en *(season);* die Temperatur, -en *(temperature)*

Mündliche Übungen

A. Hören Sie gut zu und wiederholen Sie!

1. Das Jahr hat vier Jahreszeiten. Die Jahreszeiten heißen Frühling, Sommer, Herbst und Winter.

Lerntipp
Learning Vocabulary

To remember vocabulary, you must use it. Name things as you see them in the course of your day. Label objects in your room or home, using index cards. Practice new words aloud—the use of your auditory and motor memory will quadruple your learning efficiency. Be sure to learn the gender and plural with each noun. For some, the gender and plural are predictable; study Part 1 in the Appendix.

If students ask: *cloudy* **bewölkt;** *foggy* **neblig;** *humid* **schwül;** *there's lightning* **es blitzt;** *it's pouring* **es gießt;** *stormy* **stürmisch;** *sunny* **sonnig;** *it's thundering* **es donnert;** *wet* **nass**

CD 1, Track 12

A: Read and practice in chorus several times.

2. Das Jahr hat zwölf Monate. Die Monate heißen Januar, Februar, März, April, Mai, Juni, Juli, August, September, Oktober, November und Dezember.

3. Die Woche hat sieben Tage. Die Tage heißen Montag, Dienstag, Mittwoch, Donnerstag, Freitag, Samstag und Sonntag.

B. Mustersätze

1. schön: **Es ist heute** schön.
   kühl, windig, warm
2. sehr kalt: **Es ist** sehr kalt.
   sehr heiß, schön warm, furchtbar kalt
3. toll: **Ich finde es** toll.
   gut, prima, wunderbar, furchtbar
4. Juli: **Ich bin im** Juli **geboren.**
   Januar, März, Sommer, Winter
5. 19: **Ich bin** neunzehn.
   16, 20, 27, 31

B: Act out the meaning of these adjectives.

C: After mastering this pattern, you could ask students all sorts of questions that they would answer with *yes* or *no*. Better yet, have students ask each other questions and give their own answers.

C. Wiederholung

1. **Antworten Sie mit JA!**

   BEISPIEL: Wiederholen Sie das noch einmal?
   Ja, ich wiederhole das noch einmal.

   a. Lesen Sie das auf Deutsch? c. Brauchen Sie das Buch?
   b. Lernen Sie das für morgen? d. Nehmen Sie das Heft?

2. **Antworten Sie mit NEIN!**

   BEISPIEL: Ist das die Kreide?
   Nein, das ist nicht die Kreide.

   a. Ist das die Wand?   c. Sind das die Schuhe?
   b. Ist das der Pulli?   d. Sind das die Klassenzimmer?

   BEISPIEL: Ist die Kreide gelb?
   Nein, die Kreide ist nicht gelb.

   e. Ist die Antwort richtig?   g. Ist das Wetter gut?
   f. Ist die Farbe schön?   h. Ist das typisch?

3. **Zahlen**
   a. **Wie geht's weiter?** *(Add to or subtract from a previous sum. Continue from one person to another.)*
   b. **Was kostet das?** *(Write prices on the board for others to read aloud.)*

C.4: a. **neu / alt** b. **schmutzig / sauber** c. **dünn / dick** d. **klein / groß** e. **kurz / lang**

4. **Gegenteile** *(Tell which German adjectives best describe each pair.)*

D. Fragen

1. Wie ist das Wetter hier im Winter? im Sommer? im Frühling? im Herbst?
2. Was ist der Artikel von Montag? September? Herbst? Juni? Monat? Jahr? Woche?
3. Welcher Tag ist heute? morgen?
4. Wie viele Tage hat die Woche? Wie heißen die Tage?
5. Wie viele Tage hat der September? der Oktober? der Februar?
6. Wie viele Monate hat das Jahr? Wie heißen die Monate?
7. Wie viele Wochen hat das Jahr?
8. Wie viele Jahreszeiten hat das Jahr? Wie heißen die Jahreszeiten?
9. Wie heißen die Wintermonate? die Sommermonate? die Herbstmonate?
10. Wie ist das Wetter heute? Scheint die Sonne oder regnet es?

E. Temperaturen. European thermometers use the Celsius scale. On that scale, water freezes at 0°C and boils at 100°C. Normal body temperature is about 37°C, and fever starts at about 37.6°C. To convert Fahrenheit units into Celsius, subtract 32, multiply by 5, divide by 9. To convert Celsius degrees into Fahrenheit, multiply by 9, divide by 5, add 32.

1. **Wie viel Grad Celsius sind das?** (*How many degrees Celsius? Use the thermometer as a reference.*)

   BEISPIEL: 32°F = 0°C
   Zweiunddreißig Grad Fahrenheit sind null Grad Celsius.

   100°F, 96°F, 84°F, 68°F, 41°F, 23°F, −4°F, −13°F

2. **Wie ist das Wetter?** (*What's the weather like?*)

   BEISPIEL: 12°C (zwölf Grad Celsius)
   Es ist kühl.

   21°C, 0°C, 30°C, 38°C, −10°C, −25°C

TEMPERATUREN

GRAD

Fahrenheit	Celsius	Körpertemperatur
100	38	
98.6	37	←
96	36	
95	35	
94	34	
90	32	
86	30	
84	29	
82	28	
79	26	
77	25	
72	22	
70	21	
68	20	
64	18	
59	15	
53	12	
50	10	
46	8	
41	5	
37	3	
32	0	Gefrierpunkt
28	− 2	
23	− 5	
14	−10	
5	−15	
− 4	−20	
−13	−25	

E.2: 21°C = **schön**, 0°C = **kalt**, 30°C = **sehr schön**, 38°C = **heiß**, −10°C = **sehr kalt**, − 25°C = **furchtbar kalt**

Aussprache: r; p, t, k; final b, d, g; j, h

(*Read also Part III. 1–3, 10, 17 in the Pronunciation Guide of the Workbook.*)

Hören Sie gut zu und wiederholen Sie!

[r]	**r**ichtig, **r**egnet, **r**ot, **r**osa, b**r**aun, g**r**ün, F**r**eitag, le**r**nen, hö**r**en
[ʌ]	wi**r**, vie**r**, nu**r**, ode**r**, abe**r**, saube**r**, teue**r**, Wette**r**, Somme**r**, Winte**r**
	BUT [ʌ / r] Tü**r** / Tü**r**en; Papie**r** / Papie**r**e; Jah**r** / Jah**r**e
[p]	**P**ulli, **P**lural, **p**lus, **p**rima
	AND [p] Herb**st**, Jako**b**, gel**b**, hal**b**
	BUT [p / b] gel**b** / gel**b**e; hal**b** / hal**b**e
[t]	**Th**eo, **T**ür, Doro**th**ea, Mat**th**ias, bi**tt**e
	AND [t] un**d**, **t**ausend, Bil**d**, Klei**d**, Hem**d**, Wan**d**
	BUT [t / d] Bil**d** / Bil**d**er; Klei**d** / Klei**d**er; Hem**d** / Hem**d**en; Wan**d** / Wän**d**e
[k]	**k**ühl, **k**urz, **K**uli, dan**k**e
	AND [k] sa**g**t, fra**g**t, Ta**g**
	BUT [k / g] sa**g**t / sa**g**en; fra**g**t / fra**g**en; Ta**g** / Ta**g**e
[j]	**j**a, **J**ahr, **J**anuar, **J**uni, **J**uli
[h]	**h**ören, **h**eiß, **h**at, **h**eute
[ː]	zä**h**len, ne**h**men, I**h**nen, Stu**h**l, Schu**h**

CD 1, Track 12

The **r** requires substantial practice. For additional examples, use German names: **Renate, Rita, Rainer, Rudolf, Karin, Barbara, Marion, Marika, Andreas, Friedrich, Gerhard, Hermann.**

Point out that **th** in German is [t]: **Ruth.** Final **b, d,** and **g** must be practiced repeatedly.

Frühling in Niedersachsen (*Lower Saxony*)

Looking at the weather map, have students ask each other what the weather is like in various places of Europe. **Das Wetter in Europa: 1. Wo scheint die Sonne? 2. Wo regnet es? 3. Wie warm ist es in . . . ? Ist das heiß (schön warm, kühl) oder kalt?**

Fokus — *The German Climate*

Although Germany lies between the 47th and 55th parallel north, roughly as far north as northern New England and southern Canada, its climate is generally far milder because of the effect of the Gulf Stream. Overall, Germany enjoys a temperate climate, ample rainfall throughout the year, and an absence of extreme heat and cold. In the northwest, summers tend to be cool and winters mild. Toward the east and south, the climate becomes more continental, with greater temperature differences between day and night, and summer and winter. Average daytime temperatures in Berlin are 30°F in January and 64°F in July; in Munich, they are 33°F in January and 73°F in July. Autumns are usually mild, sunny, and drier than other seasons. Between December and March, the mountainous regions of Germany can always expect snow. At the Zugspitze, the highest point in the German Alps, snow may pile up 13–16 feet. In the Black Forest, it may average 5 feet. (For information on the current weather in Germany, visit www.wetter.de.)

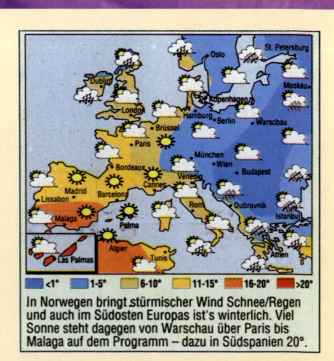

In Norwegen bringt stürmischer Wind Schnee/Regen und auch im Südosten Europas ist's winterlich. Viel Sonne steht dagegen von Warschau über Paris bis Malaga auf dem Programm – dazu in Südspanien 20°.

Gespräche + Wortschatz

Wie spät ist es?

RITA	Hallo, Axel! Wie spät ist es?
AXEL	Hallo, Rita! Es ist zehn vor acht.
RITA	Oje, in zehn Minuten habe ich Philosophie.
AXEL	Dann mach's gut, tschüss!
RITA	Ja, tschüss!
PHILLIP	Hallo, Steffi! Wie viel Uhr ist es denn?
STEFFI	Tag, Phillip! Es ist halb zwölf.
PHILLIP	Gehen wir jetzt essen?
STEFFI	O.K., die Vorlesung beginnt erst um Viertel nach eins.
HERR RICHTER	Wann sind Sie denn heute fertig?
HERR HEROLD	Um zwei. Warum?
HERR RICHTER	Spielen wir heute Tennis?
HERR HEROLD	Ja, prima! Es ist jetzt halb eins. Um Viertel vor drei dann?
HERR RICHTER	Gut! Bis später!

CD 1, Track 13

Point out that the flavoring particle **denn** conveys what English expresses through gestures and intonation. Flavoring particles often have no exact English equivalent. (see Chapter 7, Section 7.3).

Jetzt sind Sie dran! *(Based on the new vocabulary, create your own dialogue with a partner. Ask for the time and talk about your plans for the rest of the day.)*

Warm-ups: 1. **Welcher Tag ist heute?** 2. **Wie ist das Wetter heute?** 3. **Wie viel ist das?** Have some students write larger numbers on the board and have others say them in German. 4. **Was kostet das?** Have students write prices on the board and have others read them in German. 5. **Wie viel ist . . . ?** Give students a long arithmetic problem, e.g., 5 + 4 = ? − 3 = ? − 11 − ? 6. **Was sind Wörter mit A (B, D, E . . .)?** 7. **Was ist dick / dünn** (groß / klein, kurz / lang, neu / alt, sauber / schmutzig, teuer / billig)?

Wortschatz

die Uhrzeit, -en *(time of day)*

- German has a formal (see Chapter 7) and informal way of telling time. The informal system is used in everyday speech and varies somewhat from region to region. The system below is a compromise, but certain to be understood everywhere.

Es ist ein Uhr.
Es ist eins.

Es ist zwei Uhr.
Es ist zwei.

Es ist Viertel nach zwei.

Es ist halb drei.

Es ist Viertel vor drei.

Es ist zehn (Minuten) vor drei.

Es ist fünf nach vier.

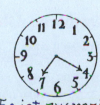

Es ist zwanzig (Minuten) nach sieben.

die Minute, -n	*minute*	morgens	*in the morning*
Sekunde, -n	*second*	mittags	*at noon*
Stunde, -n[1]	*hour*	nachmittags	*in the afternoon*
Uhr, -en	*watch, clock; o'clock*	abends	*in the evening*
Zeit, -en	*time*	Wie spät ist es?	*How late is it?*
		Wie viel Uhr ist es?	*What time is it?*

Weiteres

der Student, -en	*student (male)*
die Studentin, -nen	*student (female)*
der Kurs, -e	*course*
die Vorlesung, -en	*lecture, (university) class*
Es ist ein Uhr (zwei Uhr).[2]	*It's one o'clock (two o'clock).*
Es ist eins (zwei).	*It's one (two).*
(um) eins[2]	*(at) one o'clock*
(um) Viertel nach eins	*(at) quarter past one*
(um) halb zwei, 1.30[3]	*(at) half past one, 1:30*
(um) Viertel vor zwei, 1.45[3]	*(at) quarter to two, 1:45*
fertig	*finished, done*
jetzt	*now*
Bitte!	*here: You're welcome.*
beginnen	*to begin*
essen	*to eat*
gehen	*to go*
Tennis spielen	*to play tennis*
haben	*to have*
ich habe	*I have*
es hat	*it has*
wir	*we have*
sie } haben	*they have*
Sie	*you (formal) have*
Ich habe eine Frage.	*I have a question.*
Ich habe keine Zeit.	*I don't have time.*

---

[1] **Stunde** refers to duration or a particular class: **Die Deutschstunde ist von acht bis neun. Eine Stunde hat 60 Minuten. Uhr** refers to clock time: **Es ist 9 Uhr.**

[2] **um ein Uhr** BUT **um eins.**

[3] Until recently, there was a difference between English and German punctuation regarding time (*1:30* vs. **1.30**). Today, both styles are used. While digital clocks separate hours from minutes with a colon, newspapers and magazines commonly use a simple period.

Zum Erkennen: Oje*! (Oh no!);* denn *(flavoring particle used for emphasis);* erst *(only, not until);* warum? *(why?);* AUCH: Was tun Sie wann? *(What do you do when?);* der Kurs, -e *(course)*

Glockenturm *(bell tower)* in Innsbruck

CD 1, Track 13

Mündliche Übungen

A. Wie spät ist es?
1. 1.00: **Es ist** ein **Uhr.**
   3.00, 5.00, 7.00, 9.00, 11.00
2. 1.05: **Es ist** fünf **nach** eins.
   3.05, 9.10, 11.10, 4.20, 8.20
3. 1.15: **Es ist Viertel nach** eins.
   2.15, 4.15, 6.15, 8.15, 10.15

4. 1.30: **Es ist halb** zwei.
   2.30, 4.30, 6.30, 8.30, 10.30
5. 1.40: **Es ist** zwanzig **vor** zwei.
   5.40, 9.50, 1.50, 12.55, 4.55
6. 1.45: **Es ist Viertel vor** zwei.
   3.45, 5.45, 7.45, 9.45, 12.45

B. Wann ist die Vorlesung? *(When is the lecture?)*

1. 9.00: **Die Vorlesung ist um** neun.
   3.00, 1.00, 9.15, 12.15, 1.30, 3.30, 9.45, 12.45
2. 5: **Die Vorlesung beginnt in** fünf **Minuten.**
   2, 10, 12, 15, 20
3. morgens: **Die Vorlesung ist** morgens.
   nachmittags, abends, um acht, um Viertel nach acht, um halb neun, um Viertel vor neun.

C. Mustersätze

1. essen: Essen **Sie jetzt? Ja, ich** esse **jetzt.**
   gehen, fragen, lernen, antworten, beginnen
2. heute: **Ich spiele** heute **Tennis.**
   jetzt, morgens, nachmittags, abends, wieder
3. Sie: **Wann** sind Sie **heute fertig?**
   Horst, ich, Rolf und Maria, sie *(pl.)*
4. ich: Ich habe **keine Zeit.**
   wir, Maria, Maria und Rita

D. Wiederholung

1. **Wie ist das Wetter?**

D.1: a. **Es ist heiß.** b. **Es ist schön.** c. **Es ist windig.** d. **Es ist (sehr / furchtbar) kalt.**

a.   b.   c.   d.

2. **Wie fragen Sie?** *(Formulate the questions for these answers.)*

   BEISPIEL: Ja, ich bin müde.
               Sind Sie müde?
   a. Danke, gut.
   b. Das Buch ist grau.
   c. Nein, ich heiße nicht Fiedler.
   d. Da ist die Tür.
   e. Ja, ich spreche langsam.
   f. Das Papier kostet € 1,50.
   g. Heute ist es furchtbar heiß.
   h. Ich finde das nicht schön.
   i. Fünf plus sechzehn ist einundzwanzig.
   j. Nein, heute ist Dienstag.

D.2: a. **Wie geht's? / Wie geht es Ihnen?** b. **Welche Farbe hat das Buch?** c. **Heißen Sie Fiedler? / Sie heißen Fiedler, nicht wahr?** d. **Wo ist die Tür?** e. **Sprechen Sie langsam? / Sprechen Sie (bitte) langsam!** f. **Was kostet das Papier?** g. **Wie ist das Wetter heute?** h. **Wie finden Sie das?** i. **Wie viel ist 5 + 16?** j. **Ist heute Montag?**

3. **Und Sie?** *(Answer, then ask someone else.)*
   a. Wie alt sind Sie? **(Ich bin _____. Und Sie?)**
   b. Wo sind Sie geboren? **(Ich bin in _____ geboren. Und Sie?)**
   c. Wann sind Sie geboren? **(Ich bin im _____ geboren. Und Sie?)**

4. **Was tun Sie wann?** *(What do you do when? Use the drawings to discuss with other students what you like to do in various months and seasons.)*

    BEISPIEL: Was tun Sie im Sommer?
    Im Sommer spiele ich Tennis. Und Sie?

| Ski laufen | angeln | segeln | campen | Tennis spielen |

| joggen | reiten | schwimmen | Golf spielen | |

E. **Fragen und Antworten**

1. **Wie viele Stunden hat der Tag?** Wie viele Minuten hat die Stunde? Wie viele Sekunden hat die Minute? Wie viele Jahreszeiten hat das Jahr?

You could also write or have students write various clock times on the board and let the others read it aloud.

2. **Wie spät ist es?** Lesen Sie laut!

    8.45, 9.30, 10.15, 1.05, 2.20, 2.45, 6.59

3. **Wann essen Sie morgens, mittags und abends?** *(Ask each other when you eat your meals.)*

F. **Meine Kurse** *(Read the cue lines below, then use them to ask about your partner's schedule and to relate your own.)*

Biologie, Chemie, Deutsch, Englisch, Französisch *(French)*, Geographie, Geologie, Geschichte *(history)*, Informatik *(computer science)*, Kunst *(art)*, Latein, Mathe(matik), Musik, Philosophie, Physik, Politik, Psychologie, Soziologie, Spanisch, Sport

S1   Welche Kurse haben Sie heute?
S2   . . .
S1   Und morgen? Welche Kurse haben Sie morgen?
S2   . . .
S1   Wann haben Sie . . . ?
S2   Ich habe . . . um . . . und . . . um . . .
S1   Wie heißt der / die . . .professor(in)?
S2   . . .
S1   Ist der . . .kurs gut?
S2   . . .
S1   Wann sind Sie heute fertig?
S2   Ich bin heute um . . . fertig.

G. **Praktische Ausdrücke im Klassenzimmer** *(Useful classroom expressions. You should be able to use the following phrases.)*

Das verstehe ich nicht.	*I don't understand that.*
Ich habe eine Frage.	*I have a question.*
Ich weiß nicht.	*I don't know.*
Ist das richtig?	*Is that correct?*
Öffnen Sie das Buch auf Seite . . . !	*Open the book to page . . .*

Point out that all lists with a bar on the left are important and must be learned. Here, students already know most of the expressions. Those in **boldface** are new.

Sagen Sie das bitte noch einmal!	*Say that again, please.*
Schreiben Sie das bitte!	*Please, write that!*
(Sprechen Sie) bitte langsam!	*(Speak) slowly, please!*
Was bedeutet . . . ?	*What does . . . mean?*
Wie bitte?	*What did you say, please?*
Wiederholen Sie das bitte!	*Please, repeat that!*
Wie sagt man . . . auf Deutsch?	*How do you say . . . in German?*
Wie schreibt man das?	*How do you spell that?*

Was sagen Sie wann? *(What would you say in these situations?)*

1. You got called on in class and didn't hear the question.
2. You were unable to follow your instructor's explanation.
3. You have to ask your instructor to repeat something.
4. You want to let your instructor know that you have a question.
5. You have asked your new neighbor for his / her telephone number, but he / she is speaking much too fast.
6. You also did not catch his / her name and ask him / her to spell it.
7. In a conversation, the word **Geschwindigkeitsbegrenzung** keeps coming up. You want to ask for clarification.
8. You want to know how to say *first name* and *last name* in German.
9. You try to repeat the word and want to make sure that what you said is right.
10. Someone else asks you for the time, but you don't know.

G: 1. **Wie bitte?** 2. **Das verstehe ich nicht.** 3. **Wiederholen Sie das bitte! / Sagen Sie das bitte noch einmal!** 4. **Ich habe eine Frage.** 5. **(Sprechen Sie) bitte langsam!** 6. **Wie heißen Sie? Wie schreibt man das?** 7. **Was bedeutet** *Geschwindigkeitsbegrenzung*? 8. **Wie sagt man** *first name* **und** *last name* **auf Deutsch?** 9. **Ist das richtig?** 10. **Ich weiß nicht.**

Aussprache: ch, ig, ck, ng, gn, kn, qu, pf, ps, w, v

(Read also Part III. 5, 13–15, 19, 20–23 in the Pronunciation Guide of the Workbook.)

CD 1, Track 13

Hören Sie gut zu und wiederholen Sie!

- [k] **Ch**ristine, **Ch**ristian, **Ch**aos
- [x] a**ch**t, a**ch**thundert a**ch**tunda**ch**tzig, au**ch**, brau**ch**en, Wo**ch**e, Bu**ch**, Ba**ch**ara**ch**
- [ç] i**ch**, ni**ch**t, wirkli**ch**, wel**ch**e, schle**ch**t, Gesprä**ch**e, Bü**ch**er, **Ch**emie
- [iç] richt**ig**, wind**ig**, bill**ig**, fert**ig**, sech**z**ig, schmutz**ig**
- [ks] se**chs**, se**chs**undse**chz**ig, se**chs**hundertse**chs**undse**chz**ig
- [k] Ja**ck**e, Ro**ck**, Pi**ck**ni**ck**, di**ck**
- [ŋ] I**ng**e La**ng**e, Wolfga**ng** E**ng**el, E**ng**lisch, Frühli**ng**, la**ng**
- [gn] re**gn**et, resi**gn**ieren, Si**gn**al, Ma**gn**et
- [kn] **Kn**irps, **Kn**ie, **Kn**ut **Kn**orr
- [kv] **Qu**alität, **Qu**antität, **Qu**artett, Ä**qu**ivalent
- [pf] A**pf**el, **Pf**efferminz, Dummko**pf**, **pf**ui
- [ps] **Ps**ychologie, **Ps**ychiater, **Ps**ychoanalyse, **Ps**eudonym, Y**ps**ilon
- [v] **W**illi, **W**olfgang, **W**and, **W**ort, **w**ie, **w**as, **w**o, **w**elche
   ALSO: **V**olvo, **V**ase

Fokus — *The Benefits of Learning German*

Learning German will bring you benefits you may not have thought of before. In professional terms, you will be at an advantage regardless of whether your interests are in business, law, or academics. After all, the German economy is the strongest in Europe. Germany and Austria are active partners in the European Union, and many fields (such as music, art, literature, archaeology, philosophy, physics—to name just a few) reflect the creative work of artists and researchers from the German-speaking world. In personal terms, knowing German will open the doors to another culture. Because German and English are closely related Germanic languages, it is probable that in the course of your studies you will gain new insights into your own language as well.

Texts for the *Hören Sie zu* exercises can be found in the front of the Instructor's Edition.

HÖREN SIE ZU! TRACK 1.

Twice in every chapter, you will find listening comprehension exercises for the CD that comes with the textbook. These exercises provide you with an opportunity to listen to conversations that are as close to native speech as possible. You may want to listen to them several times. Note that it is not essential to understand every word in order to comprehend the meaning of the dialogue. However, when the passage includes vocabulary items that you have not yet learned, they are listed after the instructions, for recognition only.

Das Klassenzimmer *(Listen to the description of this class and classroom. Then select the correct response from those given below.)*

1. Das Klassenzimmer ist _____.
   a. kühl   **b.** groß   c. schmutzig
2. Das Zimmer hat _____ Fenster.
   a. vier   **b.** fünf   c. sieben
3. Die Wände sind _____.
   a. grau   b. blau   c. schwarz
4. Die _____ sind rot.
   a. Türen   b. Bücher   **c.** Stühle
5. Der Professor heißt _____.
   a. Theo Seidl   **b.** Oskar Thieme   c. Otto Brockmann
6. Die Bilder sind _____.
   a. alt   **b.** schön   c. furchtbar
7. Die Studenten lernen _____.
   a. Deutsch   b. Spanisch   c. Englisch

Video-Ecke

For accompanying exercises to the videos, see the *Video-aktiv* section of the Workbook.

- In the video *Was darf's sein?*, two friends are shopping for clothes, without much success!

Web-Ecke

- For updates, self-assessment quizzes, and online activities related to this chapter, visit the *Wie geht's?* Web site at **http://wiegehts.heinle.com**.

Rückblick: Schritte

By now, you know quite a few German words and a number of idiomatic expressions. You have learned how to pronounce German and to say a few things about yourself. You have also learned a good deal about how the German language works.

The *Rückblick* section explains the grammatical structures encountered so far. It should not lead to long, involved discussions; but if students read it at home, it should clarify much of what they have learned. For additional suggestions, see IAE.

For accompanying review exercises before exams, see the chapter reviews *(Rückblicke)* of the Workbook.

I. Nouns

1. German has three genders: MASCULINE, NEUTER, and FEMININE. Nouns are distinguished by **der, das,** and **die** in the singular. In the plural, there are no gender distinctions; the article **die** is used for all plural nouns:

der Herr, der Bleistift		Herren, Bleistifte
das Bild	**die**	Bilder
die Frau, die Tafel		Frauen, Tafeln

2. There are several ways to form the plural of nouns. You have learned how to interpret the most common plural abbreviations found in dictionaries and vocabulary lists:

das Fenster, -		Fenster
der Mantel, ¨		Mäntel
der Tag, **-e**		Tage
der Stuhl, ¨e		Stühle
das Kleid, **-er**		Kleid**er**
das Buch, ¨er	**die**	Büch**er**
die Uhr, **-en**		Uhr**en**
die Sekunde, **-n**		Sekunde**n**
die Studentin, **-nen**		Studentin**nen**
der Kuli, **-s**		Kuli**s**

3. When you learn a noun, you must also learn its gender and plural form.
4. All nouns are capitalized.

Ich brauche **B**leistifte, **K**ulis und **P**apier.

II. Pronouns

You have used the following pronouns:

ich	*I*	Ich heiße Sanders.
es	*it*	Es regnet.
wir	*we*	Wir zählen von eins bis zehn.
sie	*they*	Sind sie müde?
Sie	*you (formal)*	Wann sind Sie heute fertig?

- The pronoun **ich** is not capitalized unless it stands at the beginning of a sentence.

25

- The pronoun **Sie** (when it means *you*) is always capitalized; **Sie** is used in all formal relationships, and always when others are addressed with such titles as **Herr** and **Frau.** It is used to address one or more persons.

> Frau Thielemann, verstehen **Sie** das?
>
> Frau Thielemann und Herr Fiedler, verstehen **Sie** das?

III. Verbs

1. You have noticed that German verbs have different endings—that is, they are INFLECTED, i.e., CONJUGATED. You have used the following verb endings:

*We have also had three examples of the 3rd person sg.: **was bedeutet, es kostet, es regnet.***

ich	-e	Ich brauch**e** Papier.
wir	-en	Wir brauch**en** Papier.
sie, Sie	-en	Sie brauch**en** Papier.

2. **Sein** *(to be)* and **haben** *(to have)* are two important verbs. As in English, their forms are not regular.

ich	bin	Ich bin müde.
es	ist	Es ist spät.
sie, Sie	sind	Sie sind schnell.

ich	habe	Ich habe Zeit.
es	hat	Es hat Zeit.
sie, Sie	haben	Sie haben Zeit.

IV. Sentence structure

You have encountered three basic sentence types: STATEMENTS, QUESTIONS, and IMPERATIVES. In all of them, verb position plays a significant role.

1. Statements

   One of the most important observations you will make is that the verb is always the second element in a statement. (As you see from the examples, a SENTENCE ELEMENT can consist of more than one word.)

   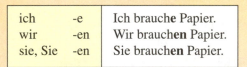

Mein Name **ist**	Dieter Schneider.
Franziska und Sebastian **sind**	hier.
Ich **finde**	das schön.
Der Rock und die Bluse **kosten**	€ 80,–.

2. Questions

   You have practiced two types of questions: INFORMATION QUESTIONS and QUESTIONS THAT ELICIT YES / NO ANSWERS.

   a. Information questions begin with a question word or phrase and ask for specific information: *what, where, how*. In information questions, too, the verb is the second element. You have learned the following question words and phrases. Note that in German all question words begin with a **w**!

Wann	**haben**	Sie Deutsch?
Was	**kostet**	das?
Wo	**ist**	der Stuhl?
Wie	**geht**	es Ihnen?
Welche Farbe	**hat**	das Buch?
Wie viel Uhr	**ist**	es?
Wie viele Tage	**hat**	die Woche?

b. Questions eliciting a yes/no response, on the other hand, begin with the verb.

Haben Sie Zeit?

Regnet es morgen?

Spielen wir heute Tennis?

Ist das richtig?

3. Imperatives

Imperatives (commands, requests, suggestions) also begin with the verb. Note that they usually conclude with an exclamation mark.

Antworten Sie bitte!

Nehmen Sie die Kreide!

Öffnen Sie das Buch!

Sagen Sie das noch einmal!

Zählen Sie von zwanzig bis dreißig!

Kapitel ①

Familie, Länder, Sprachen

Die Familie spielt „Mensch ärgere dich nicht" *("Sorry")*.

Lernziele

Vorschau
Spotlight on Germany

Gespräche + Wortschatz
Your family, yourself, and the countries
of Europe

Fokus
The Goethe Institute
Du or **Sie?**
Frankfurt am Main
German in Europe
German throughout the world

Struktur
1.1 Present tense of regular verbs
1.2 Nominative case
1.3 Sentence structure: position of subject,
     linking verbs, and predicate adjectives
1.4 Compound nouns

Einblicke
Deutschland und die Nachbarn

Video-Ecke
Minidrama: *Ganz international*
Blickpunkt: *Am Goethe-Institut*

Web-Ecke

Vorschau

Spotlight on Germany

Size: Approximately 135,800 square miles, comparable to the size of Montana; would fit twenty times into the area of the continental United States; divided into 16 federal states **(Länder).**

Population: About 82 million (including 7.3 million foreigners). After Russia, Germany is the most populous country of Europe, followed by Italy, the United Kingdom, and France.

Religion: 38% Protestant, 34% Catholic, 28% unaffiliated or other.

Geography: Divided into three major regions: the flat lowlands in the north, the central mountain region, and the southern highlands including a narrow band of the Alps.

Currency: Euro, € = 100 Cents. The former currency, the Mark (= 100 Pfennig), was phased out in 2002.

Principal cities: Berlin (pop. 3.4 million, capital); Bonn (pop. 307,000); Hamburg (pop. 1.7 million); Munich (*München*, pop. 1.3 million); Cologne (*Köln*, pop. 1 million); Frankfurt am Main (pop. 660,000); Düsseldorf (pop. 570,000); Stuttgart (pop. 588,000); Hanover (*Hannover*, pop. 515,000); Leipzig (pop. 449,000); Dresden (pop. 472,000).

Germany's sometimes turbulent history spans nearly 2,000 years. Unlike many of its neighbors, Germany did not become a centralized state until relatively late. Initially, the population consisted of various Germanic tribes, and even now their heritage gives the different regions of Germany their particular identity. The Holy Roman Empire, a loose federation of states under an emperor, lasted from 962 to 1806. During this time, the country was divided further until there were almost 350 individual political entities, some of them minuscule. Under Napoleon, they were consolidated into 32 states. In 1871, under Prussian chancellor Otto von Bismarck, Germany became a unified state for the first time. This monarchy lasted until the end of World War I, when Germany became a republic.

After the Nazi dictatorship led Germany to ruin in World War II, the country was divided into the Federal Republic of Germany, or FRG **(Bundesrepublik = BRD),** in the west, and the German Democratic Republic, or GDR **(Deutsche Demokratische Republik = DDR),** in the east. The line between the West and Communist Europe, a heavily fortified border, ran through the middle of Germany. The symbol of this division, the infamous Berlin Wall built in 1961 by the GDR, came down on November 9, 1989. On October 3, 1990, the two Germanys were officially reunited. Since then, Germans have been trying to overcome more than 40 years of living in diametrically opposed political and economic systems. Many Germans are still waiting for the day when "the wall in the minds" of people will finally fall. The cost of reunification, both socially and economically, has been much higher than anticipated. In the East, the closing of

Ask students what German cities they know or have visited, or whether they know anything special about them. As an extra activity you could look at the blank map of Germany in the *Zum Schreiben* section of the Workbook and fill it in together.

(continued on p. 30)

29

obsolete socialist enterprises has resulted in massive unemployment; in the West, taxes have increased in order to finance the high costs of reunification. However, the massive transfer of public funds from West to East (about $80 billion annually since reunification) is showing results. The telephone, rail, and road systems of the new states have been rebuilt almost completely, and the eastern part of Germany now boasts one of the most modern infrastructures in all of Europe. (For pictures and information on German cities, visit www.*[city name]*.de)

Gespräche + Wortschatz

CD 2, Track 1

Warm-ups: 1. **Wie ist das Wetter heute? Wie geht es Ihnen?** 2. **Was ist das?** Point to objects in the classroom and have students identify them. 3. **Wie ist . . . ?** Have them describe the color of various items. 4. **Ist . . . groß oder klein?** (dick / dünn, kurz / lang, schnell / langsam, neu / alt, sauber / schmutzig, teuer / billig, heiß / kalt, warm / kühl / kalt) Ask about various items, people, the weather, etc. 5. **Buchstabieren Sie . . . !** Have students spell various German words.

Remind students to read the dialogues aloud until they can do so fluently. They are not expected to memorize entire dialogues but should be prepared to answer questions about them.

The basic purpose of these dialogues is to present the chapter topic, not the grammar!

A: 1. aus Rom 2. aus Sacramento 3. in Seattle 4. zwei Schwestern und zwei Brüder 5. in zehn / Minuten 6. Flüsse (in Deutschland) 7. im Norden / Osten / Süden / Westen 8. Im Westen von Deutschland, nördlich von Bonn, am Rhein.

Am Goethe-Institut

Listen to the dialogue. Then, with a partner, act out the dialogue together.

SHARON	Roberto, woher kommst du?
ROBERTO	Ich bin aus Rom. Und du?
SHARON	Ich komme aus Sacramento, aber jetzt wohnt meine Familie in Seattle.
ROBERTO	Hast du Geschwister?
SHARON	Ja, ich habe zwei Schwestern und zwei Brüder. Und du?
ROBERTO	Ich habe nur eine Schwester. Sie wohnt in Montreal, in Kanada.
SHARON	Wirklich? So ein Zufall! Mein Onkel wohnt auch da.

Später

ROBERTO	Sharon, wann ist die Prüfung?
SHARON	In zehn Minuten. Du, wie heißen ein paar Flüsse in Deutschland?
ROBERTO	Im Norden ist die Elbe, im Osten die Oder, im Süden . . .
SHARON	. . . die Donau?
ROBERTO	Richtig! Und im Westen der Rhein. Wo liegt Düsseldorf?
SHARON	Düsseldorf? Hm. Wo ist eine Landkarte?
ROBERTO	Oh, hier. Im Westen von Deutschland, nördlich von Bonn, am Rhein.
SHARON	Ach ja, richtig! Na, viel Glück!

A. Fragen

1. Woher kommt Roberto? 2. Woher kommt Sharon? 3. Wo wohnt Sharons Familie? 4. Wie groß ist Sharons Familie? 5. Wann ist die Prüfung? 6. Was sind die Elbe, die Oder, die Donau und der Rhein? 7. Wo ist die Elbe? die Oder? die Donau? der Rhein? 8. Wo liegt Düsseldorf?

B. Jetzt sind Sie dran! *(Based on the new vocabulary, create your own dialogue with a partner. Talk about geography or about your family and where they live.)*

Fokus — *The Goethe Institute*

The Goethe Institute—since its merger with Inter Nationes officially called **"Goethe Institut Inter Nationes"**—is the official representative of German culture abroad. With approximately 130 branches in more than 76 countries, it offers German language courses and organizes lectures, exhibitions, film screenings, and readings by poets and authors. The combination of language instruction and lively cultural exchange makes the Goethe Institutes important intermediaries in international dialogue and in communicating a comprehensive image of Germany. (For further information, visit www.Goethe.de or www.inter-nationes.de.)

Wortschatz 1

Die Familie, -n *(family)*

der Bruder, ¨	*brother*	die Schwester, -n	*sister*
der Cousin, -s	*cousin*	die Kusine, -n /	*cousin*
		Cousine, -n	
der Junge, -n	*boy*	das Mädchen, -	*girl*
der Mann, ¨er	*man; husband*	die Frau, -en	*woman; wife*
der Onkel, -	*uncle*	die Tante, -n	*aunt*
der Sohn, ¨e	*son*	die Tochter, ¨	*daughter*
der Vater, ¨	*father*	die Mutter, ¨	*mother*
der Großvater, ¨	*grandfather*	die Großmutter, ¨	*grandmother*
das Kind, -er	*child*		
die Geschwister *(pl.)*	*siblings; brother and / or sister*		
die Eltern *(pl.)*	*parents*		
die Großeltern *(pl.)*	*grandparents*		

Das Land, ¨er[1]	Die Leute *(pl.)*[2]	Die Sprache, -n[3]
(country, state)	*(people)*	*(language)*
Deutschland	der Deutsche, -n / die Deutsche, -n	Deutsch
Frankreich	der Franzose, -n / die Französin, -nen	Französisch
Österreich	der Österreicher, - / die Österreicherin, -nen	Deutsch
die Schweiz	der Schweizer, - / die Schweizerin, -nen	Deutsch, Französisch, Italienisch
Italien	der Italiener, - / die Italienerin, -nen	Italienisch
Spanien	der Spanier, - / die Spanierin, -nen	Spanisch
England	der Engländer, - / die Engländerin, -nen	Englisch
Amerika	der Amerikaner, - / die Amerikanerin, -nen	Englisch
Kanada	der Kanadier, - / die Kanadierin, -nen	Englisch, Französisch

Weiteres

der Satz, ¨e	*sentence*	die Frage, -n	*question*
Berg, -e	*mountain*	Landkarte, -n	*map*
Fluss, ¨e	*river*	Prüfung, -en	*test, exam*
See, -n	*lake*	Stadt, ¨e	*city*
		Hauptstadt, ¨e	*capital city*

kommen	*to come*
liegen	*to lie (be located)*
wohnen	*to live, reside*
amerikanisch / kanadisch	*American / Canadian*
woher?	*from where?*
Ich bin / komme aus . . .	*I'm from . . . (a native of)*
im Norden / Süden / Osten / Westen[4]	*in the north / south / east / west*
nördlich / südlich / östlich / westlich von	*north / south / east / west of*
mein(e)[5]	*my*
dein(e) / Ihr(e)[5]	*your (informal / formal)*

In case you're curious:
Dad / Mom / Grandma / Grandpa = **Vati, Papa / Mutti, Mama / Oma / Opa;** *step-* = **Stief- (Stiefbruder, Stiefschwester,** etc.); *-in-law* = **Schwieger- (Schwiegervater, Schwiegermutter,** etc.), BUT **Schwager, -** *(brother-in-law)* and **Schwägerin, -nen** *(sister-in-law);* *nephew / niece* = **Neffe, -n / Nichte, -n;** *grandchild* = **Enkelkind, -er;** *great-grand-* = **Urgroß- (Urgroßeltern).**

An older alternative for **der Cousin, -s** is **der Vetter, -n.**

You might like to point out the difference between *the German* and *a German:* **der Deutsche, die Deutsche** BUT **ein Deutscher, eine Deutsche.**

Point out that it is **die Schweiz.** Other feminine examples are **die Bundesrepublik, die Slowakische Republik** or **die Slowakei, die Tschechische Republik, die Türkei** BUT **[das] Tschechien.** Some countries are plural nouns, like **die USA, die Niederlande.**

---

[1] All countries and cities are neuter unless indicated otherwise **(die Schweiz).**

[2] Many feminine nouns can be derived from masculine nouns by adding **-in**, in which case their plurals end in **-nen (der Schweizer > die Schweizerin, -nen).** BUT: **der Deutsche > die Deutsche, -n, der Franzose > die Französin, -nen.**

[3] Adjectives denoting nationality are not capitalized: **Typisch deutsch!** *(Typically German!),* BUT: **Ich spreche Deutsch** *(the German language);* **Antworten Sie auf Deutsch!** *(Answer in German!)*

[4] **im** is used with months, seasons, and points of the compass **(im Mai, im Winter, im Norden); in** is used with names of cities, countries, and continents **(in Berlin, in Deutschland, in Europa).**

[5] **mein, dein,** and **Ihr** have no ending when used before masculine and neuter nouns that are sentence subjects: **mein Vater, dein Bruder, Ihr Kind.** Before feminine and plural nouns, **meine, deine,** and **Ihre** are used: **meine Mutter, deine Schwester, Ihre Eltern.**

Point out that the words in **Zum Erkennen** are for recognition only, i.e., passive vocabulary. They are listed in the order of their appearance in the dialogue(s). Following "AUCH" are a few other words or expressions from the chapter that might help keep classroom instructions in German.

Zum Erkennen: So ein Zufall! *(What a coincidence!);* Na, viel Glück! *(Well, good luck!);* AUCH: das Pronomen, - *(pronoun);* das Subjekt, -e *(subject);* ersetzen *(to replace);* kombinieren *(to combine);* Hier fehlt was. *(Something is missing.);* Was fehlt? *(What's missing?);* Sagen Sie es anders! *(Say it differently!);* usw. = und so weiter *(etc.);* z. B. = zum Beispiel *(e.g., for example)*

Fokus — *Du or Sie?*

In forms of address, German is much more formal than English. **Du**—the cognate of the archaic English word *thou*—is used primarily for addressing children, family members, and friends. **Sie** is used with adults who are not close friends or relatives. Today, young people and university students tend to address each other automatically with the informal **du**-form; but it is still extremely rude to call older people—or even work colleagues—by **du.** When in doubt, use **Sie.** The general custom is that it is up to the person of higher age or status to suggest **duzen** instead of **siezen.** Similarly, you address a German speaker "on a first-name basis" only after you begin using the **du**-form. Up to that point, it is **Herr . . .** or **Frau . . .** to you.

Zum Thema *(Topical activity)*

The function of the *Mustersätze* is to drill new phrases and to introduce the pronunciation of some new vocabulary.

A. Mustersätze

1. Ihre Familie: **Woher kommt** Ihre Familie?
   Ihr Vater, Ihre Mutter, Ihr Onkel, Ihre Tante
2. Rom: **Ich bin aus** Rom.
   Frankfurt, Österreich, Amerika, Berlin
3. Hamburg / Norden: Hamburg **liegt im** Norden.
   Leipzig / Osten; München / Süden; Düsseldorf / Westen; Rostock / Norden
4. die Schweiz / südlich: Die Schweiz **liegt** südlich **von Deutschland**
   Dänemark / nördlich; Polen / östlich; Österreich / südlich; Luxemburg / westlich
5. Österreich / Deutsch: **In Österreich sprechen die Leute** Deutsch.
   Frankreich / Französisch; England / Englisch; Italien / Italienisch; Spanien / Spanisch.

B. Was sind sie? *(Tell what nationality the following people have.)*

CAUTION: Unlike English, German does not use an indefinite article before nationalities or references to membership in a group: **Sie ist Amerikanerin** *(an American).* **Sie ist Studentin** *(a student).* **Er ist Berliner** *(a Berliner).*

1. **Ländernamen**

B.1: a. **Luisa ist Italienerin.** b. **Lilo ist Österreicherin.** c. **Monique ist Schweizerin.** d. **Claire ist Französin.**

   BEISPIEL: Juan ist Spanier. Und Juanita?
   Juanita ist Spanierin.

   a. Antonio ist Italiener. Und Luisa?
   b. Hugo ist Österreicher. Und Lilo?
   c. Walter ist Schweizer. Und Monique?
   d. Pierre ist Franzose. Und Claire?

2. **Städtenamen**

BEISPIEL: Uwe und Margit sind aus Frankfurt.
             Uwe ist Frankfurter und Margit ist Frankfurterin.

a. Robert und Evi sind aus Berlin.
b. Klaus und Inge sind aus Hamburg.
c. Rolf und Katrin sind aus Wien.
d. Bert und Romy sind aus Zürich.

B.2: a. **Robert ist Berliner und Evi ist Berlinerin.** b. **Klaus ist Hamburger und Inge ist Hamburgerin.** c. **Rolf ist Wiener und Katrin ist Wienerin.** d. **Bert ist Züricher und Romy ist Züricherin.**

3. **Kettenreaktion: Was sind Sie?** *(Chain reaction. Ask your classmates where they are from.)*

BEISPIEL: Ich bin aus Amerika und wohne in New York. Ich bin Amerikaner(in)
             und New Yorker(in). Und Sie?
             Ich bin . . .

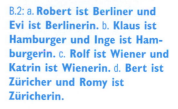

C. Familien

1. **Elkes Stammbaum** *(Look at Elke's family tree and explain who each person is.)*

BEISPIEL: Elke ist die Tochter von Jens und Ute.
             Elke ist Arndts Schwester.

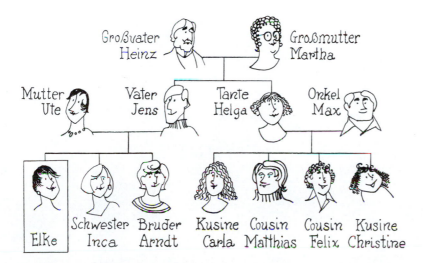

C: Ask questions about Elke's family, such as: 1. **Wie viele Kinder sind in Elkes Familie? Wie heißen sie?** 2. **Wie heißt Elkes Vater? Elkes Mutter?** 3. **Wie heißen die Großeltern?** 4. **Wie viele Geschwister / Cousins und Kusinen hat sie? Wie heißen sie?** 5. **Wer ist Onkel Max?** 6. **Wie heißt die Schwester von Elkes Vater?** 7. **Wie heißt der Mann von Ute?** 8. **Wie viele Enkelkinder** *(grandchildren)* **haben die Großeltern? wie viele Jungen? wie viele Mädchen?**

2. **Familiennamen.** Wer ist das? *(Write down various names of your immediate and extended family and pass the list on to your partner who then asks who these different people are. Take turns in inquiring about each other's family. For extra vocabulary, see the list in* Zum Erkennen *under* Wortschatz 1.)

3. **Zwei Familien**
   a. **Meine Familie** *(Taking turns, ask your partner details about his/her family, covering questions like the ones below.)*

   Wie heißt du?
   Woher kommst du? *(name your state)*
   Wie groß ist deine Familie? Wie heißen sie und wie alt sind sie?
   Wo in . . . *(name of your state)* wohnt deine Familie?
   Wo liegt . . . *(name of your state)*? (e.g., **Kalifornien liegt südlich von Oregon.**)
   Wie heißt die Hauptstadt von . . . *(name your state)*?
   Wie schreibt man das? *(spell the name of your capital)*
   Ist . . . *(name of your city)* groß oder klein? Wie viele Leute wohnen da?

Ist da ein Fluss oder ein See? der Ozean *(ocean)*? Wenn ja *(if so)*, wie heißt der
  Fluss / See / Ozean?
Sind da Berge? Wenn ja, wie heißen die Berge?
Wie ist das Wetter da im Frühling? im Sommer? im Herbst? im Winter?
Wie findest du es *(how do you like it)* in . . . *(name your city or state)*?

b. **Deine Familie** *(Take turns in reporting what you found out. While doing that, some
intentional mistakes might occur, which your partner then corrects.)*

D. **Was passt?** *(What fits? For each question or statement on the left, select one or more
appropriate responses from the right-hand column, or give your own.)*

<u>d, h</u> 1. Woher kommst du?

<u>a, i</u> 2. Wie groß ist deine Familie?

<u>c, j</u> 3. Meine Schwester wohnt in Seattle.

<u>e, f, k</u> 4. Wann ist die Prüfung?

<u>g, l</u> 5. Wo liegt Erfurt?

a. Sehr klein. Ich habe keine
   Geschwister.
b. Am Rhein.
c. Mein Onkel wohnt auch da.
d. Aus Seattle, und du?
e. Um Viertel nach zehn.
f. In zwanzig Minuten.
g. Westlich von Weimar.
h. Ich bin aus Rom.
i. Wir sind sechs.
j. Wirklich?
k. Ich weiß nicht.
l. . . .

Stadtzentrum von Erfurt

CD 2, Track 2

All pronunciation exercises are recorded on
the Lab Audio CDs. See the *Zum Hören* section of the Workbook.

Aussprache: i, a, u

*(Read also Part II. 1, 3–4, 11–13, 17, 19–20 in the Pronunciation Guide of the Work-
book.)*

1. [i:] **Ih**nen, l**ie**gen, w**ie**der, W**ie**n, Berl**i**n
2. [i] ich b**i**n, b**i**tte, K**i**nd, Geschw**i**ster, r**i**chtig

3. [a:] Frage, Sprache, Amerikaner, Spanier, Vater
4. [a] Stadt, Land, Kanada, Satz, Tante
5. [u:] gut, Bruder, Kuli, Minute, du
6. [u] Stunde, Junge, Mutter, Fluss, schmutzig, kurz
7. Wortpaare
   a. still / Stil   c. Kamm / komm   e. Rum / Ruhm
   b. Stadt / Staat   d. Schiff / schief   f. Ratte / rate

Aussprache 7: To sharpen listening skills, use variations (e.g., **still / Stil, Stil / still, still / still, Stil / Stil**), and let students tell you through signals (left hand/right hand) which one within each pair they hear.

HÖREN SIE ZU!   TRACK 2

Guten Morgen! *(Listen to the conversation between Hugo Schmidt and Monika Müller. Then decide whether the statements below are true or false according to the dialogue. Remember that you may listen as often as you wish.)*

Zum Erkennen: die Assistentin; die Arbeit *(work)*

r	1.	Hugo Schmidt ist Professor.
f	2.	Monika Müller ist Professorin.
r	3.	Monika spricht *(speaks)* Deutsch, Englisch und Spanisch.
f	4.	Monika ist aus Spanien.
f	5.	Monikas Mutter ist aus Deutschland.
f	6.	Monika ist 23.
r	7.	Der Professor braucht Monika von 2 Uhr bis 6 Uhr.
r	8.	Monika braucht Arbeit.
f	9.	Monika ist zwei Monate da.

Lerntipp
Developing Listening Comprehension

Being able to understand spoken German is probably your most important skill. Without it, you can't learn to speak it. Use class time well; listen carefully to the instructor and your classmates. Play the CD that comes with this book as often as you need to understand the dialogues and anecdotes and to complete the exercises correctly. Use the audio program in the lab, at home, or in the dormitory, and be sure to listen to the reading texts with the book closed. Take advantage of opportunities to hear German in the German Club or German House, if there is one on your campus. Listen to CDs and watch plays or movies (some can be rented in video stores). Even if you can't understand much of it in the beginning, you will be able to pick out key words and learn to "tune in" to German.

Hamburg und die Alster

Struktur

1.1 Present tense of regular verbs

1. You are already familiar with some of the PERSONAL PRONOUNS; there are four others: **du, er, sie,** and **ihr.**

	singular	plural	singular / plural
1st person	ich *(I)*	wir *(we)*	
2nd person	**du** *(you, fam.)*	**ihr** *(you, fam.)*	Sie *(you, formal)*
3rd person	**er** / es / **sie** *(he, it, she)*	sie *(they)*	

- **du** and **ihr** are intimate forms of address used with family members, close friends, fellow students, children up to the age of fourteen, and animals.
- **Sie,** which is always capitalized when it means *you,* is used with strangers, acquaintances, and people addressed with a title, e.g., **Herr** and **Frau.** It is used to address one or more persons. **Sie** *(you)* and **sie** *(they,* not capitalized) can be distinguished in conversation only through context.

> Herr Schmidt, wo wohnen **Sie?** Und Ihre Eltern, wo wohnen **sie?**
> *Mr. Schmidt, where do you live? And your parents, where do they live?*

- The subject pronouns **sie** *(she, it)* and **sie** *(they)* can be distinguished through the personal endings of the verb.

> **Sie** komm**t** im Mai und **sie** komm**en** im Juni.
> *She comes in May, and they come in June.*

2. The infinitive is the form of the verb that has no subject and takes no personal ending (e.g., *to learn*). Almost every German infinitive ends in **-en: lernen, antworten.** The stem of the verb is the part that precedes the infinitive ending **-en.** Thus, the stem of **lernen** is **lern-,** and that of **antworten** is **antwort-.**

English verbs have at most one personal ending in the present tense, *-s: I (you, we, they) learn,* BUT *he (it, she) learns.* In German, endings are added to the verb stem for all persons.

> stem + personal ending = present tense verb form

German verb endings vary, depending on whether the subject is in the FIRST, SECOND, or THIRD PERSON, and in the SINGULAR or PLURAL. The verb must agree with the subject. You have already learned the endings used for some persons. Here is the complete list of endings:

	singular	plural	formal (sg. / pl.)
1st person	ich lern**e**	wir lern**en**	
2nd person	du lern**st**	ihr lern**t**	Sie lern**en**
3rd person	er / es / sie lern**t**	sie lern**en**	

NOTE: The verb forms for formal *you* (**Sie**) and plural *they* (**sie**) are identical. The same holds true for **er / es / sie.** For that reason **Sie** and **es / sie** will not be listed in charts in future chapters.

The following verbs, which you already know from the *Schritte* and from this chapter, follow the model of **lernen.** Be sure to review them:

Caution: Students cannot yet be expected to use these verbs to write their own sentences, since most require objects.

beginnen	*to begin*	sagen	*to say, tell*
brauchen	*to need*	schreiben	*to write*
fragen	*to ask*	spielen	*to play*
gehen	*to go*	verstehen	*to understand*
hören	*to hear*	wiederholen	*to repeat, review*
kommen	*to come*	wohnen	*to live, reside*
liegen	*to lie, be located*	zählen	*to count*

NOTE: The bar on the left of vocabulary signals that a list is important. Any new words are **boldfaced;** learn them before you do the exercises that follow!

3. When a verb stem ends in **-d** or **-t** (**antwort-, find-**), or in certain consonant combinations (**öffn-, regn-**), an **-e** is inserted between the stem and the **-st** and **-t** endings to make these endings clearly audible.

The rule for "certain consonant combinations" is: If the stem ends in **-d, -t,** or a combination of any consonant (other than **l** or **r**) plus **n** or **m,** then the ending adds an **-e** (like **regnen / regnet, atmen / atmet**). At this level, it is probably too complex for students.

	singular	**plural**	**formal (sg./pl.)**
1st person	ich antworte	wir antworten	
2nd person	du antwortest	ihr antwortet	Sie antworten
3rd person	er / es / sie antwortet	sie antworten	

These familiar verbs follow the model of **antworten:**

finden	*to find*	öffnen	*to open*
kosten	*to cost*	regnen	*to rain*

4. The **du**-form of verbs with a stem ending in any **s**-sound (**-s, -ss, -ß, -tz, -z**) adds only a **-t** instead of **-st: ich heiße, du heißt.** Thus, the **du**-form is identical with the **er**-form of these verbs: **du heißt, er heißt.**

5. German has only one verb form to express what can be said in English in several ways.

Ich wohne in Köln.
$\begin{cases} \text{\textit{I live in Cologne.}} \\ \text{\textit{I'm living in Cologne.}} \\ \text{\textit{I do live in Cologne.}} \end{cases}$

Wo wohnst du?
$\begin{cases} \text{\textit{Where are you living?}} \\ \text{\textit{Where do you live?}} \end{cases}$

6. Even more than in English, in German the present tense is very frequently used to express future time, particularly when a time expression clearly indicates the future.

In dreißig Minuten **gehe** ich in die Stadt.   *I'm going downtown in thirty minutes.*

Er **kommt** im Sommer.   *He'll come in the summer.*

Übungen

A. *Du, ihr* oder *Sie*? (*How would you generally address these people—in the singular familiar, the plural familiar, or in a formal fashion?*)

A: 1. du 2. ihr 3. Sie 4. Sie 5. Sie 6. du 7. ihr 8. ihr 9. Sie

For additional exercises on any of the grammar points, see the exercises in the Workbook.

BEISPIEL: your brother
(I would address him with) **du**

1. your father   2. members of your family   3. your German professor
4. a store clerk   5. two police officers   6. your roommate   7. friends of your three-year-old niece   8. your classmates   9. a group of strangers who are older than you

B. For a quick introductory practice, have students add subjects to any of the familiar verbs listed under 1.2 and 1.3, e.g. **brauchen (er, wir, du, ich)**.

B. Ersetzen Sie das Subjekt! *(Replace the subject by using the words in parentheses.)*

BEISPIEL: Ich sage das noch einmal. (wir, Maria)
                 Wir sagen das noch einmal.
                 Maria sagt das noch einmal.

1. Wir antworten auf Deutsch. (Roberto, du, ich, die Mutter)
2. Ich wiederhole die Frage. (er, wir, ihr, Sie)
3. Ihr lernt die Wörter. (ich, du, die Kinder, wir)
4. Du öffnest das Buch auf Seite 3. (der Franzose, ich, ihr, sie/*sg.*)
5. Heidi Bauer geht an die Tafel. (ihr, sie/*pl.*, ich, du)
6. Brauchst du Papier und Bleistifte? (wir, ich, Sie, ihr)
7. Wie finden Sie das? (ihr, du, Ihre Familie, die Leute)

Optional English-to-German practice: 1. We're learning German. 2. I'm counting slowly. 3. Where do you *(pl. fam.)* come from? 4. They come from Canada. 5. I'm from America. 6. Do you *(sg. fam.)* answer in English? 7. No, I'll speak German. 8. She's opening the book. 9. I do need the book. 10. What does she say? 11. Do you *(sg. fam.)* understand (that)? 12. Is she repeating that? 13. Her name is Sabrina. 14. They do live in Wittenberg. (See answer key in the Appendix.)

C. Kombinieren Sie! *(Create sentences by combining items from each column.)*

BEISPIEL: Er kommt aus Kanada.

1	2	3
ich	beginnen	auf Deutsch
du	brauchen	auf Englisch
er	hören	aus . . .
es	kommen	(das) nicht
sie	kosten	Deutsch
das	lernen	heute
die Deutschvorlesung	regnen	in . . .
das Mädchen	schreiben	jetzt
wir	spielen	morgen
ihr	wohnen	(nicht) gut
Sie	zählen	Tennis
sie		um . . . Uhr
		vier Euro
		von zehn bis zwanzig

D. After students complete the dialogue, have them use it as a model for a role-playing activity.

D. Was fehlt? *(What's missing? Fill in the missing verb forms.)*

JENS   Inge und Heidi, woher __kommt__ ihr? (kommen)
HEIDI   Ich __komme__ aus Heidelberg. (kommen)
INGE   Und ich __bin__ aus Berlin. (sein)
JENS   Wirklich? Meine Großmutter __kommt__ auch aus Berlin. (kommen) Aber sie __wohnt__ jetzt in Hamburg. (wohnen) Wie __findet__ ihr es hier? (finden)
HEIDI   Wir __finden__ es hier prima. (finden)
INGE   Ich __finde__ die Berge wunderbar. (finden)
JENS   Ich auch!

1.2 Nominative case

To show the function of nouns or pronouns in a sentence, German uses a system called CASE. There are four cases in German: nominative, accusative, dative, and genitive. The NOMINATIVE CASE is the case of the subject and of the predicate noun. (The latter is discussed in Section 1.3-2, p. 42).

     In the English sentence *The boy asks the father,* the SUBJECT of the sentence is *the boy;* he does the asking. We know that *the boy* is the subject of the sentence because in English the subject precedes the verb. This is not always true in German, where the function of a word or phrase frequently depends on its form rather than on its position. In the sentence **Der Junge fragt den Vater,** the phrase **der Junge** indicates the subject, whereas **den Vater** represents a direct object (more about this in Chapter 2). In dictionaries and vocabulary lists, nouns are given in the nominative. The nominative answers the questions *who?* for persons or *what?* for objects and ideas.

Der Junge fragt den Vater.	*The boy asks the father.*
Der See ist schön.	*The lake is beautiful.*

1. The forms of the INTERROGATIVE PRONOUNS are **wer?** *(who?)* and **was?** *(what?).*

	persons	things and ideas
nom.	wer?	was?

Wer fragt den Vater?	→	**Der Junge.**
Who is asking the father?	→	*The boy.*
Was ist schön?	→	**Der See.**
What is beautiful?	→	*The lake.*

2. The nominative forms of the DEFINITE ARTICLE **der** *(the)* are already familiar. Note that the INDEFINITE ARTICLE **ein** *(a, an)* is the same for masculine and neuter nouns; it has no ending. It also has no plural: *I have a pencil,* BUT *I have pencils.*

	SINGULAR			PLURAL	
	masc.	**neut.**	**fem.**		
nom.	der	das	die	die	*the*
	ein	ein	eine	—	*a, an*
	kein	kein	keine	keine	*no, not a, not any*

This table will be augmented gradually and used to teach cases. You might make a poster-size reproduction or a transparency of it for future use.

The POSSESSIVE ADJECTIVES **mein** *(my),* **dein** *(your),* and **Ihr** *(your, formal)* follow the pattern of **ein** and **kein.**

> Die Frau, der Junge und das Mädchen sind aus Österreich.
>
> **Mein** Onkel und **meine** Tante wohnen auch da. Wo wohnen **deine** Eltern?

3. Nouns can be replaced by PERSONAL PRONOUNS. In English, we replace persons with *he, she,* or *they,* and objects and ideas with *it* or *they.* In German, the pronoun used depends on the gender of the noun.

According to *Duden:* **das Mädchen, (das Fräulein,) das Kind = es.** However, in everyday speech you also hear **sie** for **das Mädchen** (or **das Fräulein**) and **er** or **sie** for das **Kind: Er heißt Felix. Sie heißt Susi.**

Wer ist **der Mann?**	**Er** heißt Max.	*He's called Max.*
Wie heißt **das Kind?**	**Es** heißt Susi.	*She's called Susi.*
Wer ist **die Frau?**	**Sie** heißt Ute.	*She's called Ute.*
Wie ist **der See?**	**Er** ist groß.	*It's big.*
Wie ist **das Land?**	**Es** ist klein.	*It's small.*
Wie heißt **die Stadt?**	**Sie** heißt Ulm.	*It's called Ulm.*

• Note that German uses three pronouns **(er, es, sie)** for objects where English uses only one *(it).*

• Note also how similar these pronouns are to the forms of the articles:

$$der \rightarrow er; \ das \rightarrow es; \ die \rightarrow sie$$

- In the plural, there are no gender distinctions, as the definite article for all plural nouns is **die.** The pronoun for all plural nouns is **sie.**

$$\left.\begin{array}{l}\text{die Männer}\\\text{die Kinder}\\\text{die Frauen}\end{array}\right\}\textbf{sie}\ \textit{(they)} \qquad \left.\begin{array}{l}\text{die Seen}\\\text{die Länder}\\\text{die Städte}\end{array}\right\}\textbf{sie}\ \textit{(they)}$$

Übungen

E. **Ersetzen Sie die Wörter mit Pronomen!** *(Replace the nouns with pronouns.)*

BEISPIEL: Fritz   **er**
                die Landkarte   **sie**

der Vater, der Berg, das Land, die Großmutter, der Junge, die Stadt, der Bleistift, der Pulli, Österreich, der Österreicher, die Schweiz, die Schweizerin, Deutschland, das Kind, die Geschwister, die Töchter, die Söhne

> E: der Vater = er, der Berg = er, das Land = es, die Großmutter = sie, der Junge = er, die Stadt = sie, der Bleistift = er, der Pulli = er, Österreich = es, die Schweiz = sie, die Schweizerin = sie, Deutschland = es, das Kind = es, die Geschwister = sie, die Töchter = sie, die Söhne = sie

F. **Die Geographiestunde**

1. **Was ist das?** *(Describe some features of Europe, using the appropriate form of* **ein.**)

   BEISPIEL: Frankfurt / Stadt
                   Frankfurt ist eine Stadt.

   Österreich / Land; die Donau / Fluss; Italienisch / Sprache; Berlin / Stadt; der Main / Fluss; das Matterhorn / Berg; Französisch / Sprache; Luxemburg / Land; der Bodensee *(Lake Constance)* / See; Bremen / Stadt

> F.1: Österreich ist ein Land, die Donau ein Fluss, Italienisch eine Sprache, Berlin eine Stadt, der Main ein Fluss, das Matterhorn ein Berg, Französisch eine Sprache, Luxemburg ein Land, der Bodensee ein See, Bremen eine Stadt

2. **Ist das richtig?**

   a. **Geographische Namen in Europa** *(Geographical names in Europe. Ask and answer some questions about Europe, using the appropriate form of* **kein.**)

   BEISPIEL: die Donau / Land?
                   Ist die Donau ein Land?
                   Nein, die Donau ist kein Land. Die Donau ist ein Fluss.

   Frankfurt / Fluss; Frankreich / Sprache; Heidelberg / Berg; der Rhein / Stadt; die Schweiz / See; Spanien / Sprache; Bonn / Land

> F.2a: Frankfurt kein Fluss / eine Stadt; Frankreich keine Sprache / ein Land; Heidelberg kein Berg / eine Stadt; der Rhein keine Stadt / ein Fluss; die Schweiz kein See / ein Land; Spanien keine Sprache / ein Land; Bonn kein Land / eine Stadt

   b. **Geographische Namen irgendwo** *(Geographical names anywhere. Make your own statements about any geographical location and have your classmates react to them.)*

   BEISPIEL: Die Smokeys sind Berge. **Ja, das sind Berge.**
                   Der Hudson ist ein See.   **Nein, das ist kein See. Das ist ein Fluss.**

G. **Ersetzen Sie das Subjekt!**

1. **Antworten Sie mit JA!** *(A curious neighbor asks you questions about the new family in the neighborhood. Answer positively, using pronouns.)*

   BEISPIEL: Die Eltern kommen aus Italien, nicht wahr?
                   Ja, sie kommen aus Italien.

   a. Der Sohn antwortet auf Italienisch, nicht wahr? b. Die Tochter versteht Deutsch, nicht wahr? c. Das Kind ist fünf Jahre alt, nicht wahr? d. Die Großmutter heißt Maria, nicht wahr? e. Der Großvater wohnt auch da, nicht wahr? f. Die Familie kommt aus Rom, nicht wahr?

> G.1: a. er antwortet, b. sie versteht c. es ist d. sie heißt e. er wohnt f. sie kommt.

2. **Persönliche Antworten mit Pronomen** *(Personal answers with pronouns. Ask another student the following types of questions, which can vary. He or she answers and then returns the question.)*

   BEISPIEL: Wann beginnt . . . (z.B. dein Tag)?
                   Mein Tag? Er beginnt morgens um sechs. Und dein Tag?
                   Er beginnt morgens um halb sieben.

Fokus — *Frankfurt am Main*

Located on the Main River, Frankfurt is Germany's principal transportation hub. The city boasts the country's largest train station and an airport that handles more passengers than many others in Europe. Nicknamed "Mainhattan" because of its modern skyline, Frankfurt is one of Europe's leading financial centers. Some 430 banks (including the seat of the European Central Bank), 75 consulates, and more than 3,000 international businesses have set up shop in the Frankfurt area. Frankfurt's cosmopolitan atmosphere is reflected in its population, eight international schools, and 180 non-German professional and cultural clubs. Almost one-third of its residents have non-German passports.

Thanks to its central location, Frankfurt has been hosting one of Germany's most important trade fairs **(Frankfurter Messe)** since the Middle Ages. Since Roman times, the city has been valued for its strategic position; and beginning in 1356, the emperors of the Holy Roman Empire were crowned there. The poet Johann Wolfgang von Goethe (1749–1832), for whom the city's university is named, was born in Frankfurt, and the first German national assembly met there in St. Paul's Church in 1848.

Frankfurt ist alt und modern. Hier wohnen viele Menschen aus aller Welt.

a. Wann beginnt . . . (z.B. die Deutschvorlesung)?
b. Wie heißt . . . (z.B. das Deutschbuch)?
c. Welche Farbe hat . . . (z.B. dein Kuli)?
d. Welche Farbe hat . . . (z.B. deine Jacke)?
e. Wo ist . . . (z.B. das Fenster)?
f. Wie viele . . . hat . . . (z.B. Monate / das Jahr)?

3. **Blitzreaktionen** (*Fast responses. Say one of the German words you have learned. Someone else will quickly repeat the word with its article and make a statement about it, using the proper pronoun.*)

   BEISPIEL: Hemd
   Das Hemd. Es ist weiß.

G.3: This could be done as group competition. Whichever team answers correctly first, gets a point.

1.3 Sentence structure

1. In English, the subject usually precedes the verb, and more than one element may do so.

                   1   2
   They **are learning** German at the Goethe Institute.
   At the Goethe Institute they **are learning** German.

As you know, in German statements and information questions, the verb is always the second sentence element.

            1   2
Sie **lernen** Deutsch am Goethe-Institut.

Inverted word order is very common. The first sentence element either functions as connector to the previous sentence, or draws attention to a particular concept.

In contrast to English, however, only one sentence element may precede the verb, and this element is not necessarily the subject. If an element other than the subject precedes the verb, *the verb stays* in the second position and *the subject follows* the verb. This pattern is called INVERTED WORD ORDER.

$$\overset{2}{\text{Deutsch}} \ \textbf{lernen} \ \overset{1}{\text{sie}} \ \text{am Goethe-Institut.}$$

Am Goethe-Institut **lernen** sie Deutsch.

2. The verbs **sein** *(to be)* and **heiß**en *(to be called)* are LINKING VERBS. They normally link two words referring to the same person or thing, both of which are in the nominative: the first is the subject, the other a PREDICATE NOUN.

subject   predicate noun

Der Herr **ist**   Schweizer.

Er **heiß**t   Stefan Wolf.

The verbs **sein** and **heißen** work like an equal sign: **Er ist Schweizer (Er = Schweizer). Er heißt Stefan Wolf (Er = Stefan Wolf).** This is the best time to practice this concept and the absence of **ein** before nationalities. Practice sentences like *He's an Austrian, I'm an American,* etc.

The verb **sein** can be complemented not only by a predicate noun, but also by a PREDICATE ADJECTIVE. Both are considered part of the verb phrase. This is an example of a typical and important feature of German sentence structure: when the verb consists of more than one part, the inflected part (V1)—that is, the part of the verb that takes a personal ending—is the second element in the sentence, as always. However, the uninflected part (V2) stands at the very end of the sentence as a verb complement.

Stefan Wolf **ist** auch **Schweizer.**

Er **ist** heute **sehr müde.**

V1   V2

REMEMBER: In German, no indefinite article is used before nationalities: **Er ist Schweizer** *(an inhabitant of Switzerland).*

Übungen

H. Draw students' attention to the change in meaning or nuance that is a consequence of the change in word order.

H. Sagen Sie es anders! *(Say it differently. Begin each sentence with the word or phrase in boldface.)*

BEISPIEL: Mein Cousin kommt **morgen.**
              Morgen kommt mein Cousin.

H: 1. Jetzt bin ich am Goethe-Institut. 2. Hier sprechen die Leute nur Deutsch. 3. In zehn Minuten haben wir eine Prüfung in Geographie. 4. Auf Seite 162 findest du die Landkarte. 5. Im Süden ist die Donau. 6. Nördlich von Bonn liegt Düsseldorf. 7. Mir geht es gut. 8. Um halb drei spielen wir Tennis. 9. Im April regnet es oft. 10. Heute scheint die Sonne wieder.

1. Ich bin **jetzt** am Goethe-Institut.
2. Die Leute sprechen **hier** nur Deutsch.
3. Wir haben **in zehn Minuten** eine Prüfung in Geographie.
4. Du findest die Landkarte **auf Seite 162.**
5. Die Donau ist **im Süden.**
6. Düsseldorf liegt **nördlich von Bonn.**
7. Es geht **mir** gut.
8. Wir spielen **um halb drei** Tennis.
9. Es regnet oft **im April.**
10. Die Sonne scheint **heute** wieder.

I: 1. Er ist Italiener. 2. Er ist Amerikaner. 3. Sie ist Spanierin. 4. Er ist Engländer 5. Sie sind Amerikanerinnen. 6. Sie sind Schweizerinnen. 7. Sie sind Kanadier. 8. Er ist Schweizer. 9. Sie ist Österreicherin 10. Sie ist Liechtensteinerin.

I. Welche Nationalität? *(Professor Händel of the Goethe Institute is determining the nationality of his summer-school students. Follow the model.)*

BEISPIEL: Pierre kommt aus Marseille.
              Er ist Franzose.

1. Roberto kommt aus Florenz. 2. Sam kommt aus Houston. 3. Carla kommt aus Madrid. 4. James kommt aus Manchester. 5. Maria und Caroline kommen aus Nashville. 6. Monique und Simone kommen aus Lausanne. 7. John und Donna kommen aus Montreal. 8. Felix kommt aus Bern. 9. Eva kommt aus Wien. 10. Mirjam kommt aus Vaduz.

1.4 Compound nouns

In German, two or three simple words are frequently combined to create a new one, like **Fingerhut** (a "hat" that protects your finger = *thimble*), **Menschenfreund** (a friend of human beings = *philanthropist*), or **Stinktier** (an animal that stinks = *skunk*). The last component determines the gender and the plural form.

> das Land + **die Karte** = **die** Land**karte, -n**
> die Kinder + **das Mädchen** = **das** Kinder**mädchen, -**
> der Arm + das Band + **die Uhr** = **die** Armband**uhr, -en**
> schreiben + **der Tisch** = **der** Schreib**tisch, -e**
> klein + **die Stadt** = **die** Klein**stadt, ̈e**

Übung

J. Was bedeuten die Wörter und was sind die Artikel? *(Determine the meaning and gender of the following words.)*

> **BEISPIEL:** Schokoladentafel
> **die Schokoladentafel;** *chocolate bar*

Wochentag, Neujahr, Sommerbluse, Frühlingswetter, Altstadt, Bergsee, Wörterbuch, Sprechübung, Familienvater, Jungenname, Zimmertür, Hosenrock, Hemdbluse, Hausschuh, Handschuh, Deutschstunde, Wanduhr, Uhrzeit

Zusammenfassung *(Summary)*

K. Hoppla, hier fehlt was! *(Oops, something is missing here.)*

> This is the first of many activities in which you will try to find missing information with the help of a partner. Each of you has a chart—one appears below, the other in Section 11 of the Appendix. Each chart has information the other person needs. Do not look at your partner's chart! Always start by asking about the first blank on the left; fill it in, and then proceed to the next. Take turns asking questions until both charts are complete.

Wer sind sie? *(Take turns asking each other for the missing names, nationalities, places of residence, and ages of the persons listed. Follow the example.)*

S1:

Name	Nationalität	Wohnort	Alter
Toni	Schweizer	Bern	32
Katja	Deutsche	Ulm	21
Pia	Österreicherin	Graz	61
Nicole	Französin	Lyon	26
Pierre	Franzose	Dijon	52
Mario	Italiener	Rimini	25
Maria	Spanierin	Madrid	17
Tom	Kanadier	Halifax	28
Amy	Amerikanerin	Miami	49

> **BEISPIEL:** **S1** Wer ist Schweizer?
> **S2** Toni ist Schweizer? Und woher kommt Toni?

> **BEISPIEL:** **S1** Toni kommt aus Bern. Wie alt ist er?
> **S2** Er ist 32.

For additional practice on word compounds, see the *Zum Schreiben* section of the Workbook.

Students can form many other compound nouns, e.g., **Wintermantel (Sommer-, Regen-), Deutschkurs (Französisch-, Englisch-), Kinderbuch (-bild, -pullover).** This exercise can be done throughout the course. Additional vocabulary-building exercises are found in the various *Zum Schreiben* sections of the Workbook.

J: weekday **(der)**, New Year's **(das)**, summer blouse **(die)**, spring weather **(das)**, old center of town **(die)**, mountain lake **(der)**, dictionary **(das)**, oral exercise **(die)**, father of the family **(der)**, boy's name **(der)**, room door **(die)**, culottes **(der)**, shirt-like blouse **(die)**, house shoe, slipper **(der)**, glove **(der)**, German class **(die)**, wall clock **(die)**, time **(die)**.

Lerntipp
Reading German Texts

First, read for general content, without worrying about unfamiliar words and phrases. Then reread carefully and always finish a paragraph, or at least a sentence, before looking up an unfamiliar word or phrase. Look up as little as possible; it is often possible to determine meaning from context. Underline and pronounce the words in question, but do not scribble the English translation into the text. It will only distract you from the German. Finally, read the text a third time, after having guessed or looked up all the underlined words. See how many of them you remember. Try to learn them now, at least passively, to avoid looking them up repeatedly. If a word or phrase still remains unclear, circle it and ask your instructor instead of spending more time on it.

Bregenz am Bodensee

L: 1. Morgen kommen meine Eltern.
2. Mein Vater ist Franzose und meine
Mutter ist Österreicherin. 3. In Frankreich
sprechen sie Französisch und in Österreich
sprechen sie Deutsch. 4. Frankreich ist
(liegt) westlich von Deutschland und
Österreich ist (liegt) südlich von
Deutschland. 5. Ich verstehe Französisch
und Deutsch, aber ich antworte auf
Englisch. 6. Woher kommst du? 7. Ich bin
(komme) aus Texas. 8. Da ist Thomas.
Thomas ist Amerikaner. 9. Er lernt
Spanisch. 10. Ich finde es hier schön
(schön hier), aber ich bin sehr müde.

L. Sprachstudenten. Auf Deutsch bitte!

The translation exercises in this summary section always include material introduced in this chapter and possible previous ones. Watch carefully for differences between English and German patterns.

1. Tomorrow my parents are coming. 2. My father is (a) French(man), and my mother is (an) Austrian. 3. In France they speak French, and in Austria they speak German. 4. France is west of Germany, and Austria is south of Germany. 5. I do understand French and German, but I answer in English. 6. Where are you *(fam.)* from? 7. I'm from Texas. 8. There's Thomas. Thomas is (an) American. 9. He's learning Spanish. 10. I think it's beautiful here, but I am very tired.

Fokus — *German in Europe*

Thanks to geography, history, and economics, German is one of the principal languages of Europe. Some 92 million Europeans are native speakers, and millions more speak German as a second language. In many schools in western and northern Europe—in Scandinavia and France in particular—German is a required foreign language. In Greece, Spain, and Turkey, German is widely spoken, mainly because of southern European "guest workers" **(Gastarbeiter)** who brought German back to their countries, as well as the millions of German tourists who flock to the Mediterranean every year.

Farther east, German has a long tradition. The Austro-Hungarian Empire, in which German was the official language, encompassed large areas of central and eastern Europe. Today, after decades of Soviet domination, young people in Poland, the Czech Republic, Slovakia, and Hungary are rediscovering old links to German culture. Of course, the opportunities offered by the powerful economies of neighboring Austria and Germany are an added incentive. In Russia alone, 1.6 million students are learning German, and in the other countries of the former Soviet Union German is taught widely.

At the beginning of the century, German—not English—was the primary language of science, philosophy, and psychology. Although the German language has since seen growing competition from English, it will remain one of the most widely understood languages in Europe.

Einblicke *(Insights)*

The reading texts expand on the chapter topic. All vocabulary that is to become active is listed under *Wortschatz 2*. Learn these words well; they will recur in future exercises and activities. Following *Wortschatz 2*, a pre-reading section *(Vor dem Lesen)* introduces each reading selection. It proceeds from one to several activities composed of all sorts of general and personal questions to *Was ist das?*, a short set of cognates and compounds from the reading that you should be able to pronounce and recognize but do not have to master actively.

Lesestrategie: Read for Key Words

Ask students to read the *Lerntipp* on p. 43.

Don't worry about not understanding everything you read. Use the vocabulary you have learned in this chapter to identify the key words that will help you understand what the passage is about.

Wortschatz 2

der Ausländer, -	*foreigner*
Mensch, -en	*human being, person; (pl.) people*
Nachbar, -n / die Nachbarin, -nen	*neighbor*
Teil, -e	*part*
arbeiten	*to work*
so . . . wie . . .	*as . . . as . . .*
ungefähr	*about, approximately*
wichtig	*important*

Deutschland

DIE ZEITSCHRIFT IN 15 SPRACHEN
- •DEUTSCH
- •ENGLISCH
- •FRANZÖSISCH
- •PORTUGIESISCH
- •SPANISCH
- •POLNISCH
- •RUMÄNISCH
- •UNGARISCH
- •RUSSISCH
- •UKRAINISCH
- •TÜRKISCH
- •IWRITH
- •ARABISCH
- •CHINESISCH
- •JAPANISCH

AUSSERDEM IM INTERNET:
http://www.government.de
INTERNET-SERVICE IN:
- •ENGLISCH
- •FRANZÖSISCH
- •SPANISCH

Vor dem Lesen *(Pre-reading section)*

A. Die Europakarte *(Look at the map of Europe in front of the book. Then work out the answers to the questions below.)*

1. Wie viele Nachbarn hat Deutschland? Wie heißen sie?
2. Wo liegt Dänemark? Belgien? Spanien? Frankreich? Italien? Schweden? . . .
3. Wie heißt die Hauptstadt von Deutschland? Dänemark? Belgien? Frankreich? Spanien? Italien? Finnland? Norwegen? Schweden? England? Polen? . . .
4. Welche Sprachen sprechen die Europäer?
5. Wo in Europa sprechen Leute Deutsch als Muttersprache *(as their native tongue)*?

B. Was ist das? *(As your instructor pronounces the following words, guess their meaning in English.)*

der Bankier, Europäer, Großteil, Tourismus; (das) Europa, Sprachenlernen; die Millionen, Muttersprache, Politik; die USA *(pl.)*; Belgisch, Dänisch, Finnisch, Griechisch, Holländisch, Luxemburgisch, Norwegisch, Polnisch, Portugiesisch, Schwedisch, Tschechisch, Ungarisch; studieren; europäisch, interessant, lange

B: By reading aloud this short list of words, students will have a chance to notice the difference in pronunciation of these cognates and compounds and also gain some passive knowledge of vocabulary used in the reading.

C. Ausländer in Deutschland (*Foreigners in Germany. By looking at the statistics below, determine where some of Germany's foreigners are from, how many there are, and what language they speak.*)

1. Woher kommen die Ausländer in Deutschland? 2. Wie viele kommen aus . . . (Italien, den Niederlanden, den USA usw.)? 3. Was ist ihre (*their*) Muttersprache?

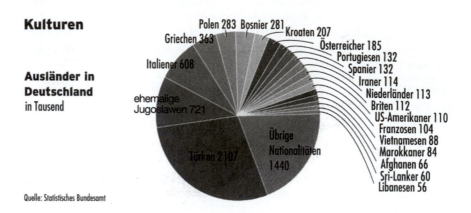

Kulturen

Ausländer in Deutschland
in Tausend

Griechen 363
Polen 283 Bosnier 281 Kroaten 207
Österreicher 185
Portugiesen 132
Spanier 132
Italiener 608
Iraner 114
Niederländer 113
Briten 112
US-Amerikaner 110
ehemalige Jugoslawen 721
Franzosen 104
Vietnamesen 88
Marokkaner 84
Afghanen 66
Sri-Lanker 60
Libanesen 56
Türken 2107
Übrige Nationalitäten 1440

Quelle: Statistisches Bundesamt

CD 2, Track 4

Deutschland und die Nachbarn

of course

by far not

as
of the

in / this way

trade
more than / in the
most of the / of the
abroad
tells
translator

at home / in school / fluently
as never before

Europa hat viele Länder und viele Sprachen. In Deutschland hören Sie natürlich° Deutsch. Aber die Nachbarn im Norden sprechen Dänisch, Schwedisch, Norwegisch und Finnisch. Die Nachbarn im Osten sprechen Polnisch und Tschechisch und im Westen sprechen sie Holländisch und Französisch. Im Süden von Europa sprechen die Menschen Italienisch, Spanisch, Portugiesisch und Griechisch; und das sind noch lange nicht° alle Sprachen!

Deutsch ist sehr wichtig. Ungefähr 92 Millionen Europäer sprechen Deutsch als° Muttersprache: die Deutschen, Österreicher, Liechtensteiner, ein Großteil der° Schweizer und ein Teil der Luxemburger und Belgier. Viele Ausländer arbeiten oder studieren in Deutschland, Österreich und in der° Schweiz und lernen so° auch Deutsch. Sehr viele Menschen in Europa sprechen zwei oder drei Sprachen. Sie finden das interessant und auch wichtig für Tourismus, Handel° und Politik. In Westeuropa wohnen ungefähr 350 Millionen Menschen; das sind mehr Menschen als° in den° USA und in Kanada zusammen. Die meisten° Länder sind ein Teil der° Europäischen Union (EU). Viele Europäer wohnen und arbeiten im Ausland°. Ein Beispiel ist Familie Breughel. Marcel Breughel erzählt°: „Ich bin aus Brüssel und meine Frau Nicole ist Französin. Sie ist Dolmetscherin° und ich bin Bankier. Wir wohnen schon zwei Jahre in Frankfurt. Wir finden es hier sehr schön. Wir haben zwei Kinder, Maude und Dominique. Sie sprechen zu Hause° Französisch, aber in der Schule° sprechen sie fließend° Deutsch. Das finde ich toll. Das Sprachenlernen ist heute so wichtig wie nie zuvor°."

Nach dem Lesen (*Post-reading section*)

A. Richtig oder falsch?

_r_	1.	In Europa hören Sie viele Sprachen.
_f_	2.	Alle Europäer sprechen Schwedisch.
_f_	3.	Ungefähr 920 000 Europäer sprechen Deutsch.
_r_	4.	Die Liechtensteiner sprechen Deutsch als Muttersprache.
_f_	5.	In Westeuropa wohnen so viele Menschen wie in Kanada und in den USA zusammen.
_f_	6.	Alle Länder in Europa sind ein Teil der EU.
_f_	7.	In Deutschland wohnen keine Ausländer.
_f_	8.	Herr und Frau Breughel sind Bankiers.
_f_	9.	Herr Breughel ist Franzose.

Optional practice: 1. **z.B. (das) Europa > es.** (Deutschland, Teil, Berlin, Menschen, Norden, Deutsch, Sprache, Nachbar, Europäerin) 2. **Was bedeuten die Wörter und was sind die Artikel?** Menschenzahl, Nachbarland, Zimmernachbar, Satzteil, Stadtteil, Teilzeit, Stadtmensch. 3. **z.B. Herr und Frau Watzlik sind aus Warschau. > Er ist Warschauer/Pole; sie ist Warschauerin/Polin.** Okko und Antje sind aus Amsterdam. Pierre und Nadine sind aus Paris. Bjorn und Christina sind aus Oslo; etc.

___f___ 10. Familie Breughel wohnt schon fünf Jahre in Frankfurt.

___r___ 11. Sie finden es da sehr schön.

___f___ 12. Die Eltern und die Kinder sprechen zu Hause Deutsch.

B. Die Deutschlandkarte *(Look at the map of Germany on the inside cover of the book. Then answer the questions below.)*

1. Welche Flüsse, Seen und Berge gibt es *(are there)* in Deutschland?
2. Wo liegt die Nordsee? die Ostsee? die Insel *(island)* Rügen? die Insel Helgoland? Wo liegen die Ostfriesischen Inseln?
3. Wo liegt . . . ? *(Ask each other about the location of various towns in Germany.)*

C. Wo sprechen die Leute auch Deutsch? *(Use the information from the preceding* Fokus-*section and from the pre-reading passage "German in Europe" to complete the statements about where German is spoken throughout the world.)*

1. Ungefähr 92 Millionen _____ sprechen Deutsch als *(as)* Muttersprache.
   a. Deutsche   b. Holländer   **c.** Europäer
2. Auch in Griechenland, in _____ und in der Türkei verstehen sehr viele Menschen Deutsch.
   a. Spanien   b. Sizilien   c. Andorra
3. Deutsch hat auch eine Tradition in Polen und _____.
   a. Portugal   b. Irland   **c.** Ungarn
4. In Russland _____ mehr als 1,6 Millionen Menschen Deutsch.
   a. brauchen   **b.** lernen   c. wiederholen
5. Viele Amerikaner, _____, Chilenen, Argentinier und Brasilianer kommen ursprünglich *(originally)* aus Deutschland.
   a. Kanadier   b. Schweizer   c. Liechtensteiner

D. Kurzgespräch *(A brief conversation. Imagine you are being interviewed. How do you respond to the reporter's questions?)*

1. Guten Tag! Wie heißen Sie? 2. Woher kommen Sie? 3. Warum sind Sie hier?
4. Was ist Ihre Muttersprache? 5. Sprechen Ihre Eltern oder Großeltern Deutsch?
6. Sprechen Sie noch andere Sprachen? 7. Wie heißt Ihr Deutschbuch? 8. Wie heißt Ihr Professor? 9. Lernen Sie viel? 10. Wie finden Sie Deutsch?

4. **Wie viele Menschen wohnen in** Bonn (Köln, Frankfurt/Main, Düsseldorf, Stuttgart, Leipzig, Dresden)? If you like, you could also introduce how to read numbers in the millions, e.g.: **In Berlin wohnen 3,4 Millionen, in Hamburg 1,7 Millionen und in München 1,3 Millionen Menschen.**

B: To foster listening skills, have students look only at the map while you read the questions aloud. Point out the difference between **der See** (lake, e.g., der Bodensee) and **die See** (sea, e.g., die Nordsee, Ostsee) – **die See** is not active vocabulary!

For a listing of the various Indo-Germanic languages, see Chapter 1 in the *Zum Schreiben* section of the Workbook.

Dein Christus ein **Jude**,
dein Auto ein **Japaner**,
deine Pizza *italienisch*,
deine Demokratie GRIECHISCH,
dein Kaffee brasilianisch,
dein Urlaub *türkisch*,
deine Zahlen **arabisch**,
deine Schrift *lateinisch*,
und dein Nachbar nur ein Ausländer?

HÖREN SIE ZU! Track 3.

Europäer in Deutschland (*Many foreign nationals have chosen to live in Germany. Listen to the four speakers, and then circle the letter of the response that correctly completes the statement.*)

Zum Erkennen: zuerst (*first of all*); komisch (*strange*)

VITTORIO
1. Vittorio ist _____.
   a. 20   b. 29   **c.** 21
2. Seine Eltern sind aus _____.
   a. Portugal   **b.** Italien   c. Spanien

MANUEL
3. Manuel ist aus _____.
   a. Spanien   b. Portugal   c. Italien
4. Er wohnt schon _____ Jahre in Deutschland.
   a. 34   **b.** 33   c. 23

MARIA
5. Maria wohnt in _____.
   a. Frankfurt   b. Dresden   **c.** Düsseldorf
6. Sie und ihre Familie sind _____.
   a. Griechen   b. Italiener   c. Türken

JOSÉ
7. José ist Professor in _____.
   a. Frankfurt   **b.** Bonn   c. Düsseldorf
8. Seine Frau ist aus _____.
   a. Berlin   b. Erfurt   c. Köln

Fokus — *German Throughout the World*

Even though Germany was never an important colonial power, German language and culture have reached all regions of the globe. Looking for new opportunities, millions of Germans emigrated to the Americas, especially to the United States, Canada, Chile, Argentina, and Brazil. Nearly a fourth of the U.S. population claims German ancestry, and some 300 German-language periodicals are still published there.

In Asia, German language, literature, and philosophy continue to be popular subjects at universities; thousands of exchange scholars and students from the Far East have studied in Germany. When Japan opened up to the West in the late 1800s, it borrowed heavily from German law and science. At the turn of the century, the Chinese city of Qindao was under German administration and consequently has many German buildings— and the best beer in China.

Although Germany only briefly controlled a handful of African colonies—Togo, Cameroon, and Namibia (formerly South West Africa)—the impact of those years as well as the influence of German missionaries and doctors can still be found in some regions. German is taught at all levels throughout Africa. Worldwide, 20 million people are learning German as a second language.

Video-Ecke

*   The *Minidrama* „Ganz international" shows two students who make a pleasant discovery and proceed to talk about their families.

*   The *Blickpunkt* „Am Goethe-Institut" takes you to one of the many locations of this renowned, international language school. At the Goethe Institute in Berlin, you'll meet some of the students who tell you about themselves, and also get introduced to one of their guest families.

Note, every chapter has one short episode that is acted out, the *Minidrama*. In addition, about every other chapter has a more spontaneous section, the *Blickpunkt,* that is intended to provide a more authentic cultural background on the chapter topic. Its vocabulary is not as controlled. Accompanying exercises can be found in the *Video-aktiv* section of the Workbook.

Web-Ecke

*   For updates, self-assessment quizzes, and online activities related to this chapter, visit the ***Wie geht's?*** Web site at **http://wiegehts.heinle.com**. You will meet some real German families, visit a few German cities, check their current situation, and learn about some of Germany's neighbors and partners in the European Union.

Besides these Web activities, the home page also offers a list of interesting Web sites. As some of them are rather complex and only in German, they probably are too difficult for a beginning student, but the Web activities are geared to this level.

Kapitel ②

Lebensmittel und Geschäfte

Im Supermarkt

Lernziele

Vorschau
Shopping and store hours

Gespräche + Wortschatz
Grocery shopping

Fokus
Weights and measures
Breads, sausages, and cheeses
Flower power
Pedestrian areas
Regensburg

Struktur
2.1 Present tense of **sein** and **haben**

2.2 Accusative case and n-nouns
2.3 Sentence structure: verb complements,
    negation, and coordinating conjunctions

Einblicke
Geschäfte und Einkaufen

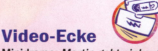

Video-Ecke
Minidrama: *Martin geht einkaufen*

Web-Ecke

Vorschau

Shopping and Store Hours

As much as the development of American-style supermarkets and discount chains has changed the way Europeans shop, customs still differ considerably from those in North America. Many people shop daily or several times a week, frequently going on foot or by bicycle rather than by car. With competition from supermarket chains, grocery sections (**Lebensmittelabteilungen**) in department stores, and large discount stores in shopping centers (**Einkaufszentren**) on the outskirts of towns, the traditional corner grocery store (**Tante-Emma-Laden**) is disappearing rapidly. Specialty stores such as butcher shops, bakeries, or fruit and vegetable stores continue to thrive, however, and many towns have retained open-air farmers' markets. Consumers value the freshness of the products and the personal atmosphere.

Customers usually bring their own shopping bags (**Einkaufstaschen**) to stores and shops or buy reusable cloth bags or plastic bags (**Plastiktüten**) at the checkout counter. They also bag their purchases themselves. Grocery store clerks sit rather than stand when checking out customers. People generally pay in cash (**Bargeld**). Checks and credit cards are rarely accepted, although some supermarkets have introduced ATM links to their cash registers. The amount shown on the price tag always includes tax.

Recycling laws require stores to take back all packaging materials; completely recyclable products are marked with a green dot.

Until 1996, store hours in Germany were regulated by a rigid shop closing law that permitted shopping only during regular business hours and a few hours on Saturday. Despite stiff opposition from owners of small shops and trade unions, the law was finally liberalized. Stores can now be open from 6:00 A.M. to 8:00 P.M.,

(continued on p. 52)

Es gibt immer weniger *(fewer and fewer)* Tante-Emma-Läden.

Monday through Friday, and until 4:00 P.M. on Saturday (on the four Saturdays before Christmas even until 6 P.M.). However, many small neighborhood stores still prefer to close for one or two hours in the early afternoon, generally from 1:00 P.M. to 3:00 P.M. There are no twenty-four–hour supermarkets in Germany. The only place to shop after hours—and all day Sunday—is at gas stations. Airports and almost all train stations also have shops that are open beyond the normal store hours.

Gespräche + Wortschatz

CD 2, Track 5

Warm-ups: 1. **Wo sprechen sie was?** z.B. Deutschland: In Deutschland sprechen sie Deutsch 2. **Wie geht's weiter?** z.B. Dezember: Januar (April, Juni . . .) 3. **Nennen Sie** *(name)* **den Plural**: z.B. der Deutsche: die Deutschen (Engländer, Franzose, Französin, Amerikaner, Student, Studentin, Sprache, Land, Stadt, Fluss, See, Berg) 4. **Wie spät ist es?** *(Have various times ready on the board.)*

Students may be curious about **im Lebensmittelgeschäft** vs. **in der Bäckerei.** Don't try to explain; tell them they will learn the reasons for this difference later.

In the metric system, a pound is about 10 percent heavier than an American pound (500 g rather than 450 g). To convert approximately U.S. pounds to metric pounds: deduct 10 percent (120 lbs. – 12 = 108 lbs.); metric pounds to U.S. pounds: add 10 percent (108 lbs. + 11 = 119 lbs).

125 g = 1 Viertelpfund, 250 g = 1 halbes Pfund, 500 g = 1 Pfund, 1000 g = 1 Kilo(gramm). As a quick-and-easy measurement guide, some cookbooks round off the following figures: 1 oz. = 30 g; 1 lb. = 500 g; 2 lbs. = 1 kg; 4 cups = 1 liter.

A: 1. etwas Obst 2. 90 Cent das Pfund, 45 Cent das Stück 3. 2 Pfund Bananen, 6 Orangen 4. 2 Kilo Äpfel 5. €8,10 6. 6 Brötchen 7. der Apfelstrudel 8. 4 Stück 9. Schokoladenplätzchen 10. nein

Im Lebensmittelgeschäft

> Listen to the dialogue. Then, with a partner, act out the dialogue together.

VERKÄUFER Guten Tag! Was darf's sein?
OLIVER Ich hätte gern etwas Obst. Haben Sie denn keine Bananen?
VERKÄUFER Doch, da drüben.
OLIVER Was kosten sie?
VERKÄUFER 90 Cent das Pfund.
OLIVER Und die Orangen?
VERKÄUFER 45 Cent das Stück.
OLIVER Gut, zwei Pfund Bananen und sechs Orangen bitte!
VERKÄUFER Sonst noch etwas?
OLIVER Ja, zwei Kilo Äpfel bitte!
VERKÄUFER €8,10 bitte! Danke! Auf Wiedersehen!

In der Bäckerei

VERKÄUFERIN Guten Morgen! Was darf's sein?
SIMONE Guten Morgen! Ein Schwarzbrot und sechs Brötchen bitte!
VERKÄUFERIN Sonst noch etwas?
SIMONE Ja, ich brauche etwas Kuchen. Ist der Apfelstrudel frisch?
VERKÄUFERIN Natürlich, ganz frisch.
SIMONE Gut, dann nehme ich vier Stück.
VERKÄUFERIN Ist das alles?
SIMONE Ich möchte auch ein paar Plätzchen. Was für Plätzchen haben Sie heute?
VERKÄUFERIN Zitronenplätzchen, Schokoladenplätzchen, Butterplätzchen . . .
SIMONE Hm . . . Ich nehme 300 Gramm Schokoladenplätzchen.
VERKÄUFERIN Noch etwas?
SIMONE Nein, danke. Das ist alles.
VERKÄUFERIN Das macht dann €9,55 bitte.

A. Fragen

1. Was braucht Oliver? 2. Was kosten die Bananen? die Orangen? 3. Wie viele Bananen und wie viele Orangen kauft er? 4. Was kauft er noch? 5. Was kostet alles zusammen? 6. Wie viele Brötchen möchte Simone? 7. Was ist frisch? 8. Wie viel Stück Apfelstrudel kauft sie? 9. Was für Plätzchen kauft sie? 10. Kauft sie sonst noch etwas?

B. Jetzt sind Sie dran! *(With a partner, create your own dialogue between a customer and a salesperson.)*

Fokus — *Weights and Measures*

In Europe—as in most of the world—the metric system is used to measure distance, volume, and weight. One exception is the older measurement **Pfund,** which is half a kilogram (500 grams), or a little more than the U.S. pound (454 grams). When shopping for food at the market, you can ask for **100 Gramm Leberwurst, ein halbes Pfund Salami,** or **ein Kilo Äpfel.** Liquids are measured by the liter, which is a little more than a quart. In cooking or baking, scales are preferred over cups and spoons, as weighing is more precise: a cup of sugar weighs about 200 grams; a cup of flour 150 grams; a tablespoon **(Esslöffel)** 12 grams; a teaspoon **(Teelöffel)** 5 grams. One ounce equals 28.3 grams.

Wortschatz I

Die Lebensmittel *(pl.)* *(groceries)*

der			die		
	Apfel, ⸚	*apple*		Banane, -n	*banana*
	Fisch, -e	*fish*		Bohne, -n	*bean*
	Jogurt, -s	*yoghurt*		Butter	*butter*
	Kaffee, -s	*coffee*		Cola	*cola drink*
	Käse, -	*cheese*		Erbse, -n	*pea*
	Kuchen, -	*cake*		Erdbeere, -n	*strawberry*
	Saft, ⸚e	*juice*		Gurke, -n	*cucumber*
	Salat, -e	*lettuce, salad*		Karotte, -n	*carrot*
	Tee, -s	*tea*		Limonade, -n	*soft drink*
	Wein, -e	*wine*		= Limo, -s	
				Marmelade, -n	*jam*
das	Bier, -e	*beer*		Milch	*milk*
	Brot, -e	*bread*		Orange, -n	*orange*
	Brötchen, -	*roll*		Tomate, -n	*tomato*
	Ei, -er	*egg*		Wurst, ⸚e	*sausage*
	Fleisch	*meat*		Zitrone, -n	*lemon*
	Gemüse, -	*vegetable(s)*			
	Obst	*fruit*			
	Plätzchen, -	*cookie*			
	Wasser	*water*			

Cola can also be neuter. In southern Germany, Austria, and Switzerland, **Jogurt** is frequently used with **das**; it can also be spelled as **Joghurt.**

Limonade (or **Limo**) is a soft drink and not the same as *lemonade.* Regular *lemonade* would be **Zitronensaft**; if carbonated, it's **Zitronenlimonade.**

Weiteres

der	Markt, ⸚e	*(farmers') market*
	Supermarkt, ⸚e	*supermarket*
	Verkäufer, -	*sales clerk*
das	Geschäft, -e	*store*
	Kaufhaus, ⸚er	*department store*
	Pfund, -e; ein Pfund[1]	*pound; one pound (of)*
	Stück, -e; ein Stück[1]	*piece; one piece (of)*
die	Bäckerei, -en	*bakery*
	Buchhandlung, -en	*bookstore*
	allerlei	*all sorts of, various*
	alles	*everything, all*
	Das ist alles.	*That's all. That's it.*

Füllhorn Öko-Erbsen und Karotten
tiefgefroren
300-g-Packung
€1,29

---

[1] One says **ein Pfund Fleisch, zwei Pfund Fleisch; ein Stück Kuchen, zwei Stück Kuchen.** Remember also **ein Euro, zwei Euro.**

Additional food-related vocabulary will be taught in Chapter 3.

dann	*then (temporal)*
doch	*yes, sure, certainly, of course*
es gibt[2]	*there is, there are*
etwas . . .	*a little, some . . .*
	(used with sg. collective nouns)
frisch	*fresh*
gern[3]	*gladly*
Ich esse / trinke gern . . . [3]	*I like to eat / drink . . .*
Ich esse / trinke nicht gern . . . [3]	*I don't like to eat / drink . . .*
Ich hätte gern . . . [4]	*I would like (to have) . . .*
Ich möchte . . . [4]	*I would like (to have) . . .*
glauben	*to believe, think*
kaufen / verkaufen	*to buy / to sell*
machen	*to make, do*
suchen	*to look for*
natürlich	*of course*
was für (ein) . . . ?[5]	*what kind of (a) . . . ?*
zusammen	*together*

The combination of **gern** + verb can be practiced with English cues: *I like to read, I like to write, I like to play, etc.*

In case you are curious: *apricot* **die Aprikose, -n;** *asparagus* **der Spargel;** *broccoli* **der Brokkoli, *pl.;*** *(fancy) cake* **die Torte, -n;** *cherry* **die Kirsche, -n;** *chocolate* **die Schokolade, -n;** *hot chocolate* **der Kakao;** *corn* **der Mais;** *cornflakes* **die Cornflakes, *pl.;*** *grape* **die Traube, -n;** *grapefruit* **die Grapefruit, -s;** *liver sausage* **die Leberwurst;** *melon* **die Melone, -n;** *oatmeal* **die Haferflocken, *pl.;*** *onion* **die Zwiebel, -n;** *pancake* **der Pfannkuchen, -;** *peach* **der Pfirsich, -e;** *peanut butter* **die Erdnussbutter;** *pear* **die Birne, -n;** *pineapple* **die Ananas, -;** *spinach* **der Spinat;** *waffle* **die Waffel, -n;** *whole-grain granola* **das Müsli**

If students ask: *Brussel sprouts* **der Rosenkohl;** *candy* **der Bonbon, -s;** *cauliflower* **der Blumenkohl;** *kiwi* **die Kiwi, -s** *mango* **die Mango, -s;** *plum* **die Pflaume, -n;** *radish* **das Radieschen, -**

---

[2] See Struktur 2.2-1d.

[3] To express that you like to do something, use **gern** with the main verb: **ich esse gern Obst; er trinkt gern Cola.** If you dislike something, use **nicht gern**, which normally precedes the direct object: **ich esse nicht gern Erbsen; sie trinken nicht gern Milch.**

[4] **möcht-** and **hätt-** are subjunctive verb forms that will be explained in Chapters 13–14: **ich möchte, du möchtest, er möchte, wir möchten, ihr möchtet, sie möchten; ich hätte, du hättest, er hätte, wir hätten, ihr hättet, sie hätten.**

[5] Treat this phrase as you would treat **ein** by itself: **Das ist ein Kuchen. Was für ein Kuchen? Das ist eine Wurst. Was für eine Wurst?** There's no **ein** in the plural: **Das sind Plätzchen. Was für Plätzchen?** Don't use **für** in answers to a **was für**-question: **Was für Obst essen Sie gern? Ich esse gern Bananen.**

Zum Erkennen: Was darf's sein? *(May I help you?);* da drüben *(over there);* Sonst noch etwas? *(Anything else?);* das Kilo / zwei Kilo *(kilogram, two kilos);* der Apfelstrudel *(apple strudel);* AUCH: der Akkusativ, -e; verneinen *(to negate);* jemand *(somebody);* Das stimmt (nicht). *That's (not) true.*

Zum Thema

A. Mustersätze
1. Bananen: **Ich esse gern** Bananen.
   Äpfel, Erdbeeren, Orangen, Gurken, Jogurt
2. Fisch: **Die Kinder essen nicht gern** Fisch.
   Salat, Tomaten, Karotten, Gemüse, Eier
3. Cola: **Wir trinken gern** Cola.
   Limo, Kaffee, Tee, Bier, Wein
4. Obst: **Ich hätte gern etwas** Obst.
   Brot, Fleisch, Marmelade, Käse, Wurst
5. Bananen: **Haben Sie keine** Bananen?
   Erdbeeren, Bohnen, Erbsen, Zitronen, Brötchen

Griechische/Türkische Tafeltrauben hell-kernlos, Sorte: „Sultanas" HKl.I, 1-kg-Schale
1,98

B. 1. die Bohne 2. die Zitrone 3. die Erdbeere 4. das Gemüse 5. der Tee 6. die Erbse 7. die Lebensmittel

B. Was passt nicht? *(Which item does not belong in each list?)*
1. die Butter—der Käse—die Wurst—die Bohne
2. das Brötchen—die Zitrone—das Plätzchen—der Kuchen
3. die Tomate—die Erdbeere—die Gurke—der Salat
4. das Gemüse—der Apfel—die Orange—die Banane
5. das Obst—das Gemüse—der Salat—der Tee
6. der Wein—das Bier—die Erbse—die Milch
7. das Geschäft—die Lebensmittel—die Bäckerei—das Kaufhaus

C. Was bedeuten die Wörter und was sind die Artikel?

Bohnensalat, Buttermilch, Delikatessengeschäft, Erdbeermarmelade, Fischbrötchen, Kaffeemilch, Milchkaffee, Obstsalat, Orangenlimonade, Zitronenlimonade, Zitronensaft, Schreibwarengeschäft, Teewasser, Wurstbrot

D. Allerlei Lebensmittel durcheinander (*In this shopping cart, you'll find all sorts of groceries thrown together. Together with a partner, place these foods into their appropriate categories, e.g., fruits and vegetables, baked goods, milk products, meats, sweets, and beverages.*)

OBST UND GEMÜSE:

MILCHPRODUKTE:

FLEISCHWAREN:

BACKWAREN:

GETRÄNKE:

ANDERES (*other*):

C: *bean salad (**der**), buttermilk (**die**), deli store (**das**), strawberry jam (**die**), fish sandwich (**das**), (coffee) creamer (**die**), coffee au lait (**der**), fruit salad (**der**), orange softdrink (**die**), lemon softdrink (**die**), lemon juice (**der**), stationer's (**das**), tea water (**das**), open sausage sandwich (**das**)*

Optional **Artikelspiel: der, das oder die?** Name certain foods without their articles. If an item is masculine, only the men will say **der**; if feminine, the women will say **die**; if neuter, they'll all reply with **das**.

Optional **Alphabetspiel: Welche Lebensmittel gibt es mit . . . ?** Name a certain letter and ask students to quickly respond with a few German words that start with that letter, e.g., **B: Brot Butter, Banane** etc.

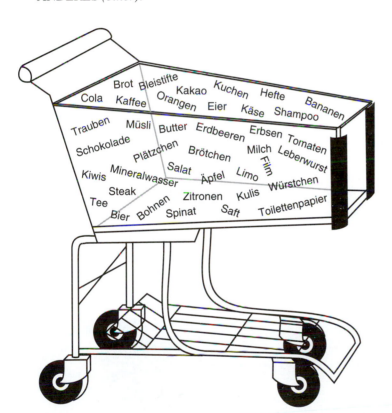

E. Was passt?

labfk 1. Ich glaube, der Fisch ist nicht frisch.
dejl 2. Möchten Sie etwas Obst?
_f_ 3. Die Bäckerei verkauft Wurst, nicht wahr?
cgh 4. Wir kaufen auch Kuchen.
abch 5. Ich trinke morgens gern Cola.

a. Wirklich?
b. Wie bitte?
c. Ich nicht.
d. Ja, gern.
e. Ja, bitte.
f. Natürlich nicht.
g. Prima!
h. Wir auch.
i. Richtig.
j. Nein, danke.
k. Doch.
l. Nein, das ist alles.
m. Schade.
n. . . .

F. **Interview**. Was essen und trinken Sie gern? (*Interview a classmate to find out what foods he / she likes and what his / her eating habits are.*)
1. Was für Obst essen Sie gern (nicht) gern?
2. Was für Gemüse essen Sie (nicht) gern?
3. Essen Sie viel Fisch und Fleisch?
4. Essen Sie gern Süßigkeiten? Wenn ja, was?
5. Was trinken Sie oft?

For the time being, let students use the **Sie**-form, as they have not had the **du**-form of **essen** yet.

CD 2, Track 6

Aussprache: e, o

(*Read also Part II. 2, 5, 14–16, 18, and 21 in the Pronunciation Guide of the Workbook.*)
1. [e:] **geh**en, n**eh**men, K**ä**se, G**e**genteil, Am**e**rika, T**ee**
2. [e] **e**s, spr**e**chen, G**e**schäft, M**e**nsch, H**e**md
3. [o:] **oh**ne B**oh**nen, **o**der, gr**o**ß, **O**bst, Br**o**t
4. [o] k**o**mmen, d**o**ch, **O**sten, N**o**rden, S**o**nne
5. Wortpaare
   a. *gate* / geht   d. den / denn
   b. *shown* / schon   e. Ofen / offen
   c. zähle / Zelle   f. Bonn / Bann

Fokus — *Breads, Sausages, and Cheeses*

When Germans think of **Brot,** they probably think first of a firm, heavy loaf of rye bread **(Schwarzbrot)** and not of the soft white bread so common in America. In Germany, white loaves and rolls are prized for their crisp crust. There are more than 300 varieties of bread in Central Europe, including bread made from a mixture of wheat and rye **(Graubrot)** or of cracked rye and wheat grains **(Vollkornbrot),** and bread with linseed **(Leinsamenbrot)** or sunflower seeds **(Sonnenblumenkernbrot).** For Germans, bread is the most important staple— on average they eat four slices of bread and one roll per day.

The traditional German supper, appropriately called **Abendbrot,** usually consists of bread with cheese, sausage, or cold cuts **(Aufschnitt).** Germany offers a wide variety of cheeses and sausages, which often carry the names of the place of origin: **Allgäuer** (cheese), **Frankfurter, Thüringer** (both sausages). Others are named after ingredients: **Butterkäse, Schimmelkäse, Leberwurst.** Many Germans also eat bread and cheese for breakfast.

Die Deutschen, Österreicher und Schweizer essen gern Brot.

HÖREN SIE ZU! TRACK 4

Essen und Trinken (*Listen to three students tell what they like and don't like to eat and drink. Then note which foods and beverages each student mentions; write H for Hanjo, M for Martina, and D for Dirk. Not all the available slots will be filled.*)

Zum Erkennen: also (*well*); manchmal (*sometimes*); Kartoffeln (*potatoes*)

Hören Sie zu! HANJO isst gern Äpfel, Orangen, Bananen, Erdbeeren, Fisch; trinkt gern Cola, Saft, Bier. 2. MARTINA isst gern Fleisch, Kartoffeln, Gemüse, Kuchen; trinkt gern Tee; trinkt nicht gern Kaffee. 3. DIRK isst nicht gern Gemüse (Karotten, Erbsen, Gurken); trinkt nicht gern Milch, Cola.

ESSEN			TRINKEN		
gern	**nicht gern**		**gern**	**nicht gern**	
_____ Äpfel	_____ Gemüse		_____ Tee	_____ Kaffee	
_____ Bananen	_____ Gurken		_____ Kaffee	_____ Bier	
_____ Kartoffeln	_____ Karotten		_____ Kakao	_____ Wein	
_____ Kuchen	_____ Erbsen		_____ Milch	_____ Milch	
_____ Erdbeeren	_____ Fisch		_____ Saft	_____ Cola	
_____ Orangen	_____ Bananen		_____ Bier	_____ Wasser	
_____ Gemüse	_____ Jogurt		_____ Cola	_____ Tee	
_____ Fisch	_____ Pizza		_____ Mineralwasser	_____ Kakao	
_____ Fleisch	_____ Käsebrot		_____ Limonade	_____ Eiswasser	

Struktur

2.1 Present tense of *sein (to be)* and *haben (to have)*

	sein		haben	
1st person	ich bin	wir sind	ich habe	wir haben
2nd person	du bist	ihr seid	du hast	ihr habt
3rd person	er ist	sie sind	er hat	sie haben

Übung

A. Ersetzen Sie das Subjekt!

> BEISPIEL: Haben Sie Zeit? (du)
> **Hast du Zeit?**

1. Ich bin schon fertig. (er, wir, sie/*sg.*)
2. Sind Sie müde? (du, ihr, sie/*pl.*)
3. Sie hat die Landkarte. (ich, er, wir)
4. Haben Sie Papier? (sie/*sg.*, ihr, du)
5. Wir sind Amerikaner. (er, sie/*pl.*, ich)
6. Er hat eine Frage. (ich, wir, Sie)
7. Seid ihr aus Düsseldorf? (Sie, du, sie/*sg.*)
8. Er hat Orangensaft. (sie/*pl.*, ich, ihr)

Müller
ACE Drink
Orangen-Karotten-Zitronen,
Blutorange oder
Multivitamin
je 500-ml-Becher
€ 0,70

2.2 Accusative case and n-nouns

The accusative case has two major functions: it is the case of the direct object and it follows certain prepositions.

1. In the English sentence *The boy asks the father*, the DIRECT OBJECT of the sentence is *the father*. He is being asked; he is the target of the verb's action. We determine the direct

object by asking *who or what* is directly affected by the verb's action. In other words, the person you see, hear, or ask, or the thing you have, buy, or eat is the direct object.

Der Junge fragt den Vater.	*The boy asks the father.*
Ich kaufe den Kuchen.	*I buy the cake.*

a. The accusative forms of the INTERROGATIVE PRONOUN are **wen?** *(whom?)* and **was?** *(what?).* You now know two cases for this pronoun.

	persons	things and ideas
nom.	wer?	was?
acc.	wen?	was?

Wen fragt der Junge?	→	**Den Vater.**
Whom does the boy ask?	→	*The father.*
Was kaufe ich?	→	**Den Kuchen.**
What am I buying?	→	*The cake.*

b. Of the articles, only those for masculine nouns have special forms for the accusative. In the other genders, the nominative and accusative are identical in form.

		SINGULAR		PLURAL
	masc.	**neut.**	**fem.**	
nom.	der	das	die	die
	ein	ein	eine	—
	kein	kein	keine	keine
acc.	**den**	**das**	**die**	**die**
	einen	**ein**	**eine**	—
	keinen	**kein**	**keine**	**keine**

This pattern is true of all possessive adjectives, but these are the only ones introduced so far.

PETER   Der Käse, das Obst, die Wurst und die Brötchen sind frisch.
PETRA   Dann kaufe ich den Käse, das Obst, die Wurst und die Brötchen.
PETER   Aber wir brauchen keinen Käse, kein Obst, keine Wurst und keine Brötchen!

• The POSSESSIVE ADJECTIVES **mein, dein,** and **Ihr** follow the pattern of **ein** and **kein:**

Brauchen Sie mein**en** Bleistift?

Nein danke, ich brauche Ihr**en** Bleistift nicht.

c. German has a few masculine nouns that have an **-n** or **-en** ending in all cases (singular and plural) except in the nominative singular. They are called N-NOUNS. Note how they are listed in vocabularies and dictionaries: the first ending refers to the singular for cases other than the nominative, the second one to the plural. You are already familiar with all of the n-nouns below.

der Franzose, **-n,** -n[1]	*Frenchman*
Herr, **-n,** -en	*gentleman*
Junge, **-n,** -n	*boy*
Mensch, **-en,** -en	*human being, person*
Nachbar, **-n,** -n	*neighbor*
Student, **-en,** -en	*student*

[1] *REMINDER*: The bar on the left of vocabulary signals that a list is important. Any new features are **bold-faced;** learn them before you do the exercises that follow!

	singular	plural
nom.	der Student	die Studenten
acc.	**den Studenten**	die Studenten

Der Herr heißt Müller.   Fragen Sie Herr**n** Müller!

Da kommt ein Student.   Fragen Sie den Student**en**!

d. Verbs that elicit accusative objects are called TRANSITIVE. (Some verbs are IN-TRANSITIVE, i.e., they cannot take a direct object: **gehen** *to go*.) Here are some familiar transitive verbs:

brauchen	*to need*	mögen / möcht-	*would like*
essen	*to eat*	nehmen	*to take*
finden	*to find*	öffnen	*to open*
fragen	*to ask*	sagen	*to say*
haben	*to have*	schreiben	*to write*
hören	*to hear*	sprechen	*to speak, talk*
kaufen	*to buy*	suchen	*to look for*
lernen	*to learn*	trinken	*to drink*
lesen	*to read*	verkaufen	*to sell*
machen	*to make, do*	verstehen	*to understand*
es gibt	*there is, there are*		

Many students need to develop a sense of the accusative case. It may help to go through the list of these verbs. Point out that they take or even require objects in English, too. If you say *I need* or *I would like*, someone is bound to ask *What?* What you need, buy, sell, take, etc., is the direct object of the verb.

Students cannot yet use **essen, lesen,** or **nehmen** in the 2nd and 3rd person singular (see Chapter 3).

Sie kauft den Rock und die Bluse.

Schreiben Sie den Satz!

Ich esse einen Apfel und eine Banane.

Wir haben einen Supermarkt und ein Kaufhaus.

Das Geschäft verkauft keinen Fisch und kein Fleisch.

Have students identify the accusatives in each example.

• The idiom **es gibt** is always followed by the accusative case in the singular or in the plural.

Es gibt hier einen Markt.   *There's a market here.*

Es gibt auch Lebensmittelgeschäfte.   *There are also grocery stores.*

The pronoun **es** is the subject of the sentence. What "there is," is in the accusative. **Es gibt** implies a general, unspecified existence—unlike **hier ist** or **da ist,** which points to a specific item.

Gibt es hier einen Markt?   *Is there a market here (in town)?*

Ja, es gibt einen Markt.   *Yes, there's a market.*

Wo ist ein Markt?   *Where is a market?*

Da ist ein Markt.   *There's a market. (There it is.)*

2. ACCUSATIVE PREPOSITIONS are always followed by the accusative case. Here are those used most frequently:

durch	*through*	Britta kommt **durch die Tür.**
für	*for*	Das Obst ist **für den Kuchen.**
gegen	*against*	Was hast du **gegen meinen Bruder?**
ohne	*without*	Wir essen das Brötchen **ohne den Käse.**
um	*around*	Wir gehen **um den See.**
	at (time)	Wir kommen **um 12 Uhr.**

- Some prepositions may be contracted with the definite article. These forms are especially common in everyday speech.

> durch + das = **durchs**
> für + das = **fürs**
> um + das = **ums**

NOTE: A sentence can contain two accusatives, one the direct object and the other the object of a preposition.

Sie kauft den Fisch für den Fischsalat.

Übungen

B. Wiederholen Sie die Sätze noch einmal mit *ein* und *kein*!

BEISPIEL: Er kauft den Bleistift, das Buch und die Landkarte.
Er kauft einen Bleistift, ein Buch und eine Landkarte.
Er kauft keinen Bleistift, kein Buch und keine Landkarte.

1. Sie möchte den Rock, das Kleid und die Bluse.
2. Du brauchst das Hemd, die Hose und den Pullover.
3. Ich esse das Brötchen, die Orange und den Apfel.
4. Wir fragen den Herrn, die Frau und das Mädchen.
5. Öffnen Sie bitte die Tür und das Fenster!
6. Kauft ihr den Kuchen, das Brot und die Brezel *(pretzel)?*

If students have difficulties with C and E because they can't remember the genders of the nouns used, point out how crucial it is to learn the article with the noun. Ask them to state the article of each noun before giving the accusative form.

C. Einkaufen *(You're making small talk while shopping with friends. Substitute the nouns in parentheses.)*

BEISPIEL: Wir kaufen den Saft. (Salat)
Wir kaufen den Salat.

1. Möchtest du das Fleisch? (Gemüse, Obst, Schwarzbrot)
2. Die Wurst essen wir nicht. (Marmelade, Tomate, Gurke)
3. Meine Schwester trinkt keinen Saft. (Limonade, Cola, Wasser)
4. Hast du den Tee? (Saft, Milch, Käse)
5. Gibt es hier eine Buchhandlung? (Markt, Delikatessengeschäft, Kaufhäuser)
6. Fragen Sie den Herrn! (Junge, Mensch, Student, Studenten/*pl.*)
7. Den Verkäufer verstehe ich nicht! (Verkäuferin, Nachbar, Kind)
8. Haben Sie keinen Jogurt? (Saft, Eier, Limo)

Sarotti
Schokolade
verschiedene Sorten

100-g-Tafel   € -.39

Aus der Käsetheke:
Galbani Mozzarella
italienischer Weichkäse,
45 % Fett i. Tr.
100 g   € -.99

Aus der Käsetheke:
Galbani Gorgonzola
50 % Fett i. Tr., 100 g

€ -.99

D. Umzug (*Moving. You are giving instructions to the movers who are bringing your belongings into your new apartment. Use the cues.*)

> **BEISPIEL:** durch / Zimmer
> **Durch das Zimmer bitte!**

1. gegen / Wand
2. um / Tisch
3. ohne / Bücher
4. durch / Tür
5. ohne / Stuhl
6. für / Kinderzimmer (*pl.*)
7. gegen / Fenster (*sg.*)
8. um / Ecke (*f.*)

D: 1. gegen die Wand 2. um den Tisch 3. ohne die Bücher 4. durch die Tür 5. ohne den Stuhl 6. für die Kinderzimmer 7. gegen das Fenster 8. um die Ecke

E. Sagen Sie es noch einmal! (*Replace the noun following the preposition with another noun.*)

> **BEISPIEL:** Ich suche etwas für meinen Vater. (Mutter, Kind)
> **Ich suche etwas für meine Mutter.**
> **Ich suche etwas für mein Kind.**

1. Wir gehen durch die Geschäfte. (Supermarkt, Kaufhaus, Bäckerei)
2. Er kommt ohne das Bier. (Wein, Cola, Kaffee, Käsebrot, Salat)
3. Was haben Sie gegen den Herrn? (Verkäuferin, Mädchen, Junge, Nachbarin)
4. Wiederholen Sie das für Ihren Großvater! (Bruder, Schwester, Nachbar, Eltern)

Optional practice: Play a memory game. Write the title of a recipe on the board, e.g., for a salad **(ein Salat):** Begin with the question **Was kaufen Sie für den Salat?** One student answers **Ich kaufe Tomaten für den Salat.** He/she then asks a classmate **Was kaufen Sie/kaufst du noch?** He/she might continue, **Ich kaufe Tomaten und Gurken für den Salat,** etc. Students keep adding to the list.

F. Was darf's sein? Kombinieren Sie! (*You are a salesperson in a clothing store. Ask your customers—a. a friend, b. a stranger, and c. two of your relatives—what kind of items they need.*)

> **BEISPIEL:** Was für einen Pullover möchten Sie?

1	2	3	4
was für (ein)	Rock	brauchen	du
	Hemd	möchten	ihr
	Jacke	suchen	Sie
	Schuhe		
	. . .		

G. Was kaufen Sie? (*Working with a partner, answer each question with four to six items, drawing on all the vocabulary you have had so far. Use articles whenever necessary.*)

> **BEISPIEL:** Sie sind im Supermarkt. Was kaufen Sie?
> **Wir kaufen einen Kuchen, eine Cola, ein Pfund Butter, ein Stück Käse, etwas Obst, etwas Jogurt . . .**

1. Sie sind in der Bäckerei. Was kaufen Sie?
2. Sie sind im Kaufhaus. Was kaufen Sie?
3. Sie sind in der Buchhandlung. Was kaufen Sie?

G: This also could be done as a competition between groups of students. Who can find the largest number of items?

H. Wie bitte? Hier hört jemand (*someone*) schlecht.

1. **Ihr Großvater** (*Your grandfather, who is hard of hearing and forgetful, always wants you to repeat whatever you say. What questions does he ask?*)

> **BEISPIEL:** Rudi hat heute eine Prüfung.
> **Wer hat eine Prüfung?**
> **Was hat Rudi?**

a. Vater hört den Nachbarn.
b. Matthias fragt Tante Martha.
c. Die Mutter kauft Obst.
d. Die Kinder möchten einen Apfel.
e. Helga und Britta verstehen die Engländer nicht.
f. Wir lernen Deutsch.
g. Ich suche eine Landkarte.

H.1: a. Wer hört den Nachbarn? Wen hört der Vater? b. Wer fragt Tante Martha? Wen fragt Matthias? c. Wer kauft Obst? Was kauft die Mutter? d. Wer möchte einen Apfel? Was möchten die Kinder? e. Wer versteht die Engländer nicht? Wen verstehen Helga und Britta nicht? f. Wer lernt Deutsch? Was lernen wir? g. Wer sucht eine Landkarte? Was suche ich / Was suchst du?

Optional activity: **Was hast du dabei?**
(What did you bring along?) Have students
ask each about the content of their
(hand)bag. By using **Ich habe . . .** or
da gibt es . . . they'll automatically use
the accusative. Be prepared to help with
certain vocabulary.

2. **Auch Sie hören schlecht**. *(You are having difficulty understanding your partner. As he or she makes statements about shopping or anything else, ask for details.)*

   BEISPIEL: Bei ALDI *(at ALDI)* gibt es heute Vollkornbrot für 99 Cent.
   Wo gibt es Brot?
   Was für Brot gibt es?
   Was kostet es?

I. **Einkaufen für eine Party** *(You are organizing a party for a friend. At the grocery store, buy the ingredients for a fruit salad, soft drinks, etc. Always ask the clerk for the price of each item to make sure that anything you are buying is within your limited budget. Try to include phrases like "half a pound, a quarter of a pound, a kilo," and "a dozen," i.e.,* **ein halbes Pfund, ein Viertelpfund, ein Kilo, ein Dutzend***).*

   S1   Guten Tag! Was darf's sein?
   S2   Ich brauche . . . und . . . Was kosten / kostet . . . ?
   S1   . . .
   S2   Und was kosten / kostet . . . ?
   S1   . . .
   S2   Gut, dann nehme ich . . . und . . .
   S1   Sonst noch etwas?
   S2   . . .
   S1   . . . Euro bitte!

Fokus — *Flower Power*

Germans are very fond of having fresh flowers in their homes. When invited for coffee / tea or dinner, guests usually bring their hosts a bouquet. The flowers, however, have to be carefully chosen: red roses, for example, carry the message of romantic love, while white chrysanthemums are considered funeral flowers. The gift of flowers (or some other small present) eliminates the need for a thank-you note, but a follow-up telephone call is very much appreciated.

Blumenmarkt in Freiburg

2.3 Sentence structure

1. Verb complements

   As you know from Chapter 1, predicate nouns and predicate adjectives are verb complements (V2). Sometimes objects or another verb also become part of the verb phrase, i.e., VERB COMPLEMENTS, and in that combination they complete the meaning of the main verb (V1). Verb complements usually stand at the end of the sentence.

Sie **sprechen Deutsch.**		Wir **gehen essen.**		
Sie **sprechen** gut **Deutsch.**		Wir **gehen** gern **essen.**		
Sie <u>**sprechen**</u> wirklich gut <u>**Deutsch.**</u>		Wir <u>**gehen**</u> mittags gern <u>**essen.**</u>		
V1	V2	V1	V2	

2. Negation

   a. **Kein**

   Kein *(no, not a, not any)* is the negative of **ein** and therefore takes the same endings as **ein**. It negates nouns that in an affirmative statement or question would be preceded by **ein** or by no article at all.

preceded by **ein:**	Hast du **einen** Bleistift?
	Nein, ich habe **keinen** Bleistift.
	No, I don't have a pencil.
unpreceded:	Haben Sie Geschwister?
	Nein, ich habe **keine** Geschwister.
	No, I don't have any brothers or sisters.

   b. **Nicht**

   Nicht *(not)* is used when **kein** cannot be used. It can negate an entire sentence, or just part of it. Its position is determined as follows:

   • When negating an entire statement, **nicht** generally stands at the end of that sentence or clause. It always follows the <u>subject and verb;</u> also, it usually follows <u>noun and pronoun objects</u> and expressions of <u>definite time.</u>

subject and verb:	*Sie schreiben* **nicht.**
noun object:	Ich brauche *die Landkarte* **nicht.**
pronoun object:	Ich brauche *sie* **nicht.**
definite time:	Ich brauche sie *heute* **nicht.**

   • When **nicht** negates a particular sentence element, it usually comes right before that element. Such elements commonly include <u>adverbs,</u> including adverbs of general time; <u>prepositional phrases;</u> and <u>verb complements (V2).</u>

adverbs:	Ich kaufe das **nicht** *gern.*[1]
	Ich kaufe das **nicht** *hier.*
	Ich kaufe das **nicht** *oft.*
prepositional phrase:	Ich kaufe das **nicht** *im Geschäft.*
	Ich kaufe das **nicht** *auf dem Markt.*
verb complements:	Ich gehe heute **nicht** *essen.*
	Ich spiele heute **nicht** *Tennis.*
	Ich heiße **nicht** *Beyer.*
	Das ist **nicht** *mein Buch.*
	Das Obst ist **nicht** *billig.*

Ich kaufe das nicht gern. Similarly, **Ich kaufe Käse nicht gern** (emphasizing that you <u>don't really like to buy</u> cheese). The more common way is **Ich kaufe nicht gern Käse** (emphasizing that you don't particularly care to buy cheese). Both sentences are acceptable, but there is a fine difference in emphasis. The word at the end of the sentence is emphasized the most.

If students ask, explain that the function of **Tennis** as a verb complement overrides its function as a direct object – hence **Tennis** is the final element rather than **nicht.**

---

[1] BUT: with **nicht gern** + noun, the word order is usually **Ich esse nicht gern** *Käse.* **Ich trinke nicht gern** *Buttermilch.*

- The following chart shows the most frequent pattern for the placement of **nicht:**

S	V1	O	definite time expression	other adverbs or adverbial phrases	V2.
			↑ **nicht**		

Wir spielen heute **nicht** mit den Kindern Tennis.

c. **Kein** vs. **nicht**

- Use **kein** when the noun has an indefinite article or no article at all.

noun + indefinite article:	Ich kaufe *ein Brot.*
	Ich kaufe **kein** Brot.
unpreceded noun:	Ich kaufe *Milch.*
	Ich kaufe **keine** Milch.

- Use **nicht** when the noun is preceded by a definite article or a possessive adjective.

noun + definite article:	Ich kaufe *das Brot.*
	Ich kaufe *das Brot* **nicht.**
noun + possessive adj.:	Das ist *mein Buch.*
	Das ist **nicht** *mein Buch.*

d. **Ja, nein, doch**

COMPARE:	Hast du das Buch?	**Ja!**	*Yes.*
		Nein!	*No.*
	Hast du das Buch **nicht?**	**Doch!**	*Of course I do.*

- **Doch** is an affirmative response to a negative question or statement.

Wohnt Erika Schwarz **nicht** in Salzburg?	**Doch!**
Haben Sie **keine** Swatch-Uhren?	**Doch,** hier sind sie.
Ich glaube, sie wohnt **nicht** in Salzburg.	**Doch,** sie wohnt dort.

3. Coordinating conjunctions

Two independent clauses can be joined into one sentence by means of COORDINATING CONJUNCTIONS. Each of the two clauses keeps the original word order.

aber	*but, however*	Wir essen Fisch, aber sie essen Fleisch.
denn	*because, for*	Sie kauft Obst, denn es ist frisch.
oder	*or*	Nehmen Sie Brot oder möchten Sie Brötchen?
und	*and*	Ich kaufe Wurst und er kauft Käse.

Übungen

J: 1. keine Erdbeeren 2. keinen Gurkensalat
3. keine Limo 4. keinen / kein Jogurt
5. kein Stück Brot 6. kein Wurstbrötchen
7. kein Glas Milch 8. keinen Apfel

J. Die Nachbarin (*Every time you visit your elderly neighbor, she insists that you eat or drink something. Use the negative **kein**.*)

BEISPIEL: Möchten Sie eine Banane?
Möchten Sie keine Banane?

1. Nehmen Sie Erdbeeren? 2. Essen Sie Gurkensalat? 3. Trinken Sie Limo? 4. Essen Sie Jogurt? 5. Möchten Sie ein Stück Brot? 6. Nehmen Sie ein Wurstbrötchen? 7. Trinken Sie ein Glas Milch? 8. Möchten Sie einen Apfel?

K. Das stimmt nicht! (*That's not true. A recent acquaintance has confused you with someone else. Correct his/her misconceptions, using **nicht**. Enact this situation with a partner, then switch roles. You may use the cues in brackets or your own.*)

BEISPIEL: Ihr Name ist [Fiedler], nicht wahr?
Nein, mein Name ist nicht [Fiedler]. Mein Name ist [Fiedel].

1. Sie heißen [Watzlik], nicht wahr? 2. Sie kommen aus [Polen], nicht wahr? 3. Ihre Familie wohnt in [Mecklenburg], nicht wahr? 4. Ihr Onkel und Ihre Tante sprechen [Mecklenburgisch], nicht wahr? 5. Ihr Bruder wohnt in [Thüringen], nicht wahr? 6. Sie studieren [Musik], nicht wahr? 7. Sie trinken gern [Tomatensaft], nicht wahr? 8. Sie essen gern [Fleischsalat], nicht wahr?

L. Nein!!!

1. **Mein kleiner Bruder.** Alles, was ich sage, verneint *(negates)* er. *(To get your attention, your little brother—played by your partner—negates everything you say. Use either **nein** or **kein**.)*

   a. Heute ist es heiß. b. Die Sonne scheint. c. Da drüben *(over there)* ist ein Geschäft. d. Das Geschäft verkauft Limonade und Eistee. e. Die Cola ist kalt. f. Ich möchte ein Käsebrötchen. g. Ich esse das Käsebrötchen! h. Ich bin Vegetarier *(vegetarian)*. i. Ich esse gern Käse. j. Käse ist gesund *(healthy / healthful)*. k. Wir gehen jetzt in eine Buchhandlung. l. Vater braucht eine Landkarte und einen Stadtplan *(city map)*. m. Er braucht die Landkarte! n. Ich finde das Amerikabuch schön. o. Wir haben Zeit. p. Ich lese gern Bücher. q. Das ist ein Spanischbuch. r. Heinz lernt Spanisch. s. Er studiert in Madrid. t. Ich brauche einen Kalender *(calendar)*. u. Ich finde den Städtekalender gut. v. Der Kalender ist billig. w. Ich möchte den Kalender! x. Wir brauchen Bleistifte und Kulis.

2. **Nein aus Protest** *(This time, make your own statements, which your partner negates out of protest. Take turns.)*

M. *Ja, **nein** oder **doch**?*

BEISPIEL: Ist der Rhein im Westen von Deutschland?   **Ja!**
Ist der Rhein im Osten von Deutschland?   **Nein!**
Ist der Rhein nicht im Westen von Deutschland?   **Doch!**

1. Sprechen die Österreicher nicht Deutsch?
2. Hat Deutschland viele Nachbarn?
3. Ist Bonn die Hauptstadt von Deutschland?
4. Ist Wien nicht die Hauptstadt von Österreich?
5. Hamburg liegt in Norddeutschland, nicht wahr?
6. Gibt es in Deutschland keine Supermärkte?
7. Sind 600 Gramm ein Pfund?
8. Ein Viertelpfund ist nicht 125 Gramm, oder?
9. Ein Kilogramm ist ein halbes Pfund, nicht wahr?

N. Blitzreaktionen *(Quick reactions. Ask your partner all sorts of questions, which he/she quickly answers with **ja, nein** or **doch**.)*

BEISPIEL: Du kommst aus . . . , nicht wahr?   **Ja! / Nein!**
Du hast keine Geschwister, oder?   **Doch! / Nein!**

O. Eine Postkarte *(After your first week in Bremen, you are writing a brief postcard to a friend. Join the two sentences with the conjunctions indicated.)*

Hallo Frank!
1. Ich schreibe nicht viel. Ich habe keine Zeit. *(because)*
2. Ich finde es hier schön. Ich lerne auch sehr viel. *(and)*
3. Meine Zimmerkolleginnen/Zimmerkollegen *(roommates)* kommen aus Kanada und sprechen Französisch. Sie verstehen nicht viel Deutsch. *(but)*
4. Am Sonntag spielen wir zusammen Minigolf. Wir gehen in die Stadt. *(or)*

L.1: a. nicht heiß b. scheint nicht c. kein Geschäft d. keine Limonade und keinen Eistee e. nicht kalt f. kein Käsebrötchen g. das Käsebrötchen nicht h. kein Vegetarier i. nicht gern j. nicht gesund k. in keine Buchhandlung / nicht in eine Buchhandlung l. keine Landkarte und keinen Stadtplan m. Keine Landkarte / die Landkarte nicht n. nicht schön o. keine Zeit p. nicht gern q. kein Spanischbuch r. nicht Spanisch s. nicht in Madrid t. keinen Kalender u. nicht gut v. nicht billig w. den Kalender nicht x. keine Bleistifte und keine Kulis

M: 1. doch 2. ja 3. nein 4. doch 5. ja 6. doch 7. nein 8. doch 9. nein

O: 1. weil ich keine Zeit habe 2. und ich lerne auch sehr viel 3. aber sie verstehen nicht viel Deutsch 4. oder wir gehen in die Stadt

Fokus — *Pedestrian Areas*

Most European cities have developed a pedestrian area **(Fußgängerzone)** in the center of town. Since cars are prohibited, these areas are free of traffic noise and exhaust fumes—a great improvement in the quality of life in dense urban centers. During business hours, and especially on Saturday mornings, pedestrian areas are packed with shoppers. During the summer, cafés spill out onto the sidewalks, and street musicians add to the atmosphere. The prime real estate along pedestrian areas has provided property owners with an incentive to refurbish older buildings, which typically combine apartments in the upper stories and businesses on the ground floor.

Fußgängerzone in Regensburg

Zusammenfassung

P. Hoppla, das haben sie hier wohl nicht! *(Oops, it looks as if they don't have that here! You and your partner are looking for certain groceries in the supermarket, but discover that you can't find them right away. Address your partner with questions about items that might or might not be visible in the picture on p. 67. Take turns and keep track of what you find.)*

picture on p. 67

BEISPIEL:	S1	Hier gibt es kein Brot, oder?
	S2	Doch, da gibt es Brot. Aber ich sehe keinen Wein.
	S1	Nein, ich sehe auch keinen Wein. Gibt es hier . . . ?

Hier gibt es . . .	Hier gibt es kein / keine / keinen . . .

Q. Im Lebensmittelgeschäft. Auf Deutsch bitte!

1. What would you like? 2. What kind of vegetables do you have today? 3. I think I'll take two pounds of beans. 4. The eggs are fresh, aren't they?—Of course. 5. We don't need (any) eggs. 6. But we need some fish and lettuce. 7. I'm not eating any fish. 8. Do you have any carrot juice? 9. Don't you like (to drink) carrot juice?—No! 10. Do you have any coke? I like to drink coke. 11. She's buying a coke and some orange juice. 12. Is that all?—No, I'd also like two pieces of strawberry cake.

Q. 1. Was möchten Sie? / Was darf's sein? 2. Was für Gemüse haben Sie heute? 3. Ich glaube, ich nehme zwei Pfund Bohnen. 4. Die Eier sind frisch, nicht wahr? — Natürlich! 5. Wir brauchen keine Eier. 6. Aber wir brauchen etwas Fisch und Salat. 7. Ich esse keinen Fisch. 8. Haben Sie Karottensaft? 9. Trinkst du nicht gern Karottensaft? — Nein! 10. Haben Sie Cola? Ich trinke gern Cola. 11. Sie kauft eine Cola und etwas Orangensaft. 12. Ist das alles? — Nein, ich möchte auch zwei Stück Erdbeerkuchen.

Einblicke

Lesestrategie: Understanding Spoken Words

This text is a spoken dialogue. After you have finished the pre-reading activities, listen to the dialogue without reading the text. Then play the dialogue again, following along the text. Now, listen to the dialogue one more time, without the text. You'll probably understand everything the last time around.

Wortschatz 2

der Durst	*thirst*
Hunger	*hunger*
das Glas, ¨er; ein Glas¹	*glass; a glass (of)*
Würstchen, -²	*hot dog*
die Apotheke, -n³	*pharmacy*
Blume, -n	*flower*
Drogerie, -n³	*drugstore*
Tasse, -n; eine Tasse¹	*cup; a cup (of)*
Ach du liebes bisschen!	*Good grief! My goodness! Oh dear!*
Bitte, bitte!	*You're welcome.*
ein paar⁴	*a few, some (used with plural nouns)*
montags (dienstags . . .)	*on Mondays (Tuesdays, . . .)*
offen / zu	*open / closed*
warum?	*why?*
Ich gehe . . . einkaufen.	*I go shopping . . .*
Ich habe Hunger / Durst.	*I'm hungry / thirsty.*

¹ **Möchten Sie *ein Glas Milch*** (*a glass of milk*) **oder *eine Tasse Kaffee*** (*a cup of coffee*)?

² All nouns ending in **-chen** are neuter. The suffix makes diminutives of nouns, i.e., it makes them smaller. They often have an umlaut, but there is no additional plural ending: **der Bruder, das Brüderchen; die Schwester, das Schwesterchen; das Glas, das Gläschen; die Tasse, das Tässchen**

³ A **Drogerie** sells over-the-counter drugs, cosmetics, toiletries, and a variety of other items found in American drugstores and is headed by a druggist (**Drogist / in**) trained in a three-year apprenticeship. An **Apotheke** sells prescription and nonprescription drugs and is staffed by a university-trained pharmacist (**Apotheker / in**) and trained assistants.

⁴ *Ein paar* **Tomaten**, *ein paar* **Äpfel** (*pl.*) BUT *etwas* **Kaffee**, *etwas* **Butter** (*sg.* collective noun)

Vor dem Lesen

A. Die Einkaufsliste (*In the following text you'll meet Carolyn, an American student in Germany. Consult her shopping list on facing page, where she has checked what she needs. Then complete the sentences below. Several correct answers are possible.*)

1. **Was hat Carolyn und was braucht sie nicht?**

   Sie hat noch etwas _____ und ein paar _____ . Sie braucht kein(e / en) _____ .

2. **Was hat sie nicht und was kauft sie?**

   Carolyn hat kein(e / en) _____ . Sie kauft ein paar _____ , ein Pfund _____ und etwas _____ .

B. Allerlei Geschäfte (*Ask your partner questions about the various stores. Take turns.*)

1. Wo gibt es Kaffee und Kuchen? Was gibt es da noch? Ab wann sind sie morgens offen?
2. Wohin gehst du, wenn du ein paar Blumen brauchst? Von wann bis wann ist das Blumengeschäft offen? Kannst du die E-Mail-Adresse buchstabieren?
3. Wo gibt es Medizin? Von wann bis wann sind sie offen? Gibt es eine Telefonnummer oder eine E-Mail-Addresse?
4. Wo verkaufen sie Weine? Kannst du das buchstabieren? Von wann bis wann sind sie offen? Wann haben sie zu? Haben sie eine Internetseite?
5. Welches Geschäft entwickelt (*develops*) Filme? Wie ist ihre Telefonnummer? Haben sie eine Internetseite?

C. Was ist das?

das Auto, Café, Einkaufen, Einkaufszentrum, Spezialgeschäft; die Boutique, Medizin; romantisch

CD 2, Track 8

Geschäfte und Einkaufen

dorm kitchen

Carolyn ist Studentin. Sie studiert ein Jahr in Regensburg. In der Studentenheimküche° findet sie zwei Regensburger Studenten, Ursula und Peter.

CAROLYN: Guten Morgen! Mein Name ist Carolyn.

URSULA: Freut mich. Das ist Peter und ich heiße Ursula.

PETER: Guten Morgen, Carolyn! Woher kommst du?

CAROLYN: Ich komme aus Colorado.

are eating breakfast / just now

PETER: Du, wir frühstücken° gerade°. Möchtest du eine Tasse Kaffee?

CAROLYN: Ja, gern. Ich habe wirklich Hunger.

URSULA: Hier hast du ein Stück Brot, etwas Butter und Marmelade.

CAROLYN: Danke!

PETER: Etwas Milch für den Kaffee?

CAROLYN: Ja, bitte.

PETER: Auch ein Ei?

CAROLYN: Nein, danke.—Hm, das Brot ist gut! Wo gibt es hier Geschäfte?

corner / butcher shop

URSULA: Um die Ecke° gibt es ein Lebensmittelgeschäft, eine Metzgerei° und auch eine Drogerie.

*In the south, the word **Metzgerei** is prevalent. Elsewhere you commonly hear **Fleischerei***

CAROLYN: Prima! Ich brauche auch Medizin.

URSULA: Da findest du auch eine Apotheke.

CAROLYN: Ist das Lebensmittelgeschäft sehr teuer?

PETER: Billig ist es nicht. Wir gehen oft in die Stadt, denn da findest du alles. Da gibt es Spezialgeschäfte, Supermärkte und auch Kaufhäuser. Es gibt auch ein Einkaufszentrum.

cathedral

URSULA: Regensburg ist wirklich sehr schön. Es ist alt und romantisch und um den Dom° gibt es viele Boutiquen.

watch

PETER: Ich finde die Fußgängerzone prima, denn da gibt es keine Autos, nur Fußgänger. Da beobachte° ich gern die Leute.

mean

URSULA: Du meinst° die Mädchen.

So what!

PETER: Na und°!

URSULA: Wir gehen auch manchmal in ein Café und essen ein Stück Kuchen.

to the

PETER: Oder wir gehen an die Donau zur° "Wurstküche", essen ein paar Würstchen und trinken ein Glas Bier.

farmers

URSULA: Samstags ist Markt. Da verkaufen die Bauern° Obst, Gemüse, Eier und Blumen. Alles ist sehr frisch.

CAROLYN: Und wann sind die Geschäfte offen?

PETER: Die Kaufhäuser sind von morgens um neun bis abends um acht offen, ein paar Boutiquen nur bis um halb sieben.

CAROLYN: Gut, dann gehe ich heute Abend einkaufen.

That won't work.

PETER: Das geht nicht.°

CAROLYN: Warum nicht?

PETER: Heute ist Samstag. Samstags sind die Geschäfte nur bis um vier offen und sonntags sind sie hier draußen° zu.

out here

CAROLYN: Aber nicht die Kaufhäuser, oder?

PETER: Doch!

CAROLYN: Ach du liebes bisschen! Dann gehe ich jetzt einkaufen. Danke fürs Frühstück!

PETER: Bitte, bitte!

Fokus — *Regensburg*

Regensburg is one of the few larger medieval cities in Germany not seriously damaged during World War II. Founded by the Celts around 500 B.C., it was later the site of a Roman military outpost called *Castra Regina,* dating back to A.D. 179. During the Middle Ages, the imperial diet of the Holy Roman Empire held occasional sessions there. After 1663, the city was the seat of a perpetual diet, the first attempt to establish a permanent German parliament.

Today Regensburg's old center is largely intact and contains fine examples of Romanesque, Gothic, and baroque architecture. Its two most famous landmarks are the Gothic cathedral and a 12th-century stone bridge that spans the Danube. The city's main sources of income are tourism, the electronics industry, and a BMW plant. The university, founded in 1962, has a significant impact on the cultural and economic life of the city.

Nach dem Lesen

A. Was passt wo? *(Find the correct places for the listed words.)*

Apotheke, einkaufen, Hunger, Kaffee, Kuchen, Kaufhäuser, Lebensmittelgeschäft, samstags, Studenten, Studentin

1. Carolyn ist _Studentin_. 2. Peter und Ursula sind auch _Studenten_. 3. Carolyn hat wirklich _Hunger_. 4. Um die Ecke gibt es ein _Lebensmittelgeschäft_ und eine _Apotheke_. 5. Die Leute im Café essen _Kuchen_ und trinken _Kaffee_. 6. Von Montag bis Freitag sind die _Kaufhäuser_ bis abends um acht offen. 7. _Samstags_ sind die Geschäfte nur bis um vier offen. 8. Carolyn geht jetzt _einkaufen_.

B. Verneinen Sie die Sätze!

1. Sie möchte ein Ei.
2. Sie möchte Milch für den Kaffee.
3. Die Kaufhäuser sind samstags zu.
4. Verkauft die Drogerie Medizin?
5. Das Lebensmittelgeschäft ist billig.
6. Gibt es da Autos?
7. Das glaube ich.
8. Die Blumen sind frisch.
9. Ich brauche Blumen.

C. Was bedeuten die Wörter und was sind die Artikel?

Söhnchen, Töchterchen, Stühlchen, Tischchen, Heftchen, Flüsschen, Mäntelchen, Höschen, Stündchen, Teilchen, Blümchen

D. Kurzgespräche *(Together with your partner, prepare one of the following brief dialogues. Then present it to the class.)*

1. **Neu in . . .**
   *A foreign exchange student comes to your university. You are in the cafeteria making small talk. He / she asks you all sorts of questions, including questions about stores and shopping hours, a farmers' market or flea market (**der Flohmarkt**), your shopping habits, etc.*

Optional practice: Richtig oder falsch? 1. Carolyn ist Amerikanerin. (R) 2. Ursula und Peter frühstücken. (R) 3. Es gibt Kaffee und Fisch. (F) 4. Die Drogerie verkauft Medizin. (F) 5. Ursula und Peter gehen oft in die Stadt. (R) 6. In Regensburg gibt es keine Fußgängerzone. (F) 7. Auf dem Markt kaufen die Leute Obst, Gemüse, Eier und Blumen. (R) 8. Samstag sind die Geschäfte nicht offen. (F) 9. Sonntags ist da draußen alles zu. (R)

B: 1. kein Ei 2. keine Milch 3. nicht zu 4. keine Medizin 5. nicht billig 6. keine Autos 7. ich nicht 8. nicht frisch 9. keine Blumen

C: Point out that all diminutives end in -chen (or -lein) and are NEUTER.

Optional practice: **Stellen Sie Fragen mit *wer, wen oder was!*** z.B. Peter beobachtet die Leute: Wer beobachtet die Leute? Wen beobachtet er? (Carolyn ist Studentin. In der Studentenheimküche findet sie zwei Regensburger Studenten. Um die Ecke findest du eine Apotheke. Die Bauern verkaufen Obst, Gemüse und Blumen.)

2. **Im Kaufhaus**

You want to buy an item of clothing in a department store. Describe to the salesclerk what you are looking for. After viewing and commenting on several items the clerk has shown you (e.g., one is too small, one too big, one too expensive, etc.), decide whether or not to buy. If you do not buy it, explain your reasons. If you do buy it, of course, you must pay before you leave!)

HÖREN SIE ZU!   TRACK 5

Neu in Regensburg *(Listen to the conversation between two students. Then decide whether the statements below are true or false according to the information in the dialogue.)*

Zum Erkennen: Sag mal! *(Say)*; nachher *(afterwards)*

___f___ 1. Ursula wohnt schon zwanzig Jahre in Regensburg.
___r___ 2. Claudia ist aus Passau.
___f___ 3. Claudia braucht Schuhe.
___r___ 4. Ursula geht heute nachmittag einkaufen.
___r___ 5. Sie geht um drei Uhr.
___f___ 6. Ursula braucht Jeans und ein Sweatshirt.
___f___ 7. Dann gehen sie ein paar Würstchen essen.

Video-Ecke

- In the *Minidrama* "Martin geht einkaufen," Martin knows exactly what he needs to buy, but somehow he misses out on the most essential item. How does this happen?

Web-Ecke

- For updates, self-assessment quizzes, and online activities related to this chapter, visit the **Wie geht's?** Web site at **http://wiegehts.heinle.com**. You will visit a German supermarket and an Austrian clothing store, and go on a virtual shopping tour, purchasing various items. You'll also tour Regensburg, take a closer look at a German map, and convert kilometers into miles.

Kapitel ③

Im Restaurant

Café am Bismarckplatz in Regensburg

Lernziele

Vorschau
Eating in and out

Gespräche + Wortschatz
Meals and restaurants

Fokus
Where to eat
Regional specialties
Friends and acquaintances
Cafés and coffee houses
Table manners
Wines from Germany, Austria, and
 Switzerland

Struktur
3.1 Verbs with vowel changes
3.2 Dative case

Einblicke
Man ist, was man isst.

Video-Ecke
Minidrama: *Und für Sie die Nummer 27*
Blickpunkt: *Was gibt's zu essen?*

Web-Ecke

Vorschau

Eating In and Out

Until the end of World War II, cooking in the German-speaking countries varied substantially from region to region, as each region's cuisine was noticeably influenced by its neighbors. Austrian cooking, for example, absorbed a strong Hungarian component, whereas Bavarian cooks in turn borrowed from Austria. Swiss-German cuisine incorporates many aspects of French and Italian culinary arts. Although retaining its regional differences, German cooking has meanwhile been influenced by the cuisines from around the world. Overseas travel and a large number of foreign residents have brought all kinds of culinary delights to markets and restaurants.

Germans are sometimes said to be especially fond of heavy, rich foods. However, compared to the lean postwar period, when only quantity mattered, Germans have developed a sophisticated taste and a sharp awareness of variety and quality in their diet. Health-food shops (**Reformhäuser**) and organic food stores (**Bio-Läden**) can be found almost everywhere.

Food preparation is no longer the sole domain of women. More and more German men have ventured into the kitchen, and many assume responsibility for shopping and cooking on weekends. Those Germans who prefer to eat out can choose from a wide range of restaurants, including Greek, Italian, Spanish, Chinese, Thai, and a wide range of other international fares. Fast food also has gained great popularity. Pizza delivery and American hamburger outlets are available in most cities, and Turkish snack bars can be found even in small towns. Traditional German **Imbiss** continues, of course, to offer a quick snack of sausage with fries (**Bratwurst mit Pommes**).

Restaurant customs in Germany, Austria, and Switzerland differ somewhat from those of North America. Guests usually seat themselves, and if the restaurant is crowded, it is acceptable to share a table with strangers after asking for permission: **Entschuldigen Sie, können wir uns dazusetzen?** Before eating, diners usually wish each other a pleasant meal (**Guten Appetit!** or **Mahlzeit!**). The appropriate response is **Danke, gleichfalls!** Salads are not eaten before but with the main course. Germans, like most Europeans, don't drink coffee with a meal, only afterwards. Also, water is never served automatically; guests are expected to order mineral water or another beverage. There are no free refills. A service charge (**Bedienung**) of 10 to 15 percent and the value-added tax (**Mehrwertsteuer**) are always included in the price of the meal. Although a tip (**Trinkgeld**) is not necessary, it is customary to add a small amount to round up the total. After asking for the bill, (**Zahlen, bitte!**), diners give the money, including the tip, directly to the server. Often diners are asked whether everything goes on one bill or whether they want to pay by Dutch treat (**Zusammen oder getrennt?**). Most restaurants do not accept credit cards.

Ask students what German, Austrian, or Swiss dishes they know. Which ones they like and which ones they don't like. Bringing in pictures from magazines or handing out menus might also be interesting. Maybe somebody in the class could bake something from a German recipe or you could go to a German restaurant. Which food items are cognates?

You could ask students about the ads below, i.e., the names of the restaurants, where they are located and when they are open, their telephone number, and anything else that's special about them.

Gespräche + Wortschatz

Im Restaurant

CD 2, Track 9

Warm-ups: 1. **Was essen / trinken Sie (nicht) gern?** 2. **Welche Getränke und Lebensmittel gibt es mit F, B, K, S, E, W?** (z.B. F: Fisch). 3. **Was ist das Gegenteil von** kaufen, offen, frisch, billig, klein, langsam, im Süden, Westen? 4. **Was ist der Artikel von** Blume, Glas, Tasse, Markt, Geschäft, Bäckerei, Kaufhaus, Zeit, Familie, Tag, Woche, Jahr, Kleidung, Farbe? 5. **Welche Länder gibt es** in Europa? Wie heißen die Hauptstädte? Welche Sprachen sprechen welche Leute? 6. **Wie alt sind Sie?** Haben Sie Geschwister? Wie viele? Wie heißen sie? *(Ask about other family members.)*

> Listen to the dialogue. Then, with a partner, act out the dialogue together.

AXEL Herr Ober, die Speisekarte bitte!
OBER Hier bitte!
AXEL Was empfehlen Sie heute?
OBER Die Menüs sind alle sehr gut.
AXEL Gabi, was nimmst du?
GABI Ich weiß nicht. Was nimmst du?
AXEL Ich glaube, ich nehme Menü 1: Schnitzel und Kartoffelsalat.
GABI Und ich hätte gern Menü 2: Rinds-rouladen mit Kartoffelklößen.
OBER Möchten Sie etwas trinken?
GABI Ein Glas Apfelsaft, und du?
AXEL Mineralwasser. *(Der Ober kommt mit dem Essen.)* Guten Appetit!
GABI Danke, gleichfalls . . . Hm, das schmeckt.
AXEL Das Schnitzel auch.

Später

GABI Wir möchten zahlen bitte!
OBER Ja, bitte. Alles zusammen?
GABI Ja. Geben Sie mir die Rechnung bitte!
AXEL Nein, nein, nein!
GABI Doch, Axel! Heute bezahle ich.
OBER Also, einmal Menü 1, einmal Menü 2, ein Apfelsaft, ein Mineralwasser, zwei Tassen Kaffee. Sonst noch etwas?
AXEL Ja, ein Brötchen.
OBER Das macht €30,30 bitte.
GABI *(Sie gibt dem Ober €40,–.)* 32 Euro bitte.
OBER Und acht Euro zurück. Vielen Dank!

A: 1. der Ober 2. die Menüs 3. Axel bestellt Menü 1 und Gabi Menü 2. 4. Gabi trinkt (ein Glas) Apfelsaft und Axel Mineralwasser. 5. die Rechnung 6. Gabi 7. €30,30 8. €1,70, das ist nicht viel. 9. Ich gebe normalerweise . . .

A. Fragen

1. Wer bringt die Speisekarte? 2. Was empfiehlt der Ober? 3. Was bestellen Gabi und Axel? 4. Was trinken sie? 5. Was bringt der Ober am Ende? 6. Wer zahlt? 7. Was kostet alles zusammen? 8. Wie viel Trinkgeld *(tip)* gibt *(gives)* Gabi dem Ober? Ist das viel? 9. Wie viel Trinkgeld geben Sie normalerweise *(normally)?* **(Ich gebe normalerweise . . . Prozent.)**

B. Jetzt sind Sie dran! *(With a partner, create your own dialogue between a waiter and a customer.)*

Wortschatz 1

Tell students not to use **Oberin** for *waitress,* as that means *Mother Superior* and also *head nurse,* but not *waitress.*

Das Restaurant, -s *(restaurant)*

der Kellner, -[1]	waiter	die Bedienung[1]	server; service
Ober, -[1]		Gabel, -n	fork
Löffel, -	spoon	Mensa	student cafeteria
Teller, -	plate	Rechnung, -en	check / bill

das Café, -s	*café*	die Serviette, -n	*napkin*	
Messer, -	*knife*	Speisekarte, -n[2]	*menu*	

Das Essen *(food, meal)*

der Nachtisch	*dessert*	die Pommes (frites) *(pl.)*	*(French) fries*
Pfeffer	*pepper*	Suppe, -n	*soup*
Pudding	*pudding*	das Eis[3]	*ice cream*
Reis	*rice*	Salz	*salt*
Zucker	*sugar*	Frühstück	*breakfast*
die Kartoffel, -n	*potato*	Mittagessen	*lunch, midday meal*
Nudel, -n	*noodle*	Abendessen	*supper*
Pizza, -s	*pizza*		

Students also like to go to the *cafeteria,* nicknamed **die Cafete.**

Weiteres

Herr Ober![1]	*Waiter!*
Was gibt's zum Frühstück (Mittagessen . . .)?	*What's for breakfast (lunch . . .)?*
Guten Appetit!	*Enjoy your meal!*
Danke, gleichfalls!	*Thanks, the same to you!*
etwas (zu essen)	*something (to eat)*
nichts (zu trinken)	*nothing (to drink)*
noch ein(e)	*another*
viel / viele[4]	*much / many*
wie viel? / wie viele?[4]	*how much? / how many?*
zu Hause / nach Hause[5]	*at home / (toward) home*
bestellen	*to order*
(be)zahlen[6]	*to pay (for)*
bleiben	*to remain, stay*
bringen	*to bring*
empfehlen	*to recommend*
frühstücken	*to eat breakfast*
schmecken	*to taste*
Das schmeckt (gut)!	*That's good! That tastes good!*
Das schmeckt (mir).	*I like it; i.e., I like the way it tastes.*
Ich mag kein(e / en) . . .	*I don't like (to eat / drink) . . .*
Ich möchte / hätte gern . . .	*I would like to have . . .*
(Ich möchte) zahlen bitte!	*I'd like to pay.*

[1] **Herr Ober!** is used to address a waiter, whereas **der Ober** and **der Kellner / die Kellnerin** are job descriptions, usually for someone working in a fancy restaurant. **Bedienung** refers to service in a restaurant. Waitresses are no longer summoned by calling **Fräulein!** *(Miss!)* Now diners usually use **Entschuldigen Sie!, Hallo!,** or a hand signal to catch a server's attention.

[2] Note that **die Speisekarte** *(regular menu with prices)* is not the same as thing as **das Menü** *(a complete meal, usually including soup and dessert)*

[3] **Eis** means both *ice* and *ice cream.* If you ask for **Eis** in a restaurant, you will get ice cream. Ice water is not served in German-speaking countries.

[4] **viel** Obst *(sg. collective noun)*, **Wie viel** Obst? BUT **viele** Äpfel *(pl.)*, **Wie viele** Äpfel?

[5] Ich bin **zu Hause** BUT Ich gehe **nach Hause.** (See Struktur 3.2-3.)

[6] The verbs **zahlen** and **bezahlen** are mostly used interchangeably. They both mean *to pay for* as well as *to pay:* **Er (be)zahlt die Rechnung.** Although most Germans would say **Zahlen bitte!,** you might also hear **Ich möchte (be)zahlen.**

Zum Erkennen: das (Tages)menü, -s *(daily special)*; das Schnitzel, - *(veal cutlet)*; der Kartoffelsalat; die Rindsroulade, -n *(stuffed beef roll)*; der Kartoffelkloß, ⸚e *(potato dumpling)*; das Mineralwasser; (ein)mal *(once)*; AUCH: der Dativ, -e; das Objekt, -e; die Präposition, -en; vergleichen *(to compare)*; Was noch? *(What else?)*; zurück *(back)*

Fokus — *Where to Eat*

In smaller towns, hotels are often the best place to eat. A **Gasthof, Gasthaus,** or **Gastwirtschaft** is—or includes—a restaurant serving complete meals. Since many restaurants serve hot food only at lunch and dinner times, the selection in the afternoon or late at night is usually limited. Whereas older people still take **Kaffee und Kuchen** in cafés, young people flock to pubs **(Kneipen)** for a drink or small meal. To avoid fancy places with astronomical prices, check the menus that are usually posted outside by the entrance.

Zum Thema

A. Mustersätze

1. die Speisekarte: **Herr Ober,** die Speisekarte **bitte!**
   ein Glas Mineralwasser, eine Tasse Kaffee, ein Stück Kuchen, ein Eis, die Rechnung
2. eine Tasse: **Ich brauche** eine Tasse.
   einen Teller, einen Löffel, ein Messer, eine Gabel
3. ein Glas Mineralwasser: **Ich hätte gern** ein Glas Saft.
   eine Tasse Kaffee, eine Tasse Tee, ein Glas Limonade, einen Teller Suppe
4. gut: **Das Schnitzel schmeckt** gut.
   auch gut, wunderbar, nicht schlecht, furchtbar
5. ein Eis: **Zum Nachtisch nehme ich** ein Eis.
   Schokoladenpudding, etwas Käse, ein Stück Apfelkuchen, ein paar Erdbeeren

*A.3: Point out that many families have shallow soup bowls the size of a dinner plate; hence the term **ein Teller Suppe.***

B. Was passt nicht?

1. der Teller—das Messer—die Speisekarte—die Gabel
2. das Frühstück—der Nachtisch—das Mittagessen—das Abendessen
3. das Salz—der Zucker—der Pfeffer—die Serviette
4. die Rechnung—die Kartoffeln—die Nudeln—der Reis
5. das Café—der Appetit—das Restaurant—die Mensa
6. bestellen—empfehlen—sein—zahlen

B: 1. die Speisekarte 2. der Nachtisch 3. die Serviette 4. die Rechnung 5. der Appetit 6. sein

C. Was bedeuten die Wörter und was sind die Artikel?

Frühstückstisch, Kaffeetasse, Fleischgabel, Buttermesser, Teelöffel, Suppenlöffel, Suppenteller, Kartoffelsuppe, Schokoladenpudding, Jogurteis

*C: breakfast table **(der)**, (coffee) cup **(die)**, meat fork **(die)**, butter knife **(das)**, teaspoon **(der)**, soup spoon **(der)**, soup plate **(der)**, potato soup **(die)**, chocolate pudding **(der)**, frozen yoghurt **(das)***

D. Was passt?

<u>bdi</u>   1. Die Suppe ist eiskalt.
<u>cdf</u>   2. Der Kartoffelsalat schmeckt prima.
<u>ehjkm</u>   3. Möchten Sie etwas zum Nachtisch?
<u>l</u>   4. Guten Appetit!
<u>gh</u>   5. Möchtest du nichts trinken?

a. Danke schön!
b. Wirklich?
c. Freut mich.
d. Das finde ich auch.
e. Ja, bitte.
f. Ja, wirklich.
g. Doch!
h. Nein, danke.
i. Ja, sie schmeckt furchtbar.
j. Ja, gern.
k. Natürlich.
l. Danke, gleichfalls.
m. Ja, ich hätte gern ein Eis.
n. . . .

E. Die Speisekarte

If possible, bring in other real menus to show.

Ratskeller

Tagesmenü:

I.	Nudelsuppe, Schnitzel und Kartoffelsalat, Eis	€ 12,20
II.	Gemüsesuppe, Rindsrouladen mit Kartoffelklößen, Eis	14,60

Tagesspezialitäten:[1]

Bratwurst und Sauerkraut	6,50
Hering mit Zwiebeln, Äpfeln, Gurken und Kartoffeln	7,90
Omelett mit Schinken, Bratkartoffeln, Salat	8,–
Putensteak mit Mais und Preiselbeeren	8,80
Kalbsleber, Erbsen und Karotten, Pommes frites	9,75
Hühnchen mit Weinsoße, Reis, Salat	10,50
Schweinebraten, Kartoffelbrei, Salat	11,20
Sauerbraten, Spätzle, Salat	12,75
Gemischte Fischplatte, Kartoffeln, Salat	13,25

Suppen:

Gulaschsuppe, Bohnensuppe, Erbsensuppe, Linsensuppe, Kartoffelsuppe, Tomatensuppe	2,50

Salate:

Grüner Salat, Tomatensalat, Gurkensalat, Bohnensalat	2,80

Getränke:

Mineralwasser	1,–	Tee	1,80
Apfelsaft	1,75	Kaffee	2,–
Limonade	1,75	Espresso	2,50
Cola	1,80	Cappuccino	3,50
Bier (0,2 l)[2]	1,40		
Wein (0,2 l)	2,20		

Nachtisch:

Schokoladenpudding	1,80	Käsekuchen	2,55
Apfelkompott	1,80	Apfelstrudel	2,80
Vanilleeis mit Erdbeeren	2,50	Kirschtorte	3,60
Rote Grütze mit Sahne	3,25	Sachertorte	3,80

[1] In case you are curious: **die Vorspeise, -n** (*hors d'oeuvre, appetizer*); **das Hauptgericht, -e** (*main dish*); **der Hering, -e** (*herring*); **das Omelett, -s** (*omelet*); **der Schinken, -** (*ham*); **die Bratkartoffeln** (*pl.*) (*fried potatoes*); **das Putensteak, -s** (*turkey steak*); **die Preiselbeeren** (*pl.*) (*type of cranberries*); **die Kalbsleber** (*calves liver*); **das Hähnchen, -** (*chicken*); **die Soße,** -n (*sauce, gravy*); **der Schweinebraten** (*pork roast*); **der Kartoffelbrei** (*mashed potatoes*); **der Sauerbraten** (*marinated pot roast*); **die Spätzle** (*pl.*) (*tiny Swabian dumplings*); **die . . . platte, -n** (*. . . platter*); **die Linsen** (*pl.*) (*lentils*); **das Getränk, -e** (*beverage*); **der Espresso, -s; der Cappuccino, -s; das Kompott, -e** (*stewed fruit*); **die Rote Grütze** (*berry sauce thickened with corn starch*); **die (Schlag)sahne** (*[whipped] cream*).

[2] A liter is a little more than a quart. 0,2 l, therefore is approximately three-fourths of a cup.

1. Was hat Menü eins? Menü zwei? Was haben die Menüs zum Nachtisch? 2. Was für Suppen gibt es? was für Salate? was für Getränke? 3. Was kostet eine Tasse Kaffee? ein Cappuccino? ein Glas Apfelsaft / Limo? ein Teller Suppe? ein Salat? 4. Was finden Sie besonders gut / nicht gut auf der Speisekarte?

1. **Wir möchten bestellen!** (*We would like to order. In groups of two to four students, take turns ordering from the menu.*)

2. **Zahlen bitte!** (*Ask for the check. Tell the server what you had, e.g.,* **Einmal Bratwurst . . .** *and let him / her figure out what you owe. Round up your bill to include an appropriate tip.*)

CD 2, Track 10

F. Was noch? *(What else? Together with your partner, see how many items you can find for each word or phrase below. Compare your results with those of others.)*

BEISPIEL: ein Stück . . .
Ich möchte ein Stück Brot.

1. ein Stück . . .   5. etwas . . .
2. ein Glas . . .   6. ein Pfund . . .
3. eine Tasse . . .   7. viel . . .
4. ein paar . . .   8. viele . . .

G. Kombinieren Sie! *(With your partner, make compound nouns with the following words. Then compare your list with that of others.)*

BEISPIEL: der Kuchen
der Kirschkuchen, die Kuchengabel

1. die Wurst   2. der Pudding   3. die Suppe   4. der Wein   5. das Obst   6. Wasser
7. Kaffee

Aussprache: ü

(Read also Part II. 22–28 in the Pronunciation Guide of the Workbook.)
1. [ü:] über, Tür, für, Frühling, Prüfung, Gemüse, südlich, grün, natürlich, müde
2. [ü] Flüsse, Würste, Stück, Jürgen Müller, München, fünf, fünfundfünfzig
3. Wortpaare
   a. vier / für
   b. missen / müssen
   c. Stuhl / Stühle
   d. Mutter / Mütter
   e. fühle / Fülle
   f. Goethe / Güte

Grotemeyer's **Sahne Torten**
Schwarzwälder Kirsch,
Käse-Sahne,
Schokoladen-Sahne
tiefgefroren
1.200 g Packung
€ 3.99

HÖREN SIE ZU!   TRACK 6

Im Gasthaus *(Find out what Jürgen, Helga, and Michael are ordering for dinner. Put their initials by the foods and beverages they order, then add up their total bill to see whether the waitress calculated it correctly.)*

Zum Erkennen: früh *(early)*; das Getränk, -e *(beverages)*; einmal *(one order of)*

Getränke		Essen		Nachtisch	
____	Limonade	H	Schnitzel	____	Apfelkuchen
H	Apfelsaft	____	Rindsroulade	M	Vanilleeis
____	Bier	J	Pizza	____	Reispudding
M	Mineralwasser	M	Würstchen	J	Schokoladenpudding
J	Cola	____	Fisch	H	Käsekuchen
Das kostet:					
€ 1,75		€ 7,50		€ 2,50	
1,50		5,–		1,40	
1,20		6,25		2,–	
		Alles zusammen:		€ 29,10	

Struktur

3.1 Verbs with vowel changes

Some very common verbs have a stem-vowel change in the SECOND and THIRD PERSON singular. These changes will be clearly noted in all vocabulary lists like this: **sprechen (spricht).**

	e > i **sprechen** *to speak*	e > ie **sehen** *to see*	a > ä **fahren** *to drive*	au > äu **laufen** *to walk, run*
ich	spreche	sehe	fahre	laufe
du	**sprichst**	**siehst**	**fährst**	**läufst**
er	**spricht**	**sieht**	**fährt**	**läuft**
wir	sprechen	sehen	fahren	laufen
ihr	sprecht	seht	fahrt	lauft
sie	sprechen	sehen	fahren	laufen

Siehst du Dresden auf der Landkarte?

Dieter **fährt** nach Dresden.

A few verbs in this group have additional, consonant changes:

	nehmen *to take*	**werden** *to become, get*
ich	nehme	werde
du	**nimmst**	**wirst**
er	**nimmt**	**wird**
wir	nehmen	werden
ihr	nehmt	werdet
sie	nehmen	werden

You need to know the following common verbs with stem-vowel changes:

essen	**isst**	*to eat*	lesen	**liest**	*to read*
empfehlen	**empfiehlt**	*to recommend*	nehmen	**nimmt**	*to take; to have*
fahren	**fährt**	*to drive*			*(food)*
geben	**gibt**	*to give*	sehen	**sieht**	*to see*
gefallen	**gefällt**	*to please,*	sprechen	**spricht**	*to speak*
		be pleasing	tragen	**trägt**	*to carry; to wear*
helfen	**hilft**	*to help*	werden	**wird**	*to become, get*
laufen	**läuft**	*to walk, run*			

Note that the second and third person singular forms of **essen** and **lesen** are identical (**du / er isst, du / er liest**). As you know from Chapter 1, the **du**-form of verbs with a stem ending in any s-sound (**-s, -ß, ss, -tz, -z**) adds only a **t**-ending instead of an **-st**: lese > du liest; heißen > du heißt.

Übungen

A. Ersetzen Sie das Subjekt!

> **BEISPIEL:**   Der Ober trägt die Teller. (ich)
> **Ich trage die Teller.**

1. Fahren Sie zum Kaufhaus? (wir, er, ihr, du)
2. Wir nehmen Nudelsuppe. (er, ich, sie/*pl.*, du)
3. Ich werde müde. (das Kind, wir, sie/*sg.*, sie/*pl.*)
4. Sie empfehlen das Schnitzel. (der Ober, ich, du, Axel)
5. Sehen Sie die Apotheke nicht? (du, ihr, er, die Leute)
6. Sprechen Sie Deutsch? (er, du, sie/*pl.*)
7. Hilfst du heute nicht? (ihr, Sie, sie/*sg.*)
8. Lesen Sie gern Bücher? (du, ihr, er, sie/*pl.*)

B: 1. er hilft 2. sie nimmt 3. er empfiehlt 4. sie laufen 5. sie liest 6. sie fährt 7. sie sieht 8. er/sie gibt

B. Was tun sie? *(Answer freely, telling what others do. Use pronouns and stem-changing verbs.)*

> **BEISPIEL:**   Ich esse schnell. Und Ihr Großvater?
> **Er isst sehr langsam.**

1. Ich helfe gern. Und Ihr Nachbar?
2. Ich nehme Apfelstrudel. Und Gabi?
3. Ich empfehle den Schweinebraten *(pork roast)*. Und der Ober?
4. Ich laufe langsam. Und Ihr Bruder oder Ihre Schwester?
5. Ich lese gern. Und Ihre Mutter?
6. Ich fahre im Sommer nach Deutschland. Und Ihre Familie?
7. Ich sehe alles. Und Ihre Nachbarin?
8. Ich gebe gern Hausaufgaben. Und Ihr(e) [Englisch]professor(in)?

C. Und du? *(Choose a classmate whom you don't know well, and find out what he / she likes.)* Follow the model and try to vary your responses. At the end, report to the class what you found out.)

1. **Was isst du gern?** *(Before doing this exercise, glance at the menu and the food vocabulary you have had in this chapter and in Chapter 2.)*

> **BEISPIEL:**   S1 Ich esse gern . . . (z.B. Fischbrötchen.). Und du, isst du gern . . . ?
> S2 Ja, ich esse gern . . . / Nein, ich esse nicht gern . . .
> S1 Magst du . . . (z.B. Linsensuppe)?
> S2 Ja, ich esse gern . . . / Nein, ich mag kein(e/en) . . . ?
> S1 Was magst du auch nicht gern?
> S2 Ich esse nicht gern . . . / Ich mag kein(e/en) . . .

2. **Was trägst du gern?** *(Before doing this exercise, review the list of clothing in pre-unit 3.)*

> **BEISPIEL:**   S1 Ich trage gern . . . (z.B. Jeans). Und du, trägst du auch gern . . . ?
> S2 Natürlich trage ich gern . . . (z.B. Jeans). / Nein, ich trage keine . . . (z.B. Jeans).
> S1 Was trägst du noch (nicht) gern?
> S2 Ich trage (nicht) gern . . . / Ich mag kein(e / en) . . . / Ich hasse *(hate)* . . .

Biergarten in München

Ask students whether there are beer gardens or garden restaurants in their town, where they and their friends love to hang out, and what they usually order.

D. Umfrage (*Survey. In small groups, ask the following questions and afterwards report back to the class. In case you need it:* everybody = **jeder**, nobody = **niemand.**)

1. Wer spricht hier . . . (z.B. Französisch)?
2. Wer läuft hier sehr gern?
3. Wer liest den/das/die . . . (z.B. *den Wallstreet Journal* or *die New York Times*)?
4. Wer sieht gern . . . (z.B. "ER")?
5. Wer isst gern . . . (z.B. Bratwurst)?
6. Wer mag kein(e/en) . . . (z.B. Fisch)?
7. Wer trinkt gern . . . (z.B. Buttermilch)?
8. Wer trinkt kein(e/en) . . . (z.B. Alkohol)?
9. Wer trägt gern . . . (z.B. lila)?
10. Wer hat ein(e/en) . . . (z.B. Auto)?

3.2 Dative case

The dative case has three major functions in German: it is the case of the INDIRECT OBJECT, it follows certain verbs, and it follows certain prepositions.

1. In English the INDIRECT OBJECT is indicated in two ways:

   • through word order: *The boy gives **the father** the plate.*

   • with a preposition: *The boy gives the plate **to the father.***

   In German this function is expressed through case and word order. You can determine the indirect object by asking *for whom* or *in reference to whom* (or occasionally *what*) the action of the verb is taking place.

   Der Junge gibt **dem Vater** den Teller. *The boy gives the father the plate.*

Emphasize that, unlike English, German does <u>not</u> use *to* or *for* for indirect objects.

Point out that students have already used the dative forms of **ich (mir)** and **Sie (Ihnen).**

a. The dative form of the INTERROGATIVE PRONOUN is **wem?** *(to whom?).*

	persons	things and ideas
nom.	wer?	was?
acc.	wen?	was?
dat.	**wem?**	—

You may wish to point out the colloquial English phrase *Who does the boy give the plate to?*

Wem gibt der Junge den Teller? → **Dem Vater.**

To whom does the boy give the plate? → *To the father.*

b. The dative forms of the DEFINITE and INDEFINITE ARTICLES are as follows:

	SINGULAR			PLURAL
	masc.	**neut.**	**fem.**	
nom.	der ein kein	das ein kein	die eine keine	die — keine
acc.	den einen keinen			
dat.	**dem einem keinem**	**dem einem keinem**	**der einer keiner**	**den — keinen**

Der Ober empfiehlt **dem** Vater, **der** Mutter und **den** Kindern das Schnitzel. Er bringt **dem** Kind einen Löffel, aber er gibt **einem** Kind kein Messer und keine Gabel.

- The POSSESSIVE ADJECTIVES **mein, dein,** and **Ihr** follow the pattern of **ein** and **kein:**

    Was empfiehlt er Ihr**em** Vater und Ihr**er** Mutter?

    Er empfiehlt mein**em** Vater und mein**er** Mutter den Fleischsalat.

The dative-plural **n**-ending needs a lot of practice. Give students familiar nouns; have them give you the dative-plural form in short sentences.

- In the dative plural, all nouns add an **-n** ending, unless the plural form already ends in **-n** or **-s.**

    die Väter / den Väter**n**

    die Kinder / den Kinder**n**

    die Äpfel / den Äpfel**n**

    BUT: die Eltern / den Eltern

    die Mädchen / den Mädchen

    die Kulis / den Kulis

- N-nouns also have an **-n** or **-en** ending in the dative singular, as they do in the accusative singular:

    Das Eis schmeckt dem Herr**n** und

    dem Student**en.**

Such verbs include **bringen, empfehlen, geben, kaufen, öffnen, sagen, schreiben, verkaufen.** Point out that the verbs listed here can have two objects in English, too. Give English sample sentences and have students identify the dative and the accusative object.

c. Many verbs can have both accusative and dative objects. Note that the direct object is usually a thing and the indirect object a person.

    Der Ober bringt dem Kind den Apfelstrudel.

    The waiter brings the child the apple strudel.

    Er empfiehlt der Studentin den Sauerbraten.

    He recommends the marinated pot roast to the student.

Note the difference in meaning:

Der Onkel trägt der Tante die Lebensmittel. BUT Der Onkel trägt die Tante.

d. In sentences with two objects, the direct object, <u>if it is a noun,</u> generally follows the indirect object.

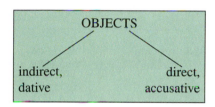

Der Kellner bringt dem Herrn den Tee.

2. Dative verbs

Some verbs take only dative objects; a few such verbs are:

antworten	*to answer*	**gehören**	*to belong to*
danken	*to thank*	glauben	*to believe*
gefallen	*to please, be pleasing*	helfen	*to help*
		schmecken	*to taste*

CAUTION: Gefallen is usually not used to talk about food but rather to say that a city, a picture, an item of clothing, or a person is pleasing to you. **Schmecken** is used with food and beverages.

Der Bruder antwortet der Kusine.	*The brother answers (gives an answer to) the cousin.*
Alex dankt der Kellnerin.	*Alex thanks (gives thanks to) the waitress.*
Der Mantel gehört dem Mädchen.	*The coat belongs to the girl.*
Ich glaube dem Jungen.	*I believe the boy.*
Ich helfe dem Nachbarn.	*I'm helping (giving help to) the neighbor.*
Die Mensa gefällt den Studenten.	*The students like the cafeteria (the cafeteria pleases the students).*
Die Salate gefallen den Studenten.	*The students like the salads (the salads are pleasing the students).*
Das Schnitzel schmeckt den Leuten.	*People like the Schnitzel (i.e., the way it tastes).*

3. Dative prepositions

These prepositions are always followed by the dative case:

aus	out of	Sie kommt **aus** dem Geschäft.
	from (a place of origin)	Er ist **aus** Berlin.
außer	besides	**Außer** dem Café ist alles zu.
bei	at, for (a company)	Sie arbeitet **bei** VW.
	near, by	Die Drogerie ist **beim** Markt.
	at the home of, with	Er wohnt **bei** Familie Angerer.
mit	with	Ich schreibe **mit** einem Kuli.
	together with	Alex kommt **mit** Gabi.
nach	after (time)	Kommst du **nach** dem Mittagessen?
	to (cities, countries, continents)	Fahrt ihr auch **nach** Österreich?
	to (used idiomatically)	Gehen Sie **nach** Hause!
seit	since	Sie wohnen **seit** Mai in Ulm.
	for (time)	Sie wohnen **seit** drei Tagen da.[1]
von	of	Das Gegenteil **von** billig ist teuer.
	from	Wir fahren **von** Ulm nach Hamburg.
	by (origin)	Das Bild ist **von** Albrecht Dürer.
zu	to (in the direction of)	Sie fährt **zum** Supermarkt.
	at (used idiomatically)	Sie sind **zu** Hause.
	for (purpose)	Was gibt es **zum** Nachtisch?

[1] **Seit** translates as *for* in English when it expresses duration of time (three minutes, one year) that began in the past and still continues in the present: *They have been living there for three days.*

- In everyday speech, some of the dative prepositions are usually contracted with the definite article.

| bei + dem = **beim** | zu + dem = **zum** |
| von + dem = **vom** | zu + der = **zur** |

- Pay particular attention to the contrasting use of these pairs of prepositions:

Sie fährt **zum** (to the) Supermarkt.

Fahrt ihr **nach** (to) Deutschland?

Wir fahren **von** (from) Salzburg nach München.

Er kommt **aus** (from) Salzburg.

Gehen Sie **nach** Hause (home)!

Sie sind nicht **zu** Hause ([at] home).

Übungen

E. Sagen Sie die Sätze im Plural! (Restate the sentences below, making the phrases in boldface plural.)

BEISPIEL: Wir sprechen mit **dem Kanadier**.
             Wir sprechen mit den Kanadiern.

1. Er lernt seit **einem Jahr** Deutsch. (drei) 2. Das Restaurant gehört **dem Schweizer.** 3. Sie kommen aus **dem Geschäft.** 4. Nach **einem Monat** bezahlt er die Rechnung. (zwei) 5. Ich gehe nur mit **dem Kind.** 6. Die Stadt gefällt **dem Engländer.** 7. Der Ober kommt mit **der Serviette.** 8. Wir sprechen mit **dem Nachbarn.** 9. Das Geschäft ist bei **dem Restaurant.** 10. Der Kuchen schmeckt **dem Studenten.**

F. Ersetzen Sie das Dativobjekt!

BEISPIEL: Die Bedienung bringt dem Kind ein Eis. (Großvater)
             Die Bedienung bringt dem Großvater ein Eis.

1. Die Kellnerin empfiehlt dem Vater die Rouladen. (Bruder, Spanier, Schweizer)

Point out that **nach Hause** does not follow the rule that "**nach** is used for cities, countries, continents."

E: 1. seit drei Jahren
   2. den Schweizern
   3. aus den Geschäften
   4. nach zwei Monaten
   5. mit den Kindern
   6. den Engländern
   7. mit den Servietten
   8. mit den Nachbarn
   9. bei den Restaurants
   10. den Studenten

2. Der Junge gibt der Mutter ein Bild. (Schwester, Studentin, Frau)
3. Der Ober bringt den Eltern das Essen. (Leute, Amerikaner/*pl.*, Studenten/*pl.*)
4. Die Drogerie gehört meiner Großmutter. (Großvater, Eltern, Familie)
5. Axel dankt dem Bruder. (Schwester, Vater, Leute)
6. Meine Großmutter hilft meinem Vater. (Mutter, Kusinen, Cousins)

G. Sagen Sie es noch einmal! *(Replace the nouns following the prepositions with the words suggested.)*

    BEISPIEL: Eva geht zum Lebensmittelgeschäft. (Apotheke)
                         Eva geht zur Apotheke.

1. Paula kommt aus dem Kaufhaus. (Drogerie, Café, Mensa)
2. Seit Sonntag ist er wieder hier. (zwei Tage, eine Stunde, ein Monat)
3. Wir sprechen mit dem Großvater. (Frau, Mädchen, Großeltern)
4. Ich wohne bei meinen Eltern. (Bruder, Schwester, Familie)
5. Er möchte etwas Salat zu den Rouladen. (Schnitzel, Suppe, Würstchen/*pl.*, Fleisch)
6. Nach dem Mittagessen spielen sie Tennis. (Frühstück, Kaffee, Deutschstunde)
7. Außer meinem Bruder sind alle hier. (Vater, Mutter, Nachbar, Studentin)
8. Tante Liesl bleibt bei den Kindern. (Cousin, Kusine, Töchter)

H. Wer, wem oder was? *(At your friend's graduation party, you are talking to a friend. Because of the loud music, you can't hear him / her. Ask what he / she said.)*

    BEISPIEL: Oskar gibt dem Bruder die Bücher.
                         Wer gibt dem Bruder die Bücher? — Oskar!
                         Wem gibt Oskar die Bücher? — Dem Bruder!
                         Was gibt Oskar dem Bruder? — Die Bücher!

1. Der Nachbar verkauft Onkel Willi den BMW.
2. Onkel Willi gibt dem Jungen den BMW.
3. Großmutter empfiehlt Irene ein paar Tage Ferien *(vacation)*.
4. Die Kinder zahlen der Mutter die Hotelrechnung.
5. Der Vater glaubt den Leuten die Geschichte *(story)* nicht.

I. Hoppla, hier fehlt was! Was gehört wem? *(You and your partner are helping another friend unpack after a family move. Work together to figure out what belongs to whom. One of you looks at and completes the chart below, the other one works with the chart in Section 11 of the Appendix.)*

S1:

	Bruder	**Schwester**	**Mutter**	**Vater**	**Großeltern**
Bild	x				
Bücher					x
Tennishose				x	
Hausschuhe				x	
Pulli		x			
Ringe *(pl.)*			x		
T-Shirts		x			
Mantel			x		
Messer *(sg.)*	x				
Gläser					x

    BEISPIEL: **S1**   Wem gehören die Hausschuhe?
                   S2   Die Hausschuhe gehören dem Vater. Und wem gehört das Bild?
                   S1   Das Bild gehört dem Bruder.

If students have difficulties with Exercise G because they can't remember the genders of the nouns used, remind them how crucial it is to learn the article with the noun. Ask them to state the article of each noun before giving the dative form.

H: 1. Wer verkauft Onkel Willi den BMW? Wem verkauft der Nachbar den BMW? Was verkauft der Nachbar Onkel Willi? 2. Wer gibt dem Jungen den BMW? Wem gibt Onkel Willi den BMW? Was gibt Onkel Willi dem Jungen? 3. Wer empfiehlt Irene ein paar Tage Ferien? Wem empfiehlt Großmutter ein paar Tage Ferien? Was empfiehlt Großmutter Irene? 4. Wer zahlt der Mutter die Hotelrechnung? Wem zahlen die Kinder die Hotelrechnung? Was zahlen die Kinder der Mutter? 5. Wer glaubt den Leuten die Geschichte nicht? Wem glaubt der Vater die Geschichte nicht? Was glaubt der Vater den Leuten nicht?

J: Point out that the phrases with dative pronouns should be treated as idioms for now. Personal pronouns (including the dative) will be presented in Chapter 5.

J.2: a. Frau Bayer gefällt das Land. b. Meinem Vater gefällt die Stadt. c. Meiner Mutter gefällt der Süden. d. Meiner Schwester gefallen die Seen. e. Meinen Geschwistern gefallen die Berge. f. Meinen Großeltern gefällt der Student. g. Dem Studenten gefallen meine Großeltern. h. Deutsch gefällt mir. i. Die Bratwurst schmeckt mir. / Mir scheckt die Bratwurst. j. Der Schweinebraten schmeckt Julia / Julia schmeckt der Schweinebraten. k. Der Fisch schmeckt meinen Freunden. / Meinen Freunden schmeckt der Fisch. l. Ich mag keinen Fisch. m. Magst du Fisch? n. Ich esse gern Fisch. o. Die Fischplatte schmeckt besonders gut.

J. Was gefällt wem?

1. **Ersetzen Sie das Dativobjekt!**

   a. Das Restaurant gefällt dem Onkel. (Tante, Großmutter, Kinder, Geschwister, Student, Studentin, Studenten)

   b. Aber die Preise gefallen der Familie nicht. (Frau, Leute, Nachbar, Herren)

2. **Gefallen, schmecken, mögen.** Auf Deutsch bitte!

   BEISPIEL: My cousin likes Hamburg.
   Hamburg gefällt meinem Cousin.

   a. Ms. Bayer likes the country. b. My father likes the city. c. My mother likes the South. d. My sister likes the lakes. e. My brothers and sisters like the mountains. f. My grandparents like the student. g. The student likes my grandparents. h. I like German **(mir).** i. I like the Bratwurst **(mir).** j. Julia likes the pork roast. k. My friends like the fish. l. I don't like fish. m. Do you like fish? n. I love to eat fish. o. The fish platter tastes especially good.

K. Was kaufen wir wem? *(The Christmas season is approaching, and you and your partner are coming up with ideas for presents for the whole family, e.g., brothers and sisters, parents and grandparents, uncles and aunts. Draw on all the vocabulary you have had so far plus any from the gift box below. Respond to each other's suggestions.)*

   BEISPIEL: S1   Braucht deine Mutter Schreibpapier?
                    S2   Nein. Sie hat Schreibpapier. Ich kaufe meiner Mutter kein Schreibpapier.
                    S1   Gefallen deinem Vater Kochbücher?
                    S2   Ja, sehr. Gut, ich kaufe meinem Vater ein Kochbuch.

die Kamera
das Handy *(cell phone)*
der Gürtel *(belt)*   die Kassette
                       das Parfüm
die Krawatte *(tie)*   die Bluse   die Blumen
das Video   das Fotoalbum
das Schreibpapier   das Kochbuch *(cookbook)*
               die Ohrringe
die Handtasche *(handbag)*   der Ring
eine Flasche Wein *(a bottle of wine)*   der Kalender
             das Portemonnaie *(wallet)*
der Pullover   die Uhr   die CD
das Taschenmesser *(pocket knife)*   die Kette *(necklace)*

L. *Nach Hause* und *zu Hause*

1. **Was fehlt?**
   a. Heute essen wir <u>zu Hause</u> .
   b. Jürgen ist nicht <u>zu Hause</u> .
   c. Er kommt oft spät <u>nach Hause</u>.
   d. Morgen bleibt er <u>zu Hause</u> .
   e. Wir arbeiten gern <u>zu Hause</u> .
   f. Geht ihr um sechs <u>nach Hause</u> ?
   g. Bringst du die Großeltern <u>nach Hause</u> ?

2. **Umfrage** (*Survey. In small groups, ask the following questions and afterwards report back to the class. In case you need it*: everybody = **jeder**, nobody = **niemand.**)

   a. Wer wohnt zu Hause?
   b. Wer kommt nur ab und zu (*once in a while*) nach Hause?
   c. Wer hat zu Hause einen Hund (*dog*)? eine Katze (*cat*)? einen Vogel (*bird*)?
   d. Wer hilft zu Hause gern in der Küche (*in the kitchen*)?
   e. Wer arbeitet zu Hause viel im Garten (*in the yard*)?
   f. Wer schreibt viel nach Hause?
   g. Wer geht zu Hause einkaufen?
   h. Wem schmeckt das Essen zu Hause besonders gut?
   i. Wer kommt zu Hause oft spät nach Hause?

L.2: For question c you might want to ask them some specifics about their pets, including the name, age, etc. When asking **Haben Sie einen Vogel?,** point out that that also means *Are you nuts / crazy?*

The animals are not active vocabulary!

M. Die Präpositionen *mit, bei, aus, von, nach* und *zu.* (*Use contractions when appropriate.*)

1. Gehst du <u>zur</u> Buchhandlung? — Nein, ich gehe <u>ins</u> Kaufhaus. (*to the / to the*)
2. Das Kaufhaus ist <u>bei</u> Café Kranzler. (*by*)
3. Christl arbeitet <u>bei</u> VW. (*at*)
4. Julia fährt heute <u>nach</u> Leipzig und Philipp <u>nach</u> Dresden. (*to*)
5. Sind Sie auch <u>aus</u> Norddeutschland? (*from*)
6. Antonio kommt <u>aus</u> Rom und wohnt <u>bei</u> Familie Dinkelacker. (*from / at the home of*)
7. Herr Dinkelacker fährt morgen <u>von</u> Frankfurt <u>nach</u> Stuttgart. (*from / to*)
8. Er fährt <u>mit</u> der Familie. (*together with*)
9. Der Hund bleibt <u>bei</u> den Nachbarn. (*at the home of*)

Zusammenfassung

N. **Bilden Sie Sätze!**

BEISPIEL: das / sein / für / Onkel
Das ist für den Onkel.

1. Ober / kommen / mit / Speisekarte
2. Mutter / kaufen / Kind / Apfelsaft
3. Student / empfehlen / Studentin / Apfelkuchen
4. er / sehen / Großvater / nicht
5. kommen / du / von / Mensa?
6. Familie / fahren / nicht / nach Berlin
7. arbeiten / du / auch / bei / Delikatessengeschäft Dallmayr?
8. die Mutter / kaufen / Kinder / schnell / ein paar / Pommes (frites)

N: Discuss synthetic exercises. Tell students that they will have to modify the verbs and add articles to the key words given in order to make complete sentences. 1. Der Ober kommt mit der Speisekarte. 2. Die Mutter kauft dem Kind (den) Apfelsaft. 3. Der Student empfiehlt der Studentin (den) Apfelkuchen. 4. Er sieht den Großvater nicht. 5. Kommst du von der Mensa? 6. Die Familie fährt nicht nach Berlin. 7. Arbeitest du auch beim Delikatessengeschäft Dallmayr? 8. Die Mutter kauft den Kindern schnell ein paar Pommes (frites).

Lerntipp
Reviewing for Tests

If you have taken full advantage of all class sessions, kept up with your work, and reviewed your lessons regularly, you should not have to spend much time preparing for tests. Concentrate on the areas that give you the most trouble. Use the *Rückblicke* sections in this textbook and in the Workbook for efficient reviewing. Go over the vocabulary lists of the chapters that will be covered by the test; make sure you know genders and plurals of nouns. Mark any words you seem to have trouble remembering; review them again. Begin your review early enough so that you can clarify any questions with your instructor.

O. Guten Appetit! Was fehlt?

1. Zum Essen braucht man ein— Messer und eine Gabel.   2. Suppe isst man mit einem Esslöffel *(tablespoon)* und für den Kaffee braucht man einen Kaffeelöffel. 3. Wir haben kein— Messer, keine Gabel und keinen Löffel *(sg.)*.   4. Gibt es hier kein— Salz und keinen Pfeffer?   5. Doch, das Salz steht bei dem Pfeffer.   6. Jetzt habe ich alles außer einer Speisekarte.   7. Der Ober empfiehlt der Studentin den Schweinebraten.   8. Nach dem Essen bringt er ein— Eis und einen Kaffee. 9. Das Restaurant gefällt den Studenten *(pl.)*.   10. Aber sie haben etwas gegen die Preise.   11. Wir sprechen von dem Professor und von der Prüfung.   12. Ich bestelle noch eine Cola.   13. Hier trinke ich die Cola aus einem Glas, aber zu Hause aus der Flasche *(f., bottle)*.   14. Da kommt der Ober mit der Rechnung.   15. Ohne die Rechnung geht's nicht.   16. Danke für das Mittagessen!

P. In der Mensa. Auf Deutsch bitte!

1. We're going with the students through the cafeteria.   2. They're from Hamburg. They're Hamburgers.   3. Paul lives with *(at the home of)* a family, and Helga lives at home.   4. Helga, what are you having?   5. I think I'll take the roast (**der Braten**), peas and carrots, and a glass of juice.   6. Would you *(formal)* like a piece of cake for dessert?   7. No, I'm not eating any cake because it's fattening (**dick machen**).   8. I have no knife, no fork, and no spoon.   9. Paul brings the student *(f.)* a knife, a fork, a spoon, and (some) ice cream.   10. Whose ice cream is that? (To whom does the ice cream belong?)   11. Would you *(fam.)* like some ice cream with a cookie?   12. She thanks the student *(m.)*.   13. Who's paying for (the) lunch?

P: 1. Wir gehen mit den Studenten durch die Mensa. 2. Sie sind aus Hamburg. Sie sind Hamburger. 3. Paul wohnt bei einer Familie und Helga wohnt zu Hause. 4. Helga, was nimmst du? 5. Ich glaube, ich nehme den Braten, Erbsen und Karotten und ein Glas Saft. 6. Möchten Sie ein Stück Kuchen zum Nachtisch? 7. Nein, ich esse keinen Kuchen, denn er macht dick. 8. Ich habe kein Messer, keine Gabel und keinen Löffel. 9. Paul bringt der Studentin ein Messer, eine Gabel, einen Löffel und etwas Eis. 10. Wem gehört das Eis? 11. Möchtest du etwas Eis mit einem Plätzchen? 12. Sie dankt dem Studenten. 13. Wer bezahlt das Mittagessen?

Wiener Schnitzel und Kartoffelsalat

Fokus — *Regional Specialties*

"Food and drink are the glue that keep body and soul together," claims an old Viennese saying. This sentiment is popular in all German-speaking countries.

German cooking has many regional specialties. In addition to excellent hams and sausages, there are numerous fish dishes, such as Helgoland lobster, **Hamburger Matjestopf** *(pickled herring with sliced apples and onion rings in a sour-cream sauce)*, Berlin eel soup, or Black Forest trout. Other regional dishes include **Sauerbraten** *(marinated pot roast)* from the Rhineland, **Kasseler Rippchen** *(smoked loin of pork)*, or Bavarian **Spanferkel** *(suckling pig)*, and **Leberkäs** *(meat loaf made from minced pork)*. In the South, dumplings and pasta dishes (e.g., **Spätzle**) are popular. Germany also boasts a large variety of pastries, such as **Schwarzwälder Kirschtorte, Frankfurter Kranz** *(a rich cake ring decorated with whipped cream and nuts)*, or **Thüringer Mohnkuchen**

(poppy-seed cake). A favorite summer dessert is **Rote Grütze** *(berries and their juices thickened with sago starch and served with vanilla sauce or cream)*.

Most famous among Austrian dishes are **Schnitzel, Gulasch,** and a variety of salted and smoked meats, as well as dumplings. But desserts like **Strudel, Palatschinken** *(dessert crêpes)*, **Kaiserschmarren** *(pancake pulled to pieces and sprinkled with powdered sugar and raisins)*, or **Sachertorte** delight visitors even more. Swiss cooking has also developed many specialties of its own, such as **Geschnetzeltes** *(minced veal in a cream sauce)*, **Berner Platte** *(dish with a variety of hams and sausages)*, or **Rös(ch)ti** *(fried potatoes with bacon cubes)*. The most famous Swiss dish is probably the cheese fondue **(Käsefondue),** a reminder that Switzerland produces a great variety of excellent cheeses (e.g., **Gruyère, Emmentaler, Appenzeller**).

Einblicke

Lesestrategie: Finding the Topic of a Passage

The first sentence of a paragraph often summarizes what will come next. Make sure you understand these thematic introductions clearly, and the rest of the passage should be easier to follow.

Wortschatz 2

der Freund, -e	*(a close) friend; boyfriend*
die Freundin, -nen	*(a close) friend; girlfriend*
Flasche, -n; eine Flasche . . .	*bottle; a bottle of . . .*
Hand, ¨-e	*hand*
besonders	*especially*
gewöhnlich	*usual(ly)*
man	*one (they, people), you*
manchmal	*sometimes*
nicht nur . . . , sondern auch	*not only . . . but also . . .*
überall	*everywhere*
vielleicht	*perhaps*
dick machen	*to be fattening*
schlafen (schläft)	*to sleep*

Make students aware that the German pronoun **man** is used only in the singular: *one speaks, they speak, people speak* = **man spricht.** They should not confuse **man** with the noun **der Mann: Hier spricht man Deutsch.** *There one speaks German.* **Der Mann spricht Deutsch.** *The man speaks German.*

Vor dem Lesen

A. Persönliche Fragen *(Personal questions. Work in pairs: At the exit of your cafeteria, a marketing specialist who is studying what college students eat and drink asks you to answer some questions. Play each role in turns.)*

1. Wann frühstückst du morgens? Wann isst du mittags und wann abends?
2. Wann isst du warm, mittags oder abends?
3. Wenn du Wasser trinkst, trinkst du Mineralwasser oder Leitungswasser *(tap water)*?
4. Trinkst du dein Wasser mit oder ohne Eiswürfel *(ice cubes)*?

5. Isst du gewöhnlich Nachtisch? Wenn ja *(if so)*, was besonders gern?

6. Zählst du beim Essen die Kalorien?

7. Isst du schnell oder langsam?

8. Gehst du manchmal ins Café, ins Kaffeehaus oder in eine Kneipe *(pub)*? Wenn ja, wo, wann und was bestellst du gern?

9. Trinkst du Wein oder Bier? Wenn ja, wann? Wenn nicht, was trinkst du auf *(at)* Partys?

10. Ist das, was du isst, immer gesund *(always healthy)*? Wenn nein, warum isst du es?

B. Allerlei Restaurants *(What do these ads tell you about the various restaurants?)*

1. Wo gibt es deutsche Küche? chinesische Spezialitäten? französische Delikatessen? Und wo bekommt man auch Bier vom Fass *(beer on draught)*?

2. Wo sind diese vier Restaurants?

3. Wie ist ihre Telefonnummer?

4. Von wann bis wann sind sie offen?

5. Welches Restaurant verkauft auch außer Haus *(has pick-up service)*?

6. Welches Restaurant hat Gruppenmenüs? Wie alt ist das Restaurant?

7. Welche Reklame *(ad)* gefällt Ihnen besonders gut? Warum?

8. Wo möchten Sie gern einmal essen? Warum?

NOTE: As you can see in the advertisement for LA CORNICHE, the German spelling reform is not followed everywhere. Frequently, you will still find the old **"ß"** where it now should be an **"ss,"** e.g., **In Berlin läßt es sich leben wie „Gott in Frankreich"** *(In Berlin, you can live like a king, lit.: "like God in France")*.

C. Was ist das?

der Kaffeeklatsch; die Großstadt, Pasta, Schule; die Kartoffelchips (*pl*).; relativ, voll

Man ist, was man isst.

CD 2, Track 12

Germans generally do NOT place a comma after the penultimate item in a series: **Die Deutschen, Österreicher und Schweizer beginnen den Tag . . .**

Die Deutschen, Österreicher und Schweizer beginnen den Tag gewöhnlich mit einem guten° Frühstück. Zum Frühstück gibt es Brot oder Brötchen, Butter, Marmelade, vielleicht auch ein Ei, etwas Schinken oder Käse und manchmal auch etwas Jogurt oder Müsli. Dazu° trinkt man Kaffee, Milch, Obstsaft, Tee oder Kakao.

    Mittags isst man gewöhnlich warm. Um die Zeit sind die Schulen aus und die Kinder kommen zum Mittagessen nach Hause. Manche Büros° machen mittags zu. Viele Leute essen mittags zu Hause. Andere° gehen nicht nach Hause, sondern in die Kantine° oder in ein Restaurant. Im Restaurant gibt es gewöhnlich ein Tagesmenü. Das ist oft besonders gut und billig. Außer Bratwurst, Omelett oder Hühnchen° findet man natürlich auch Lokalspezialitäten, wie zum Beispiel Hamburger Matjestopf° oder bayrische Schweinshax'n° mit Knödeln°. Zum Mittagessen trinkt man gern Saft, Limonade oder Mineralwasser, vielleicht auch ein Glas Wein oder Bier, aber kein Leitungswasser° und auch keinen Kaffee. Kaffee trinkt man manchmal nach dem Essen. Egal wo°, überall findet man etwas Besonderes°. Probieren° Sie die Spezialitäten! Nehmen Sie auch das Messer in die rechte° Hand und die Gabel in die linke° Hand, und dann Guten Appetit! Noch etwas: Manchmal sitzen° auch andere Leute bei Ihnen am° Tisch. Das ist oft sehr interessant. Fürs Mittagessen braucht man gewöhnlich Zeit. Leute mit nur wenig° Zeit gehen zur Imbissbude°. Da gibt es Bratwurst, Fischbrötchen, Pizza, Pasta, Schaschlik° oder auch Hamburger mit Pommes (frites). In Großstädten findet man gewöhnlich auch McDonald's oder Burger King. Schnell essen ist manchmal nicht schlecht, aber ein Mittagessen ist das für die meisten° Leute nicht.

    Nachmittags sieht man viele Menschen in Cafés. Da sitzen sie gemütlich° bei einer Tasse Kaffee und reden°. Kaffeeklatsch gibt es aber nicht nur im Café oder einer Konditorei°, sondern auch zu Hause. Besonders sonntags kommt man oft mit Freunden zusammen zu einer Tasse Kaffee und einem Stück Kuchen.

    Abends zum Abendbrot° isst man gewöhnlich kalt und nicht so viel wie mittags. Man sagt: Mit einem vollen Bauch° schläft man schlecht; und was man abends isst, macht dick. So gibt es nur etwas Brot mit Quark° oder Käse, Wurst oder Fisch, ein paar Tomaten oder saure Gurken. Dazu gibt es vielleicht eine Tasse Tee oder ein Bier. Abends öffnet man auch gern eine Flasche Wein für Freunde. Dazu gibt es Salzstangen° oder Kartoffelchips.

    Den meisten Deutschen, Österreichern und Schweizern ist wichtig, was sie essen. Wie bei uns° essen sie relativ viel Obst, Salat und Gemüse. Auch haben sie etwas gegen Farbstoffe° und Konservierungsmittel°. Sie glauben: „Man ist, was man isst."

Glosses (right margin):
good
With it
some offices
Others
company cafeteria
chicken
(see *Fokus*)
Bavarian pig's knuckles / dumplings
tap water
no matter where / something special / try / right / left
sit
at the
little / snack bar
shish kebabs
most
leisurely
talk
pastry shop
evening meal
full stomach
curd cheese
pretzel sticks
as we do here
food coloring / preservatives

Fokus — *Friends and Acquaintances*

Germans consciously distinguish between friends (**Freunde**) and acquaintances (**Bekannte**). This is based on the belief that there are only a few real friends among so many people. Genuine friendships are considered special and often last for a lifetime.

Gemütlich frühstücken ist wichtig.

Nach dem Lesen

A. Welche Antwort passt? *(Fill in the correct answer according to the text.)*
1. Zum Frühstück gibt es _____.
   a Sauerbraten   c. viel Obst und Gemüse
   b. Kuchen und Plätzchen   d. Brot, Butter und Marmelade
2. Mittags essen die Schulkinder _____.
   a. in der Schule   c. im Restaurant
   b. zu Hause   d. etwas Besonderes
3. Zum Mittagessen trinkt man gern _____.
   a. Kaffee, Milch oder Tee   c. Mineralwasser
   b. Eiswasser   d. Kakao
4. Zum Abendessen isst man gewöhnlich _____.
   a. Kaffee und Kuchen   c. Suppe, Fleisch und Gemüse
   b. Brot, Wurst und Käse   d. Salzstangen und Kartoffelchips
5. Die Deutschen, Österreicher und Schweizer essen _____ Obst und Gemüse.
   a. nicht viel   c. nur
   b. kein   d. gern

B. Guten Appetit! Was fehlt?

1. Ich beginne den Tag gewöhnlich mit einem guten Frühstück: mit einem Brötchen, einem Ei und einer Tasse Tee.   2. Gehst du mittags nach Hause? 3. Ja, zu Hause ist es nicht so teuer.   4. Bei den Preisen esse ich gern zu Hause.   5. Warum gehst du nicht zur Mensa?   6. Das Essen schmeckt mir nicht.   7. Manchmal gehe ich zu einer Imbissbude *(f.)*.   8. Dann esse ich nichts außer einer Bratwurst und die Cola trinke ich schnell aus der Flasche. 9. Oft habe ich keinen Hunger.   10. Dann esse ich nur einen Apfel oder eine Banane.   11. Möchtest du etwas Brot mit einem Stück Käse?   12. Es ist von dem Bio-Laden und hat keine Konservierungsmittel *(pl.)*!

C. Vergleichen Sie! *(With a classmate, make two lists that compare German and North American food and drink preferences. Draw on all the vocabulary you have had so far.)*

If students ask: *bacon* **der Speck;** *doughnut* **der Krapfen, -;** *boiled egg* **das gekochte Ei, -er;** *fried egg* **das Spiegelei, -er;** *scrambled egg* **das Rührei, -er;** *hamburger* **der Hamburger, -;** *honey* **der Honig;** *mustard* **der Senf;** *open-faced sandwich* **das belegte Brot, -e / Brötchen, -;** *toast* **das Toastbrot, -e**

	DEUTSCHLAND, SCHWEIZ ÖSTERREICH	NORDAMERIKA
Zum Frühstück:		
Zum Mittagessen:		
Zum Abendessen:		

Fokus — *Cafés and Coffee Houses*

Cafés and **Konditoreien** *(pastry shops)* are favorite places for conversation or for breaks in shopping excursions. They serve coffee, tea, and hot chocolate, along with a great variety of delicious cakes and pastries. In Austria, many people have a favorite café (**das Kaffeehaus**), where they can relax over such items as **Kaffee mit Schlag** *(coffee with whipped cream)* or a piece of **Linzertorte** *(jam-filled tart)*. The tradition of the coffee house goes back to the early 1700s, when it was the preferred meeting place not only of the literati, reformers, artists, and philosophers, but also of middle-class society.

Hm, da bekommt man Appetit.

D. Die Pizzeria *(Taking turns, ask your partner about DANTE's pizza ad, and find out how he/she likes pizza.)*

1. Wie heißt die Pizzeria? 2. Wo ist sie? 3. Was ist die Telefonnummer? 4. Was ist die Faxnummer? 5. Gibt es eine E-Mail? 6. Was ist der Mindestbestellwert *(minimum order)*? 7. Was macht das Pizza-Taxi? 8. Wer sitzt und wer flitzt *(is rushing)*? 9. Von wann bis wann sind sie offen? 10. Haben Sie einen Ruhetag *(a day when they're closed)*? 11. Bestellen Sie manchmal auch Pizza? Wenn ja, wo? 12. Was für Pizza bestellen Sie gern? 13. Was kostet eine Pizza? 14. Essen Sie Pizza mit Messer und Gabel oder mit der Hand?

Fokus — *Table Manners*

Whenever Europeans eat something that needs to be cut, they hold the knife in the right hand and the fork in the left throughout the meal—rather than shifting the fork to the right hand after cutting. (It is said that American spies during World War II could be identified by their different food-cutting habits.) If no knife is needed, the left hand rests on the table next to the plate, not in the lap. To signal that a person is finished eating, the knife and fork are placed parallel and diagonally on the plate.

Beim Mittagessen

E. Wie isst man das? *(Show how you would eat the following foods.)*

Suppe, Salat, Bratwurst, Hühnchen, Putenfleisch *(turkey meat)*, Sauerbraten, Schnitzel, Spagetti, Erbsen, Spargel *(asparagus)*, Kartoffelbrei *(mashed potatoes)*, Fondue, Eis, Erdbeeren

F. Kurzgespräche *(Together with your partner, prepare one of the following brief dialogues. Then present it to the class.)*

1. **An der Uni**

   You have just met another student in the cafeteria for the first time and inquire how he/she likes it here. Very much, he/she answers. The other student then asks you whether the soup tastes good. You reply that it is not bad, but too hot. You ask how your fellow student likes the chicken. He/she replies that it doesn't taste particularly good and is cold. You say the food is usually cold.

2. **Im Restaurant**

   You and a friend are in a German restaurant. The server asks what you would like, and you ask what he/she recommends. He/she mentions a particular dish. Both you and your friend order, each choosing a soup, a main dish, and a salad. The server asks what you would like to drink, and you order beverages. Use the menu from Exercise E.

G. Essgewohnheiten *(Eating habits. Write 8–10 sentences, describing when you eat, what you eat and drink at various meals, and what you like and dislike.)*

Optional tongue twisters **(Zungenbrecher):** 1. Selten ess' ich Essig *(vinegar).* Ess' ich Essig, ess' ich Essig mit Salat. 2. Klaus Knopf liebt Knödel, Klöße, Klöpse *(meat balls).* Knödel, Klöße, Klöpse liebt Klaus Knopf.

Optional practice: 1. **Ersetzen Sie das Subjekt!** (Ich schlafe schlecht. Mittags essen wir warm. Sie nehmen die Gabel in die linke Hand. Ich sehe keine Imbissbude.) 2. **Sagen Sie es anders!** (Viele Leute essen **mittags** in der Kantine. Das Tagesmenü ist **gewöhnlich** gut und billig. Man geht **natürlich** manchmal auch zur Imbissbude. Man braucht manchmal viel Zeit **fürs Mittagessen.** Qualität ist **den Deutschen** oft wichtiger als Quantität.)

HÖREN SIE ZU!   TRACK 7

Gäste zum Wochenende *(Listen to Kai and Gerda's plans for their weekend guests, Ruth and Uwe. Then read the questions below and select the correct response.)*

Zum Erkennen: die Forelle *(trout);* genug *(enough)*

1. Ruth und Uwe kommen am _____.
   a. Sonntag um vier   **b.** Samstag Nachmittag   c. Sonntag zum Kaffee
2. Gerda macht einen _____.
   a. Quarkkuchen   b. Apfelkuchen   **c.** Erdbeerkuchen
3. Zum Abendessen gibt es _____.
   a. Kartoffelsalat und Würstchen   **b.** Fondue, Brot und Wein   c. Eier, Wurst und Käse
4. Uwe isst gern _____.
   a. Jogurt   b. Schwarzbrot   c. Erdbeerkuchen
5. Zum Mittagessen machen sie _____.
   a. eine Nudelsuppe   b. Fleisch und Gemüse   **c.** Fisch mit Kartoffelsalat
6. Zum Nachtisch gibt's _____.
   a. Äpfel und Orangen   b. Quark   **c.** Obstsalat
7. Kai fährt _____.
   a. zum Supermarkt   b. zum Markt   c. zur Bäckerei
8. Gerda kauft Eier, _____.
   a. Jogurt und Kaffee   b. Obstsalat und Plätzchen   c. Gemüse und Blumen

Video-Ecke

- The *Minidrama* "Und für Sie die Nummer 27" takes place in a garden restaurant where three friends are ordering a meal. The food seems to be delicious, but for one, it is not what she thought she ordered. What now?

- *Blickpunkt* "Was gibt's zu essen?" introduces us to the manager of a **Pension** who shows us what she serves her guests for breakfast. After driving by various international restaurants in Berlin, she also takes us to one of her favorite places, where we have a chance to see the chef in action.

Web-Ecke

- For updates, self-assessment queries, and online activities related to this chapter, visit the *Wie geht's?* Web site at **http://wiegehts.heinle.com**. You'll visit several different restaurants and cafés in Germany and Austria, and check out a few sites that will show you some of the subtleties of dining out in Germany.

Fokus — *Wines from Germany, Austria, and Switzerland*

All in all, there are 13 German wine-growing regions, but most of Germany's wine is produced in western and southwestern Germany. Especially the wines from the Rhine and Moselle rivers **(Rheinwein** and **Moselwein)** are famous around the world. In Switzerland, 18 of the 23 cantons grow wine, which leads one to believe that wine is to the Swiss what beer is to the Bavarian. In Austria, there are excellent vineyards along the Danube around Vienna. Wines are classified as **Tafelwein** (*table or ordinary wine*), **Qualitätswein** (*quality wine*), and **Qualitätswein mit Prädikat** (*superior wine*).

Rückblick: Kapitel 1 – 3

The review sections give a periodic summary of material that has been introduced in the preceding chapters. They are intended for reference and as a preparation for quizzes, tests, and finals. Review exercises for both vocabulary and structure can be found in the Workbook, with a corresponding answer key in the back.

I. Verbs

1. Forms: PRESENT TENSE

   a. Most verbs inflect like **danken:**

   p. 36

singular	plural
ich dank**e**	wir dank**en**
du dank**st**	ihr dank**t**
er dank**t**	sie dank**en**

   b. Verbs whose stem ends in **-d, -t,** or certain consonant combinations inflect like **antworten,** e.g., arbeiten, bedeuten, finden, kosten, öffnen, regnen.

   p. 37

singular	plural
ich antwort**e**	wir antwort**en**
du antwort**est**	ihr antwort**et**
er antwort**et**	sie antwort**en**

   c. Some verbs have vowel changes in the second and third person singular, e.g., essen, geben, helfen, nehmen, werden; empfehlen, lesen; gefallen, tragen.

   p. 81

	e > i **sprechen**	e > ie **sehen**	a > ä **fahren**	au > äu **laufen**
ich	spreche	sehe	fahre	laufe
du	sprichst	siehst	fährst	läufst
er	spricht	sieht	fährt	läuft

   d. Some verbs are irregular in form:

   pp. 57, 81

	haben	**sein**	**werden**	**essen**	**nehmen**
ich	habe	bin	werde	esse	nehme
du	hast	bist	wirst	isst	nimmst
er	hat	ist	wird	isst	nimmt
wir	haben	sind	werden	essen	nehmen
ihr	habt	seid	werdet	esst	nehmt
sie	haben	sind	werden	essen	nehmen

2. Usage

   a. German has only one verb to express what English says with several forms:

   p. 37

   Er **antwortet** meinem Vater.
   { *He **answers** my father.*
     *He **is answering** my father.*
     *He **does answer** my father.* }

b. The present tense occasionally expresses future time.

Im Mai **fährt** sie nach Aachen.   { *She **is going** to Aachen in May.*
                                       *She **will be going** to Aachen in May.*

II. Nouns and pronouns

1. You have learned three of the four German cases.

pp. 38, 42   a. The NOMINATIVE is the case of the subject:

Da kommt **der Ober. Er** bringt das Essen.

It is also used for PREDICATE NOUNS following the linking verbs **heißen, sein,** and **werden.**

Der Herr **heißt** Oskar Meyer.
Er **ist**   Wiener.
Er **wird** Vater.

p. 57   b. The ACCUSATIVE is the case of the direct object:

Wir fragen **den Freund**.

It follows these prepositions: durch, für, gegen, ohne, um

p. 83   c. The DATIVE is the case of the indirect object:

Rotkäppchen bringt **der Großmutter** den Wein.

It follows these prepositions: aus, außer, bei, mit, nach, seit, von, zu

It also follows these verbs: antworten, danken, gefallen, gehören, glauben, helfen, schmecken.

Nouns in the dative plural have an **-n** ending unless the plural ends in **-s**:

die Freunde / den Freunde**n**   BUT   die Kulis / den Kulis

pp. 58, 84   d. N-nouns

Some masculine nouns have an **-n** or **-en** ending in all cases (singular and plural) except in the nominative singular:

der Franzose, **-n, -n**   der Mensch, **-en, -en**
der Herr, **-n, -en**   der Nachbar, **-n, -n**
der Junge, **-n, -n**   der Student, **-en, -en**

Der Junge fragt den Nachbarn. Der Nachbar antwortet dem Junge**n**.

2. These are the case forms of the DEFINITE and INDEFINITE ARTICLES:

p. 84

	SINGULAR			PLURAL
	masc.	**neut.**	**fem.**	
nom.	der ein kein	das ein kein	die eine keine	die — keine
acc.	den einen keinen			
dat.	dem einem keinem	dem einem keinem	der einer keiner	den — keinen

Mein, dein, and **Ihr** follow the pattern of **ein** and **kein.**

3. These are the case forms of the INTERROGATIVE PRONOUNS:
p. 84

	persons	things and ideas
nom.	wer?	was?
acc.	wen?	was?
dat.	wem?	—

III. Sentence structure

1. Verb position

   a. In a German statement, the verb must be the second GRAMMATICAL ELEMENT. p. 41
   The element before the verb is not necessarily the subject.

$$\begin{array}{cc} 1 & 2 \end{array}$$

Ich **sehe** meinen Vater morgen.

Morgen **sehe** ich meinen Vater.

Meinen Vater **sehe** ich morgen.

   b. A verb phrase consists of an INFLECTED VERB and a COMPLEMENT that com- p. 42
   pletes its meaning. Such complements include predicate nouns, predicate adjectives,
   some accusatives, and other verbs. When the verb phrase consists of more than one
   part, the inflected part (V1) is the second element in a statement, and the other part
   (V2) stands at the very end of the sentence.

Das **ist** **meine Schwester**.
Du **bist** **prima**.
Er **spielt** sehr gut **Tennis**.
Jetzt **gehen** wir schnell **essen.**
V1   V2

2. Negation

   a.
   > nicht + (ein) = kein
   p. 63

   Möchten Sie **ein** Eis?   Nein, ich möchte **kein** Eis.
   Möchten Sie Erdbeeren?   Nein, ich möchte **keine** Erdbeeren.

   b.
   > S V1 0 definite time expression   other adverbs or adverbial phrases V2.
   > ↑
   > nicht

   Wir spielen heute **nicht** mit den Kindern Tennis.

3. Clauses

   Coordinate clauses are introduced by COORDINATING CONJUNCTIONS:

   > aber, denn, oder, und
   p. 64

   Coordinating conjunctions do not affect the original word order of the two sentences.

   Ich bezahle den Kaffee **und** du bezahlst das Eis.

Kapitel (4)

Feste und Daten

Feuerwerk *(fireworks)* zu Silvester in Innsbruck

Lernziele

Vorschau
Holidays and vacations

Gespräche + Wortschatz
Celebrations and the calendar

Fokus
Congratulations
German holidays
Traditions
Wine festivals, harvest time, and traditional garb

Struktur
4.1 Present perfect with **haben**

4.2 Present perfect with **sein**
4.3 Subordinating conjunctions

Einblicke
Deutsche Feste

Video-Ecke
Minidrama: *Das hat es bei uns nicht gegeben*

Web-Ecke

102

Vorschau

Holidays and Vacations

One of the most pleasant aspects of life in Germany, Switzerland, and Austria is the large number of secular and religious holidays (**Feiertage**) that are celebrated. There are, for example, two holidays each on Christmas and on Easter. In combination with a weekend and a couple of vacation days, these holidays make it easy to visit family in other parts of the country, to go skiing, or to go to the countryside for a few days.

Ask on which holidays schools, shops, banks, etc. are closed in this country. How much vacation does the average worker get here? How does that affect families whose kids are off for a long summer?

Lebkuchenherzen als Geschenk für den Freund oder die Freundin

Secular holidays include New Year's Eve and New Year's Day (**Silvester** and **Neujahr**), May Day or Labor Day (**Maifeiertag** or **Tag der Arbeit**), and national holidays marked by parades, speeches, and fireworks. On October 3 (**Tag der deutschen Einheit**), Germany commemorates its reunification in 1990. Austria, in turn, celebrates its independence from the Allied occupation in 1955 on October 26 (**Nationalfeiertag**). Switzerland's **Bundesfeiertag** on August 1 is based on the country's founding in 1291. Besides Christmas (**Weihnachten**), Good Friday (**Karfreitag**), and Easter (**Ostern**), religious holidays include Ascension Day (**Christi Himmelfahrt**) and Pentecost (**Pfingsten**) throughout Germany, Austria, and Switzerland. Additional religious holidays, such as Epiphany (**Heilige Drei Könige**), Corpus Christi (**Fronleichnam**), and All Saints' Day (**Allerheiligen**), are observed only in those states and areas where the majority of the population is Catholic.

The combination of very generous vacations (**Urlaub**) — up to six weeks for wage earners — and of the many holidays has reduced the average number of working days in Germany to about 197 per year, compared with 230 in the United States and 238 in Japan. Germans feel that frequent holidays and generous vacations improve efficiency and productivity. Recently, however, some concerns have arisen about the competitiveness of German workers in the global economy, especially as some unions have been able to reduce the work-week to less than 40 hours.

German enthusiasm for vacation travel has created some problems, such as overcrowding on highways when school vacations (**Ferien**) begin and end. To alleviate this situation, a system of rotating and staggered school vacations was developed in the various federal states, so that no state — with the exception of Bavaria — always has very late or very early vacations.

Gespräche + Wortschatz

CD 3, Track 1

Am Telefon

CHRISTA	Hallo, Michael!
MICHAEL	Hallo, Christa! Wie geht's dir denn?
CHRISTA	Nicht schlecht, danke. Was machst du am Wochenende?
MICHAEL	Nichts Besonderes. Warum?
CHRISTA	Klaus hat übermorgen Geburtstag und wir geben eine Party.
MICHAEL	Super! Aber bist du sicher, dass Klaus übermorgen Geburtstag hat? Ich glaube, sein Geburtstag ist am siebten Mai.
CHRISTA	Quatsch! Klaus hat am dritten Mai Geburtstag. Und Samstag ist der dritte.
MICHAEL	Na gut. Wann und wo ist die Party?
CHRISTA	Samstag um sieben bei mir. Aber nichts sagen! Es ist eine Überraschung.
MICHAEL	O.K.! Also, bis dann!
CHRISTA	Tschüss! Mach's gut!

Klaus klingelt bei Christa

CHRISTA	Grüß dich, Klaus! Herzlichen Glückwunsch zum Geburtstag!
KLAUS	Wie bitte?
MICHAEL	Ich wünsche dir alles Gute zum Geburtstag.
KLAUS	Tag, Michael! . . . Hallo, Gerda! Kurt und Sabine, ihr auch?
ALLE	Wir gratulieren dir zum Geburtstag!
KLAUS	Danke! So eine Überraschung! Aber ich habe heute nicht Geburtstag. Mein Geburtstag ist am siebten.
CHRISTA	Wirklich?—Ach, das macht nichts. Wir feiern heute.

A. Richtig oder falsch?

f	1.	Michael hat Geburtstag.
f	2.	Klaus hat vor einem Monat Geburtstag gehabt.
r	3.	Am 3. Mai gibt es eine Party.
r	4.	Klaus hat am 7. Mai Geburtstag.
r	5.	Die Party ist bei Christa.
f	6.	Zum Geburtstag sagt man "Grüß dich!"
f	7.	Klaus gratuliert zum Geburtstag.
r	8.	Alle gratulieren.

B. Jetzt sind Sie dran! *(With a partner, create your own dialogue. Talk about weekend plans and any upcoming events, possibly a birthday party.)*

Fokus — *Congratulations*

Herzlichen Glückwunsch! or **Alles Gute zum Geburtstag!** are the most accepted and popular ways of saying *Happy birthday!* The first two words (or the plural, **Herzliche Glückwünsche**) suit almost any occasion, be it a birthday, an engagement, a wedding, the birth or christening of a baby, church confirmation or communion, or an anniversary. Germans make a lot of fuss over the celebration of birthdays. Quite contrary to American custom, the "birthday kid" in Germany is expected to throw his/her own party. Surprise parties, however, are popular with students. Coming-of-age and special birthdays (18, 25, 30, 40, 50, etc.) are considered particularly important—the older you get, the more elaborate the celebration.

Wortschatz 1

Die (Ordinal)zahl, -en *(ordinal number)*

1. **erste**[1]	9. neunte	17. **siebzehnte**
2. zweite	10. zehnte	18. achtzehnte
3. **dritte**	11. elfte	19. neunzehnte
4. vierte	12. zwölfte	20. zwanzigste
5. fünfte	13. dreizehnte	21. einundzwanzigste
6. sechste	14. vierzehnte	22. zweiundzwanzigste
7. **siebte**	15. fünfzehnte	30. dreißigste
8. **achte**	16. **sechzehnte**	

Das Datum, die Daten *(calendar date)*

Welches Datum ist heute?	*What's the date today?*
Heute ist der erste Mai (1.5.).[2]	*Today is the first of May (5/1).*
Wann haben Sie Geburtstag?	*When is your birthday?*
Ich habe am ersten Mai (1.5.) Geburtstag.[2]	*My birthday is on the first of May.*
Wann sind Sie geboren?	*When were you born?*
Ich bin 1980 geboren.[3]	*I was born in 1980.*
Ich bin am 1.5.1980 geboren.	*I was born on May 1, 1980.*
Die Ferien sind vom . . . bis zum . . .	*The vacation is from . . . until . . .*

Instead of **Welches Datum ist heute?,** the following two expressions are also quite common (but a little more difficult): **Was für ein Datum ist heute? Der Wievielte ist heute? Den Wievielten haben wir heute?**

Das Fest, -e *(fest, festival)*

der	Feiertag, -e[4]	*holiday*	die	Feier, -n	*celebration, party*
	Geburtstag, -e	*birthday*		Party, -s	*party*
	Sekt	*champagne*		Überraschung, -en	*surprise*
das	Geschenk, -e	*present, gift*	die	Ferien *(pl.)*[4]	*vacation*
	bekommen	*to get, receive*		singen	*to sing*
	dauern	*to last (duration), take*		tanzen	*to dance*
	denken	*to think*		tun[5]	*to do*
	feiern	*to celebrate, party*		überraschen	*to surprise*
	gratulieren	*to congratulate*		wünschen	*to wish*
	schenken	*to give (a present)*			

anniversary **das Jubiläum, Jubiläen;** *graduation* **Abschluss, ⸚e;** colloquial for *party* **die Fete, -n**

FESTE FEIERN IN WESTFALEN

Weiteres

gerade	*just, right now*
noch	*still; else*
sicher	*sure(ly), certain(ly)*
gestern / vorgestern	*yesterday / the day before yesterday*
morgen / übermorgen	*tomorrow / the day after tomorrow*
am Wochenende	*on the weekend*
Wie lange?	*How long?*
vor einer Woche[6]	*a week ago*
Das gibt's doch nicht!	*I don't believe it! / That's impossible!*
So eine Überraschung!	*What a surprise!*
Vielen / herzlichen Dank!	*Thank you very much!*
Danke schön! / Bitte schön!	*Thanks a lot! / You're welcome!*
Nichts zu danken!	*You're welcome! / My pleasure.*
zu Ostern / Weihnachten / Silvester	*at/for Easter / Christmas / New Years' Eve*
zum Geburtstag	*on/for the birthday*
Alles Gute!	*All the best!*
Alles Gute zum Geburtstag!	*Happy birthday!*
Herzlichen Glückwunsch (zum Geburtstag)!	*Congratulations (on your birthday)!*

Ich gratuliere dir/Ihnen . . . !	*Congratulations . . . !*
Ich wünsche dir/Ihnen . . . !	*I wish you . . . !*
Herzliche Glückwünsche!	*Best wishes!*
Viel Glück!	*Good luck!*
Gute Besserung!	*Get well soon!*
Frohe / Fröhliche Weihnachten!	*Merry Christmas!*
Ein gutes Neues Jahr!	*Have a good New Year!*
(Ein) schönes Wochenende!	*Have a nice weekend!*

1 From 1 to 19, the ordinal numbers have a **-te(n)** ending. Starting with 20, they end in **-ste(n)**. Note the irregularities within the numbers.

2 In writing dates, Americans give the month and then the day: *5/1 (May 1), 1/5 (January 5)*. Germans give the day first and then the month. The ordinal number is followed by a period: **1.5. (1. Mai), 5.1. (5. Januar).** Thus **1.5.** reads **der erste Mai,** and **5.1.** reads **der fünfte Januar.** Note the **-en** after **am, vom,** and **zum:** am erst**en** Mai, vom neunt**en** Juli bis zum achtzehnt**en** August.

3 German traditionally does not use a preposition when simply naming a year: **Ich bin 1980 geboren.** *I was born in 1980.*

4 **Feiertag** refers to a special day, a holiday, and can be in either the singular or the plural, whereas **Ferien** refers to school or university vacation time. A (paid) vacation from work is **der Urlaub.**

5 The present tense forms of **tun** are: **ich tue, du tust, er tut, wir tun, ihr tut, sie tun.**

6 **vor** meaning *ago* is PREpositional rather than POSTpositional as it is in English: **vor einem Monat** *(a month ago),* **vor zwei Tagen** *(two days ago).*

Zum Erkennen: nichts Besonderes *(nothing special);* Quatsch! *(Nonsense!);* na gut *(all right);* klingeln *(here: to ring the doorbell);* Grüß dich! *(Hi! Hello!);* AUCH: das Sternzeichen, - *(sign of the zodiac);* der Ferienkalender, - *(vacation schedule);* das Partizip, -ien *(participle);* der Infinitiv, -e; das Hilfsverb, -en *(auxiliary verb);* der Nebensatz, ¨e *(subordinate clause);* verbinden *(to connect)*

Write several dates on the board (**31.12., 1.4., 7.6.,** etc.), have the students repeat the dates after you. Then point to the dates at random; let individual students read them. Then go to Exercise A.

Zum Thema

A. Sagen Sie das Datum!

1. **Kettenreaktion.** Welches Datum haben wir? *(Chain reaction. Start with any date, then name the next two.)*

   BEISPIEL: Heute ist der 2. Juli.
   Morgen ist der 3. Juli und übermorgen ist der 4. Juli.

2. **Nationalfeiertage in Europa** *(Say when these European countries celebrate their national holidays.)*

   BEISPIEL: Irland (3.3.)
   Der Nationalfeiertag in Irland ist am dritten März.

   a. Griechenland (25.3.)   b. England (23.4.)   c. Italien (2.6.)   d. Dänemark (5.6.)
   e. Portugal (10.6.)   f. Luxemburg (23.6.)   g. Frankreich (14.7.)   h. Belgien (21.7.)
   i. Deutschland (3.10.)   j. Spanien (12.10.)

B. Der Spielplan. Was spielt wann und wo? (*Schedule of performances. You work at a ticket office representing four of Bremen's theaters. Give patrons information about dates and times of upcoming performances. Read aloud!*)

BEISPIEL: S1 Am zweiten um acht gibt es im Theater am Goetheplatz *Die Zauberflöte*, einen Film von Ingmar Bergmann.
S2 Und im Schauspielhaus oder in der Concordia?
S1 Im Schauspielhaus *Die Gerechten* von Albert Camus, und in der Concordia *Appetit* von Urs Dietrich.

B: In addition, you could ask other questions, e.g., about the particular days of the week (**Was für ein Tag ist der erste [Oktober]?—Der erste ist ein Mittwoch.**) or when students repeat phrases (**Wann spielen sie das noch mal?—Am . . . um . . .).**

BREMER THEATER

Oktober	Theater am Goetheplatz	Schauspielhaus	Brauhaus	Concordia
1 Montag	bis 2. Okt täglich um 18 Uhr. Kino 46 DIE ZAUBERFLÖTE ein Film von Ingmar Bergmann			
2 Dienstag		20.00 DIE GERECHTEN Albert Camus	20.30 GESTOCHEN SCHARFE POLAROIDS Mark Ravenhill	20.00 APPETIT Urs Dietrich
3 Mittwoch	19.30-22.45 DIE ZAUBERFLÖTE W. A. Mozart	19.30 VOLKSVERNICHTUNG ODER MEINE LEBER IST SINNLOS	16.00 ZWEI MONSTER Gertrud Pigor	15., 16., 17. u. 18. Okt, 10.30 Die TOCHTER DES GANOVENKÖNIGS
4 Donnerstag			20.30 ROTER OKTOBER-VIDEO-ABEND I	
5 Freitag		20.00 DIE GERECHTEN Albert Camus	16.00 ZWEI MONSTER 20.30 FREUD'S BABY	29. und 30. Okt., 10.30 ZWEI MONSTER
6 Samstag	19.00-22.00 PIQUE DAME P. I. Tschaikowskij	19.30 VOLKSVERNICHTUNG ODER MEINE LEBER IST SINNLOS	23.00 programme plaisir supersexyswingsounds	20.00 APPETIT Urs Dietrich
7 Sonntag	19.30-22.45 DIE ZAUBERFLÖTE W. A. Mozart	20.00 DIE GERECHTEN Albert Camus	16.00 ZWEI MONSTER 20.30 GESTOCHEN SCHARFE POLAROIDS	29. Sept. bis 14. Okt.
8 Montag	Di, 9. Okt., 9.00 Uhr: Radio Bremen 2 präsentiert: NOACH, NATHAN DER WEISE, SCHÖNE BESCHERUNGEN			Theater statt Teneriffa Herbstferien
9 Dienstag			20.30 ALEXANDER OSANG liest	

B: Although official time will not be taught until Chapter 7, students should be able to guess the times shown here.

C. Was sagen Sie? (*Find out how your partner would respond to the following situations. Take turns.*)

1. Ein Freund oder eine Freundin hat heute Geburtstag.
2. Sie haben Geburtstag. Ein Freund oder eine Freundin aus der Schule telefoniert und gratuliert Ihnen.
3. Sie schreiben Ihrer Großmutter zu Weihnachten.
4. Sie haben einen Aufsatz (*paper*) geschrieben. Sie haben nicht viel Zeit gebraucht und doch ein „A" bekommen.
5. Sie haben mit einer Freundin in einem Restaurant gegessen. Die Freundin zahlt fürs Essen.
6. Sie sind im Supermarkt gewesen und haben viel gekauft. Die Tür zu Ihrem Studentenheim ist zu. Ein Student öffnet Ihnen die Tür.

7. Ihre Eltern haben Ihnen etwas Schönes zu Weihnachten geschenkt.

8. Sie haben eine Million Euro gewonnen.

9. Sie danken Ihrem Zimmernachbarn, weil er Ihnen geholfen hat. Was antwortet der Nachbar?

10. Ein Freund fragt, ob Sie zu einer Party kommen möchten.

11. Ihre beste Freundin sagt, dass sie im Herbst ein Jahr nach Deutschland geht.

12. Sie studieren in Deutschland. Ein Regensburger Student fragt, ob Sie Weihnachten bei seiner *(his)* Familie feiern möchten.

13. Sie haben Weihnachten bei Familie Huber gefeiert. Sie fahren wieder nach Hause. Was sagen Sie zu Herrn und Frau Huber?

14. Ihr Cousin hat die Grippe *(flu)*.

D. Geburtstage und Sternzeichen *(Birthdays and signs of the zodiac. Find out about your partner's birthday and the ones of his/her family members. What are their signs of the zodiac?)*

D: You could also ask students to report findings to the class. Note: students can report to the class about family members only if they use proper names; **Peters Mutter/Vater/Bruder ist . . . ; sein/ihr** is new.

BEISPIEL: S1   Wann hast du Geburtstag und was bist du?
             S2   Ich habe am 25. Dezember Geburtstag. Ich bin Steinbock. Und du?
             S1   Mein Geburtstag ist am 21. Januar. Ich bin Wassermann.
             S2   Wann ist dein Vater (deine Mutter usw.) geboren?
             S1   Er ist am 21. Juni geboren. Er ist Zwilling.

Note **die Waage, die Jungfrau.** All other signs of the zodiac are masculine.

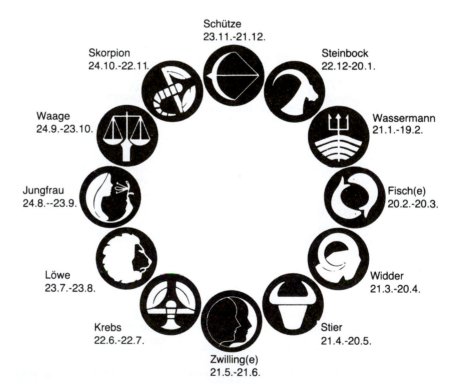

E. Ferien in Deutschland *(Ask each other about vacations in Germany and elsewhere. Alternate.)*

1. Was für Ferien gibt es in Deutschland?

2. Von wann bis wann sind die Osterferien in Bayern? die Pfingstferien *(Pentecost holidays)* in Baden-Württemberg? die Sommerferien in Berlin und in Schleswig-Holstein? die Herbstferien in Niedersachsen? die Weihnachtsferien in Hessen? . . .

3. Was für Ferien gibt es hier (in den USA, in Kanada . . .)? Wann sind sie? Wie lange dauern sie?

4. Wann beginnen die nächsten *(next)* Ferien? Wann enden sie? Was tun Sie dann?

Land	Winter	Früjahr/Ostern	Himmelfahrt/Pfingsten	Sommer	Herbst	Weihnachten
Baden-Württemberg	-	25.04. - 29.04.	02.06. - 13.06.	27.07. - 09.09.	02.11. - 03.11.	23.12. - 05.01.
Bayern	-	17.04. - 29.04.	13.06. - 24.06.	27.07. - 11.09.	30.10. - 04.11.	27.12. - 08.01.
Berlin	29.01. - 09.02.	20.04. - 06.05.	02.06./10.06. - 13.06.	20.07. - 02.09.	28.10. - 04.11.	23.12. - 02.01.
Brandenburg	31.01. - 12.02.	25.04. - 04.05.	-	20.07. - 02.09.	30.10. - 04.11.	23.12. - 02.01.
Bremen	-	03.04. - 25.04.	-	13.07. - 26.08.	23.10. - 01.11.	22.12. - 06.01.
Hamburg	-	06.03. - 18.03.	29.05. - 03.06.	20.07. - 30.08.	16.10. - 28.10.	21.12. - 02.01.
Hessen	-	10.04. - 20.04.	-	23.06. - 04.08.	02.10. - 14.10.	27.12. - 13.01.
Mecklenburg-Vorp.	07.02. - 19.02.	15.04. - 25.04.	09.06. - 13.06.	20.07. - 30.08.	23.10. - 28.10.	20.12. - 02.01.
Niedersachen	-	14.04. - 29.04.	02.06. - 13.06.	13.07. - 23.08.	19.10. - 01.11.	22.12. - 06.01.
Nordrhein-Westfalen	-	17.04. - 29.04.	-	29.06. - 12.08.	02.10. - 14.10.	22.12. - 06.01.
Rheinland-Pfalz	-	17.04. - 28.04.	-	23.06. - 04.08.	02.10. - 13.10.	22.12. - 05.01.
Saarland	-	14.04. - 29.04.	-	22.06. - 02.08.	02.10. - 14.10.	23.12. - 06.01.
Sachsen	14.02. - 26.02.	20.04. - 28.04.	10.06. - 13.06.	13.07. - 23.08.	16.10. - 27.10.	22.12. - 02.01.
Sachsen-Anhalt	17.02. - 26.02.	17.04. - 20.04.	02.06. - 10.06.	13.07. - 23.08.	23.10. - 30.10.	27.12. - 02.01.
Schleswig-Holstein	-	08.04. - 25.04.	-	20.07. - 02.09.	23.10. - 04.11.	27.12. - 06.01.
Thüringen	07.02. - 12.02.	17.04. - 29.04.	10.06. - 13.06.	13.07. - 23.08.	16.10. - 21.10.	22.12. - 06.01.

F. Deutsche Länder und Hauptstädte *(Look at the map of the various federal states of Germany. Then take turns asking each other questions about their location and their respective capitals.)*

Aussprache: ch, ck

(Read also Part III. 13–15 in the Pronunciation Guide of the Workbook.)

1. [ç]   **ich, nicht, furchtbar, vielleicht, manchmal, sprechen, Rechnung, Mädchen, Milch, durch, gewöhnlich, richtig, wichtig**

CD 3, Track 2

2. [x] a**ch,** a**ch**t, ma**ch**en, Weihna**ch**ten, au**ch,** brau**ch**en, Wo**ch**e, no**ch,** do**ch,** Bu**ch,** Ku**ch**en, Ba**ch,** Ba**ch**ara**ch**
3. [ks] se**chs,** se**chs**te
4. [k] di**ck,** Zu**ck**er, Bä**ck**er, Ro**ck,** Ja**ck**e, Frühstü**ck,** schme**ck**en
5. Wortpaare
   a. mich / misch   c. nickt / nicht   e. Nacht / nackt
   b. Kirche / Kirsche d. lochen / locken   f. möchte / mochte

HÖREN SIE ZU!   TRACK 8

Die Geburtstagsparty *(Listen to the conversation between Anke and Paul. Then answer the questions below by jotting down key words.)*

Zum Erkennen: Gute Idee! *(That's a good idea!);* es geht sicher *(it's probably all right)*

1. Wer hat am 7. Oktober Geburtstag? Claire
   Wer hat am 8. Oktober Geburtstag? Peter
2. Was möchte Paul machen? eine Party geben
3. Was tut Claire samstags bis um drei? arbeiten
4. Wo wollen sie feiern? bei Anke
5. Was bringt Paul? CDs und etwas zu essen
   Was bringt Klaus? etwas zu trinken
6. Wer telefoniert mit Peter und Claire? Anke
7. Wann beginnt die Party? um 8 Uhr

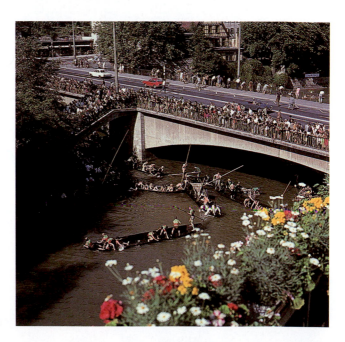

Kahnschlacht *(boat fight)* in Tübingen

Struktur

4.1 Present perfect with *haben*

1. The German PRESENT PERFECT corresponds closely in form to the English present perfect. In both languages, it consists of an inflected auxiliary verb (or "helping verb") and an unchanging past participle.

*You **have learned** that well.*	Du **hast** das gut **gelernt.**
*She **has brought** the books.*	Sie **hat** die Bücher **gebracht.**
*We **haven't spoken** any English.*	Wir **haben** kein Englisch **gesprochen.**

2. In the use of this tense, however, there is a considerable difference between English and German. In everyday conversation, English makes more use of the simple past, whereas German prefers the present perfect.

Du **hast** das gut **gelernt.**	*You **learned** that well.*
Sie **hat** die Bücher **gebracht.**	*She **brought** the books.*
Wir **haben** kein Englisch **gesprochen.**	*We **didn't speak** any English.*

The German present perfect corresponds to four past-tense forms in English:

Wir haben das gelernt.
$\left\{ \begin{array}{l} \textit{We have learned that.} \\ \textit{We learned that.} \\ \textit{We did learn that.} \\ \textit{We were learning that.} \end{array} \right.$

3. Most German verbs form the present perfect by using the present tense of **haben** (V1) with the past participle (V2). The past participle is placed at the end of the sentence or clause.

ich	**habe**	. . . gelernt	wir	**haben**	. . . gelernt
du	**hast**	. . . gelernt	ihr	**habt**	. . . gelernt
er	**hat**	. . . gelernt	sie	**haben**	. . . gelernt

4. German has two groups of verbs that form their past participles in different ways:

- T-VERBS (also called "WEAK VERBS") with the participle ending in **-t (gelernt)**
- N-VERBS (also called "STRONG VERBS") with the participle ending in **-en (gesprochen)**

Any verb not specifically identified as an irregular t-verb or as an n-verb can be assumed to be a regular t-verb.

a. The majority of German verbs are regular t-verbs. They form their past participles with the prefix **ge-** and the ending **-t.** They correspond to such English verbs as *learn, learned,* and *ask, asked.*

ge + stem + t	lernen →	ge lern t

Verbs that follow this pattern include: brauchen, danken, dauern, feiern, fragen, glauben, hören, kaufen, machen, sagen, schenken, schmecken, spielen, suchen, tanzen, wohnen, zählen.

Although lists of familiar verbs such as these are not printed in boldface, they are important. Please review these verbs.

- Verbs with stems ending in **-d, -t,** or certain consonant combinations make the final **-t** audible by inserting an **-e-.**

ge + stem + et	kosten →	ge kost et

Other verbs that follow this pattern include: antworten, arbeiten, öffnen, regnen.

- A few t-verbs are IRREGULAR (MIXED VERBS), i.e., they usually change their stem. They can be compared to such English verbs as *bring, brought,* and *think, thought.*

ge + stem (change) + t	bringen →	ge brach t

Here are the participles of familiar irregular t-verbs:

bringen	**gebracht**
denken	**gedacht**
haben	**gehabt**

b. A smaller but extremely important group of verbs, the N-VERBS, form their past participles with the prefix **ge-** and the ending **-en**. They correspond to such English verbs as *write, written,* and *speak, spoken*. The n-verbs frequently have a stem change in the past participle. Their forms are not predictable and therefore must be memorized. (Many of them also have a stem change in the second and third person singular of the present tense: **sprechen, du sprichst, er spricht.** *NOTE:* Those that do have this change are always n-verbs.)

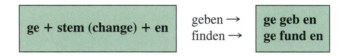

ge + stem (change) + en   geben → **ge geb en**
                                finden → **ge fund en**

For a complete alphabetical listing, see Appendix.

You will need to learn the past participles of these n-verbs:

Gesagt. Getan.

essen	**gegessen**	schlafen	**geschlafen**
finden	**gefunden**	schreiben	**geschrieben**
geben	**gegeben**	sehen	**gesehen**
heißen	**geheißen**	singen	**gesungen**
helfen	**geholfen**	sprechen	**gesprochen**
lesen	**gelesen**	tragen	**getragen**
liegen	**gelegen**	trinken	**getrunken**
nehmen	**genommen**	tun	**getan**
scheinen	**geschienen**		

5. Two groups of verbs have no **ge-**prefix.

- Inseparable-prefix verbs

   In English as in German, many verbs have been formed by the use of inseparable prefixes, e.g., *to belong, to impress, to proceed*. In both languages, the stress is on the verb, not on the prefix. The German inseparable prefixes are **be-, emp-, ent-, er-, ge-, ver-,** and **zer-.** *NOTE:* These verbs do *not* have a **ge-** prefix.

bestellen → be stell t
verstehen → ver stand en

In case students ask for an example: **Wiederholen** Sie *(repeat)* den Satz! BUT **Holen** Sie das Buch **wieder** *(get back)!* **Übersetzen** Sie *(translate)* den Satz! BUT **Setzen** Sie mit dem Boot **über** *(cross over the river)!*

Familiar t-verbs that also follow this pattern include: bedeuten, bezahlen, gehören, verkaufen, überraschen, wiederholen. *NOTE:* **über-** and **wieder-** are not always inseparable prefixes.

You will need to learn the past participles of these familiar n-verbs:

beginnen	**begonnen**	gefallen	**gefallen**
bekommen	**bekommen**	verstehen	**verstanden**
empfehlen	**empfohlen**		

- Verbs ending in **-ieren** (all of which are t-verbs):

  gratulieren   **gratuliert**

  studieren   **studiert**

Übungen

A. Geben Sie das Partizip!

BEISPIEL: fragen
                 gefragt

1. dauern, feiern, danken, wohnen, tanzen, antworten, bedeuten, kosten, öffnen, regnen, schmecken, verkaufen, bezahlen, gratulieren, denken, bringen, studieren
2. essen, finden, tun, helfen, lesen, heißen, trinken, schlafen, scheinen, singen, bekommen, empfehlen, beginnen, gefallen, verstehen

B. Geben Sie den Infinitiv!

BEISPIEL: gebracht
                 bringen

begonnen, bekommen, bezahlt, empfohlen, geantwortet, gedacht, gefallen, gefeiert, gefunden, gegessen, geglaubt, gehabt, geholfen, gelegen, genommen, geschienen, geschrieben, gesprochen, gesucht, gesungen, getan, getrunken, gratuliert, überrascht, verkauft, verstanden

C. Ersetzen Sie das Subjekt!

BEISPIEL: Ich habe eine Flasche Sekt gekauft. (er)
                 Er hat eine Flasche Sekt gekauft.

1. Du hast nichts gesagt. (ihr, man, ich)
2. Ich habe auf Englisch geantwortet. (wir, du, er)
3. Er hat Klaus Geschenke gebracht. (ihr, sie/*pl.,* ich)
4. Sie haben nur Deutsch gesprochen. (du, ihr, Robert und Silvia)

D. Was habt ihr gemacht? *(Tell your roommate what happened at Klaus' party.)*

BEISPIEL: Ich habe Klaus ein Buch gegeben. (schenken)
                 Ich habe Klaus ein Buch geschenkt.

1. Wir haben viel gefeiert. (tanzen, spielen, essen, tun, servieren)
2. Christa und Joachim haben Kuchen gekauft. (bestellen, nehmen)
3. Susanne hat Klaus gratuliert. (danken, glauben, helfen, überraschen, suchen)
4. Klaus hat viel gegessen. (arbeiten, trinken, singen, bekommen)
5. Wie gewöhnlich hat Peter nur gelesen. (schlafen, lernen, sprechen)
6. Sabine hat Helmut nicht gesehen. (fragen, antworten, schreiben)

E. Allerlei Fragen *(Ask your partner all sorts of questions, using only verbs that form the present perfect with **haben**.)*

BEISPIEL: S1   Was hast du zuletzt *(the last time)* zum Geburtstag bekommen?
                 S2   Ich habe . . . bekommen.
                 S1   Wie hat dir . . . gefallen?

4.2 Present perfect with *sein*

Whereas most German verbs use **haben** as the auxiliary in the perfect tenses, a few common verbs use **sein.** You will probably find it easiest to memorize **sein** together with the past participles of those verbs requiring it. However, you can also determine which verbs take **sein** by remembering that they must fulfill two conditions:

- They are INTRANSITIVE, i.e., they cannot take an accusative (direct) object. Examples of such verbs are: **gehen, kommen,** and **laufen.**

- They express a CHANGE OF PLACE OR CONDITION. **Sein** and **bleiben** are exceptions to this rule.

Wir **sind** nach Hause **gegangen.**	*We went home.*
Er **ist** müde **geworden.**	*He got tired.*
Ich **bin** zu Hause **geblieben.**	*I stayed home.*

CAUTION: A change in prefix or the addition of a prefix may cause a change in auxiliary because the meaning of the verb changes.

Ich **bin** nach Hause **gekommen.**	*I came home.*
Ich **habe** ein Geschenk **bekommen.**	*I received a present.*

The present perfect of the following verbs is formed with the present tense of **sein** (V1) and the past participle (V2). They are all n-verbs, although some t-verbs also take **sein.**

sein	**ist gewesen**	kommen	**ist gekommen**
bleiben	**ist geblieben**	laufen	**ist gelaufen**
fahren	**ist gefahren**	werden	**ist geworden**
gehen	**ist gegangen**		

ich	**bin**	. . . gekommen		wir	**sind**	. . . gekommen
du	**bist**	. . . gekommen		ihr	**seid**	. . . gekommen
er	**ist**	. . . gekommen		sie	**sind**	. . . gekommen

Occasionally, **fahren** takes an object. In that case, the auxiliary **haben** is used:

Sie **sind** nach Hause **gefahren.**	*They drove home.*
Sie **haben** mein Auto nach Hause **gefahren.**	*They drove my car home.*

Übungen

F: hat gegessen, hat gebracht, ist geworden, ist gewesen, ist gefallen, ist geblieben, hat gelegen, hat gesprochen, ist gelaufen, hat geholfen

F. *Sein* oder *haben*? Geben Sie das Partizip und das Hilfsverb *(auxiliary)!*

BEISPIEL: empfehlen   **hat empfohlen**
              gehen   **ist gegangen**

essen, bringen, werden, sein, gefallen, bleiben, liegen, sprechen, laufen, helfen

G. Hoppla, hier fehlt was! Wie ist das gewesen? *(How was it? Yesterday's party went very late, and you don't remember all the details. With a partner, piece together the picture. One of you looks at and completes the chart below, the other works with the chart in Section 11 of the Appendix.)*

S1:

	Ute	Eva	Max	Toni	ich	Partner/in
an alles denken		x				
mit dem Essen helfen	x					x
Getränke bringen			x		x	
den Sekt öffnen		x				
viel essen			x		x	
viel trinken			x			
schön singen				x		
etwas tanzen	x					x
mit allen sprechen						x
nichts tun				x		
nicht lange bleiben				x	x	

BEISPIEL: **S1** Was hat Ute gemacht?
           S2 Ute hat mit dem Essen geholfen und etwas getanzt. Und Eva?
           S1 Eva hat . . .

H. Ferien

1. **Michaels Sommerferien** (*Michael is explaining what he did during his last summer vacation. Use the present perfect. In each case, decide whether to use the auxiliary* **haben** *or* **sein.**)

   BEISPIEL: Im August habe ich Ferien.
                     Im August habe ich Ferien gehabt.

   a. In den Ferien fahre ich nach Zell.
   b. Ich nehme zwei Wochen frei (*take off*).
   c. Ich wohne bei Familie Huber.
   d. Das Haus liegt direkt am See.
   e. Zell gefällt mir gut.
   f. Nachmittags laufe ich in die Stadt.
   g. Manchmal gehen wir auch ins Café.
   h. Das Café gehört Familie Huber.
   i. Mittwochs hilft Renate da.
   j. Renate bringt oft Kuchen nach Hause.
   k. Ich bekomme alles frei.
   l. Sie empfiehlt die Sahnetorte.
   m. Die schmeckt wirklich gut.
   n. Den Apfelstrudel finde ich besonders gut.
   o. Renate ist in den Sommerferien bei uns.
   p. Wir werden gute Freunde.
   q. Leider regnet es viel.
   r. Wir lesen viel und hören Musik.

   H.1: a. bin gefahren b. habe genommen c. habe gewohnt d. hat gelegen e. hat gefallen f. bin gelaufen g. sind gegangen h. hat gehört i. hat geholfen j. hat gebracht k. habe bekommen l. hat empfohlen m. hat geschmeckt n. habe gefunden o. ist gewesen p. sind geworden q. hat geregnet r. haben gelesen / gehört

2. **Meine Ferien** (*Tell your partner what you did during your vacation last summer or any other time, using the present perfect with* **haben** *or* **sein.**)

I. Interview (*Find out the following information from a classmate and then tell the class what he/she said.*)
   1. wann er/sie gestern ins Bett (*to bed*) gegangen ist
   2. ob (*whether*) er/sie viel für die Deutschstunde gelernt hat
   3. wie er/sie geschlafen hat und wie lange
   4. was er/sie heute zum Frühstück gegessen und getrunken hat
   5. wie er/sie zur Uni(versität) gekommen ist, ob er/sie gelaufen oder gefahren ist
   6. wie viele Kurse er/sie heute schon gehabt hat und welche

I: To help students go through several items of this interview, demonstrate how they must transform the indirect questions into direct ones.

Focus — *German Holidays*

In German-speaking countries, Christmas Eve (**Heiligabend**) is at the center of the Christmas celebration. A late-afternoon or midnight church service is held on this day, and gifts are exchanged in the evening. In southern Germany, the **Christkind** brings the gifts around the **Christbaum,** whereas in the North, the **Weihnachtsmann** is responsible for delivering the presents. Many Germans also observe **St. Nikolaustag** on December 6 with the exchange of smaller gifts and goodies.

Nuremberg's outdoor **Christkindlmarkt** is the most famous German Christmas market. In the months before Christmas, more than 2 million visitors stroll by the market's booths, which offer Christmas decorations, candy, and toys. The smell of mulled wine, toasted almonds, and roasted chestnuts is in the air as well as the festive music of choirs and instrumentalists. Nuremberg is home to the fancy gingerbread called **Nürnberger Lebkuchen.** The traditional **Weihnachtsplätzchen** and **Stollen**—a buttery yeast bread filled with almonds, currants, raisins, and candied fruit—are other favorites at Christmas.

Abends auf dem Christkindlmarkt in Nürnberg

4.3 Subordinating conjunctions

You already know how to join sentences with a coordinating conjunction. Clauses can also be joined with SUBORDINATING CONJUNCTIONS. Subordinating conjunctions introduce a subordinate or dependent clause, i.e., a statement with a subject and a verb that cannot stand alone as a complete sentence.

because it's his birthday
that they have left already

Whereas coordinating conjunctions do not affect word order, subordinating conjunctions do. German subordinate clauses are always set off by a comma, and the inflected verb (V1) stands at the very end.

1. Six common subordinating conjunctions are:

In case students ask, both **denn** and **weil** mean *because*. Whereas **denn** (Ch. 1) is a coordinating conjunction and has no effect on word order, **weil** is a subordinating conjunction that influences the position of the main verb. **Denn** cannot begin a sentence, but **weil** can.

bevor	*before*
dass	*that*
ob	*if, whether*[1]
obwohl	*although*
weil	*because*
wenn	*if, when(ever)*[1]

[1] When it is possible to replace *if* with *whether,* use **ob;** otherwise use **wenn.**

Ich $\boxed{\text{kaufe}}$ ein Geschenk.

Ich frage Helga, **bevor** ich ein Geschenk **kaufe.**

I'll ask Helga before I buy a present.

Klaus $\boxed{\text{hat}}$ Geburtstag.

Sie sagt, **dass** Klaus morgen Geburtstag **hat.**

She says that Klaus has his birthday tomorrow.

$\boxed{\text{Ist}}$ sie sicher?

Ich frage, **ob** sie sicher **ist.**

I ask whether she is sure.

Sie $\boxed{\text{hat}}$ nicht viel Zeit.

Sie kommt zur Party, **obwohl** sie nicht viel Zeit **hat.**

She's coming to the party although she doesn't have much time.

Er $\boxed{\text{trinkt}}$ gern Sekt.

Wir bringen eine Flasche Sekt, **weil** er gern Sekt **trinkt.**

We are bringing a bottle of champagne because he loves to drink champagne.

Ich $\boxed{\text{habe}}$ Zeit.

Ich komme auch, **wenn** ich Zeit **habe.**

I'll come, too, if I have time.

NOTE: The subject of the dependent clause almost always follows the subordinating conjunction. When a sentence with inverted word order becomes a dependent clause, the subject moves to the position immediately after the conjunction.

Morgen hat **Klaus** Geburtstag.

Ich glaube, dass **Klaus morgen** Geburtstag hat.

2. Information questions can become subordinate clauses by using the question word (**wer? was? wie? wo?** etc.) as a conjunction and putting the verb last.

Wie $\boxed{\text{schmeckt}}$ der Salat?

Sie fragt, **wie** der Salat **schmeckt.**

She asks how the salad tastes.

Wo $\boxed{\text{sind}}$ die Brötchen?

Sie fragt, **wo** die Brötchen **sind.**

She asks where the rolls are.

Note the similarity with English:

Where $\boxed{\text{are}}$ *the rolls?*

*She asks **where** the rolls **are.***

3. Yes/no questions require **ob** as a conjunction.

$\boxed{\text{Schmeckt}}$ der Salat gut?

Sie fragt, **ob** der Salat gut schmeckt.

She asks whether the salad tastes good.

$\boxed{\text{Sind}}$ die Würstchen heiß?

Sie fragt, **ob** die Würstchen heiß sind.

She asks whether the franks are hot.

Lerntipp
Having the Last Word

When listening or reading, pay special attention to the end of the sentence, which often contains crucial sentence elements. As Mark Twain wrote in *A Connecticut Yankee in King Arthur's Court:* "Whenever the literary German dives into a sentence, that is the last we are going to see of him till he emerges on the other side of the Atlantic with his verb in his mouth."

gehabt

4. Subordinate clauses as the first sentence element

If the subordinate clause precedes the main clause, the inflected verb of the main clause—the second sentence element—comes right after the comma. In that case, the entire subordinate clause is the first sentence element.

1   2

Ich **komme**, wenn ich Zeit habe.

Wenn ich Zeit habe, **komme** ich.

5. The present perfect in subordinate clauses

In subordinate clauses in the present perfect, the inflected verb **haben** or **sein** (V1) stands at the end of the sentence.

Er hat eine Geburtstagskarte bekommen.

Er sagt, **dass** er eine Geburtstagskarte bekommen **hat.**

Er ist überrascht gewesen.

Er sagt, **dass** er überrascht gewesen **ist.**

Übungen

J. Verbinden Sie die Sätze!

BEISPIEL: Eva geht zur Bäckerei. Sie braucht noch etwas Brot. *(because)*
Eva geht zur Bäckerei, weil sie noch etwas Brot braucht.

1. Der Herr fragt die Studentin. Kommt sie aus Amerika? *(whether)*
2. Die Stadt gefällt den Amerikanern. Sie ist alt und romantisch. *(because)*
3. Eine Tasse Kaffee tut gut. Man ist müde. *(when)*
4. Rechnen Sie alles zusammen! Sie bezahlen die Rechnung. *(before)*
5. Wir spielen nicht Tennis. Das Wetter ist schlecht. *(if)*
6. Sie hat geschrieben. Sie ist in Österreich gewesen. *(that)*
7. Ich habe Hunger. Ich habe gerade ein Eis gegessen. *(although)*
8. Ich arbeite bei Tengelmann. Ich brauche Geld. *(because)*

K. Beginnen Sie mit dem Nebensatz! *(Begin with the subordinate clause.)*

BEISPIEL: Ich trinke Wasser, wenn ich Durst habe.
Wenn ich Durst habe, trinke ich Wasser.

1. Ich habe ein Stück Käse gegessen, weil ich Hunger gehabt habe.
2. Ich verstehe nicht, warum die Lebensmittel Farbstoffe brauchen.
3. Ihr habt eine Party gegeben, weil ich 21 geworden bin.
4. Ich finde (es) prima, dass ihr nichts gesagt habt.
5. Ich bin nicht müde, obwohl wir bis morgens um sechs gefeiert haben.

L. Sagen Sie die Sätze noch einmal!

1. **Er sagt, dass . . .** *(A friend has just come back from Luxembourg. Tell the class what he has observed. Follow the model.)*

BEISPIEL: Luxemburg ist wirklich schön.
Er sagt, dass Luxemburg wirklich schön ist.

a. Die Luxemburger sprechen Französisch, Deutsch und Letzeburgisch.
b. Letzeburgisch ist der Luxemburger Dialekt.
c. Er hat den Geburtstag auf einer Burg *(in a castle)* gefeiert.
d. Das ist einfach toll gewesen.
e. In Luxemburg gibt es viele Banken.
f. Den Leuten geht es wirklich sehr gut.
g. Überall sieht man BMWs und Citroëns.

J: 1. ob sie . . . kommt 2. weil sie . . . ist 3. wenn man . . . ist 4. bevor Sie . . . bezahlen 5. wenn das Wetter . . . ist 6. dass sie . . . gewesen ist 7. obwohl ich . . . gegessen habe 8. weil ich . . . brauche

K: 1. Weil ich Hunger gehabt habe, habe ich . . . 2. Warum die Lebensmittel Farbstoffe brauchen, verstehe ich . . . 3. Weil ich 21 geworden bin, habt ihr . . . 4. Dass ihr nichts gesagt habt, finde ich . . . 5. Obwohl wir . . . gefeiert haben, bin ich . . .

L. 1: Er sagt, . . . a. dass die Luxemburger Französisch . . . sprechen b. dass Letzeburgisch der Luxemburger Dialekt ist c. dass er den Geburtstag auf einer Burg gefeiert hat d. dass das einfach toll gewesen ist e. dass es in Luxemburg viele Banken gibt f. dass es den Leuten wirklich sehr gut geht g. dass man überall BMWs und Citroëns sieht

2. **Sie fragt, ...** *(Your mother wants to know about Carla's graduation party. Follow the model.)*

   BEISPIEL: Wer ist Carla?
   Sie fragt, wer Carla ist.

   a. Wo wohnt Carla? b. Wie viele Leute sind da gewesen? c. Wie lange hat die Party gedauert? d. Was habt ihr gegessen und getrunken? e. Mit wem hast du getanzt? f. Wie bist du nach Hause gekommen?

L.2. Sie fragt, ... a. wo Carla wohnt b. wie viele Leute da gewesen sind c. wie lange die Party gedauert hat d. was ihr gegessen und getrunken habt e. mit wem du getanzt hast f. wie du nach Hause gekommen bist

3. **Sie fragt, ob ...** *(Your parents are celebrating their 30th anniversary, and your sister is in charge of the party. Now she asks whether you and your brothers have completed the tasks she assigned a week ago.)*

   BEISPIEL: Hast du Servietten gekauft?
   Sie fragt, ob du Servietten gekauft hast.

   a. Seid ihr gestern einkaufen gegangen?   b. Hat Alfred Sekt gekauft?   c. Haben wir jetzt alle Geschenke?   d. Habt ihr den Kuchen beim Bäcker *(baker)* bestellt? e. Hat Peter mit den Nachbarn gesprochen?   f. Hat Alfred die Kamera gefunden?

L.3. Sie fragt, ... a. ob ihr gestern einkaufen gegangen seid b. ob Alfred Sekt gekauft hat c. ob wir jetzt alle Geschenke haben d. ob ihr den Kuchen beim Bäcker bestellt habt e. ob Peter mit den Nachbarn gesprochen hat f. ob Alfred die Kamera gefunden hat

Fokus — *Traditions*

Germany is a thoroughly modern industrial society, but it also has many traditions rooted in its long history. Some of these are carried on not only out of reverence for the past, but possibly also to foster tourism, which contributes significantly to the German economy.

Every year millions of visitors flock to Munich's **Oktoberfest,** the world's biggest beer festival. The tradition began with a royal wedding more than 150 years ago. Similar festivals on a much smaller scale take place elsewhere, with amusement park rides and game booths. In late summer and early fall, wine festivals **(Winzerfeste)** are celebrated in wine-growing regions, especially along the Rhine, Main, and Moselle rivers, where wine production plays an important economic role.

Some towns attract visitors by recreating historical events in their carefully preserved surroundings. The **Meistertrunk** in Rothenburg ob der Tauber recalls an event from the Thirty Years' War (1618–1648). Landshut recruits many of its residents in the reenactment of the 1475 wedding of the son of Duke Ludwig to a Polish princess **(die Fürstenhochzeit).** The **Rattenfänger von Hameln** *(The Pied Piper of Hamelin)* commemorates the Children's Crusade of 1284, when 130 of the town's children mysteriously vanished.

Carnival time—the German version of Mardi Gras—starts on November 11, at 11:11, and ends with Ash Wednesday. It has its roots in the pre-Christian era and was intended to cast out the demons of winter. Celebrated in the South as **Fasching** and along the Rhine as **Karneval,** it ends just before Lent, with parades and merry-making in the streets. Much more could be mentioned here, as there are all sorts of celebrations taking place in the various regions throughout the year, all expressions of the enjoyment of life.

Der Rattenfänger von Hameln

Zwei Clowns beim Karneval in Köln

Zusammenfassung

M. Was haben Sie gestern gemacht? Schreiben Sie 8–10 Sätze im Perfekt!

  BEISPIEL: Ich habe bis 10 Uhr geschlafen. Dann . . .

N. Die Abschlussparty

 1. **Wir planen eine Abschlussparty.** *(With one or several partners, work out a plan for your cousin's graduation party. Be prepared to outline your ideas.)*
 Sagen Sie, . . . !

 a. wann und wo die Party ist   b. wie lange sie dauert   c. wer kommt   d. was Sie trinken und essen   e. was Sie noch brauchen

 2. **Wie ist die Party gewesen?** *(Describe what happened at the party.)*

O: You might assign different chapters for each of the partners.

O. Rückblick auf die Gespräche *(Looking back on the dialogues. With your partner, pick the dialogues of any of the pre-units or chapters you have read so far and report what people talked about.)*

  KAPITEL 1:   Sharon hat Roberto gefragt, woher er kommt. Er hat gesagt, dass er aus Rom kommt und dass er eine Schwester in Montreal hat. Dann hat Roberto Sharon gefragt, wann die Prüfung ist. Sie hat gesagt, dass sie in zehn Minuten ist und hat Roberto viel Glück gewünscht.

P. Die Geburtstagsfeier. Auf Deutsch bitte!

1. The day before yesterday I gave a birthday party. 2. Did Volker and Bettina come? 3. Yes, they came, too. 4. My friends brought presents. 5. My father opened a bottle of champagne. 6. How long did you *(pl. fam.)* celebrate? 7. Until three o'clock. We danced, ate well, and drank a lot of Coke. 8. The neighbors said that the music was too loud **(laut).** 9. Did you *(sg. fam.)* hear that? 10. Yesterday a neighbor came and spoke with my parents. 11. I liked the party.

P: 1. Vorgestern habe ich eine Geburtstagsparty/-feier gegeben. 2. Sind Volker und Bettina gekommen? 3. Ja, sie sind auch gekommen. 4. Meine Freunde haben Geschenke gebracht. 5. Mein Vater hat eine Flasche Sekt geöffnet. 6. Wie lange habt ihr gefeiert? 7. Bis um drei. Wir haben getanzt, gut gegessen und viel Cola getrunken. 8. Die Nachbarn haben gesagt, dass die Musik zu laut gewesen ist. 9. Hast du das gehört? 10. Gestern ist ein Nachbar/eine Nachbarin gekommen und hat mit meinen Eltern gesprochen. 11. Die Party/Feier hat mir gefallen.

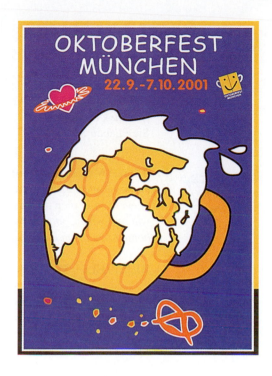

Einblicke

Lesestrategie: Understanding a Text Through Images

In this text, Carolyn talks about her exchange year in Germany. She uses pictures to illustrate her presentation. Use the pictures to better understand the text. What do the images tell you about the different events Carolyn describes?

Wortschatz 2

das Lied, -er	*song*
die Kerze, -n	*candle*
dort	*(over) there*
eigentlich	*actual(ly)*
ein bisschen	*some, a little bit (+ sing.)*
immer	*always*
laut	*loud, noisy*
lustig	*funny, amusing*
(noch) nie	*never (before)*
verrückt	*crazy*
fallen (fällt), ist gefallen	*to fall*
studieren[1]	*to study a particular field, be a student at a university*
Glück / Pech haben	*to be (un)lucky*
Glück / Pech gehabt!	*I was (you were, she was, etc.) (un)lucky!*
Spaß machen[2]	*to be fun*
Das macht (mir) Spaß.[2]	*That's fun.*

»Ich tue, was mir Spaß macht«

[1] **Ich studiere** *(I am a student)* in Heidelberg. **Ich studiere** Kunst und Geschichte *(i.e., art and history are my majors).* BUT **Ich lerne** Deutsch und Französisch *(i.e., I'm taking these languages).* **Ich lerne** gerade Vokabeln *(i.e., I'm learning / studying, possibly for a test).*

[2] Learn this like an idiom! **Tanzen macht Spaß,** *(Dancing is fun.);* **Das macht mir/ihm/uns/ihnen Spaß.** *(I/he/we/they love [to do] it.);* **Macht es dir Spaß?** *(Do you enjoy (doing) it?)*

Vor dem Lesen

A. Fragen

1. Welche religiösen Feste feiern wir hier (in den USA, in Kanada . . .)?   2. Gibt es hier historische Feste? Wenn ja, welche?   3. Wann gibt es hier Karussells, Buden *(booths),* Spaß für alle?   4. Was machen die Leute hier gern am 4. Juli? Was machen Sie / haben Sie gemacht?

B. Allerlei Musikalisches um die Weihnachtszeit. Wohin gehen wir? *(All sorts of musical entertainment during the Christmas season. Look at the Leipzig calendar of events and then discuss with your partner what performances might interest you and why. Compare the theater program with what is typically offered in your home town or on campus during that time.)*

BEISPIEL: **S1**   Welche Oper möchtest du sehen?
　　　　　　S2   Ich möchte . . . sehen. / Ich möchte keine Oper sehen, aber ich gehe gern ins Konzert.

Spielpläne

Oper Leipzig

29. 11.	19.30 Uhr	Les Contes d'Hoffmann
30. 11.	10.30 Uhr	Salome
1. 12.	19.00 Uhr	Bruckner 8 *(Ballet)*
2. 12.	18.00 Uhr	Tannhäuser
5. 12.	19.30 Uhr	Hänsel und Gretel
6. 12.	19.30 Uhr	Bruckner 8 *(Ballet)*
7. 12.	19.30 Uhr	Hänsel und Gretel
8. 12.	19.00 Uhr	Bruckner 8 *(Ballet)*
9. 12.	18.00 Uhr	Salome
12. 12.	19.30 Uhr	Bruckner 8 *(Ballet)*
13. 12.	19.30 Uhr	Rigoletto
14. 12.	19.30 Uhr	Salome
15. 12.	19.00 Uhr	Carmen
16. 12.	11.00 Uhr	Hänsel und Gretel
	17.00 Uhr	Hänsel und Gretel
20. 12.	19.30 Uhr	Schwanensee *(Ballet)*
21. 12.	19.30 Uhr	Hänsel und Gretel
22. 12.	17.00 Uhr	Hänsel und Gretel
23. 12.	18.00 Uhr	Schwanensee *(Ballet)*

Neues Gewandhaus

1. 12.	16.00 Uhr	Salonorchester CAPPUCCINO Vorweihnachtliche Impressionen
	17.00 Uhr	Orgelstunde zum 1. Advent
2. 12.	11.00 Uhr	Salonorchester CAPPUCCINO Vorweihnachtliche Impressionen
	20.00 Uhr	Großes Konzert für UNICEF
3. 12.	16.00 Uhr	Adventskonzert
6./7./8. 12.	19.30 Uhr	Großes Konzert
	19.00 Uhr	G. F. Händel: Messias (Teil I – III)
8. 12.	16.00 Uhr	Orgelstunde zum 2. Advent
9. 12.	18.00 Uhr	Kammermusik
10. 12.	16.00 Uhr	Adventskonzert
12. 12.	20.00 Uhr	Konzert für den American Football Club „Leipzig Lions" J. S. Bach: Weihnachtsoratorium (I–III)
15. 12.	16.00 Uhr	Familienkonzert: Hänsel und Gretel
16. 12.	18.00 Uhr	Kammermusik
17. 12.	16.00 Uhr	Adventskonzert
20./21. 12.	20.00 Uhr	Musik aus Hollywood-Filmen

C: As pointed out earlier, it might be very helpful to quickly read these words aloud in class — possibly as a chain reaction — since their pronunciation is often quite different from the English. Reading them aloud also helps students to recognize relatively easy, but still unfamiliar vocabulary.

C. Was ist das?

der Prinz, Studentenball, Vampir; das Kostüm, Musikinstrument, Weihnachtsessen, Weihnachtslied; die Adventszeit, Brezel, Flamme (in Flammen), Kontaktlinse, Konversationsstunde, Prinzessin, Weihnachtsdekoration, Weihnachtspyramide, Weihnachtszeit; Ende Juli; ins Bett fallen; authentisch, enorm viel, exakt, historisch, Hunderte von, wunderschön

Deutsche Feste

(Carolyn berichtet° für die Konversationsstunde.)

CD 3, Track 4   reports

Wie ihr gehört habt, habe ich gerade ein Jahr in Deutschland studiert. Ich bin erst° vor einem Monat wieder nach Hause gekommen, weil ich dort mit der Uni erst Ende Juli fertig geworden bin. Es ist wunderschön gewesen. Ich habe viel gesehen und viel gelernt. Heute habe ich ein paar Bilder gebracht.

only

Im September bin ich mit Freunden beim Winzerfest° in Bacharach am Rhein gewesen. Da haben wir Wein getrunken und gesungen. Abends haben wir von einem Schiff den „Rhein in Flammen" gesehen, mit viel Feuerwerk° und Rotlicht°. Ich habe immer gedacht, dass die Deutschen etwas steif° sind. Aber nicht, wenn sie feiern! So lustig und verrückt habe ich sie° noch nie gesehen. Zwei Wochen später sind wir zum Oktoberfest nach München gefahren. Im Bierzelt° haben wir Brezeln gegessen und natürlich auch Bier getrunken. Die Musik ist mir° ein bisschen zu laut gewesen. Was mir aber besonders gefallen hat, war° der Trachtenzug° zur Wies'n°.

vintage festival

fireworks / red light of torches

stiff

them

...tent

for me

was / parade in traditional garb / festival grounds

Im Oktoberfestzelt

Halloween gibt es in Deutschland nicht, aber dafür° gibt es im Februar den Fasching. Das ist so etwas wie° Mardi Gras in New Orleans, mit Umzügen° und Kostümen. Ich bin als Vampir zu einem Studentenball gegangen. Wir haben lange getanzt und morgens bin ich dann todmüde° ins Bett gefallen.

instead

like / parades

dead-tired

Außer diesen° Festen gibt es natürlich noch viele Feiertage. Weihnachten war besonders schön. Beim Christkindlmarkt in Nürnberg gibt es Hunderte von Buden° mit Weihnachtsdekorationen, Kerzen, Spielzeug°, Lebkuchen und auch Buden mit Glühwein°. Den Weihnachtsengel° habe ich dort gekauft; der Nussknacker° und die Weihnachtspyramide kommen aus dem Erzgebirge. In der Adventszeit hat man nur einen Adventskranz°. Den Weihnachtsbaum sehen die Kinder erst am 24. Dezember, am Heiligabend. Aber dann bleibt er gewöhnlich bis zum 6. Januar im Zimmer.

these

booths

toys / mulled wine

...angel / nutcracker

...wreath

Zu Weihnachten bin ich bei Familie Fuchs gewesen. Bevor das Christkind die Geschenke gebracht hat, haben wir Weihnachtslieder gesungen. Am 25. und 26. Dezember sind alle Geschäfte zu. Die zwei Feiertage sind nur für Familie und Freunde. Das

Nussknacker aus dem Erzgebirge

goose / red cabbage

at midnight / church bells
rang / Happy New Year!

finde ich eigentlich gut. Zum Weihnachtsessen hat es Gans° mit Rotkraut° und Knödeln gegeben. Die Weihnachtsplätzchen und der Stollen haben mir besonders gut geschmeckt.

Silvester habe ich mit Freunden gefeiert. Um Mitternacht° haben alle Kirchenglocken° geläutet° und wir haben mit Sekt und „Prost Neujahr!"° das neue Jahr begonnen.

Landshuter Fürstenhochzeit

forget / medieval

knights

tournaments / glasses

in the Middle Ages

every

more than

Das Bild hier ist von der Fürstenhochzeit in Landshut. Da bin ich im Juni gewesen. Das vergesse° ich nie. Viele Landshuter haben mittelalterliche° Kleidung getragen und alles ist sehr authentisch gewesen: die Ritter°, Prinzen und Prinzessinnen, die Musikinstrumente und Turniere°. Man ist historisch so exakt, dass Leute mit Brillen° Kontaktlinsen tragen, weil es im Mittelalter° noch keine Brillen gegeben hat. Übrigens habe ich Glück gehabt, weil man das Fest nur alle° vier Jahre feiert.

Ich habe immer gedacht, dass die Deutschen viel arbeiten. Das tun sie, aber sie haben auch enorm viele Feiertage, viel mehr als° wir. Und Feiern in Deutschland macht Spaß.

Fokus — *Wine Festivals, Harvest Time, and Traditional Garb*

- Germany's largest wine festival, the Sausage Fair **(Wurstmarkt)** in Bad Dürkheim—between Mannheim and Kaiserslautern—dates back to the year 1442 and attracts more than 500,000 visitors annually. Aside from Bacharach, big wine festivals are also held in Koblenz, Mainz, Assmannshausen, Trier, and Bingen.

- Germans don't have a Thanksgiving holiday with traditional foods like cranberry sauce and pumpkin pie.

Instead, churches and rural communities celebrate Harvest Thanksgiving **(Erntedankfest)** with special services and harvest wreaths.

- Traditional folk-style dresses **(Trachten)** are still worn in rural areas of Germany, Austria, and Switzerland, but only on church holidays, for weddings, and on similar occasions. Special clubs **(Trachtenvereine)** try to keep the tradition alive.

Nach dem Lesen

A. Was hat Carolyn gesagt? *(Match the sentence fragments from the two groups.)*

<u> f </u> 1. Wie ihr gehört habt, . . .

<u> e </u> 2. Ich bin erst vor einem Monat wieder nach Hause gekommen, . . .

<u> g </u> 3. Ich habe immer gedacht, . . .

<u> c </u> 4. Im Bierzelt haben wir . . .

<u> d </u> 5. Der Weihnachtsbaum bleibt . . .

<u> a </u> 6. Bevor das Christkind die Geschenke gebracht hat, . . .

<u> b </u> 7. Was mir besonders gut gefallen hat, . . .

<u> h </u> 8. Man ist historisch so exakt, . . .

a. haben wir Weihnachtslieder gesungen.

b. war die Fürstenhochzeit in Landshut.

c. Brezeln gegessen.

d. bis zum 6. Januar im Zimmer.

e. weil ich dort mit der Uni erst Ende Juli fertig geworden bin.

f. habe ich gerade ein Jahr in Deutschland studiert.

g. dass die Deutschen etwas zu steif sind.

h. dass Leute mit Brillen Kontaktlinsen tragen.

Optional activity: Richtig oder falsch? 1. Carolyn hat einen Monat in Deutschland studiert. (F) 2. Das Semester dort ist bis Ende Juli gegangen. (R) 3. Im Herbst feiert man das Winzerfest und das Oktoberfest. (R) 4. Auf dem Oktoberfest haben die Leute viel Wein getrunken. (F) 5. Der Fasching ist im Sommer. (F) 6. Die Kinder sehen den Weihnachtsbaum am 1. Advent. (F) 7. Der Nürnberger Christkindlmarkt ist populär. (R) 8. In Landshut feiert man alle vier Jahre die Landshuter Fürstenhochzeit. (R) 9. Weil sie es schön finden, tragen alle Landshuter Kontaktlinsen. (F)

B. Feiern in Deutschland *(Complete these sentences with the appropriate verb in the present perfect. Use each verb once.)*

bringen, fahren, feiern, gefallen, gehen, haben, kaufen, kommen, sein, studieren

1. Carolyn <u>ist</u> vor einem Monat nach Hause <u>gekommen</u>. 2. Sie <u>hat</u> ein Jahr in Deutschland <u>studiert</u>. 3. Es <u>ist</u> wunderbar <u>gewesen</u>. 4. Sie <u>hat</u> ein paar Bilder zur Deutschstunde <u>gebracht</u>. 5. Im September <u>ist</u> sie mit Freunden zum Winzerfest nach Bacharach <u>gefahren</u>. 6. Zum Fasching <u>ist</u> sie als Vampir zu einem Studentenball <u>gegangen</u>. 7. Die Weihnachtszeit <u>hat</u> Carolyn besonders gut <u>gefallen</u>. 8. In Nürnberg <u>hat</u> sie einen Weihnachtsengel <u>gekauft</u>. 9. Sie <u>hat</u> Weihnachten bei der Familie Fuchs <u>gefeiert</u>. 10. Mit der Landshuter Fürstenhochzeit <u>hat</u> sie Glück <u>gehabt</u>, weil man das Fest nur alle vier Jahre feiert.

Optional practice: Geben Sie das Partizip! z.B. geben: hat gegeben (hören, werden, sehen, lernen, sprechen, trinken, singen, denken, Spaß machen, essen, heißen, fallen, bleiben, dekorieren, haben, finden, schmecken, beginnen, liegen, tragen, arbeiten)

C. Interview. Fragen Sie einen Nachbarn/eine Nachbarin, . . . !

1. wie und wo er/sie das (Ernte)dankfest *(Thanksgiving)* feiert
2. wie er/sie gewöhnlich Weihnachten (oder Hannukah) feiert
3. was für Geschenke er/sie gewöhnlich bekommt und was er/sie der Familie schenkt
4. wie und wo er/sie das letzte Silvester gefeiert hat
5. ob er/sie zum 4. Juli auch Kracher *(firecrackers)* gehabt oder ein Feuerwerk gesehen hat

Optional vocabulary: der Schlips, -e *tie,* **Gürtel, -** *belt,* **Schlafanzug, ̈e** *pajamas;* **das Nachthemd, -en** *nightgown,* **Parfüm, -e** *perfume;* **die Rose, -n, Kassette, -n, CD, -s.**

D. Kurzgespräche *(Together with your partner, prepare one of the following brief dialogues. Then present it to the class.)*

1. **Krankenbesuch** *(sick visit)*

   One of your very best friends has been quite sick. You stop by to visit. Your friend expresses his/her surprise. You have also brought a little present (a book, flowers, cookies, for example). Your friend is very pleased and thanks you. You respond appropriately and wish him/her a speedy recovery.

2. **Ich komme!**

   Your Mom (**Mutti**) calls you up and asks whether you have plans for the weekend. She is driving through the town where you are studying and would like to see you **(dich).** You are surprised and pleased. It is your mother's birthday, and you wish her a happy birthday. Tell her you have bought a present and that she will get it when she comes. You conclude the conversation.

E. Zwei Feiertage *(Jot down some key words about two of the holidays Carolyn mentions, then write three to five sentences about each.)*

BEISPIEL: Winzerfest
                 Bacharach am Rhein, September, Wein, singen

E: Lends itself to small-group activity. Assign one holiday to each group, or a different holiday to each member of a group. Reports can be oral or written.

Carolyn ist zum Winzerfest nach Bacharach gefahren. Bacharach liegt am Rhein. Das Winzerfest ist im September. Die Leute haben Wein getrunken, gesungen und getanzt. Es ist sehr lustig gewesen.

1. Rhein in Flammen
2. Oktoberfest
3. Fasching

4. Weihnachtszeit
5. Silvester
6. Fürstenhochzeit in Landshut

HÖREN SIE ZU!   TRACK 9

Das Straßenfest *(Listen to what Bibi tells Matthias about their local street fair. Then select the correct response from those given below.)*

Zum Erkennen: Was gibt's? *(What's up?)*; niemand *(nobody)*; Krimskrams *(this and that)*; Spiele *(games)*; Jung und Alt *(all ages, young and old)*

1. Matthias ist bei Bibi gewesen, aber niemand hat _____ geöffnet.
   a. das Fenster   b. die Garage   **c.** die Tür
2. Bei Bibi hat es am _____ ein Straßenfest gegeben.
   a. Freitag   **b.** Samstag   c. Sonntag
3. Bibi findet das eigentlich _____ ganz gut.
   a. nie   **b.** immer   c. noch
4. Bibi hat mit _____ beim Straßenfest geholfen.
   a. Matthias   **b.** den Eltern   c. dem Bruder
5. Der Vater hat _____.
   a. Würstchen verkauft   b. mit den Kindern gespielt
   c. mit den Tischen und Stühlen geholfen
6. Abends haben die Leute ein bisschen _____.
   a. Pech gehabt   **b.** getanzt   c. geschlafen

Video-Ecke

- The *Minidrama* "Das hat es bei uns nicht gegeben" takes you to the family of Mr. and Mrs. Winter, who are preparing for the Christmas holidays. While the son and daughter have plans of their own, the parents are longing for the good old days and complain about the lack of family spirit. A surprising discovery puts their nostalgic memories into perspective.

Web-Ecke

- For updates, self-assessment quizzes, and online activities related to this chapter, visit the ***Wie geht's?*** Web site at **http://wiegehts.heinle.com**. You will visit Munich and the Oktoberfest, learn about German holiday customs, and visit shopping sites to select presents for your friends.

Kapitel ⑤

In der Stadt

Schloss Belvedere in Wien

Vorschau

Spotlight on Austria

Area: Approximately 32,400 square miles, about the size of Maine.

Population: About 8 million, 98 percent German-speaking; ethnic minorities include some 50,000 Croats in the Burgenland, 20,000 Slovenes in southern Carinthia, and small groups of Hungarians, Czechs, Slovaks, and Italians.

Religion: 78 percent Catholic, 5 percent Protestant, 17 percent other.

Geography: The Alps are the dominant physical feature, covering all of the narrow western part of the country and much of its central and southern regions. The Danube Valley and the Vienna Basin lie in the northeastern part of the country.

Currency: Euro, 1 € = 100 Cents. The former Austrian currency, the Schilling (= 100 Groschen), was phased out in 2002.

Principal cities: Vienna (**Wien** pop. 1.6 million, capital); Graz (pop. 250,000), Linz (pop. 213,000); Salzburg (pop. 143,000); Innsbruck (pop. 120,000).

The history of Austria and that of the Habsburg family were closely linked for nearly 650 years. Rudolf von Habsburg started the dynasty in 1273, when he was elected emperor of the Holy Roman Empire (962–1806). Over the course of several centuries, the Habsburg empire grew to include Flanders, Burgundy, Bohemia, Hungary, and large areas of the Balkans. These acquisitions were made not only through war, but also through shrewdly arranged marriages (**Heiratspolitik**) with other European ruling houses. The Holy Roman Empire ended with the Napoleonic wars, yet members of the Habsburg family ruled until the end of World War I. In 1918, the defeated Austro-Hungarian Empire was carved up into independent countries: Austria, Hungary, Czechoslovakia, Yugoslavia, and Romania. In 1938, after several political and economic crises, Hitler annexed the young Austrian republic into the Third Reich. After World War II, the country was occupied by the Allies until 1955, when Austria regained its sovereignty and pledged neutrality. During the Cold War, the country belonged to neither the Warsaw Pact nor to NATO.

Ask students whether they have been to Austria and what they associate with the different cities mentioned here. What prominent Austrians do they know? In the *Zum Schreiben* section of the Workbook, there is also a blank map of Austria. Let them fill in the blanks to check their geography.

Since the end of World War II, Austria has been actively involved in international humanitarian efforts. Hungary's decision in 1989 to allow East German refugees to cross their border into Austria was a contributing factor to the fall of the Berlin Wall. Austria has also joined the process of European integration. In 1995, the country became a member of the European Union. Finally, there also is a domestic movement to give up neutrality and join NATO. (For pictures and information on Austrian cities, visit www.*[city name]*.at).

In der Innenstadt von Innsbruck

Gespräche + Wortschatz

CD 3, Track 5

Entschuldigen Sie! Wo ist . . . ?

TOURIST	Entschuldigen Sie! Können Sie mir sagen, wo das Hotel Sacher ist?
WIENER	Erste Straße links hinter der Staatsoper.
TOURIST	Und wie komme ich von da zum Stephansdom?
WIENER	Geradeaus, die Kärntner Straße entlang.
TOURIST	Wie weit ist es zum Dom?
WIENER	Nicht weit. Sie können zu Fuß gehen.
TOURIST	Danke!
WIENER	Bitte schön!

Warm-ups: 1. Welches Datum ist das? Ist das Ihr Geburtstag? z.B. Das ist der I. Mai. Ich habe am 3. August Geburtstag. *(Write various dates on the board: have students answer.)* **2. Nennen Sie das Partizip!** (arbeiten, bekommen, beobachten, bedeuten, bleiben, denken, gefallen, fahren, fallen, finden, gehen, gratulieren, helfen, laufen, lesen, singen, tragen, tun, überraschen)

Like in previous chapters, you could have students act out the dialogue with a partner.

Da drüben!

TOURIST	Entschuldigung! Wo ist das Burgtheater?
HERR	Es tut mir Leid. Ich bin nicht aus Wien.
TOURIST	Verzeihung! Ist das das Burgtheater?
DAME	Nein, das ist nicht das Burgtheater, sondern die Staatsoper. Fahren Sie mit der Straßenbahn zum Rathaus! Gegenüber vom Rathaus ist das Burgtheater.
TOURIST	Und wo hält die Straßenbahn?
DAME	Da drüben links.
TOURIST	Vielen Dank!
DAME	Bitte sehr!

A: 1. hinter der Staatsoper 2. geradeaus, die Kärntner Straße entlang 3. einen Herrn 4. nein 5. mit der Straßenbahn 6. da drüben links 7. das Rathaus

A. Fragen

1. Wo ist das Hotel Sacher?   2. Wie kommt man von der Staatsoper zum Stephansdom?   3. Wen fragt der Tourist im zweiten Gespräch?   4. Ist der Herr Wiener?   5. Wie kommt der Tourist zum Burgtheater?   6. Wo ist die Haltestelle?   7. Was ist gegenüber vom Burgtheater?

B. Jetzt sind Sie dran! *(With a partner, create your own dialogue asking for any place in your city.)*

Fokus — *Viennese Landmarks*

- **Hotel Sacher** is probably the best-known hotel in Vienna. One of the reasons for its popularity is its famous café, for which a rich, delicious cake **(Sachertorte)** has been named.

- Vienna's Opera **(Staatsoper),** inaugurated in 1869, was built in the style of the early French Renaissance and is one of the foremost European opera houses.

- A masterpiece of Gothic architecture, St. Stephen's **(Stephansdom)** dates from the 12th century. Its roof of colored tile and its 450-foot-high spire make it the landmark of Vienna.

- In 1776, Emperor Joseph II declared Vienna's **Burgtheater** Austria's national theater. The Burgtheater has always been devoted to classical drama and has developed a stylized mode of diction, giving it an aura of conservatism. Most of the ensemble, numbering more than a hundred, have lifetime contracts.

Das Wiener Burgtheater

Wortschatz 1

Der Stadtplan, ⸚e *(city map)*

der Bahnhof, ⸚e	*train station*	die Bank, -en	*bank*
Bus, -se	*bus*	Bibliothek, -en	*library*
Dom, -e	*cathedral*	Brücke, -n	*bridge*
Park, -s	*park*	Haltestelle, -n	*(bus etc.) stop*
Platz, ⸚e	*place; square*	Kirche, -n	*church*
Weg, -e	*way; trail*	Post	*post office*
das Auto, -s	*car*	Schule, -n	*school*
Fahrrad, ⸚er	*bike*	Straße, -n	*street*
Hotel, -s	*hotel*	Straßenbahn, -en	*streetcar*
Kino, -s	*movie theater*	U-Bahn	*subway*
das Museum, Museen	*museum*	die Universität, -en	*university*
Rathaus, ⸚er	*city hall*	Uni, -s	
Schloss, ⸚er	*palace*		
Taxi, -s	*taxi*		
Theater, -	*theater*		

Note, a student nickname for **die Bibliothek** is **die Bib.** Also, **U-Bahn** stands for **Untergrundbahn,** and **S-Bahn** for **Schnellbahn** *(a suburban commuter train)*

Weiteres

der Tourist, -en	*tourist*
die Dame, -n	*lady*
besichtigen	*to tour, visit (palace, etc.)*

halten (hält), gehalten[1]	*to stop; to hold*
zeigen	*to show*
zu Fuß gehen, ist zu Fuß gegangen	*to walk*
Entschuldigen Sie!	*Excuse me!*
Entschuldigung! / Verzeihung!	
Es tut mir Leid.	*I'm sorry.*
Ich möchte zum/zur . . .	*I would like to go to . . .*
Können Sie mir sagen, wo . . . ist?	*Can you tell me where . . . is?*
Wie kommt man von hier zum/zur . . . ?	*How do you get from here to . . . ?*
Gibt es hier in der Nähe . . . ?	*Is there . . . nearby?*
in der Nähe von (+ *dat.*)	*near (in the vicinity of)*
die erste Straße links / rechts	*first street to the left/right*
(immer) geradeaus	*(keep) straight ahead*
an/am . . . vorbei	*past the . . .*
(den Fluss) entlang	*along (the river)*
bis Sie . . . sehen	*until you see . . .*
da drüben	*over there*
dorthin	*to there*
gegenüber von (+ *dat.*)	*across from*
nah / weit	*near / far*
sondern	*but (on the contrary)*
Sie können zu Fuß gehen.	*You can walk.*
Fahren Sie mit dem Bus!	*Take the bus!*

[1] When **halten** is intransitive (i.e., without an accusative object), it means *to come to a stop:* Der Bus **hält** da drüben. When it is transitive, it means *to hold:* **Halten** Sie mir bitte das Buch!

The difference between **sondern** and **aber** will be discussed in Struktur 5.3.

Point out that **fahren** expresses *to go* when a vehicle is involved.

Zum Erkennen: hinter *(behind);* die Oper, -n *(opera house);* AUCH: das Hauptwort, ¨er *(noun);* das Modalverb, -en *(modal auxiliary);* variieren *(to vary);* direkt dorthin *(right to it)*

Zum Thema

A. Mustersätze

1. das Theater / die Oper: **Das ist nicht** das Theater, **sondern** die Oper.
   das Rathaus / die Universität; das Museum / die Bibliothek; die Bank / die Post; die Bushaltestelle / die Straßenbahnhaltestelle
2. zur Universität: **Können Sie mir sagen, wie ich** zur Universität **komme?**
   zum Rathaus, zur Bibliothek, zum Museum, zur Schulstraße
3. erste / links: **Die** erste **Straße** links.
   zweite / rechts; dritte / links; vierte / rechts
4. die Straßenbahn: **Fahren Sie mit** der Straßenbahn!
   der Bus, das Auto, das Fahrrad, die U-Bahn, das Taxi
5. da drüben: **Die Straßenbahn hält** da drüben.
   da drüben rechts, beim Bahnhof, in der Nähe vom Park, gegenüber vom Theater

B: *cathedral square* **(der)**, *pedestrian way* **(der)**, *bicycle path* **(der)**, *palace hotel* **(das)**, *tourist town* **(die)**, *church festival* **(das)**, *school vacation* **(die)**, *student cinema* **(das)**, *train station drugstore* **(die)**, *university parking lot* **(der)**, *parking meter* **(die)**

B. Was bedeuten die Wörter und was sind die Artikel?

Domplatz, Fußgängerweg, Fahrradweg, Schlosshotel, Touristenstadt, Kirchenfest, Schulferien, Studentenkino, Bahnhofsdrogerie, Universitätsparkplatz, Parkuhr

C: 1. das Kino 2. der Weg 3. die U-Bahn 4. der Stadtplan 5. schade 6. halten

C. Was passt nicht?

1. der Bus—das Taxi—das Fahrrad—das Kino
2. das Theater—der Weg—das Museum—die Bibliothek
3. die U-Bahn—die Bank—die Post—das Rathaus
4. die Straße—die Brücke—der Stadtplan—der Platz

5. da drüben — gegenüber von — in der Nähe von — schade
6. fahren — zu Fuß gehen — halten — laufen

D. Wo ist . . . ? *(Working with a partner, practice asking for and giving directions to various places on campus.)*

S1   Entschuldigen Sie! Wo ist . . . ?
S2   . . .
S1   Und wie komme ich dorthin?
S2   . . .
S1   Gibt es hier in der Nähe . . . ?
S2   . . .
S1   Vielen Dank!
S2   . . . !

If students ask: building **das Gebäude, -;** *dorm* **das Studentenheim, -e;** *gym* **die Turnhalle, -n;** *lab* **das Labor, -s;** *office* **das Büro, -s;** *parking lot* **der Parkplatz, ̈-e;** *stadium* **das Stadion, Stadien**

E.   **Fragen zum Stadtplan von Winterthur** *(With your partner, using the formal Sie, practice asking and giving directions from one place to another. Start out at the information office at the train station.)*

BEISPIEL: Entschuldigung! Können Sie mir sagen, wie ich zum Technikum *(technical university)* komme?
Das Technikum ist in der Technikumstrasse. Gehen Sie am Bahnhof vorbei und links in die Technikumstrasse. Dann gehen Sie immer geradeaus, bis Sie rechts das Technikum sehen.

See additional exercise with a different map and questions for directions in the Zum Schreiben *section of the Workbook.*

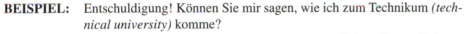

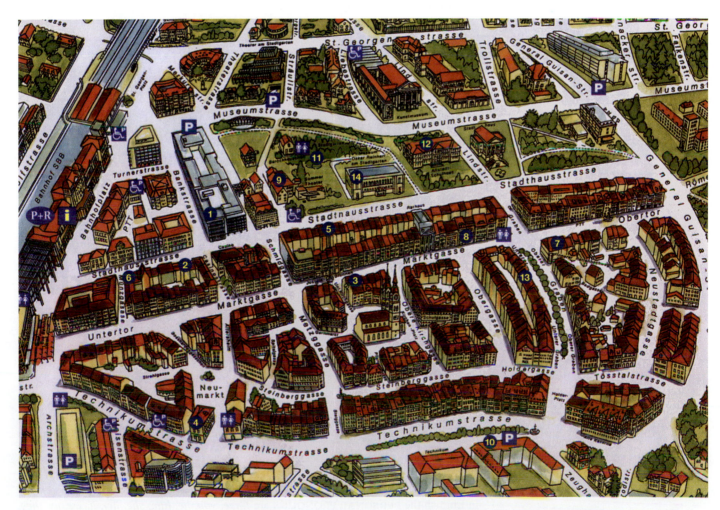

1. Kaufhaus	2. Metzgerei	3. Möbelladen	4. Hotel	5. Fotogeschäft	6. Sportgeschäft	7. Drogerie
8. Bank	9. Theater	10. Technikum	11. Stadtpark	12. Schule	13. Post	14. Museum

CD 3, Track 6

Aussprache: ö

(Read also Part II. 29–36 in the pronunciation guide of the Workbook.)

1. [ö:] **Ö**sterreich, Br**ö**tchen, G**oe**the, sch**ö**n, gew**öh**nlich, franz**ö**sisch, h**ö**ren
2. [ö] **ö**ffnen, **ö**stlich, k**ö**nnen, L**ö**ffel, zw**ö**lf, n**ö**rdlich, m**ö**chten
3. Wortpaare
   - a. kennen / können
   - b. Sehne / Söhne
   - c. große / Größe
   - d. schon / schön
   - e. Sühne / Söhne
   - f. Höhle / Hölle

HÖREN SIE ZU!   TRACK 10

Touristen in Innsbruck *(Listen to this conversation between two tourists and a woman from Innsbruck. Then complete the sentences below with the correct information from the dialogue.)*

Zum Erkennen: uns *(us)*; das Goldene Dachl *(The Golden Roof, a fifteenth-century burgher house)*; das Konzert *(concert)*; erst *(only)*; Viel Spaß! *(Have fun!)*

1. Die Touristen fragen, wo _das Goldene Dachl_ ist.
2. Es ist _nicht_ sehr weit. Sie können _zu Fuß_ gehen.
3. Bei der Brücke _beginnt_ die Fußgängerzone.
4. Da geht man _geradeaus_, bis man links zum Dachl kommt.
5. Der Dom ist _in der Nähe vom_ Dachl.
6. Das Konzert beginnt _um fünf_.
7. Vor dem Konzert möchten die Touristen _die Maria-Theresia-Straße entlanglaufen_.
8. Von der Maria-Theresia-Straße sieht man wunderbar _die Berge_.
9. Sie sollen nicht *(are not supposed to)* zu spät zum Dom gehen, weil _da heute furchtbar viele Leute sind_.

Das Goldene Dachl in Innsbruck

Struktur

5.1 Personal pronouns

1. In English the PERSONAL PRONOUNS are *I, me, you, he, him, she, her, it, we, us, they,* and *them*. Some of these pronouns are used as subjects, others as direct or indirect objects, or objects of prepositions.

SUBJECT:	*He is coming.*
DIRECT OBJECT:	*I see **him**.*
INDIRECT OBJECT:	*I give **him** the book.*
OBJECT OF A PREPOSITION:	*We'll go without **him**.*

The German personal pronouns are likewise used as subjects, direct or indirect objects, or objects of prepositions. Like the definite and indefinite articles, personal pronouns have special forms in the various cases. You already know the nominative case of these pronouns. Here are the nominative, accusative, and dative cases together.

	singular					plural			sg. / pl.
nom.	ich	du	er	es	sie	wir	ihr	sie	Sie
acc.	mich	dich	ihn	es	sie	uns	euch	sie	Sie
dat.	mir	dir	ihm	ihm	ihr	uns	euch	ihnen	Ihnen

SUBJECT:	**Er** kommt.
DIRECT OBJECT:	Ich sehe **ihn.**
INDIRECT OBJECT:	Ich gebe **ihm** das Buch.
OBJECT OF A PROPOSITION:	Wir gehen ohne **ihn.**

- Note the similarities between the definite article of the noun and the pronoun that replaces it.

	masc.	neut.	fem.	pl.
nom.	der Mann = **er**	das Kind = **es**	die Frau = **sie**	die Leute = **sie**
acc.	den Mann = **ihn**	das Kind = **es**	die Frau = **sie**	die Leute = **sie**
dat.	**dem** Mann = **ihm**	**dem** Kind = **ihm**	der Frau = **ihr**	den Leuten = **ihnen**

2. As in English, the dative object usually precedes the accusative object, unless the accusative object is a pronoun. If that is the case, the accusative object pronoun comes first.

Ich gebe **dem Studenten** den Kuli.	*I'm giving the student the pen.*
Ich gebe **ihm** den Kuli.	*I'm giving him the pen.*
Ich gebe ihn **dem Studenten.**	*I'm giving it to the student.*
Ich gebe ihn **ihm.**	*I'm giving it to him.*

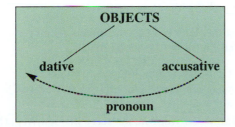

Übungen

A. Ersetzen Sie die Hauptwörter durch Pronomen! (*Replace each noun with a pronoun in the appropriate case.*)

BEISPIEL: den Bruder   **ihn**

1. der Vater, dem Mann, den Großvater, dem Freund, den Ober
2. die Freundin, der Großmutter, der Dame, die Frau, der Familie
3. die Eltern, den Herren, den Frauen, die Freundinnen, den Schweizern
4. für die Mutter, mit den Freunden, gegen die Studenten, außer dem Großvater, ohne den Ober, von den Eltern, zu dem Mädchen, bei der Großmutter

B. Kombinieren Sie mit den Präpositionen! Was sind die Akkusativ- und Dativformen?

> **BEISPIEL:**   ich (ohne, mit)
> **ohne mich, mit mir**

1. er (für, mit)
2. wir (durch, von)
3. Sie (gegen, zu)
4. du (ohne, bei)
5. ihr (für, außer)
6. sie/*sg.* (um, nach)
7. sie/*pl.* (für, aus)
8. es (ohne, außer)

C. Was fehlt?

1. **Geben Sie die Pronomen!** *(Complete the sentences with the appropriate German case forms of the suggested pronouns.)*

> **BEISPIEL:**   Sie kauft _____ das Buch. *(me)*
> **Sie kauft mir das Buch.**

a. Siehst du _____? *(them, him, her, me, us)*
b. Geben Sie es _____! *(him, me, her, us, them)*
c. Sie braucht _____. *(you/sg. fam., you/pl. fam., you/formal, me, him, them, us)*
d. Wie geht es _____? *(him, them, you/formal, her, you/sg. fam., you/pl. fam.)*
e. Der Ober hat _____ das Eis gebracht. *(you/sg. fam., you/pl. fam., us, him, her, me, you/formal)*
f. Hat die Party _____ überrascht? *(you/formal, me, you/sg. fam., us, her, him, you/pl. fam.)*

2. **Fragen und Antworten** *(Working with a partner, complete the following sentences.)*

S1   Siehst du __sie__? *(them)*
S2   Nein, aber sie sehen __uns__. *(us)*
S1   Gehört das Buch __dir__? *(you/sg. fam.)*
S2   Nein, es gehört __ihm__. *(him)*
S1   Glaubst du __ihm__? *(him)*
S2   Nein, ich glaube __euch__. *(you/pl. fam.)*
S1   Sie sucht __dich__. *(you/sg. fam.)*
S2   Ich suche __sie__. *(her)*
S1   Hilft er __uns__? *(us)*
S2   Nein, er hilft __ihnen__. *(them)*
S1   Zeigst du __uns__ die Kirche? *(us)*
S2   Ja, ich zeige sie __euch__. *(you/ pl. fam.)*

D. Antworten Sie! Ersetzen Sie die Hauptwörter!

> **BEISPIEL:**   Wo ist **das Hotel? Es** ist da drüben. (Bank)
> **Wo ist die Bank? Sie ist da drüben.**

1. Wo ist **die Post?** Da ist **sie.** (Dom, Rathaus, Apotheke)
2. Ist **das Museum** weit von hier? Nein, **es** ist nicht weit von hier. (Kirche, Geschäft, Platz)
3. Zeigen Sie **der Dame** den Weg? Ja, ich zeige **ihr** den Weg. (Mann, Leute, Touristin)
4. Helfen Sie **dem Herrn?** Ja, ich helfe **ihm.** (Kind, Damen, Touristin)
5. Haben Sie **die Straßenbahn** genommen? Ja, ich habe **sie** genommen. (Bus, U-Bahn, Taxi)
6. Wie hat dir **die Stadt** gefallen? **Sie** hat mir gut gefallen. (Hotel, Universität, Park)

E. Variieren Sie die Sätze!
1. **Es tut mir Leid.**
   a. He's sorry. b. She's sorry. c. They're sorry. d. Are you (3×) sorry? e. We aren't sorry. f. Why are you *(sg. fam.)* sorry? g. I was sorry. h. We weren't sorry.

2. **Wien gefällt mir.**

a. They like Vienna. b. Do you (3×) like Vienna? c. He doesn't like Vienna. d. We like Vienna. e. I liked Vienna. f. How did you *(sg. fam.)* like Vienna? g. Who didn't like Vienna? h. She didn't like Vienna.

F. Fragen und Antworten mit Pronomen *(Ask your partner all sorts of questions which he/she answers freely with the proper pronouns.)*

> **BEISPIEL:** Wie geht es . . . (dir, deiner Freundin)?
> **Es geht mir gut.**
> **Es geht ihr nicht so gut.**

1. Wie geht es . . . (Andreas, Stefanie, Andreas und Stefanie usw.)?
2. Hast du mit . . . (Kevin, Mirjam, Sabine und Karin usw.) gesprochen?
3. Wie gefällt/gefallen dir . . . (die Uni, der Campus, Paul, Paul und Paula usw.)?
4. Wie findest du . . . (die Bibliothek, die Restaurants, Toni, Toni und Anne usw.)?
5. Habt ihr schon einmal . . . (den Park, das Rathaus, die Museen usw.) besichtigt?
6. Zeigst du . . . (deinem Onkel, deinem Onkel und deiner Tante, Helga und mir usw.) die Stadt?
7. Glaubst du alles, was . . . (ich, wir, er und ich, die Leute usw.) sage/sagt/sagen?

G. Wer bekommt was?

1. **Wem gibt sie was?** *(Carolyn has just cleaned out her closet and is going to give away all the souvenirs from her European trip. Explain whom she is going to give them.)*

> **BEISPIEL:** ihrer Schwester / die Bilder
> **Sie gibt ihrer Schwester die Bilder.**
> **Sie gibt ihr die Bilder.**
> **Sie gibt sie ihrer Schwester.**
> **Sie gibt sie ihr.**

a. ihrem Vater / den Stadtplan b. ihren Großeltern / die Landkarte c. ihrer Mutter / den Zuckerlöffel d. ihrer Schwester / das Kleingeld *(small change)* e. Eva / die CD von den Toten Hosen f. Markus und Charlotte / die Poster g. dir / das T-Shirt

2. **Wem schenkst du was?** *(Ask your partner what presents he/she gives for Christmas or Hannukah. Follow the pattern.)*

> **BEISPIEL:** Ich schenke meinem Vater ein Wörterbuch.
> Ich schenke ihm ein Wörterbuch.
> Ich schenke es ihm.

5.2 Modal auxiliary verbs

1. Both English and German have a small group of MODAL AUXILIARY VERBS that modify the meaning of another verb. Modal verbs express such ideas as the permission, ability, necessity, obligation, or desire to do something.

dürfen	*to be allowed to, may*
können	*to be able to, can*
müssen	*to have to, must*

sollen	*to be supposed to*
wollen	*to want to*
mögen	*to like*

Ich soll
Sie schön
grüßen...

(Marginal notes:)

2. a. Wien gefällt ihnen. b. Gefällt dir/euch/Ihnen Wien? c. Wien gefällt ihm nicht. d. Wien gefällt uns. e. Wien hat mir gefallen. f. Wie hat dir Wien gefallen? g. Wem hat Wien nicht gefallen? h. Wien hat ihr nicht gefallen.

Instead of giving students English text cues, you could give them names and have them respond with pronouns. 1. **Es tut mir Leid.** (Mark, Barbara, Holger und Birgit) 2. **Es tut ihm nicht Leid.** (Karin, Rolf, meinem Mann und mir, meinem Vater und meiner Mutter) 3. **Wien gefällt mir.** (Andreas und mir, meinen Freunden und deinen Freunden, meinem Onkel, meiner Tante, Herrn und Frau Meyer)

Optional English-to-German practice: 1. Did you *(3x)* thank him? 2. We congratulated her. 3. I surprised them. 4. We'll show you *(3x)* the palace. 5. Did they answer you *(pl. fam.)*? 6. I wrote (to) you *(sg. fam.)*. 7. Are you *(sg. fam.)* going to give him the present? 8. She doesn't believe me.

G.1: a. Sie gibt ihrem Vater den Stadtplan (ihm den Stadtplan, ihn ihrem Vater, ihn ihm). b. Sie gibt ihren Großeltern die Landkarte (ihnen die Landkarte, sie ihren Großeltern, sie ihnen). c. Sie gibt ihrer Mutter den Zuckerlöffel (ihr den Zuckerlöffel, ihn ihrer Mutter, ihn ihr). d. Sie gibt ihrer Schwester das Kleingeld (ihr das Kleingeld, es ihrer Schwester, es ihr). e. Sie gibt Eva die CD (ihr die CD, sie Eva, sie ihr). f. Sie gibt Markus und Charlotte die Poster (ihnen die Poster, sie Markus und Charlotte, sie ihnen). g. Sie gibt dir das T-Shirt (es dir).

- The German modals are irregular in the singular of the present tense:

	dürfen	können	müssen	sollen	wollen	mögen / möchten	
ich	darf	kann	muss	soll	will	mag	möchte
du	darfst	kannst	musst	sollst	willst	magst	möchtest
er	darf	kann	muss	soll	will	mag	möchte
wir	dürfen	können	müssen	sollen	wollen	mögen	möchten
ihr	dürft	könnt	müsst	sollt	wollt	mögt	möchtet
sie	dürfen	können	müssen	sollen	wollen	mögen	möchten

> **Möchte(n)** is the subjunctive form of **mögen.** The indicative form of **mögen** is not used in this text, since it usually occurs in negative sentences and without a dependent infinitive. Students are already learning several ways to express liking: **gefallen, gern** + verb, **etwas schön / gut finden.** For additional practice, give students English cues: *I like to sleep, I like the city, I would like a cup of tea, I would like an apple, I like the store, I like to read,* etc.

> If students use the English equivalents *to be able to, to have to,* and *to be allowed to* rather than *can, must,* and *may,* they'll avoid certain problems, e.g., **Ich muss gehen.** *I have to go.;* **Ich muss nicht gehen.** *I don't have to go,* NOT: *I must not go;* **Du darfst gehen.** *You're allowed to go.;* **Du darfst nicht gehen.** *You're not allowed to go.* = *You must not go.*

- The **möchte**-forms of **mögen** occur more frequently than the **mag**-forms. **Mögen** is usually used in a negative sentence.

Ich **möchte** eine Tasse Tee.	*I would like (to have) a cup of tea.*
Ich **mag** Kaffee nicht.	*I don't like coffee.*

2. Modals are another example of the two-part verb phrase. In statements and information questions, the modal is the inflected second element of the sentence (VI). The modified verb (V2) appears at the very end of the sentence in its infinitive form.

Er **geht** nach Hause.			*He's going home.*
Er **darf** nach Hause	gehen.		*He may (is allowed to) go home.*
Er **kann** nach Hause	gehen.		*He can (is able to) go home.*
Er **muss** nach Hause	gehen.		*He must (has to) go home.*
Er **soll** nach Hause	gehen.		*He is supposed to go home.*
Er **will** nach Hause	gehen.		*He wants to go home.*
Er **möchte** nach Hause	gehen.		*He would like to go home.*
V1		V2	

CAUTION:

- The English set of modals is frequently supplemented by such forms as *is allowed to, is able to, has to.* The German modals, however, do not use such supplements. They follow the pattern of *may, can,* and *must:* **Ich muss gehen.** *(I must go.)*

- The subject of the modal and of the infinitive are always the same: **Er will nach Hause gehen.** *(He wants to go home.)* The English *He wants you to go home* cannot be imitated in German. The correct way to express this idea is **Er will, dass du nach Hause gehst.**

> **Ihr sollt gehen** always expresses *you're supposed to go* (outer compulsion), NOT *you should go* (inner compulsion). *Should* must be avoided at this point, since it is a subjunctive form. Students may grasp this if you refer to the Bible: *Thou shalt not kill* (a command), NOT *you shouldn't kill* (an appeal to one's conscience).

3. Modals can be used without an infinitive, provided the modified verb is clearly understood. This structure is common with verbs of motion.

> Musst du zum Supermarkt?—Ja, ich **muss,** aber ich **kann** nicht.

4. Watch these important differences in meaning:

> Because modals use two different forms in the present perfect, we have avoided sentences with modals in that tense. The simple past of the modals will be discussed in Chapter II.

a. **Gern** vs. **möchten**

> Ich **esse gern** Kuchen. BUT Ich **möchte** ein Stück Kuchen **(haben).**

The first sentence says that I am generally fond of cake *(I like to eat cake).* The second sentence implies a desire for a piece of cake at this particular moment *(I'd like a piece of cake).*

> If students ask: **Ich möchte gern ein Stück Kuchen (haben).** *I really would like (to have) a piece of cake.*

b. **Wollen** vs. **möchten**

Notice the difference in tone and politeness between these two sentences:

> Ich **will** Kuchen. BUT Ich **möchte** Kuchen.

The first might be said by a spoiled child *(I want cake),* the second by a polite adult *(I would like cake).*

5. Modals in subordinate clauses

   a. Remember that the inflected verb stands at the very end of clauses introduced by subordinate conjunctions such as **bevor, dass, ob, obwohl, wenn,** and **weil.**

   Sie sagt, **dass** du nach Hause gehen **kannst.**

   Du kannst nach Hause gehen, **wenn** du **möchtest.**

   b. If the sentence starts with the subordinate clause, then the inflected verb of the main sentence (the modal) follows right after the comma.

   Du **kannst** nach Hause gehen, wenn du möchtest.

   Wenn du möchtest, **kannst** du nach Hause gehen.

In a dependent clause, two-part verb structures appear in the sequence V2 V1.

Übungen

H. Ersetzen Sie das Subjekt!

BEISPIEL: Wir sollen zum Markt fahren. (ich)
Ich soll zum Markt fahren.

1. Wir wollen zu Hause bleiben. (er, sie/*pl.*, du, ich)
2. Sie müssen noch die Rechnung bezahlen. (ich, ihr, du, Vater)
3. Du darfst zum Bahnhof kommen. (er, ihr, die Kinder, ich)
4. Möchtet ihr ein Eis haben? (sie/*pl.*, du, er, das Mädchen)
5. Können Sie mir sagen, wo das ist? (du, ihr, er, die Damen)

I. Am Sonntag *(Say what these people will do on Sunday.)*

BEISPIEL: Carolyn spricht nur Deutsch. (wollen)
Carolyn will nur Deutsch sprechen.

1. Volker und Silvia spielen Tennis. (wollen)
2. Paul fährt mit ein paar Freunden in die Berge. (möchten)
3. Friederike bezahlt Rechnungen. (müssen)
4. Helmut hilft Vater zu Hause. (sollen)
5. Herr und Frau Ahrendt besichtigen Schloss Schönbrunn. (können)
6. Die Kinder gehen in den Zoo. (dürfen)

J. Besucher *(Visitors)*

1. **Stadtbesichtigung** *(Sightseeing in town. Mitzi and Sepp are visiting their friends Heike and Dirk in Salzburg. Dirk tells Mitzi and Sepp what Heike wants to know.)*

   Beginnen Sie mit **Heike fragt, ob . . .** !

   a. Könnt ihr den Weg in die Stadt allein finden?
   b. Wollt ihr einen Stadtplan haben?
   c. Möchtet ihr zu Fuß gehen?
   d. Soll ich euch mit dem Auto zum Stadtzentrum bringen?
   e. Müsst ihr noch zur Bank?

J.1: Heike fragt, ob . . .
a. ihr . . . finden könnt
b. ihr . . . haben wollt
c. ihr . . . gehen möchtet
d. ich . . . bringen soll
e. ihr . . . müsst

2. **Fragen** *(Mitzi has several questions. Report what she is asking.)*

   Beginnen Sie mit **Mitzi fragt, wo (was, wie lange, wann, wer) . . .** !

   a. Wo kann man hier in der Nähe Blumen kaufen?
   b. Was für ein Geschenk sollen wir für den Vater kaufen?

J.2: Mitzi fragt, . . . a. wo man . . . kaufen kann b. was für ein Geschenk wir . . . kaufen sollen c. wie lange wir . . . bleiben dürfen d. wann wir . . . sein müssen e. wer . . . will

Wenn du dein ganzes Leben lang glücklich sein willst, musst du gute Freunde haben.

c. Wie lange dürfen wir hier bleiben?

d. Wann müssen wir abends wieder hier sein?

e. Wer will mit in die Stadt?

K. Hoppla, hier fehlt was! Feiern in Wien. *(You, your partner, and some friends are checking out Vienna's calendar of events. You've each talked with different members of the group. Express your preferences. One of you looks at and completes the chart below, the other one works with the chart in Section 11 of the Appendix.)*

S1:

WER?	WAS?	WARUM?	WANN?	INFORMATION?
Dieter	bei den Wiener Festwochen in Wien sein	Er kann nicht genug Opern und Theaterstücke sehen.	10.5.–1.6.	www.festwochen.at
Dieter + ich	Silvester in Wien feiern	Es ist eine Mega-Open-Air-Party mit Walzermusik. (müssen)	vom 31.12.-1.1.	www.wien-event.at
Sonja	das Museum moderner Kunst besichtigen	Es soll alles von Picasso bis Warhol haben.	ab *(starting)* 15.9.	www.mumok.at
Karen	zum Christkindlmarkt am Rathausplatz	Sie kauft Weihnachtsdekorationen. (wollen)	vom 17.11.-24.12	www.christkindlmarkt.at
Karen + Charlie	zum Wiener Eistraum gehen	Da dürfen die Leute auf dem Eis vorm Rathaus tanzen.	sechs Wochen ab Ende Januar	www.wien-event.at

BEISPIEL: **S1** Wer möchte bei den Wiener Festwochen in Wien sein?

S2 Dieter möchte bei den Wiener Festwochen in Wien sein.

S1 Und warum?

S2 Er kann nicht genug Opern und Theaterstücke sehen.

L. Have students complete the dialogue with a classmate or in small groups, then compare answers to see how the meaning is affected by the modal chosen.

L. Welches Modalverb passt? *(Work with a partner to complete the dialogue. several answers are possible.)*

UWE Uta, _____ du mit mir gehen? Ich _____ einen Stadtplan kaufen.

UTA Wo _____ wir einen Stadtplan bekommen?

UWE Die Buchhandlung _____ Stadtpläne haben.

UTA Gut, ich gehe auch. Ich _____ zwei Bücher für meinen Bruder kaufen.

UWE _____ wir zu Fuß gehen oder _____ wir mit dem Fahrrad fahren?

UTA Ich _____ mit dem Fahrrad fahren. Dann _____ wir noch zur Bank. Die Bücher sind bestimmt nicht billig. _____ du nicht auch zur Bank?

UWE Ja, richtig. Ich _____ eine Rechnung bezahlen.

Optional English-to-German practice: 1. He wants to see the cathedral. 2. They have to go to the post office. 3. I can't read that. 4. You *(pl. fam.)* are supposed to speak German. 5. You *(sg. fam.),* may order a piece of cake. 6. She's supposed to study **(lernen).** 7. We have to find the way. 8. Can't you *(3x)* help me? 9. We'd like to drive to Vienna. 10. Are we allowed to see the palace? (See answer key in the Appendix.)

M. Was machst du morgen? *(Using the modals, ask a partner what he/she wants to, has to, is supposed to, would like to do tomorrow. In the responses you may use some of the phrases below or choose your own expressions.)*

BEISPIEL: Was möchtest du morgen tun?

Ich möchte morgen Tennis spielen.

einen Pulli kaufen	einkaufen gehen	nach . . . fahren
Pizza essen gehen	Rechnungen bezahlen	zu Hause bleiben
viel lernen	ein Geschenk für . . . kaufen	das Schloss besichtigen
ein Buch lesen	meine Eltern überraschen	

Fokus — *Viennese Landmarks (continued)*

- The **Hofburg** is almost a self-contained city within the city of Vienna. For two-and-a-half centuries (until 1918), it was the residence of the Austrian emperors. It now houses the Museum of Art and Ethnography, the portrait collection of the National Library, the treasury, the Spanish Riding Academy, and the federal chancellor's residence.
- **Schönbrunn** was the favorite summer residence of the Empress Maria Theresa *(Maria Theresia),* who ruled Austria, Hungary, and Bohemia from 1740 to 1780. Her daughter Marie Antoinette, who was beheaded during the French Revolution, spent her childhood there. It was Schönbrunn where Mozart dazzled the empress with his talents. During the wars of 1805 and 1809, Napoleon used it as his headquarters. Franz Joseph I, emperor of Austria from 1848 to 1916, was born and died at Schönbrunn, and Charles I, the last of the Habsburgs, abdicated there in 1918, when Austria became a republic. To this day, the parks of Schönbrunn feature some of the best-preserved French-style baroque gardens.
- The **Prater** is a large amusement park with a giant Ferris wheel and many modern rides, a stadium, fairgrounds, race tracks, bridle paths, pools, and ponds.

Das Riesenrad im Prater

5.3 *Sondern* vs. *aber*

German has two coordinating conjunctions corresponding to the English *but.*

aber	*but, however*
sondern	*but on the contrary, but rather*

- **Sondern** implies *but on the contrary* and occurs frequently with opposites. It must be used when the first clause is negated and the two ideas are mutually exclusive.

sondern or **aber**?
↓
Is the first clause negated? → NO → **aber:** Das Restaurant ist teuer, **aber** gut.
↓
YES
↓
Are the two ideas mutually exclusive? → NO → **aber:** Das Restaurant ist nicht teuer, **aber** gut.
↓
YES
↓
sondern: Das Restaurant ist nicht teuer, **sondern** billig.

- **Nicht nur . . . , sondern auch . . .**

Das Restaurant ist **nicht nur** gut, **sondern auch** billig.

The restaurant is not only good, but also inexpensive.

Übungen

N. *Sondern* **oder** *aber?* *(Insert the appropriate conjunction.)*

1. Wien ist sehr schön, _aber_ Salzburg gefällt mir besser *(better)*.
2. Die Straßenbahn hält nicht hier, _sondern_ gegenüber von der Post.
3. Gehen Sie beim Theater nicht rechts, _sondern_ geradeaus!
4. Die Kirche ist nicht alt, _sondern_ neu.
5. Das Rathaus ist nicht besonders schön, _aber_ sehr alt.
6. Das ist kein Museum, _sondern_ eine Bibliothek.
7. Die Mensa ist billig, _aber_ nicht gut.

Fokus — *Jugendstil*

Jugendstil (*art nouveau, Sezessionsstil* in Austria) is a style of art that emerged toward the end of the 19th century and flourished until World War I. It broke with previous historical styles, combining romantic and almost sentimental fidelity to nature with symbolic and abstract ornamentation. The school's influence brought about changes not only in art, but in the applied arts, including fashion, architecture, jewelry, sculpture, poetry, music, theater, and dance. Munich, Darmstadt, Brussels, Paris, Nancy, and Vienna were all centers of the movement. Gustav Klimt emerged as the leader of the "secession" in Austria.

„Der Kuss *(The Kiss)*" von Gustav Klimt

Zusammenfassung

O. Kombinieren Sie! *(Create questions by combining items from each column. Then ask different classmates and have them give you an answer, using a modal.)*

BEISPIEL: **S1** Wann möchtet ihr essen gehen?
  S2 Ich möchte jetzt gehen. Und ihr?
  S3 Wir möchten um halb eins gehen.

1	2	3	4
wann	dürfen	du	nach Österreich fahren
warum	können	man	nach Hause gehen
was	möchten	wir	in die Stadt (Mensa . . .) gehen
wem	müssen	ihr	schön (billig . . .) essen
wen	sollen	sie	zu Fuß gehen
wer	wollen	Sie	mit dem Bus fahren
wie lange		das	jetzt tun
		. . .	schenken
			dauern
			haben
			sein
			. . .

P. Wie geht's weiter? *(Use the statements below as models to tell a partner something about yourself. You may modify the sentences as needed. Then take turns.)*

BEISPIEL: Ich esse nicht gern Karotten, aber . . .
Ich esse nicht gern Karotten, aber Bohnen finde ich gut.

1. Ich trinke nicht gern Cola, aber . . .
2. Wir besichtigen nicht das Museum, sondern . . .
3. Die Straßenbahn hält nicht hier, sondern . . .
4. Es gibt keinen Bus, aber . . .
5. Er kann uns heute die Stadt nicht zeigen, aber . . .
6. Ich bin nicht in Wien geblieben, sondern . . .
7. Ihr lernt nicht Spanisch, sondern . . .

Q. Wo ist eine Bank? Auf Deutsch bitte!

1. Excuse me *(formal),* can you tell me where there's a bank?   2. I'm sorry, but I'm not from Vienna.   3. Whom can I ask?   4. Who can help me?   5. May I help you?   6. I'd like to find a bank.   7. Near the cathedral (there) is a bank.   8. Can you tell me whether that's far from here?   9. You can walk (there), but the banks close (are closed) in 20 minutes.   10. Take the subway or a taxi!

Fokus — *Vienna*

Originally, Vienna **(Wien)** was a Roman settlement. The city's fate was linked to its geographical location on the Danube and at the gateway to the plains of eastern Europe. Here merchants met where ancient trade routes crossed; crusaders passed through on their way to the Holy Land; and in 1683, at the walls and gates of this city, the Turks had to abandon their hope of conquering the heart of Europe.

The center of Vienna **(die Innenstadt)** dates from medieval times. As late as the 1850s, it was surrounded by horseshoe-shaped walls. The city reached its zenith of power and wealth as the capital of the Austro-Hungarian Empire during the reign of Emperor Franz Josef (1848–1916), when it developed into one of Europe's most important cultural centers. Composers such as Haydn, Mozart, Beethoven, Schubert, Brahms, Bruckner, Johann and Richard Strauss, Mahler, and Schönberg have left a lasting imprint on the city's cultural life. The psychoanalyst Freud, the writers Schnitzler, Zweig, and von Hofmannsthal, as well as the painters Klimt and Kokoschka laid the intellectual and artistic foundation of the 20th century. Today, Vienna ranks among the leading convention cities in the world. It is headquarters for the International Atomic Energy Agency, the Organization of Petroleum Exporting Countries (OPEC), and the United Nations Industrial Development Organization (UNIDO); it is one of the three UN

Restaurantterrasse vom Haashaus beim Stephansdom

headquarters, alongside New York and Geneva. When the Iron Curtain was in place, Vienna served as a bridge between the West and the Communist countries of Eastern Europe. With this situation having become obsolete in 1989, the city is now trying to hold its ground against such tough competitors as Prague or Budapest. The country's membership in the European Union means new opportunities for Vienna as an economic and increasingly political community.

Einblicke

Lesestrategie: Reading a Letter

Letters are often very "conversational" in tone and tend to use informal language. As you read the text, look for examples of informal language, such as abbreviations, frequent use of flavoring particles (e.g., **ja**), and casual idioms.

Wortschatz 2

bekannt	*well-known*
Das macht nichts.	*That doesn't matter.*
einmal	*once, (at) one time*
gemütlich	*pleasant, cozy, convivial*
genug	*enough*
hoffentlich	*hopefully; I hope*
interessant	*interesting*
leider	*unfortunately*
lieb[1]	*dear*
stundenlang[2]	*for hours*
bummeln, ist gebummelt	*to stroll*

[1] Lieb**e** Eltern, lieb**e** Elisabeth, lieb**er** Michael

[2] Also: **jahrelang, monatelang, wochenlang, tagelang,** etc.

Vor dem Lesen

A. **Auf Reisen** *(Traveling. Read the list below and pick out the five most important things you like to do when you travel. Compare your travel interests with those of your partner. What do you have in common and where do you differ?)*

___ zu Fuß durch die Stadt gehen   ___ die Bibliothek besichtigen

___ mit Leuten sprechen   ___ Schlösser besichtigen

___ Souvenirs kaufen   ___ Kirchen besichtigen

___ in Museen gehen   ___ Karten schreiben

___ in die Oper gehen   ___ tanzen gehen

___ in Restaurants gehen   ___ lange schlafen

___ McDonalds finden   ___ mit dem Taxi fahren

___ mit der Familie telefonieren   ___ fotografieren

B. **Wohin gehen wir?** *(Look with your partner at the following entertainment offers. Then decide where you'd like to go and why.)*

C. Was ist das?

der Sport, Stopp; das Gästehaus; die Studentengruppe, Winterresidenz; zentral

CD 3, Track 8

Grüße° aus Wien

greetings

Liebe Eltern!

Jetzt muss ich euch aber wirklich wieder einmal schreiben! Ich habe so viel gesehen, dass ich gar nicht weiß, wo ich beginnen soll. Vor einer Woche war° ich mit unserer Studentengruppe noch in Passau. Von dort sind wir mit dem Schiff die Donau hinuntergefahren°. Wir haben einen Stopp in Linz gemacht und haben die Stadt, das Schloss und den Dom besichtigt. Dann sind wir mit dem Schiff weiter bis nach Wien gefahren. Die Weinberge°, Burgen° und besonders Kloster° Melk haben mir sehr gut gefallen. Das Wetter ist auch sehr schön gewesen.

was

traveled down

vineyards / castles / monastery

Jetzt sind wir schon ein paar Tage in Wien. Ich finde es toll hier! Unser Gästehaus liegt sehr zentral und wir können alles zu Fuß oder mit der U-Bahn erreichen°. So viel bin ich noch nie gelaufen! Am Freitag sind wir stundenlang durch die Innenstadt gebummelt. Die Geschäfte in der° Kärntner Straße sind sehr teuer, aber man muss ja° nichts

reach

in the / (flavoring particle)

Kloster Melk an der Donau

Letters for friends and relatives usually start with **Liebe(r) . . .** and end with **Viele liebe Grüße, Dein(e)/Euer/ Eure . . .** More formal letters may begin with **Sehr geehrter Herr/geehrte Dame . . .** or **Sehr geehrte Damen und Herren**, followed by a comma. Common phrases to end such a letter are **Mit freundlichen Grüßen** or **Mit freundlichem Gruß! Ihr(e) . . .**

elevator
went to the top of the tower
Magic Flute

of the / emperors / riding academy
white horses
riding / art

small restaurant

kaufen. Wir haben natürlich auch den Stephansdom besichtigt und sind mit dem Aufzug° im Turm hinaufgefahren°. Von dort kann man Wien gut sehen. Am Abend haben wir Mozarts *Zauberflöte*° in der Oper gesehen.

Am Samstag haben wir die Hofburg besichtigt. Das ist einmal die Winterresidenz der° Habsburger Kaiser° gewesen. Dort ist auch die Spanische Reitschule° und man kann die Lipizzaner° beim Training sehen. Das haben wir auch getan. Wirklich prima! Da ist das Reiten° kein Sport, sondern Kunst°. Am Abend sind wir mit der Straßenbahn nach Grinzing gefahren und haben dort Marks Geburtstag mit Musik und Wein gefeiert. Die Weinstube° war sehr gemütlich.

Note, according to the new spelling reform, **du, euch, dein,** and **euer** are not capitalized in letters, but the formal *you* and *your* **(Sie, Ihnen, Ihr)** are. The same holds true for the end of a letter, but not everybody abides by these rules. Many, including the authors of this book, still prefer to end a letter the old-fashioned way, especially when addressing grand-parents who might find **"Euer Michael"** still more respectful. It's really up to your discretion.

Lipizzaner beim Training in der Spanischen Reitschule

ethnology / an art museum
ferris wheel

almost over
monuments

traffic

simply

Hungary
we get going again

Heute besichtigen wir das Museum für Völkerkunde° und die Sezession° und später wollen ein paar von uns noch zum Prater. Das Riesenrad° dort soll toll sein. Morgen früh wollen wir noch zum Schloss Schönbrunn, der Sommerresidenz der Habsburger; und dann ist unsere Zeit in Wien auch schon fast um°.

Wien ist wirklich interessant. Überall findet man Denkmäler° oder Straßen mit bekannten Namen wie Mozart, Beethoven, Johann Strauß usw. Aber ihr dürft nicht denken, dass man hier nur Walzer hört und alles romantisch ist. Wien ist auch eine Groß-stadt mit vielen Menschen und viel Verkehr°. Es gefällt mir hier so gut, dass ich gern noch ein paar Tage bleiben möchte. Das geht leider nicht, weil wir noch nach Salzburg und Innsbruck wollen. Eine Woche ist einfach° nicht lange genug für so eine Reise. Nach Budapest können wir leider auch nicht. Nun, das macht nichts. Hoffentlich komme ich im Frühling einmal nach Ungarn°.

So, jetzt muss ich schnell frühstücken und dann geht's wieder los°! Tschüss und viele liebe Grüße!

Euer Michael

Nach dem Lesen

A. Wer, was oder wo ist das? *(Match the descriptions with the places or people in the list below.)*

die Donau, Grinzing, die Hofburg, die Kärntner Straße, Linz, Melk, Passau, der Prater, Schloss Schönbrunn, die Spanische Reitschule, die Staatsoper, der Turm vom Stephansdom

1. Hier hat die Flussfahrt nach Wien begonnen.
2. Auf diesem *(on this)* Fluss kann man mit dem Schiff bis nach Wien fahren.

3. Hier haben die Habsburger Kaiser im Sommer gelebt.
4. Hier gibt es ein Barockkloster. Es ist sehr bekannt.
5. Da haben die Studenten einen Stopp gemacht und die Stadt besichtigt.
6. Hier kann man schön bummeln, aber die Geschäfte sind sehr teuer.
7. Von dort kann man ganz Wien sehen.
8. Das ist einmal die Winterresidenz der *(of the)* Habsburger Kaiser gewesen.
9. Hier kann man die Lipizzaner trainieren sehen.
10. Hier kann man Mozarts *Zauberflöte* sehen.
11. Hier gibt es ein Riesenrad.
12. Dort kann man gemütlich essen und Wein trinken.

A: 1. Passau 2. die Donau 3. Schloss Schönbrunn 4. Melk 5. Linz 6. die Kärntner Straße 7. der Turm vom Stephansdom 8. die Hofburg 9. die Spanische Reitschule 10. die Staatsoper 11. der Prater 12. Grinzing

Fokus — *Heurigen Wine*

Located on the outskirts of Vienna, Grinzing is probably the best-known Heurigen wine village. Young, fresh wine **(der Heurige)** is sold by wine growers in their courtyards or houses, some of which have been turned into restaurants **(Weinstuben** or **Heurigenschänken).**

B. *Sondern* **oder** *aber*? *(Insert the appropriate conjunction.)*
1. Das Gästehaus ist nicht sehr elegant, __aber__ es liegt zentral.
2. Wir sind nicht mit dem Bus gefahren, __sondern__ viel gelaufen.
3. Bei der Spanischen Reitschule ist das Reiten kein Sport, __sondern__ Kunst.
4. Die Geschäfte in der Kärntner Straße sind teuer, __aber__ sie gefallen mir.

C. **Fahrt** *(trip)* **nach Österreich** *(Mr. Schubach tells about his travel plans. Use modal verbs.)*

BEISPIEL: Ihr fahrt mit uns mit dem Schiff bis nach Wien. (müssen)
Ihr müsst mit uns mit dem Schiff bis nach Wien fahren.

1. Unsere Fahrt beginnt in Passau. (sollen)
2. In Linz machen wir einen Stopp. (wollen)
3. Meine Frau besichtigt das Kloster Melk. (möchten)
4. Vom Schiff sieht man viele Weinberge und Burgen. (können)
5. Wir bleiben fünf Tage in Wien. (wollen)
6. Dort gibt es viel zu sehen. (sollen)
7. Man hat natürlich gute Schuhe dabei *(along)*. (müssen)
8. Ich laufe aber nicht so viel. (dürfen)
9. Meine Frau bummelt gemütlich durch die Kärntner Straße. (möchten)
10. Ich sehe viele Museen. (wollen)

C: 1. soll . . . beginnen
2. wollen . . . machen
3. möchte . . . besichtigen
4. kann . . . sehen 5. wollen . . . bleiben
6. soll . . . geben 7. muss . . . dabei haben
8. darf . . . laufen 9. möchte . . . bummeln
10. will . . . sehen

Passau is a *German* city situated near the border with Austria and the Czech Republic. It is the starting point for regular steamer service down the Danube to Vienna and the Black Sea.

For a colorful and more detailed map of Vienna, visit the Internet at www.wien.at. Then click on *Tourism > English > city maps > overview map of the old city Vienna*. The map you find there gives you a nice impression of Vienna, and, when printed out, even helps when asking for directions.

D. Stadtplan von Wien

1. **Wo ist das?** (*In groups of two or three, make a list of all the locations in Vienna mentioned throughout this chapter. Find them on the map and ask each other about their location, giving just a brief description.*)

   BEISPIEL: Wo ist die Oper?
   Am Opernring, in der Nähe vom Burggarten.

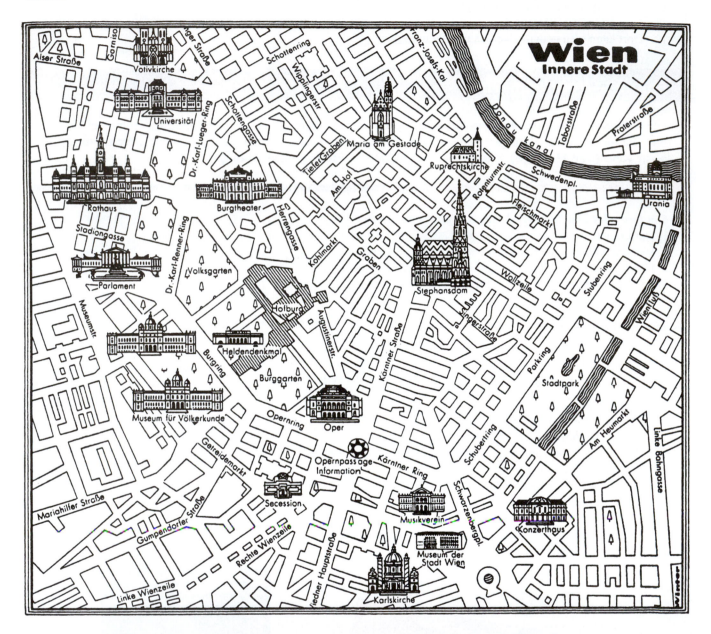

Optional practice: **Ersetzen Sie die Hauptwörter durch Pronomen! z.B. Er zeigt der Dame den Weg: Er zeigt ihr den Weg. Er zeigt ihn ihr.** (Er zeigt den Eltern den Stadtplan. Wir zeigen dem Touristen das Rathaus. Ich zeige der Studentin die Museen. Ich zeige dem Kind den Park.)

2. **Wie kommt man dorthin?** (*Now practice asking and giving directions from one place to another.*)

   BEISPIEL: vom Stephansdom zur Oper
   Entschuldigen Sie bitte! Können Sie mir sagen, wie ich von hier zur Oper komme?
   Gern. Gehen Sie immer geradeaus die Kärntner Straße entlang! Sie sehen dann die Oper rechts.

   a. von der Oper zur Hofburg
   b. von der Hofburg zur Uni
   c. von der Uni zum Parlament
   d. vom Parlament zum Musikverein
   e. vom Musikverein zum Donaukanal
   f. vom Donaukanal zur Praterstraße

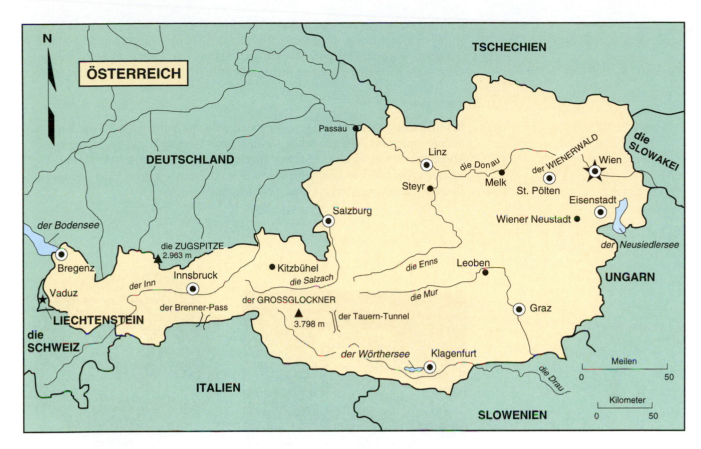

E. Etwas Geographie. Sehen Sie auf die Landkarte von Österreich und beantworten Sie die Fragen! Arbeiten Sie mit einem Partner!

1. Wie viele Nachbarländer hat Österreich? Wie heißen sie und wo liegen sie?
2. Wie heißt die Hauptstadt von Österreich? Wie heißen ein paar Städte in Österreich?
3. Welche Flüsse gibt es in Österreich? An welchem Fluss liegt Wien? Salzburg? Innsbruck? Linz? Graz? (**. . . liegt am/an der . . .**)
4. Welcher See liegt nicht nur in Österreich, sondern auch in Deutschland und in der Schweiz? Welcher See liegt zum Teil in Österreich und zum Teil in Ungarn? An welchem See liegt Klagenfurt?
5. Wo liegt der Brenner-Pass? der Großglockner? der Tauern-Tunnel?

F. Interview. Fragen Sie einen Nachbarn/eine Nachbarin, . . . !

1. ob er/sie schon einmal in Wien gewesen ist; wenn ja, was ihm/ihr in Wien besonders gut gefallen hat (**Was hat dir . . . ?**);
wenn nein, was er/sie einmal in Wien sehen möchte
2. ob er/sie in einer Großstadt oder Kleinstadt wohnt
3. ob die Stadt eine Altstadt hat und ob sie schön ist
4. ob es dort eine Straßenbahn, eine U-Bahn oder Busse gibt
5. welche Denkmäler und Straßen mit bekannten Namen es gibt
6. was ihm/ihr dort besonders gefällt und was nicht
7. ob er/sie schon einmal in einem Schloss gewesen ist; wenn ja, wo; wenn nein, welches Schloss er/sie einmal sehen möchte

F: Have students work in pairs, or use the questions as guidelines for a written assignment.

G. Kurzgespräche (*Together with your partner, prepare one of the following brief dialogues. Then present it to the class.*)

1. **Im Kaffeehaus**

You and a friend are in a Viennese coffee house. Your friend suggests visiting the *Museum für Völkerkunde*. You ask someone at the table next to yours where the museum is located. You find out that it is not too far away, but that unfortunately it is closed today. You respond politely. Your friend suggests an alternative activity (strolling along the Kärntner Straße, visiting the Riding Academy or St. Stephen's Cathedral, etc.). Discuss how to reach your destination. Then consider what you might want to do in the evening (**heute Abend**): go to Grinzing or the Prater, etc.

2. **Souvenirs aus Wien**

Before leaving Vienna, you and a friend are souvenir hunting but have a hard time finding something. What could one bring home? You might end up buying some **Mozartkugeln** or a piece of **Sacher Torte;** but instead of taking them home, you eat them yourself. You decide that that's O.K. and that it was delicious. Some post-cards (**Karten**) would be fine, too, but of what?

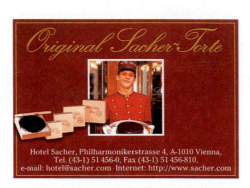

H. Grüße von zu Hause. Schreiben Sie 8–10 Sätze an Michael!

BEISPIEL: Lieber Michael! Danke für deinen Brief *(letter)*! Wie ich sehe, hast du Spaß in Wien gehabt . . . Hier zu Hause ist es kalt und es regnet viel . . . Viele liebe Grüße! Dein(e) . . .

 **HÖREN SIE ZU!**   TRACK 11

Schon lange nicht mehr gesehen! *(Listen to the conversation between Uwe and Erika, then answer the questions. You do not need to write complete sentences.)*

Zum Erkennen: schon lange nicht mehr *(not for a long time);* Bergwanderungen *(mountain hikes)*

1. Wo ist Uwe gewesen? in Österreich
2. Mit wem ist er gefahren? mit Jürgen
3. Wie ist das Wetter gewesen? wunderbar, es hat nur einmal geregnet
4. Wo ist Maria Alm? in der Nähe von Salzburg
5. Was haben sie dort gemacht? Bergwanderungen
6. Wo sind sie noch gewesen? in Salzburg
7. Was haben sie dort besichtigt? die Burg und den Dom
8. Wann will Uwe nach Wien? im Oktober
9. Warum muss Erika gehen? Ihre Vorlesung beginnt in fünf Minuten.

Video-Ecke

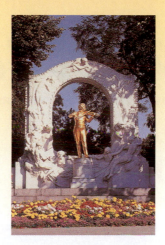

- The *Minidrama* "Wie komme ich zur Staatsoper?" shows a young man looking for the State Opera, where he wants to buy tickets for a Pavarotti concert. An older woman and a street merchant aren't much help. Then his friend shows up, only to tell him that the concert is sold out. However, the street vendor has a solution.

- *Blickpunkt* "Besuch in Österreich" brings you to Vienna, where a Viennese waiter tells you about everything he loves in his city. We also have a brief look at Salzburg and other sites to get a good impression of why Austria is so popular.

Web-Ecke

- For updates, self-assessment quizzes, and online activities related to this chapter, visit the **Wie geht's?** Web site at **http://wiegehts.heinle.com**. You will visit Vienna, check into the Hotel Sacher, and meet the Vienna Boys' Choir and some of Austria's famous composers. You will also visit Linz and take a trip up the Danube toward Passau, Germany.

Kapitel (6)

Wohnen

Jugendstilhaus in Dresden

Lernziele

Vorschau
Housing

Gespräche + Wortschatz
Housing and furniture

Fokus
Shared living arrangements
Homes and houses
Friedensreich Hundertwasser
Public transportation and city life
High German and dialects

Struktur
6.1 Two-way prepositions
6.2 Imperatives
6.2 **Wissen** and **kennen**

Einblicke
Schaffen, sparen, Häuschen bauen

Video-Ecke
Minidrama: *Kein Zimmer für Studenten*
Blickpunkt: *Bei Viktor zu Hause*

Web-Ecke

152

Vorschau

Housing

After World War II, West Germany suffered an acute housing shortage, not only because so many buildings had been destroyed, but also because of the large number of refugees who moved west. Rebuilding in the sixties and seventies created high-rise apartment clusters (**Wohnsilos**) that mushroomed around the old cities, often contrasting sharply with the traditional architecture. Fortunately, many people have rediscovered the beauty of older buildings. Along came subsidies and tax incentives that have made it possible to restore and modernize them. More recently, the new housing developments have attempted to harmonize with the landscape and to conform to local building styles. Strict zoning laws prevent the loss of open space and agricultural land, but they also make it more difficult to add housing.

With the end of the Cold War and the collapse of the eastern economies, another wave of people moved west, which again created a housing crisis. Students, young couples, large families, and foreign nationals have great difficulties finding affordable accommodations.

You could talk about the picture on p. 152, how it differs from houses in the students' neighborhood and where there might be similar houses in their own city. Also, ask what students usually expect in a furnished apartment, what extra expenses they have to count on, what they expect from their landlord, and what the landlord expects from them.

In the former German Democratic Republic (GDR, East Germany), two-thirds of the housing units dated back to the time before World War II, often lacking modern sanitary facilities and heating systems. Since reunification, many of the old housing units have been renovated, and new modern homes and apartments are being built everywhere. Although real estate is expensive in Germany, nine out of ten Germans would prefer to own their own home or condominium (**Eigentumswohnung**); homeownership is encouraged by various forms of governmental help, such as tax incentives.

Apartments are advertised by the number of rooms. Those who want to rent a three-bedroom apartment with a living room and a dining room need a **Fünf-zimmerwohnung**; bathroom and kitchen are excluded from the room count. Furnished apartments are relatively rare. "Unfurnished" is usually to be taken literally. There are no built-in closets, kitchen cabinets, appliances, light fixtures, and other conveniences. Tenants are responsible for furnishing and maintaining their apartments, including interior painting and decorating, and may have to pay a monthly **Wohngeld** for a janitor, garbage removal, building maintenance, and the like. Heating may or may not be included in the rent or **Wohngeld** and is advertised accordingly as **warm** or **kalt**.

Die Dreiflüssestadt Passau liegt an der Grenze zu Österreich.

Gespräche + Wortschatz

CD 3, Track 9

Warm-ups: 1. **Was ist der Artikel von . . . ?** *(Refer to clothing and food.)* 2. **Was ist der Plural von** Bus, Brücke, Kino, Museum, . . . ? 3. **Können Sie mir sagen,** wie spät es ist? welches Datum heute ist? was für ein Tag heute ist? auf welcher Seite vom Buch wir sind?

Point out that, as mentioned in the *Vorschau,* **kalt** means "without electricity." The renter pays for that.

Wohnung zu vermieten

INGE	Hallo, mein Name ist Inge Moser. Ich habe gehört, dass Sie eine Zweizimmerwohnung zu vermieten haben. Stimmt das?
VERMIETER	Ja, in der Nähe vom Dom.
INGE	Wie alt ist die Wohnung?
VERMIETER	Ziemlich alt, aber sie ist renoviert und schön groß und hell. Sie hat sogar einen Balkon.
INGE	In welchem Stock liegt sie?
VERMIETER	Im dritten Stock.
INGE	Ist sie möbliert oder unmöbliert?
VERMIETER	Unmöbliert.
INGE	Und was kostet die Wohnung?
VERMIETER	€ 550.
INGE	Ist das kalt oder warm?
VERMIETER	Kalt.
INGE	Oh, das ist ein bisschen zu teuer. Vielen Dank! Auf Wiederhören!
VERMIETER	Auf Wiederhören!

In der WG (Wohngemeinschaft)

INGE	Euer Haus gefällt mir!
HORST	Wir haben noch Platz für dich. Komm, ich zeige dir alles! . . . Hier links ist unsere Küche. Sie ist klein, aber praktisch.
INGE	Wer kocht?
HORST	Wir alle: Jens, Gisela, Renate und ich.
INGE	Und das ist das Wohnzimmer?
HORST	Ja. Es ist ein bisschen dunkel, aber das ist O.K.
INGE	Eure Sessel gefallen mir.
HORST	Sie sind alt, aber echt bequem. Oben sind dann vier Schlafzimmer und das Bad.
INGE	Nur ein Bad?
HORST	Ja, leider! Aber hier unten ist noch eine Toilette.
INGE	Was bezahlt ihr im Monat?
HORST	Jeder 200 Euro.
INGE	Nicht schlecht! Und wie kommst du zur Uni?
HORST	Kein Problem. Ich gehe zu Fuß.
INGE	Klingt gut!

You could also have students create their own questions and ask each other for the answer.

A. Richtig oder falsch?

_r_ 1. In der Nähe vom Dom gibt es eine Wohnung zu vermieten.
_f_ 2. Die Wohnung hat vier Zimmer.
_f_ 3. Die Wohnung ist etwas dunkel.
_f_ 4. Die Wohnung liegt im Parterre.
_r_ 5. Horst wohnt in einer WG.
_f_ 6. Das Haus hat drei Schlafzimmer.
_f_ 7. Sie fahren mit der U-Bahn zur Uni.
_f_ 8. Für das Haus bezahlen die Studenten 100 Euro pro Person.
_r_ 9. Horst möchte, dass Inge auch dort wohnt.
_f_ 10. Aber das gefällt Inge nicht.

B. Jetzt sind Sie dran! *(With a partner, create your own dialogue, pretending you are hunting for an apartment or house. Talk about prices, individual rooms, whether utilities are included or not, location, and how to get from there to the university.)*

Fokus — *Shared Living Arrangements*

Students and other young people often choose to live in **WGs** or **Wohngemeinschaften** *(shared housing).* Moving into an apartment or house—often with complete strangers—is quite common, as rooms in dormi- tories **(Studenten[wohn]heime)** are scarce and one-room apartments often too expensive for tight budgets.

Wortschatz 1

Das Haus, ̈er *(house)*

Das Studentenheim, -e *(dorm)*

Die Wohnung, -en *(apartment)*

der Balkon, -s	*balcony*	die Ecke, -n	*corner*
Baum, e	*tree*	Garage, -n	*garage*
Flur, -e	*hallway*	Küche, -n	*kitchen*
Garten, ̈	*garden, yard*	Toilette, -n	*toilet*
Keller, -	*basement*		
das Bad, ̈er	*bathroom*		
Dach, ̈er	*roof*	im Bad / in der Küche	*in the bathroom / kitchen*
Zimmer, -	*room*		
Arbeitszimmer, -	*study*	im Keller	*in the basement*
Esszimmer, -	*dining room*	im Parterre	*on the first floor (ground level)*
Schlafzimmer, -	*bedroom*		
Wohnzimmer, -	*living room*	im ersten Stock	*on the second floor*

Note: **das Parterre,** BUT **der Stock.**

Die Möbel *(pl.)* *(furniture)*

der Fernseher, -	*TV set*	das Bett, -en	*bed*
Kühlschrank, ̈e	*refrigerator*	Radio, -s	*radio*
Schrank, ̈e	*closet, cupboard*	Regal, -e	*shelf, bookcase*
Schreibtisch, -e	*desk*	Sofa, -s	*sofa*
Sessel, -	*armchair*	Telefon, -e	*telephone*
Stuhl, ̈e	*chair*	die Kommode, -n	*dresser*
Teppich, -e	*carpet*	Lampe, -n	*lamp*
Tisch, -e	*table*		
Vorhang, ̈e	*curtain*		

Weiteres

im Monat	*per month*
oben / unten	*up(stairs) / down(stairs)*
hell / dunkel	*bright, light / dark*
praktisch	*practical(ly)*

There are two verbs with the infinitive **hängen.** The t-verb means *to hang (up)* something somewhere, the n-verb, that something *is hanging* somewhere.

(un)bequem	*(un)comfortable; (in)convenient*
sogar	*even*
ziemlich	*quite, rather*
baden	*to take a bath; to swim*
duschen	*to take a shower*
hängen, gehängt	*to hang (up)*
hängen, gehangen	*to hang (be hanging)*
kochen	*to cook*
legen	*to lay, put (flat)*
liegen, gelegen	*to lie (be lying flat)*
mieten / vermieten	*to rent / to rent out*
setzen	*to set, put*
sitzen, gesessen	*to sit (be sitting)*
stehen, gestanden	*to stand (be standing)*
stellen	*to stand, put (upright)*
waschen (wäscht), gewaschen	*to wash*
das Problem, -e	*problem*
(Das ist) kein Problem.	*(That's) no problem.*
(Das) klingt gut!	*(That) sounds good.*
(Das) stimmt!	*(That's) true. / (That's) right.*
Auf Wiederhören!	*Good-bye! (on the phone)*

Zum Erkennen: renoviert *(renovated);* (un)möbliert *([un]furnished);* die WG, -s / Wohngemeinschaft, -en *(shared housing);* echt *(really);* jeder *(each one);* AUCH: der Imperativ, -e, der Blick (auf + *acc.*) *view of;* im Dachgeschoss *(on the attic floor);* im Erdgeschoss *(on the ground level);* beschreiben *(to describe)*

Fokus — *Homes and Houses*

When German-speakers say "first floor" (**erste Etage** or **erster Stock**), they mean what North Americans call the *second floor*. Either **das Parterre** or **das Erdgeschoss** is used to denote the ground floor, or North American first floor. In elevators, remember to press "E" (for **Erdgeschoss**) or "0" to get to the exit.

Homes and apartments usually have a foyer and a hallway (**der Flur**), with doors leading to the various rooms. For privacy's sake, many Germans prefer to keep doors shut—this also holds true in the workplace and institutions like the university, where people prefer to work with doors closed. Sheer, pretty curtains (**Gardinen**) are also a typical feature that permits people to see out, but prevents others from looking in. In addition, some houses have outside shutters (**Rolläden** or **Rollos**) that can be rolled down over the windows. Traditional half-timbered houses (**Fachwerkhäuser**) often have colorful shutters that swing shut on hinges.

Zum Thema

A. Mustersätze

1. das Haus: Das Haus **gefällt mir.**
   das Wohnzimmer, die Küche, das Bad, der Garten
2. der Sessel: **Wie gefällt dir** der Sessel?
   das Sofa, der Teppich, das Regal, das Radio
3. die Möbel: Die Möbel **gefallen mir.**
   Sessel, Stühle, Vorhänge, Schränke

4. sehr praktisch: **Die Wohnung ist** sehr praktisch.
   schön hell, ziemlich dunkel, zu klein, schön sauber, sehr gemütlich, furchtbar
   schmutzig, wirklich bequem
5. unten: **Die Wohnung ist** unten.
   oben, im Parterre, im ersten Stock, im zweiten Stock, im dritten Stock

B. Beschreiben Sie die Wohnung! *(Together with a partner, describe what furniture you see in the various rooms of this apartment.)*

BEISPIEL: Im Bad gibt es ein Klo, ein Waschbecken . . .

In case you are curious: *bathtub* **die Badewanne, -n**; *closet* **der Kleiderschrank, ̈-e**; *computer* **der Computer, -**; *diningroom cabinet* **das Büfett, -s**; *dishwasher* **die Spülmaschine, -n**; *fireplace* **der Kamin, -e**; *kitchen cabinet* **der Küchenschrank, ̈-e**; *microwave* **die Mikrowelle, -n (coll.)**; *mirror* **der Spiegel, -**; *night stand* **der Nachttisch, -e**; *oven* **der Ofen ̈-**; *patio* **die Terrasse, -n**; *piano* **das Klavier, -e**; *range* **der Herd, -e**; *shower* **die Dusche, -n**, *sink* **das Waschbecken, -**

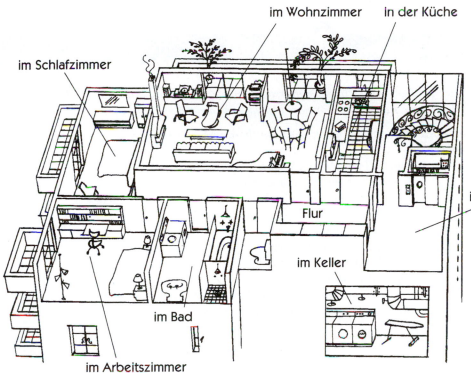

im Wohnzimmer   in der Küche
im Schlafzimmer
im Treppenhaus
Flur
im Keller
im Bad
im Arbeitszimmer

In case students ask: *answering machine* **der Anrufbeantworter, -**; *cell phone* **das Handy, -s**; *elevator* **der Aufzug, ̈-e**; *john* **das Klo, -s**; *pool* **der Swimmingpool, -s**; *stairwell* **das Treppenhaus**; *toaster* **der Toaster, -**

C. Kein Haus / keine Wohnung ohne Maschinen *(Working in small groups, report what machines or appliances you have or don't have, what you need, and what you would like to have.)*

D. Was bedeuten die Wörter? Was ist ihr Artikel und ihr Plural?

Balkontür, Bücherregal, Dachgeschosswohnung, Duschvorhang, Elternschlafzimmer, Kinderbad, Farbfernseher, Küchenfenster, Kochecke, Liegestuhl, Schlafsofa, Schreibtischlampe, Sitzecke, Stehlampe, Wandlampe, Waschecke, Wohnzimmerteppich

D: *balcony door* (**die** / -türen), *bookshelf* (**das** / -regale), *attic apartment* (**die** / -wohnungen), *shower curtain* (**der** / -vorhänge), *master bedroom* (**das** / -zimmer), *children's bath* (**das** / -bäder), *color TV* (**der** / -fernseher), *kitchen window* (**das** / -fenster), *cook's nook / cooking area* (**die** / -ecken), *lounge chair* (**der** / -stühle), *sofa sleeper* (**das** / -sofas), *desk lamp* (**die** / -lampen), *corner bench seating arrangement* (**die** / -ecken), *standard lamp* (**die** / -lampen), *wall lamp* (**die** / -lampen), *vanity area* (**die** / -ecken), *livingroom carpet* (**der** / -teppiche)

E. Interview. Fragen Sie einen Nachbarn/eine Nachbarin, . . . !
1. ob er/sie eine Wohnung hat oder ob er/sie zu Hause, im Studentenheim oder in einer WG wohnt; wenn nicht zu Hause, wie viel Miete er/sie bezahlt
2. ob er/sie Mitbewohner *(housemates)*, einen Zimmerkollegen oder eine Zimmerkollegin *(roommate)* hat; wenn ja, wie sie heißen
3. wie sein Zimmer ist und was für Möbel er/sie im Zimmer hat
4. ob er/sie eine Küche hat; wenn ja, was es in der Küche gibt und wer kocht
5. was man vom Zimmerfenster sehen kann
6. wie lange er/sie schon da wohnt
7. wie er/sie zur Uni kommt

CD 3, Track 10

Aussprache: ei, au, eu, äu

(Read also Part II. 37–39 in the pronunciation guide of the Workbook.)

1. [ai] w**ei**t, l**ei**der, **ei**gentlich, z**ei**gen, f**ei**ern, bl**ei**ben
2. [au] **au**f, bl**au**grau, B**au**m, K**au**fhaus, br**au**chen, l**au**fen
3. [oi] **eu**ch, h**eu**te, t**eu**er, L**eu**te, Fr**eu**nde, H**äu**ser, B**äu**me
4. Wortpaare
   a. *by* / bei   c. *mouse* / Maus   e. aus / Eis
   b. *Troy* / treu   d. Haus / Häuser   f. euer / Eier

HÖREN SIE ZU!   TRACK 12

Hier Müller! *(Listen to the conversation between Inge and Mrs. Müller. Then decide whether the statements below are true or false according to the dialogue.)*

Zum Erkennen: nett *(nice);* teilen *(to share);* na gut *(well, good);* Bis bald! *(See you soon!)*

r	1. Inge ist Frau Müllers Tochter.
f	2. Frau Müller hat ein Zimmer gefunden.
r	3. Das Zimmer ist in der Schillerstraße.
f	4. Inges Telefonnummer ist 91 68.
r	5. Wohnungen sind sehr teuer.
r	6. Inge hat Horst vor ein paar Tagen gesehen.
f	7. Sie teilt jetzt ein Zimmer mit Horst.
f	8. Inge zahlt 140 Euro im Monat.
r	9. Sie kann mit dem Fahrrad zur Uni fahren.
f	10. Am Wochenende kommt sie nach Hause.

Struktur

6.1 Two-way prepositions

You have learned some prepositions that are always followed by the dative and some that are always followed by the accusative. You will now learn a set of prepositions that sometimes take the dative and sometimes the accusative.

1. The basic meanings of the nine TWO-WAY PREPOSITIONS are:

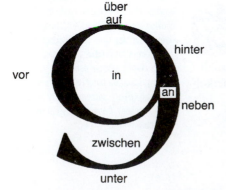

an	*to up to, at (the side of), on (vertical surface)*
auf	*on (top of, horizontal surface), onto*
hinter	*behind*
in	*in, into, inside of*
neben	*beside, next to*
über	*over, above; about*
unter	*under, below*
vor	*before, in front of*
zwischen	*between*

Most of these prepositions may be contracted with articles. The most common contractions are:

an + das = **ans**	in + das = **ins**
an + dem = **am**	in + dem = **im**
auf + das = **aufs**	

To practice the meaning of the prepositions, give students sentences in English and have them state the appropriate German preposition: 1. *My car is in front of the house.* **(vor)** 2. *I left my books on top of the car.* **(auf)** 3. *I saw them when I went to the window.* **(an)**

CAUTION: The preposition **vor** precedes a noun (**vor dem Haus**). The conjunction **bevor** introduces a clause (. . . , **bevor du das Haus mietest**).

2. **Wo?** vs. **wohin?**

   a. German has two words to ask *where:* **wo?** (*in what place?*) and **wohin?** (*to what place?*). **Wo** asks about LOCATION, where something is, or an activity within a place. **Wohin** asks about DESTINATION OR A CHANGE OF PLACE.

      LOCATION: **Wo** ist Horst?   *Where's Horst? (in what place)*

      DESTINATION: **Wohin** geht Horst?   *Where's Horst going? (to what place)*

   b. The difference between location and destination also plays a role in determining the case following two-way prepositions. If the question is **wo?,** the <u>dative</u> is used. If the question is **wohin?,** the <u>accusative</u> is used.

      Wo ist Horst?   → **In der** Küche.   *Where's Horst?*   → *In the kitchen.*

      Wohin geht Horst? → **In die** Küche.   *Where's Horst going?* → *To the kitchen.*

woher *(from where),* introduced in Chapter 1, denotes origin.

Demonstrate the difference between ACTIVITY IN A PLACE by walking back and forth in the classroom, then CHANGE OF PLACE by walking out of the room.

wo?	LOCATION	→	<u>dative</u>
wohin?	DESTINATION	→	<u>accusative</u>

3. The difference lies entirely in the verb!

   • Some verbs denoting LOCATION OR ACTIVITY WITHIN A PLACE (**wo?** → dative) are: hängen, kaufen, kochen, lesen, liegen, schlafen, sein, sitzen, spielen, stehen, studieren, tanzen, trinken, wohnen

   • Typical verbs implying DESTINATION OR A CHANGE OF PLACE OR MOTION TOWARD a point (**wohin?** → accusative) are: bringen, fahren, gehen, hängen, kommen, laufen, legen, setzen, stellen, tragen

4. Some important verb pairs

To give students practice in determining whether the <u>dative</u> or the <u>accusative</u> must be used, give them English sentences and have them state the proper case in German: e.g., *The library is next to the dorm. She's going into the cafeteria. He sits down next to a friend. Put your books on the floor.*

N-VERBS / LOCATION → <u>dative</u>	T-VERBS / CHANGE OF PLACE → <u>accusative</u>
hängen, gehangen *(to be hanging)*	hängen, gehängt *(to hang up)*
liegen, gelegen *(to be lying [flat])*	legen, gelegt *(to lay down, put [flat])*
sitzen, gesessen *(to be sitting)*	setzen, gesetzt *(to set down)*
stehen, gestanden *(to be standing)*	stellen, gestellt *(to put [upright])*

   • Note that the four n-verbs are all intransitive (i.e., they do not take a direct object). The four t-verbs, on the other hand, are transitive (i.e., they do take a direct object).

      Der Mantel hat **im** Schrank gehangen.

      Ich habe den Mantel **in den** Schrank gehängt.

CAUTION: Although **legen, setzen,** and **stellen** are all sometimes translated as *to put,* they are <u>not interchangeable</u>!

      Sie **stellt** den Stuhl an die Wand. *(upright position)*

      Sie **legt** das Heft auf den Tisch. *(flat position)*

      Er **setzt** das Kind auf den Stuhl. *(sitting position)*

5. Summary

WOHIN?

WO?

WOHIN?	Die Tante hängt den Teppich **über das** Balkongeländer (. . . *banister*).
WO?	Der Teppich hängt **über dem** Balkongeländer.
WOHIN?	Die Mutter stellt die Leiter *(ladder)* **an die** Wand.
WO?	Die Leiter steht **an der** Wand.
WOHIN?	Das Kind legt den Teddy **auf die** Bank *(bench)*.
WO?	Der Teddy liegt **auf der** Bank.
WOHIN?	Das Auto fährt **neben das** Haus.
WO?	Das Auto steht **neben dem** Haus.
WOHIN?	Das Kind läuft **hinter die** Mutter.
WO?	Das Kind steht **hinter der** Mutter.
WOHIN?	Der Hund läuft **vor das** Auto.
WO?	Der Hund steht **vor dem** Auto.
WOHIN?	Der Großvater nimmt die Pfeife *(pipe)* **in den** Mund *(mouth)*.
WO?	Der Großvater hat die Pfeife **im** Mund.
WOHIN?	Das Huhn *(chicken)* läuft **unter die** Bank **zwischen die** Bankbeine (. . . *legs*).
WO?	Das Huhn sitzt **unter der** Bank **zwischen den** Bankbeinen.

In addition to the drawings, you could act out situations: 1. Ich gehe an die Tafel. Ich stehe . . . 2. Ich lege das Buch auf den Tisch. Es liegt . . . 3. Ich stelle den Stuhl hinter den Tisch. Er steht . . . 4. Ich werfe das Papier in den Papierkorb. Es liegt . . . 5. Ich hänge das Bild an die Wand. Es hängt . . . 6. Ich lege das Heft unter das Buch. Es liegt . . . 7. Die Kreide fällt vom Tisch. Sie liegt vor (unter, auf . . .) 8. Ich gehe zwischen den Tisch und die Tafel. Ich stehe . . .

Note also these uses of **an, auf,** and **in!** You are already familiar with most of them:

Die Stadt liegt **am** Rhein/**an der** Donau.	*The city is on the Rhine/on the Danube.*
Sie spielen **auf der** Straße.	*They're playing in the street.*
Sie leben **in** Deutschland/**in der** Schweiz.	*They live in Germany/in Switzerland.*
Sie leben **in** Stuttgart/**im** Süden.	*They live in Stuttgart/in the South.*
Sie wohnen **in der** Schillerstraße.	*They live on Schiller Street.*
Sie wohnen **im** Parterre/**im** ersten Stock.	*They live on the first/second floor.*

- With feminine or plural names of countries, **in** is used rather than **nach** to express *to.*

  Wir fahren **in die Schweiz/in die Bundesrepublik.**

  Wir fahren **in die USA/in die Vereinigten Staaten.**

  BUT: Wir fahren **nach Österreich/nach Deutschland.**

The preposition **zu** *is introduced in Chapter 3.*

- If you plan to see a film or play, or to attend a church service, **in** must be used; **zu** implies going *in the direction of, up to,* BUT NOT *into a place.*

Wir gehen **zum Kino.**	*(just to look outside and see what's playing, or to meet somebody there)*
Wir gehen **ins Kino.**	*(to go inside and see a movie)*

Übungen

A. Sagen Sie es noch einmal! (*Replace the nouns following the prepositions with the words suggested.*)

A: Remind students that most nouns end in **-n** in the dative plural.

BEISPIEL: Der Bleistift liegt unter dem Papier. (Jacke)
Der Bleistift liegt unter der Jacke.

1. Die Post ist neben der Bank. (Bahnhof, Kino, Apotheke)
2. Ursula kommt in die Wohnung. (Küche, Esszimmer, Garten)
3. Die Mäntel liegen auf dem Bett. (Sofa, Kommode, Stühle)
4. Mein Schlafzimmer ist über der Küche. (Wohnzimmer, Garage, Bad)
5. Willi legt den Pullover auf die Kommode. (Bett, Schreibtisch, Sessel)

B. Wo bekommt man das? (*Where can you get the following items? Start with the underlined phrase. Repeat the information by saying where each of the people below are going to get those items.*)

BEISPIEL: Frau Müller braucht etwas Butter und Käse. (Supermarkt)
Butter und Käse bekommt man im Supermarkt.
Frau Müller geht in den Supermarkt.

1. Silvia sucht ein paar Bücher. (Bibliothek)
2. Oliver will ein paar CDs. (Kaufhaus)
3. Conni braucht Parfüm (*perfume*) und Shampoo. (Drogerie)
4. Andreas braucht Medizin. (Apotheke)
5. Lisa sucht ein paar Schuhe. (Schuhgeschäft)
6. Steffen hat viele Bücher, aber keine Regale. (Möbelgeschäft)
7. Oma Schütz ist müde vom Einkaufen und möchte eine Tasse Kaffee und Kuchen. (Café)

Optional practice: **Fragen an die Studenten:** 1. Wo schläft man? 2. Wo kocht man? 3. Wohin tut man Lebensmittel wie Milch, Butter und Käse? 4. Wo essen Sie gewöhnlich? 5. Wo machen Sie ihre Hausaufgaben? 6. Wo sitzen Sie gewöhnlich mit Ihren Freunden?

C. Wo sind Sie wann? (*Report where you are at certain times. You may use the locations in the last column or come up with ideas of your own.*)

BEISPIEL: Morgens   **Morgens bin ich gewöhnlich in der Bibliothek.**

1	2	3	4	5
morgens	fahren	gern	an	Badewanne (*f.*)
mittags	gehen	gemütlich	auf	Berge
abends	liegen	gewöhnlich	in	Bett
am Wochenende	sein	manchmal	vor	Bibliothek
(über)morgen	sitzen	nicht		Computer (*m.*)
im Sommer . . .	sprechen	oft		Fernseher
wenn ich Hunger habe	. . .	stundenlang		Garten
wenn ich faul (*lazy*) bin				Sofa
wenn ich lernen muss				Kühlschrank
wenn ich baden will				Swimmingpool
wenn ich müde bin				Kino
wenn ich keine Zeit habe				Vorlesung(en) . . .

D. Wieder zu Hause (*After you and your family come home from a camping trip, your mother has many questions. Form her questions with **wo** or **wohin**!*)

BEISPIEL: Vater ist in der Garage.   **Wo ist Vater?**
Jochen geht in den Garten.   **Wohin geht Jochen?**

D: 1. Wo ist das Handy? 2. Wo liegt der Rucksack? 3. Wohin legt Marita die Schlafsäcke? 4. Wohin hängt Gabi den Mantel? 5. Wo sind die Regenmäntel? 6. Wo liegen die Jacken? 7. Wohin haben Gabi und Günther die Lebensmittel gebracht? 8. Wohin hat Günther die Milch gestellt? 9. Wo hat Gabi den Schuh gefunden? 10. Wo liegt der Hund?

1. Das Handy ist im Auto.
2. Der Rucksack (*backpack*) liegt im Flur.
3. Marita legt die Schlafsäcke (*sleeping bags*) aufs Bett.
4. Gabi hängt den Mantel über den Stuhl.
5. Die Regenmäntel sind auf dem Balkon.
6. Die Jacken liegen in der Ecke.
7. Gabi und Günther haben die Lebensmittel in die Küche gebracht.
8. Günther hat die Milch in den Kühlschrank gestellt.
9. Gabi hat den Schuh unter dem Baum gefunden.
10. Der Hund liegt auf dem Sofa.

E. Ein paar Fragen, bevor Sie gehen! *(Before you leave for a vacation, answer the questions your house sitter is asking you.)*

BEISPIEL: Wo ist das Telefon? (an / Wand)
             An der Wand!

1. Wo darf ich schlafen? (auf / Sofa; in / Arbeitszimmer)
2. Wohin soll ich meine Kleider hängen? (in / Schrank; an / Wand; über / Stuhl)
3. Wo gibt es ein Lebensmittelgeschäft? (an / Ecke; neben / Bank; zwischen / Apotheke und Café)
4. Wo können die Kinder spielen? (hinter / Haus; unter / Baum; auf / Spielplatz)
5. Wohin gehen sie gern? (in / Park; an / Fluss; in / Kino)
6. Wohin soll ich die Katze tun? (vor / Tür *[outside]*; in / Garten; auf / Balkon; in / Garage)

F. Wir bekommen Besuch. *(Tell what you still have to do; fill in the blanks with the correct form of the definite article. Use contractions where possible.)*

1. Die Gläser sind _in der_ Küche. *(in the)*   2. Ich muss die Gläser _ins_ Wohnzimmer bringen und sie _auf den_ Tisch stellen. *(into the, on the)*   3. Der Wein ist noch _im_ Keller. *(in the)*   4. Wir müssen die Teller _neben die_ Gläser stellen. *(next to the)*   5. Ich muss _in die_ Küche gehen und die Wurst und den Käse _auf den_ Teller *(sg.)* legen. *(into the, on the)*   6. Haben wir Blumen _im_ Garten? *(in the)*   7. Wir stellen die Blumen _auf das_ Tischchen *(sg.)* _vorm_ Sofa. *(on the, in front of the)*   8. Sind die Kerzen _im_ Schrank? *(in the)*   9. Nein, sie stehen _auf der_ Kommode. *(on the)*

G. Bei Lotte

1. **Wohin sollen wir das stellen?** *(Lotte is moving into a new house. She is telling the movers where they are supposed to put things.)*

    BEISPIEL: Schreibtisch / an / Wand
                Stellen Sie den Schreibtisch an die Wand!

    a. Computer *(m.)* / auf / Schreibtisch
    b. Schrank / in / Ecke
    c. Lampe / neben / Bett
    d. Stuhl / an / Tisch
    e. Regal / unter / Uhr
    f. Bild / auf / Regal
    g. Nachttisch / vor / Fenster
    h. Bett / zwischen / Tür / und / Fenster

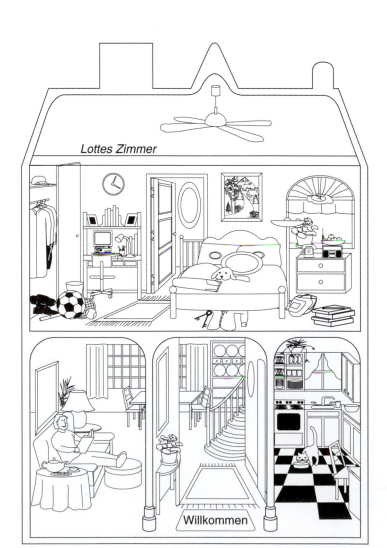

2. **Was ist wo?** *(Make 10 statements about the picture of Lotte's house, telling where things are standing, lying, or hanging.)*

    BEISPIEL: Der Schreibtisch steht an der Wand.

3. **Wo sind nur meine die Schlüssel?** *(Lotte has lost her keys. Looking at the drawing of the house, ask her about specific places she may have put them. Lotte will answer each question negatively until finally you guess right. Enact this scene with a partner. Ask at least five questions using two-way prepositions.)*

    BEISPIEL: Hast du sie auf den Schreibtisch gelegt?
                Nein, sie liegen nicht auf dem Schreibtisch.

H. Mensch, wo ist mein Handy (*cell phone*)? (*Your partner can't find his/her cell phone. Looking at the drawing of Lotte's home or just simply around the classroom, ask him/her about specific places where it might have been put. Your partner will answer each question negatively until finally you guess right. Ask at least five questions using two-way prepositions.*)

> **BEISPIEL:**   Hast du es neben die Blumen im Flur gelegt?
> **Nein, es liegt nicht neben den Blumen im Flur.**

I. Mein Zimmer / meine Wohnung / mein Studentenheim
(*Describe your room, apartment, or dorm in 8–10 sentences. Use a two-way preposition to each sentence.*)

Fokus — *Friedensreich Hundertwasser*

Friedrich Stowasser, called Friedensreich Hundertwasser (1928–2000), is a well-known Austrian painter, graphic artist, and architect. In his ecologically oriented writings, he vehemently opposes contemporary architecture, which he describes as "an aesthetic void" "a desert of uniformity," and "criminal sterility." Since no straight lines exist in nature, he also rejects them in his art, referring to them as "something cowardly drawn with a ruler, without thought or feeling." His architecture echoes that conviction, as exemplified by the Hundertwasser House in Vienna and the Hundertwasser Church in Bärnbach near Graz, whose exterior is uneven and constructed of various materials to symbolize the vicissitudes of life. Its processional path leads through multiple gates that bear a variety of symbols from other religions as a mark of respect.
(See www.hundertwasserhaus.at)

Hundertwasser-Haus in Wien

6.2 Imperatives

You are already familiar with the FORMAL IMPERATIVE which addresses one individual or several people. You know that the verb is followed by the pronoun **Sie:**

> Herr Schmidt, **lesen Sie** das bitte!
>
> Herr und Frau Müller, **kommen Sie** später wieder!

1. The FAMILIAR IMPERATIVE has two forms: one for the singular and one for the plural.

   a. The singular usually corresponds to the **du**-form of the verb WITHOUT the pronoun **du** and WITHOUT the **-st** ending:

du schreibst	du tust	du antwortest	du fährst	du nimmst	du isst	du liest
Schreib!	**Tu!**	**Antworte!**	**Fahr!**	**Nimm!**	**Iss!**	**Lies!**

> *NOTE*:   **lesen** and **essen** retain the **s** or **ss** of the verb stem. **Lies! Iss!**
>
> • Verbs ending in **-d, -t, -ig,** or in certain other consonant combinations USUALLY have an **-e** ending in the **du**-form.
>   **Finde** es! **Antworte** ihm! **Entschuldige** bitte! **Öffne** die Tür!

The complete rule is: if the stem ends in **-m** or **-n** preceded by a consonant other than **-l-** and **-r-**, the imperative of the **du**-form ends in **-e.**

- Verbs with vowel changes from **a > ä** in the present singular DO NOT make this change in the imperative. Verbs that change from **e > i(e)** do retain this change, however.

    Fahr langsam! **Lauf** schnell!

    Nimm das! **Iss** nicht so viel! **Sprich** Deutsch! **Lies** laut! **Sieh** mal!

b. The plural corresponds to the **ihr**-form of the verb WITHOUT the pronoun **ihr**.

Note that with the spelling reform, the sharp **s**-sound after a short vowel is spelled **ss** (instead of **ß**).

ihr schreibt	ihr tut	ihr antwortet	ihr fahrt	ihr nehmt	ihr esst	ihr lest
Schreibt!	**Tut!**	**Antwortet!**	**Fahrt!**	**Nehmt!**	**Esst!**	**Lest!**

Legt den Teppich vors Sofa!   *Put the carpet in front of the couch.*

Stellt die Kommode an die Wand!   *Put the dresser against the wall.*

Hängt das Bild neben die Tür!   *Hang the picture next to the door.*

2. English imperatives beginning with *Let's . . .* are expressed in German as follows:

    Sprechen wir Deutsch!   *Let's speak German.*

    Gehen wir nach Hause!   *Let's go home.*

3. Here is a summary chart of the imperative.

In case questions arise, the imperative of **sein** and **werden** are: **Seien Sie! Seid! Sei! / Werden Sie! Werdet! Werde!**

An INFINITIVE can also be used as an imperative, especially on signs: **Langsam fahren! Nicht mit dem Fahrer sprechen!**

Schreiben Sie!	Schreib!	Schreibt!	Schreiben wir!
Antworten Sie!	Antworte!	Antwortet!	Antworten wir!
Fahren Sie!	**Fahr!**	Fahrt!	Fahren wir!
Nehmen Sie!	**Nimm!**	Nehmt!	Nehmen wir!
Essen Sie!	**Iss!**	Esst!	Essen wir!
Lesen Sie!	**Lies!**	Lest!	Lesen wir!

Frau Schmidt,   **schreiben Sie** mir!

Helga,   **schreib** mir!

Kinder,   **schreibt** mir!

Schreiben wir Lisa!

NOTE: The German imperative is usually followed by an EXCLAMATION POINT.

Übungen

J. Geben Sie den Imperativ! *(First form the singular and then the plural familiar.)*

    BEISPIEL: Bleiben Sie bitte!
    Bleib bitte!
    Bleibt bitte!

1. Fragen Sie ihn!
2. Entschuldigen Sie bitte!
3. Bitte helfen Sie uns!
4. Zeigen Sie uns den Weg!
5. Geben Sie mir die Landkarte!
6. Fahren Sie immer geradeaus!
7. Wiederholen Sie das bitte!
8. Halten Sie da drüben!
9. Hören Sie mal!
10. Schlafen Sie gut!
11. Essen Sie einen Apfel!
12. Trinken Sie eine Cola!

K. Geben Sie Befehle! *(Form formal and familiar commands, using the phrases below.)*

> BEISPIEL: an die Tafel gehen   **Gehen Sie an die Tafel!**
> **Geh an die Tafel!**
> **Geht an die Tafel!**

1. die Kreide nehmen 2. ein Wort auf Deutsch schreiben 3. von 1 bis 10 zählen
4. wieder an den Platz gehen 5. das Deutschbuch öffnen 6. auf Seite 150 lesen
7. mit dem Nachbarn auf Deutsch sprechen 8. mir einen Kuli geben 9. nach Hause
gehen 10. das nicht tun

K: Additional practice: bitte kommen, jetzt beginnen, Golf spielen, schön feiern, zusammen singen, auch tanzen, nicht so schnell laufen, im See baden, schwimmen gehen, das wieder finden, auf Deutsch antworten, nicht so viel arbeiten, die Wohnung mieten, ihm danken, den Dom besichtigen, die Suppe empfehlen, mal sehen, nicht so viel essen

L. Was tun? *(Decide with your friend what to do with the rest of the day.)*

> BEISPIEL: zu Hause bleiben   **Bleiben wir zu Hause!**

1. in die Stadt gehen 2. an den See fahren 3. durch die Geschäfte bummeln 4. eine
Pizza essen 5. das Schloss besichtigen 6. ins Kino gehen

M. Noch mehr Befehle! *(Address three commands to each of the following below.)*

> BEISPIEL: an einen Touristen   **Fahren Sie mit dem Bus!**
> **Gehen Sie immer geradeaus!**
> **Fragen Sie dort noch einmal!**

1. an einen Taxifahrer/eine Taxifahrerin
2. an einen Kellner/eine Kellnerin
3. an ein paar Freunde oder Klassenkameraden *(classmates)*
4. an einen Bruder/eine Schwester
5. an ein paar Kinder

M: These individual commands will vary, of course, from student to student.

N. Bitte tue, was ich sage! *(Ask your partner to do what you say. Give each other 5–10 different classroom commands that are to be followed, e.g., opening the book at a certain page, reading something fast or slowly, etc.)*

N: We already did something similar at the end of the *Schritte,* but now students understand what they only recognized as "useful classroom instructions" before. Also, they can now use the **du-** and **ihr-** forms of the imperative.

6.3 *Wissen* and *kennen*

In German, two verbs correspond to the English to *know.*

kennen, gekannt	*to know (to be acquainted with a person or thing)*
wissen, gewusst	*to know a fact (the fact is often expressed in a subordinate clause)*

Remind students not to confuse the forms of **kennen** and **können.**

Whereas **kennen** is regular in the present tense, the forms of **wissen** are very similar to the forms of the modals.

ich	weiß
du	weißt
er	weiß
wir	wissen
ihr	wisst
sie	wissen

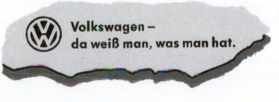

Ich **kenne** das Buch.	BUT	Ich **weiß, dass** es gut ist.
Ich **kenne** den Lehrer.	BUT	Ich **weiß, dass** er aus Salzburg ist.
		Ich **weiß** seine Telefonnummer.

Übungen

O. Kennen oder wissen? *(Fill in the appropriate forms.)*

ANGELIKA	Entschuldigen Sie! __Wissen__ Sie, wo die Wipplinger Straße ist?
DAME	Nein. Ich __kenne__ Wien gut, aber das __weiß__ ich nicht.
MICHAEL	Danke! Du, Angelika, __weißt__ du, wie spät es ist?
ANGELIKA	Nein, aber ich __weiß__, dass ich Hunger habe.
MICHAEL	Hallo, Holger und Sabine! Sagt mal, __kennt__ ihr Angelika?
SABINE	Ja, natürlich.
MICHAEL	Wir haben Hunger. __Wisst__ ihr, wo es hier ein Restaurant gibt?
HOLGER	Ja, da drüben ist die „Bastei Beisl". Wir __kennen__ es nicht, aber wir __wissen__, dass es gut sein soll.
MICHAEL	__Wisst__ ihr was? Gehen wir essen!

P. Was weißt du und wen kennst du? *(Ask your partner 10 questions about certain people or certain things, which he/she will answer in a complete German sentence. Include also questions in the present perfect.)*

BEISPIEL:	Kennst du den Herrn da?	**Natürlich kenne ich ihn.**
	Weißt du, dass er gestern Geburtstag gehabt hat?	**Nein, das habe ich nicht gewusst.**

Fokus — *Public Transportation and City Life*

Visitors from America are often astounded at the efficient and far-reaching public transportation networks in German cities. Most large cities have extensive subway lines **(U-Bahn-Linien)** that connect with suburban commuter trains **(S-Bahn)**. Bikes are usually permitted on board during off-peak hours. Trains and stations are generally cleaner and safer than those in the United States.

German urban transport operates on the honor system. Passengers are required to validate their own tickets **(Fahrkarten entwerten)** by inserting them into machines that stamp the time and date. People who evade paying **(Schwarzfahrer)** have to reckon with random checks by plainclothes employees and stiff fines. Buses and streetcars complement the subway system, making for dense networks that reach outlying suburbs. At each stop, a schedule is posted, and buses usually arrive within a few minutes of the given time. Most large cities also have night buses **(Nachtbusse)**, which run on special routes all night long.

All cities have some form of public transportation, usually heavily subsidized in an effort to limit pollution and congestion in city centers. Monthly and yearly tickets are available with reduced rates for commuters, students, and senior citizens.

Zusammenfassung

Q. Hoppla, wo soll das hin? Umzug *(Moving. You and a friend—your partner—are moving into new apartments right next to each other and are helping each other move. Both apartments are shown below. First, your partner will tell you where to put everything. He/she should be as specific as possible and keep track of his/her directions. Write the name or abbreviation of each item into the spot where it should go, or draw it in. Then tell your partner where to put your belongings.)*

MÖBEL: Stuhl, Schreibtisch, Bücher, Computer, Telefon, Lampe, Regal, Fernseher, Radio, Kühlschrank, Kommode, Nachttisch, Schrank, Sessel, Bild, Tisch, Pflanze *(f., plant)*, Spiegel *(m., mirror)* usw.

1. **Wohin soll das?**

BEISPIEL:	S1	Wohin soll der Teppich?
	S2	Leg den Teppich ins Wohnzimmer vors Sofa!
	S1	Und die Lampe?
	S2	Stell die Lampe rechts neben das Sofa!

2. **Ist alles da, wo es sein soll?** *(When you are through with furnishing both apartments, each partner checks with the other whether directions have been followed for each of the respective apartments.)*

    BEISPIEL: **S1** Liegt der Teppich im Wohnzimmer vorm Sofa?
                S2 Ja, ich habe den Teppich vors Sofa gelegt.
                S1 Steht die Lampe rechts neben dem Sofa?
                S2 Ja, ich habe die Lampe rechts neben das Sofa gestellt.
                    (OR: Nein, ich habe die Lampe links neben das Sofa gestellt.)

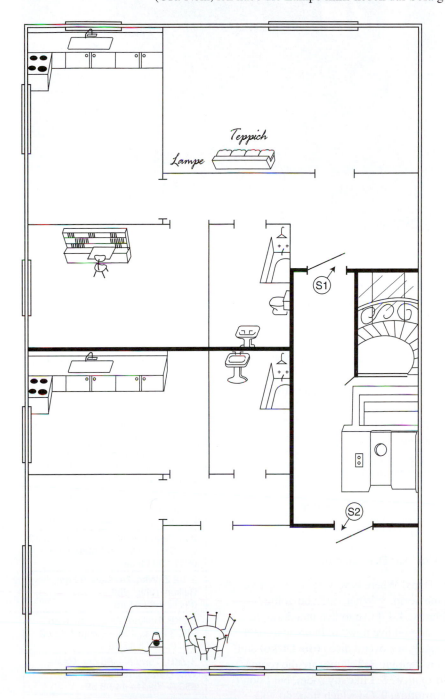

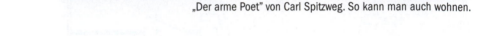

„Der arme Poet" von Carl Spitzweg. So kann man auch wohnen.

You could ask the students to describe how this "poor poet" lives or ask questions: 1. Wie gefällt Ihnen das Zimmer? 2. Was tut der Poet im Bett? 3. Was liegt neben dem Bett? 4. Warum hat er einen Regenschirm *(umbrella)* überm Bett? Was glauben Sie? 5. Wo ist die Wohnung? 6. Möchten Sie als Student so eine Wohnung mieten?

R. Zu vermieten *(For rent. Read the rental ads below, then choose one that is "yours." Your partner will inquire about it. Answer his / her questions, based on the ad. If some of the information is not given in the ad, make it up. Reverse roles.)*

S1   Ich habe gelesen, dass Sie eine Wohnung zu vermieten haben. Wo ist die Wohnung?
S2   . . .
S1   Können Sie mir die Wohnung etwas beschreiben *(describe)*?
S2   Ja, gern. Sie hat . . .
S1   Gibt es auch . . . ?
S2   . . .
S1   Wie weit ist es zu . . . ?
S2   . . .
S1   Und was kostet die Wohnung?
S2   . . .

R: In case students ask: **Whg = Wohnung, qm = Quadratmeter** *(square meter)* **teilmöbliert** *(partly furnished),* **ruhig** *(quiet),* **WC = Wasserklosett** *(toilet),* **ZKB = Zimmer Küche Bad, Bauernhof** *(farm),* **pro Woche** *(per week)*

VERMIETUNGEN
1-Zi-Whg in Uninähe, 25 qm, möbl., schön u. hell, Dusche/WC, 200,— warm. 0941 / 70 63 22
1-Zi-Neubauwhg an Student/in, ca. 29 qm, teilmöbl., zentral, 250,— kalt, ab 1.11.02. 0941 / 4 28 62
2 Zi-Dachgeschoss, Altstadt, ca. 50 qm, 315,— kalt, ab Februar '03. 0941 / 99 06 86
2 1/2 Zi-Whg, Neubau, 60 qm, Balkon, ruhig, 280,—. 0941 / 4 63 61 45
3-ZKB, Balkon, 72 qm, auch an WG 3 Pers., 425,—, zum 1.12.02 frei. 0941 / 5 17 76
3-ZKB, Terrasse, 98 qm, Gäste-WC, Garage, Keller, Kaltmiete 550,—. 0941 / 44 98 69
Bungalow, 120 qm, 4-ZKB, Garten, Terrasse, Sauna, 750,—. 0941 / 4 70 04
2-Zi-Whg auf Bauernhof, 50 qm, Garten, Tiere kein Problem, gegen 10 Stunden Arbeit pro Woche. 0941 / 57 65 98

S. An der Uni. Auf Deutsch bitte!

1. Hello, Hans! Where have you been? 2. I've been in the dorm. 3. Where are you going?—To the library. 4. I'd like to live in a dorm, too. 5. Where do you live now? 6. In an apartment. Unfortunately it's over a disco **(die Disko)** and next to a restaurant. 7. Tell me, are the rooms in the dorm nice? 8. I like my room, but I don't like the furniture. 9. On which floor do you live?—On the third floor. 10. Do you know how much it costs?—180 Euro a month. 11. There's Rico. 12. Who's that? From where am I supposed to know him? (Where am I supposed to know him from?) 13. I didn't know that you don't know him. 14. Let's say hello.

S: 1. Hallo, Hans! Wo bist du gewesen? 2. Ich bin im Studentenheim gewesen. 3. Wohin gehst du? – in die / zur Bibliothek. 4. Ich möchte auch in einem Studentenheim wohnen. 5. Wo wohnst du jetzt? 6. In einer Wohnung. Leider ist sie über einer Disko und neben einem Restaurant. 7. Sag mal / Sag mir, sind die Zimmer im Studentenheim schön? 8. Mein Zimmer gefällt mir, aber die Möbel gefallen mir nicht. 9. In welchem Stock wohnst du? – Im 2. Stock. 10. Weißt du, wie viel es kostet? – 180 Euro im Monat. 11. Da ist Rico. 12. Wer ist das? Woher soll ich ihn kennen? 13. Ich habe nicht gewusst, dass du ihn nicht kennst. 14. Sagen wir „Hallo" / „Guten Tag"!

Einblicke

Lesestrategie: Comparison and Contrast

This passage compares life in a city with life in the country. As you read the passage, make note of the arguments for and against each type of living. Try to determine whether the text seems to favor one way of life over the other.

Wortschatz 2

das Reihenhaus, ⸚er	*townhouse*
die Arbeit	*work*
die Eigentumswohnung, -en	*condo*
am Abend	*in the evening*
am Tag	*during the day*
aufs Land / auf dem Land(e)	*in(to) the country(side)*
ausgezeichnet	*excellent*
außerdem	*besides (adverb)*
fast	*almost*
leicht	*easy, easily (lit. light)*
schwer	*hard, difficult (lit. heavy)*
mitten in (+ *acc. / dat.*)	*in the middle of*
noch nicht	*not yet*
trotzdem	*nevertheless, in spite of that*
bauen	*to build*
leben[1]	*to live*
lieben	*to love*
sparen	*to save (money, time)*

[1] Note the difference between **leben** (*to live, literally: to be alive*) and **wohnen** (*to reside*): Dürer hat in Nürnberg **gelebt**. Er **lebt** nicht mehr. Er hat in dem Haus da drüben **gewohnt**.

Vor dem Lesen

A. **Blick auf** *(glance at)* **den Marktplatz** *(How many sentences can you and your partner form about the typical city scene on p. 170, using the two-way prepositions* in, auf, unter, über, vor, hinter, an, neben, zwischen? *Which examples include the accusative and which the dative? Compare your sentences with those of your fellow students.)*

B. **Fragen**

1. Leben die meisten Leute *(most people)* hier in Wohnungen oder in Häusern mit Garten? 2. Wo ist Bauland *(building lot[s])* teuer? Wissen Sie, wo es nicht so teuer ist? 3. Was für öffentliche Verkehrsmittel *(public transportation)* gibt es hier? 4. Wie kommen die meisten Leute zur Arbeit? Wie kommen Sie zur Uni? Braucht man hier unbedingt *(necessarily)* ein Auto? 5. Gibt es hier Schlafstädte *(bedroom communities)*, von wo die Leute morgens in die Stadt und abends wieder nach Hause fahren? 6. Wohin gehen oder fahren die Leute hier am Wochenende?

C. **Was ist das?**

der Arbeitsplatz, Biergarten, Clown, Dialekt, Münchner, Musiker, Spielplatz, Stadtpark, Wanderweg; das Boot, Feld, Konsulat; die Energie, Mietwohnung, Wirklichkeit; frei, idyllisch, pünktlich; Ball spielen, eine Pause machen, picknicken

Auf dem Marktplatz

CD 3, Track 12

Schaffen, sparen, Häuschen bauen

saying / Swabia / standard German

work hard

most

little

dream of

dream

to the outskirts / move

out(side)

commute back and forth / money

sidewalks

with them

goes window-shopping

there's something going on / sidewalk
   artists

„Schaffe, spare, Häusle baue" ist ein Spruch° aus Schwaben°. Auf Hochdeutsch° heißt es „Schaffen°, sparen, Häuschen bauen." Der Spruch aus Schwaben ist nicht nur typisch für die Schwaben, sondern für die meisten° Deutschen, Österreicher und Schweizer.

In den drei Ländern leben viele Menschen, aber es gibt nur wenig° Land. Die meisten wohnen in Wohnungen und träumen von° einem Haus mit Garten. Für viele bleibt das aber nur ein Traum°, denn in den Städten ist Bauland sehr teuer. Es gibt auch nicht genug Bauland, weil man nicht überall bauen darf.

Oft muss man an den Stadtrand° oder aufs Land ziehen°, wo mehr Platz ist und wo Land noch nicht so teuer ist. Aber nicht alle möchten so weit draußen° wohnen und stundenlang hin- und herpendeln°. Das kostet Energie, Zeit und Geld°. Abends kommt man auch nicht so leicht ins Kino oder ins Theater. Das Leben auf dem Land ist oft idyllisch, aber nicht immer sehr bequem.

In der Stadt kann man eigentlich sehr gut leben. Die Wohnungen sind oft groß und schön. Man braucht nicht unbedingt ein Auto, weil alles in der Nähe liegt. Fast überall gibt es Bürgersteige° und Fahrradwege, und die öffentlichen Verkehrsmittel sind ausgezeichnet. Die Busse kommen relativ oft und pünktlich. In Großstädten gibt es auch Straßenbahnen, U-Bahnen und S-Bahnen. Damit° können Sie nicht nur aus der Stadt oder durch die Stadt, sondern auch mitten ins Zentrum, in die Fußgängerzone fahren, wo die Leute am Tag einkaufen und am Abend gern bummeln gehen. Man sieht ein bisschen in die Schaufenster° und geht vielleicht in eine Bar oder ein Café. Auf den Straßen ist im Sommer fast immer etwas los°. Es gibt Straßenkünstler°, Musiker und Clowns.

Idyll auf dem Land. Haus mit Strohdach *(thatched roof)* in Schleswig-Holstein

Wenn man in der Stadt wohnt, kann man aber auch leicht aufs Land fahren. Viele tun das gern und oft. Am Wochenende fährt man gern einmal an die See° oder in die Berge. *ocean* Überall zwischen Wäldern° und Feldern findet man Wanderwege und Fahrradwege. Dort *woods* findet man auch leicht ein Restaurant, wo man gemütlich Pause machen kann.

Man muss aber nicht unbedingt aufs Land fahren, wenn man ins Grüne° will. Fast alle *out into nature* Städte, ob groß oder klein, haben Stadtparks. Die Münchner z.B. lieben ihren Englischen Garten. Dort gibt es nicht nur Wanderwege, sondern auch Spielplätze und Bänke, Biergärten, Wiesen° zum Picknicken und zum Ballspielen und einen See mit Bootchen. *meadows*

Die meisten leben eigentlich gern in der Stadt, entweder in einer Eigentumswohnung oder einer Mietwohnung. In der Stadt gibt es viel zu sehen und zu tun. Alles ist ziemlich nah, nicht nur der Arbeitsplatz, die Geschäfte und die Schulen, sondern auch die Theater, Kinos, Museen und Parks. Viele träumen trotzdem von einem Haus mit Garten. Sie wissen, dass sie schwer arbeiten und sparen müssen, wenn der Traum Wirklichkeit werden soll. Und das tun auch viele.

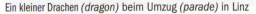

Ein kleiner Drachen *(dragon)* beim Umzug *(parade)* in Linz

Im Münchner Hofgarten

Nach dem Lesen

Optional activity: **Was ist das?**
1. Bauland 2. eine Wohnung 3. ein Bürger-steig 4. öffentliche Verkehrsmittel 5. eine Fußgängerzone 6. ein Straßenkünstler 7. die Innenstadt 8. ein Häuschen im Grünen

A. Richtig oder falsch? Wenn falsch, sagen Sie warum!

  _r_   1. In Deutschland, in Österreich und in der Schweiz gibt es nicht viel Bauland, besonders nicht in den Städten.

  _f_   2. Die meisten Leute dort wohnen in einem Haus mit Garten.

  _r_   3. Auf dem Land ist Bauland nicht so teuer wie in der Stadt.

  _f_   4. Das Leben auf dem Land ist sehr bequem.

  _f_   5. In allen Städten gibt es Straßenbahnen, eine U-Bahn und eine S-Bahn.

  _r_   6. Mit den öffentlichen Verkehrsmitteln kann man durch die Stadt fahren.

  _f_   7. Überall in Wäldern und Feldern gibt es Fahrradwege und Fußgängerzonen.

  _r_   8. In der Fußgängerzone kann man am Tag einkaufen, am Abend bummeln gehen und manchmal Musik hören.

  _f_   9. Im amerikanischen Konsulat in München kann man picknicken.

  _r_ 10. Wenn man ein Haus kaufen oder bauen möchte, muss man schwer arbeiten und lange sparen.

B: 1. in einer 2. In (den) 3. an den, aufs 4. Auf den 5. an der 6. in die 7. auf dem 8. in der, in der 9. nach der, ins 10. Im

B. Haus oder Wohnung? *(Fill in the appropriate two-way prepositions and articles. Use contractions where possible.)*

1. Die meisten Deutschen wohnen _____ Wohnung. 2. _____ Städten ist Bauland sehr teuer. 3. Der Traum vom Häuschen mit Garten hat viele _____ Stadtrand *(out-skirts, sg. m.)* oder ____ Land gebracht. 4. _____ Feldern stehen jetzt Reihenhäuser. 5. Die Reihenhäuser sind manchmal direkt _____ Straße. 6. Morgens fahren viele _____ Stadt. 7. Das Leben _____ Land kann unbequem sein. 8. Viele bleiben _____ Stadt, weil dort alles _____ Nähe ist. 9. _____ Arbeit fahren sie dann noch einmal ___ Zentrum *(n.)* 10. ____ Zentrum ist fast immer etwas los.

C. In der Großstadt *(You have never been to Munich before. Ask questions about the city, using **wo** or **wohin.**)*

> **BEISPIEL:**   <u>In Großstädten</u> gibt es eine U-Bahn.
>   **Wo gibt es eine U-Bahn?**

1. Mit der U-Bahn kann man <u>mitten in die Fußgängerzone</u> fahren.
2. <u>Dort</u> kann man immer schön bummeln.
3. Abends kann man <u>ins Kino</u> gehen.
4. Wenn man ins Grüne will, geht man <u>in den Park.</u>
5. <u>Dort</u> gibt es überall Wege und Bänke.

You could point out on a map where dialects such as **Schwäbisch, Bairisch, Fränkisch, Thüringisch, Sächsisch, Mecklenburgisch,** or **Friesisch** are spoken.

Fokus — *High German and Dialects*

"Joden Dach, wie jeit es Ihne?" sagt der Kölner.

"Tachchen, wie jeht et Ihnen?" sagt der Berliner.

"Moin, moin, wie geiht Di dat?" sagt der Hamburger.

"Griaß Gott, wia geht's Eana?" sagt der Bayer.

Germany has numerous dialects. These are much older than the standard "High German" (**Hochdeutsch**) that you hear nearly everywhere today. In some regions, there are movements to keep regional dialects alive. North German Radio, for example, broadcasts short daily sermons in Low German (**Plattdeutsch**), whereas some Bavarian newspapers include a regular feature in Bavarian. Some dialects are staging a comeback in song, literature, and theater. Children always learn the dialect first—automatically. However, they also need to master standard German so as not to be at a disadvantage in school and on the job market. "High German" is understood everywhere in Germany.

D. *Kennen* oder *wissen?*

1. <u>Kennen</u> Sie den Spruch „Schaffe, spare, Häusle baue"?
2. <u>Wissen</u> Sie, wie viele Leute in Deutschland auf dem Land leben?
3. <u>Kennen</u> Sie den Englischen Garten?
4. <u>Wisst</u> ihr, dass es überall Fahrradwege gibt?
5. Ich habe nicht <u>gewusst</u>, dass es in der Stadt so viele Fußgängerwege gibt.
6. <u>Kennst</u> du Herrn Jakob? Nein, aber Hans <u>kennt</u> ihn.
7. <u>Weißt</u> du, dass er mit seinen 80 Jahren immer noch viel wandert?

C: 1. Wohin kann man mit der U-Bahn fahren? 2. Wo kann man schön bummeln? 3. Wohin kann man abends gehen? 4. Wohin geht man, wenn man ins Grüne will? 5. Wo gibt es überall Wege und Bänke?

E. Was ist typisch auf dem Land und in der Stadt? *(Work with two or three other students. Some groups list the advantages of city life and the disadvantages of country life, while the others do the reverse. Then compare; which group has the more convincing arguments?)*

Optional tongue twister (**Zungenbrecher):** Wer nichts weiß und weiß, dass er nichts weiß, weiß mehr als der, der *(the one who)* nichts weiß und nicht weiß, dass er nichts weiß.

viel Platz · Busse · Wälder · Gockelhahn *(rooster)* · alles in der Nähe · Fußgängerzonen · S-Bahn · viele Menschen · Theater · Imbissbuden · Kinos · Bürgersteige · Schaufensterbummeln · Geschäfte · Felder · Ruhe *(quiet)* · Straßenkünstler · Kühe *(cows)* · Wiesen · Straßenbahn · Pferde *(horses)* · viel Verkehr · wandern · Bauernhof *(farm)* · einkaufen · U-Bahn

F. Wo möchten Sie wohnen, und warum?

1. **Schreiben Sie!** Hier wohne ich gern. *(Write three to four sentences describing where you would like to live and why. Include one phrase or word from each group below.)*

   BEISPIEL: Ich möchte in einem Reihenhaus mitten in San Franzisko wohnen. Da komme ich leicht zur Arbeit und zum Ozean. Man braucht nicht unbedingt ein Auto.

1	2
in einer WG	mitten in . . .
in einer (Miet)wohnung	in der Nähe von . . .
in einer Eigentumswohnung	am Stadtrand von . . .
in einem Reihenhaus	im . . . Stock
in einem Haus mit Garten	auf dem Land . . .

2. **Meinungsumfrage** *(Opinion poll. Ask each other about your lifestyle preferences now and later. Give reasons why. Your instructor then polls the entire class to determine what choices have been made.)*

   BEISPIEL: S1 Wo möchtet ihr jetzt wohnen, in der Stadt oder auf dem Land?
   S2 Ich möchte [auf dem Land] wohnen, weil . . .
   S3 [Ich auch.]
   S1 Und wenn ihr Kinder habt?
   S2 Dann möchte ich [auch dort wohnen, weil es ruhig ist.]
   S1 Und wenn ihr alt seid?
   S3 [Dann vielleicht in der Stadt.]

Knochenhauer Amtshaus

G. Kurzgespräche *(Together with your partner, prepare one of the following brief dialogues. Then present it to the class.)*

1. **Einladung zum Mittagessen**

   You have been invited to a classmate's house for dinner, but you are quite late. You introduce yourself to his/her mother, who asks you to come in (**herein**). You apologize repeatedly for being so late, while she maintains it doesn't matter. When you hand her the flowers you have brought, she thanks you and says that dinner is ready.

2. **Wo ist das Knochenhauer Amtshaus?**

   You are visiting Hildesheim and want to see the well-known *Knochenhauer Amtshaus,* a 16th-century guild house. You stop a Hildesheimer and ask where the building is. He/she replies that it is at the Marktplatz, across from city hall. Your informant asks whether you see the pedestrian area over there; he/she directs you to walk along that street and turn right at the pharmacy. The *Marktplatz* is nearby (**ganz in der Nähe**). You thank the stranger and say good-bye.

HÖREN SIE ZU!   TRACK 13

Die Großeltern kommen. *(Listen to the message that Mrs. Schmidt has left for her children on the answering machine. Then indicate which chores each child has been asked to do; write S for Sebastian, M for Mareike, and J for Julia. Finally, note briefly what the children are NOT supposed to do.)*

1. **Wer soll was tun?**
   - _S_ zum Supermarkt fahren
   - _M_ einen Schokoladenpudding machen
   - _S_ Bratwurst und Käse kaufen
   - _J_ den Großeltern zeigen, wo sie schlafen
   - _J_ zum Blumengeschäft fahren
   - _M_ Kartoffeln kochen
   - _J_ Blumen ins Esszimmer stellen
   - _S_ 20 Euro aus dem Schreibtisch nehmen
   - _S_ Mineralwasserflaschen zum Supermarkt bringen
   - _J_ die Kleidung der *(of the)* Großeltern in den Schrank hängen
   - _S_ Wein in den Kühlschrank stellen

2. **Was sollen die Kinder nicht tun?**
   a. das Radio nicht zu laut spielen
   b. den Apfelkuchen nicht essen

Video-Ecke

- The *Minidrama* "Kein Zimmer für Studenten" shows two students who are hunting for an affordable apartment, but they are having a hard time finding something. Suddenly, they discover their dream place in the ads: a studio apartment that's centrally located, large enough for two, and within their price range. Will this be their lucky day?

- *Blickpunkt* "Bei Viktor zu Hause" introduces us to Victor, who lives in Berlin-Zehlendorf. We meet him at the subway station, from where he proceeds to bike home, showing us his neighborhood and then his home. He introduces us to his family and gives us a tour of his home.

Web-Ecke

- For updates, self-assessment quizzes, and online activities related to this chapter, visit the *Wie geht's?* Web site at **http://wiegehts.heinle.com**. You will have a chance to choose a German house to live in, go furniture hunting, and place the furniture throughout your new home. You will also visit Stuttgart and use its public transportation system.

Kapitel ⑦

Auf der Bank und im Hotel

Brauchen Sie Geld? Hier bitte!

Lernziele

Vorschau
The story of the *Deutsche Mark*

Gespräche + Wortschatz
(Formal) time, banking, and hotel
accommodations

Fokus
Exchange offices and credit cards
Hotel names
Accommodations and tourist information
Youth hostels
Luxembourg

Struktur
7.1 **Der-** and **ein**-words
7.2 Separable-prefix verbs
7.3 Flavoring particles

Einblicke
Übernachtungsmöglichkeiten

Video-Ecke
Minidrama: *Ihren Ausweis bitte!*

Web-Ecke

Vorschau

The Story of the *Deutsche Mark*

Despite a West German economic boom that began in the 1950s and continued for nearly 40 years, this recent prosperity has been accompanied by a fear of inflation. The concern is rooted in the conditions that plagued Germany after World War I, when it experienced what was probably the worst inflation of any modern industrialized country. The mark had so little value that people needed pushcarts to transport the piles of money needed to buy groceries, as a single loaf of bread cost billions of marks. In the aftermath of World War II, the Western Allies replaced the **Reichsmark** (RM) with the **Deutsche Mark** (DM) to hold inflation in check, to reduce the enormous war debt, and to instill economic confidence. The Soviet Union followed suit with the introduction of the **Mark** (M) in the Moscow-controlled East German zone. Boosted by the Marshall Plan, the West German economy experienced dramatic growth, while the Soviets stripped East German factories of machinery and shipped it east. Nevertheless, the German Democratic Republic (GDR) economy became one of the strongest in the Eastern Bloc, yet always lagged behind the capitalist West. The difference in economic efficiency accelerated in the two decades before the collapse of the GDR in 1989.

On July 2, 1990, three months before the German reunification, Bonn undertook one of the biggest financial bail-outs in history with a currency union **(Währungsunion).** GDR citizens were allowed to exchange up to 6,000 Eastmark for DM at a rate of 1:1; savings above these amounts were converted at a rate of 2:1. This meant that after the exchange **(Umtausch),** the average savings of a three-member GDR household of 27,000 M became DM 13,500. The introduction of the much-desired, strong West German Mark had a devastating impact on the East German economy by driving much of the industry out of competition overnight and throwing large numbers of employees out of work. This situation required huge cash infusions from West to East, increasing inflationary pressure in all of Germany. The staunchly independent German central bank **(Bundesbank),** which is charged with ensuring monetary stability, raised interest rates to the highest level in decades. The bank reluctantly lowered them only after the worst recession since World War II hit Germany in the early 1990s.

The introduction of the euro, the new all-European currency, in 1999 for institutional transactions meant the beginning of the end of the **Deutsche Mark,** symbol of German economic power and stability in the second half of the 20th century. In the beginning of the year 2002, the Euro replaced the DM in everyday transactions.

If you have some old German or Austrian money, some Swiss francs, or new euros, bring it to class. Ask students to check the current exchange of the dollar to the euro.

To be precise, children until the age of 14 were allowed to exchange up to 2,000 DM at a rate of 1:1, people aged 15–59 up to 4,000 DM, and people older than 60 up to 6,000 DM. All salaries and pensions were also converted at a rate of 1:1.

177

178   Kapitel 7   Auf der Bank und im Hotel

Gespräche + Wortschatz

CD 4, Track I

Warm-ups: 1. **Was ist das Gegenteil von:** immer, oben, links, bequem, hell, leicht, nah, offen, schnell, Tag, mieten, zu Fuß gehen? 2. **Was für Zimmer gibt es in einem Haus?** Was gibt es im Wohnzimmer, in der Küche . . .? 3. **Nennen Sie den Plural von:** Bank, Fahrrad, Museum, Haus, Wohnung, Studentenheim, Bad, Bett, Ecke, Kommode, Regal, Schrank, Telefon, Teppich, Vorhang, Dach, Keller!

As the book went to press, the euro was slightly less than a dollar. Ask students, if they know what the exchange rate is today. How much would € 1 million be in U.S. / Canadian currency?

Auf der Bank

TOURISTIN	Guten Tag! Können Sie mir sagen, wo ich Geld umtauschen kann?
ANGESTELLTE	Am Schalter 1.
TOURISTIN	Vielen Dank! *(Sie geht zum Schalter 1.)* Guten Tag! Ich möchte Dollar in Euros umtauschen. Hier sind meine Reiseschecks.
ANGESTELLTE	Darf ich bitte Ihren Pass sehen?
TOURISTIN	Hier.
ANGESTELLTE	Unterschreiben Sie bitte hier, dann gehen Sie dort zur Kasse! Da bekommen Sie Ihr Geld.
TOURISTIN	Danke! *(Sie geht zur Kasse.)*
KASSIERER	324 Euro 63: einhundert, zweihundert, dreihundert, zehn, zwanzig vierundzwanzig Euro und dreiundsechzig Cent.
TOURISTIN	Danke! Auf Wiedersehen!

An der Rezeption im Hotel

EMPFANGSDAME	Guten Abend!
GAST	Guten Abend! Haben Sie ein Einzelzimmer frei?
EMPFANGSDAME	Für wie lange?
GAST	Für zwei oder drei Nächte; wenn möglich ruhig und mit Bad.
EMPFANGSDAME	Leider haben wir heute nur noch ein Doppelzimmer, und das nur für eine Nacht. Aber morgen wird ein Einzelzimmer frei. Wollen Sie das Doppelzimmer sehen?
GAST	Ja, gern.
EMPFANGSDAME	Zimmer Nummer 12, im ersten Stock rechts. Hier ist der Schlüssel.
GAST	Sagen Sie, kann ich meinen Koffer einen Moment hier lassen?
EMPFANGSDAME	Ja, natürlich. Stellen Sie ihn da drüben in die Ecke!
GAST	Danke! Noch etwas, wann machen Sie abends zu?
EMPFANGSDAME	Um 24.00 Uhr. Wenn Sie später kommen, müssen Sie klingeln.

A: 1. die Touristin 2. auf der Bank 3. zum Schalter I 4. den Pass 5. an der Kasse 6. 324 Euro (und 63 Cent) 7. ein Einzelzimmer 8. für 2 oder 3 Nächte 9. ein Doppelzimmer im I. Stock 10. den Schlüssel 11. da drüben in der Ecke 12. um 24.00 Uhr

You might also ask students to retell the content of the dialogue, each is responsible for one.

A. Fragen

1. Wer möchte Geld umtauschen? 2. Wo ist sie? 3. Wohin muss sie gehen? 4. Was muss die Touristin der Angestellten zeigen? 5. Wo bekommt sie ihr Geld? 6. Wie viele Euros bekommt sie? 7. Was für ein Zimmer möchte der Gast? 8. Für wie lange braucht er es? 9. Was für ein Zimmer nimmt er und wo liegt es? 10. Was gibt die Dame an der Rezeption dem Gast? 11. Wo kann der Gast seinen Koffer lassen? 12. Wann macht das Hotel zu?

B. Jetzt sind Sie dran! *(With a partner, create your own dialogue as it could happen at a bank counter or the reception desk of a hotel.)*

Wortschatz 1

Die Uhrzeit *(time of day)*

- The formal (official) time system is like the one used by the military. The hours are counted from 0 to 24, with 0 to 11 referring to A.M. and 12 to 24 referring to P.M. The system is commonly used in timetables for trains, buses, planes, etc., on radio and television, and to state business hours of stores and banks.

16.05 Uhr = sechzehn Uhr fünf		*4:05 P.M.*
16.15 Uhr = sechzehn Uhr fünfzehn		*4:15 P.M.*
16.30 Uhr = sechzehn Uhr dreißig		*4:30 P.M.*
16.45 Uhr = sechzehn Uhr fünfundvierzig		*4:45 P.M.*
17.00 Uhr = siebzehn Uhr		*5:00 P.M.*

Midnight can be referred to as **24.00 Uhr** or **0.00 (null) Uhr.**

- Note that in newspapers and advertisement, German usually separates hours and minutes by a period instead of a colon (**16.05 Uhr** BUT *4:05 P.M.*) However, with the popularity of digital time, the use of the colon has also become very common (**16:05 Uhr** AND *4:05 P.M.*).

Die Bank, -en *(bank)*

der Ausweis, -e	*identification card (ID)*
Dollar, -(s)	*dollar*
Pass, ̈e	*passport*
Schalter, -	*counter, ticket window*
(Reise)scheck, -s	*(traveler's) check*
das Geld	*money*
Bargeld	*cash*
Kleingeld	*change*
die Kasse, -n	*cashier's window (lit. cash register)*

Das Hotel, -s *(hotel)*

der Ausgang, ̈e	*exit*	das Einzelzimmer, -	*single room*
Eingang, ̈e	*entrance*	Doppelzimmer, -	*double room*
Gast, ̈e	*guest*	Gepäck	*baggage, luggage*
Koffer, -	*suitcase*	die Nacht, ̈e	*night*
Schlüssel, -	*key*	Nummer, -n	*number*
		Tasche, -n	*bag; pocket*

Wer spart, kann große Sprünge machen.
BfG: Die Bank für Gemeinwirtschaft.

Fokus — *Exchange Offices and Credit Cards*

Currency can be exchanged and traveler's checks cashed in at banks and post offices. Exchange offices **(Wechselstuben)** are open daily at all major railroad stations, airports, and border crossings.

The popularity of credit cards **(Kreditkarten)** is increasing in the German-speaking countries, although many small businesses and restaurants still do not accept them. So-called eurocheque cards to withdraw cash from banks or ATMs **(Geldautomaten)** and to pay bills in shops, restaurants, and hotels are used by Europeans throughout Europe. If you have your four-digit PIN number, you can use your Visa or American Express card in European ATMs, but the banks will usually charge you a 2.5 percent transaction fee and the current interest rate on the date of transaction. Even though the exchange rate might be good, it is usually more advantageous to exchange traveler's checks at a bank.

Die Geschäfte **sind** alle **auf / zu** (**offen / geschlossen**). Sie **machen** bald **auf / zu** (BUT NOT **offen / geschlossen**).

Einlösen and **umtauschen** are separable-prefix verbs. Until they are discussed in the grammar section of this chapter, avoid using these verbs in separated forms.

Weiteres

bald	*soon*
frei	*free, available*
auf / zu	
geöffnet / geschlossen	*open / closed*
laut / ruhig	*loud / quiet(ly)*
möglich	*possible*
einen Moment	*(for) just a minute*
Wann machen Sie auf / zu?	*When do you open / close?*
einen Scheck ein·lösen	*to cash a check*
um·tauschen	*to exchange*
wechseln	*to change; to exchange*
lassen (lässt), gelassen	*to leave (behind)*
unterschreiben, unterschrieben	*to sign*
Das glaube ich nicht.	*I don't believe that*
Das ist doch nicht möglich!	*That's impossible (lit. not possible)!*
Das kann doch nicht wahr sein!	*That can't be true!*
Quatsch!	*Nonsense!*
Vorsicht!	*Careful!*
Pass auf! Passt auf! Passen Sie auf!	*Watch out!*
Warte! Wartet! Warten Sie!	*Wait!*
Halt!	*Stop!*

Zum Erkennen: die Angestellte, -n *(clerk, employee, f.);* die Empfangsdame, -n *(receptionist);* klingeln *(here: to ring the doorbell);* AUCH: der Dienst, -e *(service);* sparen *(to save [money / time])*

Zum Thema

A. Mustersätze

1. Geld wechseln: **Wo kann ich hier** Geld wechseln?
   Dollar umtauschen, einen Scheck einlösen, Reiseschecks einlösen
2. Pass: **Darf ich bitte Ihren** Pass **sehen?**
   Scheck, Reisescheck, Ausweis
3. Dollar: **Können Sie mir das in** Dollar **geben?**
   Euro, Franken, Kleingeld, Bargeld
4. mein Auto: **Wo kann ich** mein Auto **lassen?**
   meinen Schlüssel, mein Gepäck, meinen Koffer, meine Tasche
5. 24.00 Uhr: **Wir machen um** 24.00 Uhr **zu.**
   22.00 Uhr, 22.15 Uhr, 22.30 Uhr, 22.45 Uhr, 23.00 Uhr

B. Was bedeuten die Wörter und was sind die Artikel?

B: *exit door* **(die),** *guest pass* **(der),** *money exchange* **(der),** *piece of luggage* **(das),** *handbag* **(die),** *hotel entrance* **(der),** *key to a suitcase* **(der),** *nighttime pharmacy* **(die),** *nightgown* **(das),** *night person* **(der),** *passport number* **(die),** *checkbook* **(das),** *savings book* **(das),** *pocket money* **(das),** *flashlight* **(die),** *latchkey child* **(das)**

Ausgangstür, Gästeausweis, Geldwechsel, Gepäckstück, Handtasche, Hoteleingang, Kofferschlüssel, Nachtapotheke, Nachthemd, Nachtmensch, Passnummer, Scheckbuch, Sparbuch, Taschengeld, Taschenlampe, Schlüsselkind

C. Ich brauche Kleingeld. *(With a partner, practice asking for a place where you can get change. Take turns and vary your responses.)*

S1   Ich habe kein Kleingeld. Kannst du mir . . . wechseln?
S2   Nein, . . .
S1   Schade!
S2   Aber du kannst . . .
S1   Wo ist . . . ?
S2   . . .
S1   Danke schön!
S2   . . .

D. Im Hotel *(With a partner, practice inquiring about a hotel room. Take turns and be sure to vary your responses.)*

S1   Guten . . . ! Haben Sie ein . . . mit . . . frei ?
S2   Wie lange wollen Sie bleiben?
S1   . . .
S2   Ja, wir haben ein Zimmer im . . . Stock.
S1   Was kostet es?
S2   . . .
S1   Kann ich es sehen?
S2   . . . Hier ist der Schlüssel. Zimmernummer . . .
S1   Sagen Sie, wo kann ich . . . lassen?
S2   . . .
S1   Und wann machen Sie abends zu?
S2   . . .

E. Wie spät ist es? *(Ralf loves his new digital watch. Kurt prefers his old-fashioned one with hands. As Ralf says what time it is, Kurt confirms it in a more casual way. Work with a classmate. Take turns.)*

> **BEISPIEL:**   14.15 Auf meiner Uhr ist es vierzehn Uhr fünfzehn.
> **Bei mir ist es Viertel nach zwei.**

1. 8.05	4. 13.25	7. 19.40	10. 23.59
2. 11.10	5. 14.30	8. 20.45	11. 00.01
3. 12.30	6. 17.37	9. 22.50	12. 02.15

E: 1. fünf nach acht 2. zehn nach elf 3. halb eins 4. fünf vor halb zwei 5. halb drei 6. sieben nach halb sechs 7. zwanzig for acht 8. Viertel vor neun 9. zehn vor elf 10. eine Minute vor zwölf / Mitternacht 11. eine Minute nach zwölf / Mitternacht 12. Viertel nach zwei

F. Öffnungszeiten. Wann sind diese Restaurants und Kunstgalerien offen?

Gasthaus BAUER
1., Schottenbastei 4, Tel.:533 6128
Mo-Fr 9-24 Uhr, warme Küche bis 21 Uhr,
Café MUSEUM 1., Friedrichstraße 6,
Tel.: 56 52 02
tgl. 7-23 Uhr; Alt-Wiener Kaffeehaus

ZUR WEINPERLE
9., Alserbachstraße 2, Tel.: 34 32 52
Mo-Fr 9-21.30 Uhr, Sa 9-14.30 Uhr.
Café CENTRAL, 1., Herrengasse 14 (im inside Palais Ferstel), Tel.: 535 41 76
Mo-Sa 10-22 Uhr.

SCHNITZELWIRT
7., Neubaugasse 52, Tel.: 93 37 71
Mo-Sa 10-22 Uhr, warme Küche 11.30-14.30 Uhr und 17.30-22 Uhr.
SCHWEIZERHAUS 2., Prater, Straße des
1. Mai 116, Tel.: 218 01 52
tgl. 10-24 Uhr, mitten im Wurstelprater.

GALERIE NÄCHST ST. STEPHAN
1., Grünangergasse 1, Tel.: 512 12 66
Mo-Fr 10-18 Uhr, Sa 11-14 Uhr,
GALERIE HUMMEL
1., Bäckerstraße 14, Tel.: 512 12 96
Di-Fr 15-18 Uhr, Sa 10-13 Uhr.

GALERIE PETER PAKESCH
1., Ballgasse 6, Tel.: 52 48 14 und
3., Ungargasse 27, Tel.: 713 74 56
Di-Fr 14-19 Uhr, So 11-14 Uhr,
GALERIE STEINEK
1., Himmelpfortgasse 22, Tel: 512 87 59
Di-Fr 13-18 Uhr, Sa 10-12 Uhr.

G. Was sagen Sie? *(Working with a partner, react to the following situations with an appropriate expression, using each expression only once. Take turns.)*

> **BEISPIEL:**   Da kommt ein Auto wie verrückt um die Ecke!
> **Vorsicht!**

1. Hier kostet ein Hotelzimmer 110 Euro.
2. Ich habe ein Zimmer für 240 Euro im Monat gefunden.
3. Du, die Vorlesung beginnt um 14.15 Uhr und es ist schon 14.05 Uhr!

Other familiar expressions of disbelief are: **Stimmt das?, Wirklich?, Das gibt's doch nicht!** or **Ach du liebes bisschen!** You could also mention **Du spinnst (wohl)!** *(You're crazy!)* or **Mach keine Witze!** *(Stop joking!)* Another expression of warning could be **Achtung!** *(Watch out!)*

4. Sie bummeln mit einem Freund durch die Stadt. Ihr Freund will bei Rot *(at a red light)* über die Straße laufen.
5. Sie sind auf einer Party und es macht Ihnen viel Spaß. Aber morgen ist eine Prüfung und Sie hören, dass es schon zwei Uhr ist.
6. Sie lernen auf einer Party einen Studenten kennen. Sie hören, dass sein Vater und Ihr Vater als Studenten Freunde gewesen sind.
7. Sie stehen mit einer Tasse Kaffee an der Tür. Die Tür ist zu. Ein Freund möchte hereinkommen.
8. Ein Freund aus Deutschland will die Kerzen auf seinem Weihnachtsbaum anzünden *(light)*. Sie sind sehr nervös.

H. Interview. Fragen Sie einen Nachbarn/eine Nachbarin, . . .
1. wo man hier Bargeld oder Kleingeld bekommt
2. wo man hier Franken *(Swiss currency)* oder Euros bekommen kann
3. ob er/sie weiß, wie viele Franken/Euros man für einen Dollar bekommt
4. wie er/sie bezahlt, wenn er/sie einkaufen geht: bar, mit einem Scheck oder mit einer Kreditkarte
5. wie er/sie bezahlt, wenn er/sie reist *(travels)*
6. was er/sie tut, wenn er/sie kein Geld mehr hat
7. ob er/sie schon einmal etwas gewonnen hat; wenn ja, was und wie *(die Lotterie)*

CD 4, Track 2

Aussprache: ei, ie

(Read also Part 11.37, 40–41 in the Pronunciation Guide of the Workbook.)

1. [ei] s**ei**t, w**ei**ßt, bl**ei**bst, l**ei**der, fr**ei**, **Rai**ner M**ey**er, **Bay**ern
2. [ie] w**ie**, w**ie** v**ie**l, n**ie**, l**ie**ben, l**ie**gen, m**ie**ten, l**ie**s, s**ie**h, D**ie**nstag
3. v**ie**ll**ei**cht, **Bei**sp**ie**l, bl**ei**ben / bl**ie**ben, h**ei**ßen / h**ie**ßen, W**ie**n / W**ei**n, W**ie**se / w**ei**ß
4. Wortpaare

   a. See / Sie   c. biete / bitte   e. leider / Lieder
   b. beten / bieten   d. Miete / Mitte   f. Mais / mies

HÖREN SIE ZU!   TRACK 14

Eine Busfahrt *(Listen to the discussion between these American exchange students in Tübingen and their professor before taking a bus trip early in their stay. Then complete the statements below according to the dialogue.)*

Zum Erkennen: abfahren *(to depart);* das Konto *(account);* die Jugendherberge *(youth hostel);* also *(in other words);* Briefmarken *(stamps)*

1. Der Professor und die Studenten wollen am <u>am Montag</u> um <u>7 Uhr</u> abfahren.
2. Sie sind von <u>Montag</u> bis <u>Mittwoch</u> in der Schweiz.
3. Sie sind von <u>Donnerstag</u> bis <u>Samstag</u> in Österreich.
4. Sie sollen heute noch <u>zur Bank</u> gehen.
5. Die Jugendherbergen und <u>das Essen</u> sind schon bezahlt.
6. Sie brauchen nur etwas Geld, wenn sie <u>Eis, Cola, Postkarten</u> oder <u>Briefmarken</u> kaufen wollen.
7. <u>Museen</u> und <u>Schlösser</u> sind auch schon bezahlt.
8. Manchmal braucht man Kleingeld für <u>Toiletten</u>.

Dieses Blumengeschäft ist auch am Sonntag offen.

Struktur

7.1 *Der-* and *ein-*words

1. **Der**-words

   This small but important group of limiting words is called DER-WORDS because their case endings are the same as those of the definite articles **der, das, die.**

der, das, die	*the, that (when stressed)*
dieser, -es, -e	*this, these*
jeder, -es, -e	*each, every (sg. only, pl.* **alle***)*
mancher, -es, -e	*many a (sg.); several, some (usually pl.)*
solcher, -es, -e	*such (usually pl.)*
welcher, -es, -e	*which*

CAUTION: The singular of **solcher** usually is **so ein,** which is not a **der**-word but an **ein**-word: **so ein Hotel** (*such a hotel*) BUT **solche Hotels** (*such hotels*).

COMPARE the endings of the definite article and the **der**-words!

		masc.	neut.	fem.	pl.
nom.		der dies**er** welch**er**	das dies**es** welch**es**	die dies**e** welch**e**	die dies**e** welch**e**
acc.		den dies**en** welch**en**			
dat.		dem dies**em** welch**em**	dem dies**em** welch**em**	der dies**er** welch**er**	den dies**en** welch**en**

It might be helpful to translate these sentences into English. They can be used in reverse (English to German) during the next period.

nom.	Wo ist **der** Schlüssel?—**Welcher** Schlüssel? **Dieser** Schlüssel?
acc.	Hast du **den** Kofferschlüssel gesehen?—Wie soll ich **jeden** Schlüssel kennen?
dat.	Kannst du ihn mit **dem** Schlüssel öffnen?—Mit **welchem** Schlüssel?
plural	Gib mir **die** Schlüssel!—Hier sind **alle** Schlüssel. **Manche** Schlüssel sind vom Haus, **solche** Schlüssel zum Beispiel.
BUT	Der Kofferschlüssel ist **so ein** Schlüssel. Hast du **so einen** Schlüssel?

2. **Ein**-words

POSSESSIVE ADJECTIVES are called **ein**-words because their case endings are the same as those of the indefinite article **ein** and the negative **kein.**

If students need help in telling whether **ihr** is a dative pronoun or a possessive adjective (and which one of the three), give them examples such as the following: 1. Ich gebe **ihr** das Buch. Ich habe **ihr** Buch. 2. Sie bringen **ihr** Blumen. Sie bringen **ihre** Blumen. 3. Das ist Ruth. Ich habe **ihr** Heft. 4. Wir fahren zu Müllers. Wo ist **ihre** Adresse? 5. Guten Tag, Herr Fiedler! Wie geht es **Ihrer** Frau?

mein	*my*	**unser**	*our*
dein	*your (sg. fam.)*	**euer**	*your (pl. fam.)*
sein	*his / its*	**ihr**	*their*
ihr	*her / its*	**Ihr**	*your (sg./pl. formal)*

COMPARE the endings of the indefinite article and the **ein**-words!

		masc.	neut.	fem.	pl.
nom.		ein mein unser	ein mein unser	ein**e** mein**e** unser**e**	kein**e** mein**e** unser**e**
acc.		ein**en** mein**en** unser**en**			
dat.		ein**em** mein**em** unser**em**	ein**em** mein**em** unser**em**	ein**er** mein**er** unser**er**	kein**en** mein**en** unser**en**

When **unser** and **euer** have an ending, the **-e-** is often dropped (**unsre, eure**), especially in colloquial speech.

CAUTION: The **-er** of uns**er** and eu**er** is not an ending!

- **Ein**-words have no endings in the masculine singular nominative and in the neuter singular nominative and accusative.

nom.	Hier ist **ein** Pass. Ist das **mein** Pass oder **dein** Pass?
acc.	Braucht er **keine** Kreditkarte?—Wo hat er **seine** Kreditkarte? Hat sie **einen** Ausweis?—Natürlich hat sie **ihren** Ausweis. Haben Sie **Ihren** Ausweis?
dat.	In welcher Tasche sind die Schlüssel?—Sie sind in **meiner** Tasche. Oder sind die Schlüssel in **einem** Koffer?—Sie sind in **Ihrem** Koffer.
plural	Wo sind die Schecks?—Hier sind **unsere** Schecks und da sind **eure** Schecks.

Translate into English! This can be used in reverse (or as a quiz) in the next period.

Übungen

A. Ersetzen Sie die Artikel!

1. **Der**-Wörter

   BEISPIEL: die Tasche *(this)*
   diese Tasche

A.1 – 2: Use variations of these exercises during several class periods until students have mastered the **der-** and **ein**-words.

   a. das Gepäck *(every, which, this)*
   b. der Ausweis *(this, every, which)*
   c. die Nummer *(which, every, this)*
   d. die Nächte *(some, such, these)*

   e. an dem Schalter *(this, which, each)*
   f. an der Kasse *(this, every, which)*
   g. mit den Schecks *(these, some, all)*

2. **Ein**-Wörter

   BEISPIEL: die Gäste *(your/3×)*
   deine / euere / Ihre Gäste

A.2: To make the practice of the possessive adjective more meaningful, do it with some of your own and the students' belongings: e.g., **Ist das Ihr Bleistift? Nein, das ist sein Bleistift.**

   a. der Pass *(my, her, no, his)*
   b. das Bargeld *(our, her, their)*
   c. die Wohnung *(my, our, your/3×)*

   d. neben den Koffer *(your/3×, our, their)*
   e. in dem Doppelzimmer *(no, his, your/3×)*
   f. mit den Schlüsseln *(your/3×, my, her)*

3. **Der**- und **ein**-Wörter

   BEISPIEL: Das Bad ist klein. *(our)*
   Unser Bad ist klein.

Additional practice: **Bilden Sie Sätze! BEISPIEL: *except for our bag* Wir haben alles außer unserer Tasche.** e.g., *for his guest, after every meal, around their house, to your (pl. fam.) apartment, without my money, since that day, out of our suitcase, through this exit, from some people, into which restaurant, near this bridge, with your (sg. fam.) ID.*

   a. Das Zimmer hat einen Fernseher. *(each, my, his, our)*
   b. Bitte bringen Sie den Koffer zum Auto! *(this, her, our, my)*
   c. Ich kann die Schlüssel nicht finden. *(your/3×, our, some, my)*
   d. Darf ich das Gepäck hier lassen? *(her, his, this, our)*
   e. Der Ober kennt den Gast. *(each, our, this, your/3×)*
   f. Die Taschen sind schon vor dem Ausgang. *(our, all, some, my)*
   g. Den Leuten gefällt das Hotel nicht. *(these, some, such)*
   h. Du kannst den Scheck auf der Bank einlösen. *(this, my, every, such a, your/sg. fam.)*

B. Dias von einer Deutschlandreise *(Slide show from a trip to Germany)*

1. Auf <u>diesem</u> Bild seht ihr <u>meine</u> Freunde aus Holland. 2. Das sind <u>ihr</u> Sohn
   this   *my*   *their*

Heiko und <u>ihre</u> Tochter Anke. 3. In <u>welcher</u> Stadt ist <u>diese</u> Kirche?
     their   *which*   *this*

4. <u>Solche</u> Kirchen gibt es in Norddeutschland. 5. <u>Dieses</u> Haus ist sehr
   Such   *This*

alt, aber nicht <u>jedes</u> Haus in Neubrandenburg ist so alt. 6. Ich finde
      every

<u>solche</u> Häuser sehr schön; Müllers wohnen in <u>so einem</u> Haus. 7. Und
such   *such a*

hier sind <u>mein</u> Onkel Thomas und <u>meine</u> Tante Hilde. 8. Ist das
      my   *my*

nicht <u>euer</u> Auto da vor <u>diesem</u> Hotel?
    your (pl. fam.)   *this*

HOTEL VIER TORE
NEUBRANDENBURG

C. Ruck, zuck! Wem gehört das? *(One person claims to own everything. Quickly correct him/her and tell whose property it is. You may mention the items suggested or think of your own.)*

> BEISPIEL: Das ist mein Buch. (Heft, Bleistift, Jacke, Tasche, Schlüssel usw.)
> **Quatsch! Das ist nicht dein Buch; das ist mein (ihr, sein) Buch.**

7.2 Separable-prefix verbs

1. English has a number of two-part verbs that consist of a verb and a preposition or an adverb.

> *Watch out! Hurry up! Come back!*

In German, such verbs are called SEPARABLE-PREFIX verbs. You are already familiar with two of them:

> **Passen** Sie **auf! Hören** Sie **zu!**

Their infinitives are **aufpassen** and **zuhören.** The prefixes **auf** and **zu** carry the main stress: **auf'·passen, zu'·hören.** From now on, we will identify such separable-prefix verbs by placing a raised dot (·) between the prefix and the verb in vocabulary lists: **auf·passen, zu·hören.**

Tell students to kick the separable prefix to the end of the sentence or clause, just like the soccer player.

- These verbs are separated from the prefixes when the inflected part of the verb is the first or second sentence element: in imperatives, questions, and statements.

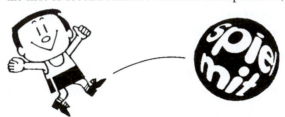

> **Hören** Sie bitte **zu!**
> **Hören** Sie jetzt **zu?**
> Warum **hören** Sie nicht **zu?**
> Wir **hören** immer gut **zu.**
>   V1   V2

- These verbs are NOT SEPARATED from the prefix when the verb stands at the end of a sentence or clause: with modals, in the present perfect, and in subordinate clauses. Note, however, that in the present perfect the **-ge-** of the past participle is inserted between the stressed prefix and the participle.

> Ich soll immer gut **zuhören.**
>
> Ich habe immer gut **zugehört.**
>
> Ich weiß, dass ich immer gut **zuhöre.**
>
> Ich weiß, dass ich immer gut **zuhören** soll.
>
> Ich weiß, dass ich immer gut **zugehört** habe.

2. Knowing the basic meanings of some of the most frequent separable prefixes will help you derive the meanings of some of the separable-prefix verbs.

You may want to point out that there are numerous compounds with **hin-** and **her-:** Ich gehe **hinaus (hinauf, hinein, hinüber).** Er kommt **heraus (herauf, herein, herüber).** In colloquial speech: **raus, rauf, rein, rüber.**

ab-	*away, off*	**mit-**	*together with, along with*
an-	*to, up to*	**nach-**	*after, behind*
auf-	*up, open*	**um-**	*around, over, from one to the other*
aus-	*out, out of*	**vor-**	*ahead, before*
ein-	*into*	**vorbei-**	*past, by*
her-	*toward (the speaker)*	**zu-**	*closed*
hin-	*away from (the speaker)*	**zurück-**	*back*

BEISPIEL:	**an·**kommen	*to arrive (come to)*
	her·kommen	*to come (toward the speaker)*
	herein·kommen	*to come in (toward the speaker)*
	heraus·kommen	*to come out (toward the speaker)*
	hin·kommen	*to get there (away from the point of reference)*

mit·kommen	to come along
nach·kommen	to follow (come after)
vorbei·kommen	to come by
zurück·kommen	to come back

You will need to learn these common separable-prefix verbs:

an·rufen, angerufen	to call, phone
auf·machen	to open
auf·passen	to pay attention, watch (out)
auf·schreiben, aufgeschrieben	to write down
auf·stehen, ist aufgestanden	to get up
aus·gehen, ist ausgegangen	to go out
ein·kaufen	to shop
ein·lösen	to cash (in)
mit·bringen, mitgebracht	to bring along
mit·gehen, ist mitgegangen	to go along
mit·kommen, ist mitgekommen	to come along
mit·nehmen, mitgenommen	to take along
um·tauschen	to exchange
vorbei·gehen, ist vorbeigegangen (an, bei)	to pass (by)
zu·hören (+ dat.)	to listen
zu·machen	to close
zurück·kommen, ist zurückgekommen	to come back

Point out that **vorbeigehen** uses the preposition **bei** or **an** + dative if followed by an object: Kommt ihr **vorbei?** BUT Ich gehe **an** der Uni **vorbei.** Kommst du **bei** der Drogerie **vorbei?**

CAUTION: Not all verbs with prefixes are separable, e.g., **unterschreiben, wiederholen.** Here the main stress is on the verb, not on the prefix: **unterschrei'ben, wiederho'len.** Remember also the inseparable prefixes **be-, ent-, er-, ge-, ver-,** etc. (Chapter 4, Struktur 4.1). They never stand alone.

Übungen

D. Was bedeuten diese Verben? (*Knowing the meanings of the basic verbs and the prefixes, can you tell what these separable-prefix verbs mean?*)

1. abgeben, abnehmen
2. ansprechen
3. aufbauen, aufgeben, aufstehen, aufstellen
4. ausarbeiten, aushelfen, aus(be)zahlen
5. heraufkommen, herauskommen, herüberkommen, herunterkommen
6. hinaufgehen, hinausgehen, hineingehen, hinuntergehen
7. mitgehen, mitfahren, mitfeiern, mitsingen, mitspielen
8. nachkommen, nachlaufen, nachmachen
9. vorbeibringen, vorbeifahren, vorbeikommen
10. zumachen
11. zurückbekommen, zurückbleiben, zurückbringen, zurückgeben, zurücknehmen, zurücksehen

Mach's nach!

D: 1. *to hand in, take off* 2. *to address, speak to* 3. *to build up, give up, get up, put in place* 4. *to work out, help out, pay out* 5. *to come up, come out, come over, come down* 6. *to go up, go out, go in, go down* 7. *to go along, drive along, join in celebrating, sing along, join in playing* 8. *to follow, run after, imitate* 9. *to bring by, drive by, come by* 10. *to close* 11. *to get back, stay back, bring back, give back, take back, look back*

E. Noch einmal. Wiederholen Sie die Sätze ohne Modalverb!

> **BEISPIEL:**   Sie soll ihm zuhören.
> **Sie hört ihm zu.**

1. Wir dürfen am Wochenende ausgehen. 2. Wann musst du morgens aufstehen? 3. Wollt ihr mit mir einkaufen gehen? 4. Ich soll Wein mitbringen. 5. Er will morgen zurückkommen. 6. Ich möchte dich gern mitnehmen. 7. Du kannst das Geld umtauschen. 8. Er will an der Universität vorbeigehen. 9. Können Sie bitte die Fenster aufmachen? 10. Ihr sollt gut aufpassen.

F. Am Telefon (*Report to a brother what your mother is telling or asking you about tomorrow's family reunion.*)

> **BEISPIEL:**   Sie möchte wissen, ob Rainer und Wolfgang die Kinder mitbringen.
> **Bringen Rainer und Wolfgang die Kinder mit?**
> Sie sagt, dass die Tante auch mitkommt.
> **Die Tante kommt auch mit.**

1. Sie sagt, dass wir abends alle zusammen ausgehen.
2. Sie möchte wissen, ob du deine Kamera mitbringst.
3. Sie möchte wissen, wann die Bank aufmacht.
4. Sie sagt, dass sie noch etwas Geld umtauscht.
5. Sie sagt, dass sie dann hier vorbeikommt.

G. Das tut man. (*Say what things one needs to do before checking out of a hotel.*)

> **BEISPIEL:**   früh aufstehen
> **Man steht früh auf.**

1. die Koffer zumachen 2. das Gepäck zur Rezeption mitnehmen 3. den Schlüssel zurückgeben 4. vielleicht ein Taxi anrufen 5. vielleicht einen Reisescheck einlösen

H. Hoppla, hier fehlt was! Fertig für die Reise? (*Work with a partner to find out whether various family members have finished their tasks. Take turns asking questions until you have both completed your lists. One list is below, the other in Section 11 of the Appendix.*)

S1:

Vater	bei der Bank vorbeigehen	Ja, gestern.
Vater	Geld umtauschen	Ja.
Mutter	Kamera mitbringen	Ja, ich glaube.
Mutter	die Nachbarn anrufen	Nein.
Thomas	die Telefonnummer aufschreiben	Ja, ich glaube.
Thomas	die Garagentür zumachen	Nein, noch nicht.
Carla	bei der Post vorbeigehen	Ja, gestern.
Carla	die Fenster zumachen	Nein, noch nicht.
Kinder	den Fernseher ausmachen (*turn off*)	Ja.
Kinder	die Lichter (*lights*) ausmachen	Nein, noch nicht.
ich	ein paar Bücher mitnehmen	Ja.

> **BEISPIEL:**   **S1**   Ist Vater bei der Bank vorbeigegangen?
> **S2**   Ja, er ist gestern bei der Bank vorbeigegangen. Haben die Kinder den Fernseher ausgemacht?
> **S1**   Ja, sie haben den Fernseher ausgemacht.

I. Geben Sie alle vier Imperative!

> **BEISPIEL:** Die Tür aufmachen
> **Machen Sie die Tür auf!**
> **Mach die Tür auf!**
> **Macht die Tür auf!**
> **Machen wir die Tür auf!**

1. jetzt aufstehen
2. in der Stadt einkaufen
3. den Scheck noch nicht einlösen
4. genug Bargeld mitbringen
5. das Gepäck mitnehmen
6. mit ihnen mitgehen
7. bei der Bank vorbeigehen
8. trotzdem zuhören
9. wieder zurückkommen

Optional English-to-German practice:
1. You *(sg. fam.)* didn't close your book.
2. Listen! *(formal)* 3. They came back on the weekend. 4. Are you *(pl. fam.)* going out soon? 5. I don't know if she's coming along. 6. Do you *(sg. fam.)* know when she went out? 7. I exchanged our money. 8. Whom did you *(formal)* bring along? (See answer key in the Appendix.)

J. Nein, das tue ich nicht! (*Your partner is not very cooperative and makes all sorts of statements that he/she won't do this or that. You plead with him/her not to be so stubborn and do it anyway. Try to use the verbs listed in* Struktur 7.2 *of this chapter, then follow the example. Take turns.*)

> **BEISPIEL:** Nein, ich rufe sie nicht an!
> **Ach, ruf(e) sie doch bitte an! Du hast sie doch immer angerufen.**

K. Interview. Fragen Sie einen Nachbarn/eine Nachbarin, . . . !
1. wann er/sie heute aufgestanden ist
2. wann er/sie gewöhnlich am Wochenende aufsteht
3. wohin er/sie gern geht, wenn er/sie ausgeht
4. wo er/sie einkauft
5. was er/sie heute mitgebracht hat (drei Beispiele bitte!)

Optional practice: **Wissen Sie, . . . ?**
1. wo man Schecks einlösen kann 2. was man alles aufmachen kann (z.B. einen Schrank) 3. wo man aufpassen muss (z.B. auf der Straße) 4. was man aufschreibt 5. was man auf eine Reise mitnimmt, etc.

Fokus — *Hotel Names*

Germany, Austria, and Switzerland have many small hotels (**Gasthöfe** or **Gasthäuser**), a type of accommodation that first appeared around monasteries toward the end of the Middle Ages. Many of them still have names that refer to the Bible: *Gasthof Engel* (angel); *Gasthof Drei Könige* (the three kings were symbols of travel); *Gasthof Rose* or *Lilie* (both flowers represent the Virgin Mary); *Gasthof Lamm* (the Lamb of God). After a postal system began to develop in the 1400s, names such as *Gasthof Goldenes Posthorn, Alte Post, Neue Post,* and *Zur Post* became common.

„Gasthof zur Post" in Kochel am See

7.3 Flavoring particles

In everyday speech, German uses many FLAVORING WORDS (or intensifiers) to convey what English often expresses through gestures or intonation, e.g., surprise, admiration, or curiosity. When used in these contexts, flavoring particles have no exact English equivalent. Here are some examples:

aber	*expresses admiration, or intensifies a statement*
denn	*expresses curiosity, interest (usually in a question)*
doch	*expresses concern, impatience, assurance*
ja	*adds emphasis*

Euer Haus gefällt mir **aber!**	*I do like your house*
Die Möbel sind **aber** schön!	*Isn't this furniture beautiful!*
Was ist **denn** das?	*What (on earth) is that?*
Wie viel kostet **denn** so etwas?	*(Just) how much does something like that cost?*
Das weiß ich **doch** nicht.	*That I don't know*
Frag **doch** Julia!	*Why don't you ask Julia!*
Du kennst **doch** Julia?	*You do know Julia, don't you?*
Euer Garten ist **ja** super!	*(Wow,) your garden is great!*
Ihr habt **ja** sogar einen Pool!	*(Hey,) you even have a pool!*

Übung

L. Im Hotel. Auf Englisch bitte!

> **BEISPIEL:**   Haben Sie denn kein Einzelzimmer mehr frei?
> *Don't you have any single room available?*

1. Hier ist ja der Schlüssel!
2. Das Zimmer ist aber schön!
3. Es hat ja sogar einen Balkon!
4. Hat es denn keine Dusche?
5. Wir gehen doch noch aus?
6. Hast du denn keinen Hunger?
7. Komm doch mit!
8. Ich komme ja schon!
9. Lass doch den Mantel hier!
10. Wohin gehen wir denn?

Fokus — Accommodations and Tourist Information

Frühstückspension Elisabeth Dalhaus

Berenbrock 51
59348 Lüdinghausen
Tel. 02591/33 38, Fax 70547

Bauernhof

Auf dem Bauernhof mit alten Linden und Diele mit offenem Kamin, finden Sie Ruhe und können Kraft tanken. Im „besten Zimmer" wird zum Frühstück Selbstgemachtes serviert: Marmeladen, Butter, Honig, Brot, Eier und Milch. Ideal für Familien ist „Mutters Etage" mit 2 Schlafzimmern und eigenem Bad. 8 Betten, Mehrbettzimmer möglich!
In der Nähe: Dortmund-Ems-Kanal, Burg Vischering, Badesee, Hallenbad, Rosengarten, Reitmöglichkeiten

When looking for accommodations in a German city, you can choose from a wide range of prices and comfort, from campgrounds to luxury hotels. A **Pension** usually offers a simple room with a sink; toilets and showers are shared. Homes offering inexpensive **Fremdenzimmer,** or rooms for tourists, are common in rural areas and can be spotted by a sign saying **Zimmer frei.** Breakfast is usually included in the price of accommodation, regardless of the price category. In the interest of public safety, hotel guests are required by law to fill out a form providing home address, date of birth, and other personal information.

To find accommodations, travelers can rely on a town's tourist information office **(Touristeninformation).** Usually located in train stations or city centers, the offices offer standard tourist information as well as the reservation of rooms in hotels or private homes **(Zimmervermittlung).**

Zusammenfassung

M. Bilden Sie Sätze! *(Use the verb form suggested.)*

> **BEISPIEL:**   Eva / gestern / ausgehen / mit Willi *(present perfect)*
> **Eva ist gestern mit Willi ausgegangen.**

1. man / umtauschen / Geld / auf / eine Bank *(present tense)*
2. welch- / Koffer *(sg.)* / du / mitnehmen? *(present tense)*
3. einkaufen / ihr / gern / in / euer / Supermarkt? *(present tense)*
4. unser / Nachbarn *(pl.)* / zurückkommen / vor einer Woche *(present perfect)*
5. wann / ihr / aufstehen / am Sonntag? *(present perfect)*
6. ich / mitbringen / dir / mein / Stadtplan *(present perfect)*
7. vorbeigehen / noch / schnell / bei / Apotheke! *(imperative / sg. fam.)*
8. zumachen / Schalter / um 17.30 Uhr! *(imperative / formal)*
9. umtauschen / alles / in Dollar! *(imperative/pl. fam.)*

M: 1. Man tauscht (das) Geld auf einer Bank um. 2. Welchen Koffer nimmst du mit? 3. Kauft ihr gern in eu(e)rem Supermarkt ein? 4. Unsere Nachbarn sind vor einer Woche zurückgekommen. 5. Wann seid ihr am Sonntag aufgestanden? 6. Ich habe dir meinen Stadtplan mitgebracht. 7. Geh noch schnell bei der Apotheke vorbei! 8. Machen Sie den Schalter um 17.30 Uhr zu! 9. Tauscht alles in Dollar um!

N. Gedächtnisspiel *(Memory game. In a small group, one of your classmates starts with a statement using verbs such as **mitbringen** or **umtauschen**. One student starts, the next one repeats and adds to it, and so on. When your memory fails, you're out. Let's see who wins!)*

> **BEISPIEL:**   Ich bringe Blumen mit.
> Ich bringe Blumen und Wein mit.
> Ich bringe, Blumen, Wein und Salzstangen mit.

O. An der Rezeption. Auf Deutsch bitte!

1. All (the) hotels are full **(voll).** 2. Look (**sehen,** *sg. fam.*), there's another hotel. 3. Let's ask once more. 4. Do you *(formal)* still have a room available? 5. Yes, one room without (a) bath on the first floor and one room with (a) shower **(Dusche)** on the second floor. 6. Excellent! Which room would you *(sg. fam.)* like? 7. Give *(formal)* us the room on the second floor. 8. Where can I leave these suitcases? 9. Over there. But don't go yet. 10. May I please see your ID? 11. Yes. Do you cash traveler's checks?—Of course. 12. Did you see our restaurant?—Which restaurant? 13. This restaurant. From each table you can see the sea. 14. You don't find a restaurant like this (such a restaurant) everywhere. 15. That's true.

O: 1. Alle Hotels sind voll. 2. Sieh, da ist noch ein Hotel! 3. Fragen wir noch einmal! 4. Haben Sie noch ein Zimmer frei? 5. Ja, ein Zimmer ohne Bad im Parterre und ein Zimmer mit Dusche im ersten Stock. 6. Ausgezeichnet! Welches Zimmer möchtest du? 7. Geben Sie uns das Zimmer im ersten Stock. 8. Wo kann ich diese Koffer lassen? 9. Da drüben. Aber gehen Sie noch nicht! 10. Darf ich bitte Ihren Ausweis sehen? 11. Ja, lösen Sie Reiseschecks ein? – Natürlich! 12. Haben Sie unser Restaurant gesehen? – Welches Restaurant? 13. Dieses Restaurant. Von jedem Tisch können Sie die See / das Meer sehen. 14. Sie finden so ein Restaurant nicht überall. 15. Das stimmt.

Einblicke

Lesestrategie: Understanding a Series of Directions

This reading describes how to make a room reservation in different types of accommodation. Use what you know about this activity in your own country to follow along with the explanations. Also, think about why hotels and youth hostels may have different ways of working with their guests.

Wortschatz 2

der Gasthof, ∸e	*small hotel*
Wald, ∸er	*forest, woods*
die Jugendherberge, -n	*youth hostel*
Pension, -en	*boarding house; hotel*
Reise, -n	*trip*
einfach	*simple, simply*
meistens	*mostly, usually*
an·kommen, ist angekommen[1]	*to arrive*
an·nehmen, angenommen	*to accept*
kennen lernen	*to get to know, meet*
packen	*to pack*
reisen, ist gereist	*to travel*
reservieren	*to reserve*
übernachten	*to spend the night*
Das kommt darauf an.	*That depends.*

NOTE: After the spelling reform, the verb **kennen** *in* **kennenlernen** *no longer functions as a separable prefix: Er hat sie hier* **kennen gelernt** *(NOT:* **kennengelernt**). *He met her here.*

Point out that **übernachten** *works like* **wiederholen** *and* **unterschreiben;** *here* **über-** *is an inseparable prefix.*

[1] Two-way prepositions take the dative with **an·kommen: Er ist am Bahnhof / in der Stadt angekommen.**

Vor dem Lesen

A. Fragen

1. Wo kann man in den USA / in Kanada gut übernachten? 2. Wie heißen ein paar Hotels oder Motels? 3. Was gibt es in einem Hotelzimmer? 4. Was kostet ein Zimmer in einem Luxushotel in New York oder San Franzisko? 5. Wo kann man frühstücken? Kostet das Frühstück extra? 6. Haben Sie schon einmal in einer Jugendherberge übernachtet? Wenn ja, wo? 7. Gehen Sie gern campen? Wenn ja, warum; wenn nein, warum nicht?

B. Allerlei Hotels Wo möchten Sie übernachten? *(Together with your partner, compare the various hotels listed below and decide which one to recommend to your parents who are going to visit you in Regensburg.)*

HOTEL	ADRESSE	TEL.	PREIS									
Am Peterstor	Fröhliche-Türkenstr. 12	5 45 45	50,11		TV		Fahrstuhl	Frühstücksbüfett				P · Hund
Apollo	Neuprüll 17	91 05-0	81,81	Tel.	Radio·TV		Fahrstuhl	Frühstücksbüfett	Sauna+Solarium	P · P · Hund		
Bischofshof	Krauterermarkt 3	58 46-0	166,17	Tel. · MINI BAR	Radio·TV		Rollstuhl · Fahrstuhl · Nachtportier · Frühstücksbüfett · DIÄT			P · Hund		
Courtyard by Marriott	Frankenstr. 28	8 10 10	96,63	Tel. · MINI BAR	Radio·TV · Airc. · Modem		Fahrstuhl · Nachtportier · Frühstücksbüfett · DIÄT		Sauna · BAR · P	Hund		
Münchner Hof	Tändlergasse 9	58 44-0	102,26	Tel. · MINI BAR	TV		Fahrstuhl · Nachtportier · Frühstücksbüfett			P · Hund		
Orphee	Wahlenstr. 1	59 60 20	107,37	Tel. · MINI BAR	Radio·TV	Modem	Frühstücksbüfett · DIÄT	BAR	Hund			
Künstlerhaus	Alter Kornmarkt 3	57 13 4	81,81	Radio·TV								
Spitalgarten	St.-Katharinen-Platz 1	8 47 74	40,90									

SYMBOLE: 📻 = Radio, ❄ = Aircondition, ⚡ = Modemanschluss (...*connection*),

🛗 = Fahrstuhl (*elevator*), 🌙 = Nachtportier, ☕ = Frühstücksbüfett, 🧖 = Sauna + Solarium

C. Was ist das?

der Campingplatz, Evangelist; das Formular, Symbol; die Adresse, Attraktion, Bibel, Möglichkeit, Übernachtung, Übernachtungsmöglichkeit; ausfüllen; international, luxuriös, modern, primitiv, privat

Übernachtungsmöglichkeiten

CD 4, Track 4

Wo kann man gut übernachten? Nun°, das kommt darauf an, ob das Hotel elegant oder einfach sein soll, ob es zentral liegen muss oder weiter draußen° sein darf. Wer will, kann auch Gast in einem Schloss oder auf einer Burg sein.

well
farther out

In Amerika gibt es viele Hotels mit gleichen° Namen, weil sie zu einer Hotelkette° gehören, z.B. Holiday Inn oder Hilton. Bei diesen Hotels weiß man immer, was man hat, wenn man dort übernachtet. In Deutschland gibt es auch Hotels mit gleichen Namen, z.B. Hotel zur Sonne oder Gasthof Post. Aber das bedeutet nicht, dass solche Hotels innen gleich sind° Im Gegenteil°! Sie sind meistens sehr verschieden°, weil sie zu keiner Kette gehören. Ihre Namen gehen oft bis ins Mittelalter zurück. Oft sagen sie etwas über° ihre Lage° z.B. Berghotel, Pension Waldsee. Andere° Namen, wie z.B. Gasthof zum Löwen, zum Adler° oder zum Stier° sind aus der Bibel genommen. Sie sind Symbole für die Evangelisten Markus, Johannes und Lukas.

same / ...franchise

are alike inside / on the contrary / different / about
location / other
eagle / bull

Manche Hotels sind sehr luxuriös und teuer, andere sind einfach und billig. Sprechen wir von einem normalen Hotel, einem Gasthof oder Gasthaus! Wenn Sie ankommen, gehen Sie zur Rezeption. Dort müssen Sie meistens ein Formular ausfüllen und bekommen dann Ihr Zimmer: ein Einzelzimmer oder Doppelzimmer, ein Zimmer mit oder ohne Bad. Für Zimmer ohne Bad gibt es auf dem Flur eine Toilette und meistens auch eine Dusche. Das Frühstück ist gewöhnlich im Preis inbegriffen°. Übrigens hat jeder Gasthof seinen Ruhetag°. Dann ist das Restaurant geschlossen und man nimmt keine neuen Gäste an. Der Herr oder die Dame an der Rezeption kann Ihnen auch Geschäfte und Attraktionen in der Stadt empfehlen, manchmal auch Geld umtauschen. Aber Vorsicht! Auf der Bank ist der Wechselkurs° fast immer besser°.

included
day off

exchange rate
better

Wenn Sie nicht vorher° reservieren können, dann finden Sie auch Übernachtungsmöglichkeiten durch die Touristeninformation am Hauptbahnhof. Hier finden Sie nicht nur Adressen von Hotels, sondern auch von Privatfamilien und Pensionen. So eine Übernachtung ist gewöhnlich nicht sehr teuer, aber sauber und gut.

in advance

Haben Sie schon einmal in einer Jugendherberge oder einem Jugendgästehaus übernachtet? Wenn nicht, tun Sie es einmal! Sie brauchen dafür° einen Jugendherbergsausweis. So einen Ausweis können Sie aber schon vorher in Amerika oder Kanada bekommen. Fast jede Stadt hat eine Jugendherberge, manchmal in einem modernen Haus, manchmal in einer Burg oder in einem Schloss. Jugendherbergen und Jugendgästehäuser sind in den Ferien meistens schnell voll, denn alle Gruppen reservieren schon vorher. Das Übernachten in einer Jugendherberge kann ein Erlebnis° sein, weil man oft interessante Leute kennen lernt. Jugendherbergen haben nur einen Nachteil°. Sie machen gewöhnlich abends um 23.00 Uhr zu. Wenn Sie später zurückkommen, haben Sie Pech gehabt. In fast allen Großstädten gibt es Jugendgästehäuser. Wenn Sie schon vorher wissen, dass Sie fast jeden Abend ausgehen und spät nach Hause kommen, dann übernachten Sie lieber° in einem Jugendgästehaus, denn diese machen erst° um 24.00 oder 1.00 Uhr zu, und in manchen Gästehäusern kann man sogar einen Hausschlüssel bekommen.

for that

experience
disadvantage

rather / not until

Man kann natürlich auch anders° übernachten, z.B. im Zelt auf einem Campingplatz. Das macht Spaß, wenn man mit dem Fahrrad unterwegs° ist; aber das ist nichts für jeden°. Ob im Hotel oder auf dem Campingplatz, in einer Pension oder Jugendherberge, überall wünschen wir Ihnen viel Spaß auf Ihrer Reise durch Europa.

in other ways
on the road
everybody

Optional practice: **Was ist das?** 1. eine Hotelkette 2. die Rezeption 3. ein Einzelzimmer 4. der Flur 5. ein Gasthof 6. eine Jugendherberge 7. eine Pension 8. ein Waldsee 9. ein Hausschlüssel 10. Glück

Nach dem Lesen

A. Was passt? *(Choose the correct answer.)*

1. Deutsche Hotels mit gleichen Namen sind . . .
   a. immer alle gleich
   b. innen meistens nicht gleich
   c. alle aus dem Mittelalter
   d. Symbole

2. Wenn man in einem Gasthof ankommt, geht man erst . . .
   a. ins Bad
   b. ins Restaurant
   c. zur Rezeption
   d. ins Zimmer

3. Im Hotel kann man Geld umtauschen, aber . . .
   a. nur morgens
   b. nicht an der Rezeption
   c. der Wechselkurs ist meistens nicht sehr gut
   d. der Wechselkurs ist oft super

4. Das Übernachten in einer Jugendherberge kann sehr interessant sein, weil . . .
   a. Jugendherbergen in den Ferien schnell voll sind
   b. sie gewöhnlich abends um 22.00 Uhr zumachen
   c. man manchmal neue Leute kennen lernt
   d. sie immer auf einer Burg sind

5. Auf dem Campingplatz . . .
   a. gibt es eine Toilette auf dem Flur
   b. ist das Frühstück im Preis inbegriffen
   c. gibt es Zelte
   d. darf man nicht früh ankommen

Optional practice: **Geben Sie alle vier Imperative!** (bei der Information fragen, die Namen lesen, in einer Pension übernachten, ein Zimmer reservieren, ein Formular ausfüllen, einen Scheck einlösen, Geld umwechseln, jetzt frühstücken, Ihre Tasche nehmen)

B: 1. Pension 2. Campingplatz 3. Hotel 4. Jugendgästehaus 5. Gasthof 6. Jugendherberge

B. Wo sollen wir übernachten? *(Match each lodging with the corresponding description.)*

Campingplatz, Gasthof, Jugendgästehaus, Jugendherberge, Luxushotel, Pension

1. Diese Übernachtungsmöglichkeit ist meistens nicht teuer, aber doch gut. Man kann sie z.B. durch die Touristeninformation am Bahnhof finden.
2. Hier ist es besonders billig, aber wenn es viel regnet, kann es sehr ungemütlich sein.
3. Wenn man viel Geld hat, ist es hier natürlich wunderbar.
4. Diese Möglichkeit ist für junge Leute. Sie ist nicht teuer und man kann abends spät zurückkommen oder einen Schlüssel bekommen.
5. Das Übernachten kann hier sehr bequem und gemütlich sein; das Frühstück kostet nichts extra. Am Ruhetag kann man dort nicht essen.
6. Hier können Leute mit Ausweis billig übernachten, aber man darf abends nicht nach elf zurückkommen.

C. Übernachtungsmöglichkeiten. Was fehlt?

1. In <u>diesem</u> Hotel kann man gut übernachten, aber das kann man nicht von <u>jedem</u> Hotel sagen. *(this, every)*
2. Bei <u>so einem</u> Hotel wissen Sie immer, wie es innen aussieht. *(such a)*

3. <u>Manche</u> Hotels sind sehr luxuriös und teuer, <u>dieses</u> Hotel zum Beispiel. *(some, this)*
4. <u>Unser</u> Hotel ist sehr schön gewesen. *(our)*
5. Hast du schon einmal von <u>dieser</u> Pension gehört? *(this)*
6. Wie gefällt es euch in <u>eu(e)rer</u> Jugendherberge? *(your)*
7. <u>Uns(e)re</u> Jugendherberge ist in einer Burg. *(our)*
8. In <u>dieser</u> Jugendherberge gibt es noch Platz. *(this)*
9. Wollen wir auf <u>diesem</u> Campingplatz übernachten? *(this)*
10. <u>Welchen</u> Campingplatz meinst du *(do you mean)*? *(which)*

D. In der Jugendherberge. Sagen Sie die Sätze noch einmal ohne Modalverb, (a) im Präsens und (b) im Perfekt!

> D: 1. kommt ihr an / seid ihr angekommen 2. lernt ihr … kennen / habt ihr … kennen gelernt 3. du bringst … mit / hast du … mitgebracht 4. geht ihr … aus / seid ihr … ausgegangen 5. macht … zu / hat … zugemacht 6. hat Pech / hat Pech gehabt

BEISPIEL: Du kannst in den Ferien vorbeikommen.
   Du kommst in den Ferien vorbei.
   Du bist in den Ferien vorbeigekommen.

1. Wann möchtet ihr ankommen?
2. In der Jugendherberge könnt ihr Leute kennen lernen.
3. Du musst natürlich einen Jugendherbergsausweis mitbringen.
4. Wollt ihr abends spät ausgehen?
5. Die Jugendherberge soll um 11 Uhr zumachen.
6. Wer spät zurückkommen möchte, kann Pech haben.

Fokus — *Youth Hostels*

Youth hostels **(Jugendherbergen)** are immensely popular among budget travelers in Germany, Switzerland, and Austria. They are open to individual travelers, groups, and families. There is no upper age limit. During peak season, however, members up to age 25 have priority. Accommodation is usually dormitory-style, with bunk beds and shared bathrooms. Many youth hostels offer laundry facilities, dining halls, and common rooms. Although they are not real hotels— many are closed during the day and have a curfew— youth hostels have reached a relatively high level of comfort for the price. Students and backpackers have come to value the hostels as places to meet other young people from around the world. If you plan on "hosteling," remember to purchase a membership card **(Jugendherbergsausweis)** before traveling overseas.

Jugendherberge in Nürnberg. Haben Sie noch Platz für zwei Leute?

E. Kofferpacken. Was nimmst du mit? *(Together with three or four students, make a list of what you take along on vacation to the various destinations. Then compare.)*

1. ans Meer   2. in die Berge   3. nach Europa

BEISPIEL: Ich habe eine Sonnenbrille mitgenommen. Und du?
Ich habe eine Sonnenbrille und meine Kamera mitgenommen.

E: This probably is done best as a class activity using the board. Like in the *Zusammenfassung,* you could also have a **Gedächtnisspiel** with this vocabulary.

These words are not active vocabulary!

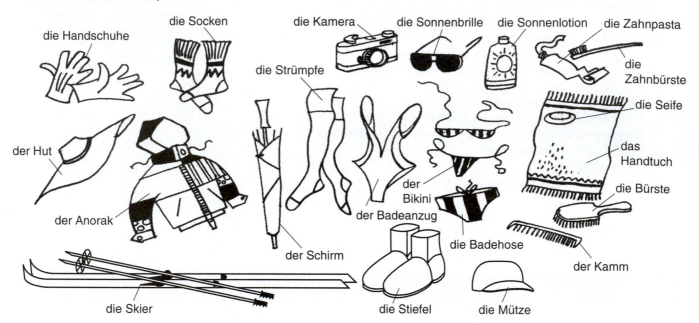

die Handschuhe · die Socken · die Kamera · die Sonnenbrille · die Sonnenlotion · die Zahnpasta · die Strümpfe · die Zahnbürste · die Seife · der Hut · das Handtuch · der Anorak · der Bikini · die Bürste · der Badeanzug · die Badehose · der Schirm · der Kamm · die Skier · die Stiefel · die Mütze

F. Kurzgespräche *(Together with your partner, prepare one of the following brief dialogues. Then present it to the class.)*

1. **Überraschung in Heidelberg**

   You are visiting your aunt in Heidelberg. As you tour the castle, you see a German student whom you got to know while you both stayed at a youth hostel in Aachen. Call out to the German student. Both of you express your disbelief that you have met again. Your friend is studying in Heidelberg; you explain why you are there. You ask whether your friend would like to go for a cola (drink), and he/she agrees.

2. **Hotelsuche in Stralsund**

   You and a friend are in Stralsund and are looking for a hotel room. You have both inquired in several places. All the hotels you saw had no available rooms at all; in desperation your friend has taken a double room that will cost you 120 Euro for one night. You both express your disbelief at your bad luck.

G. Meine Ferienreise *(Using the questions as a guideline, write a brief paragraph.)*
1. Wohin geht Ihre nächste *(next)* Reise? Wann? Wo übernachten Sie dann, und warum dort?
2. Wo sind Sie das letzte Mal *(the last time)* gewesen? Wann? Wo haben Sie übernachtet und wie hat es Ihnen gefallen?

Fokus — *Luxembourg*

The Grand Duchy of Luxembourg (**Luxemburg,** pop. 435,700), one of Europe's oldest and smallest independent countries, lies between Germany, France, and Belgium. Although it is one of the world's most industrialized nations, its heavy industry, mainly iron and steel production, has not spoiled the natural beauty of the country's rolling hills and dense forests. Almost all Luxembourgers speak Letzeburgish, a German dialect. French, German, and Letzeburgish are used in parliament. Despite close ties to their neighbors, the people of Luxembourg maintain an independent spirit, as expressed in the words of their national anthem: "Mir wölle bleiwe wat mir sin" (**Wir wollen bleiben, was wir sind**). Its capital by the same name (pop. 80,700) is a big financial and banking center and home to several European institutions, including the EURATOM (European Atomic Energy Community).

Blick auf *(view of)* Luxemburg, mit der Unterstadt an der Alzette

HÖREN SIE ZU! TRACK 15

Hotel Lindenhof *(Mr. Baumann calls the reception of Hotel Lindenhof on Lake Constance. Listen to the conversation. Then complete the sentences below with the correct information from the dialogue.)*

Zum Erkennen: die Person, -en; das Frühstücksbüfett; das Schwimmbad; Minigolf

1. Herr Baumann und seine Familie fahren im Sommer an den Bodensee . 2. Sie wollen am 10. Juli ankommen und eine Woche bleiben. 3. Sie brauchen Zimmer für vier Personen, also zwei Zimmer. 4. Die Zimmer kosten 85 Euro pro Tag. 5. Das Frühstücksbüfett kostet nichts extra. 6. Herr Baumann findet das nicht (zu) teuer . 7. Die Kinder können dort schwimmen und in der Nähe auch Minigolf und Tennis spielen. 8. Zum See ist es auch nicht weit . 9. Vom Balkon hat man einen Blick auf den See und die Alpen . 10. Er nimmt / reserviert die Zimmer.

Video-Ecke

- The *Minidrama* "Ihren Ausweis, bitte!" is the story of an American traveling salesman who tries to check into a German hotel. He is in a great hurry to exchange money because the taxi driver waits to be paid. However, he can find neither his passport nor his airline tickets. Luckily, he locates some other ID, so he can go ahead to exchange money and rent a room. As he keeps worrying about his passport, events take a few unexpected turns.

Web-Ecke

- For updates, self-assessment quizzes, and online activities related to this chapter, visit the *Wie geht's?* Web site at **http://wiegehts.heinle.com**. You will find out about various vacation options on an island in the North Sea, check the prices of a camping vacation in Germany, and learn more about the small nation of Luxembourg.

Rückblick: Kapitel 4—7

I. Verbs

1. Wissen

p. 165

Wissen, like the modals below, is irregular in the singular of the present tense. It means *to know a fact,* as opposed to **kennen,** which means *to be acquainted with a person or thing.*

singular	plural
ich weiß	wir wissen
du weißt	ihr wisst
er weiß	sie wissen

Remember that the Workbook has extensive review exercises to accompany this Rückblick.

2. Modals

pp. 137—139

	dürfen	können	müssen	sollen	wollen	mögen	möchten
ich	darf	kann	muss	soll	will	mag	möchte
du	darfst	kannst	musst	sollst	willst	magst	möchtest
er	darf	kann	muss	soll	will	mag	möchte
wir	dürfen	können	müssen	sollen	wollen	mögen	möchten
ihr	dürft	könnt	müsst	sollt	wollt	mögt	möchtet
sie	dürfen	können	müssen	sollen	wollen	mögen	möchten

The modal is the second sentence element (V1); the infinitive of the main verb (V2) stands at the end of the sentence.

Sie **sollen** ihr den Kaffee **bringen.**   *You're supposed to **bring** her the coffee.*
  V1   V2

3. Imperatives

pp. 163—164

The forms of the familiar imperative have no pronouns; the singular familiar imperative has no **-st** ending.

formal sg. + pl.	fam. sg. (du)	fam. pl. (ihr)	1st pers. pl. (let's . . .)
Schreiben Sie!	Schreib!	Schreibt!	Schreiben wir!
Antworten Sie!	Antworte!	Antwortet!	Antworten wir!
Fahren Sie!	**Fahr!**	Fahrt!	Fahren wir!
Nehmen Sie!	**Nimm!**	Nehmt!	Nehmen wir!

4. Present perfect

pp. 110—113

a. Past participles

t-verbs (weak and mixed verbs)	n-verbs (strong verbs)
(ge) + stem(change) + (e)t	(ge) + stem(change) + en
gekauft	geschrieben
gearbeitet	
gebracht	
eingekauft	mitgeschrieben
verkauft	unterschrieben
reserviert	

b. Most verbs use **haben** as the auxiliary. Those that use **sein** are intransitive (take no object) and imply a change of place or condition; **bleiben** and **sein** are exceptions to the rule.

> Wir haben Wien gesehen.
>
> Wir sind viel gelaufen.
>
> Abends sind wir müde gewesen.

5. Verbs with inseparable and separable prefixes

p. 112

a. Inseparable-prefix verbs (verbs with the unstressed prefixes **be-, emp-, ent-, er-, ge-, ver-** and **zer-**) are never separated.

> Was bedeutet das?
>
> Das verstehe ich nicht.
>
> Was empfehlen Sie?
>
> Wer bezahlt das Mittagessen?

über-, unter-, and **wieder-** can be used as separable or inseparable prefixes, depending on the particular verb and meaning.

> Übernach'tet ihr in der Jugendherberge?
>
> Unterschrei'ben Sie bitte hier!
>
> Wiederho'len Sie bitte! BUT Hol das bitte wieder!

pp. 186–187

b. Separable-prefix verbs (verbs where the prefix is stressed) are separated in statements, questions, and imperatives.

> Du **bringst** deine Schwester **mit.**
>
> **Bringst** du deine Schwester **mit?**
>
> **Bring** doch deine Schwester **mit!**

They are not separated when used with modals, in the present perfect, or in dependent clauses.

> Du **sollst** deine Schwester **mitbringen.**
>
> **Hast** du deine Schwester **mitgebracht?**
>
> Sie will wissen, ob du deine Schwester **mitbringst.**

II. Cases

pp. 39, 58, 84

1. Interrogative pronouns

nom.	wer?	was?
acc.	wen?	was?
dat.	wem?	—

pp. 183–185

2. **Der**-words and **ein**-words

Der-words have the same endings as the definite article **der**; and **ein**-words (or possessive adjectives) have the same endings as **ein** and **kein.**

dieser	solcher (so ein)		mein	unser
jeder	welcher		dein	euer
mancher	alle		sein, sein, ihr	ihr, Ihr

3. Two-way prepositions: accusative or dative?   pp. 158–160

> **an, auf, hinter, in, neben, über, unter, vor, zwischen**

The nine two-way prepositions take either the dative or the accusative, depending on the verb.

> wo?   LOCATION, activity within a place → <u>dative</u>
> wohin?   DESTINATION, motion to a place → <u>accusative</u>

Remember the difference between these two sets of verbs:

to put (upright)	Er **stellt** den Koffer neben den Ausgang.
to stand	Der Koffer **steht** neben dem Ausgang.
to put (flat), lay	**Legen** Sie den Ausweis auf den Tisch!
to lie (flat)	Der Ausweis **liegt** auf dem Tisch.

4. Summary of the three cases

	use	follows ...	masc.	neut.	fem.	pl.
nom.	SUBJECT, PREDICATE NOUN	**heißen, sein, werden**	der dieser ein mein	das dieses ein mein	die diese eine meine	die diese keine meine
acc.	DIRECT OBJECT	**durch, für, gegen, ohne, um**	den diesen einen meinen			
		an, auf, hinter, in, neben, über, unter, vor, zwischen				
dat.	INDIRECT OBJECT	**aus, außer, bei, mit, nach, seit, von, zu**	dem diesem einem meinem	dem diesem einem meinem	der dieser einer meiner	den diesen keinen meinen
		antworten, danken, gefallen, gehören, helfen, zuhören				

5. Personal pronouns   pp. 134–135

	singular					plural			sg. / pl.
nom.	ich	du	er	es	sie	wir	ihr	sie	Sie
acc.	**mich**	**dich**	**ihn**	**es**	**sie**	**uns**	**euch**	**sie**	**Sie**
dat.	**mir**	**dir**	**ihm**	**ihm**	**ihr**	**uns**	**euch**	**ihnen**	**Ihnen**

Don't confuse these pronouns with the **ein**-words (or possessive adjectives, see 2 on page 200), which are always followed by a noun.

III. Sentence structure

1. Verb position

pp. 26–27, 63   a. V1 — V2

In declarative sentences, yes/no questions, and imperatives, two-part verb phrases are split:

- the inflected part (V1) is the first or second sentence element
- the other part (V2) appears at the end of the clause.

Er **ist** hier an der Uni **Student.**
Er **ist** wirklich sehr **interessant.**
Hast du ihn schon **kennen gelernt?**
Ich **kann** jetzt nicht lange **sprechen.**
Komm doch später bei uns **vorbei!**
V1   V2

pp. 116–118   b. Subordinate clauses

- Subordinate clauses are introduced by subordinating conjunctions or interrogatives:

> bevor, dass, ob, obwohl, weil, wenn, etc.

> wer? wen? wem? was? was für ein(e)? wohin? woher? wo? wann? warum? wie? wie lange? wie viel? wie viele? etc.

- In subordinate clauses, the subject usually comes right after the conjunction, and the inflected verb (V1) is at the end of the clause.

Sie sagt, **dass** sie das Einzelzimmer **nimmt.**
Er sagt, **dass** er den Zimmerschlüssel **mitbringt.**

- Two-part verb phrases appear in the order V2 V1.

Sie sagt, **dass** er den Koffer **mitbringen soll.**

- If a subordinate clause is the first sentence element, then the inflected part of the verb in the main clause comes right after the comma, retaining second position in the overall sentence.

Ich **habe** den Schlüssel **mitgenommen,** weil das Hotel um 24.00 Uhr zumacht.

Weil das Hotel um 24.00 Uhr zumacht, **habe** ich den Schlüssel **mitgenommen.**

pp. 85, 135 2. Sequence of objects

The indirect object usually precedes the direct object, unless the direct object is a pronoun.

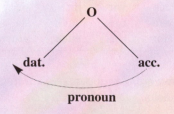

Sie gibt **dem Herrn** den Reisescheck.
Sie gibt **ihm** den Reisescheck.
Sie gibt ihn **dem Herrn.**
Sie gibt ihn **ihm.**

3. **Sondern** vs. **aber**   p. 141

Sondern must be used when the first clause is negated AND the meaning *but on the contrary* is implied.

> Er wohnt hier, **aber** er ist gerade nicht zu Hause.

> Heinz ist nicht hier, **aber** er kommt in zehn Minuten zurück.

> Heinz ist nicht hier, **sondern** bei Freunden.

NOTE: Review exercises for both vocabulary and structures can be found in the Workbook.

Kapitel ⑧

Post und Reisen

Das Reisen mit dem ICE ist schnell und bequem.

Lernziele

Vorschau
Spotlight on Switzerland

Gespräche + Wortschatz
Postal service, phones, and travel

Fokus
Phoning and postal services
Train travel
Car travel
William Tell
Switzerland's mountain world
Switzerland and its languages
Hermann Hesse

Struktur
8.1 Genitive case
8.2 Time expressions
8.3 Sentence structure: types and sequence of adverbs, the position of **nicht**

Einblicke
Touristen in der Schweiz
Hermann Hesse, *Im Nebel*

Video-Ecke
Minidrama: *Die Schweizer Post ist schnell*
Blickpunkt: *Reise in die Schweiz*

Web-Ecke

Vorschau

Spotlight on Switzerland

Area: Approximately 16,000 square miles, about half the size of Indiana.

Population: About 7.1 million.

Religion: 46 percent Catholic, 40 percent Protestant, 14 percent other.

Geography: This landlocked country is clearly defined by three natural regions: the *Alpine ranges* that stretch from the French border south of Lake Geneva diagonally across the southern half of Switzerland and include the world-renowned resorts of the Bernese Oberland, Zermatt, and St. Moritz in the Inn River valley; the plateaus and valleys of the *midland* between Lake Geneva and Lake Constance; and the mountains of the *Jura* in the northernmost section of the Alps.

Currency: Schweizer Franken, 1 sfr = 100 Rappen or Centimes.

Principal Cities: Capital Berne (*Bern*, pop. 127,470), Zurich (*Zürich*, pop. 361,555), Basel (pop. 174,000), Geneva (*Genf*, pop. 176,000), Lausanne (pop. 124,465).

Isolated and protected by its relative inaccessibility, Switzerland developed as a nation without major hindrance over a span of 700 years. It was founded in 1291, when the cantons of Uri, Schwyz, and Unterwalden formed an alliance against the ruling House of Habsburg. Over time, the original confederation grew into a nation of 26 cantons (states). These cantons maintain considerable autonomy, with their own constitutions and legislatures. The 1848 constitution merged the old confederation into a single state by eliminating all commercial barriers and establishing a common postal service, military, legislature, and judiciary.

Despite its small size, few natural resources, and ethnic diversity, Switzerland is one of the most stable nations in the world. Its stability can be attributed to its high standard of living, the conservative character of its people, and the country's neutrality in the two world wars. Switzerland has stubbornly adhered to the principle of neutrality—to the extent of staying out of NATO and the European Union; it joined the United Nations only in 2002, with a narrow margin of 12 cantons voting for and 11 against the approval. Switzerland's stability and bank-secrecy law continue to attract capital from all over the world, although revelations during the 1990s about the role of Swiss banks in holding gold stolen by the Nazis during World War II have tarnished the image of these renowned financial institutions.

Switzerland is active in the Council of Europe and several specialized agencies of the United Nations (UN). The seat of the League of Nations after World War I, Switzerland is now home to the UN's Economic and Social Council, the International Labor Organization, the World Health Organization, the World Council of Churches, and the International Red Cross. Founded in Geneva in 1864, the Red Cross derived its universally recognized symbol from the inverse of the Swiss flag, a white cross on a red background. (For pictures and information on a Swiss city, visit www.[city name].ch.)

Museum für Völkerkunde.
Flügellöwe. Als Göttersänfte in Prozessionen mitgeführt
Bali, Indonesien.

205

Gespräche + Wortschatz

Warm-ups: 1. **Können Sie mir sagen,** wie spät es ist? welches Datum heute ist? wo ich … lassen kann? (z.B. S1: Wo kann ich das Buch lassen? – S2: Leg es auf den Tisch!) In a chain reaction, have students ask each other where they can leave certain things. Whoever answers, asks the next question. 2. **Welche Verben beginnen mit** an-, auf-, ein-, mit-, um-, vor-, bei-, zu-, zurück-; be-, emp-, ent-, ge-, über-, ver-, wieder-? 3. **Geben Sie die Imperativformen von:** hier bleiben, bitte entschuldigen, langsam sprechen, schön schlafen, nicht so viel essen, laut lesen, den Scheck einlösen, hier unterschreiben!

Although Switzerland so far chose not to convert its franc to the euro, one euro equals about 1.60 Swiss francs.

Like in previous chapters, you could have students act out the dialogue with a partner.

Auf der Post am Bahnhof

UTA Ich möchte dieses Paket nach Amerika schicken.

HERR Normal oder per Luftpost?

UTA Per Luftpost. Wie lange dauert das denn?

HERR Ungefähr eine Woche. Füllen Sie bitte diese Paketkarte aus! … Moment, hier fehlt noch Ihr Absender.

UTA Ach ja! … Noch etwas. Ich brauche eine Telefonkarte.

HERR Für fünf, 10 oder 20 Franken?

UTA Für 20 Franken. Vielen Dank!

CD 4, Track 5

Am Fahrkartenschalter in Zürich

ANNE Wann fährt der nächste Zug nach Interlaken?

FRAU In 10 Minuten. Abfahrt um 11.28 Uhr, Gleis 2.

ANNE Ach du meine Güte! Und wann kommt er dort an?

FRAU Ankunft in Interlaken um 14.16 Uhr.

ANNE Muss ich umsteigen?

FRAU Ja, in Bern, aber Sie haben Anschluss zum InterCity mit nur 24 Minuten Aufenthalt.

ANNE Gut. Geben Sie mir bitte eine Hin- und Rückfahrkarte nach Interlaken!

FRAU Erster oder zweiter Klasse?

ANNE Zweiter Klasse.

Das Postpaket Schnell und sicher

Zug		IC 118 ✕ [4]	518 ✕	1720	[4]	IC 120 ✕ [4]	1520 ⚤	1822 ⚤	[4]
Zürich HB		10 03	10 07	10 28		11 03	11 07	11 28	
Baden				10 45				11 45	
Brugg (Aargau)				10 53				11 53	
Aarau			10 35	11 07			11 35	12 07	
Olten	24016		10 44	11 15			11 44	12 15	
Olten	24000			10 47				11 47	
Biel/Bienne				11 33				12 33	
Lausanne								13 48	
Genève				13 05					

Zug		IC 721 ⚤	2521		EC 73 ✕ [7]	[4] ⚤	1866		IC 725 🛏
Basel SBB		10 00	10 11	10 29	11 00		11 29		12 00
Liestal			10 21	10 46			11 46		
Olten		10 26	10 43	11 11	11 26		12 11		12 26
Olten		10 28	10 48	11 17	11 28		12 17		12 28
Langenthal			11 00	11 29			12 29		
Herzogenbuchsee			11 06	11 35			12 35		
Burgdorf			11 18	11 47			12 47		
Bern		11 10	11 14	11 35	12 04	12 10	12 14	13 04	13 10
Bern	24004	11 28 ←		12 28 ↙		12 28			13 28
Interlaken West		12 16		13 16		13 16			14 16

A: 1. am Bahnhof 2. nach Amerika 3. per Luftpost 4. ungefähr eine Woche 5. eine Paketkarte 6. der Absender 7. eine Telefonkarte 8. fünf, 10 oder 20 Franken 9. nach Interlaken 10. in 10 Minuten / Abfahrt 11.28 Uhr, Ankunft 14.16 Uhr 11. in Bern 12. eine Hin- und Rückfahrkarte 2. Klasse

A. Fragen

1. Wo ist die Post? 2. Wohin will Uta ihr Paket schicken? 3. Wie schickt sie es? 4. Wie lange soll das dauern? 5. Was muss man bei einem Paket ins Ausland (*abroad*) ausfüllen? 6. Was fehlt auf der Paketkarte? 7. Was braucht Uta noch? 8. Was kosten Telefonkarten? 9. Wohin will Anne fahren? 10. Wann fährt der Zug ab und wann kommt er in Interlaken an? 11. Wo muss Anne umsteigen? 12. Was für eine Karte kauft sie?

B. Jetzt sind Sie dran!
Diesmal (*this time*) stehen Sie am Fahrkartenschalter. Bereiten Sie Ihr eigenes Gespräch mit Ihrem Partner/Ihrer Partnerin vor (*prepare your own dialogue*) und präsentieren Sie es dann vor der Klasse!

S1 Wann gehen Flüge nach . . .?
S2 Zu welcher Tageszeit möchten Sie denn fliegen?
S1 Ich muss um . . . in . . . sein.
S2 Es gibt einen Flug um . . .
S1 Hat er eine Zwischenlandung?
S2 Ja, in . . . Dort haben Sie . . . Aufenthalt.
S1 Muss ich umsteigen?
S2 . . .
S1 . . . Dann geben Sie mir bitte eine Hin- und Rückflugkarte nach . . . !

Wortschatz I

Die Post *(post office, mail)*

Das Telefon, -e *(telephone)*

der Absender, -	*return address*	die Adresse, -n	*address*
Brief, -e	*letter*	(Ansichts)karte, -n	*(picture) postcard*
Briefkasten, ⸚	*mailbox*	Briefmarke, -n	*stamp*
		E-Mail, -s	*e-mail*
das Fax, -e	*fax*	Postleitzahl, -en	*zip code*
Handy, -s	*cell(ular) phone*	Telefonkarte, -n	*telephone card*
Paket, -e	*package, parcel*	Telefonnummer, -n	*telephone number*
Postfach, ⸚er	*PO box*	Vorwahl, -en	*area code*

If students ask: *collect call* **das R-Gespräch, -e;** *mail carrier* **der Briefträger, - / Postbote, -n, -n;** *plain postcard* **die Postkarte, -n.** Also: **das Internet; das Ticket, -s**

Although Germans say **Briefmarken** for stamps, foreigners will often look in vain for the word in a German post office, where the official word **Postwertzeichen** prevails instead.

Fokus — *Phoning and Postal Services*

Placing calls in the German-speaking countries is still not inexpensive, but call-by-call providers, where you pre-dial a certain number, have made it much more affordable. Even local calls are charged according to minutes spent on line. The introduction of wireless phones (**Handys**) has made a big difference in communication habits. People are using cell phones everywhere. On the road, however, motor vehicle operators are not allowed to use phones unless they are permanently installed in the car.

Most public phone booths (**Telefonzellen**) require a phone card (**Telefonkarte**), which can be bought at post offices and newspaper stands. Since hotels usually add a substantial surcharge for phone calls, travelers often find it cheaper to use a long-distance calling card or to place calls from a post office. Post offices in European countries offer a far greater range of services than in the United States or Canada. For example, it is possible to open a bank account with the post office, wire money, buy traveler's checks, and send a telegram or fax. However, the post office no longer has a monopoly on mail-delivery services; UPS and FedEx trucks have become a familiar sight in Europe.

der Wagen BUT **das Auto**

Die Reise, -n *(trip)*

der Aufenthalt, -e	*stopover, stay*	das Flugzeug, -e	*plane*
Bahnsteig, -e	*platform*	Gleis, -e	*track*
Fahrplan, ⸚e	*schedule*	die Abfahrt, -en	*departure*
Flug, ⸚e	*flight*	Ankunft, ⸚e	*arrival*
Flughafen, ⸚	*airport*	Bahn, -en	*railway, train*
Wagen, -	*car; railroad car*	Fahrkarte, -n	*ticket*
Zug, ⸚e	*train*	(Hin- und) Rück- fahrkarte, -n	*round-trip ticket*
		Fahrt, -en	*trip, drive*

Weiteres

ab·fahren (fährt ab), ist abgefahren (von)	*to leave, depart (from)*
ab·fliegen, ist abgeflogen (von)	*to take off, fly (from)*
aus·steigen, ist ausgestiegen	*to get off*
ein·steigen, ist eingestiegen	*to get on (in)*
um·steigen, ist umgestiegen	*to change (trains, etc.)*
besuchen	*to visit*
einen Satz bilden	*to form a sentence*
erzählen	*to tell*
fehlen	*to be missing / lacking*
fliegen, ist geflogen	*to fly*
landen, ist gelandet	*to land*
schicken	*to send*
telefonieren	*to call up, phone*

in einer Viertelstunde	*in a quarter of an hour*
in einer halben Stunde	*in half an hour*
in einer Dreiviertelstunde	*in three-quarters of an hour*
mit dem Zug / der Bahn fahren, ist gefahren	*to go by train*
Ach du meine Güte!	*My goodness!*
Na und?	*So what?*
Das ist doch egal.	*That doesn't matter. It's all the same to me.*
Das sieht dir (ihm, ihr, ihnen) ähnlich.	*That's typical of you (him, her, them).*
Das freut mich (für dich).	*I'm happy (for you).*
Gott sei Dank!	*Thank God!*

Also: **mit dem Bus / mit dem Fahrrad / mit der U-Bahn fahren** *to go by bus / bike / subway*

Students are already familiar with expressions like. **Schade!, Das tut mir Leid., Ach du liebes bisschen!, Das macht (doch) nichts., Pech / Glück gehabt!**, or **Das ist ja prima / toll / furchtbar . . . !** If you like, you could introduce **Du Glückspilz!** *You lucky thing!*, **Du Pechvogel!** *You unlucky thing!*, **Um Gottes willen!** *For heaven's sake!*, **Das ist wirklich zu dumm!** *That's really too bad!*, **Das geschieht dir recht**. *That serves you right.*

Zum Erkennen: normal *(regular);* per Luftpost *(by airmail);* die Paketkarte, -n *(parcel form);* aus·füllen *(to fill out);* noch etwas *(one more thing, something else);* der nächste / letzte Zug nach *(the next / last train to);* der Anschluss, ⸚e *(connection);* die Klasse, -n; AUCH: der Anhang *(appendix);* der Ausdruck, ⸚e *(expression);* der Genitiv, -e; die Gruppe; -n *(group);* die Liste, -n; die Tabelle, -n *(chart);* benutzen *(to use);* ergänzen *(to add to);* jemandem eine Frage stellen *(to ask sb. a question);* heraus·finden *(to find out);* korrigieren *(to correct);* präsentieren *(to present);* überprüfen *(to check);* Bereiten Sie Ihr eigenes Gespräch vor! *(Prepare your own dialogue!);* Wechseln Sie sich ab! *(Take turns!);* diesmal *(this time);* einer von Ihnen *(one of you);* der/die andere *(the other one);* die anderen *(the others)*

Fokus — *Train Travel*

Trains are a popular means of transportation in Europe, not only for commuting but also for long-distance travel. The rail network is extensive, and trains are generally clean, comfortable, and on time. Domestic InterCity **(IC)** and international EuroCity **(EC)** trains connect all major western European cities. In Germany, the high-speed InterCityExpress **(ICE),** which travels at speeds up to 280 km/h (175 mph), is an attractive alternative to congested highways. Business people can make or receive phone calls on board and even rent conference rooms equipped with fax machines. Non-European residents can benefit from a *Eurailpass,* which permits unlimited train—and some bus and boat—travel in most European countries, or from a *German Railpass,* which is less expensive but limited to Germany; both passes must be purchased outside of Europe. Larger train stations provide a wide range of services for the traveler, including coin-operated lockers **(Schließfächer)** or checked luggage rooms **(Gepäckaufgabe).**

Zum Thema

A. Allerlei Fragen

1. Was kostet es, wenn man einen Brief innerhalb von *(within)* Amerika oder Kanada schicken will? Wie lange braucht ein Brief innerhalb der Stadt? nach Europa?
2. Was muss man auf alle Briefe, Ansichtskarten und Pakete schreiben? Schreiben Sie oft Briefe? Wenn ja, wem? Schicken Sie oft E-Mails oder Faxe an Ihre Freunde? Was ist Ihre E-Mail-Adresse?
3. In Deutschland sind Briefkästen gelb. Welche Farbe haben die Briefkästen hier? Wo findet man sie?
4. Wo kann man hier telefonieren? Gibt es Telefonkarten? Wenn ja, wo bekommt man sie?
5. Haben Sie ein Handy? Wenn ja, wann und benutzen Sie es besonders viel?
6. In Deutschland darf man beim Autofahren nur mit einem im Auto eingebauten *(built-in)* Handy sprechen. Wie ist das hier? Benutzen Sie Ihr Handy beim Autofahren? Ist es eingebaut? Warum ist das Telefonieren beim Autofahren so gefährlich *(dangerous)*?
7. Wie reisen Sie gern und wie nicht? Warum?
8. Wohin sind Sie zuletzt *(the last time)* gereist? Sind Sie geflogen oder mit dem Wagen gefahren?
9. Was ist das Gegenteil von abfahren? abfliegen? einsteigen? Abfahrt? Abflug?
10. Wie heißt der Ort *(place),* wo Züge abfahren und ankommen? wo Flugzeuge abfliegen und landen? wo Busse halten?

A: Have students prepare answers in small groups, then ask the class some of these questions. When students of the same age speak to each other, they should address each other with **du!**

B. Was bedeuten die Wörter und was sind ihre Artikel?

Adressbuch, Abfahrtszeit, Ankunftsfahrplan, Bahnhofseingang, Busbahnhof, Busfahrt, Flugkarte, Flugschalter, Flugsteig, Gepäckkarte, Mietwagen, Nachtzug, Paketschalter, Postfachnummer, Speisewagen, Telefonrechnung

B: *address book* **(das)**, *departure time* **(die)**, *schedule of arrivals* **(der)**, *train station entrance* **(der)**, *bus depot* **(der)**, *bus trip* **(die)**, *plane ticket* **(die)**, *flight ticket counter* **(der)**, *gate* **(der)**, *luggage claim ticket* **(die)**, *rental car* **(der)**, *night train* **(der)**, *parcel post counter* **(der)**, *PO box number* **(die)**, *dining car* **(der)**, *telephone bill* **(die)**

C. Was fehlt? Finden Sie die Antworten auf dem Fahrplan!

> *NOTE:* 1 km = 0.62 miles. Here is an easy way to convert kilometers to miles: divide the km figure in half, and add a quarter of that to the half. Thus, 80 km ÷ 2 = 40 + 10 = 50 miles.

km	Stuttgart–Zürich		Zug	E3504	D83	D381	D383			D85	D389		D87	D385	E3309	D387
0	Stuttgart Hbf	740			6 48	7 31	9 34			12 44	14 26		17 32	18 26	20 06	
26	Böblingen					7 53	9 56			13 06	14 48		17 55	18 48	20 29	
67	Horb				7 34	8 20	10 24			13 33	15 15		18 21	19 15	21 00	
110	Rottweil				8 05	8 59	10 54			14 02	15 52		18 51	19 45	21 36	
138	Tuttlingen				8 26	9 17	11 13			14 21	16 11		19 09	20 11	21 55	
172	Singen (Hohentwiel)				8 49	9 42	11 37			14 45	16 35		19 32	20 35	22 22	
			Zug						D2162	×1)						
	Singen (Hohentwiel)	730		6 31	8 55	9 49	11 44		12 43	14 51	16 44		19 37	20 44		22 44
192	Schaffhausen			6 49	9 10	10 05	12 00		12 58	15 07	17 00		19 52	21 00		23 00
			Zug	1559	(EC 83)				IC 357	(EC 85)			(IC 87)			
	Schaffhausen	24032		7 02	9 12	10 09	12 09		13 09	15 09	17 09		19 55	21 09		23 09
238	Zürich HB			7 47	9 47	10 47	12 47		13 47	15 47	17 47		20 31	21 47		23 47

1. Von Stuttgart nach Zürich sind es __238 km__ Kilometer.
2. Der erste Zug morgens fährt um __6.48 Uhr__ Uhr und der letzte *(last)* Zug abends um __20.06 Uhr__ Uhr.
3. Die Reise von Stuttgart nach Zürich geht über __Schaffhausen__.
4. Wenn man um 6.48 Uhr von Stuttgart abfährt, ist man um __9.47 Uhr__ Uhr in Zürich.
5. Die Fahrt dauert ungefähr __drei__ Stunden.

D. Jeder hat Probleme.

1. **So geht's** *(that's the way it goes)!* Lesen Sie die folgenden *(following)* Sätze laut!

Was sagen Sie zu Daniels Pech? Wechseln Sie sich ab *(take turns)!*

a. Daniel hat von seinen Eltern zum Geburtstag ein Auto bekommen.
b. Das Auto ist nicht ganz neu.
c. Aber es fährt so schön ruhig und schnell, dass er gleich am ersten Tag einen Strafzettel *(ticket)* bekommen hat.
d. Am Wochenende ist er in die Berge gefahren, aber es hat immer nur geregnet.
e. Es hat ihm trotzdem viel Spaß gemacht, weil er dort eine Studentin kennen gelernt hat.
f. Auf dem Weg zurück ist ihm jemand in sein Auto gefahren. Totalschaden *(total wreck)!*
g. Daniel hat aber nur ein paar Kratzer *(scratches)* bekommen.

Fokus — *Car Travel*

A U.S. or Canadian driver's license (**der Führerschein**) can be used in the German-speaking countries. Most traffic signs are identical to those in the United States and Canada; others are self-explanatory. Unless otherwise indicated, the driver approaching from the right has the right-of-way. As a rule, right turns at a red light are prohibited, as is passing on the right. The speed limit (**Tempolimit** or **Geschwindigkeitsbegrenzung**) in cities and towns is generally 50 km/h (31 mph), and on the open road 100 km/h (62 mph). Except for certain stretches, there is no official speed limit on the freeway (**die Autobahn**), but drivers are recommended (**die Richtgeschwindigkeit**) not to exceed 130 km/h (81 mph). The driving style is generally more aggressive than in North America.

Europcar Inter rent

RAIL ROAD

Raus aus dem Zug, rein ins Auto!

h. Er hat übrigens seit ein paar Tagen eine Wohnung mitten in der Stadt. Sie ist gar nicht teuer.

i. Er möchte das Mädchen aus den Bergen wiedersehen, aber er kann sein Adressbuch mit ihrer Telefonnummer nicht finden.

j. Momentan geht alles schief *(wrong)*. Er kann auch sein Portemonnaie *(wallet)* nicht finden.

k. Noch etwas. Die Katze *(cat)* des Nachbarn hat seine Goldfische gefressen *(ate)*.

l. Sein Bruder hat übrigens eine Operation gehabt. Aber jetzt geht es ihm wieder gut und er ist wieder zu Hause.

2. **Und wie geht's mir?** Erzählen Sie Ihrer Gruppe, wie es Ihnen geht! Jeder hat wenigstens *(at least)* ein Problem. Was sagen die anderen dazu *(the others to that)*?

Aussprache: e, er

Lesen Sie auch Teil II. 8–10 in *Zur Aussprache* im *Arbeitsbuch*.

1. [ə] Adresse, Ecke, Haltestelle, bekommen, besuchen, eine halbe Stunde
2. [ʌ] aber, sauber, schwer, euer, unser, Zimmernummer, Uhr, vor, nur, unter, über, außer, wiederholen
3. Wortpaare

    a. Studenten / Studentin
    b. Touristen / Touristin
    c. diese / dieser
    d. arbeiten / Arbeitern
    e. lese / Leser
    f. mieten / Mietern

CD 4, Track 6

HÖREN SIE ZU!   TRACK 16

Weg zur Post

Zum Erkennen: Na klar! *(Sure!);* endlich mal *(finally);* das Papierwarengeschäft, -e *(office supply store);* Lass sie wiegen! *(Have them weighed!)*

Richtig oder falsch?

f	1. Bill muss endlich mal an Claudias Eltern schreiben.
f	2. Claudia möchte wissen, wo man Papier, Ansichtskarten und Briefmarken bekommt.
r	3. Bei Schlegel in der Beethovenstraße gibt es Briefpapier.
f	4. Postkarten findet man nur in Drogerien.
r	5. Gegenüber vom Stadttheater ist die Post.
f	6. Bill kauft heute Briefmarken und geht morgen zum Bahnhof.
f	7. Er soll zur Post gehen und Claudia Briefmarken mitbringen.

Struktur

8.1 Genitive case

The genitive case has two major functions: it expresses possession or another close relationship between two nouns and it follows certain prepositions.

1. The English phrases *the son's letter* and *the date of the letter* are expressed by the same genitive construction in German.

> Das ist **der Brief des Sohnes.**   *That's the son's letter.*
>
> Was ist **das Datum des Briefes?**   *What's the date of the letter?*

a. The genitive form of the INTERROGATIVE PRONOUN **wer** is **wessen** *(whose)*. The chart below shows all four cases of the interrogative pronouns.

	persons	things and ideas
nom.	wer?	was?
acc.	wen?	was?
dat.	wem?	—
gen.	**wessen?**	—

The interrogative pronoun **wessen** *is always followed (eventually) by a noun:* **Wessen Sohn? Wessen (furchtbar langer) Brief?**

Wessen Brief ist das?   *Whose letter is that?*

Der Brief des Sohnes!   *The son's letter.*

b. The genitive forms of the DEFINITE and INDEFINITE ARTICLES complete this chart of articles:

Der Planet der Ideen

	SINGULAR masc.	neut.	fem.	PLURAL
nom.	der ein kein	das ein kein	die eine keine	die — keine
acc.	den einen keinen			
dat.	dem einem keinem	dem einem keinem	der einer keiner	den — keinen
gen.	des eines keines	des eines keines	der — keiner	der — keiner

c. The genitive case is signaled not only by the forms of the articles, but also by a special ending for MASCULINE and NEUTER nouns in the singular.

- Most one-syllable nouns and nouns ending in **-s, -ss, -ß, -z, -tz,** or **-zt,** add **-es:**

  der Zug   das Geld   der Ausweis   der Pass   der Platz

  des Zug**es**   **des** Geld**es**   **des** Ausweis**es**   **des** Pass**es**   **des** Platz**es**

- Nouns with more than one syllable add only an **-s:**

  des Flughafen**s**   *of the airport, the airport's*

  des Wagen**s**   *of the car, the car's*

  NOTE: German uses NO apostrophe for the genitive!

- N-nouns have an **-n** or **-en** ending in ALL CASES except in the nominative singular. A very few n-nouns have a genitive **-s** as well.

der Franzose, **-n**, -n	**des** Franzose**n**
Herr, **-n**, -en	Herr**n**
Junge, **-n**, -n	Junge**n**
Mensch, **-en**, -en	Mensch**en**
Nachbar, **-n**, -n	Nachbar**n**
Student, **-en**, -en	Student**en**
Tourist, **-en**, -en	Tourist**en**
Name, **-n(s)**, -n	Name**ns**

Note how n-nouns are listed in vocabularies and dictionaries: the first ending usually refers to the accusative, dative, and genitive singular; the second one to the plural.

d. FEMININE NOUNS and PLURAL NOUNS have no special endings in the genitive.

die Reise	**der** Reise
die Reisen	**der** Reisen

e. Proper names usually add a final **-s:**

Annemarie**s** Flug	*Annemarie's flight*
Frau Strobel**s** Fahrt	*Ms. Strobel's trip*
Wien**s** Flughafen	*Vienna's airport*

In colloquial speech, however, **von** is frequently used instead of the genitive of a name: **die Adresse von Hans.**

f. Nouns in the genitive NORMALLY FOLLOW the nouns they modify, whereas proper names precede them.

> Er liest den Brief **der Tante.**
>
> Er liest **Annemaries** Brief.
>
> Er liest **Herrn Müllers** Brief.

The only exception to this rule about NO apostrophe for the genitive occurs when a proper name ends in **-s, -z, -tz,** or **-x: Hans' Adresse.** In written language, such genitives of names also take the ending **-ens: Schulzens Auto, Lorenzens Reisepläne.**

CAUTION: Even though the use of the possessive adjectives **mein, dein,** etc. inherently show possession, they still have the genitive case along with the noun.

Das ist **mein** Onkel.	*That's my uncle.*
Das ist der Koffer **meines Onkels.**	*That's my uncle's suitcase (the suitcase of my uncle).*
Er ist der Bruder **meiner Mutter.**	*He's my mother's brother (the brother of my mother).*

2. These prepositions are followed by the genitive case:

(an)statt	*instead of*	Ich nehme oft den Bus **(an)statt der Straßenbahn.**
trotz	*in spite of*	**Trotz des Wetters** bummele ich gern durch die Stadt.
während	*during*	**Während der Mittagspause** gehe ich in den Park.
wegen	*because of*	Heute bleibe ich **wegen des Regens** *(rain)* hier.

Während is also used as a subordinating conjunction: **Während ich hier bin, lerne ich viel Deutsch.**

In colloquial speech, **trotz** and **wegen** are also used with the dative, e.g., **trotz dem Wetter, wegen dem Regen.**

Übungen

A. Im Reisebüro *(at the travel agency).* Überprüfen Sie *(check)* noch einmal, ob Ihr Assistent die Reise nach Bern auch gut vorbereitet hat!

> BEISPIEL: Wo ist die Liste der Touristen? (Hotel/*pl.*)
> **Wo ist die Liste der Hotels?**

1. Wie ist der Name des Reiseführers *(tour guide)*? (Schloss, Dom, Museum, Straße, Platz, Tourist, Touristin, Franzose, Französin)
2. Wo ist die Telefonnummer des Hotels? (Gästehaus, Pension, Gasthof, Jugendherberge)

Simple introductory exercise: **z.B. das Buch: des Buches** 1. das Heft, der Pass, die Reise, der Scheck, das Taxi, der Ausweis, die Nacht, der Name 2. welche Bank, dieses Hotel, jeder Wagen, alle Flughäfen, manche Studenten, solche Leute 3. deine Geschwister, ihre Tante, unser Auto, euer Haus, sein Telefon, seine Telefonkarte, so ein Wagen, so eine Bahn

3. Wo ist die Adresse dieser Dame? (Gast, Mädchen, Junge, Herr, Herren, Student, Studenten)

4. Wann ist die Ankunft unserer Gruppe? (Bus, Zug, Flugzeug, Reiseführerin, Gäste)

5. Haben Sie wegen der Reservierung *(reservation)* angerufen? (Zimmer, Schlüssel/*sg.*, Gepäck, Adresse, Theaterkarten)

6. Wir fahren trotz des Gewitters *(thunderstorm).* (Wetter, Regen/*m.*, Eis, Feiertag, Ferien)

7. Christiane Binder kommt statt ihrer Mutter mit. (Vater, Bruder, Onkel, Nachbar, Nachbarin, Geschwister)

B: Have each student write five sentences (e.g., **Die Farbe des Wagens ist rot.**), and then share them with the class. Column 5 can be various things: an adjective, noun, name, pronoun, or a phrase.

B. Bilden Sie Sätze mit dem Genitiv! Benutzen Sie Wörter von jeder Liste!

BEISPIEL: Die Abfahrt des Zuges ist um 19.05 Uhr.

Optional English-to-German practice: 1. Is that Eva's train? 2. Do you know the number of the platform? 3. No. Where's the departure schedule [of the trains]? 4. Her train leaves in a few minutes. 5. Take along Kurt's package. 6. Kurt is a student and a friend of a friend *(f.).* 7. Eva, do you have the student's *(m.)* address? 8. No, but I know the name of the dorm. 9. I'll take (bring) it to him during the holidays. 10. Because of the exams, I don't have time now. 11. I'll send you a postcard instead of a letter. 12. And I'll send you an e-mail instead of a postcard. (See answer key in the Appendix.)

1	2	3		4	5
die Farbe	d-	Wagen	Gasthof	ist	_____
der Name	dies-	Bus	Ausweis	gefällt	
die Adresse	mein-	Zug	Pass	. . .	
die Nummer	unser-	Bahnsteig	Reisescheck		
das Zimmer	. . .	Koffer	Flug		
das Gepäck		Tasche	Frau		
die Abfahrt		Haus	Herr		
der Preis		Wohnung	Freund(in)		
die Lage *(location)*		Hotel	Tourist(in)		
. . .		Pension	Gäste		
		Berge	. . .		
		Postfach			
		. . .			

C: When students are familiar with the genitive, you can reverse this exercise: **Wer ist Ihr Großvater? Er ist der Vater meines Vaters.**

C. Wer ist diese Person und wie heißt sie? Fragen Sie Ihren Partner/Ihre Partnerin!

BEISPIEL: Wer ist der Vater deiner Mutter?
Der Vater meiner Mutter ist mein Großvater. Er heißt Paul.

1. Wer ist der Sohn deines Vaters? 2. Wer ist die Mutter deiner Mutter? 3. Wer ist die Tochter deiner Mutter? 4. Wer sind die Söhne und Töchter deiner Eltern? 5. Wer ist der Sohn deines Urgroßvaters *(great-grandfather)*? 6. Wer ist der Großvater deiner Mutter? 7. Wer ist die Schwester deiner Mutter? 8. Wer ist der Mann deiner Tante? 9. Wer ist die Tochter deines Großvaters?

D: First ask questions such as these of individual students, using anything they have with them or on them. Then have them form pairs or small groups, and ask each other similar questions.

D. Wem gehört das? Fragen Sie Ihren Partner/Ihre Partnerin!

BEISPIEL: Gehört die Jacke deinem Freund?
Nein, das ist nicht die Jacke meines Freundes. Das ist meine Jacke.

Gehört das Hemd deinem Bruder? die Uhr deiner Mutter? das Buch deinem Professor? die Tasche deiner Freundin? die Post deinem Nachbarn? der Kuli Frau . . . *(name a student)*? das Heft Herrn . . . *(name a student)*? usw.

Fokus — *William Tell*

William Tell (**Wilhelm Tell**) is a legendary Swiss folk hero and a universal symbol of resistance to oppression. In 1307, he purportedly refused to obey the commands of the tyrannical Austrian bailiff, Gessler, who then forced him to shoot an arrow through an apple on his son's head. Tell did so, but later took revenge by killing Bailiff Gessler. That event was the beginning of a general uprising of the Swiss against the Habsburgs, the ruling dynasty since 1273. In 1439, when the Habsburgs tried to bring Switzerland back under Austrian rule, the Confederation broke free of the Empire. The story of Tell's confrontation with Gessler inspired Friedrich Schiller's drama *Wilhelm Tell* (1804) and Rossini's opera *Guillaume Tell* (1829).

8.2 Time expressions

1. Adverbs of time

   a. To refer to SPECIFIC TIMES, such as *yesterday evening* or *tomorrow morning*, combine one word from group A with another from group B. The words in group A can be used alone, whereas those in group B must be used in combinations: **gestern Abend, morgen früh.**

Note spelling reform changes: **gestern abend > gestern Abend.** Point out capitalization rules with nouns: **der Morgen, (Nach)mittag, Abend, die Nacht; heute Morgen, morgen Mittag;** BUT **morgens, mittags, nachmittags, abends, nachts.**

A

vorgestern	*the day before yesterday*
gestern	*yesterday*
heute	*today*
morgen	*tomorrow*
übermorgen	*the day after tomorrow*

B

früh, Morgen[1]	*early, morning*
Vormittag[2]	*midmorning (9–12 A.M.)*[4]
Mittag	*noon (12–2 P.M.)*
Nachmittag	*afternoon (2–6 P.M.)*
Abend[3]	*evening (6–10 P.M.)*
Nacht[3]	*night (after 10 P.M.)*[4]

[1] **heute früh** is used in southern Germany, **heute Morgen** in northern Germany; both mean *this morning.* BUT *Tomorrow morning* is always **morgen früh.**

[2] The expressions in this column are commonly combined with the days of the week. In that combination—except for **früh**—they combine to make a compound noun: **Montagmorgen, Dienstagvormittag, Donnerstagabend** BUT **Montag früh.**

[3] German distinguishes clearly between **Abend** and **Nacht:** Wir sind **gestern Abend** ins Kino gegangen. Ich habe **gestern Nacht** schlecht geschlafen. **Heute Nacht** can mean *last night* or *tonight* (whichever is closer), depending on context.

[4] The times may vary somewhat, but these are reasonable guidelines.

Heute fliege ich von New York ab.
Morgen früh bin ich in Frankfurt.
Übermorgen fahre ich nach Bonn.
Montagabend besuche ich Krauses.
Dienstagnachmittag fahre ich mit dem Zug zurück.

   b. Adverbs such as **montags** and **morgens** don't refer to specific time (a specific *Monday* or *morning*), but rather imply that events USUALLY OCCUR (more or less regularly), for example, *on Mondays* or *in the mornings, most mornings.* The following new expressions also belong to this group: **täglich** *(daily),* **wöchentlich** *(weekly),* **monatlich** *(monthly),* and **jährlich** *(yearly, annually).*

montags, dienstags, mittwochs, donnerstags, freitags, samstags, sonntags; morgens, vormittags, mittags, nachmittags, abends, nachts, montagmorgens, dienstagabends[1], **täglich, wöchentlich, monatlich, jährlich**

[1] Note the difference in spelling: Kommst du **Dienstagabend?** Nein, **dienstagabends** kann ich nicht.

Sonntags tue ich nichts, aber **montags** arbeite ich schwer.

Morgens und **nachmittags** gehe ich zur Uni. **Mittags** spiele ich Tennis.

Freitagabends gehen wir gern aus und **samstagmorgens** stehen wir dann nicht so früh auf.

Ich muss **monatlich** 500 Euro zahlen.

2. Other time expressions

a. The accusative of time

To refer to a DEFINITE point in time (**wann?**) or length of time (**wie lange?**), German often uses time phrases in the accusative, without any prepositions. Here are some of the most common expressions:

wann?		wie lange?	
jeden Tag	*each day*	zwei Wochen	*for two weeks*
diese Woche	*this week*	einen Monat	*for one month*

Haben Sie diese Woche Zeit?   *Do you have time this week?*

Die Fahrt dauert zwei Stunden.   *The trip takes two hours.*

Ich bleibe zwei Tage in Zürich.   *I'll be in Zurich for two days.*

b. The genitive of time

To refer to an INDEFINITE point in time (in the past or future), German uses the genitive:

eines Tages   *one day, some day*

Eines Tages ist ein Fax gekommen.   *One day, a fax came.*

Eines Tages fahre ich in die Schweiz.   *Some day, I'll go to Switzerland.*

The following new expressions also belong into this group:

Anfang / Ende der Woche[2]   *at the beginning / end of the week*

Mitte des Monats[2]   *in the middle of the month*

[2]Anfang / Mitte / Ende **des Monats** BUT: Anfang / Mitte / Ende **Mai**

c. Prepositional time phrases

You are already familiar with the following phrases:

an	am Abend, am Wochenende, am Montag, am 1. April
bis	bis morgen, bis 2.30 Uhr, bis (zum) Freitag, bis (zum) Januar
für	für morgen, für Freitag, für eine Nacht
in	im Juli, im Sommer, in einem Monat; in 10 Minuten, in einer Viertelstunde, in einer Woche, in einem Jahr
nach	nach dem Essen, nach einer Stunde
seit	seit einem Jahr, seit September
um	um fünf (Uhr)
von . . . bis	vom 1. Juni bis (zum) 25. August; von Juli bis August
vor	vor einem Monat, vor ein paar Tagen
während	während des Sommers, während des Tages

- Two-way prepositions usually use the <u>dative</u> in time expressions: Wir fahren **in einer Woche** in die Berge. **Am Freitag** fahren wir ab.

- German uses **seit** plus the present tense to describe an action or condition that began in the past and is still continuing in the present. English uses the present perfect progressive to express the same thing: **Er wohnt seit zwei Jahren hier.** *(He has been living here for two years.)*

Übungen

E. Ein Besuch *(visit).* Was fehlt?

1. Sven ist *vor einer Woche* angekommen. *(one week ago)*
2. Wir sind *Donnerstagabend um sieben (Uhr)* abgefahren. *(Thursday evening at 7 o'clock)*
3. Er ist *neun Stunden* geflogen. *(for nine hours)*
4. Ich habe ihn schon *ein Jahr (lang)* nicht mehr gesehen. *(for one year)*
5. Er schläft *morgens* gewöhnlich nicht lange. *(in the morning)*
6. Aber er hat *Freitagmorgen bis um elf (Uhr)* geschlafen. *(Friday morning until 11 A.M.)*
7. Er bleibt noch ungefähr *eine Woche* bei uns. *(for one week)*
8. *Vorgestern* sind wir bei meiner Tante gewesen. *(the day before yesterday)*
9. *Heute Abend* gehen wir ins Kino. *(this evening)*
10. *Morgen früh* kommen Erika und Uwe vorbei. *(tomorrow morning)*
11. *Morgen Mittag* gehen wir alle essen. *(tomorrow at noon)*
12. *Am Nachmittag* bummeln wir etwas durch die Stadt. *(in the afternoon)*
13. Was wir *übermorgen* tun, weiß ich noch nicht. *(the day after tomorrow)*
14. *Jeden Tag / täglich* machen wir etwas Besonderes. *(every day)*
15. *(Am) Samstagmorgen, Samstagvormittag* fahren wir ab. *(on Saturday morning)*
16. Schade, dass Sven *in einer Woche* schon wieder zu Hause sein muss. *(in one week)*

F. Bei mir *(at my place).* Erzählen Sie Ihrer Gruppe, wie das bei Ihnen ist! Benutzen Sie Wörter von den Listen oder ergänzen Sie, was Sie brauchen!

BEISPIEL: Morgens trinke ich gewöhnlich Kaffee, aber heute Morgen habe ich Tee getrunken.

1	2	3	4	5	6
morgens	gewöhnlich	ausgehen	aber	letzte Woche	zu Hause bleiben
(nach)mittags	manchmal	in der Bibliothek arbeiten		diese Woche	meine Familie besuchen
(freitag)abends	meistens	die Wohnung putzen		vor ein paar Tagen	ins Konzert gehen
sonntags	oft	fernsehen *(watch TV)*		(vor)gestern	ein Buch lesen
während der Woche	immer	einkaufen gehen		gestern Abend	Tee trinken
am Wochenende	nie	E-Mails schreiben		heute Morgen	Musik hören
jeden Tag	. . .	im Internet surfen		(über)morgen	. . .
. . .		Kaffee trinken		. . .	
		. . .			

G. Allerlei Märkte in Bern. Finden Sie mit Ihrem Partner/Ihrer Partnerin heraus, wann es welchen Markt wo gibt! Geben Sie die Antwort auf Deutsch und auf Englisch!

BEISPIEL: Weihnachtsmarkt
täglich im Dezember
every day in December

MÄRKTE
MARCHÉS
MARKETS

www.markt-bern.ch

BERN – DIE MÄRITSTADT

① WARENMARKT: AUF DEM WAISENHAUSPLATZ, DAS GANZE JAHR ÜBER JEDEN DIENSTAG UND SAMSTAG. VON ANFANGS APRIL BIS OKTOBER AUCH AM DONNERSTAG MIT ABENDVERKAUF.

② GEMÜSE-, FRÜCHTE- UND BLUMENMARKT: DAS GANZE JAHR AUF DEM BUNDES- UND BÄRENPLATZ UND DEN ANGRENZENDEN GASSEN, JEDEN DIENSTAG UND SAMSTAG VORMITTAGS. AUF DEM BÄRENPLATZ VON APRIL BIS OKTOBER TÄGLICH.

③ FLEISCHMARKT: DIENSTAG UND SAMSTAG VORMITTAGS, MÜNSTERGASSE.

④ HANDWERKMARKT: JEDEN ERSTEN SAMSTAG DES MONATS, MÜNSTERPLATZ.

⑤ FLOHMARKT: AUF DEM MÜHLEPLATZ IN DER MITTE JEDEN DRITTEN SAMSTAG DES MONATS VON MAI BIS OKTOBER.

⑥ GERANIENMARKT: NACH MITTE MAI AUF DEM BUNDESPLATZ, NUR VORMITTAGS.

ZWIEBELMARKT: AM VIERTEN MONTAG DES NOVEMBERS IN DER GANZEN STADT.

⑦ WEIHNACHTSMARKT: DEZEMBER TÄGLICH, MÜNSTER UND WAISENHAUSPLATZ.

8.3 Sentence structure

1. Types of adverbs

   You have already encountered various adverbs and adverbial phrases. They are usually divided into three major groups.

   a. ADVERBS OF TIME, answering the questions **wann? wie lange?**

      am Abend, am 2. April, am 4. Montag, Anfang März, bis Mai, eine Woche, eines Tages, ein paar Minuten, Ende des Monats, heute, im Juni, immer, jetzt, manchmal, meistens, montags, Mitte Juli, morgens, nie, oft, stundenlang, täglich, um zwölf, vor einer Woche, während des Winters usw.

   b. ADVERBS OF MANNER, answering the question **wie?**

      gemütlich, langsam, laut, mit der Bahn, ohne Geld, schnell, zu Fuß, zusammen usw.

   c. ADVERBS OF PLACE, answering the questions **wo? wohin? woher?**

      auf der Post, bei uns, da, dort, hier, im Norden, zu Hause, mitten in der Stadt, überall, nach Berlin, nach Hause, auf die Post, zur Uni, aus Kanada, von Amerika, aus dem Flugzeug usw.

2. Sequence of adverbs

   If two or more adverbs or adverbial phrases occur in one sentence, they usually follow the sequence TIME, MANNER, PLACE.

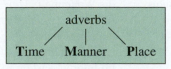

Er kann das Paket **morgen mit dem Auto zur Post** bringen.
              T   M   P

Since **studenlang** means *for hours,* let students figure out the meaning of **tagelang, wochenlang, monatelang, jahrelang.**

- If there is more than one time expression, general time references precede specific time references:

  Er bringt das Paket **morgen** **um neun Uhr** zur Post.

- Like other sentence elements, adverbs and adverbial phrases may precede the verb.

  Morgen kann er das Paket mit dem Auto zur Post bringen.
  Mit dem Auto kann er das Paket morgen zur Post bringen.
  Zur Post kann er das Paket morgen mit dem Auto bringen.

3. Position of **nicht**

   As you already know from Chapter 2, Section 2.3, **nicht** usually comes <u>after adverbs of definite time</u> but <u>before other adverbs, such as adverbs of manner or place</u>.

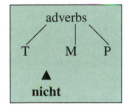

Er bringt das Paket ▲.
Er bringt das Paket ▲ mit.
Er kann das Paket ▲ mitbringen.
Er kann das Paket **morgen** ▲ mitbringen.
Er kann das Paket **morgen** ▲ **mit dem Auto** mitbringen.
Er kann das Paket **morgen** ▲ **mit dem Auto zur Post** bringen.

Übungen

H. **Sagen Sie das noch einmal!** Benutzen Sie die adverbialen Ausdrücke *(adverbial expressions)* in der richtigen Reihenfolge *(in the proper sequence)*!

Fokus — *Switzerland's Mountain World*

Not surprisingly, Switzerland has a number of popular and fashionable mountain resorts. The glacier village of **Grindelwald** in the Bernese Oberland is a favorite base for mountain climbers and skiers. **St. Moritz,** south of Davos, is nestled in the Upper Inn Valley next to a lake. Twice host to the Winter Olympics (1928 and 1948), the resort has become a jet-set sports mecca. Another fashionable area is **Saas Fee,** northeast of Zermatt. The village allows no motor vehicles to spoil its magnificent setting facing the great Fee glacier.

Besides the **Matterhorn** (14,692 ft.), the most famous Swiss peaks are the **Jungfrau, Mönch,** and **Eiger** (all around 13,000 ft.). A tunnel, almost 4.5 miles long, leads steeply up to the **Jungfraujoch** terminus (11,333 ft.). Its observation deck offers a superb view of the surrounding mountains and the lakes of central Switzerland. From there, on a very clear day, even the Black Forest in southern Germany can be spotted.

Blick aufs Matterhorn

H: 1. Er kommt heute Abend mit dem Bus in Wien an. 2. Sie reist ohne ihre Familie nach Deutschland. 3. Deine Jeans liegen seit drei Tagen da drüben auf dem Sofa. 4. Wir fahren am Sonntag mit der Bahn zu meiner Tante. 5. Gehst du heute Nachmittag zu Fuß in die Stadt? 6. Ich kaufe die Eier samstags billig auf dem Markt. 7. Wir wollen morgen Abend zusammen ins Kino gehen. 8. Ihr müsst in einer Viertelstunde in den Zug nach Nürnberg umsteigen. 9. Sie lässt die Kinder ein paar Tage bei den Großeltern in St. Gallen.

BEISPIEL: Ich kaufe die Briefmarken. (auf der Post, morgen)
Ich kaufe die Briefmarken morgen auf der Post.

1. Er kommt an. (heute Abend, in Wien, mit dem Bus)
2. Sie reist. (nach Deutschland, ohne ihre Familie)
3. Deine Jeans liegen auf dem Sofa. (da drüben, seit drei Tagen)
4. Wir fahren. (zu meiner Tante, am Sonntag, mit der Bahn)
5. Gehst du? (zu Fuß, in die Stadt, heute Nachmittag)
6. Ich kaufe die Eier. (samstags, auf dem Markt, billig)
7. Wir wollen ins Kino gehen. (zusammen, morgen Abend)
8. Ihr müsst umsteigen. (in einer Viertelstunde, in den Zug nach Nürnberg)
9. Sie lässt die Kinder in St. Gallen. (bei den Großeltern, ein paar Tage)

I. So kann man's auch sagen. Beginnen Sie jeden Satz mit dem fettgedruckten *(boldfaced)* Satzteil und sagen Sie es dann auf Englisch!

BEISPIEL: Wir bleiben **während der Ferien** gewöhnlich zu Hause.
Während der Ferien bleiben wir gewöhnlich zu Hause.
During vacations, we usually stay home.

1. Wir haben gewöhnlich keine Zeit **für Reisen.**
2. Manfred hat **gerade** mit seiner Schwester in Amerika gesprochen.
3. Sie ist **seit einer Woche** bei ihrem Bruder in Florida.
4. Wir wollen sie alle **am Wochenende** besuchen *(visit).*
5. Das finde ich **schön.**

J: nicht in die Berge; die Berge nicht; nicht gesagt, nicht diesen Winter (diesen Winter nicht), nicht sehr teuer; weiß nicht; nicht so müde; nicht gern; nicht mit dem Auto; nicht lange; nicht so heiß; nicht so langweilig; nicht nach Spanien, nicht mit

If students need more practice, have them negate: Hast du die Paketkarte ausgefüllt? Haben Sie das Fax geschickt? Haben Sie Petras E-Mail-Adresse? Sie hat den Brief mit Luftpost geschickt. Wollen wir zu Fuß zum Bahnhof gehen? Sie fahren gern mit dem Bus. Er kann morgen kommen. Olaf hat Tante Irma besucht. Dieser Zug fährt nach Basel.

J. Ferienwünsche. Verneinen Sie *(negate)* die Sätze mit **nicht!**

GISELA   Ich möchte diesen Winter in die Berge fahren.
OTTO   Gefallen dir die Berge?
GISELA   Das habe ich gesagt. Warum fliegen wir diesen Winter nach Korsika? 279 Euro ist sehr teuer.
OTTO   Ich weiß.
GISELA   Im Flugzeug wird man so müde.
OTTO   Ich fliege gern.
GISELA   Ich möchte aber mit dem Auto fahren.
OTTO   Mittags kannst du lange in der Sonne liegen.
GISELA   Morgens und nachmittags ist die Sonne so heiß.
OTTO   In den Bergen ist es so langweilig.
GISELA   Gut. Wenn wir nach Spanien fliegen, komme ich mit.

KORSIKA INSEL DER SCHÖNHEIT **TRAUM-URLAUB**

K. Das stimmt nicht. Lesen Sie mit Ihrem Partner/Ihrer Partnerin, welche Busreisen es zwischen Weihnachten und Silvester gibt! Ihr Partner/Ihre Partnerin sagt dann etwas, was nicht stimmt, und Sie korrigieren *(correct)* es! Wechseln Sie sich ab *(take turns)*!

BEISPIEL: Die 7-Tage-Busreise zu Silvester in die Schweiz kostet 299 Euro.
Nein, sie kostet nicht 299 Euro, sondern 619 Euro.

In case students ask: **der Wirt, -e** *inn keeper,* **HP** = **Halbpension** *breakfast and evening meal,* **Ausflüge** *excursions,* **ÜF** = **Übernachtung + Frühstück** *overnight stay and breakfast,* **das Hallenbad, ¨er** *inside pool,* **der Sportler, -** *sportsman,* **gebührenfrei** *tollfree,* **buchen** *to book,* **der Prospekt, -e** *brochure,* **kostenlos** *free*

Zusammenfassung

L. Hoppla, hier fehlt was! Schon lange nicht mehr gesehen!—Es ist September und Sie erzählen Ihrem Partner/Ihrer Partnerin, was Ihre Freunde während der Ferien gemacht haben. Finden Sie heraus, was Sie nicht wissen! Einer von Ihnen *(one of you)* sieht auf die Tabelle unten, der andere *(the other one)* auf die Tabelle im Anhang *(appendix)*, Teil 11.

S1:

Wer	Wann / Wie lange	Wie / Obj. + Präposition	Wo und was
Lucian	*(Wann) ein paar Wochen*	gemütlich	durch Italien reisen
Christl	ein- Monat	*(Wie) bei einer Gastfamilie*	*(Wo) in Amerika sein*
Steffi	dies- Sommer	*(Wie) wegen ihrer Prüfung*	zu Hause bleiben
Nina + Kim	*(Wann) während der Ferien*	mit dem Schiff	*(Wo) von Passau bis Wien fahren*
Ben + Michi	jed- Nachmittag	zusammen	*(Wo) in einer Pizzeria arbeiten*
Günther	im August	*(Wie) trotz des Wetters / dem Wetter*	*(Wo) auf der Insel Rügen campen*
Jutta	*(Wann) vom 1. bis 31. Juli*	als Au-Pair	in London arbeiten
Nicole	vor einer Woche	*(Wie) wieder*	*(Wo) von Griechenland zurückkommen*
Yvonne	*(Wann) morgens*	meistens	im Fitnessstudio trainieren
Jochen	*(Wann) mittags*	*(Wie) gewöhnlich*	im Restaurant jobben

BEISPIEL: **S1** Ich weiß, dass Lucian gemütlich durch Italien gereist ist. Aber wann?

S2 Das weiß ich nicht genau. Ich weiß nur, dass er ein paar Wochen gereist ist. Und hast du gehört, was Christl gemacht hat? Sie ist . .

M. Frau Köchli. Bilden Sie Sätze!

BEISPIEL: Hauptstadt / Schweiz / sein / Bern
Die Hauptstadt der Schweiz ist Bern.

1. Tante / unsere Freunde / leben / hier in Bern
2. leider / ich / nicht / wissen / die / Adresse / diese Tante
3. Name / Dame / sein / Köchli
4. wegen / dieser Name / ich / nicht / können / finden / Frau Köchli
5. statt / eine Köchli / da / sein / viele Köchlis
6. du / nicht / wissen / Telefonnummer / eure Freunde?

M: 1. Die Tante unserer Freunde lebt hier in Bern. 2. Leider weiß ich die Adresse dieser Tante nicht. 3. Der Name der Dame ist Köchli. 4. Wegen dieses Namens kann ich Frau Köchli nicht finden. 5. Statt einer Köchli sind da viele Köchlis. 6. Weißt du die Telefonnummer eurer Freunde nicht?

7. Die Nummer steht im Adressbuch meiner Frau. 8. Ich kann Inges Adressbuch nicht finden. 9. Eines Tages findet Inge es hoffentlich wieder. 10. Könnt ihr mir den Namen eines Hotels empfehlen? 11. Trotz der Preise brauchen wir ein Hotelzimmer. 12. Während der Feiertage hast du Probleme wegen der Touristen.

7. Nummer / stehen / in / Adressbuch / meine Frau
8. ich / nicht / können / finden / Inge / Adressbuch
9. ein Tag / Inge / es / hoffentlich / wieder / finden
10. können / ihr / mir / empfehlen / Name / ein Hotel?
11. trotz / Preise *(pl.)* / wir / brauchen / Hotelzimmer
12. während / Feiertage / du / haben / Probleme *(pl.)* / wegen / Touristen

Fokus — *Switzerland and Its Languages*

European cars usually carry a small sticker indicating the country of origin: *D* stands for Germany, *A* for Austria, and *CH* for Switzerland. The abbreviation *CH* stands for the Latin *Confoederatio Helvetica*, a reference to the Celtic tribe of the Helvetii who settled the territory of modern Switzerland when Julius Caesar prevented them from moving to Gaul (today's France). The neutral choice of *CH* is a good example of how the Swiss avoid giving preference to one of their four national languages.

Roughly 70 percent of the Swiss speak a dialect of Swiss-German **(Schwyzerdütsch)**; 20 percent speak French; and 9 percent Italian. A tiny minority (1 percent) speaks Romansh **(Rätoromanisch).**

Most Swiss people understand two or three—some even all four—of these languages. This quadrilingualism goes back to the time when the Romans colonized the area. Over time, tribes from present-day Italy, France, and Germany migrated to the region. Romansh is a Romance language that has evolved little from Vulgar Latin and is spoken mainly in the remote valleys of the Grisons (canton *Graubünden*). Although it became one of the four official languages in 1938, Romansh has been under constant pressure from the other major languages in surrounding areas. The fact that Romansh is not one language but a group of dialects (including **Ladin**) makes it even harder to preserve.

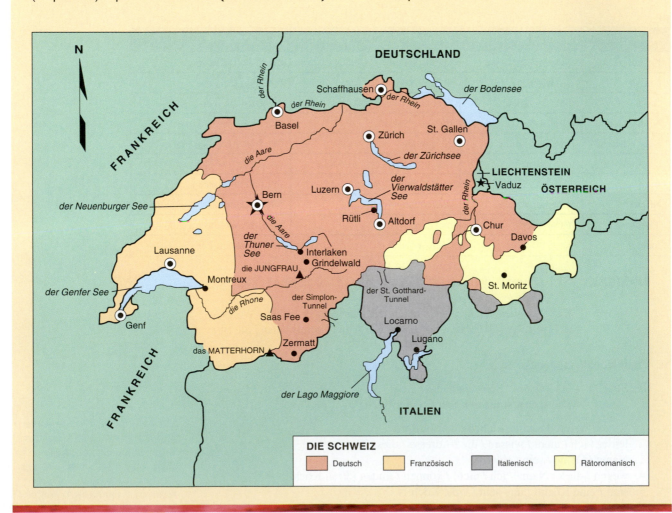

N. Mein Alltag *(my daily life).* Schreiben Sie 8–10 Sätze über *(about)* Ihren Alltag, zum Beispiel wann Sie aufstehen, wann Sie essen, wann Sie zur Schule / Uni gehen, welche Klassen Sie wann haben, was Sie abends und am Wochenende tun usw.! Benutzen Sie so viele Zeitausdrücke wie möglich *(as possible)*!

BEISPIEL: Ich bin fast jeden Tag an der Uni. Morgens stehe ich um sechs auf . . .

Einblicke

Lesestrategie: Ein Land, drei Meinungen *(opinions)*

Drei Touristen in der Schweiz (Felix, Frau Weber und Frau Lorenz) beschreiben ihre Reiseerlebnisse. Lesen Sie den Text und vergleichen Sie *(compare)* die drei Reisen! Was hat den drei Leuten am besten gefallen? Gibt es etwas, was ihnen nicht so gut gefallen hat?

Wortschatz 2

das Dorf, ¨er	*village*
Schnäppchen, -	*bargain*
die Gegend, -en	*area, region*
Geschichte, -n	*history; story*
herrlich	*wonderful, great*
hinauf·fahren (fährt hinauf), ist hinaufgefahren	*to go or drive up (to)*
weiter·fahren (fährt weiter), ist weitergefahren	*to drive on, keep on driving*

Vor dem Lesen

A. Etwas Geographie. Sehen Sie auf die Landkarte der Schweiz und beantworten Sie die Fragen!
1. Wie heißen die Nachbarländer der Schweiz? Wo liegen sie?
2. Wie heißt die Hauptstadt der Schweiz?

Since **weiterfahren** means *to drive on, to keep on driving,* let students guess what these words mean: **weitergehen, weitergeben, weiterfliegen, weiterlesen, weiterreisen, weiterschlafen.**

Im Stadtzentrum von Bern

3. Nennen Sie ein paar Schweizer Flüsse, Seen und Berge! Welcher Fluss fließt weiter *(flows on)* nach Deutschland / nach Frankreich? Welcher See liegt zwischen der Schweiz und Deutschland / Italien / Frankreich?
4. Wo liegt Bern? Basel? Zürich? Luzern? Genf? Lausanne? Zermatt? Lugano? St. Moritz? Davos? Saas Fee? Grindelwald?
5. Wo spricht man Deutsch? Französisch? Italienisch? Rätoromanisch?
6. Was assoziieren Sie mit der Schweiz?

B. Besuch in Bern. Lesen Sie mit Ihrem Partner/Ihrer Partnerin, wie man als Tourist Bern kennen lernen kann: zu Fuß, mit dem Bus oder mit dem Schlauchboot *(rubber boat)*! Stellen Sie einander *(each other)* Fragen und beantworten Sie sie!

BEISPIEL: Wo beginnt die Stadtrundfahrt mit dem Schlauchboot?
             Sie beginnt am Schwellenmätteli.

Stadtrundfahrt

Stadtrundfahrt durch Bern unter kundiger lokaler Führung mit Besichtigung des Rosengartens, des Bärengrabens, des Zeitglockenturms, des Münsters sowie des Botschaftsviertels.

1.11.–31. 3.	Sa	**14.00 Uhr**
1. 4.–31.10.	täglich	**14.00 Uhr**
Preis	*Erwachsene*	CHF 24.—
	Kinder 6–16 Jahre	CHF 12.—
Dauer	*2 Stunden*	
Treffpunkt	**Bahnhof, Tourist Center**	

Stadtrundfahrt im Schlauchboot

Lernen Sie Bern aus einer unbekannten Perspektive kennen. Die Schlauchbootrundfahrt führt Sie vorbei an mächtigen Sandsteinbrücken und blumengeschmückten Häusern. (Rundfahrt in Zusammenarbeit mit Berger Aktiv-Reisen)

2.6.–30.9.	Di, Do, Sa, So	**17.00 Uhr**
Preis	*Erwachsene*	CHF 30.—
	Kinder 6–16 Jahre	CHF 20.—
Dauer	*1½ Stunden*	
Treffpunkt	**Schwellenmätteli**	

Altstadtbummel

Ein(e) sprachkundige(r) Stadtführer(in) begleitet Sie auf einer Entdeckungsreise durch die Berner Altstadt (UNESCO Welterbe) und führt Sie zu den schönsten Sehenswürdigkeiten der Bundesstadt.

1.6.–30.9.	täglich	**11.00 Uhr**
Preis	*Erwachsene*	CHF 14.—
	Kinder 6–16 Jahre	CHF 7.—
Dauer	*1½ Stunden*	
Treffpunkt	**Bahnhof, Tourist Center**	

C. Was ist das?

der Film, Besucher, Kanton, Wintersport; das Kurzinterview, Panorama; die Alpenblume, Arkade, Bergbahn, Konferenz, Nation, Rückreise, Schneeszene, Viersprachigkeit; bergsteigen gehen, faszinieren, filmen; autofrei, elegant

CD 4, Track 8

Touristen in der Schweiz

In Kurzinterviews mit Touristen in Altdorf, Bern und Saas Fee hören wir, was Besuchern in der Schweiz besonders gefällt:

wooden bridge

created their confederation

outdoor performances
national holiday / parades

FELIX: Ich finde die Gegend um den Vierwaldstätter See besonders interessant wegen ihrer Geschichte. Gestern bin ich in Luzern gewesen und auch über die Holzbrücke° aus dem Jahr 1408 gelaufen. Heute früh bin ich mit dem Schiff von Luzern zum Rütli gefahren, wo 1291 die drei Kantone Uri, Schwyz und Unterwalden ihren Bund geschlossen° haben und die Schweiz als eine Nation begonnen hat. Dann bin ich weitergefahren nach Altdorf zum Wilhelm-Tell-Denkmal und heute Abend gehe ich zu den Wilhelm-Tell-Freilichtspielen°. Dieses Wochenende ist hier auch Bundesfeier° mit Umzügen° und Feuerwerk. Dann geht's wieder zurück mit dem Zug. Die Fahrt durch die Berge ist einfach herrlich.

FRAU WEBER: Mir gefällt Bern wegen seiner Arkaden und Brunnen°. Mein Mann und ich fahren fast jedes Jahr im Juni oder Juli in die Schweiz. Auf unserer Fahrt kommen wir gewöhnlich durch Bern und bleiben hier ein paar Tage. Wenn wir Glück haben, ist gerade Flohmarkt° oder Handwerksmarkt°. Da haben wir schon manches Schnäppchen gemacht. Morgen fahren wir weiter nach Grindelwald, ins Berner Oberland. Wir wollen mit der Bergbahn zum Jungfraujoch hinauffahren und von dort oben den Blick auf die Berge genießen°. Trotz der vielen Touristen ist das Berner Oberland immer wieder schön. Haben Sie gewusst, dass man fast alle Schneeszenen der James-Bond-Filme im Berner Oberland gefilmt hat? Auf der Rückreise haben wir Aufenthalt in Zürich, wo mein Mann mit den Banken zu tun hat. Der See mit dem Panorama der Berge ist herrlich. Während der Konferenzen meines Mannes bummle ich gern durch die Stadt. Die Geschäfte in der Bahnhofstraße sind elegant, aber teuer.

fountains

flea market / crafts fair

enjoy

Zürich mit Blick auf den Limmat und den Zürichsee

FRAU LORENZ: Die Viersprachigkeit der Schweiz fasziniert uns. Unsere Reise hat in Lausanne begonnen, wo wir Französisch gesprochen haben. Jetzt sind wir hier in Saas Fee bei Freunden. Mit uns sprechen sie Hochdeutsch, aber mit der Familie Schwyzerdütsch. Saas Fee ist nur ein Dorf, aber wunderschön. Es ist autofrei und in den Bergen kann man überall wandern und bergsteigen gehen. Wegen der Höhenlage° gibt es viele Alpenblumen und Gämsen° und oben auf den Gletschern° kann man sogar während des Sommers immer noch Ski laufen gehen. Übermorgen fahren wir weiter nach St. Moritz, wo man viel Rätoromanisch hört. Am Ende der Reise wollen wir noch nach Lugano, wo das Wetter fast immer schön sein soll und die Leute Italienisch sprechen. Vier Sprachen in einem Land, das ist schon toll.

altitude
mountain goats / glaciers

Nach dem Lesen

A. Richtig oder falsch? Wenn falsch, sagen Sie warum!

  <u>f</u>   1. Felix findet die Gegend um den Bodensee so interessant wegen ihrer Geschichte.

  <u>f</u>   2. Die Schweiz hat 1691 als Nation begonnen.

  <u>r</u>   3. Felix ist wegen des Wilhelm-Tell-Denkmals und der Freilichtspiele in Altdorf.

  <u>f</u>   4. Frau Weber und ihr Mann fahren jeden Winter ins Berner Oberland.

  <u>r</u>   5. Während ihrer Reise bleiben sie gewöhnlich ein paar Tage in Bern, weil ihnen die Stadt so gut gefällt.

  <u>r</u>   6. An Markttagen haben sie dort schon manches Schnäppchen gemacht.

  <u>f</u>   7. Herr Weber hat in Zürich oft mit der Universität zu tun.

Optional practice: 1. Sind Sie schon einmal in der Schweiz gewesen? Wann? Wo? 2. Wann ist bei uns Nationalfeiertag? Wie feiern wir ihn? 3. Wann hat unser Land als Nation begonnen? 4. Wohin geht man hier zum Wintersport? Wo ist es besonders teuer? Wie kommt man dorthin *(to that place)*? 5. Wo gibt es Gletscher? 6. Was für eine Uhr haben Sie? Woher kommt sie? Wie finden Sie Swatch-Uhren?

_f_   8. Zürich ist eine Stadt am Genfer See mit dem Panorama der Berge.

_r_   9. Familie Lorenz ist fasziniert von den Sprachen der Schweiz.

_f_ 10. Mit ihren Freunden in Saas Fee sprechen sie Rätoromanisch.

_f_ 11. Am Ende der Reise fahren sie noch nach Lausanne.

_f_ 12. In Lausanne spricht man Italienisch.

B. Etwas Geschichte. Lesen Sie laut!

B: This practices reading dates, which was presented in Chapter 4, Wortschatz I.

1. Im Jahr 1291 schlossen Uri, Schwyz und Unterwalden am Rütli einen Bund.
2. Luzern ist 1332 dazu gekommen *(here: joined it)* und Zürich 1351. 3. 1513 hat es 13 Kantone gegeben. 4. Heute, 20___ *(add current year)*, sind es 26 Kantone.
5. 1848 ist die Schweiz ein Bundesstaat geworden. 6. Im 1. Weltkrieg (1914–1918) und im 2. Weltkrieg (1939–1945) ist die Schweiz neutral geblieben. 7. Trotz ihrer Tradition von Demokratie können die Frauen der Schweiz erst seit 1971 in allen Kantonen wählen *(vote)*. 8. Seit 1981 gibt es offiziell auch keine Diskriminierung der Frau mehr.

C. Die Eidgenossenschaft *(The Swiss Confederacy).* Wiederholen Sie die Sätze mit den Ausdrücken in Klammern. Manchmal gibt es mehrere Möglichkeiten.

BEISPIEL: Viele Touristen fahren in die Schweiz. (jedes Jahr)
Viele Touristen fahren jedes Jahr in die Schweiz.
Jedes Jahr fahren viele Touristen in die Schweiz.

1. Felix findet die Gegend um den Vierwaldstätter See interessant. (wegen ihrer Geschichte)
2. Felix ist mit einem Schiff zum Rütli gefahren. (von Luzern)
3. Die drei Kantone Uri, Schwyz und Unterwalden haben ihren Bund am Rütli geschlossen. (1291)
4. Viele Touristen wollen Wilhelm Tells Denkmal sehen. (natürlich)
5. In der Schweiz feiert man die Bundesfeier. (jedes Jahr am 1. August)
6. Felix ist noch einen Tag geblieben. (wegen dieses Festes)

D. Welche Frage gehört zu welcher Antwort?

_e_	1. Hier hat die Schweiz als Nation begonnen.	a. Sprechen Ihre Freunde zu Hause Rätoromanisch?
_j_	2. In der Bahnhofstraße.	b. Sprechen Sie mit Ihren Freunden Schwyzerdütsch?
_c_	3. Mein Mann hat dort mit Banken zu tun.	c. Warum fahren Sie nach Zürich?
_i_	4. Mit der Bergbahn.	d. Warum fahren Sie nach Lugano?
_b_	5. Nein, Hochdeutsch.	e. Warum fasziniert Sie die Gegend um den Vierwaldstätter See?
_a_	6. Nein, Schwyzerdütsch.	f. Warum gibt es in Altdorf ein Feuerwerk?
_h_	7. Gut, besonders wegen ihrer Arkaden und Brunnen.	g. Was hat Sie nach Saas Fee gebracht?
_f_	8. Wegen der Bundesfeier.	h. Wie gefällt Ihnen die Stadt Bern?
_d_	9. Wegen des Wetters.	i. Wie kommt man zum Jungfraujoch?
_g_	10. Wir haben hier Freunde.	j. Wo gehen Sie in Zürich bummeln?

E. Kurzgespräche. Erzählen Sie den anderen von Ihrer Reise! Was sagen sie dazu *(to that)*?

1. **Die Heimreise** *(trip home)*

   The weather was awful. Your plane arrived two hours late **(mit zwei Stunden Verspätung)** and departed five hours late. You arrived at two o'clock in the morning. Your suitcase wasn't there. There were no buses into town. You didn't have enough cash for a cab. You phoned your father. You got home at 4 A.M. You were very tired.

2. **Im Schwyzerhüsli**

   Staying overnight: You and your friend arrived in Schaffhausen on the Rhine. You inquired at three hotels, but they had no rooms available. They sent you to the *Schwyzerhüsli*. There they had some rooms. Since you were very tired, you went to bed early **(ins Bett).** There was a party in the hotel until midnight. Then cars drove by. It was very loud. At 4 A.M. your neighbors got up, talked in the hallway **(im Gang)** and got into their car. You couldn't sleep any more, got up too, and left. What a night!

HÖREN SIE ZU!   TRACK 17

Im Reisebüro

Zum Erkennen: Skilift inbegriffen *(ski lift included);* die Broschüre, -n *(brochure)*

Was stimmt?
1. Ulrike und Steffi möchten im _____ reisen.
   a. August   **b.** März   c. Januar
2. Sie wollen _____.
   a. wandern   b. bergsteigen gehen   **c.** Ski laufen gehen
3. Ulrike reserviert ein Zimmer im Hotel _____.
   a. Alpenrose   **b.** Alpina   c. Eiger
4. Ulrike und Steffi fahren mit der Bahn bis _____.
   a. Bern   **b.** Interlaken   c. Grindelwald
5. Sie kommen um _____ Uhr an ihrem Ziel *(destination)* an.
   a. 12.16   b. 12.30   **c.** 1.00
6. Sie fahren am _____ um _____ nach Hause zurück.
   a. 15. / zwei   b. 14. / drei   c. 16. / sechs

Fokus — *Hermann Hesse*

Hermann Hesse (1899–1962) was awarded the Nobel Prize for literature in 1946. Although born in Germany, he became a Swiss citizen at the outbreak of World War I. The first stage of his writing began with his romantic rendering of the artist as a social outcast. At the beginning of the war, the strain of his pacifist beliefs and domestic crises led him to undergo psychoanalysis, which gave a new dimension to his work. The novels *Demian, Siddharta*, and *Steppenwolf* were influenced by his readings of Nietzsche, Dostoyevsky, Spengler, and Buddhist mysticism, and are based on his conviction that people must discover their own nature. A third phase began in 1930, balancing the artist's rebellion against the constraints of social behavior. After 1943, when his name was put on the Nazi blacklist, he quit writing novels and concentrated on poems, stories, and essays that articulated a humanistic spirit reminiscent of Goethe's *Weltbürgertum (world citizenship)*. They also reflect Hesse's faith in the spirituality of all mankind, for which he coined the term *Weltglaube*.

Im Nebel

strange / fog	Seltsam°, im Nebel° zu wandern!
lonely	Einsam° ist jeder Busch und Stein,
	Kein Baum sieht den andern,
	Jeder ist allein.
was / world	Voll von Freunden war° mir die Welt°,
when / light	Als° noch mein Leben licht° war;
	Nun, da der Nebel fällt,
visible	Ist keiner mehr sichtbar°.
truly / wise	Wahrlich°, keiner ist weise°,
	Der nicht das Dunkel kennt,
inescapably / quietly	Das unentrinnbar° und leise°
separates	Von allen ihn trennt°.

Seltsam, im Nebel zu wandern!
Leben ist Einsamkeit.
Kein Mensch kennt den andern,
Jeder ist allein.

Hermann Hesse

Beginning with this chapter, the final *Fokus* section will include a short poem for enrichment and enjoyment. Begin by reading the poem aloud, so that students get a feel for the rhythm and intonation.

These poems are considered extra reading and not as a substitute for the *Einblicke* readings. The latter are closely tied to the chapter grammar and also introduce new active vocabulary.

Fragen über das Gedicht *(about the poem)*

1. Was ist typisch, wenn es neblig *(foggy)* ist?
2. Wo sind oft die Freunde im Nebel des Lebens?
3. Wie ist das Leben ohne Freunde?
4. Warum ist manchmal eine Zeit der Dunkelheit auch wichtig?
5. Wie ist die Stimmung *(mood)* dieses Gedichts?
6. Wie gefällt Ihnen das Gedicht? Warum?

Video-Ecke

- The *Minidrama* "Die Schweizer Post ist schnell" shows two young ladies as they are walking with their bags to the train station. They are on time, until it occurs to them that they forgot to inform their Swiss friend to pick them up in Davos. Since they don't have any coins, one of them decides to ask for change at the post office and to buy stamps at the same time. The other one starts writing post-cards out of boredom. By the time they have the money to make that important call, the two have missed the train.

- *Blickpunkt* "Reise in die Schweiz" introduces us to a travel agent who shows us around in Switzerland, with all its beauty and diversity. She talks also briefly about the four languages spoken there and how to get around inexpensively by train.

Web-Ecke

- For updates, self-assessment quizzes, and online activities related to this chapter, visit the *Wie geht's?* Web site at **http://wiegehts.heinle.com**. You will see some statistics about Switzerland, take a trip to Saas-Fee, and find out about some of Switzerland's popular export items.

Kapitel ⑨

Hobbys

Fahrradfahrt an der Donau bei Passau

Lernziele

Vorschau
Sports and clubs in the German-speaking countries

Gespräche + Wortschatz
Physical fitness and leisure time

Fokus
Telephone courtesies
Animal and food talk (some idiomatic
   expressions)
Schrebergärten
Vacationing
Rose Ausländer

Struktur
9.1 Endings of preceded adjectives
9.2 Reflexive verbs
9.3 Infinitives with **zu**

Einblicke
Freizeit—Lust oder Frust?
Rose Ausländer: *Noch bist du da*

Video-Ecke
Minidrama: *Lachen ist die beste Medizin*

Web-Ecke

Vorschau

Sports and Clubs in the German-Speaking Countries

Sports are very popular in Germany, Austria, and Switzerland, not only with spectators, but with amateur athletes as well. Whereas professional sports are big business like anywhere else, one out of three people belongs to a sports club **(Sportverein)**. The German Sports Federation **(Deutscher Sportbund)** has more than 75,000 affiliated sports clubs. It sponsors such programs as **Trimm dich** and **Sport für alle** with competitions in running, swimming, cycling, and skiing. Millions of people participate in these events every year. Soccer **(Fußball)** is as important in Europe as football, baseball, and basketball are in North America. Other popular sports are **Handball** and winter sports such as skating and ice hockey. Tennis is also becoming more popular, but usually requires membership in a club in order to play. The successes of Steffi Graf, Boris Becker, Michael Stich, and Martina Hingis have given tennis a tremendous boost. Although not as popular as in the United States, golf is also becoming more common. **Volksmärsche**, as group-hiking events, are open to the public.

You might ask students if they are familiar with any of the great athletes in the German-speaking countries, e.g., Steffi Graf, Boris Becker, etc. Also, in the *Zum Schreiben* section of the Workbook, there is a report on bike tours. Ask students where they can go biking in their own community and where one could take actual bike trips like the one mentioned in the Workbook.

High schools and universities are not involved in competitive sports; for that purpose, students usually join a sports club. Such organizations are basically autonomous, but the government provides some support for those with insufficient funds. This applies particularly to the former East Germany, where an effort has been made to set up independent clubs. In the 1970s and 1980s, these clubs did not exist; instead, the East German government spent a great deal of money on making sports accessible to every citizen, seeking out young talents early and training them in special boarding schools—a practice that led to considerable success in the Olympics.

In addition to sports clubs, there are associations promoting all kinds of leisure activities, ranging from dog breeding and pigeon racing to gardening, crafts, music, and dancing. Clubs devoted to regional traditions and dress **(Trachtenvereine)** and centuries-old rifle associations **(Schützenvereine)**—with their own emblems, uniforms, and ceremonial meetings—keep old traditions alive and draw thousands to their annual festivals.

Marathonlauf in Bern

231

Gespräche + Wortschatz

CD 4, Track 9

Am Telefon

FRAU SCHMIDT	Hier Schmidt.
ANNEMARIE	Guten Tag, Frau Schmidt. Ich bin's, Annemarie.
FRAU SCHMIDT	Tag, Annemarie!
ANNEMARIE	Ist Thomas da?
FRAU SCHMIDT	Nein, tut mir Leid. Er ist gerade zur Post gegangen.
ANNEMARIE	Ach so. Können Sie ihm sagen, dass ich heute Abend nicht mit ihm ausgehen kann?
FRAU SCHMIDT	Ja, sicher. Was ist denn los?
ANNEMARIE	Ich bin krank. Mir tut der Hals weh und ich habe Kopfschmerzen.
FRAU SCHMIDT	Das tut mir aber Leid. Gute Besserung!
ANNEMARIE	Danke. Auf Wiederhören!
FRAU SCHMIDT	Wiederhören!

Bis gleich!

YVONNE	Bei Mayer.
DANIELA	Hallo, Yvonne! Ich bin's, Daniela.
YVONNE	Tag, Daniela! Was gibt's?
DANIELA	Nichts Besonderes. Hast du Lust, Squash zu spielen oder schwimmen zu gehen?
YVONNE	Squash? Nein, danke. Ich habe noch Muskelkater von vorgestern. Ich kann mich kaum rühren. Mir tut alles weh.
DANIELA	Lahme Ente! Wie wär's mit Schach?
YVONNE	O.K., das klingt gut. Kommst du zu mir?
DANIELA	Ja, bis gleich!

A. Wie geht's weiter?

1. Annemaries Freund heißt . . .   2. Annemarie spricht mit . . .   3. Thomas ist nicht zu Hause, weil . . .   4. Annemarie kann nicht mit ihm . . .   5. Annemaries Hals . . .   6. Sie hat auch . . .   7. Am Ende eines Telefongesprächs sagt man . . . 8. Danielas Freundin heißt . . .   9. Yvonne will nicht Squash spielen, weil . . . 10. Sie hat aber Lust, . . .

B. Jetzt sind Sie dran!
Diesmal sind Sie am Telefon. Sie rufen Ihren Freund/Ihre Freundin an und fragen Sie, ob er/sie Lust hat, etwas zu tun. Aber Sie haben Pech, denn er/sie hat schon Pläne *(plans)* oder ist krank. Wechseln Sie sich ab!

S1	Hier . . .
S2	Tag, . . . ! Ich bin's, . . . Sag mal, hast du Lust, . . . ?
S1	Nein, ich kann nicht . . .
S2	Warum nicht? Was ist los?
S1	Ich bin krank. Mir tut/tun . . . weh.
S2	. . . Wie lange hast du schon . . .schmerzen?
S1	Seit . . .
S2	Hoffentlich . . . Gute Besserung!
S1	. . .

Fokus — *Telephone Courtesies*

When answering the phone, German-speakers usually identify themselves with their last names. If you were answering your own phone, you would say *Hier . . .* (plus your own name). If you were answering someone else's phone, say Ms. Schmidt's, you would say *(Hier) bei Schmidt.* Only afterwards do you say *Guten Tag!* or *Hallo!* If you are the one making the call, you usually give your own name before asking for the person you are trying

to reach: *Guten Abend, hier spricht . . .* (or *Ich bin's, . . .*). *Kann ich bitte mit . . . sprechen?* or *Ich möchte gern . . . sprechen.* The answer might be *Einen Moment bitte!* or *. . . ist nicht da. Kann ich ihm/ihr etwas ausrichten* (take a message)? When ending a phone conversation formally, say *Auf Wiederhören!* (lit. until we hear each other again). Friends may simply say *Tschüss!*, *Mach's gut!*, *Bis bald!*, or *Bis gleich!*

Wortschatz 1

Der Körper, - *(body)*

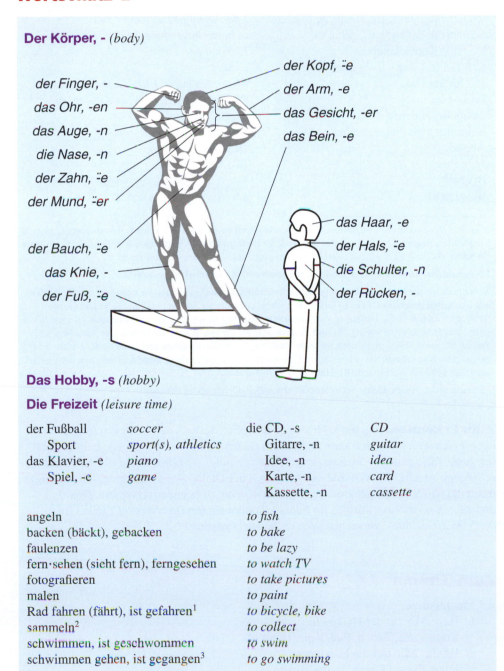

der Finger, -
das Ohr, -en
das Auge, -n
die Nase, -n
der Zahn, ̈e
der Mund, ̈er

der Bauch, ̈e
das Knie, -
der Fuß, ̈e

der Kopf, ̈e
der Arm, -e
das Gesicht, -er
das Bein, -e

das Haar, -e
der Hals, ̈e
die Schulter, -n
der Rücken, -

Point out that **Haare** is usually used in the plural, and also that **Knie** *(sg.)* and **Knie** *(pl.)* are spelled alike but are pronounced differently: [i:] **das Knie** BUT [i̇:] **die Knie.**

If students ask: *back* **der Rücken, -;** *bosom* **der Busen, -;** *bottom / behind* **der Po(po), -s / Hintern, -;** *cheek* **die Backe, -n;** *chest / breast* **die Brust, ̈e;** *chin* **das Kinn;** *elbow* **der Ell(en)bogen, -;** *eyebrow* **die Augenbraue, -n;** *eyelash* **die Wimper, -n;** *fingernail* **der Fingernagel, ̈** *forehead* **die Stirn;** *index finger* **der Zeigefinger, -;** *shoulder* **die Schulter, -n;** *stomach* **der Magen, -;** *thumb* **der Daumen, -;** *toe* **die Zehe, -n;** *toenail* **der Fußnagel, ̈;** *tongue* **die Zunge, -n**

Das Hobby, -s *(hobby)*
Die Freizeit *(leisure time)*

der Fußball	soccer	die CD, -s	CD
Sport	sport(s), athletics	Gitarre, -n	guitar
das Klavier, -e	piano	Idee, -n	idea
Spiel, -e	game	Karte, -n	card
		Kassette, -n	cassette

If students ask: *cello* **das Cello, -s;** *coin* **die Münze, -n;** *drum* **die Trommel, -n;** *organ* **die Orgel, -n;** *recorder* **die Blockflöte, -n;** *stein* **der Bierkrug, ̈e;** *trumpet* **die Trompete, -n;** *violin* **die Geige, -n**

angeln	to fish
backen (bäckt), gebacken	to bake
faulenzen	to be lazy
fern·sehen (sieht fern), ferngesehen	to watch TV
fotografieren	to take pictures
malen	to paint
Rad fahren (fährt), ist gefahren[1]	to bicycle, bike
sammeln[2]	to collect
schwimmen, ist geschwommen	to swim
schwimmen gehen, ist gegangen[3]	to go swimming

Also popular are the card game **Skat** and nine-pin bowling **(Kegeln)** without the headpin, although U.S.-style bowling is also "in." The **Fußball-Bundesliga** is the "first division" of German soccer, consisting of the 18 best teams.

Ski laufen (läuft), ist gelaufen[1]   *to ski*
Ski laufen gehen, ist gegangen[3]   *to go skiing*
spazieren gehen, ist gegangen[3]   *to go for a walk [lit.: walking]*
(Dame, Schach) spielen[1]   *to play (checkers, chess)*
(Freunde) treffen (trifft), getroffen   *to meet, get together (with friends)*
Sport treiben, getrieben[1]   *to engage in sports*
wandern, ist gewandert   *to hike*

Weiteres

gesund / krank   *healthy / sick, ill*
fantastisch   *fantastic, great, super*
andere   *others*
die anderen   *the others*
zuerst / danach   *first / then*
Lust haben (hat), gehabt, zu . . .   *to feel like doing something*
Ich habe (keine) Lust, Tennis zu spielen.   *I don't feel like playing tennis.*
Schmerzen haben (hat), gehabt   *to hurt / have some pain*
Ich habe Kopfschmerzen.   *I have a headache.*
weh·tun (tut weh), wehgetan   *to hurt*
Mir tut der Hals weh.   *My throat hurts. I have a sore throat.*
Was ist los?   *What's the matter? What's going on?*
nichts Besonderes[4]   *nothing special*
Nein, das geht (heute) nicht.   *No, that won't work (today).*
Ach so.   *Oh, I see.*
Ja, sicher.   *Yes, sure.*
Bis bald!   *See you soon!*
Bis gleich!   *See you in a few minutes!*

[1] In each of these combinations, **fahren, laufen, spielen, treiben** function as V1, while the other word, the verb complement, functions as V2: Ich **fahre** viel **Rad.** Sie **läuft** gern **Ski.** Wir **spielen** immer **Schach.** Sie **treiben** nie **Sport.** *(I bike a lot. She loves to ski. We always play chess. They never do any sports.)*

[2] **Ich samm(e)le, du sammelst, er sammelt, wir sammeln, ihr sammelt, sie sammeln.**

[3] Note the difference between **schwimmen** and **schwimmen gehen** *(to swim / to go swimming)*, or **Ski laufen** and **Ski laufen gehen** *(to ski / to go skiing)*. In each second example, **gehen** functions as V1 and the other (here: **schwimmen** or **Ski laufen**) as V2. **Schwimmst** du gern? Ja, ich **gehe** gern **schwimmen.** *(Do you like to swim? Yes, I like to go swimming.)* / **Lauft** ihr gern **Ski?** Ja, wir **gehen** gern **Ski laufen.** *(Do you like to ski? Yes, we like to go skiing).* In this list, the same holds true for **spazieren gehen** and could be done with verbs like **angeln, Rad fahren:** Sie **gehen** viel im Park **spazieren.** Morgen **geht** er **angeln.** *(Tomorrow, he goes fishing.)* / Ich **gehe** am Wochenende **Rad fahren.** *(I go biking a lot.)*

[4] Similarly **nichts** Neues, **nichts** Schlechtes OR **etwas** Besonderes, **etwas** Schönes.

Zum Erkennen: Ich bin's. *(It's me.);* Ich habe Muskelkater. *(My muscles are sore. I have a charley horse.);* Ich kann mich kaum rühren. *(I can hardly move.);* Lahme Ente! *(lit. lame duck, someone with no pep);* Wie wär's mit . . . ? *(How about . . . ?);* zu mir *(to my place);* AUCH: die Aktivität, -en *(activity);* der Dialog, -e; die Endung, -en *(ending);* das reflexive Verb, -en; an·kreuzen *(to mark with an x);* beenden *(complete, finish);* diskutieren *(to discuss);* folgen *(to follow);* kommentieren *(to comment);* teilen (in + acc.) *(to divide into);* versuchen *(to try);* fehlend *(missing)*

Zum Thema

A. **Mustersätze**
1. Hals: **Mir tut** der Hals **weh.**
   Kopf, Zahn, Bauch, Fuß, Knie, Hand
2. Hände: **Mir tun die** Hände **weh.**
   Füße, Finger, Ohren, Beine, Augen

Note that **treffen** can be used as listed or reflexively, as listed in *Struktur* 9-2: **Ich treffe** ein *paar* Freunde. BUT **Ich treffe mich mit** ein paar Freunden. At this point, the reflexive verbs should be avoided.

Another way of saying **Ich gehe gern Ski laufen** *(I like to go skiing)* is **Ich gehe gern zum Skilaufen.** In that case, **Skilaufen** is capitalized and one word, since it is used as a noun.

Also like **sammeln:** bummeln, angeln, wechseln, tun

A: Rather than giving students the cue words, you could use gestures or have students supply their own words.

3. Kopf: **Ich habe** Kopf**schmerzen.**
   Hals, Zahn, Bauch, Ohren
4. Squash: **Hast du Lust,** Squash **zu spielen?**
   Tennis, Fußball, Klavier, CDs, Karten, Schach

B. Was tun Sie dann? Beenden Sie die Sätze mit einer Antwort von der Liste oder mit Ihren eigenen Worten!

_____ 1. Wenn ich Kopfschmerzen habe, . . .
_____ 2. Wenn mir die Füße wehtun, . . .
_____ 3. Wenn mir der Bauch wehtut, . . .
_____ 4. Wenn ich Halsschmerzen habe, . . .
_____ 5. Wenn ich Augenschmerzen habe, . . .
_____ 6. Wenn ich krank bin, . . .
_____ 7. Wenn ich gestresst bin, . . .
_____ 8. Wenn ich nicht schlafen kann, . . .

a. bleibe ich im Bett.
b. esse ich Nudelsuppe / nichts.
c. gehe ich ins Bett / in die Sauna.
d. gurgele _(gargle)_ ich.
e. gehe ich nicht spazieren.
f. mache ich die Augen zu.
g. meditiere ich.
h. nehme ich Aspirin / Vitamin C.
i. sehe ich nicht fern.
j. rufe ich einen Arzt _(doctor)_ an.
k. trinke ich Tee.
l. trinke ich heiße Milch / Zitrone mit Honig _(honey)._

B: For a follow-on personalization activity, you could have students ask each other in pairs **Was machst du, wenn du Kopfschmerzen hast (wenn dir die Füße weh tun . . .)?,** etc.

Fokus — _Animal and Food Talk (Some Idiomatic Expressions)_

As in the case of **Lahme Ente!** in the dialogue, names of animals are frequently used in everyday speech to characterize people—often in a derogatory way: **Ich Esel!** or **Du Affe!** _(donkey, monkey) for someone who made a mistake or behaves in a silly manner;_ **Du hast einen Vogel!** or **Bei dir piept's!** _(You're cuckoo);_ **Fauler Hund!** _(dog) for someone lazy;_ **Du Brummbär!** _(grumbling bear) for someone grumpy;_ **(Das ist) alles für die Katz'!** if everything is useless or in vain; **Du Schwein!** _(pig)_ for someone who is messy or a scoundrel. **Schwein haben,** however, has quite a different meaning: _to be lucky._ In addition, names of food are used in special expressions: **Das ist doch Käse!** _(That's nonsense);_ **Das ist mir Wurst!** _(I don't care!);_ or **Alles Banane?** _(Everything all right?);_ **Es ist alles in Butter!** _Everything is ok!;_ **Das ist doch Sahne!** _That's ok!_

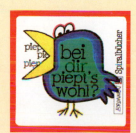

C. Was tust du gern in deiner Freizeit? Lesen Sie mit Ihrem Partner/Ihrer Partnerin die drei Listen und kreuzen Sie an *(check)*, was Sie gern in Ihrer Freizeit tun! Fragen Sie danach andere in der Klasse und finden Sie heraus, was sie angekreuzt haben! Welche fünf Aktivitäten sind besonders populär?

BEISPIEL: S1   Ich lese gern, und du?
            S2   Ich auch. Ich spiele auch gern Videospiele, und du?
            S1   Ich nicht. Ich spiele lieber *(rather)* Klavier . . .

Germans also say **Ping-Pong** instead of **Tischtennis.** The word **Federball** is generally used for recreation and **Badminton** for competitions. **Rollschuhlaufen** is plain *roller skating;* inline skating is **Inlineskating** or **Rollerblading.** to rollerblade = **inlineskaten** *(I like to go rollerblading.* **Ich gehe gern inlineskaten.***)*

Ich . . . gern

❏ backen
❏ campen
❏ diskutieren
❏ essen
❏ faulenzen
❏ fernsehen
❏ joggen
❏ kochen
❏ lesen
❏ malen
❏ reisen
❏ schwimmen
❏ tanzen
❏ träumen *(dream)*
❏ im Garten arbeiten
❏ im Internet surfen
❏ . . .

Ich gehe gern . . .

❏ angeln
❏ bergsteigen *(mountain climbing)*
❏ Geschäfte bummeln
❏ Rad fahren
❏ reiten *(horseback riding)*
❏ Rad fahren
❏ Rollschuh laufen *(roller-skating)*
❏ Schlittschuh laufen *(ice-skating)*
❏ (Wasser)ski laufen
❏ segelfliegen *(gliding)*
❏ segeln *(sailing)*
❏ spazieren
❏ wandern
❏ windsurfen
❏ ins Kino
❏ zum Fitnessstudio
❏ . . .

Ich spiele gern . . .

❏ Basketball
❏ Federball *(badminton)*
❏ Fußball
❏ Volleyball
❏ Golf
❏ Minigolf
❏ Tennis
❏ Tischtennis
❏ Karten
❏ Schach
❏ Computerspiele
❏ Videospiele
❏ Flöte *(flute)*
❏ Gitarre
❏ Klavier
❏ Schlagzeug *(the drums)*
❏ . . .

D. Interview. Fragen Sie einen Nachbarn/eine Nachbarin, . . . !

1. ob er/sie als Kind ein Instrument gelernt hat; wenn ja, welches Instrument und ob er/sie es heute noch spielt
2. ob er/sie gern singt; wenn ja, was und wo (in der Dusche oder Badewanne, im Auto oder Chor)
3. was für Musik er/sie schön findet (klassische oder moderne Musik, Jazz, Rock-, Pop-, Country- oder Volksmusik)
4. ob er/sie viel fernsieht; wenn ja, wann gewöhnlich und was
5. ob er/sie oft lange am Telefon spricht; wenn ja, mit wem
6. wie lange er/sie jeden Tag vor dem Computer sitzt und warum

CD 4, Track 10

Aussprache: l, z

Lesen Sie auch Teil III. 8–10 in *Zur Aussprache* im Arbeitsbuch!

1. [l]   laut, leicht, lustig, leider, Hals, Geld, malen, spielen, fliegen, stellen, schnell, Ball, hell
2. [ts] zählen, zeigen, zwischen, zurück, zuerst, Zug, Zahn, Schmerzen, Kerzen, Einzelzimmer, Pizza, bezahlen, tanzen, jetzt, schmutzig, trotz, kurz, schwarz, Salz, Schweiz, Sitzplatz
3. Wortpaare
   a. *felt* / Feld   c. *plots* / Platz   e. seit / Zeit
   b. *hotel* / Hotel   d. Schweiß / Schweiz   f. so / Zoo

HÖREN SIE ZU! TRACK 18

Beim Arzt

Zum Erkennen: passieren *(to happen);* war *(was);* der Ellbogen, - *(elbow);* hoch·legen *(to put up [high]);* (Schmerz)tabletten *([pain] pills)*

Was fehlt?

1. Kim geht zum Arzt, weil ihr _das Knie_ wehtut. 2. Sie ist mit ihrer Freundin im Harz _Ski laufen_ gegangen. 3. Am letzten Tag ist sie _gefallen_. 4. Sie darf ein paar Tage nicht _laufen_. 5. Sie soll das Bein _hoch legen_. 6. Der Arzt gibt ihr ein paar _Schmerztabletten_ mit. 7. Kim kann bald wieder _schwimmen_ oder _spazieren gehen_. 8. Wenn Kim in einer Woche immer noch Schmerzen hat, soll sie _zurückkommen_.

Skipause oberhalb *(above)* Innsbruck

Struktur

9.1 Endings of adjectives preceded by *der-* and *ein*-words

1. PREDICATE ADJECTIVES and ADVERBS do not have endings.

Willi fährt schnell.	*Willi drives fast.*
Willi ist schnell.	*Willi is quick.*

2. However, ADJECTIVES PRECEDING A NOUN (attributive adjectives) do have an ending that varies with the preceding article and with the noun's case, gender, and number.

Der schnelle Fahrer *(m.)* ist mein Bruder.	*The fast driver is my brother.*
Mein Bruder ist ein schneller Fahrer.	*My brother is a fast driver.*
Er hat ein schnelles Auto *(n.).*	*He has a fast car.*

If you compare the tables below, you will readily see that there are only FOUR DIF-FERENT endings: **-e, -er, -es,** and **-en.**

a. Adjectives preceded by a definite article, or **der**-word:

	masculine			neuter			feminine			plural		
nom.	der	neue	Wagen	das	neue	Auto	die	neue	Farbe	die	neuen	Ideen
acc.	den	neuen	Wagen	das	neue	Auto	die	neue	Farbe	die	neuen	Ideen
dat.	dem	neuen	Wagen	dem	neuen	Auto	der	neuen	Farbe	den	neuen	Ideen
gen.	des	neuen	Wagens	des	neuen	Autos	der	neuen	Farbe	der	neuen	Ideen

b. Adjectives preceded by an indefinite article, or **ein**-word:

	masculine			neuter			feminine			plural		
nom.	ein	neuer	Wagen	ein	neues	Auto	eine	neue	Farbe	keine	neuen	Ideen
acc.	einen	neuen	Wagen	ein	neues	Auto	eine	neue	Farbe	keine	neuen	Ideen
dat.	einem	neuen	Wagen	einem	neuen	Auto	einer	neuen	Farbe	keinen	neuen	Ideen
gen.	eines	neuen	Wagens	eines	neuen	Autos	einer	neuen	Farbe	keiner	neuen	Ideen

Comparing the two preceding tables, you can see:

• Adjectives preceded by the definite article or any **der**-word have either an **-e** or **-en** ending.

• Adjectives preceded by the indefinite article or any **ein**-word have two different adjective endings WHENEVER **ein** HAS NO ENDING: **-er** for masculine nouns and **-er** for neuter nouns. Otherwise the **-en** ending predominates and is used in the masculine accusative singular, all datives and genitives, and all plurals.

after **der**-words

	masc.	neut.	fem.	pl.
nom.		-e		
acc.				
dat.		-en		
gen.				

after **ein**-words

	masc.	neut.	fem.	pl.
nom.	-er	-es	-e	
acc.		-es	-e	
dat.		-en		
gen.				

Or, to put it in another way, the endings are:

• in the NOMINATIVE and ACCUSATIVE SINGULAR
—after **der, das, die,** and **eine** ⟶ **-e**
—after **ein** with masc. nouns ⟶ **-er**
with neut. nouns ⟶ **-es**

• in ALL OTHER CASES ⟶ **-en**
(incl. masc. accusative sg., all datives and genitives, and all plurals)

Der große Ball, das schöne Spiel und die neue CD sind gut.

Das ist ein guter Preis für so ein fantastisches Geschenk.

Das sind keine teuren Geschenke.

NOTE: Adjective endings are not difficult to remember if you understand the following basic principle: in the nominative and the accusative, one of the words preceding the noun must convey information about its gender, number, and case. If an article does not do so, then the adjective must. For example, **der** is clearly masculine nominative; therefore, the adjective can take the minimal ending **-e. Ein,** however, does not show gender or case; therefore, the adjective must do so.

3. If two or more adjectives precede a noun, all have the same ending.

Das sind keine groß**en**, teur**en** Geschenke.

> When adding an ending, a few adjectives, like **teuer** and **dunkel**, drop the -e- in their stem: **Das Geschenk ist teuer. Das sind teu(e)re Geschenke. Das Zimmer ist dunkel. Das ist ein dunkles Zimmer.** In the case of **teuer,** that drop is totally optional.

Übungen

A. Familienfotos. Sagen Sie, was man auf dem Bild vom 50. Jubiläum Ihrer Großeltern sieht!

> A: You could also have students repeat these sentences, using both adjectives in the same sentence, e.g., **Das ist mein Onkel Max mit seinen drei wilden, kleinen Kindern.**

BEISPIEL: Das ist mein Onkel Max mit seinen drei Kindern. (wild, klein)
Das ist mein Onkel Max mit seinen drei wilden Kindern.
Das ist mein Onkel Max mit seinen drei kleinen Kindern.

1. Das ist Tante Jutta mit ihrem Freund aus London. (verrückt, englisch)
2. Hier sitzen wir alle an einem Tisch und spielen Monopoly. (groß, rund)
3. Das ist Oma mit ihrem Porsche *(m.)*. (teuer, rot)
4. Die Farbe dieses Autos gefällt mir. (toll, schnell)
5. Das ist wirklich ein Geschenk! (wunderbar, fantastisch)
6. Opa hat ein Fahrrad bekommen. (schön, neu)
7. Jetzt kann er mit seinen Freunden Fahrrad fahren. (viel, alt)
8. Das hier ist unser Hund *(dog, m.)*. (klein, braun)
9. Das ist wirklich ein Hündchen *(n.)*. (lieb, klein)
10. Wegen des Wetters haben wir nicht im Garten gefeiert. (schlecht, kalt)

> Optional activity: Have students bring magazine photos to class. Then, as a group activity, have them describe their photos to classmates, using adjectives.

B. Die neue Wohnung. Lesen Sie den Dialog mit den Adjektiven!

BEISPIEL: Ist der Schrank neu? (groß)
Ist der große Schrank neu?

S1 Ist dieser Sessel bequem? (braun)
S2 Ja, und das Sofa auch. (lang)
S1 Die Lampe gefällt mir. (klein)
  Woher hast du diesen Teppich? (fantastisch)
  Und wo hast du dieses Bild gefunden? (supermodern)
S2 In einem Geschäft. (alt)
  Wenn du willst, kann ich dir das Geschäft mal zeigen. (interessant)
S1 Ist es in der Müllergasse *(f.)*? (klein)
S2 Ja, auf der Seite. (link-)
S1 Während der Woche habe ich keine Zeit. (nächst-)
  Sind diese Möbel teuer gewesen? (schön)
S2 Natürlich nicht. Für solche Möbel gebe ich nicht viel Geld aus. (alt)

Mercedes-Benz
Ihr guter Stern auf allen Straßen.

C. Inge zeigt Jens ihr Zimmer. Jens stellt Fragen und kommentiert *(comments)*. Bilden Sie aus zwei Sätzen einen Satz!

BEISPIEL: Woher kommt dieses Schachspiel? Es ist interessant.
Woher kommt dieses interessante Schachspiel?

1. Weißt du, was so ein Schachspiel kostet? Es ist chinesisch.
2. Bist du Schachspielerin? Spielst du gut? *(add ein!)*
3. Ich bin kein Schachspieler. Ich spiele nicht gut.
4. Woher hast du diese Briefmarkensammlung? Sie ist alt.
5. Mein Vater hat auch eine Sammlung. Sie ist groß.
6. Sammelst du solche Briefmarken auch? Sie sind normal.
7. Was machst du mit so einer Briefmarke? Sie ist doppelt *(double)*.
8. Darf ich diese Briefmarke haben? Sie ist ja doppelt!

> C: 1. ein chinesisches Schachspiel 2. eine gute Schachspielerin 3. kein guter Schachspieler 4. diese alte Briefmarkensammlung 5. eine große Sammlung 6. solche normalen Briefmarken 7. mit so einer doppelten Briefmarke 8. diese doppelte Briefmarke 9. diese tollen Bilder 10. der kleine Junge 11. was für ein fantastisches Gesicht 12. die dunkelbraunen Augen 13. mit meiner billigen Kamera 14. ein bekannter, deutscher Tennisspieler 15. trotz des schlechten Wetters 16. wegen meines kaputten Knies

9. Hast du diese Bilder gemacht? Sie sind toll.
10. Wer ist der Junge? Er ist klein.
11. Was für ein Gesicht! Es ist fantastisch!
12. Die Augen gefallen mir! Sie sind dunkelbraun.
13. Mit meiner Kamera ist das nicht möglich. Sie ist billig.
14. Und das hier ist ein Tennisspieler, nicht wahr? Er ist bekannt und kommt aus Deutschland.
15. Weißt du, dass wir gestern trotz des Wetters Fußball gespielt haben? Das Wetter ist schlecht gewesen.
16. Leider kann ich wegen meines Knies nicht mehr mitspielen. Das Knie ist kaputt.

D: Alternatively, divide the class into two groups, one giving the first response and the other the second.

D. Ist das nicht schön? Ihr Partner/Ihre Partnerin findet etwas besonders gut. Sagen Sie ihm/ihr, dass Sie das auch finden und stellen Sie danach eine Frage wie beim Mustersatz! *(according to the model)!*

1. **BEISPIEL:**   Ist der Pullover nicht warm?
   Ja, das ist ein warmer Pullover.
   Woher hast du den warmen Pullover?

   a. Ist das Hemd nicht elegant?
   b. Ist die Uhr nicht herrlich?
   c. Ist der Hut *(hat)* nicht verrückt?

2. **BEISPIEL:**   Ist das Hotel nicht gut?
   Ja, das ist ein gutes Hotel.
   Wo hast du von diesem guten Hotel gehört?

   a. Ist die Pension nicht wunderbar?
   b. Ist der Gasthof nicht billig?
   c. Ist das Restaurant nicht gemütlich?

D.3: a. ein großer, moderner Supermarkt; so große, moderne Supermärkte b. ein neues, kleines Handy; so neue, kleine Handys c. eine alte, interessante Kitche; so alte, interessante Kirchen

3. **BEISPIEL:**   Ist das alte Schloss nicht herrlich?
   Ja, das ist ein altes, herrliches Schloss.
   Ich gehe gern in so alte, herrliche Schlösser.

   a. Ist der große Supermarkt nicht modern?
   b. Ist das neue Handy nicht klein?
   c. Ist die alte Kirche nicht interessant?

4. **Und jetzt finden Sie etwas gut (oder nicht so gut).** Was sagt Ihr Partner/Ihre Partnerin dazu *(about it)*? Wechseln Sie sich ab!

   BEISPIEL: Ist unser Professor nicht gut?
   Ja, es ist ein guter Professor.
   Von einem guten Professor kann man viel lernen.

E. Allerlei Beschreibungen *(descriptions)*

1. **Petras Wohnung.** Ergänzen Sie die fehlenden *(missing)* Adjektivendungen!

   a. Petra wohnt in einem toll_en_ Haus im neu_en_ Teil unserer schön_en_ Stadt. b. Ihre klein_e_ Wohnung liegt im neunt_en_ Stock eines modern_en_ Hochhauses *(high-rise)*. c. Sie hat eine praktische___ Küche und ein gemütlich_es_ Wohnzimmer. d. Von dem groß_en_ Wohnzimmerfenster kann sie unsere ganz_e_ Stadt und die viel_en_ Brücken über dem breit_en_ *(wide)* Fluss sehen. e. Petra liebt ihre Wohnung wegen des schön_en_ Blickes *(view, m.)* und der billig_en_ Miete. f. In ihrem hell_en_ Schlafzimmer stehen ein einfach_es_ Bett und ein klein_er_ Nachttisch mit einer klein_en_ Nachttischlampe. g. An der Wand steht ein braun_er_ Schreibtisch und über dem braun_en_ Schreibtisch hängt ein lang_es_ Regal mit ihren viel_en_ Büchern. Petra findet ihre Wohnung schön.

2. **Bilder in diesem Buch.** Finden Sie jeder *(each)* zwei Bilder in diesem Buch und beschreiben Sie sie Ihrem Partner/Ihrer Partnerin! Benutzen Sie ein Adjektiv in jedem Satz!

3. **Meine Wohnung**. Schreiben Sie 8–10 Sätze mit ein oder zwei Adjektiven in jedem Satz!

Fokus — *Schrebergärten*

Many German city-dwellers are passionate gardeners, spending their summers in "garden colonies" or community gardens, assemblages of small garden plots in the middle or on the outskirts of large urban areas. The orthopedist Daniel Schreber (1808–1861) of Leipzig founded the garden movement in the 19th century as a means for workers to supplement their incomes and defuse urban angst. Today the gardens primarily provide an opportunity for recreation, as well as fresh flowers and home-grown vegetables and fruit.

Im Schrebergarten, für Stadtmenschen eine Oase im Grünen

9.2 Reflexive verbs

If the subject and one of the objects of a sentence are the same person or thing, a reflexive pronoun must be used for the object. In the English sentence, *I see myself in the picture,* the reflexive pronoun *myself* is the accusative object. *(Whom do I see?—Myself.)* In the sentence, *I am buying myself a CD,* the pronoun *myself* is the dative object. *(For whom am I buying the CD?—For myself.)*

In German, only the third person singular and plural have a special reflexive pronoun: **sich.** *The other persons use the accusative and dative forms of the personal pronouns, which you already know.*

> **COMPARE:** Ich sehe meinen Bruder auf dem Bild.
> Ich sehe **mich** auf dem Bild.
> Ich kaufe meinem Bruder eine CD.
> Ich kaufe **mir** eine CD.

nom.	ich	du	er / es / sie	wir	ihr	sie	Sie
acc.	mich	dich					
			sich	uns	euch	sich	sich
dat.	mir	dir					

Since only the 1st and 2nd person sg. distinguish between dative and accusative by FORM, they are stressed in examples and exercises.

1. Many verbs you have already learned CAN BE USED REFLEXIVELY, although the English equivalent may not include a reflexive pronoun:

- The reflexive pronoun USED AS THE DIRECT OBJECT (ACCUSATIVE):

sich fragen	*to wonder*	**sich treffen**	*to meet, gather*
sich legen	*to lie down*	usw.	
sich sehen	*to see oneself*		

Ich frage **mich,** ob das richtig ist.	*I wonder (ask myself) whether that's right.*
Ich lege **mich** aufs Sofa.	*I lie down on the sofa.*
Ich sehe **mich** im Spiegel.	*I see myself in the mirror.*

- The reflexive pronoun used AS THE INDIRECT OBJECT (DATIVE):

Optional practice: Was wünschst du dir zum Geburtstag? z.B. **Ich wünsche mir eine Uhr. Und du?**

sich bestellen	**sich nehmen**	
sich kaufen	**sich wünschen**	*to wish*
sich kochen	usw.	

Ich bestelle **mir** ein Eis.	*I am ordering ice cream (for myself).*
Ich koche **mir** ein Ei.	*I'm cooking myself an egg.*
Ich wünsche **mir** ein Auto.	*I'm wishing for a car (for myself).*

2. Some verbs are ALWAYS REFLEXIVE, or are reflexive when they express a certain meaning. Here are some important verbs that you need to know.

sich an·hören	*to listen to*
sich an·sehen, angesehen	*to look at*
sich an·ziehen, angezogen	*to put on (clothing), get dressed*
sich aus·ziehen, ausgezogen	*to take off (clothing), get undressed*
sich um·ziehen, umgezogen	*to change (clothing), get changed*
sich baden	*to take a bath*
sich beeilen	*to hurry*
sich duschen	*to take a shower*
sich erkälten	*to catch a cold*
sich (wohl) fühlen	*to feel (well)*
sich (hin·)legen	*to lie down*
sich kämmen	*to comb one's hair*
sich konzentrieren	*to concentrate*
sich (die Zähne / Nase) putzen	*to clean (brush one's teeth / blow one's nose)*
sich rasieren	*to shave*
sich (hin·)setzen	*to sit down*
sich waschen (wäscht), gewaschen	*to wash (oneself)*

It is important for students to realize that reflexive pronouns play exactly the same role as nouns or personal pronouns in a sentence, i.e., they function as accusative (direct) objects, dative (indirect) objects, or objects of prepositions. Remind students not to confuse **sich legen** *(to lie down)* and **liegen** *(to be lying down),* or **sich setzen** *(to sit down)* and **sitzen** *(to be sitting).*

Setz dich (hin)!	*Sit down.*
Warum müsst ihr euch beeilen?	*Why do you have to hurry?*
Ich fühle mich nicht wohl.	*I don't feel well.*
Letzte Woche hat sie sich erkältet.	*Last week she caught a cold.*
Wir treffen uns mit Freunden.	*We're meeting with friends.*

- With some of these verbs, the reflexive pronoun may be EITHER THE AC-CUSATIVE OR THE DATIVE OBJECT. If there are two objects, then the person (the reflexive pronoun) is in the dative and the thing is in the accusative.

Ich wasche **mich.**	*I wash myself.*
Ich wasche **mir** die Haare.	*I wash my hair.*
Ich ziehe **mich** an.	*I'm getting dressed.*
Ich ziehe **mir** einen Pulli an.	*I'm putting on a sweater.*

3. In English, possessive adjectives are used to refer to parts of the body: *I'm washing my hands*. In German, however, the definite article is usually used together with the reflexive pronoun in the dative.

*I'm washing **my** hands.*	Ich wasche **mir die** Hände.
*She's combing **her** hair.*	Sie kämmt **sich die** Haare.
*Brush **your** teeth.*	Putz **dir die** Zähne!

REMEMBER: When there are two object pronouns, the accusative precedes the dative!

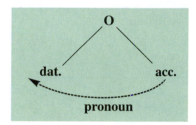

Ich wasche **mir die Hände.**	Ich wasche **sie mir.**
Du kämmst **dir die Haare.**	Du kämmst **sie dir.**
dat. acc.	acc. dat.

Hör dir das an!

Übungen

F. Antworten Sie mit JA!

1. **Singular**

BEISPIEL: Soll ich mir die Hände waschen?
Ja, waschen Sie sich die Hände!
Ja, wasch dir die Hände!

a. Soll ich mich noch umziehen?   d. Soll ich mich jetzt setzen?
b. Soll ich mir die Haare kämmen?   e. Soll ich mir die Bilder ansehen?
c. Soll ich mir ein Auto kaufen?

Du kannst dir auch mal wieder die Ohren waschen.

2. **Plural**

BEISPIEL: Sollen wir uns die Hände waschen?
Ja, waschen Sie sich die Hände!
Ja, wascht euch die Hände!

a. Sollen wir uns ein Zimmer mieten?   d. Sollen wir uns die Kassetten anhören?
b. Sollen wir uns ein Haus bauen?   e. Sollen wir uns die Briefmarken
c. Sollen wir uns in den Garten setzen?   ansehen?

Students might find it amusing if you teach them the following verse to the melody from the "Volga Boatman": **Zieht euch warm an, zieht euch warm an, denn die Kälte greift den Darm an"** (attacks the intestines)!

blub, blub und sich
wohl fühlen, wie ein Fisch
im Wasser.

Park Hotel blub und blub Badeparadies.

G. Was fehlt?

1. Kinder, zieht __euch__ warm an!
2. Einen Moment, ich muss __mir__ die Nase putzen.
3. Gestern haben wir __uns__ ein Klavier gekauft.
4. Setzen Sie __sich__ bitte!
5. Peter, konzentrier __dich__!
6. Kinder, erkältet __euch__ nicht!
7. Ich habe __mir__ zum Geburtstag ein Schachspiel gewünscht.
8. Willst du __dir__ etwas im Radio anhören?
9. Junge, fühlst du __dich__ nicht wohl?
10. Möchten Sie __sich__ die Hände waschen?
11. Bestellst du __dir__ auch ein Stück Kuchen?
12. Ich setze __mich__ gemütlich in den Garten.

H. Hoppla, hier fehlt was! Jeder hat seine Routine. Finden Sie mit Ihrem Partner/Ihrer Partnerin heraus, was die anderen morgens tun! Einer von Ihnen sieht auf die Tabelle unten, der andere auf die Tabelle im Anhang, Teil 11.

S1:

	Zuerst	Dann	Danach
ELKE	s. duschen s. die Haare waschen	s. kämmen s. die Zähne putzen	s. in die Küche setzen s. ein Ei kochen gemütlich frühstücken s. Musik anhören
HORST	s. schnell anziehen joggen gehen	s. duschen s. umziehen s. vor den Spiegel stellen	s. die Haare kämmen s. rasieren Joghurt und Müsli essen
SUSI	zu lange schlafen schnell aufstehen	s. schnell anziehen s. nicht kämmen	ihre Sachen nicht finden etwas zu essen mitnehmen
INGO	s. das Gesicht waschen s. eine Tasse Kaffee machen s. anziehen	s. an den Computer setzen s. die E-Mails ansehen	s. wieder hinlegen s. nicht beeilen

Optional English-to-German practice:
1. Otto, get dressed! 2. Christian, hurry!
3. Anne und Sabrina, are you putting on a sweater? 4. We still have to brush our teeth. 5. Peter, comb your hair! 6. I don't feel well. 7. Today we're all going jogging. 8. Yes, but I've caught a cold. 9. Then lie down (sg. fam.).! (See answer key in the Appendix.)

1. **So ist es bei Elke, Horst, Susi und Ingo.**

    BEISPIEL: S1 Was macht Horst morgens?
                S2 Horst zieht sich schnell an und geht joggen. Dann . . .

2. **Und bei mir?**

    BEISPIEL: S1 Ich bin wie (like) . . . Zuerst . . . Danach . . .
                S2 Wirklich? Ich bin wie . . . Zuerst . . . Danach . . .

I. Und du, was machst du den ganzen Tag? Fragen Sie Ihren Partner/Ihre Partnerin, was er/sie zu einer gewissen (certain) Zeit des Tages tut! Wenn möglich, benutzen Sie in Ihren Fragen und Antworten reflexive Verben! Machen Sie sich Notizen (take notes) und erzählen Sie dann der Klasse, was Sie herausgefunden haben!

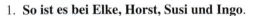

    BEISPIEL: S1 Was machst du abends um zehn?
                  S2 Abends um zehn höre ich mir die Nachrichten an. Und du?
                  S1 Um diese Zeit lege ich mich ins Bett . . .

9.3 Infinitive with *zu*

English and German use infinitives with **zu** (*to*) in much the same way.

    Es ist interessant **zu reisen.**   *It's interesting to travel.*

    Ich habe keine Zeit gehabt **zu essen.**   *I didn't have time to eat.*

Although the spelling reform makes it optional to separate the infinitive phrase from the main clause without a comma, we prefer to stick to the old rule for clarity's sake, i.e., keep the comma.

1. In German, if the infinitive is combined with other sentence elements, such as a direct object or an adverbial phrase, a comma usually separates the infinitive phrase from the main clause.

Haben Sie Zeit, eine Reise **zu** machen?   *Do you have time to take a trip?*

Note that in German the infinitive comes at the end of the phrase.

2. If a separable-prefix verb is used, the **-zu-** is inserted between the prefix and the verb.

> prefix + **zu** + verb

Es ist Zeit ab**zu**fahren.   *It's time to leave.*

CAUTION: No **zu** after modals! Wir **müssen** jetzt **abfahren.**

3. Infinitive phrases beginning with **um** explain the purpose of the action described in the main clause.

Wir fahren nach Hessen, **um** unsere Oma **zu** besuchen.   *(in order to visit . . .)*
Rudi geht ins Badezimmer, **um** sich **zu** duschen.   *(in order to take a shower)*

MISEREOR

„Die Menschen
haben gelernt,
zu schwimmen wie die Fische
und zu fliegen wie die Vögel,
aber wie Brüder
zusammenzuleben
haben sie nicht
gelernt"
M. L. King

Übungen

J. Wie geht's weiter?

> **BEISPIEL:**   Hast du Lust . . . ? (sich Kassetten anhören)
> **Hast du Lust, dir Kassetten anzuhören?**

1. Dort gibt es viel . . . (sehen, tun, fotografieren, zeigen, essen)
2. Habt ihr Zeit . . . ? (vorbeikommen, die Nachbarn kennen lernen, faulenzen, euch ein paar Bilder ansehen)
3. Es ist wichtig . . . (aufpassen, sich konzentrieren, Sprachen lernen, Freunde haben, Sport treiben)
4. Es ist interessant . . . (ihm zuhören, Bücher sammeln, mit der Bahn fahren, mit dem Flugzeug fliegen)
5. Es hat Spaß gemacht . . . (reisen, wandern, singen, spazieren gehen, aufs Land fahren, Freunde anrufen)

K. Bilden Sie Sätze!

1. heute / wir / haben / nicht viel / tun
2. es / machen / ihm / Spaß // sich mit Freunden treffen
3. sie *(sg.)* / müssen / noch / einlösen / Scheck
4. ich / haben / keine Zeit // Geschichten / sich anhören *(pres. perf.)*
5. du / haben / keine Lust // mit uns / Ski laufen gehen? *(pres. perf.)*
6. möchten / du / fernsehen / bei uns?
7. wir / möchten / kaufen / neu / Auto
8. es / sein / sehr bequem // hier / sitzen
9. ich / sein / zu müde // Tennis spielen
10. du / sollen / anrufen / dein- / Kusine

J.5: In English, the present perfect isn't used very often in such constructions; the simple past is much more common.

K: 1. Heute haben wir nicht zu tun.
2. Es macht ihm Spaß, sich mit Freunden zu treffen. 3. Sie muss noch einen Scheck einlösen. 4. Ich habe keine Zeit gehabt, mir (die) Geschichten anzuhören. 5. Hast du keine Lust gehabt, mit uns Ski laufen zu gehen? 6. Möchtest du bei uns fernsehen? 7. Wir möchten (uns) ein neues Auto kaufen. 8. Es ist sehr bequem, hier zu sitzen. 9. Ich bin zu müde, (um) Tennis zu spielen. 10. Du sollst deine Kusine anrufen.

L. So bin ich. Sprechen Sie mit den anderen über Ihre Hobbys und Ihre Freizeit!
1. Ich habe keine Lust . . .
2. Ich habe nie Zeit . . .
3. Mir macht es Spaß . . .
4. Ich finde es wichtig . . .
5. Ich finde es langweilig *(boring)* . . .
6. Als *(as)* Kind hat es mir Spaß gemacht . . .
7. Ich brauche das Wochenende gewöhnlich, um . . .
8. Ich lerne Deutsch, um . . .

M. Was tue ich gern? Teilen Sie *(divide)* die Klasse in zwei Mannschaften *(teams)*. Eine Mannschaft denkt an *(of)* ein Hobby. Die andere Mannschaft versucht *(tries)* dann mit bis zu 10 Fragen herauszufinden, was dieses Hobby ist. Nach 10 Fragen wechselt sich die Mannschaft ab!

Fokus — *Vacationing*

In contrast to many North Americans who take their vacation days in short breaks combined with a holiday and one or two weekends, Germans are more likely to view their annual vacation as the year's major event. With relatively high incomes and a minimum of three to four weeks' paid vacation **(Urlaub)** each year, Germans are among the world's greatest travelers. Many head south to the beaches of southern France, Spain, Italy, Greece, Turkey, and North Africa. Others opt for educational trips, such as language courses abroad or cultural tours. Favorite destinations include Thailand, Kenya, and North America. Those who wish to stay closer to home may take bike tours or spend a week on a farm in the countryside.

Ferien auf dem Bauernhof

Zusammenfassung

N. Rotkäppchen und der Wolf. Was fehlt?

1. Es hat einmal eine gute Mutter mit ihrem kleinen Mädchen in einem ruhigen Dorf gewohnt. 2. Sie hat zu ihrer kleinen Tochter gesagt: „Geh zu deiner alten Großmutter und bring ihr diese gute Flasche Wein und diesen frischen Kuchen!

3. Aber du musst im dunkl<u>en</u> Wald aufpassen, weil dort der groß<u>e</u> bös<u>e</u> *(bad)* Wolf wohnt." 4. Das klein<u>e</u> Mädchen ist mit seiner groß<u>en</u> Tasche in den grün<u>en</u> Wald gegangen. 5. Auf dem dunkl<u>en</u> Weg ist der bös<u>e</u> Wolf gekommen und hat das klein<u>e</u> Mädchen gefragt, wo seine alt<u>e</u> Großmutter lebt. 6. Er hat dem gut<u>en</u> Kind auch die wunderbar<u>en</u> Blumen am Weg gezeigt. 7. Dann hat der furchtbar<u>e</u> Wolf die arm<u>e</u> *(poor)* Großmutter gefressen *(devoured)* und hat sich in das bequem<u>e</u> Bett der alt<u>en</u> Frau gelegt. 8. Das müd<u>e</u> Rotkäppchen ist in das klein<u>e</u> Haus gekommen und hat gefragt: „Großmutter, warum hast du so groß<u>e</u> Ohren? Warum hast du so groß<u>e</u> Augen? Warum hast du so einen groß<u>en</u> Mund?" 9. Da hat der bös<u>e</u> Wolf geantwortet: „Dass ich dich besser fressen kann!" 10. Nun *(well)*, Sie kennen ja das Ende dieser bekannt<u>en</u> Geschichte *(story, f.)*! 11. Der Jäger *(hunter)* hat den dick<u>en</u> Wolf getötet *(killed)* und dem klein<u>en</u> Mädchen und seiner alt<u>en</u> Großmutter aus dem Bauch des tot<u>en</u> *(dead)* Wolfes geholfen.

O. Hallo, Max! Auf Deutsch bitte!

1. What have you been doing today? 2. Oh, nothing special. I listened to my old cassettes. 3. Do you feel like going swimming (taking a swim)? 4. No, thanks. I don't feel well. I have a headache and my throat hurts. Call Stephan. 5. Hello, Stephan! Do you have time to go swimming? 6. No, I have to go to town **(in die Stadt)** in order to buy (myself) a new pair of slacks and a warm coat. Do you feel like coming along? 7. No, I already went shopping this morning. I bought (myself) a blue sweater and a white shirt. 8. Too bad. I've got to hurry. 9. OK, I'm going to put on my swim trunks **(die Badehose)** and go swimming. Bye!

O: 1. Was hast du heute gemacht / getan? 2. Oh, nichts Besonderes. Ich habe mir meine alten Kassetten angehört. 3. Hast du Lust, schwimmen zu gehen? 4. Nein, danke. Ich fühle mich nicht wohl. Ich habe Kopfschmerzen und der Hals tut mir weh. Ruf (doch) Stephan an! 5. Hallo, Stephan! Hast du Zeit, schwimmen zu gehen? 6. Nein, ich muss in die Stadt (fahren / gehen), um mir eine neue Hose und einen warmen Mantel zu kaufen. Hast du Lust mitzukommen? 7. Nein, ich bin heute früh / Morgen schon einkaufen gewesen / gegangen. Ich habe mir einen blauen Pullover und ein weißes Hemd gekauft. 8. Schade! Ich muss mich beeilen. 9. O.K., gut, ich ziehe mir die Badehose an und gehe schwimmen. Tschüss! / Auf Wiederhören!

Drachenflieger *(hang-gliders)* vor dem Abflug

Einblicke

Lesestrategie: Freizeit

Was machen Sie in der Freizeit? Schreiben Sie eine kurze Liste von Freizeitaktivitäten, die *(which)* Sie gern machen! Dann lesen Sie, wie man in Deutschland die Freizeit verbringt *(spends)*.

Wortschatz 2

der Urlaub	*(paid) vacation*
das Leben[1]	*life*
die Musik	*music*
ander- *(adj.)*[2]	*other, different*
anders *(adv.)*[2]	*different(ly)*
beliebt	*popular*
ganz	*whole, entire(ly), all*
etwas (ganz) anderes	*something (totally) different*
(genauso) wie . . .	*(just) like . . .*
aus·geben (gibt aus), ausgegeben	*to spend (money)*
sich entspannen	*to relax*
sich erholen	*to recuperate*
erleben	*to experience*
sich fit halten (hält), gehalten	*to keep in shape*
sich langweilen	*to get (or be) bored*
vor·ziehen, vorgezogen	*to prefer*

[1] In German, **Leben** is normally used only in the singular: Sport ist wichtig **in ihrem Leben** *(in her life, in their lives)*.

[2] Note the various uses of *other:* Das Leben auf dem Land ist **anders** *(different)*. Es ist **ein anderes** *(a different kind of)* **Leben**. In *Wortschatz 1* you also learned two additional forms of *other:* Manche Leute leben gern in der Stadt, **andere** *(others)* gern auf dem Lande. Ich liebe es dort, aber **die anderen** *(the others)* finden es furchtbar.

A.1: In the United States, people work an average of 230 days a year, in Japan 238 days.

Vor dem Lesen

A. Allerlei Fragen

1. Wie viele Stunden die Woche *(per week)* arbeitet man in den USA / in Kanada? 2. Wie viele Wochen Urlaub hat man im Jahr? 3. Was tun die Amerikaner / Kanadier in ihrer Freizeit? 4. Was ist der Nationalsport hier? 5. Was sind andere populäre Sportarten? 6. Wohin fahren Sie gern in den Ferien? 7. Sind Ferien für Sie gewöhnlich Lust oder Frust? Warum?

B. Ferientipps.
Finden Sie mit ihrem Partner/Ihrer Partnerin auf Seite 249 heraus, wo diese Kurorte *(health resorts)* sind, was sie zu bieten *(offer)* haben und was das kostet! Wenn Sie wollen, besuchen Sie den Kurort im Internet. Was klingt besonders interessant und warum?

Kurort	Wo liegt das?	Was bieten sie dort?	Preis
BAD DRIBURG			
BAD NENNDORF			
BAD REICHENHALL			
BAD TÖLZ			
OBERSTDORF			
ROTTACH-EGERN			

C. Was ist das?

der Arbeiter, Freizeitboom, Freizeitfrust, Musikklub, Urlaubstag; das Fernsehen, Gartenhäuschen, Gartenstück, Industrieland, Musikfestspiel, Privileg, Thermalbad; die Aerobik, Autobahn, Disko, Kulturreise, Massage, Schönheitsfarm; mit sich bringen, planen; deutschsprachig, frustriert, überfüllt

Kurorte, wo man sich erholen kann.

Freizeit—Lust oder Frust?

CD 4, Track 12

Vor hundert Jahren war es° das Privileg der reichen° Leute, nicht arbeiten zu müssen. Die Arbeiter in den deutschsprachigen Ländern haben zu der Zeit aber oft noch 75 Stunden pro Woche gearbeitet. Urlaub für Arbeiter gibt es erst seit 1919: zuerst nur drei Tage im Jahr. Heute ist das anders. Die Deutschen arbeiten nur ungefähr 197 Tage im Jahr, weniger als° die Menschen in fast allen anderen Industrieländern. Außer den vielen Feiertagen haben sehr viele Leute fünf oder sechs Wochen Urlaub im Jahr. So ist die Freizeit ein sehr wichtiger Teil des Lebens und mehr als° nur Zeit, sich vom täglichen Stress zu erholen.

    Was tut man mit der vielen Freizeit? Natürlich ist Fernsehen sehr wichtig. Viele sitzen mehr als zwei Stunden pro Tag vorm Fernseher. Auch Sport ist sehr populär, nicht nur das Zusehen°, sondern auch das aktive Mitmachen°, um sich fit zu halten. Heute sind Aerobik, Squash oder Windsurfen genauso „in" wie Tennis und Golf. Fußball ist bei den Deutschen und Österreichern, wie überall in Europa, der Nationalsport. Auch Handball und Volleyball sind in den deutschsprachigen Ländern sehr beliebt.

    Die Menschen sind gern draußen° in der Natur. An Wochenenden fahren sie oft mit dem Zug oder mit dem Auto aufs Land und gehen spazieren, fahren Rad oder wandern. Danach setzt man sich in ein schönes Gartenrestaurant und entspannt sich. Im Sommer gehen sie oft ins öffentliche Schwimmbad oder fahren an einen schönen See. Sie sind auch viel im Garten. Wenn sie in einer Stadtwohnung leben, können sie sich ein kleines Gartenstück pachten° und dort Blumen und Gemüse ziehen°. Viele bauen sich dort ein Gartenhäuschen, wo sie sich duschen, umziehen oder entspannen können.

    Die Deutschen sind reiselustig°. Immer wieder zieht es sie hinaus in die Ferne, z.B. nach Spanien, Griechenland oder Frankreich. Sie geben fast ein Sechstel° des Touristikumsatzes° der ganzen Welt aus. Manche machen Kulturreisen, um Land und Leute kennen zu lernen, in Museen zu gehen oder sich auf einem der vielen Festspiele Musik anzuhören. Andere reisen, um Sprachen zu lernen oder einmal etwas ganz anderes zu tun, etwas Neues zu erleben. Viele fahren in den warmen Süden, um sich in die Sonne zu legen und schön braun wieder nach Hause zu kommen. Andere ziehen es vor, zu einem Kurort oder einer Schönheitsfarm zu gehen, um sich mit Thermalbädern, Massagen und Hautpflege° verwöhnen zu lassen°.

    Und die jungen Leute? Außer den oben genannten° Aktivitäten macht es ihnen besonders Spaß, sich mit Freunden zu treffen und in Kneipen°, Diskos, Cafés, Musikklubs oder ins Kino zu gehen. Auch gehen sie gern bummeln oder einkaufen.

100 years ago, it was / rich

less than

more than

watching / participation

outdoors

lease / grow

travel-hungry
one sixth
here: travel dollars

skin care / let themselves be spoiled
above-mentioned
pubs

Inlineskaten und Bergsteigen sind nichts für jeden.

Dieser ganze Freizeitboom bringt aber auch Probleme mit sich. Manche langweilen sich, weil sie nicht wissen, was sie mit ihrer Freizeit machen sollen. Andere sind frustriert, wenn sie auf der Autobahn in lange Staus° kommen oder die Züge überfüllt sind. Manchmal muss man eben° etwas planen. Man muss ja nicht am ersten oder letzten° Urlaubstag unterwegs° sein. Und wenn man seine Ruhe° haben will, darf man nicht in der Hauptsaison° zu den bekannten Ferienplätzen fahren. Sonst° wird Freizeitlust zum Freizeitfrust.

traffic jams
just / last
on the road / peace and quiet
high season / otherwise

Nach dem Lesen

A. Was passt?

a. im Garten
b. vorm Fernseher
c. Staus
d. den vielen Feiertagen
e. mit ihrer Freizeit
f. sich da richtig wohl fühlen

g. sich ein kleines Gartenstück zu pachten
h. zu erholen
i. anzuhören
j. arbeiten zu müssen
k. schön braun zurückzukommen
l. in Diskos

Optional: Working in groups of two to four, students underline all the infinitives with **zu** *that they can find in the text. See which group can find the most.*

  j   1. Vor hundert Jahren war es das Privileg der reichen Leute, nicht . . .

  d   2. Heute haben sehr viele Leute außer . . . auch noch fünf oder sechs Wochen Urlaub im Jahr.

  h   3. Die Freizeit ist mehr als nur Zeit, sich vom Stress . . .

  b   4. Viele Leute sitzen über zwei Stunden am Tag . . .

  a   5. Andere arbeiten gern . . .

  g   6. Wer keinen Garten hat, hat die Möglichkeit, . . .

  f   7. Wenn das Wetter schön ist, kann man . . .

  i   8. Manche machen Kulturreisen, um sich zum Beispiel auf einem der vielen Musikfeste Musik . . .

  k   9. Andere fahren in den warmen Süden, um . . .

  l   10. Junge Leute gehen gern . . .

  c   11. Am Anfang und am Ende der Ferien sind die Autobahnen oft überfüllt *(overcrowded)* und es gibt . . .

  e   12. Für manche Leute ist Freizeit ein Problem, weil sie nicht wissen, was sie . . . tun sollen.

B. Ich ziehe es vor, . . . Beim Thema Freizeit haben Sie und Ihr Partner/Ihre Partnerin ganz andere Ideen. Folgen Sie *(follow)* dem Beispiel!

BEISPIEL: Ich habe Lust, . . . (baden gehen, hier bleiben usw.)
Ich habe Lust, baden zu gehen. Und du?
Ich ziehe es vor, hier zu bleiben.

1. Nach der Vorlesung habe ich Zeit, . . . (Tennis spielen, mein Buch lesen usw.)
2. Mir gefällt es, . . . (durch Geschäfte bummeln und einkaufen, nichts ausgeben usw.)
3. Ich habe Lust, diesen Sommer . . . (in den Süden fahren, nach Norwegen reisen usw.)
4. Ich finde es schön, abends . . . (in einen Musikklub gehen, sich Musik im Radio anhören usw.)
5. Meine Freunde und ich haben immer Lust, . . . (windsurfen gehen, in den Bergen wandern usw.)
6. Mir ist es wichtig, . . . (immer etwas Neues erleben und Leute kennen lernen, sich mit Freunden gemütlich hinsetzen usw.)

C. **Kreativurlaub.** Mal etwas ganz anderes in den Ferien. Lesen Sie die Ferienangebote *(vacation offers)* mit ihrem Partner/Ihrer Partnerin und finden Sie heraus, ob das etwas für ihn/sie ist! Erzählen Sie dann der Klasse, was ihm/ihr besonders gefällt!

1. Wo gibt es Sprachkurse in Französisch? Wie viele Stunden sind Sie da in der Klasse und wie viele Stunden Praxis *(practice)* bekommen Sie in der Woche?
2. Wo kann man Segelfliegen lernen? Wie lange braucht ein Anfänger *(beginner)*, bevor er/sie allein fliegen kann? Von wann bis wann gibt es Intensivkurse?
3. Wo kann man Husky-Safaris und Rentierschlittenfahrten *(trips with a reindeer sled)* erleben? Wie wär's mit (Ski)langlauf *(cross-country skiing)*? Haben Sie das schon einmal gemacht? Wenn ja, wo?
4. Wo gibt es auch Skilanglauf? Von wann bis wann sind die Skikurse? Wie wär's mit Kanufahren? Ist das etwas für Sie? Haben Sie das schon einmal gemacht? Wenn ja, wo?
5. Wo gibt es Kunstkurse? Ist das etwas für Sie? Wann gibt es diese Kurse?
6. Wer verkauft Auszeiten *(time-outs)*, wo man die Natur erleben kann? Wo gibt es diese Auszeiten? Ist das etwas für Sie? Warum (nicht)?
7. Wo gibt es Kurse für kreatives Schreiben? Ist das etwas für Sie? Warum (nicht)?
8. Wohin gehen die Skiflüge von Hamburg? Ist das etwas für Sie? Wenn ja, wohin? Was kostet eine solche Woche Skiurlaub? Ist das billig oder teuer?

D. Kurzgespräche. Bereiten Sie mit Ihrem Partner/Ihrer Partnerin einen der beiden Dialoge vor und präsentieren Sie ihn danach vor der Klasse!

1. **Ich bin's, Tante Elisabeth!**

Your aunt Elisabeth, who lives in Zurich, calls. You answer the phone, greet her, and ask how she and Uncle Hans are doing. She says how they are and asks about you. You tell her you've caught a cold and aren't feeling very well. She expresses her sympathy and asks whether you'd like to visit them during [spring break]. Do you want to accept? If so, your aunt says that she's glad, and she reminds you to tell her when you are going to arrive. You both say good-bye.

2. **Hier Reisebüro Eckhardt!**

You call a travel agency, *Reisebüro Eckhardt*. An employee answers the phone and connects you with an agent. You ask the agent about trains to Zurich. He/she wants to know when you want to go. You tell him/her on [March 17]. He/she says that you need to reserve a seat (**einen Platz reservieren**). He/she says it costs [€ 120,-]; you tell him/her to reserve a seat. The agent asks when you want the tickets, and you reply that you'll come by on [Wednesday]. You both say good-bye.

Since you will be departing for Zurich from Stuttgart, the travel agent will use the schedule on p. 210 to tell you about your options, depending on what time of day you would like to travel. You also ask him/her about the return schedule and the cost of a round-trip ticket.

HÖREN SIE ZU! TRACK 19

Eine tolle Radtour

Zum Erkennen: im Büro *(at the office);* das Mietfahrrad, ¨er *(rent-a-bike);* ab·holen *(to pick up);* die Zahnradbahn *(cogwheel-railway);* das Panorama; die Talfahrt *(descent);* die Fähre, -n *(ferry)*

Richtig oder falsch?

- f 1. Weil Sabrina bei der Post arbeitet, möchte sie in den Ferien etwas ganz anderes tun.
- r 2. Im Frühling hat sie eine Radtour um den Bodensee gemacht.
- f 3. Sie hat diese Tour mit ihrer Familie gemacht.
- f 4. In Lindau haben sie ihre Fahrräder abgeholt.
- r 5. Am ersten Tag sind sie bis nach Heiden gekommen.
- r 6. Am zweiten Tag haben sie eine schnelle Talfahrt bis an den See gehabt.
- f 7. Die zweite Nacht haben sie in Bregenz übernachtet.
- f 8. Am dritten Tag hat sie eine Fähre zurück nach Friedrichshafen gebracht.
- r 9. Sie sind in den paar Tagen in drei Ländern gewesen.
- f 10. Die Tour hat mit Übernachtungen 233 Franken gekostet.
- f 11. Zum Mittagessen haben sie meistens nichts gegessen.
- r 12. Mit so einer Radtour hält man sich fit.

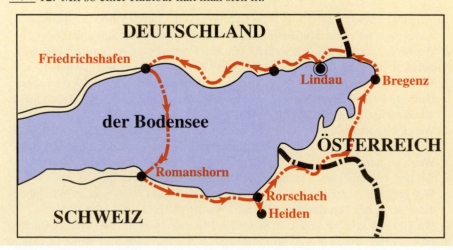

Fokus — *Rose Ausländer*

Rose Ausländer was one of Germany's most prominent writers of her time. Born into a Jewish family in 1907 in the German-speaking town of Czernowitz, Ukraine, she was transported to a Nazi-guarded ghetto in 1941 and emerged four years later to tell her story. After developing her writing talent during two decades of self-imposed exile in the United States, she returned to Europe in the mid-1960s to settle and publish in Düsseldorf. Themes of persecution, emigration, and loneliness marked her work, which appeared in collections of poetry: *Blinder Sommer* (1956), *Inventar* (1972), and *Ein Stück weiter* (1979), and in her outstanding volume of poetry and prose, *Ohne Visum* (1974). She died in Düsseldorf in 1988.

Noch bist du da

Wirf° deine Angst	Noch	throw
in die Luft°	duftet° die Nelke°	air / is fragrant / carnation
	singt die Drossel°	thrush (bird)
Bald	noch darfst du lieben	
ist deine Zeit um°	Worte verschenken	up
bald	noch bist du da	
wächst° der Himmel°		grows / sky
unter dem Gras	Sei° was du bist	be
fallen deine Träume	Gib was du hast	
ins Nirgends°		into nowhere

Rose Ausländer

Fragen zum Gedicht

1. Rose Ausländer weiß, am Ende des Lebens steht der Tod *(death)*. Was will sie uns mit dem Gedicht sagen? Was sollen wir tun?
2. Das Gedicht hat kein Komma und keinen Punkt *(period)*. Warum nicht? Was denken Sie?
3. Was wollen Sie noch erleben, bevor Ihr Leben zu Ende ist?

Video-Ecke

- The *Minidrama* "Lachen ist die beste Medizin" shows Daniela at home with the flu. Her mother is caring for her, and her father tries to cheer her up. Surprisingly, her friend drops in with her arm in a cast. Perhaps Daniela is not so bad off after all?

Web-Ecke

- For updates, self-assessment quizzes, and online activities related to this chapter, visit the *Wie geht's?* Web site at **http://wiegehts.heinle.com**. You will prepare a trip to Frankfurt, make hotel reservations, and plan an excursion. You can also learn about Germany's soccer team and buy tickets for a game. Finally, you have the opportunity to do some guided Internet search on your own.

Kapitel ⑩

Unterhaltung

Szene aus Paul Hindemiths Oper *Cardillac*

Lernziele

Vorschau
The magic of the theater

Gespräche + Wortschatz
Entertainment

Fokus
German film
The world of music
The art scene
German television
German cabaret
Wolf Biermann

Struktur
10.1 Verbs with prepositional objects
10.2 Da- and wo-compounds
10.3 Endings of unpreceded adjectives

Einblicke
Wer die Wahl hat, hat die Qual.
Wolf Biermann: *Ach, Freund, geht es nicht auch dir so?*

Video-Ecke
Minidrama: *Kino? Ja, bitte!*
Blickpunkt: *Das Hebbel Theater*

Web-Ecke

Vorschau

The Magic of the Theater

Theater plays a central role in the cultural life of Germany, Austria, and Switzerland. As in other European countries, the German government has traditionally subsidized the fine arts; but with recent budget cuts, many theater directors are beginning to rely more heavily on corporate sponsorship.

Germany has more than 400 stages, with the leading theaters in such metropolises as Berlin, Hamburg, and Munich. But even medium-sized and small cities have their own repertory theaters as well. Some date back to the 18th century, when—before Germany was united as a country—many local sovereigns founded their own court theaters. By the 19th century, a number of towns and cities had established theaters as public institutions. Theaters were, after all, a major source of entertainment.

Today, theater continues to be popular. Works by William Shakespeare, Jean-Baptiste Molière, Johann Wolfgang von Goethe, Friedrich Schiller, Bertolt Brecht, Max Frisch, and Friedrich Dürrenmatt continue to draw large audiences, as do works by women authors such as Elfriede Jelinek and Gerlind Reinshagen. States and local governments subsidize tickets in public venues; and most houses offer reduced ticket prices for students, seniors, and the unemployed. An active children's theater thrives across the country, with marionettes especially drawing delighted crowds.

Municipal theaters in medium-sized cities usually also offer ballet, musicals, and operas. Among the latter, not only the traditional famous German-language operas (e.g., Beethoven's *Fidelio*, Mozart's *Die Zauberflöte*, or Richard Strauss's *Der Rosenkavalier*) retain their popularity, but also other international and modern operas (e.g., Puccini's *La Bohème* or Alban Berg's *Wozzeck*). In the summer, many cities invite to music, theater, ballet, and open-air film festivals. Broadway musicals have met with similar success, with special musical theaters dedicated to performing British composer Andrew Lloyd Webber's *Das Phantom der Oper, Cats, Starlight Express,* or *Die Schöne und das Biest,* and newer musicals such as *Mozart* and *Verdi,* a pop-adaptation with music and lyrics by Elton John and Tim Rice. At the same time, German stages have supported experiments in the tradition of dance by artists such as Oskar Schlemmer, Gret Palucca, and Pina Bausch with her world-famous Wuppertal Dance Theater.

Entertainment in Germany can, but does not have to have a traditional-rustic touch. The Love Parade in Berlin is an example of a more recent German "folk festival," a mega-event that regularly attracts thousands of fans of techno music to the German capital from all over Europe on the second weekend in July. There is also a varied club scene, where you can dance the night away. The latest thing for night-owls are literature parties and open-air film festivals.

You could ask students to read the dates below aloud in German. In addition, you might initiate classroom discussion on which of these German cultural figures they are already familiar with.

Life data of celebrities from the German-speaking countries: Goethe (1749 – 1832), Schiller (1759 – 1805), Brecht (1898 – 1956), Frisch (1911 – 1991), Dürrenmatt (1921 – 1990), Jelinek (1946), Reinshagen (1926), Beethoven (1770 – 1827), Mozart (1756 – 1791), Strauss (1864 – 1949), Berg (1885 – 1935), Schlemmer (1888 – 1943), Palucca (1902 – 1993), Bausch (1940).

Gespräche + Wortschatz

CD 5, Track 1

Explain that *Gute Zeiten, schlechte Zeiten* is a popular German soap opera taped in the Berlin-Babelsberg Studios.

Warm-ups: 1. **Was kann man in der Freizeit tun?** 2. **Was muss der Artikel sein?** Wintersportfest, Flugschalter, Kunstmuseumseingang, Klavierlehrerin, Sektglas, Tischtennistisch, Samstagnachmittagfußballspiel, Nachthemd, Bierbauch, Stuhlbein, Zahnfleisch, Haarfarbe, Gitarrenmusik, Fax-Adresse? 3. **Welches Verb passt?** z.B. Bummler: bummeln (Anruf, Aufpasser, Bedeutung, Besucher, Gefühl, Gepäck, Langschläfer, Maler, Fotograf, Reise, Sammler, Schwimmer, Skiläufer, Spaziergänger, Wunsch) 4. **Geben Sie drei Imperative! z.B. sich setzen: Setzen Sie sich! Setzt euch! Setz dich!** (s. abwechseln, s. beeilen, s. fit halten, s. kämmen, s. die Ohren putzen) 5. **Im Kaufhaus.** Was sehen Sie sich an oder was kaufen Sie sich?

Blick in die Zeitung

SONJA   Du, was gibt's denn heute Abend im Fernsehen?

THEO   Keine Ahnung. Sicher nichts Besonderes.

SONJA   Mal sehen! *Gute Zeiten, schlechte Zeiten,* einen Dokumentarfilm und einen Krimi.

THEO   Dazu habe ich keine Lust.

SONJA   Vielleicht gibt's was im Kino?

THEO   Ja, *Planet der Affen, Das Tier im Manne* und *Shrek.*

SONJA   Hab' ich alle schon gesehen.

THEO   Im Theater gibt's *Der kaukasische Kreidekreis* von Brecht.

SONJA   Nicht schlecht. Hast du Lust?

THEO   Ja, das klingt gut. Gehen wir!

An der Theaterkasse

THEO   Haben Sie noch Karten für heute Abend?

DAME   Ja, erste Reihe erster Rang links und Parkett rechts.

THEO   Zwei Plätze im Parkett! Hier sind unsere Studentenausweise.

DAME   10 Euro bitte!

SONJA   Wann fängt die Vorstellung an?

DAME   Um 20.15 Uhr.

Während der Pause

THEO   Möchtest du eine Cola?

SONJA   Ja, gern. Aber lass mich zahlen! Du hast schon die Programme gekauft.

THEO   Na gut. Wie hat dir der erste Akt gefallen?

SONJA   Prima. Ich habe das Stück schon mal in der Schule gelesen, aber noch nie auf der Bühne gesehen.

THEO   Ich auch nicht.

DER KAUKASISCHE KREIDEKREIS

von Bertolt Brecht
Musik von Paul Dessau

A: 1. *Gute Zeiten, schlechte Zeiten,* einen Dokumentarfilm, einen Krimi 2. Nein. 3. Nein, das/den hat er schon gesehen. 4. *Der kaukasische Kreidekreis.* 5. Ja, im I. Rang links und Parkett rechts. 6. Im Parkett. 7. Um 20.15 Uhr. 8. Sie trinken eine Cola. 9. Sonja. 10. Aus der Schule.

A. Fragen

1. Was gibt's im Fernsehen? 2. Gefällt das Theo? 3. Hat Theo Lust, sich *Planet der Affen* anzusehen? 4. Was gibt's im Theater? 5. Gibt es noch Karten für dieses Stück? 6. Wo sind Theos und Sonjas Plätze? 7. Wann fängt die Vorstellung an? 8. Was tun Theo und Sonja während der Pause? 9. Wer bezahlt dafür *(for it)?* 10. Woher kennt Sonja das Stück schon?

B. Jetzt sind Sie dran! Sehen Sie sich mit Ihrem Partner/Ihrer Partnerin die Zeitung an, um herauszufinden, was es im Fernsehen, im Kino und im Theater gibt. Vielleicht machen Sie auch Pläne und gehen zur Kino- oder Theaterkasse oder Sie gehen zur Videothek *(video store)* und holen sich *(get)* ein oder zwei Videos.

Since students probably don't have newspapers available, ask them to just pretend and invent the details.

Staudte (1906 – 1984), Beyer (1932), Fassbinder (1946 – 1982), Herzog (1942), v. Trotta (1942), Dörrie (1955), Schlöndorff (1939), Grass (1927), Petersen (1941), Emmerich (1955), Wenders (1945), Szabó (1938), Polanski (1933), Annaud (1943), Tykwer (1965), Petzold (1960)

Fokus — *German Film*

During the early days of film, the Ufa studios in the Berlin suburb of Potsdam-Babelsberg were second only to Hollywood in churning out world-class productions, including such classics as *Nosferatu, Metropolis,* and *Der blaue Engel.* When the Nazis took power, film production continued, although many prominent directors and actors turned their backs on Germany, emigrating to the United States and elsewhere. After the war, those studios were taken over by Defa, whose films were subject to the approval of GDR authorities and have become a bridge to the past. Among Defa's best known films are Wolfgang Staudte's *Der Untertan* and Frank Beyer's *Jakob der Lügner.*

Beginning in the 1960s, a new wave of young West German filmmakers seized the world's attention. Directors such as Rainer Werner Fassbinder (*Die Ehe der Maria Braun*), Werner Herzog (*Stroszek*), Margarethe von Trotta (*Rosa Luxemburg*), Doris Dörrie (*Männer*), Volker Schlöndorff (*Die Blechtrommel,* based on a novel for which Günter Grass received the Nobel Prize in 1999), and Wolfgang Petersen (*Das Boot*) produced critically acclaimed movies. Many German directors continue to work closely with Hollywood. Examples are Roland Emmerich (*Independence Day*), and Wim Wenders (*Wings of Desire*). Whereas many critics lament the domination of American blockbusters (most of which are dubbed), German film has been experiencing a renaissance, with co-productions of István

Das Boot, von Wolfgang Petersen

Szabo's *Taking Sides,* Roman Polanski's *Pianist,* or Jean-Jacques Annaud's Stalingrad epic *Duel—Enemy at the Gates.* Despite internationally renowned achievements such as Tom Tykwer's *Run Lola Run* and Christian Petzold's *The State I Am In,* the German film industry is struggling. The market share of German films in the cinemas is currently only approximately 10–15 percent. It all increasingly seems to happen on television rather than in the cinema. Babelsberg Studio in Potsdam is now relying heavily on television productions and major international movies. The strategy seems to be paying off.

Wortschatz 1

Die Unterhaltung (entertainment)

der Anfang, ⸚e	beginning, start	die Kunst, ⸚e	art
Autor, -en	author	Oper, -n	opera
Chor, ⸚e	choir	Pause, -n	intermission, break
Film, -e	film, movie		
Komponist, -en, -en	composer	Vorstellung, -en	performance
Krimi, -s	detective story	Werbung	advertising
Maler, -	painter(-artist)	Zeitschrift, -en	magazine
Roman, -e	novel	Zeitung, -en	newspaper
Schauspieler, -	actor		
das Ballett, -s	ballet	dumm	stupid, silly
Ende	end	komisch	funny (strange, comical)
Gemälde, -	painting		
Konzert, -e	concert	langweilig	boring
Orchester, -	orchestra	nächst- / letzt-	next / last
Programm, -e	(general) program; channel	spannend	exciting, suspenseful
Stück, -e	play, piece (of music or ballet)	traurig / lustig	sad / funny
		klatschen	to applaud
		lachen / weinen	to laugh / to cry
		lächeln	to smile

Weiteres

der Anfang / das Ende	beginning / end
am Anfang / am Ende	in the beginning / at the end
der Blick (in / auf + *acc.*)	glance (at), view (of)
vor kurzem	recently
an·fangen (fängt an), angefangen	to start, begin
an·machen / aus·machen	to turn on / to turn off
sich entscheiden, entschieden	to decide
ersetzen	to replace
vergessen, vergessen	to forget
Was gibt's im Fernsehen?	What's (playing) on television?
Keine Ahnung!	No idea!
(Das ist doch) unglaublich!	That's unbelievable. That's hard to believe.
(Das ist ja) Wahnsinn!	That's crazy / awesome / unbelievable!
Das ärgert mich.	That makes me mad.
Jetzt habe ich aber genug.	That's enough. I've had it.
Ich habe die Nase voll.	I'm fed up (with it).
Das hängt mir zum Hals(e) heraus.	I'm fed up (with it).

Zum Erkennen: die Reihe, -n *(row);* im Rang *(in the balcony);* im Parkett *(in the orchestra);* der Akt, -e; AUCH: die Ausstellung, -en *([art] exhibit / show);* das Da- / Wo-Kompositum *(da- / wo-compound);* die Leseratte, -n *(bookworm);* der Lieblingsplatz, ⸚e *(favorite place);* die Rolle, -n *(role, part);* die Statistik, -en; bewerten *(to rate);* sich holen *(to get);* vorausgehend *(preceding);* Das hängt mir zum Hals heraus. *(I'm fed up [with it].)*

Zum Thema

A. Am Frühstückstisch. Beenden Sie die Sätze!

1. Auf diesem Bild gehört die . . . zu einem guten Frühstück.
2. Das ist natürlich Werbung für . . .

3. Ich . . . *(know)* diese Zeitung *(nicht)*.

4. Auf dem Frühstückstisch sieht man . . .

5. Ich esse morgens gern . . .

6. Wenn ich Zeit habe, lese ich . . .

7. Diese Woche liest man in den Zeitungen viel über *(about)* . . .

8. Ich interessiere mich besonders für *(am interested in)* . . .

9. Am . . . ist die Zeitung immer sehr dick.

B. Hoppla, hier fehlt was! Was spielt wo und wann? Sehen Sie sich mit Ihrem Partner/Ihrer Partnerin den Spielplan an und finden Sie heraus, was Sie nicht wissen! Einer von Ihnen sieht sich die Tabelle unten an, der andere die Tabelle im Anhang, Teil 11. Entscheiden Sie sich dann, was Sie sehen wollen und warum!

S1:

Wo	Was?	Wann?
Volksbühne	**Macbeth,** Schauspiel von William Shakespeare	19.30
Urania-Theater	**Eine Nacht in Venedig,** Operette von Johann Strauss	20.15
Metropol-Theater	**West Side Story,** Musical von Leonard Bernstein	19.00
Im Dom	**Jedermann,** Schauspiel von Hugo von Hofmannsthal	15.00
Philharmonie	**Original Wolga-Kosaken,** Lieder und Tänze	15.30
Konzerthaus	**Flamenco-Festival,** mit Montse Salazar	20.00
Komödie	**Jahre später, gleiche Zeit,** Komödie von Bernhard Slade	16.00
Kammerspiele	**Carmina Burana,** von Carl Orff	17.30
Filmbühne 1	**Das Versprechen,** von Margarethe von Trotta	19.30
Filmbühne 2	**Das Boot,** von Wolfgang Petersen	22.00

1. **BEISPIEL:**   **S2**   Was gibt's heute in der Philharmonie?
    S1   Die Wolga-Kosaken.
    S2   Und wann?
    S1   Um halb vier . . . und im Dom gibt's . . .
    S2   O ja, wann denn?
    S1   . . .

2. **BEISPIEL:**   **S1**   Hast du . . . schon gesehen / gehört? Das ist ein(e) von . . .
    S2   Ja / Nein, . . . aber . . .
    S1   Dann hast du Lust . . . ?
    S2   . . .
    S2   Gut, . . .

C. Allerlei Fragen

1. Lesen Sie gern? Sind Sie eine Leseratte *(bookworm)?* Wenn ja, was für Bücher interessieren Sie? Wie viele Bücher haben Sie in den letzten drei Monaten gelesen? Welche Autoren finden Sie besonders gut? Welche Zeitungen und Zeitschriften lesen Sie gern? Lesen Sie auch Comics?

2. Wo kann man hier Theaterstücke, Opern oder Musicals sehen? Haben Sie dieses Jahr ein interessantes Stück oder ein gutes Musical / eine gute Oper gesehen? Wenn ja, wo und welche(s)? Wie hat es/sie Ihnen gefallen?

3. Gehen Sie manchmal in ein Rock-, Jazz- oder Popkonzert? Mögen Sie klassische Musik? Welche Komponisten oder Musikgruppe hören Sie gern?

4. Wer von Ihnen singt gern? Wer singt im Chor? Wer spielt im Orchester oder in einer Band? Wer von Ihnen spielt ein Instrument?

C: Consult the newspaper for current offerings in your area. Also come prepared with names of composers and painters and titles of plays and / or operas.

5. Wer hat schon mal eine Rolle *(role, part)* in einem Theaterstück gespielt? Was für eine Rolle?

6. Wie gefällt Ihnen abstrakte Kunst? Welche Maler finden Sie gut? Gehen Sie manchmal zu Kunstausstellungen *(art shows)?* Wenn ja, wo? Wessen Gemälde gefallen Ihnen (nicht)? Malen Sie auch? Wenn ja, was malen Sie gern?

7. Was kann man hier noch zur *(for)* Unterhaltung tun?

D. Was gibt's Interessantes?

1. **Im CineStar.** Sehen Sie sich mit Ihrem Partner/Ihrer Partnerin das Programm vom "CineStar" an und entscheiden Sie sich, was Sie sehen wollen und zu welcher Zeit. Was kosten die Karten? Vergessen Sie nicht, donnerstags gibt's Premieren zum Schnupperpreis *(at bargain prices)!*

2. **Einfach toll / furchtbar!** Sprechen Sie in kleinen Gruppen über einen Film, ein Stück, ein Konzert oder etwas anderes, was Sie vor kurzem gesehen haben und sagen Sie, wie es Ihnen gefallen hat! Wenn Sie es noch nicht gesehen haben, erzählen Sie, was Sie darüber gehört oder gelesen haben!

E. Mein Lieblingsplatz *(favorite place)*. Sehen Sie sich mit den anderen die folgende *(following)* Liste an und erzählen Sie den anderen, wo Sie sich besonders wohl fühlen und entspannen können! Warum dort? Vielleicht ist dieser Lieblingsplatz nicht auf dieser Liste.

1. im Billardsalon
2. unter einem Baum im . . .
3. am Strand *(beach)* von . . .
4. in meinem Zimmer
5. in der Badewanne
6. im Fitnessstudio
7. in der Bibliothek
8. in unserer Garage
9. vorm Computer
10. im Café / Kaffeehaus . . .

F. Kurzgespräche. Bereiten Sie mit Ihrem Partner/Ihrer Partnerin einen der beiden Dialoge vor und präsentieren Sie ihn danach vor der Klasse!

1. **Im Buchladen**

You are in a bookstore. As the clerk approaches you, tell him/her you need a present for someone, maybe a good book about art, music, the theater, or film. He/she shows you several ones that he/she says are very nice, but you don't like any of them. Finally, you find something that's just right, including the price. You take it.

2. **Die Notizen** *(class notes)*

You have lent your notebook with class notes to a classmate [give him/her a name] who has failed to return it as promised—again. Not only that, but this classmate has passed the notebook on to a third person who is supposed to return it to you. You have called there and didn't get an answer. You are trying to prepare for a test. Tell your roommate your tale of woe and vent your anger about the situation.

Aussprache: r, er

Sehen Sie auch Teil II. 9 und III. 11 in *Zur Aussprache* im Arbeitsbuch!

CD 5, Track 2

1. [r] **r**ot, **r**osa, **r**uhig, **r**echts, **R**adio, **R**egal, **R**eihe, **R**oman, P**r**ogramm, Do**r**f, Konze**r**t, Fah**r**t, Gita**rr**e, t**r**au**r**ig, k**r**ank, He**rr**en
2. [ʌ] Orchest**er**, Theat**er**, Mess**er**, Tell**er**, ab**er**, leid**er**, hint**er**, unt**er**, üb**er**, wied**er**, weit**er**
3. [ʌ / r] Uh**r** / Uh**r**en; Oh**r** / Oh**r**en; Tü**r** / Tü**r**en; Cho**r** / Chö**r**e; Auto**r** / Auto**r**en; Klavie**r** / Klavie**r**e
4. Wortpaare
   a. *ring* / Ring
   b. *Rhine* / Rhein
   c. *fry* / frei
   d. *brown* / braun
   e. *tear* / Tier
   f. *tour* / Tour

Die Litfasssäule zeigt, was es an Unterhaltung gibt.

HÖREN SIE ZU! TRACK 20

Biedermann und die Brandstifter

Zum Erkennen: mal eben *(just for a minute)*; die Inszenierung *(production)*; die Hauptrolle, -n *(leading role)*; die Einladung, -en *(invitation)*

Richtig oder falsch?

f	1.	Christians Vater hat ihm zwei Theaterkarten gegeben.
r	2.	Christian fragt seinen Freund Daniel, ob er mitkommen möchte.
f	3.	Die Plätze sind in der 2. Reihe vom 1. Rang.
f	4.	Die Vorstellung beginnt um halb sieben.
f	5.	Christian muss sich noch die Haare waschen.
r	6.	Wenn Daniel sich beeilt, können sie noch schnell zusammen essen.
f	7.	Sie treffen sich an der Straßenbahnhaltestelle in der Breslauer Straße.

Fokus — *The World of Music*

Composers from the German-speaking countries have played no small role in shaping the world of music. Johann Sebastian Bach is one of the preeminent German composers. His rich work, including passions and secular concertos, is universally praised for its beauty and perfection. Other important composers of the baroque period are George Frideric Handel and Georg Philipp Telemann.

Wolfgang Amadeus Mozart, another musical genius, dominated the classical period, and Ludwig van Beethoven laid the foundations for the Romantic Movement. The final choral movement of Beethoven's Ninth Symphony, "Ode to Joy," was chosen as the European anthem. Composers Franz Schubert, Felix Mendelssohn-Bartholdy, Robert Schumann, Carl Maria von Weber, Richard Wagner, and Johannes Brahms all regarded their works as following in the tradition of

Die Semperoper am Dresdner Theaterplatz

Beethoven. Through the interpretation of their music, pianists like Clara Wieck (wife of Robert Schumann) and Elly Ney, violinist Anne-Sophie Mutter, and clarinetist Sabine Meyer have gained international acclaim in a previously male-dominated field.

Great innovators have also influenced the modern era. Gustav Mahler is a link between the lyrical impulse of the Romantic Movement and the more ironic attitudes of the arts in the 20th century. Richard Strauss pioneered musical drama; Paul Hindemith and Carl Orff established new standards in choral music; and Arnold Schönberg introduced the 12-tone system of composition. Contemporary composers Bernd-Alois Zimmermann, Hans Werner Henze, and Karlheinz Stockhausen have all stretched the horizons of the avant-garde.

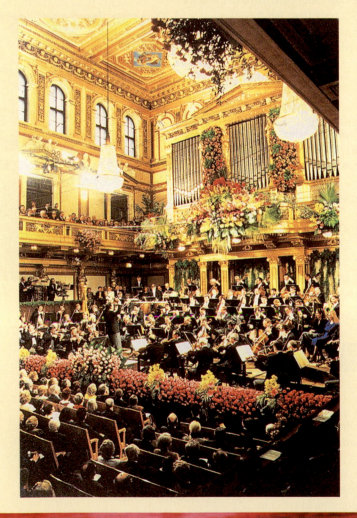

Neujahrskonzert in Wien

Bach (1685–1750), Händel (1685–1759), Telemann (1681–1767), Mozart (1756–1791), Beethoven (1770–1827), Schubert (1797–1828), Mendelssohn-Bartholdy (1809–1847), Schumann (1810–1856), Weber (1786–1826), Wagner (1813–1883), Brahms (1833–1897), Wieck (1819–1896), Ney (1882–1968), Mutter (1963), Meyer (1960), Mahler (1860–1911), Strauss (1864–1949), Hindemith (1895–1963), Orff (1895–1982), Schönberg (1874–1951), Zimmermann (1918–1970), Henze (1926), Stockhausen (1928).

Struktur

10.1 Verbs with prepositional objects

In both English and German, a number of verbs are used together with certain prepositions. These combinations often have special idiomatic meanings.

I'm thinking of my vacation. I'm waiting for my flight.

Since the German combinations differ from English, they must be memorized.

<table>
<tr><td>denken an (+ acc.)</td><td>to think of / about</td></tr>
<tr><td>schreiben an (+ acc.)</td><td>to write to</td></tr>
<tr><td>sich freuen auf (+ acc.)</td><td>to look forward to</td></tr>
<tr><td>sich vor·bereiten auf (+ acc.)</td><td>to prepare for</td></tr>
<tr><td>warten auf (+ acc.)</td><td>to wait for</td></tr>
<tr><td>sich ärgern über (+ acc.)</td><td>to get annoyed / upset about</td></tr>
<tr><td>lächeln über (+ acc.)</td><td>to smile about</td></tr>
<tr><td>sich entscheiden über (+ acc.)</td><td>to decide on / about</td></tr>
<tr><td>sich entscheiden gegen (+ acc.)</td><td>to decide against</td></tr>
<tr><td>sich informieren über (+ acc.)</td><td>to inform oneself / find out about</td></tr>
<tr><td>sich interessieren für (+ acc.)</td><td>to be interested in</td></tr>
<tr><td>erzählen von (+ dat.)</td><td>to tell about</td></tr>
<tr><td>halten von (+ dat.)</td><td>to think of, be of an opinion</td></tr>
<tr><td>sprechen von (+ dat.) / über (+ acc.)</td><td>to talk of / about</td></tr>
</table>

You may need to point out the difference between a separable-prefix verb (**aufstehen**) and verbs commonly used in combination with a preposition (**warten auf**). **Er steht früh auf.** (Nothing follows **auf**; it's a V2, i.e., part of the verb infinitive.) BUT **Ich warte auf dem Bahnsteig auf den Zug.** (**auf** is followed by an object of the preposition; the infinitive is **warten.**)

WIR FREUEN UNS AUF SIE!
Mo.-Fr. 9 - 20 Uhr
Jeden Samstag von 9 - 16 Uhr!

NOTE: In these idiomatic combinations, two-way prepositions most frequently take the accusative.

Er denkt an seine Reise.	*He is thinking about his trip.*
Sie schreibt an ihre Eltern.	*She is writing to her parents.*
Freut ihr euch aufs Wochenende?	*Are you looking forward to the weekend?*
Ich bereite mich auf eine Prüfung vor.	*I'm preparing for an exam.*
Ich warte auf ein Telefongespräch.	*I'm waiting for a phone call.*
Ich ärgere mich über den Brief.	*I'm upset about the letter.*
Über so etwas Dummes kann ich nur lächeln.	*I can only smile about something stupid like that.*
Informier dich über das Programm!	*Find out about the program.*
Interessierst du dich für Sport?	*Are you interested in sports?*
Erzählt uns von euerem Flug!	*Tell us about your flight.*
Was hältst du denn von dem Film?	*What do you think of the movie?*
Sprecht ihr von *Shrek*?	*Are you talking about Shrek?*

Remind students that the preposition **von** after **erzählen** and **halten** is not a two-way preposition but is always followed by the dative; likewise, remind them that **für** always takes the accusative.

CAUTION: These idiomatic combinations, **an, auf, über,** etc., are not separable prefixes, but prepositions followed by nouns or pronouns in the appropriate cases:

Ich **rufe** dich morgen **an.**	BUT	Ich **denke an** dich.
I'll call you tomorrow.		*I'm thinking of you.*

Note also these two different uses of **auf:**

Ich warte **auf den** Zug.	BUT	Ich warte **auf dem** Zug.
For what? For the train.		*Where? On (top of) the train.*

Übungen

A: These sentences can be used with different objects or in a quick English-German drill: 1. **s. interessieren für:** Sprachen, Philosophie, Bücher, Theater . . . 2. **sprechen von:** Geld, Land, Politik, Autos . . . 3. **erzählen von:** Universität, Schweiz, Ferien, Museum . . . 4. **denken an:** Blumen, Prüfung, Werbung, Wochenende . . . 5. **warten auf:** Student, Antwort, Rechnung, Freund . . . 6. **s. freuen auf:** Schiffsreise, Fußballspiel, Postkarte . . . 7. **s. ärgern über:** Konzert, Film, Fernsehprogramm . . . 8. **halten von:** Werbung, Maler, Gemälde, Theaterstück . . .

A. Sagen Sie es noch einmal! Ersetzen Sie die Hauptwörter!

> **BEISPIEL:**   Sie warten auf den Zug.
> (Telefongespräch)
> **Sie warten auf das Telefongespräch.**

1. Wir interessieren uns für Kunst. (Sport, Musik)
2. Er spricht von seinem Urlaub. (Bruder, Hobbys)
3. Sie erzählt von ihrem Flug. (Familie, Geburtstag)
4. Ich denke an seinen Brief. (Ansichtskarte, Name)
5. Wartest du auf deine Familie? (Gäste, Freund)
6. Freut ihr euch auf das Ballett? (Vorstellung, Konzert)
7. Ich habe mich über das Wetter geärgert. (Junge, Leute)
8. Was haltet ihr von der Idee? (Gemälde, Maler)

B. Die Afrikareise. Was fehlt?

1. Meine Tante hat_an_ mein_en__Vater geschrieben. 2. Sie will uns_von_ ihr_er___ Reise durch Afrika erzählen. 3. Wir freuen uns_auf_ ihr_en___ Besuch *(m.)*. 4. Meine Tante interessiert sich sehr_für_ Afrika. 5. Sie spricht hier im Museum_über / von_ ihr_e/en__ Fahrten. 6. Sie malt auch gern und ist_über_ Kunst gut informiert. 7. Ich denke gern_an__ sie. 8. Mein Vater ärgert sich_über_ sie, wenn sie nicht schreibt. 9. Sie hält einfach nicht viel_von_ Briefen und sie hat keinen Computer, aber sie ruft uns manchmal an.

Optional English-to-German practice: 1. I am looking forward to the art show. 2. Have you found out about the tickets? 3. We have talked about the show, but then I didn't think of the date. 4. Please don't wait for me *(pl. fam.)*, but go without me. 5. You *(pl. fam.)* know I'm not interested in art. 6. Why do you get so upset about this painter? 7. I'm not upset, but I know this painter and I don't think much of his paintings. 8. The whole town is talking about him. (See answer key in the Appendix.)

C. Hört euch das an! Erzählen Sie den anderen von drei Situationen, wo Sie sich vor kurzem gefreut oder geärgert haben! Vergessen Sie nicht zu sagen, wie Sie sich fühlen!

> **BEISPIEL:**   Wisst ihr, das Autohaus hat mein Auto schon dreimal repariert *(repaired)*. Ich habe viel Geld dafür *(on it)* bezahlt und es läuft immer noch nicht richtig. Jetzt habe ich aber die Nase voll!

D. So beende ich die Sätze. Und du? Beenden Sie die Sätze mit Präpositionen wie **an, auf, für, über** oder **von!** Fragen Sie dann die anderen, wie sie sie beendet haben!

> **BEISPIEL:**   Ich lächele nur . . .
> **Ich lächele nur über solche dummen Fragen.**

1. Ich denke oft . . .
2. Ich warte . . .
3. Ich schreibe gern . . .
4. Ich interessiere mich . . .
5. Ich freue mich . . .
6. Ich ärgere mich manchmal . . .
7. Ich spreche gern . . .
8. Ich halte nicht viel . . .
9. Ich muss mich . . . vorbereiten.
10. Es ist schwer, sich . . . zu entscheiden.

Fokus — *The Art Scene*

As in other parts of Europe, early painting in the German-speaking countries was devoted to religious works, especially altar pieces. In the 16th century, Albrecht Dürer became the first important portrait painter; he also developed landscape painting and is regarded as the inventor of etching. His contemporaries include Lucas Cranach and Hans Holbein. Although painting followed the trends of western European art, it did not reach another high point until the 19th century. Caspar David Friedrich's landscapes are representative of the romantic era. Following the Congress of Vienna, the Biedermeier period introduced its idyllic settings; and towards the turn of the century came the Viennese Secession (or **Jugendstil**) with Gustav Klimt.

Early-20th-century artists conveyed the fears and dangers of the times through expressionism. Two examples are Oskar Kokoschka, who reflected the anxious, decadent atmosphere of prewar Vienna, and Paul Klee, who ventured into abstract art. Others, including Käthe Kollwitz, Max Beckmann, and Otto Dix, exercised sharp social criticism through their sculptures and canvasses. The rise of the Nazis, who denounced most modern art as "degenerate," put an abrupt end to this creative period. In the second half of the century, Germany's art scene again came alive, with representatives like Joseph Beuys, who turned visual art into action, Rebecca Horn, who presents sculptures as performances, and Markus Lüpertz, whose representational painting wants to convey a "drunken, rapturous" feeling of life.

If students ask: **die Messe** = *(trade) fair*

Maske, von Paul Klee

Dürer (1471 – 1528), Cranach (1472 – 1553), Holbein the Younger (1497 – 1543), Friedrich (1774 – 1840), Klimt (1910 – 1962), Kokoschka (1866 – 1980), Klee (1879 – 1940), Kollwitz (1867 – 1945), Beckmann (1884 – 1950), Dix (1891 – 1969), Beuys (1921 – 1986), Horn (1944), Lüpertz (1941).

In case students ask: 1. After the defeat of Napoleon in 1814, the victorious European monarchs convened at the **Congress of Vienna** (1814 – 1815) to create a new European order. The mastermind of the diplomatic gathering was Austria's Prince Metternich. 2. **Biedermeier** is a central and eastern European style that flourished between 1815 and 1848. The name comes from a popular cartoon character, "Papa Biedermeier," who symbolized quiet, comfortable bourgeois domesticity. 3. For information about the **Jugendstil,** see the *Fokus* section in Chapter 5.

10.2 *Da-* and *wo-*compounds

1. **Da**-Compounds

In English, pronouns following prepositions can refer to people, things, or ideas:

I'm coming with him.   I'm coming with it.

In German, this is not the case; pronouns following prepositions refer only to people:

Ich komme **mit ihm (mit meinem Freund).**

If you wish to refer to a thing or an idea, you must use a **da**-COMPOUND.

Ich komme **damit (mit unserem Auto).**

Most accusative and dative prepositions (except **außer, ohne,** and **seit**) can be made into **da**-compounds. If the preposition begins with a vowel (**an, in,** etc.), it is used with **dar-:**

Compare with English *thereafter, thereupon, therein, thereby,* etc.

dafür	*for it (them)*	**darauf**	*on it (them)*
dagegen	*against it (them)*	**darin**	*in it (them)*
damit	*with it (them)*	**darüber**	*above / about it (them)*
danach	*after it (them)*	usw.	

Wer weiß schon genau, woraus ein Hamburger besteht?

Können Sie mir sagen, wo ein Briefkasten ist? — Ja, sehen Sie die Kirche dort? **Daneben** ist eine Apotheke, **dahinter** ist die Post und **davor** ist ein Briefkasten mit einem Posthorn **darauf.**

2. **Wo**-compounds

The interrogative pronouns **wer, wen,** and **wem** refer to people.

Von wem sprichst du?   *About whom are you talking? (Who are you talking about?)*

Auf wen wartet ihr?   *For whom are you waiting? (Who are you waiting for?)*

In questions about things or ideas, **was** is used. If a preposition is involved, however, a **wo**-COMPOUND is required. Again, if the preposition begins with a vowel, it is combined with **wor-.**

Compare with English *wherefore, whereby, wherein, whereto,* etc.

wofür?	*for what?*	**worauf?**	*on what?*
wogegen?	*against what?*	**worüber?**	*above, about what?*
womit?	*with what?*	usw.	

To help students figure out when to use **da**- or **wo**-compounds, give them a dozen or so English sentences and have them give you a compound or a pronoun: *I have a pen. I'm writing with it* **(damit).** *With what am I writing* **(womit)?** *I'm talking with my friend* **(mit ihm).** *With whom am I talking* **(mit wem)?**

Wovon sprichst du?   *About what are you talking? (What are you talking about?)*

Worauf wartet ihr?   *For what are you waiting? (What are you waiting for?)*

REMEMBER: To ask where something is located, use the question word **wo,** regardless of the answer expected: **Wo ist Peter?** To ask where someone is going, use **wohin** (NOT <u>wo</u> combined with <u>nach</u> or <u>zu</u>!): **Wohin ist Peter gegangen?** To ask where a person is coming from, use **woher** (NOT <u>wo</u> combined with <u>aus</u> or <u>von</u>!): **Woher kommt Peter?**

Übungen

E. Wo ist nur mein Adressbuch? Helfen Sie Ihrem Partner/Ihrer Partnerin, es zu finden! Benutzen Sie dabei immer ein **Da**-Kompositum *(da-compound)!*

> **BEISPIEL:** auf dem Sofa
> **Vielleicht liegt es darauf.**

neben dem Bett, vor dem Telefon, hinter der Lampe, auf dem Esstisch, in der Tasche, unter den Fotos, zwischen den Zeitungen und Zeitschriften, . . .

E: daneben, davor, dahinter, darauf, darin, darunter, dazwischen

F. Noch einmal bitte! Ersetzen Sie die fettgedruckten *(boldfaced)* Wörter mit einem **Da**-Kompositum oder mit einer Präposition mit Pronomen!

F: 1. danach 2. damit 3. für sie 4. dagegen 5. von ihnen 6. darauf 7. dahinter 8. zwischen ihnen 9. davon 10. darin 11. an ihn 12. darauf

> **BEISPIEL:** Hans steht neben Christa.   **Er steht neben ihr.**
> Die Lampe steht neben dem Klavier.   **Sie steht daneben.**

1. Was machst du **nach den Ferien**?
2. Bist du auch **mit dem Bus** gefahren?
3. Er hat das Gemälde **für seine Frau** gekauft.
4. Was hast du **gegen Skilaufen**?
5. Das Paket ist **von meinen Eltern** gewesen.
6. Die Karten liegen **auf dem Tisch**.
7. Die Kinder haben **hinter der Garage** gespielt.
8. Anja hat **zwischen Herrn Fiedler und seiner Frau** gesessen.
9. Was halten Sie **von dem Haus**?
10. Ist die Faxnummer **im Adressbuch**?
11. Wir denken oft **an unseren kranken Freund**.
12. Freust du dich auch **auf unsere Fahrt**?

Kombinieren Sie mit da- und wo-! z.B. für: dafür / wofür? (durch, gegen, um, an, auf, hinter, in, neben, über, unter, vor, zwischen, aus, bei, mit, nach, von, zu). Practice the formation of **da-** and **wo**-compounds for several days in one-minute drills.

G. Das Klassentreffen *(class reunion).* Sie erzählen Ihrer Großmutter/Ihrem Großvater (Ihrem Partner/Ihrer Partnerin) von einem Klassentreffen, aber er/sie hört schlecht und möchte, dass Sie alles wiederholen. Tun Sie das und wechseln Sie sich nach jedem Verb ab! Jeder darf einmal schwerhörig *(hard of hearing)* sein.

	Horst	Claire	Max + Eva	Gerd + Elke
sprechen über	Sport	Arbeit	Familie	Schulzeit
denken an	Golf spielen	Mittagspause	Urlaub	Vergangenheit *(f., past)*
schreiben an	Golftrainer	Freunde	Reisebüro	Schulfreunde
warten auf	Freundin	Post	Antwort	Klassentreffen *(n.)*
s. freuen auf	jedes Spiel	Besuch	Seereise	Wiedersehen
s. interessieren für	nichts anderes	Kunst	Sprachen	alles
s. informieren über	Wetter	Ausstellungen	Städte in Amerika	Lehrer
s. ärgern über	jeden Fehler	Boss	Kinder	Essen

Exaggerating questions and responses, using **da-** and **wo**-compounds, can also be effective. Bring along a rubber snake, spider, mouse, or any other creepy crawler / or show pictures of them. Write the German equivalent on the board (**Schlangen, Spinnen, Mäuse, Ratten,** etc.). Begin with full-sentence prompts, like **Ich habe Angst vor Schlangen** *(acting scared),* then students are generally able to create their own sentences just with partial cues (e.g., **Angst haben vor**).
S1 of class: Wir haben Angst vor Spinnen.
S2: Wovor habt ihr Angst?
S1: *(louder!)* Vor Spinnen!
S1: Ach so! Davor!

> **BEISPIEL:**
> **S1** Claire spricht über die Arbeit.
> **S2** Worüber spricht Claire?
> **S1** Über die Arbeit.
>
> **S1** Claire ärgert sich über ihren Boss.
> **S1** Über wen ärgert sie sich?
> **S2** Über ihren Boss.

H. Wie bitte? Ihr Partner/Ihre Partnerin sagt Ihnen etwas, aber Sie hören nicht genau hin und gehen ihm/ihr mit Ihren vielen Fragen etwas auf die Nerven. In den Sätzen benutzt er nur Verben von der Liste im Teil 10.1 der Grammatik *(grammar)*. Wechseln Sie sich ab!

BEISPIEL: S1   Ich freue mich auf die nächste Woche.
　　　　　　　　S2   Worauf freust du dich?
　　　　　　　　S1   Ach, darauf!

　　　　　　　　S1   Ich freue mich auf meinen Onkel und meine Tante.
　　　　　　　　S2   Auf wen freust du dich?
　　　　　　　　S1   Ach, auf sie!

10.3 Endings of unpreceded adjectives

You already know how to deal with adjectives preceded by either **der-** or **ein-**words. Occasionally, however, adjectives are preceded by neither; they are then called UNPRECEDED ADJECTIVES. The equivalent in English would be adjectives preceded by neither *the* nor *a(n):*

We bought fresh fish and fresh eggs.

1. Unpreceded adjectives take the endings that the definite article would have, if it were used.

der frische	Fisch	**das** frische	Obst	**die** frische	Wurst	**die** frischen	Eier
frisch**er**	Fisch	frisch**es**	Obst	frisch**e**	Wurst	frisch**e**	Eier

	masculine	neuter	feminine	plural
nom.	frisch**er** Fisch	frisch**es** Obst	frisch**e** Wurst	frisch**e** Eier
acc.	frisch**en** Fisch	frisch**es** Obst	frisch**e** Wurst	frisch**e** Eier
dat.	frisch**em** Fisch	frisch**em** Obst	frisch**er** Wurst	frisch**en** Eiern
gen.[1]	(frisch**en** Fisches)	(frisch**en** Obstes)	(frisch**er** Wurst)	frisch**er** Eier

[1] The genitive singular forms are relatively rare, and the masculine and neuter forms of the genitive are irregular.

Heute Abend gibt es heiß**e** Suppe, holländisch**en** Käse, frisch**e** Brötchen und frisch**es** Obst.

- If there are several unpreceded adjectives, all have the same ending.

　　Ich wünsche dir schön**e,** interessant**e** Ferien.

2. Several important words are often used as unpreceded adjectives in the plural:

Bücher sind wie große Ferien.

andere	*other*
einige	*some, a few (pl. only)*
mehrere	*several (pl. only)*
viele	*many*
wenige	*few*

　　Wir haben uns mehrer**e** modern**e** Gemälde angesehen.

　　Sie haben einig**en** jung**en** Leuten gefallen, aber mir nicht.

- Usually neither **viel** (*much*) nor **wenig** (*little, not much*) has an ending in the singular, but these words are often used as unpreceded adjectives in the plural.

  Viele Studenten haben **wenig** Geld, aber nur **wenige** Studenten haben **viel** Zeit.

- Numerals, **mehr**, and **ein paar** have no endings. The same holds true for a few colors, such as *purple* and *pink* (**lila, rosa**), and adjectives like **Frankfurter, Berliner, Schweizer,** etc.

  The adjective **prima** also never has an ending.

  Da sind **drei** junge **Wiener** Studenten mit **ein paar** kurzen Fragen.

  Haben Sie noch **mehr** graues oder blaues Papier?

  Was mache ich mit diesem alten **rosa** Pullover?

Übungen

I. Ersetzen Sie die Adjektive!

BEISPIEL: Das sind nette Leute. (verrückt)
Das sind verrückte Leute.

1. Ich trinke gern schwarzen Kaffee. (heiß, frisch)
2. Sie braucht dünnes Papier. (billig, weiß)
3. Er schreibt tolle Bücher. (spannend, lustig)
4. Heute haben wir wunderbares Wetter. (ausgezeichnet, furchtbar)
5. Dort gibt es gutes Essen. (einfach, gesund)
6. Hier bekommen wir frischen Fisch. (wunderbar, gebacken)
7. Er hat oft verrückte Ideen. (dumm, fantastisch)

J. Wiederholen Sie die Sätze noch einmal, aber diesmal ohne den Artikel!

BEISPIEL: Der holländische Käse ist ausgezeichnet.
Holländischer Käse ist ausgezeichnet.

1. Die deutschen Zeitungen haben auch viel Werbung.
2. Der Mann will mit dem falschen Geld bezahlen.
3. Sie hat das frische Brot gekauft.
4. Er hat den schwarzen Kaffee getrunken.
5. Wir haben die braunen Eier genommen.

6. Er ist mit seinen alten Tennisschuhen auf die Party gegangen.
7. Sie trinken gern das dunkle Bier.
8. Auf der Party haben sie diese laute Musik gespielt.
9. Er erzählt gern solche traurigen Geschichten.
10. Sie hat Bilder der bekannten Schauspieler.

K. Ein Brief an Freunde. Was fehlt?

Liebe_ Gudrun, lieber_ Bill! 1. Seit gestern bin ich mit ein paar anderen_ Studenten in Dresden. 2. Eine wunderbare_ Stadt mit alter_ Tradition *(f.)!* 3. Im Zentrum gibt es viele_ schöne_ Gebäude mit barocken_ Fassaden *(pl.)*. 4. Die Ruine der Frauenkirche erinnert an *(reminds of)* furchtbare_ Zeiten. 5. Bis zum Jahr 2006 will man sie mit alten_ und neuen_ Steinen wieder aufgebaut haben *(have rebuilt)*. 6. Gestern haben wir zwei alte_ Dresdener kennen gelernt. 7. Sie haben uns einige interessante_ Geschichten aus alter_ und neuer_ Zeit erzählt. 8. Mit ihnen sind wir abends an der Elbe entlang gelaufen, mit herrlichem_ Blick auf *(m.)* die Stadt. 9. Danach haben wir im Ballhaus Watzke gegessen, einer alten_ Brauerei *(brewery)* mit guter_ Atmosphäre *(f.)* und gutem_ Bier. 10. Für heute Abend haben wir billige_ Karten für die Oper bekommen. Wie ihr seht, es geht mir gut. Viele Grüße! Eure Anne

L. Das mache ich gern. Und du? Beenden Sie die folgenden Sätze mit Hauptwörtern und Adjektiven ohne vorausgehenden *(proceeding)* Artikel! Fragen Sie dann die anderen in der Gruppe, wie das bei ihnen ist!

BEISPIEL: Ich singe gern . . .
Ich singe gern alte Lieder.

1. Ich esse gern . . .
2. Ich trinke gern . . .
3. Ich sammle gern . . .
4. Ich lese gern . . .
5. Ich trage gern . . .
6. Ich sehe gern . . .
7. Ich finde . . . prima.
8. Ich möchte . . .

Fokus — *German Television*

German public television and radio are run by independent public corporations. The main channels are ARD (or **I. Programm**) and ZDF (or **2. Programm**). Together they produce a third regional channel that concentrates on regional affairs and educational programming. Since 1985 these public corporations have been participating in additional ventures, for example, in 3-SAT, a ZDF joint venture with the Swiss and Austrian broadcasting corporations. Public broadcasting gets most of its funding from fees that owners of radios and television sets are required to pay. Revenues from advertising are becoming increasingly important.

The two major private German television networks are RTL and SAT-I, which show mainly sports, entertainment, and feature films. Other private broadcasters include, among others, PRO-7, DSF, KIKA-ARTE, VOX, VIVA, KABEL-1, and the all-news channel N-TV.

Their programs are transmitted by satellite and cable but can also be received over regular frequencies. These broadcasters are operated by consortia—mostly publishing companies—and advertising is their sole source of revenue. Supposedly, the average German watches a little more than three hours of television each day. (See also www.hoerzu.de)

Zusammenfassung

M. Bilden Sie ganze Sätze!

1. wie lange / du / warten / — / ich? *(pres. perf.)*
2. ich / sich freuen / — / Reise nach Spanien *(pres.)*
3. er / sich ärgern / — / Film *(pres. perf.)*
4. wo- / ihr / sich interessieren? *(pres.)*
5. wollen / sich kaufen / du / einig- / deutsch / Zeitschriften? *(pres.)*
6. in London / wir / sehen / mehrer- / interessant / Stücke *(pres. perf.)*
7. während / Pause / wir / trinken / billig / Sekt *(pres. perf.)*
8. Renate / schon / lesen / ein paar / spannend / Krimi *(pres. perf.)*
9. am Ende / viel / modern / Stücke / Leute / nicht / klatschen / lange *(pres.)*

N. Ein alter Film: Das Dschungelbuch

Stellen Sie Fragen darüber mit 10 verschiedenen *(different)* Interrogativpronomen, zum Beispiel mit **wer?, wen?, wem?, wessen?, wann?, wo?, wonach?, wogegen?** usw.!

Das Dschungelbuch

20.15 PRO 7 Waldjunge Mowgli, jetzt erwachsen°, rettet° entführte° Offizierstochter — Abenteuer° mit Jason Scott Lee, frei nach Kiplings Roman

Seit seinem fünften Lebensjahr lebt Mowgli (Jason Scott Lee) im indischen Dschungel°. Menschen kennt er nicht, seine besten Freunde sind Balu, der Bär, und der Panter Baghira. Eines Tages trifft der junge Mann die hübsche Kitty, Tochter des englischen Colonels Brydon (Sam Neill). Die beiden finden heraus, dass sie schon als Kinder zusammen gespielt haben, und sind sich sofort sehr sympathisch°. Aber auch Schurke° Boone (Cary Elwes) ist an Kitty interessiert — fast so sehr wie an den Reichtümern° der Dschungelstadt Monkey City. Er entführt das Mädchen, um Mowgli zu zwingen°, um ihn zu dem Schatz° zu bringen. **Fazit°:** Der gute Wilde im Kampf° gegen die böse Zivilisation — Stephen Sommers setzt die simple Story in herrlicher Natur mit viel Herz in Szene.

Der indische Urwald ist sein Zuhause: Mowgli (Jason Scott Lee)

Action Spannung Humor Herz

°grown-up, rescues, abducted, adventure, jungle, attractive, crook, richess, force, treasure, result, fight

O. Interessanter Besuch. Auf Deutsch bitte!

1. Two weeks ago an old friend of my father visited us. 2. He is the author of several plays. 3. I'm very interested in the theater. 4. He knows many important people, also some well-known actresses. 5. Our friend knows many other authors. 6. He spoke about them. 7. He told us some exciting stories. 8. He has just been to **(in)** Vienna. 9. He saw several performances of his new play and bought a few expensive books. 10. He's coming back in the summer. 11. We are looking forward to that. 12. We have also bought him some new novels.

M: 1. Wie lange hast du auf mich gewartet? 2. Ich freue mich auf die Reise nach Spanien. 3. Er hat sich über den Film geärgert. 4. Wofür interessiert ihr euch? 5. Willst du dir einige deutsche Zeitschriften kaufen? 6. In London haben wir mehrere interessante Stücke gesehen. 7. Während der Pause haben wir billigen Sekt getrunken. 8. Renate hat schon ein paar spannende Krimis gelesen. 9. Am Ende vieler moderner Stücke klatschen die Leute nicht lange.

O: 1. Vor zwei Wochen hat uns ein alter Freund meines Vaters besucht. 2. Er ist der Autor mehrerer Stücke. 3. Ich interessiere mich sehr fürs Theater. 4. Er kennt viele wichtige Leute, auch einige bekannte Schauspielerinnen. 5. Unser Freund kennt viele andere Autoren. 6. Er hat von ihnen gesprochen. 7. Er hat uns einige / ein paar spannende Geschichten erzählt. 8. Er ist gerade in Wien gewesen. 9. Er hat mehrere Vorstellungen seines neuen Stückes gesehen und [er hat] einige / ein paar teu(e)re Bücher gekauft. 10. Er kommt im Sommer zurück. 11. Wir freuen uns darauf. 12. Wir haben ihm auch einige / ein paar neue Romane gekauft.

Lesestrategie: Vokabeln sind wichtig.

Bevor Sie den Text lesen, lernen Sie die Wörter in *Wortschatz 2!* Machen Sie auch eine Liste von anderen Wörtern, die *(which)* mit dem Thema „Medien" zu tun haben.

Wortschatz 2

der Bürger, -	*citizen*
Einfluss, ⸚e	*influence*
Zuschauer, -	*viewer, spectator*
das Fernsehen	*television (the medium)*
die Art, -en (von)	*type (of)*
Auswahl an (+ *dat.*)	*selection, choice (of)*
Nachricht, -en	*news (on radio and television, usually pl.)*
Sendung, -en[1]	*(particular) program*
sich an·schauen	*to look at*
also	*in other words*
etwa	*about, approximately*
folgend	*following*
öffentlich / privat	*public / private*
verschieden	*different (kinds of), various*
vor allem	*mainly, especially, above all*
weder . . . noch	*neither . . . nor*

[1] Note the difference between **das Programm** and **die Sendung** as they refer to television: **das Programm** refers to a *general program* or *channel* (Was gibt's **im Abendprogramm? im 1. Programm?**). **Die Sendung** refers to a *particular program* (Ich sehe mir gern diese **Kultursendung** an).

Vor dem Lesen

A. Statistiken über junge Deutsche. Lesen Sie, was junge Deutsche über den Einfluss der Massenmedien *(mass media)* in ihrem Leben zu sagen haben! Wie ist das bei Ihnen und Ihren Klassenkameraden? (Für % liest man „Prozent".)

Wie viele Stunden sehen Sie jeden Tag fern?	Kein TV	3%	Gibt es zu viel Sex im Fernsehen und im Kino oder zu wenig?	Zu viel	38%
	1–2 Stunden	42%		Zu wenig	13%
	2–4 Stunden	28%		Genau richtig	48%
	4–6 Stunden	5%	Gibt es zu viel Gewalt *(crime)* im Fernsehen und im Kino?	Zu viel	71%
Wie viele Videos sehen Sie pro Woche?	Kein Video	46%		Zu wenig	4%
	1–2 Videos	42%		Genau richtig	25%
	3–5 Videos	10%	Wie viele Bücher haben Sie in den letzten drei Monaten gelesen?	kein Buch	41%
Wie oft sehen Sie die Nachrichten im Fernsehen?	Täglich	39%		1–2 Bücher	33%
	Manchmal	23%		3 + Bücher	25%
	Nie	4%			
Wie oft lesen Sie eine Tageszeitung?	Täglich	42%			
	Manchmal	26%			
	Nie	7%			

1. Wie ist das bei Ihnen und Ihrer Familie, bei Ihren Freunden und Mitbürgern *(fellow citizens)?* Kommentieren Sie!
2. Haben Sie einen Computer? Was tun Sie vor allem damit? Haben Sie E-Mail? Wie viele E-Mails pro Tag müssen Sie beantworten? Finden Sie das gut?
3. Können Sie ans Internet? Wenn ja, welche Rolle spielt das Internet in Ihrem Leben? Wie viele Stunden pro Tag sitzen Sie am Computer und surfen Sie im Internet? Was interessiert Sie darin besonders und was nicht? Kaufen oder verkaufen Sie manchmal Sachen im Internet? Wenn ja, wo und was für Sachen?

B. Gehen wir angeln! Lesen Sie schnell den folgenden Lesetext und finden Sie mit Ihrem Partner/Ihrer Partnerin Beispiele für Adjektive mit und ohne vorausgehenden Artikel! Wovon gibt es mehr *(more)?*

C. Was ist das?

der Haushalt, Kritiker, Medienmarkt; das Kabarett, Satellitenprogramm; die Buchproduktion, Interessengruppe, Kreativität, Tagespresse; finanzieren, registrieren; experimentell, finanziell, informativ, kulturell, politisch, staatlich kontrolliert, unterhaltend

Wer die Wahl hat, hat die Qual°.

CD 5, Track 4

Choosing isn't easy (*lit.* it's a pain).

Wie überall spielen die Massenmedien, vor allem das Fernsehen, auch in Deutschland eine wichtige Rolle. Fast jeder Haushalt hat heute einen oder zwei Fernseher und die Auswahl an Sendungen ist groß und wird jedes Jahr größer°. Zu den Hauptprogrammen kommen Programme aus Nachbarländern und auch privates Fernsehen und interessante Kabel- und Satellitenprogramme. Die privaten Sender° leben natürlich von der Werbung. Aber um das öffentliche Fernsehen zu finanzieren, müssen die Deutschen ihre Fernseher und Radios registrieren und monatliche Gebühren° zahlen. Werbung gibt es auch, aber nicht nach acht Uhr abends und selten während Filmsendungen. Sie kommt vor allem vor dem Abendprogramm und dauert fünf bis 10 Minuten. Damit° die Leute den Fernseher dann nicht einfach ausmachen, muss die Werbung natürlich unterhaltend sein.

 Das öffentliche Fernsehen ist weder staatlich noch privat kontrolliert, sondern finanziell und politisch unabhängig°. Darum kann es auch leicht Sendungen für kleine Interessengruppen bringen, z.B. Nachrichten in verschiedenen Sprachen, Sprachunterricht° für Ausländer, experimentelle Musik, politische Diskussionen und lokales Kabarett. Das deutsche Fernsehen präsentiert eigentlich eine gute Mischung aus° aktuellem° Sport und leichter Unterhaltung, von informativen Dokumentarfilmen, internationalen Filmen und kulturellen Sendungen, z.B. Theaterstücken, Opern und Konzerten.

 Manche Kritiker halten nicht viel vom Fernsehen. Sie ärgern sich zum Beispiel darüber, dass so viele amerikanische Filme, Serien° und Seifenopern° laufen, obwohl die Statistiken zeigen, dass sich die Zuschauer dafür interessieren. Neben guten und informativen Kultursendungen sind auch spannende Filme mit Sex und Gewalt gefragt°. Aber nicht nur darin sehen die Kritiker Probleme, sondern auch in der passiven Rolle der Zuschauer. Manche Menschen, vor allem Kinder, sitzen viel zu lang vorm Fernseher. Sie werden dadurch passiv und verlieren an° Kreativität.

 Trotz der Auswahl an Programmen muss das Fernsehen mit vielen anderen Medien konkurrieren°. Das Radio ist weiterhin° wichtig, denn man hört im Durchschnitt täglich zwei Stunden Radio und liest gern dabei. Viele Deutsche sind Leseratten. Die Tagespresse verkauft täglich über 30 Millionen Exemplare°. Dazu kommen fast 9 000 Zeitschriften und die zwei großen Nachrichtenmagazine *Der Spiegel* und *Focus*. Man liest auch gern Bücher. Die Buchproduktion steht international nach den USA am zweiten Platz. Mehr als° 600 000 Titel sind auf dem Markt und jedes Jahr kommen etwa 70 000 Erst- und Neuauflagen° dazu.

 Wie sich das Internet auf die Rolle des Medienmarktes auswirkt°, ist die große Frage. Denn auch diese moderne Technik konkurriert um° die Zeit der Bürger. Die Men-

(margin glosses)
bigger
stations
fees
so that
independent
…instruction
mixture of
current
series / soap operas
popular
lose in
compete / still
copies
more than
new editions
effects
competes for

schen haben heute eine enorme Auswahl, woher sie ihre Informationen bekommen und womit sie ihre Freizeit ausfüllen. Diese Wahl ist nicht immer leicht. Ja, wer die Wahl hat, hat die Qual.

Nach dem Lesen

A. Richtig oder falsch? Wenn falsch, sagen Sie warum!

<u>f</u> 1. In Deutschland spielt das Fernsehen keine wichtige Rolle.

<u>f</u> 2. Nur wenige Haushalte haben einen Fernseher.

<u>r</u> 3. Die Auswahl an Sendungen ist groß.

<u>f</u> 4. Weil die Deutschen monatliche Gebühren zahlen, gibt es im privaten Fernsehen keine Werbung.

<u>f</u> 5. Werbung läuft im öffentlichen Fernsehen nie nach sechs Uhr abends.

<u>f</u> 6. Das öffentliche Fernsehen ist staatlich kontrolliert.

<u>r</u> 7. Es hat eine gute Mischung aus verschiedenen Sendungen.

<u>f</u> 8. Manche Kritiker ärgern sich über zu viele deutsche Filme.

<u>r</u> 9. Sie denken auch, dass zu viel Fernsehen die Leute passiv macht.

<u>r</u> 10. Wie überall muss das Fernsehen mit anderen Medien konkurrieren.

<u>r</u> 11. Dazu gehören das Radio, Zeitungen, Zeitschriften und Bücher.

<u>f</u> 12. Wegen des Internets haben die Deutschen keine Zeit mehr fürs Fernsehen.

If students ask: These fees are paid to the GEZ (Gebühreneinzugszentrale).

B. Was fehlt? Ergänzen Sie die fehlenden Präpositionen!

1. Der Lesetext spricht <u>von / über</u> Deutschlands Massenmedien. 2. Wenn wir in Nordamerika fernsehen, denken wir nur <u>an</u> mögliche Kabelgebühren, aber nicht <u>an</u> Fernsehgebühren. Die Deutschen müssen <u>daran</u> denken. 3. Sie ärgern sich oft <u>über</u> diese Gebühren, aber sie können nichts <u>dagegen</u> *(against it)* tun. Sie haben keine Wahl. 4. Viele interessieren sich nicht nur <u>für</u> leichte Unterhaltung, sondern auch <u>für</u> informative Dokumentarfilme. 5. Andere warten jeden Abend <u>auf</u> die Nachrichten. 6. Sie freuen sich auch hier und da <u>auf</u> ein Theaterstück oder ein Konzert. 7. Die großen Nachrichtenmagazine sprechen nicht nur <u>von / über</u> Politik, sondern auch <u>von / über</u> Kultur und Sport. 8. Manche Leute sitzen täglich am Computer, um sich <u>über</u> alles gut zu informieren. 9. Sie stellen Fragen <u>an</u> andere Leute im Internet und warten dann <u>auf</u> ihre Antwort. 10. Ich halte nicht viel <u>von / vom</u> Fernsehen. 11. Ich bin eine Leseratte und freue mich <u>auf</u> mein nächstes *(next)* Buch. 12. <u>Wofür</u> interessieren Sie sich, für Fernsehen, Zeitungen oder Bücher?

Optional tongue twisters **(Zungenbrecher):** 1. Eine schwarze Swatch 2. Spanier lieben spannende Spiele.

C. Womit? Damit! Stellen Sie Fragen mit einem Wo-Kompositum und antworten Sie mit einem Da-Kompositum oder einer Präposition mit Pronomen!

BEISPIEL: Das deutsche Fernsehen ist unabhängig **von der Werbung.**
Wovon ist es unabhängig?—**Davon!**
Die Werbung ist abhängig **von den Käufern.**
Von wem ist sie abhängig?—**Von ihnen!**

1. Einige Kritiker halten nicht viel **vom Fernsehen.** 2. Vor allem ärgern sie sich **über die vielen amerikanischen Serien.** 3. Sie sprechen **über die Zuschauer.** 4. Sie warten jede Woche **auf die Fortsetzung** *(continuation).* 5. Diese Kritiker denken auch **an die Kinder.** 6. **Durch zu viel Fernsehen und zu viel Musik** verlieren sie an Kreativität. 7. **Fürs Hobby** haben die Leute oft keine Zeit.

C: 1. Wovon halten sie nicht viel? Davon, vom Fernsehen. 2. Worüber ärgern sie sich? Darüber, über die vielen . . . 3. Über wen sprechen sie? Über sie, über die Zuschauer. 4. Worauf warten sie jede Woche? Darauf, auf die Fortsetzung. 5. An wen denken sie auch? An sie, an die Kinder. 6. Wodurch verlieren sie an Kreativität? Dadurch, durch zu viel . . . 7. Wofür haben sie keine Zeit? Dafür, fürs Hobby.

D. Deutsches Fernsehen. Ergänzen Sie die Adjektivendungen, wo nötig *(necessary)!*

1. Das deutsch<u>e</u> Fernsehen ist eine gut<u>e</u> Mischung aus kulturell<u>en</u> Sendungen und leicht<u>er</u> Unterhaltung. 2. Man bekommt auch viel<u>e</u> interessant<u>e</u> Sendungen aus verschieden<u>en</u> Nachbarländern. 3. Das öffentlich<u>e</u> Fernsehen finanziert man durch monatlich<u>e</u> Gebühren. 4. Öffentlich<u>e</u> Sender *(pl.)* haben natürlich auch

öffentliche__ Aufgaben. 5. Sie können leicht verschiedene__ Sendungen für kleine__ Interessengruppen bringen, z.B. internationale__ Nachrichten in verschiedenen__ Sprachen oder auch lokale__ Kabarett (n.). 6. Privates__ Fernsehen gibt es auch. 7. Diese kleinen__ Sender sind natürlich abhängig von viel Werbung. 8. Beim privaten__ Fernsehen kann man auch viele__ amerikanische__ Filme sehen. 9. Kritiker sprechen von schlechter__ Qualität beim privaten__ Fernsehen. 10. Viele Deutsche sind große__ Leseratten. 11. Sie lesen alles, was ihnen in die Hände fällt, von lokalen__ Nachrichten und lokaler__ Werbung bis zu intellektuellen__ (intellectual) Nachrichtenmagazinen. 12. Sie hören aber auch gern Radio, von leichter__ bis zu klassischer__ Musik.

E. Wofür interessieren Sie sich im Fernsehen? Schauen Sie sich die Auswahl an Programmen an und bewerten Sie sie (rate them)! Wie vergleicht sich das mit der Bewertung der anderen? Benutzen Sie: 1 = sehr interessant, 2 = manchmal interessant, 3 = uninteressant!

❑ Nachrichten	❑ Konzerte	❑ Seifenopern
❑ Politik	❑ Opern	❑ Horrorfilme
❑ Reisen	❑ Krimis	❑ Dokumentarfilme
❑ Hobbys	❑ Western	❑ Geschichtsfilme
❑ Sport	❑ Theaterstücke	❑ Liebesfilme (love...)
❑ Sprachen	❑ Fernsehspiele	❑ Science-Fiction-Filme
❑ Ballett	❑ Fernsehquizze	❑ Zeichentrickfilme (cartoons)

Fokus — *German Cabaret*

The term *cabaret* (**Kabarett**) describes both a form of theatrical entertainment and the dance halls where the genre emerged in the late 19th century. Performers satirized contemporary culture and politics through skits, pantomimes, poems, and songs. During the Weimar Republic (1919–1933), this type of variety show flourished in Germany, but was then banned by the Nazis for its political nature. After World War II, the cabaret reemerged as a popular form of entertainment. Some of Germany's most popular cabarets are the *Lach- und Schießgesellschaft* in Munich, the *Floh de Cologne* in Cologne, the *Mausefalle* in Hamburg, the *Herkuleskeule* in Dresden, and the *SanftWut* in Leipzig. Berlin, home to many cabarets during the Roaring Twenties, now again has several popular ones, including the *Distel,* the *Knefzange,* and the *Wühlmäuse.*

You might want to explain the play on words in the names of these cabarets: **Lach- und Schießgesellschaft** *(a company that provokes laughter through sharpshooting with words)* derived form **Wach- und Schließgesellschaft** *(a security-alarm company);* **Floh de Cologne** *(lit. flea from Cologne)* derived from Eau de Cologne; **Mausefalle** *(mouse trap);* **Herkuleskeule** *(Hercules' club);* **SanftWut** derived from **sanfte Wut** *(gentle anger);* **Distel** *(thistle);* **Knefzange** derived from **Kneifzange** *(pincers),* here alluding to the actor Hildegard Knef; **Wühlmäuse** *(moles).*

MI   **24. Oktober**

DAS ERSTE	ZDF	SAT.1

DAS ERSTE

5.30 **Frühprogramm**
7.30 **Pumuckl TV** Kindermagazin   60-409
8.30 **Sesamstraße** Für Kinder   3-138
9.00 **Tagesschau** Nachrichten   64-409
9.03 **Kopfball** Ratespiel   300-004-867
9.30 **Ski alpin: Weltcup Herren**   821-645
live Riesenslalom, 1. Lauf. Aus Sölden/Öst.
11.00 **Tagesschau** Nachrichten   20-041
11.03 **Die magische Münze** 300-004-003
11.30 **Die Maus** Für Kinder   7-190
12.00 **Presseclub**   34-867
live Polit-Talk mit Journalisten
12.45 **Ski alpin: Weltcup Herren** 2-966-022
live Riesenslalom, 2. Lauf. Aus Sölden/Öst.
13.45 **Bilderbuch D** Kassel   4-976-119

14
14.03 **Tennis: WTA-Masters** 304-798-108
live Das Achtelfinale. Aus München
15.55 **Tagesschau**   6-460-924
16.00 **Fliege – Die Talkshow** 50-672
Thema: Vorsicht Bank!
Ohne Banken läuft in unserem
Alltag nichts mehr, ihre Macht
scheint nahezu grenzenlos.

17
17.00 **Tagesschau** Nachrichten   44-643
17.03 **ARD-Ratgeber:**   300-003-117
Bauen & Wohnen Reihe
17.55 **Verbotene Liebe**   60-892
18.25 **Marienhof**   58-057
Nik will Lucy zurückerobern.
18.54 **Das Quiz mit Jörg Pilawa**
Quizshow   408-566-386
19.49 **Das Wetter**   400-104-750
19.51 **Lottozahlen**   107-297-556
20.00 **Tagesschau** Nachrichten 86-469

LIEBESKOMÖDIE

20.15
FILM **Während du schliefst**
Liebeskomödie, USA 1995   47-573
TOP Mit Sandra Bullock, P. Gallagher
Tipp Lucy rettet Peter, in den sie schon
lange aus der Ferne verliebt ist,
das Leben. Während er im Koma
liegt, wird Lucy von dessen Verwandten für Peters Verlobte
gehalten. Die familiäre Herzlich-
keit macht es ihr unmöglich, den
Irrtum aufzuklären.   → S. 122
22.30 **Tagesthemen**   250
23.00 **Friedman** Diskussion   8-637
mit einem prominenten Gast
23.30 **Das Elend, alt zu werden** 27-328

Mi

ZDF

5.30 **Morgenmagazin**   64-053-523
9.00 **heute** Nachrichten   17-813
9.05 **Volle Kanne, Susanne** 2-472-078
Servicemagazin mit Ingo Nommsen
10.00 **heute** Nachrichten   88-356
10.03 **Forsthaus Falkenau**   307-615-542
Familienserie. Zurück nach Falkenau
10.50 **Wie gut, dass es Maria gibt**
Familienserie. Fan-Post   3-917-144
11.35 **Praxis täglich** Herbst spe- 7-470-250
zial: Asthma – Aufatmen am Meer
12.00 **Tagesschau** Nachrichten   65-960
12.15 **drehscheibe D**   7-295-989
13.00 **Tagesschau** Nachrichten   38-095
13.05 Mittagsmagazin   364-502

14.00 heute – in Deutschland   75-439
14.15 **Discovery** Triumph der   93-675
Natur – Nationalparks in Amerika
15.00 **heute/Sport**   23-052
15.10 **Streit um Drei**   8-745-746
Alltagskonflikte vor Gericht
16.00 **heute – in Europa**   95-255
16.15 **Risiko** Quiz   2-447-304

17.00 **heute/Wetter**   53-521
17.15 **hallo Deutschland**   86-453
17.45 **Leute heute** Journal   5-766-057
17.54 **NKL-Tagesmillion** 405-796-298
18.00 **Derrick**   8-203-174
Krimiserie. Familie im Feuer
18.50 **Lotto am Mittwoch** 7-882-298
19.00 **heute/Wetter**   65-182
19.25 **Die Rettungsflieger (5)**
10-tlg. Actionserie   5-153-892
Torstens Entscheidung

UNTERHALTUNG

20.15 **30 Jahre „Lustige**   22-683
Musikanten" Die große
Jubiläumsgala. Gäste u. a.: Patrick
Lindner, das Nockalm Quintett
Zur Jubiläumsgala in Rotenburg
an der Fulda haben Marianne &
Michael (Foto) heute, neben den
ehemaligen Moderatoren Lolita,
Carolin Reiber und Elmar Gunsch,
die Comedians Ingolf Lück und
Annette Frier eingeladen.

21.45 **heute-journal**   593-618
22.15 **Abenteuer Forschung**
Thema: Die Krise: 141-279
Energie. Mit Joachim Bublath

SAT.1

5.30 **Frühstücksfernsehen**   79-364-610
U. a.: täglich ran – Sport; Morning
Queen; Superball. Moderation:
Jessica Winter und Andreas Franke
9.00 Home Shopping Europe   11-821
10.00 **Hallo, Onkel Doc!**   22-937
Kinderarztserie. Familienkuss
10.15 **Tiny Toon Abenteuer** Trick 2-316-204
10.40 **Familie Feuerstein** Trick   8-956-440
11.10 **Bugs Bunny** Trickserie   4-257-223
11.35 **Police Academy** Trickserie 6-965-759
12.05 **Die Peanuts** Trickserie   405-136
12.35 **Schweine nebenan** Trickserie 72-117
13.00 **The Real Ghostbusters**   2-778
13.30 **Alf** Comedy. Das Kostümfest   5-865

14.00 **Der große Diktator** 40-141-889
Politsatire, USA 1940. Mit Charlie
Chaplin, Jack Oakie. Buch/
Regie: Charlie Chaplin   → S. 24
15.00 **Allein gegen die Zukunft** 42-117
Serie. Der Weihnachtsmann
16.00 **Star Trek –**   36-487
Das nächste Jahrhundert
Science-Fiction-Serie. Déjà vu

17.30 **ran – Basketball** BBL, 5.   7-961
Tag: Avitos Gießen – Opel Sky-
liners, Brandt Hagen – Leverkusen
18.00 **Einfach Verona! (1)**   1-020
neu 11-tlg. VIP-Magazin
Mit Verona Feldbusch
18.30 **18:30** Nachrichten mit Sport 76-117
18.45 **ran – Sport**   183-117
19.00 **ran – Bundesliga**   933-594
U. a.: FC Bayern – Kaiserslautern

ABENTEUERFILM

20.15 **Die Maske des Zorro** 49-903-570
FILM Abenteuerfilm, USA 1998
TOP Mit Antonio Banderas
Tipp Zwanzig Jahre musste Zorro in
einer Zelle schmoren, um mit Don
Montero abzurechnen, der seine
Tochter Elena entführt und groß-
gezogen hat. Zwecks Verstärkung
trainiert der alternde Kämpfer den
Charme und die Degen-Künste des
Heißsporns Alejandro.   → S. 31

22.55 **Nachrichten** Wahl   2-348-860
zum Abgeordnetenhaus in Berlin
23.10 **Planetopia**   6-216-860
Magazin. Thema: Lauschangriff –

F. Das Fernsehprogram. Schauen Sie sich das Programm auf der Linken Seite an und beantworten Sie die Fragen darüber!

1. Wann beginnt das Morgenprogramm bei den drei Sendern?
2. Wie heißen die zwei großen Nachrichtensendungen im 1. Programm (ARD) und im 2. Programm (ZDF)?
3. Welche Kinderprogramme gibt es im ARD und bei SAT.1?
4. Was gibt es über Sport, Musik, Gesundheit, Natur und Politik?
5. Wo geht es um Wohnen, die Lotterie, Home Shopping und Banken?
6. Welche amerikanischen Filme finden Sie auf diesem Programm?
7. Aus welchem Jahr ist der Film *Der große Diktator?* Welchen bekannten Schauspieler können wir darin sehen?
8. Was halten Sie von diesen Sendungen im deutschen Fernsehen?

G. Fernsehen in Deutschland und Amerika / Kanada. Schreiben Sie zwei bis vier Sätze zu jedem der folgenden Punkte!

1. Popularität
2. Auswahl an Programmen
3. Art der Programme
4. Werbung und Fernsehgebühren
5. Qualität
6. Rolle von Radio und Fernsehen

F: You could ask students to prepare this at home, since it might take some time to find everything! **1.** 5.30 Uhr **2.** Tagesschau, heute **3. ARD:** Pumuckl, Sesamstraße, Die Maus; **SAT. 1:** Tiny Toon Abenteuer, Familie Feuerstein, Bugs Bunny, Die Peanuts **4. Sport:** Ski alpin, Tennis, Basketball, Fußball; **Musik:** 30 Jahre „Lustige Musikanten"; **Gesundheit:** Praxis täglich, Hallo, Onkel Doc!; **Natur:** Discovery Nationalparks in Amerika; **Politik:** Presseclub, Tagesthemen, heute-journal **5. Wohnen:** 17.03 Uhr (ARD); **Lotterie:** 19.51 Uhr (ARD), 18.50 Uhr (ZDF); **Home Shopping:** 9.00 (SAT.1); **Banken:** 16.00 Uhr (ARD) **6.** Während du schliefst, Derrick, The Real Ghostbusters, Star Trek, etc. **7.** 1940 Charlie Chaplin

HÖREN SIE ZU!   TRACK 21

Pläne für den Abend

Zum Erkennen: ausverkauft *(sold out);* die Anzeige, -n *(advertisement)*

Was ist richtig?
1. Monika möchte gern _____ gehen.
   a. ins Kino   b. in die Bibliothek   **c.** ins Theater
2. Felix und Stefan finden das _____.
   a. eine gute Idee   b. furchtbar langweilig   c. komisch
3. Monika ruft an, um _____.
   a. Karten zu bestellen   **b.** zu fragen, ob es noch Karten gibt
   c. zu fragen, wie man zum Theater kommt
4. Sie wollen zum KARTOON gehen, weil _____.
   a. das Programm sehr interessant ist   **b.** sie dort auch essen können
   c. Monika Gutes darüber gehört hat
5. Sie wollen um _____ Uhr essen.
   a. 18.30   **b.** 19.30   c. 21.00
6. Zum KARTOON kommt man _____.
   a. zu Fuß   b. mit der U-Bahn   **c.** irgendwie *(somehow),* aber das wissen wir nicht

Fokus — *Wolf Biermann*

Wolf Biermann, songwriter and poet, was one of East Germany's most famous dissident artists. Born in the port city of Hamburg in 1936, Biermann emigrated to East Germany in 1953 because of his socialist political convictions, but he soon became disillusioned. What he had imagined as a workers' paradise soon revealed a large gap between theory and practice, and Biermann turned a venomous pen to what he saw. Armed with a worn guitar and a gravelly voice, he attacked the ruling SED party with a blend of humor and indignant rage, until it expelled him in 1976 during a tour of West Germany. Since reunification in 1990, Biermann has urged eastern Germans in particular to critically rethink the political system they have inherited.

Ach, Freund, geht es nicht auch dir so?

> Ich kann nur lieben
> <small>freedom</small>   was ich die Freiheit° habe
> <small>leave</small>   auch zu verlassen°:
> dieses Land
> diese Stadt
> diese Frau
> dieses Leben
> <small>that's why</small> Eben darum° lieben ja
> wenige ein Land
> manche eine Stadt
> viele eine Frau
>   aber das Leben alle
>
>   *Wolf Biermann*

Fragen zum Gedicht

1. Was bedeutet für Wolf Biermann das Wort „Freiheit"?
2. Was meint er damit, wenn er sagt, dass nur wenige ein Land, doch viele eine Frau lieben?
3. Warum lieben alle das Leben?
4. Wie hat sich das in Biermanns Leben gezeigt?
5. Wie bei Rose Ausländer hat auch dieses Gedicht keinen Punkt und kein Komma, nur einen Doppelpunkt *(colon)*. Was bedeutet das?
6. Warum sind manche Zeilen eingerückt *(lines indented)*?

Video-Ecke

- The Minidrama *Kino? Ja bitte!* shows Daniela waiting for her friend to take her to a special movie at the film festival. Her parents haven't been to the theater for a long time. They can hardly appreciate films as an art form. Her father seems to be lost in the sixties, and her mother is aspiring to the higher arts, such as impressionist painters. As discussion develops about the movie scene. Daniela tries very hard to teach her parents some "movie culture." Will she succeed?

- The Blickpunkt *Das Hebbel Theater* introduces us to the director of public relations at one of Berlin's alternative theaters, built in 1908 and one of the few not destroyed by war. He tells us about its repertoire and some of its unique features that attract a rather diverse audience.

Web-Ecke

- For updates, self-assessment quizzes, and online activities related to this chapter, visit the *Wie geht's?* Web site at **http://wiegehts.heinle.com**. You will discover what's playing in movie theaters in Düsseldorf, find out about Karl May and his books about a German cowboy in America, and learn about some of the rising stars of the German music scene.

Kapitel (11)

Beziehungen

Junge Leute haben Spaß im Szenelokal *(popular restaurant)* von Linz

Lernziele

Vorschau
Women and society

Gespräche + Wortschatz
Relationships and characteristics

Fokus
Love and marriage
Liechtenstein
Telling a story and encouraging the speaker
The brothers Grimm and their fairy tales

Struktur
11.1 Simple past
11.2 Conjunctions **als, wann,** and **wenn**
11.3 Past perfect

Einblicke
Gebrüder Grimm: *Rumpelstilzchen, Der alte Großvater und der Enkel*

Video-Ecke
Minidrama: *Der Märchenprinz*

Web-Ecke

Vorschau

Women and Society

Families in Germany—as in other countries—are currently confronted by profound social change. Gone is the stereotype of the woman whose life revolves around children, the kitchen, and the church **(Kinder, Küche, Kirche)**. Today, women—self-confident and highly qualified—usually want both: children and a career. Combining these two goals is not an easy task in view of new lifestyles and new forms of relationships, changes at the workplace, and a variety of obstacles ranging from a shortage of childcare facilities to a lack of financial resources. After all, most women still continue to spend three times as much time as men on housework and child-rearing; men frequently continue to hold on to old patterns of behavior while professing to believe in total equality.

Until reunification, West German women, especially those older than 30 years of age, were far less likely to have full-time jobs than their counterparts in East Germany. Only one-half of West German women worked outside the home, compared with more than 90 percent in East Germany. Women in the GDR were able to combine motherhood with full-time employment because state-run day care and other services were readily available. Staying home with a sick child was taken for granted in East Germany, and mothers were able to take as much as one year of maternity leave with full pay. The loss of these facilities and benefits, coupled with record-high unemployment, caused a drastic decline in the number of births.

Like everywhere in Europe, Germany's population is slowly shrinking and aging. Because the proportion of seniors is growing, Germany started a statutory long-term nursing care insurance plan to supplement the retirement pension scheme and a medical insurance system. With the social security system built on the principle that the younger generation secures the welfare of the old through its contributions, German laws regarding pregnancy and childbirth now reflect the conviction that women who bear and raise children are performing a task vital to society and therefore are entitled to have their social security contributions at least partially reduced and work-related childcare expenses offset against taxes. Working women are entitled to maternity leave with pay **(Mutterschaftsurlaub)** six weeks before and eight weeks after childbirth. After that, either one of the parents is

(continued on p. 282)

Two main factors contributed to the high employment rate of women in the former GDR: the need for additional income, and the law that required all able-bodied men and women to work.

You could ask students to compare this information with the situation in their own county.—If students have access to German newspapers, they could bring in various birth or wedding announcements as well as congratulations for special birthdays or anniversaries. See also the additional marriage and anniversary ad in the *Zum Schreiben* section of the Workbook.

1. Wie heißt das neue Baby? 2. Ist Jan ein Junge oder ein Mädchen? 3. Wann ist Jan geboren? 4. Wie groß und wie schwer war er bei der Geburt? Wissen Sie, wie viel das in amerikanischen Maßen *(measures)* ist? 5. Wie heißen die glücklichen Eltern?

Wir freuen uns über die Geburt unseres Sohnes

Jan

* 12. 9. 01 · 3740 g · 54 cm

Die glücklichen Eltern

Claudia und Dirk Haesloop

ZWISCHEN KIND UND KARRIERE

entitled to "parental time" or switching to part-time work up to 30 hours a week; a monthly child-raising benefit (**Erziehungsgeld**) is available for the first three years after the birth of each child. During this period, the parent who chooses to take the child-raising leave cannot be laid off. Another advantage is that the child-raising period, like the time spent caring for sick family members, counts towards the parent's pension claim. This practice aims to assess work within the home as equal to gainful employment. The shortage of childcare facilities in Germany has yet to be resolved.

Women have only had equal rights (**Gleichberechtigung**) since 1976. At that time, the constitutional clause stipulated that women could work outside the home only if the job was compatible with their family obligations. Since then, women have used equal access to schools, universities, and other training facilities to take advantage of new opportunities. Yet, while they have had the right to vote since 1918, women still occupy only a small role in the upper levels of business, government, and the universities. It is interesting that women in former East Germany have maintained some of their earlier independence: one-third of east German businesses are now owned by women, compared with less than one-fourth in the west. Even though equal pay for equal work is guaranteed by law, women's incomes are generally lower than men's, partly because women interrupt their careers for child-raising, enter the labor force later, or continue to work in lower paying positions. While women in western Germany earn about 75% as much as men, women in eastern Germany earn about 90% of what men earn. In all of Germany, however, the unemployment rate for women is higher than for men.

Gespräche + Wortschatz

CD 5, Track 5

Warm-ups: 1. Was finden Sie schön (furchtbar, langweilig, spannend, leicht, schwer)? **2. Wie viele Da-Komposita kennen Sie?** Sie haben eine Minute. **3. Wie geht's weiter?** Bilden Sie Sätze mit: heute Morgen, gestern Nachmittag, vorgestern Abend, am Wochenende, vor einem Jahr, damals, eines Tages! **4. Kombinieren Sie mit dem Genitiv, z.B. Adresse: Hotel = die Adresse des Hotels! (a. der Anfang:** Programm, Vorstellung, Ferien, Flug; **b. das Ende:** Film, Pause, Stück, Nachrichten; **c. die Telefonnummer:** Kino, Flughafen, Kaufhaus, Herr, Studentin, Student, Leute).
You might suggest a personalization activity in which students use the information about the characters presented in the dialogue to write personal ads for Sonja, Nicole, and Frank.

Jedem Tierchen sein Pläsierchen

SONJA	Nicole, hör mal! „Gesucht wird: hübsche, dynamische, zärtliche EVA. Belohnung: gut aussehender ADAM mit Herz, Ende 20, mag Antiquitäten, alte Häuser, schnelle Wagen, Tiere, Kinder."
NICOLE	Hmm, nicht schlecht, aber nicht für mich. Ich mag keine Kinder und gegen Tiere bin ich allergisch.
SONJA	Dann schau mal hier! „Es gibt, was ich suche. Aber wie finden? Künstler, Anfang 30, charmant, unternehmungslustig, musikalisch, sucht sympathische, gebildete, zuverlässige Frau mit Humor." Ist das was?
NICOLE	Ja, vielleicht. Er sucht jemanden mit Humor. Das gefällt mir; und Musik mag ich auch. Aber ob er Jazz mag?
SONJA	Vielleicht können wir sie beide kennen lernen?
NICOLE	Ich weiß nicht. Mir ist das zu dumm, Leute durch Anzeigen in der Zeitung kennen zu lernen.
SONJA	Quatsch! Versuchen wir's doch! Was haben wir zu verlieren?
NICOLE	Was meinst du, Frank?
FRANK	Ich denke ihr seid verrückt. Aber naja, jedem Tierchen sein Pläsierchen! . . . Schaut mal hier! Da will jemand einen Hund, eine Katze und einen Vogel gemeinsam abgeben.
NICOLE	Das ist alles, was wir brauchen: einen ganzen Zoo! Nein, danke!
FRANK	Wie wär's denn mit einem kleinen Hund oder einem Kätzchen?

Suche neues Zuhause für unseren kleinen Zoo. Hund, Katze und Vogel gemeinsam abzugeben, 0941/447635.

SONJA   Ich liebe Tiere, aber dafür habe ich momentan keinen Platz und auch nicht
         genug Zeit.
FRANK   Aber so ein kleines Kätzchen braucht nicht viel.
SONJA   Vielleicht später. Momentan liebe ich meine Freiheit.
FRANK   Und ihr wollt euch mit jemandem aus der Zeitung treffen?
NICOLE   Ach, davon verstehst du nichts.

> Gesucht wird: hübsche, dynamische, zärtliche EVA. Belohnung: gut aussehender ADAM mit Herz, Ende 20, mag Antiquitäten, alte Häuser, schnelle Wagen, Tiere, Kinder.

> Es gibt, was ich suche. Aber wie finden? Künstler, Anfang 30, charmant, unternehmungslustig, musikalisch, sucht sympathische, gebildete, zuverlässige Frau mit Humor.

A. Fragen

1. Was sehen sich Nicole und Sonja an? 2. Was sucht der erste Mann? 3. Wofür interessiert er sich? 4. Was hält Nicole von dem ersten Mann? 5. Was sucht der zweite Mann? 6. Was hält Nicole von der zweiten Anzeige? 7. Was meint Sonja dazu? 8. Was hält Frank von der Idee, die Männer zu treffen? 9. Was schaut sich Frank an? 10. Was mag Nicole an der ersten Tieranzeige nicht? 11. Wer von den beiden Frauen mag keine Tiere? 12. Was hält Frank von Katzen? 13. Warum will Sonja momentan nichts davon wissen? 14. Wie endet das Gespräch? 15. Meinen Sie, dass die beiden auf die Anzeigen antworten?

B. Jetzt sind Sie dran! Schauen Sie sich mit Ihrem Partner/Ihrer Partnerin Anzeigen in der Zeitung an. Es sind Anzeigen wo Leute Lebenspartner, Freunde fürs Hobby oder vielleicht auch ein Tier suchen. Reagieren Sie darauf *(react to it)*! Wechseln Sie sich ab!

A: 1. Zeitungsanzeigen 2. eine hübsche, dynamische, zärtliche EVA / Frau 3. für Antiquitäten, alte Häuser, schnelle Wagen, Tiere und Kinder 4. nicht viel, weil sie keine Kinder mag 5. eine sympathische, gebildete, zuverlässige Frau mit Humor 6. Sie gefällt ihr. / Sie findet Sie interessant. 7. Sie möchte beide kennen lernen. 8. eine verrückte Idee 9. Tieranzeigen 10. zu viele Tiere 11. Nicole 12. Er liebt sie. 13. Sie möchte frei sein. 14. Nicole meint, dass Frank davon nichts versteht. 15. Ja, das kann gut sein.

You could point out that **Liebe auf den 1. Klick** is a play on words; normally it's **Liebe auf den 1. Blick** (love at first sight).

Fokus — *Love and Marriage*

Advertising for partners in newspapers and magazines is not at all unusual in the German-speaking countries. Dating shows on television are common, and Internet chat rooms are gaining in popularity.

Changing traditions and laws reflect the increasing equality of German women. For example, women no longer automatically take the name of their husband when marrying; more and more are using hyphenated last names—a practice that was written into law only recently. Married women are not addressed with their husband's first name, but

Magazin Partnersuche per Internet

Liebe auf den 1. Klick

Partnersuche im Datennetz: Finden Singles dort den Mann/die Frau fürs Leben?

Fokus — *Love and Marriage (continued)*

with their own—for example, Christiane Binder, not Mrs. Rudolf Binder. Widowed women keep their married name, whereas divorced women are free to use their maiden name again.

For a marriage to be legally recognized, it must be performed at the office of records **(Standesamt),** usually located in the city hall. A church ceremony afterwards is still popular. Traditionally, Germans wore the engagement ring on the left hand, and then switched it to the right hand as a wedding ring. Today, the American custom of a separate engagement ring is becoming more common, but the wedding ring is still worn on the right hand.

You could mention **Polterabend,** the noisy custom the day before the wedding that calls for friends of the couple to go to the bride's house and smash old plates or pottery outside the door — probably related to the old saying **Scherben bringen Glück.** To help ensure a happy marriage, the couple sweeps up the broken pieces together.

If students ask: *engagement* **die Verlobung, -en;** *honeymoon* **die Flitterwochen (pl.);** *to separate* **s. trennen;** *to get divorced* **s. scheiden lassen;** *ambitious* **ehrgeizig;** *bitter* **verbittert;** *casual* **lässig;** *chaotic* **chaotisch;** *conservative* **konservativ;** *excentric* **exzentrisch;** *(in)flexible* **(un)flexibel;** *insecure* **unsicher;** *lacking empathy* **verständnislos;** *lacking enthusiasm* **lahm;** *optimistic* **optimistisch;** *pessimistic* **pessimistisch;** *shy* **schüchtern;** *stubborn* **stur / dickköpfig;** *successful* **erfolgreich**

Wortschatz 1

Die Beziehung, -en *(relationship)*

der Partner, -	*partner*	ledig	*single*
Wunsch, ⸚e	*wish*	verliebt (in + *acc.*)	*in love (with)*
das Vertrauen	*trust*	verlobt (mit)	*engaged (to)*
die Anzeige, -n	*ad*	(un)verheiratet	*(un)married*
Ehe, -n	*marriage*	geschieden	*divorced*
Freundschaft	*friendship*	sich verlieben (in + *acc.*)	*to fall in love (with)*
Hochzeit, -en	*wedding*	sich verloben (mit)	*to get engaged (to)*
Liebe	*love*	heiraten	*to marry,*
Scheidung, -en	*divorce*		*get married (to)*

Die Eigenschaft, -en *(attribute, characteristic)*

anhänglich	*devoted, attached*	(un)ehrlich	*(dis)honest*
attraktiv	*attractive*	(un)freundlich	*(un)friendly*
charmant	*charming*	(un)gebildet	*(un)educated*
dynamisch	*dynamic*	(un)geduldig	*(im)patient*
ernst / lustig	*serious / funny*	(un)glücklich	*(un)happy*
fleißig / faul	*industrious / lazy*	(un)kompliziert	*(un)complicated*
gut aussehend	*good-looking*	(un)musikalisch	*(un)musical*
hübsch / hässlich	*pretty / ugly*	(un)selbstständig	*(dependent)*
intelligent / dumm	*intelligent / stupid*		*independent*
jung	*young*	(un)sportlich	*(un)athletic*
liebe(voll)	*loving*	(un)sympathisch	*(un)congenial,*
nett	*nice*		*(un)likable*
reich / arm	*rich, wealthy / poor*	(un)talentiert	*(un)talented*
schick	*chic, neat*	(un)zuverlässig	*(un)reliable*
schlank	*slim*		
schrecklich	*awful*		
selbstbewusst	*self-confident*		
seltsam	*strange, weird*		
süß	*sweet, cute*		
vielseitig	*versatile*		
zärtlich	*affectionate*		

Weiteres

der Hund, -e[1]	*dog*
Vogel, ¨	*bird*
das Pferd, -e	*horse*
Tier, -e[2]	*animal*
die Katze, -n	*cat*
beid- / beide	*both / both (of them))*
damals	*then, in those days*
eigen-	*own*
gemeinsam	*together, shared; joint(ly)*
jemand[3]	*someone, somebody*
ein·laden (lädt ein), lud ein, eingeladen	*to invite*
meinen	*to think, be of an opinion*
passieren (ist)	*to happen*
träumen (von)	*to dream (of)*
vergleichen, verglichen	*to compare*
verlieren, verlor	*to lose*
versuchen	*to try*
Ach, wie süß!	*Oh, how sweet / cute!*
Das gefällt mir aber!	*I really like it.*
So ein süßes Kätzchen![4]	*Such a cute kitty!*
Was für ein hübscher Hund!	*What a pretty dog!*
Wenn du meinst.	*If you think so.*

[1] Since it is **der Hund** and **die Katze,** the personal pronoun for these are **er** and **sie!**

[2] As mentioned in a special *Fokus* note in Chapter 9, there are numerous idiomatic expressions including animals in everyday conversation, e.g., **Du hast einen Vogel!** or **Bei dir piept's!** *(You're crazy),* **Fauler Hund!** *(for someone lazy),* **(Das ist) alles für die Katz'!** *(if everything is useless or in vain).* Also, certain animals are associated with certain characteristics, e.g., **Er ist schlau wie ein Fuchs.** *(He's really pretty clever.),* **Du bist geduldig wie ein Lamm.** *(You're really patient.),* **Sie ist arbeitsam wie ein Pferd.** *(She's really working hard).*

[3] Note the use of this pronoun in the various cases: **Jemand** ist an der Tür. Er bringt **jemanden** mit. Sie spricht mit **jemandem.**

[4] As mentioned in Part I of the Appendix, all nouns ending in -**chen** are neuter. This suffix makes diminutives of nouns, i.e., they denote them as being small. In the case of people or animals, the diminutive may also indicate affection or—with people—sometimes also belittling. When adding this suffix, other changes in the noun might apply: der Hund / **das Hündchen,** der Vogel / **das Vögelchen,** die Katze / **das Kätzchen.**

Zum Erkennen: gesucht wird *(wanted);* die Belohnung *(reward);* allergisch gegen *(allergic to);* mit Humor *(with a sense of humor);* das Zuhause *(home);* der Zoo, -s; momentan *(right now, at the moment);* der Dackel, - *(dachshund);* das Halsband *(collar);* das Haustier, -e *(pet);* die Modepuppe, -n *(fashion doll);* hassen *(to hate);* ambitiös *(ambitious);* herzförmig *(heart-shaped);* kinderlieb *(loves children);* schlau *(clever; lit. sly);* silbern *(silver);* unternehmungslustig *(enterprising);* verständnisvoll *(understanding);* AUCH: das Imperfekt *(simple past);* die Konjunktion, -en *(conjunction);* das Perfekt *(present perfect);* das Plusquamperfekt *(past perfect);* Präsens *(present tense);* die Qualität, -en; das Stichwort, ¨er *(key word);* reagieren auf *(+ acc.) (to react to);* unterstreichen *(to underline);* Jedem Tierchen sein Pläsierchen. *(To each his own.)*

Schick sein,
reich sein,
cool sein - und
sonst nichts?

Zum Thema

A. Was ist das Adjektiv dazu?

der Charme, Ernst, Freund, Reichtum, Sport; das Glück, Unternehmen; die Allergie, Attraktion, Bildung, Dynamik, Dummheit, Ehrlichkeit, Faulheit, Geduld, Gemütlichkeit, Intelligenz, Komplikation, Natur, Musik, Scheidung, Selbstständigkeit, Sympathie, Zärtlichkeit, Zuverlässigkeit; sich verlieben, sich verloben, heiraten

B. Fragen
1. Was machen Sie und Ihre Freunde in der Freizeit? Worüber sprechen Sie?
2. Was für Eigenschaften finden Sie bei Freunden wichtig? Wie dürfen sie nicht sein?
3. Waren Sie schon einmal in einen Schauspieler/eine Schauspielerin oder einen Sänger/eine Sängerin verliebt? Wenn ja, in wen?
4. Was halten Sie vom Zusammenleben vor dem Heiraten? Was halten Sie vom Heiraten? Wie alt sollen Leute wenigstens *(at least)* sein, wenn sie heiraten? Finden Sie eine lange Verlobung wichtig? Warum (nicht)?
5. Sind Sie gegen etwas allergisch? Wenn ja, wogegen?

C. Anzeigen über Menschen und Tiere. Ergänzen Sie die fehlenden Adjektivendungen!

Millionär bin ich nicht. Will mein Glück auch nicht kaufen. Ich, 28 / 170, suche keine extravagante Modepuppe oder exotische Diskoqueen, sondern ein nettes natürliches Mädchen, darf auch hübsch - sein.

Tanzen, Segeln und Reisen sind meine große Liebe. Welche sympathische Frau mit Fantasie will mitmachen? Ich bin Journalist, nicht hässlich -, verständnisvoll - und mit unkonventionellen Ideen.

Sympathischer Klarinettenanfänger sucht humorvolle Leute mit Spaß und Freude am gemeinsamen Musizieren.

Man denkt, man arbeitet, man schläft, man lebt? Ist das alles? Temperamentvolle Endzwanzigerin, 180, sucht charmanten, lustigen ADAM mit vielseitigen Interessen.

Welcher nette, intelligente Mann, bis 45 Jahre jung, mag Reisen, Tanzen, Schwimmen, Skilaufen und mich? Ich: attraktives, dunkelhaariges, unternehmungslustiges Naturkind. Geschieden - Anfang 30, zwei sportliche Jungen.

Neu in Bonn: Attraktive, dynamische Psychotherapeutin, Mutter und kreative Frau mit Charme und Esprit, natürlich - und auch lustig -, sucht Kontakt zu lebensbejahenden, kultivierten, netten Leuten für Freizeit, Freundschaft und Aktivitäten.

Verloren: Kleiner, brauner Dackel mit braunem Halsband und herzförmigem, silbernem Schild. Hört auf den Namen „Fiffi"

Gefunden: Grauweiße Katze, ziemlich alt - aber sehr anhänglich -, hat ihren Weg nach Hause verloren. Sind Sie das traurige Herrchen oder Frauchen?

Zu adoptieren: Kleiner, schwarzer Pudel, zwei Jahre alt -, sucht neue Familie mit netten Kindern, geht gern mit Herrchen oder Frauchen auf lange Spaziergänge und ist auch gern bei langen Touren mit dem Auto dabei.

NOTE: In Europe the metric system is standard. Is someone who has a height of 180 cm short or tall? Figure it out yourself. Since one inch equals 2.54 cm, divide the height by 2.54 to get the number of inches. How tall are you in metric terms? Multiply your height in inches by 2.54.

Note, **das Herrchen** and **das Frauchen** refer to the dog owners in a loving way. Because of the ending **-chen,** both are neuter.

1. **Noch einmal!** Lesen Sie die Anzeigen noch einmal und sprechen Sie dann mit den anderen über die folgenden Themen!
   a. Welche Qualitäten suchen die Leute in den Anzeigen? Machen Sie eine Liste!
   b. Wie sehen die Leute sich selbst (*themselves*)? Was sagen sie und was sagen sie nicht? Machen Sie eine Liste!

2. **Freundschaft**
   a. Welche Qualitäten suchen Sie in einem Freund oder einer Freundin?
   b. Sind Freundschaften wichtig? Wenn ja, warum?
   c. Was tun Sie gern mit Ihren Freunden?

3. **Liebe.** Lesen Sie die folgende Liste verschiedener Eigenschaften! Welche fünf davon sind Ihnen beim Lebenspartner besonders wichtig? Vergleichen Sie Ihre Auswahl (*choice*) mit Listen der anderen!

__ häuslich (*domestic*)	__ natürlich	__ zuverlässig	__ schick
__ sparsam (*thrifty*)	__ ehrlich	__ zärtlich	__ tolerant
__ sportlich	__ musikalisch	__ verständnisvoll	__ dynamisch
__ kinderlieb (*loves children*)	__ ernst	__ religiös	__ lustig
__ tierlieb (*loves animals*)	__ schlau	__ ambitiös	__ reich

4. **So bin ich.** Welche fünf Eigenschaften sind typisch für Sie? Vergleichen Sie Ihre Liste mit der Liste Ihres Nachbarn/Ihrer Nachbarin!

5. **Allerlei über Tiere.** Lesen Sie die Tieranzeigen noch einmal und stellen Sie dann den anderen die folgenden Fragen! Finden Sie heraus, . . . !
   a. wer von den anderen tierlieb ist
   b. wer welche Tiere zu Hause hat
   c. wer sich welche Tiere wünscht
   d. welche Qualitäten ihnen bei Tieren wichtig sind und was sie hassen (*hate*)

Katzen-Tageskalender
Jeden Tag eine süße Katze
2002
Prall gefüllt mit 365 bunten und lustigen Bildern, dazu viele praktische Tipps und nützliche Infos

Hunde-Tageskalender
Jeden Tag ein netter Hund
2002
Prall gefüllt mit 365 bunten und lustigen Bildern, dazu viele praktische Tipps und nützliche Informationen

6. **Eigene Anzeigen.** Schreiben Sie Ihre eigene Anzeige auf der Suche (*in search for*) nach Freundschaft, einem Reisepartner / einer Reisepartnerin, nach Liebe oder einem Haustier (*pet*).

You could also have students bring in a picture of their favorite pet and tell the class about it.

D. Was sagen Sie dazu?

> You have now learned enough adjectives to express admiration for people as well as for objects or animals. Remember that the flavoring particle (or intensifier) **aber** can also express admiration (see Chapter 7, 7.3).

1. Sie haben einen besonders guten Film (Stück, Konzert, Kunstausstellung) gesehen.
2. Sie haben einen sehr netten Mann/eine sehr nette Frau kennen gelernt.
3. Sie sind auf den Turm (*tower*) eines großen Domes gestiegen und haben einen wunderbaren Blick.
4. Ein Freund hat ein sehr schönes, neues Auto.
5. Auf einem Spaziergang treffen Sie Leute mit einem Hund.
6. Sie sind bei Nachbarn eingeladen und finden ihre Tiere toll.
7. Freunde haben Sie zum Essen eingeladen. Sie haben nicht gewusst, dass Ihre Freunde so gut kochen können.
8. Ihre Freunde haben ihre neue Wohnung sehr schick möbliert.

9. Eine junge Frau mit einem süßen Baby sitzt neben Ihnen im Flugzeug.
10. Sie haben Besuch. Sie finden die Leute gut, aber nicht die Kinder.

E. Schreiben Sie acht bis neun Sätze! Beschreiben Sie sich selbst *(yourself)* oder eine andere Person!

1. So bin ich.
2. Was für ein toller (interessanter, lieber . . .) Mensch!
3. Was für ein seltsamer (langweiliger, schrecklicher . . .) Mensch!
4. Was für ein süßes (interessantes, liebes . . .) Tier!

CD 5, Track 6

Aussprache: f, v, ph, w

Lesen Sie auch Teil III. 1, 4 und 5 in *Zur Aussprache* im *Arbeitsbuch*!

1. [f]   **f**ast, **f**ertig, **f**reundlich, ö**ff**nen, Brie**f**
2. [f]   **v**erliebt, **v**erlobt, **v**erheiratet, **v**ersucht, **v**ergessen, **v**erloren, Philoso**ph**ie
3. [v]   **V**ideo, Kla**v**ier, Sil**v**ester, Pullo**v**er, Uni**v**ersität
4. [v]   **w**er, **w**en, **w**em, **w**essen, **w**arum, sch**w**arz, sch**w**er, z**w**ischen
5. Wortpaare

    a. *wine* / Wein   c. *oven* / Ofen   e. Vase / Wasser
    b. *when* / wenn   d. *veal* / viel   f. vier / wir

In case students ask: **bügeln** *to iron;*
wickeln *to diaper*

Der Moderator kocht, wäscht, bügelt –
und kann sogar Babys wickeln

Johannes B. Kerner: »Ich bin ein
perfekter Hausmann«

HÖREN SIE ZU!   TRACK 22

Leute sind verschieden. Welche zwei Adjektive — vielleicht auch mehr — beschreiben die folgenden Personen? Schreiben Sie den Anfangsbuchstaben ihrer Namen neben die Adjektive, z.B. K = Kirsten, M = Martin, O = Oliver, S = Sabine. Nicht alle Adjektive passen.

Zum Erkennen: das Krankenhaus, ¨er *(hospital)*; während *(while)*; die Katastrophe, -n; nicht einmal *(not even)*

Wie sind sie?

__ arm	S lustig	__ selbstbewusst
O attraktiv	M musikalisch	S sportlich
M faul	O nett	__ temperamentvoll
K fleißig	O populär	M unsportlich
O freundlich	M reich	K unternehmungslustig
O intelligent	O ruhig	S verständnisvoll

Struktur

11.1 Simple past *(imperfect, narrative past)*

The past tense is often referred to as the SIMPLE PAST because it is a single verb form in contrast to the perfect tenses (or „compound past tenses"), which consist of two parts, an auxiliary and a past participle.

We spoke German.   Wir **sprachen** Deutsch.

In spoken German, the present perfect is the preferred tense—especially in southern Germany, Austria, and Switzerland. Only the simple past of **haben, sein,** and the modals is common everywhere. The simple past is used primarily in continuous narratives such as novels, short stories, newspaper reports, and letters relating a sequence of events. Therefore it is often also called the "narrative past."

Again, <u>one</u> German verb form corresponds to several in English.

Sie **sprachen** Deutsch.
{
*They **spoke** German.*
*They **were speaking** German.*
*They **did speak** German.*
*They **used to speak** German.*

1. T-verbs *(weak verbs)*

T-verbs can be compared to such regular English verbs as *love / loved* and *work / worked*, which form the past tense by adding *-d* or *-ed* to the stem. To form the simple past of t-verbs, add **-te, -test, -te, -ten, -tet, -ten** to the STEM of the verb.

ich lern**te**	wir lern**ten**
du lern**test**	ihr lern**tet**
er lern**te**	sie lern**ten**

Point out that these verbs are all familiar to the students.

Verbs that follow this pattern include: angeln, anschauen, ärgern, benutzen, danken, diskutieren, entspannen, ergänzen, erholen, erleben, erzählen, faulenzen, fehlen, fragen, freuen, glauben, gratulieren, hören, interessieren, kochen, lächeln, lachen, legen, machen, malen, meinen, passieren, reisen, sagen, sammeln, schmecken, setzen, spielen, suchen, stellen, stimmen, träumen, wandern, weinen, wohnen, wünschen.

a. Verbs with stems ending in **-d, -t,** or certain consonant combinations add an **-e-** before the simple past ending.

ich arbeit**ete**	wir arbeit**eten**
du arbeit**etest**	ihr arbeit**etet**
er arbeit**ete**	sie arbeit**eten**

Verbs that follow this pattern include: antworten, baden, bedeuten, beenden, bilden, halten, heiraten, kosten, landen, mieten, öffnen, übernachten, vorbereiten, warten.

b. Irregular t-verbs (sometimes called *mixed verbs*) usually have a stem change. Compare the English *bring / brought* and the German **bringen / brachte.**

ich **brachte**	wir **brachten**
du **brachtest**	ihr **brachtet**
er **brachte**	sie **brachten**

Here is a list of the PRINCIPAL PARTS of all the irregular t-verbs that you have used thus far. Irregular present-tense forms are also noted. You already know all the forms of these verbs except their simple past. Verbs with prefixes have the same forms as the corresponding simple verbs (**brachte mit**). If you know the principal parts of a verb, you can derive all the verb forms you need!

Infinitive	Present	Simple Past	Past Participle
bringen		**brachte**	gebracht
denken		**dachte**	gedacht
haben	hat	**hatte**	gehabt
kennen		**kannte**	gekannt
wissen	weiß	**wusste**	gewusst

Modals also belong to this group. (The past participles of these verbs are rarely used.)

dürfen	darf	**durfte**	(gedurft)
können	kann	**konnte**	(gekonnt)
müssen	muss	**musste**	(gemusst)
sollen	soll	**sollte**	(gesollt)
wollen	will	**wollte**	(gewollt)

NOTE: The simple past of irregular t-verbs has the same stem change as the past participle.

Point out that "n-verb" refers to the "n" of the past participle (e.g., **gesprochen**), to make the terminology clear.

2. N-verbs *(strong verbs)*

N-verbs correspond to such English verbs as *write / wrote / written* and *speak / spoke / spoken*. They usually have a stem change in the simple past that is difficult to predict and must therefore be memorized. (Overall they fall into a number of groups with the same changes. For a listing by group, see the Appendix.) To form the simple past, add **-, -st, -, -en, -t, -en** to the IRREGULAR STEM of the verb.

ich sprach	wir sprach**en**
du sprach**st**	ihr sprach**t**
er sprach	sie sprach**en**

On page 291 is a list of the PRINCIPAL PARTS of n-verbs that you have used up to now. You already know all the forms except the simple past. Irregular present-tense forms and the auxiliary **sein** are also noted.

Infinitive	Present	Simple Past	Past Participle
an·fangen	fängt an	fing an	angefangen
an·ziehen		zog an	angezogen
beginnen		begann	begonnen
bleiben		blieb	ist geblieben
ein·laden	lädt ein	lud ein	eingeladen
empfehlen	empfiehlt	empfahl	empfohlen
entscheiden		entschied	entschieden
essen	isst	aß	gegessen
fahren	fährt	fuhr	ist gefahren
fallen	fällt	fiel	ist gefallen
finden		fand	gefunden
fliegen		flog	ist geflogen
geben	gibt	gab	gegeben
gefallen	gefällt	gefiel	gefallen
gehen		ging	ist gegangen
halten	hält	hielt	gehalten
hängen		hing	gehangen
heißen		hieß	geheißen
helfen	hilft	half	geholfen
kommen		kam	ist gekommen
lassen	lässt	ließ	gelassen
laufen	läuft	lief	ist gelaufen
lesen	liest	las	gelesen
liegen		lag	gelegen
nehmen	nimmt	nahm	genommen
rufen		rief	gerufen
schlafen	schläft	schlief	geschlafen
schreiben		schrieb	geschrieben
schwimmen		schwamm	ist geschwommen
sehen	sieht	sah	gesehen
sein	ist	war	ist gewesen
singen		sang	gesungen
sitzen		saß	gesessen
sprechen	spricht	sprach	gesprochen
stehen		stand	gestanden
steigen		stieg	ist gestiegen
tragen	trägt	trug	getragen
treffen	trifft	traf	getroffen
treiben		trieb	getrieben
trinken		trank	getrunken
tun	tut	tat	getan
vergessen	vergisst	vergaß	vergessen
vergleichen		verglich	verglichen
verlieren		verlor	verloren
waschen	wäscht	wusch	gewaschen
werden	wird	wurde	ist geworden

Have students mark the familiar principal parts in the irregular verb list of the Appendix and consult it from now on. Make them aware that there are two lists: one ARRANGED ALPHABETICALLY, the other divided into GROUPS WITH THE SAME STEM CHANGES. They should consult the list that best suits their learning style.

Learning the principal parts of n-verbs needs to be spread out over several days. Start the reading text early so that many verbs can be seen and learned in context. Stress that all forms but the simple past are already familiar.

Use this opportunity to review the participles while learning the simple past of these common verbs.

3. Sentences in the simple past follow familiar word-order patterns.

Der Zug **kam** um acht.

Der Zug **kam** um acht **an.**

Der Zug **sollte** um acht <u>**ankommen.**</u>
         V1   V2

Er wusste, dass der Zug um acht **kam.**

Er wusste, dass der Zug um acht **ankam.**

Er wusste, dass der Zug um acht <u>**ankommen sollte.**</u>
                  V2   V1

Übungen

A. Geben Sie das Imperfekt (simple past)!

BEISPIEL: feiern **feierte**

1. fragen, erzählen, klatschen, lächeln, legen, bummeln, ersetzen, wechseln, fotografieren, passieren, erleben, schicken, putzen, benutzen, versuchen, sich kämmen, sich rasieren, sich entspannen, sich ärgern, sich erholen
2. arbeiten, baden, bilden, beenden, bedeuten, kosten, antworten, übernachten, warten, vorbereiten, öffnen
3. haben, müssen, denken, wissen, können, kennen
4. nehmen, essen, vergessen, sehen, lesen, ausgeben, herausfinden, singen, sitzen, liegen, kommen, wehtun, sein, hängen, beschreiben, treiben, heißen, entscheiden, einsteigen, vergleichen, schlafen, fallen, lassen, fahren, tragen, waschen, werden, einladen

B. Ersetzen Sie die Verben!

BEISPIEL: Sie schickte das Paket. (mitbringen)
            Sie brachte das Paket mit.

1. Sie schickten ein Taxi. (suchen, bestellen, mieten, warten auf)
2. Das hatte ich damals nicht. (wissen, kennen, denken, mitbringen)
3. Wann solltet ihr zurückkommen? (müssen, wollen, dürfen, können)
4. Wir fanden es dort. (sehen, lassen, verlieren, vergessen)
5. Er dankte seiner Mutter. (antworten, zuhören, helfen, schreiben)
6. Du empfahlst den Sauerbraten. (bestellen, nehmen, wollen, bringen)

C. Wiederholen Sie die Texte im Imperfekt!

1. **Weißt du noch?** Ein Bruder und eine Schwester—Sie und Ihr Partner/Ihre Partnerin—erinnern sich (remember).

   BEISPIEL: Großvater erzählt stundenlang von seiner Kindheit (childhood).
               Großvater erzählte stundenlang von seiner Kindheit.

   a. Ich setze mich aufs Sofa und höre ihm zu. Seine Geschichten interessieren mich.
   b. Vater arbeitet viel im Garten. Du telefonierst oder besuchst gern die Nachbarn.
   c. Karin und Jörg spielen stundenlang Karten. Mutter kauft ein oder bezahlt Rechnungen.
   d. Großmutter legt sich nachmittags ein Stündchen hin und freut sich danach auf ihre Tasse Kaffee. Richtig?

2. **Haben Sie das nicht gewusst?** Ein paar Nachbarn klatschen (gossip) über Lothar und Ute.

   BEISPIEL: Hat Ute ihren Mann schon lange gekannt?
               Kannte Ute ihren Mann schon lange?

   a. Wie hat sie ihn kennen gelernt?
   b. Hast du nichts von ihrer Anzeige gewusst? Sie hat Lothar durch die Zeitung kennen gelernt.
   c. Der Briefträger (mail carrier) hat ihr einen Brief von dem jungen Herrn gebracht.
   d. Gestern haben sie Hochzeit gehabt. Sie hat Glück gehabt.
   e. Das habe ich mir auch gedacht.

3. **Schade!** Bärbel erzählt ihrer Freundin, warum sie traurig ist.

   BEISPIEL: Was willst du denn machen?
               Was wolltest du denn machen?

a. Ich will mit Karl-Heinz ins Kino gehen, aber ich kann nicht.

b. Warum, darfst du nicht?

c. Doch, aber meine Kopfschmerzen wollen einfach nicht weggehen.

d. Musst du im Bett bleiben?

e. Nein, aber ich darf nicht schon wieder krank werden. Leider kann ich nicht mit Karl-Heinz sprechen. Aber seine Mutter will es ihm sagen. Er soll mich anrufen.

4. **Wo wart ihr?** Caroline erzählt von ihrer kurzen Reise in die Schweiz.

> **BEISPIEL:** Wir sind eine Woche in Saas Fee gewesen.
> **Wir waren eine Woche in Saas Fee.**

a. Von unserem Zimmer haben wir einen Blick auf die Alpen gehabt. b. Die Pension hat natürlich Alpenblick geheißen. c. Morgens haben wir lange geschlafen, dann haben wir gemütlich gefrühstückt. d. Später bin ich mit dem Sessellift auf einen Berg gefahren und bin den ganzen Nachmittag Ski laufen gegangen. e. Wolfgang ist unten geblieben, hat Bücher gelesen und Briefe geschrieben.

C.4: a. hatten b. hieß c. schliefen, frühstückten d. fuhr, ging Ski laufen e. blieb, las, schrieb

D. **Eine vielseitige Persönlichkeit.** Geben Sie die fehlenden Verbformen im Imperfekt!

1. Else Lasker-Schüler ist eine vielseitige Persönlichkeit aus der deutschen Kunstszene. 2. Geboren 1868 in Wuppertal, _gehörte_ (gehören) sie zu einer jüdischen Familie, wo man ihr damals viel Freiheit _ließ_ (lassen). 3. 1894 _heiratete_ (heiraten) sie einen Berliner Arzt, _begann_ (beginnen) zu zeichnen *(draw)* und ihre ersten Gedichte *(poems)* zu schreiben. 4. In Berlin _brachte_ (bringen) sie 1899 ihren Sohn Paul zur Welt. 5. Bald danach _stieg_ sie aus dem bürgerlichen *(bourgeois)* Leben _aus_ (aus·steigen), _ließ_ (lassen) sich scheiden und _heiratete_ (heiraten) 1903 Herwarth Walden, den Herausgeber *(editor)* der Zeitschrift *Sturm*, mit Kontakt zu allen Künstlern Berlins. 6. Zwischen 1910 und 1930 _wurde_ (werden) sie selbst sehr bekannt. 7. Sie _lebte_ (leben) nicht nur von ihren Gedichten und ihrer Prosa, sondern auch als Grafikerin. 8. 1933 _nahmen . . ._ die Nazis ihre Zeichnungen *(drawings)* _weg_ (weg·nehmen) und sie _ging_ (gehen) ins Exil in die Schweiz, später nach Palästina.

Lasker-Schülers Porträts einiger bekannter Freunde:

Georg Trakl

George Grosz

Oskar Kokoschka

1. **Georg Trakl** (1887–1914) was an Austrian poet acutely conscious that his world, both personal and external, was breaking apart. The outbreak of war and his experience with the wounded at the front overtaxed his resources; he died from an overdose of drugs while serving as a pharmacist in the army. 2. **George Grosz** (1893–1959) was a painter, caricaturist, and graphic artist who satirized the military, industrialists, and bourgeois life and got into trouble with the Nazis because of it. Between 1932 and 1959, he lived in the United States; he died shortly after his return to Germany. 3. **Oskar Kokoschka** (1886–1980) was an Austrian painter and playwright, best known for his expressionist portraiture and the expressionist magazine *Der Sturm*, edited by Herwarth Walden. In 1938 he emigrated to England and in 1954 to Switzerland.

9. Als sie 1939 in Palästina _ankam_ (an·kommen), _war_ (sein) sie schockiert. 10. Ihr ganzes Leben lang _träumte_ (träumen) sie von einem Land, wo verschiedene Kulturen und Religionen harmonisch _zusammenlebten_ (zusammenleben). 11. Dieses Palästina _hatte_ (haben) nichts mit dem Land ihrer Träume zu tun. 12. Sie _fühlte_ (fühlen) sich dort wie im Exil. 13. So _schrieb_ (schreiben) sie 1942: „Ich bin keine Zionistin, keine Jüdin, keine Christin, ich glaube aber ein tief trauriger Mensch." 14. Lasker-Schüler _starb_ *(died)* 1945 im Alter von 77 Jahren in Jerusalem.

E. **So war das damals.** Stellen Sie Ihrem Partner/Ihrer Partnerin Fragen über frühere *(earlier)* Zeiten! Wechseln Sie sich ab! Fragen Sie, . . . !

1. wo er/sie früher wohnte

2. wo er/sie zur Schule ging

3. wie viele Leute zu Hause wohnten
4. was die Familie gewöhnlich am Wochenende machte
5. was sie in den Ferien machten
6. wie eine typische Woche aussah
7. ob er/sie Tiere zu Hause hatte; wenn ja, welche, wie sie waren und wie sie hießen
8. was ihm/ihr damals gefiel und was nicht
9. . . .

11.2 Conjunctions *als, wann, wenn*

Care must be taken to distinguish among **als, wann,** and **wenn,** all of which correspond to the English *when*.

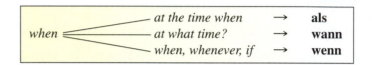

- **Als** refers to a SINGLE (OR PARTICULAR) EVENT IN THE PAST.

  Als ich gestern Abend nach Hause kam, war er noch nicht zurück.
  When I came home last night, he wasn't back yet.

- **Wann** introduces direct or indirect questions REFERRING TO TIME.

  Ich frage mich, **wann** er nach Hause kommt.
  I wonder when (or at what time) he'll come home.

- **Wenn** covers all other situations.

  Wenn du ankommst, ruf mich an!
  When you arrive, call me! (referring to a present or future event)

  Wenn er kam, brachte er immer Blumen.
  Whenever he came, he brought flowers. (repeated event in the past)

Remember that **wenn** (*if*) can also introduce a conditional clause:

  Wenn es nicht regnet, gehen wir spazieren.
  If it doesn't rain, we'll take a walk.

Point out to students that the single event can cover an extended period of time, for example **Als ich jung war, . . .**

Übungen

F. **Was fehlt:** *als, wann* oder *wenn?*
1. Wenn ihr kommt, zeigen wir euch die Bilder von unserer Reise.
2. Können Sie mir sagen, wann der Zug aus Köln ankommt?
3. Als wir letzte Woche im Theater waren, sahen wir Stefan und Sonja.
4. Sie freute sich immer sehr, wenn wir sie besuchten.
5. Sie bekommen diese Möbel, wenn sie heiraten; aber wer weiß, wann sie heiraten.
6. Als ich klein war, habe ich nur Deutsch gesprochen.

G. **Verbinden Sie die Sätze mit** *als, wann* oder *wenn!*

BEISPIEL: Sie riefen an. Ich duschte mich. *(when)*
             Sie riefen an, als ich mich duschte.

             (when) Ich duschte mich. Sie riefen an.
             Als ich mich duschte, riefen sie an.

1. Wir sahen Frau Loth heute früh. Wir gingen einkaufen. *(when)*
2. *(when)* Sie spricht von Liebe. Er hört nicht zu.
3. Sie möchte (es) wissen. Die Weihnachtsferien fangen an. *(when)*
4. *(when)* Ich stand gestern auf. Es regnete.
5. *(when)* Das Wetter war schön. Die Kinder spielten immer im Park.
6. Er hat mir nicht geschrieben. Er kommt. *(when)*

G: 1. . . . als wir einkaufen gingen
2. Wenn sie von Liebe spricht . . .
3. . . . wann die Weihnachtsferien anfangen
4. Als ich gestern aufstand . . . 5. Wenn das Wetter schön war . . . 6. . . . wann er kommt

H. Was dann? Stellen Sie den anderen Fragen mit den Konjunktionen **als, wann** oder **wenn!** Benutzen Sie dabei das Präsens *(present tense)*, Perfekt *(present perfect)* oder Imperfekt!

1. **Wo warst du als, . . . ?**

   BEISPIEL: Wo warst du, als am 11. September 2001 die Flugzeuge ins Trade Center flogen?
   Als das passierte, war ich . . .

H: The examples given with **als, wann, wenn** are only suggestions. Students should be free to formulate any questions with these interrogative pronouns.

2. **Wann warst du . . . ?**

   BEISPIEL: Wann warst du in New York?
   Ich war letzten Sommer in New York.

3. **Was tust du gewöhnlich, wenn . . . ?**

   BEISPIEL: Was siehst du dir gewöhnlich an, wenn du in New York bist?
   Ich sehe mir alles an.

I. Damals. Schreiben Sie 8–10 Sätze über eins der folgenden Themen. Benutzen Sie dabei das Imperfekt—aber jedes Verb nur einmal—und die Konjunktionen **als, wann** oder **wenn!**

1. **Eine schöne Reise.** Sagen Sie, wo Sie waren und mit wem, was Sie sahen und erlebten!

2. **Als ich klein war . . .** Beschreiben Sie etwas aus Ihrer Kindheit *(childhood)* oder Jugend *(youth)*!

   BEISPIEL: Als ich klein war, musste / wollte ich zu Fuß zur Schule gehen . . .

3. **Mein(e) . . .** Beschreiben Sie jemanden oder ein Lieblingstier *(favorite pet)*.

4. **Frauen früher.** Beschreiben Sie das Leben der Frau in früheren Zeiten!

11.3 Past perfect

1. Like the present perfect, the PAST PERFECT in both English and German is a compound form consisting of an auxiliary and a past participle, with the AUXILIARY IN THE SIMPLE PAST.

Ich **hatte** das gut **gelernt.**	*I had learned that well.*
Er **war** um 10 Uhr nach Hause **gekommen.**	*He had come home at 10 o'clock.*

Students often find it difficult to remember to use the past perfect since in English this is often replaced by the simple past. *After we saw the movie, we had dessert.* It might be helpful to study newspaper or magazine articles or literary texts to show proper usage.

ich	**hatte** . . .	gelernt	**war** . . .	gekommen
du	**hattest** . . .	gelernt	**warst** . . .	gekommen
er	**hatte** . . .	gelernt	**war** . . .	gekommen
wir	**hatten** . . .	gelernt	**waren** . . .	gekommen
ihr	**hattet** . . .	gelernt	**wart** . . .	gekommen
sie	**hatten** . . .	gelernt	**waren** . . .	gekommen

2. The past perfect is used to refer to EVENTS PRECEDING OTHER EVENTS IN THE PAST.

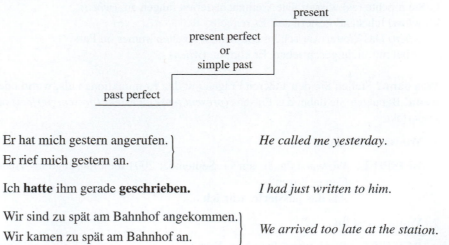

Er hat mich gestern angerufen.	*He called me yesterday.*
Er rief mich gestern an.	
Ich **hatte** ihm gerade **geschrieben.**	*I had just written to him.*
Wir sind zu spät am Bahnhof angekommen.	*We arrived too late at the station.*
Wir kamen zu spät am Bahnhof an.	
Der Zug **war** schon **abgefahren.**	*The train had already left.*

3 The conjunction **nachdem** *(after)* is usually followed by the past perfect in the subordinate clause, whereas the main clause is in the simple past or present perfect.

> **nachdem**   *after*

Nachdem er mich **angerufen hatte,** schickte ich den Brief nicht mehr ab.
Nachdem der Zug **abgefahren war,** gingen wir ins Bahnhofsrestaurant.

Übungen

J. Ersetzen Sie das Subjekt!

BEISPIEL: Sie hatten uns besucht. (du)
Du hattest uns besucht.

1. Du hattest den Schlüssel gesucht. (ihr, Sie, sie/*sg.*)
2. Sie hatten das nicht gewusst. (wir, du, ich)
3. Ich war nach Dresden gereist. (sie/*pl.,* ihr, er)
4. Sie waren auch in der Dresdener Oper gewesen. (du, ich, wir)

K. Nicht schon wieder! Auf Englisch bitte!

1. Meine Schwester wollte den Film sehen. 2. Er war ein großer Erfolg. 3. Ich hatte ihn schon zweimal gesehen. 4. Ich hatte schon lange nicht mehr so gelacht. 5. Aber meine Schwester war nicht mit mir gegangen. 6. Sie hatte nicht genug Geld gehabt. So sind wir noch einmal zusammen / gemeinsam gegangen.

L. Und dann?

1. **Bei Schneiders.** Frau/Herr Schneider — Ihr Partner/Ihre Partnerin — erzählt von einem typischen Tag bei sich zu Hause. Fragen Sie immer wieder **Und dann?,** um herauszufinden, was dann passierte! Sehen Sie, wie Frau/Herr Schneider vom Perfekt *(present perfect)* zum Plusquamperfekt *(past perfect)* wechselt? Wechseln Sie sich nach den ersten fünf Sätzen ab!

BEISPIEL: S1   Ich bin aufgestanden.
S2   Und dann?
S1   Nachdem ich aufgestanden war, habe ich mir die Zähne geputzt.

a. Ich bin aufgestanden.
b. Ich habe mir die Zähne geputzt.
c. Ich habe mich angezogen.
d. Ich habe Frühstück gemacht.
e. Alle haben sich an den Tisch gesetzt.
f. Das Telefon hat geklingelt *(rang)*.
g. Ich habe mit Helmut gesprochen.
h. Er hat die Zeitung gelesen.
i. Er ist zur Arbeit gegangen.
j. Ich habe mich an den Computer gesetzt . . .

2. **Letztes Wochenende.** Fragen Sie Ihren Partner/Ihre Partnerin, was er/sie am Wochenende gemacht hat! Benutzen Sie auch andere Verben als *(than)* in L.1!

M. So war's! Beschreiben Sie Ihr Wochenende oder Ihre Ferien. Benutzen Sie dabei die Konjunktion **nachdem!**

Zusammenfassung

N. Wiederholen Sie die Sätze im Imperfekt!

1. Lothar denkt an Sabine. 2. Er will ein paar Wochen segeln gehen. 3. Aber sie hat keine Lust dazu. 4. Er spricht mit Holger. 5. Die beiden setzen eine Anzeige in die Zeitung. 6. Ute liest die Anzeige und antwortet darauf. 7. Durch die Anzeige finden sie sich. 8. Danach hat Lothar für Sabine keine Zeit mehr. 9. Er träumt nur noch von Ute. 10. Am 24. Mai heiraten die beiden. 11. Sie laden Holger zur Hochzeit ein. 12. Die Trauung *(ceremony)* ist in der lutherischen Kirche. 13. Ute heißt vorher *(before)* Kaiser. 14. Jetzt wird sie Ute Müller. 15. Die Hochzeitsreise verbringen *(spend)* sie auf einem Segelboot.

N: 1. dachte 2. wollte segeln gehen 3. hatte 4. sprach 5. setzten 6. las, antwortete 7. fanden 8. hatte 9. träumte 10. heirateten 11. luden ein 12. war 13. hieß 14. wurde 15. verbrachten

Verliebt...
...Verlobt...
...Verheiratet

Lothar Müller
Ute Müller
geb. Kaiser

Vahrenwalder Str. 93
Hannover 1

Kirchliche Trauung am 24. Mai 2002, 15°° Uhr in der Ev.-luth.
Vahrenwalder Kirche

O. Hoppla, hier fehlt was! Unser Kätzchen. Thomas und sein Zimmerkollege haben ein Kätzchen durch eine Zeitungsanzeige gefunden, aber alles ging nicht so, wie geplant. Finden Sie mit Ihrem Partner/Ihrer Partnerin heraus, was passierte! Einer von Ihnen schaut auf die Tabelle unten, der andere auf die Tabelle im Anhang, Teil 11. Benutzen Sie dabei das Perfekt und das Plusquamperfekt!

S1:

See BEISPIEL sentences on p. 298.

	Nachdem . . .	Dann . . .
Thomas	die Anzeige lesen	den Besitzer *(owner)* anrufen
Besitzer	über die Katze erzählen	Thomas seine Adresse geben
Thomas	dorthin fahren und s. die Katze ansehen	sich in die Katze verlieben
Thomas	die Katze mit nach Hause nehmen	sie Ingo zeigen
Die Beiden	ihr etwas Milch geben	mit ihr spielen
Die Katze	sich einleben *(get used to the place)*	oft auf Ingos Bett schlafen
Die Beiden	die Katze eine Woche haben	wässrige *(watery)* Augen und eine verstopfte *(stuffed-up)* Nase bekommen
Ingo	die Katze zwei Wochen auf seinem Bett haben	richtig krank davon werden
Die Beiden	eine lange Diskussion haben	eine Anzeige in die Zeitung setzen
Besitzer	zwei Wochen ohne die Katze sein	sie sehr vermissen *(miss)*
Besitzer	auf die Anzeige antworten	die Katze zurücknehmen

BEISPIEL: S1   Was passierte, nachdem Thomas die Anzeige gelesen hatte?
S2   Nachdem Thomas die Anzeige gelesen hatte, rief er den Besitzer *(owner)* an. Der Besitzer erzählte über die Katze — und dann?
S1   Nachdem der Besitzer über die Katze erzählt hatte, . . .

P: 1. Arthur hatte an die Hochzeit seiner Tochter gedacht. 2. Als wir sie im Dezember sahen, war sie in einen charmanten, reichen Mann verliebt. 3. Sie sollten im April heiraten. 4. Ich hatte schon ein schönes Geschenk gekauft. 5. Vor zwei Wochen verlobte sie sich mit einem anderen Mann. 6. Michael ist ein armer Student an ihrer Universität. 7. Sie sagten nicht, wann sie heiraten wollten. 8. Am Wochenende rief sie ihre Eltern an. 9. Sie und Michael hatten gerade geheiratet. 10. Sie hatten ihre Eltern nicht zur Hochzeit / zur Hochzeit nicht eingeladen. 11. Arthur ärgert sich, wenn er daran denkt.

P. Die Hochzeit. Auf Deutsch bitte! Benutzen Sie das Imperfekt, wenn nicht anders gefragt!

1. Arthur had been thinking of his daughter's wedding. 2. When we saw her in December, she was in love with a charming, wealthy man. 3. They were supposed to get married in April. 4. I had already bought a beautiful present. 5. Two weeks ago she got engaged to another man. 6. Michael is a poor student at **(an)** her university. 7. They didn't say when they wanted to get married. 8. On the weekend she called her parents. 9. She and Michael had just gotten married. 10. They hadn't invited their parents to **(zu)** the wedding. 11. Arthur gets annoyed when he thinks about it.

Einblicke

Lesestrategie: Das ist typisch für Märchen.

Ein Märchen ist eine Geschichte, in der seltsame Ereignisse *(in which strange events)*, Könige und Prinzessinnen oder magische Verwandlungen *(transformations)* eine große Rolle spielen. Während Sie lesen, finden Sie Beispiele dafür im Text!

Wortschatz 2

You might point out the word **das Niemandsland** *(no man's land)*.

der König, -e	*king*
das Gold	*gold*
die Königin, -nen	*queen*
Welt	*world*
das erste (zweite . . .) Mal	*the first (second . . .) time*
zum ersten (dritten . . .) Mal	*for the first (third . . .) time*
allein	*alone*
froh	*glad, happy*
niemand[1]	*nobody, no one*
nun	*now*
plötzlich	*sudden(ly)*
sofort	*right away, immediately*
voll	*full*
geschehen (geschieht), geschah, ist geschehen	*to happen*
herein·kommen, kam herein, ist hereingekommen	*to enter, come in*
nennen, nannte, genannt	*to name*
spinnen, spann, gesponnen	*to spin*
springen, sprang, ist gesprungen	*to jump*
sterben (stirbt), starb, ist gestorben	*to die*
versprechen (verspricht), versprach, versprochen	*to promise*

[1] Just like with **jemand,** note the use of this pronoun in the various cases: Da ist **niemand** an der Tür. Er hat **niemanden** mitgebracht. Sie sprach mit **niemandem.** Das sind **niemandes** Schlüssel.

Vor dem Lesen

A. Allerlei Fragen

1. Wie beginnen viele Märchen auf Englisch? 2. Wo spielen sie? 3. Welche Personen sind typisch in einem Märchen? 4. Welche Märchen kennen Sie? 5. Haben Sie als Kind gern Märchen gelesen? Warum (nicht)?

B. Gehen wir angeln!

Lesen Sie mit Ihrem Partner/Ihrer Partnerin still (*quietly*) durch das Märchen. Wenn Sie einen Imperfekt finden, lesen Sie diesen laut und geben Sie den passenden Infinitiv dazu! Das gleiche Verb in der gleichen Verbform brauchen Sie nicht zu wiederholen. Wechseln Sie sich ab!

BEISPIEL:	S1	war	**sein**
	S2	hatte	**haben**
	S1	geschah	**geschehen**

C. Was ist das?

der Müller, Ring, Rückweg, Sonnenaufgang; das Feuer, Männchen, Spinnrad; die Nachbarschaft; testen; golden

Rumpelstilzchen

CD 5, Track 8

Es war einmal° ein Müller. Er war arm, aber er hatte eine schöne Tochter. Eines Tages geschah es, dass er mit dem König sprach. Weil er dem König gefallen wollte, sagte er ihm: „Ich habe eine hübsche und intelligente Tochter. Sie kann Stroh° zu Gold spinnen." Da sprach der König zum Müller: „Das gefällt mir. Wenn deine Tochter so gut ist, wie du sagst, bring sie morgen in mein Schloss! Ich will sie testen." Am nächsten Tag brachte der Müller seine Tochter aufs Schloss. Der König brachte sie in eine Kammer° mit viel Stroh und sagte: „Jetzt fang an zu arbeiten! Wenn du bis morgen früh nicht das ganze Stroh zu Gold gesponnen hast, musst du sterben." Dann schloss er die Kammer zu° und die Müllerstochter blieb allein darin.

°once upon a time there was

°straw

°chamber

°locked

Da saß nun das arme Mädchen und weinte, denn sie wusste nicht, wie man Stroh zu Gold spinnt. Da öffnete sich plötzlich die Tür. Ein kleines Männchen kam herein und sagte: „Guten Abend, schöne Müllerstochter! Warum weinst du denn?" „Ach", antwortete das Mädchen, „weil ich Stroh zu Gold spinnen soll, und ich weiß nicht wie." „Was gibst du mir, wenn ich dir helfe?", fragte das Männchen. „Meine goldene Kette°", antwortete das Mädchen. Das Männchen nahm die Goldkette, setzte sich an das Spinnrad und spann bis zum Morgen das ganze Stroh zu Gold. Bei Sonnenaufgang kam der König. Er freute sich, als er das viele Gold sah, denn das hatte er nicht erwartet°. Dann brachte er sie sofort in eine andere Kammer, wo noch viel mehr° Stroh lag. Er befahl° ihr, auch dieses Stroh in einer Nacht zu Gold zu spinnen, wenn ihr das Leben lieb war.

°necklace

°expected

°more / ordered

Wieder weinte das Mädchen; und wieder öffnete sich die Tür und das Männchen kam herein. „Was gibst du mir, wenn ich dir das Stroh zu Gold spinne?", fragte es. „Meinen Ring vom Finger", antwortete das Mädchen. Wieder setzte sich das Männchen ans Spinnrad und spann das Stroh zu Gold. Der König freute sich sehr, aber er hatte immer noch nicht genug. Nun brachte er die Müllerstochter in eine dritte Kammer, wo noch sehr viel mehr Stroh lag und sprach: „Wenn du mir dieses Stroh auch noch zu Gold spinnst, heirate ich dich morgen." Dabei dachte er sich: Wenn es auch nur eine Müllerstochter ist, so eine reiche Frau finde ich in der ganzen Welt nicht. Als das Mädchen allein war, kam das Männchen zum dritten Mal. Es sagte wieder: „Was gibst du mir, wenn ich dir noch einmal das Stroh spinne?" Die Müllerstochter aber hatte nichts mehr, was sie ihm geben konnte. „Dann versprich mir dein erstes Kind, wenn du Königin bist", sagte das Männchen. Die Müllerstochter wusste nicht, was sie tun sollte und sagte ja. Am nächsten Morgen heiratete sie den König und wurde Königin.

Nach einem Jahr brachte sie ein schönes Kind zur Welt. Sie hatte aber das Männchen schon lange vergessen. Da stand es aber plötzlich in ihrer Kammer und sagte: „Gib mir das Kind, wie du es mir versprochen hast!" Die Königin bekam Angst° und versprach dem

°became afraid

kingdom
living / more important than
pity
keep
messenger

Männchen das ganze Gold im Königreich°, wenn es ihr das Kind lassen wollte. Aber das Männchen sagte: „Nein, etwas Lebendes° ist mir wichtiger als° alles Gold in der Welt." Da fing die Königin an zu weinen, dass das Männchen Mitleid° bekam. „Na gut", sagte es, „du hast drei Tage Zeit. Wenn du bis dann meinen Namen weißt, darfst du das Kind behalten°."

Nun dachte die Königin die ganze Nacht an Namen und sie schickte einen Boten° über Land. Er sollte fragen, was es sonst noch für Namen gab. Am ersten Abend, als das Männchen kam, fing die Königin an mit „Kaspar, Melchior, Balthasar . . . ", aber bei jedem Namen lachte das Männchen und sagte: „Nein, so heiß' ich nicht." Am nächsten Tag fragte man die Leute in der Nachbarschaft nach Namen. Am Abend sagte die Königin dem Männchen viele komische Namen wie „Rippenbiest" und „Hammelbein", aber es antwortete immer: „Nein, so heiß' ich nicht." Am dritten Tag kam der Bote zurück und

borders

erzählte: „Ich bin bis an die Grenzen° des Königreichs gegangen, und niemand konnte mir neue Namen nennen. Aber auf dem Rückweg kam ich in einen Wald. Da sah ich ein kleines Häuschen mit einem Feuer davor. Um das Feuer sprang ein seltsames Männchen.

hopped / screamed

Es hüpfte° auf einem Bein und schrie°:

brew

> Heute back ich, morgen brau° ich,
> übermorgen hol' ich der Königin ihr Kind;
> ach, wie gut, dass niemand weiß,
> dass ich Rumpelstilzchen heiß!

Die Königin war natürlich sehr froh, als sie das hörte. Am Abend fragte sie das Männchen zuerst: „Heißt du vielleicht Kunz?" „Nein!" „Heißt du vielleicht Heinz?" „Nein!" „Heißt du vielleicht Rumpelstilzchen?" „Das hat dir der Teufel° gesagt, das hat dir der

devil
stomped
ground / sank in / grabbed
ripped / to pieces

Teufel gesagt!", schrie das Männchen und stampfte° mit dem rechten Fuß so auf den Boden°, dass es mit dem Bein bis zum Körper darin versank°. Dann packte° es den linken Fuß mit beiden Händen und riss° sich selbst in Stücke°.

retold

Märchen der Brüder Grimm (nacherzählt°)

Nach dem Lesen

A. **Rumpelstilzchen.** Erzählen Sie die Geschichte noch einmal in Ihren eigenen Worten! Benutzen Sie das Imperfekt und die folgenden Stichwörter *(key words)*!

Müller, Tochter, König, Stroh zu Gold spinnen, Kammer, sterben, weinen, Männchen, Goldkette, Spinnrad, noch mehr, heiraten, Ring, Kind, Königin, nach einem Jahr, Angst, Mitleid, behalten, einen Boten schicken, Häuschen, Feuer, springen, Teufel, auf den Boden stampfen, im Boden versinken (versank), sich selbst in Stücke reißen (riss)

B. *Als, wenn* **oder** *wann?*

1. Als die Müllerstochter das hörte, fing sie an zu weinen.
2. Immer, wenn die Königin nicht wusste, was sie tun sollte, weinte sie.
3. Wenn du mir das Stroh zu Gold spinnst, heirate ich dich morgen.
4. Das Männchen lachte nur, als die Königin fragte, ob es Melchior hieß.
5. Als die Königin den Namen Rumpelstilzchen nannte, ärgerte sich das Männchen furchtbar.
6. Wir wissen nicht genau, wann sie geheiratet haben, aber wenn sie nicht gestorben sind, dann leben sie noch heute.

Fokus — *Telling a Story and Encouraging a Speaker*

As you have seen in the reading text, many fairy tales start with the phrase **Es war einmal …** Here are some common expressions to catch a listener's attention when beginning to relate a story: **Weißt du, was mir passiert ist? Mensch, du glaubst nicht, was …! Ich muss dir was erzählen. Ich vergesse nie …**

Hast du gewusst, dass …? Hast du schon gehört, dass …? And this is what a listener might say in response to various sentences: **Wirklich? Natürlich! Klar! Und (dann)? Was hast du dann gemacht? Und wo warst du, als …? Und wie geht's weiter?**

C. Gespräch zwischen Mutter und Sohn

1. **Wusstest du das?** Lesen Sie, was die Königin ihrem Sohn nach dem Tod *(death)* des Vaters erzählt! Unterstreichen Sie *(underline)* das Plusquamperfekt!

   Jetzt, wo dein Vater gestorben ist, kann ich dir erzählen, wie es dazu kam, dass dein Vater und ich heirateten. Er wollte nie, dass du weißt, dass dein Großvater nur Müller war. Mein Vater brachte mich eines Tages hier aufs Schloss, weil er am Tag davor dem König gesagt hatte, dass ich Stroh zu Gold spinnen kann. Der König brachte mich damals in eine Kammer voll Stroh und ich sollte es zu Gold spinnen. Ich wusste natürlich nicht, wie man das macht. Weil der König gesagt hatte, dass ich sterben sollte, wenn das Stroh nicht am nächsten Morgen Gold geworden war, hatte ich große Angst und fing an zu weinen. Da kam plötzlich ein Männchen in die Kammer. Für meine Halskette wollte es mir helfen. Bevor es Morgen war, hatte es das ganze Stroh zu Gold gesponnen. Aber dein Vater brachte mich in eine andere Kammer voll Stroh. Wieder kam das Männchen und half mir, nachdem ich ihm meinen Ring gegeben hatte. Aber in der dritten Nacht hatte ich nichts mehr, was ich ihm schenken konnte. Da musste ich ihm mein erstes Kind versprechen. Am nächsten Tag heirateten wir und ich wurde Königin. Nach einem Jahr kamst du auf die Welt und plötzlich stand das Männchen vor mir und wollte dich mitnehmen. Ich hatte es aber schon lange vergessen. Als ich weinte, sagte es, dass ich dich behalten dürfte, wenn ich in drei Tagen seinen Namen wüsste *(would know)*. Am letzten Tag kam mein Bote zurück und sagte mir, dass er ein Männchen gesehen hatte, wie es um ein Feuer tanzte und schrie: „Ach, wie gut, dass niemand weiß, dass ich Rumpelstilzchen heiß'." Nachdem ich dem Männchen seinen Namen gesagte hatte, riss es sich selbst in Stücke und du durftest bei mir bleiben.

2. **Ich muss dir was erzählen.** Spielen Sie jetzt mit Ihrem Partner/Ihrer Partnerin die Rolle von Mutter und Sohn. Die Mutter erzählt die Geschichte noch einmal, aber nach jedem Satz hat der Sohn etwas zu sagen.

   BEISPIEL: Jetzt, wo dein Vater gestorben ist, kann ich dir erzählen, wie es dazu kam, dass dein Vater und ich heirateten.
   Dann erzähl mal!

Your students' response to a fairy tale as a reading text will depend on your attitude. You might discuss the genre, typical style, and features. Our students enjoyed occasional telling of familiar tales because they could understand them quite easily.

Schloss Neuschwanstein von Ludwig II. stammt aus *(dates back to)* dem 19. Jahrhundert.

D. Mensch, du glaubst nicht, was . . . ! Erzählen Sie Ihrem Partner/Ihrer Partnerin, was Ihnen . . . (an der Uni, bei der Arbeit, in den Ferien und so weiter) passiert ist! Ihr Partner/Ihre Partnerin hat zu jedem Satz etwas zu sagen.

E. Allerlei Fragen

Topics for discussion: a. die Abhängigkeit der Frau von Vater und Mann b. Frau und Baby als Handelsobjekt *(object for trade)* c. der Materialismus des Königs und Geld als Basis zur Ehe d. Rumpelstilzchens Rolle und seine Perspektive; gibt es positive Eigenschaften? e. gebrochene Versprechen und Versprechen unter Druck *(duress)* f. die soziale Funktion solcher Geschichten

1. Aus welcher Zeit kommen solche Märchen wie *Rumpelstilzchen*?
2. Warum ist *Rumpelstilzchen* ein typisches Märchen? Was ist charakteristisch für Märchen?
3. Was ist die Rolle der Frau in diesem Märchen? Sieht man die Frau auch heute noch so?
4. Was für Frauen findet man oft in Märchen? In welchen Märchen findet man starke *(strong)* Frauen? Welche Rollen spielen sie meistens?
5. Warum heiratet der König die Müllerstochter? Gibt es das heute auch noch?
6. Wie endet die Geschichte in der englischen Version? Warum? Was für Geschichten hören (oder sehen) Kinder heute? Sind sie anders? Wenn ja, wie?

Gedichte • Romane • Märchen • Love-Story • Krimi

Und was lesen *Sie*?

HÖREN SIE ZU!   TRACK 23

Vier berühmte Märchen

Zum Erkennen: brachen ab *(broke off);* schütteten *(dumped);* die Linsen *(lentils);* die Asche; auslesen *(to pick out);* der Turm *(tower);* das Spinnrad *(spinning wheel);* die Spindel *(spindle);* kaum *(hardly);* erfüllte sich° *(was fulfilled);* der Zauberspruch *(magic spell);* stach *(pricked);* schlief ein *(fell asleep)*

Welcher Text gehört zu welchem Märchen? Schreiben Sie die Nummer daneben!

<u>2</u> *Aschenputtel*   <u>1</u> *Hänsel und Gretel*   ___ *Rotkäppchen*

<u>3</u> *Dornröschen*   ___ *Rapunzel*   <u>4</u> *Schneewittchen*

Der alte Großvater und sein Enkel

Es war einmal ein steinalter° Mann. Ihm waren die Augen trüb° geworden, die Ohren taub° und die Knie zitterten° ihm. Wenn er nun am Tisch saß und den Löffel kaum halten konnte, schüttete° er Suppe auf das Tischtuch° und es floß° ihm auch etwas wieder aus dem Mund. Sein Sohn und dessen° Frau ekelten sich° davor und darum° musste sich der alte Großvater nach einiger Zeit hinter den Ofen in die Ecke setzen und sie gaben ihm sein Essen in einem irdenenen Schüsselchen°. Da saß er nun und sah traurig nach dem Tisch und die Augen wurden ihm nass°. Einmal konnten seine zittrigen° Hände das Schüsselchen nicht halten; es fiel zur Erde° und zerbrach°. Die junge Frau wurde böse°, aber er sagte nichts und seufzte° nur. Da kaufte sie ihm ein hölzernes° Schüsselchen . . .

Als sie eines Tages da so saßen, trug der kleine Enkel von vier Jahren auf der Erde kleine Brettchen° zusammen. „Was machst du da?", fragte der Vater. „Ich mache ein Schüsselchen für euch," antwortete das Kind „woraus ihr essen sollt, wenn ich groß bin." Da sahen sich Mann und Frau eine Weile° an, fingen an zu weinen, holten sofort den alten Großvater an den Tisch und ließen ihn von nun an immer mitessen, sagten auch nichts, wenn er ein bisschen verschüttete.

Märchen der Brüder Grimm (nacherzählt)

very old / dim
deaf / trembled
spilled / tablecloth / came
his / were disgusted / therefore

little earthen bowl
he cried / trembling
fell down / broke / mad
sighed / wooden

little boards

for a while

Fragen

1. Woran sieht man, dass der Großvater sehr alt ist?
2. Warum musste er beim Essen allein in der Ecke sitzen und aus einer Holzschüssel essen?
3. Woher wissen wir, dass ihm das nicht gefällt?
4. Wie kritisierte *(criticized)* der kleine Sohn die Eltern, ohne es zu wissen?
5. Was geschah danach und warum?
6. Was halten Sie von dem Märchen?
7. Haben Sie alte Menschen in Ihrer Familie? Was geschieht hier oft mit alten Menschen?
8. Warum haben uns die Brüder Grimm dieses Märchen erzählt?

The brothers Grimm, Jacob (1785–1863) and Wilhelm (1786–1859), are well remembered for their collection of fairy tales *(Märchen)*, including *Hänsel und Gretel, Schneewittchen* (Snow White), *Rotkäppchen* (Little Red Riding Hood), *Aschenputtel* (Cinderella), *Dornröschen* (Sleeping Beauty), *Rumpelstilzchen, Rapunzel, König Drosselbart* (King Thrushbeard), *Die Bremer Stadtmusikanten,* and many others. Such stories had been transmitted orally from generation to generation and were long considered typically German. Modern research has shown, however, that some of these tales originated in other countries. The story of Rapunzel, for example, had already appeared in an Italian collection in 1634; there the heroine is called "Petrosinella." The next traceable reference is from France, where the girl's name is "Persinette." Researchers assume that the story travelled to Germany and Switzerland with the Huguenots who left France after Louis XIV lifted the edict that granted them religious freedom. Jacob and Wilhelm Grimm heard many of the stories from women living in and around Kassel in northern Hesse, among them the 16-year-old Dorothea Wild, who later became Wilhelm's wife.

Jacob Grimm also wrote the first historical German grammar, in which he compared 15 different Germanic languages and analyzed their stages of development. The brothers' work on the *Deutsches Wörterbuch* was a pioneering effort that served as a model for later lexicographers. In 1840, the brothers became members of the German Academy of Sciences in Berlin.

See also the additional fairytale, *Der Froschkönig,* in the *Zum Schreiben* section of the Workbook.

- The Minidrama *Der Märchenprinz* shows Daniela reading the personal ads in a magazine. She is joined by her girlfriend who just returned from a vacation in Mexico. Seated comfortably in their favorite coffee house, Daniela can't wait to get the latest scoop on her friend's travel adventures. She had a fantastic time despite a flat tire on her bus. In telling her story, she gets so carried away that she knocks over a glass on the table. The travel bug turns out to be infectious, because Daniela is getting wanderlust, too.

- For updates, self-assessment quizzes, and online activities related to this chapter, visit the *Wie geht's?* Web site at **http://wiegehts.heinle.com**. You will read some personal ads, look behind the scenes of one couple's wedding preparations, and go sightseeing in Liechtenstein.

Rückblick: Kapitel 8—11

I. Verbs

pp. 241—243 1. Reflexive verbs

If the subject and object of a sentence are the same person or thing, the object is a reflexive pronoun. The reflexive pronouns are as follows:

See corresponding review exercises in the Workbook.

	ich	du	er / es / sie	wir	ihr	sie	Sie
acc.	mich	dich	sich	uns	euch	sich	sich
dat.	mir	dir	sich	uns	euch	sich	sich

a. Many verbs <u>can</u> be used reflexively.

> Ich habe (**mir**) ein Auto gekauft.   *I bought (myself) a car.*

b. Other verbs <u>must</u> be used reflexively, even though their English counterparts are often not reflexive.

> Ich habe **mich** erkältet.   *I caught a cold.*

c. With parts of the body, German normally uses the definite article together with a reflexive pronoun in the dative.

> Ich habe **mir die Haare** gewaschen.   *I washed my hair.*

You are familiar with the following:

s. anhören, s. anschauen, s. ansehen, s. anziehen, s. ausruhen, s. umziehen, s. ausziehen, s. baden, s. beeilen, s. duschen, s. entscheiden, s. entspannen, s. erholen, s. erkälten, s. fit halten, s. (wohl) fühlen, s. (hin)legen, s. kämmen, s. konzentrieren, s. langweilen, s. (die Nase / Zähne) putzen, s. rasieren, s. (hin)setzen, s. verlieben, s. verloben, s. waschen, s. wünschen (see also 2 below).

pp. 263—264 2. Verbs with prepositional objects

Combinations of verbs and prepositions often have a special idiomatic meaning. These patterns cannot be translated literally but must be learned.

> Er **denkt an** seine Reise.   *He's **thinking of** his trip.*

You are familiar with the following:

denken an, erzählen von, halten von, schreiben an, sprechen von, träumen von, warten auf; s. ärgern über, s. freuen auf, s. informieren über, s. interessieren für, s. vorbereiten auf.

pp. 244—245 3. Infinitive with **zu**

The use of the infinitive is similar in German and in English.

> Ich habe viel **zu** tun.
>
> Ich habe keine Zeit, eine Reise **zu** machen.
>
> Vergiss nicht, uns **zu** schreiben!

According to the revised spelling reform, this comma is now optional. Since we feel that it helps considerably in the organization of the sentence, we prefer to continue using it here.

If the infinitive is combined with other sentence elements, a COMMA separates the infinitive phrase from the main clause. If a separable prefix is used, **zu** is inserted between the prefix and the verb.

> Hast du Lust, heute Nachmittag mit**zu**kommen?

REMEMBER: Don't use **zu** with modals! (Möchtest du heute Nachmittag **mitkommen?**)

4. Summary of past tenses

Be sure to learn the principal parts of verbs (infinitive, simple past, past participle). If you know that a verb is a regular t-verb, all its forms can be predicted; but the principal parts of irregular t-verbs and n-verbs must be memorized. You must also remember which verbs take **sein** as the auxiliary verb in the perfect tenses.

a. The perfect tenses   pp. 295–296

   • Past participles.

t-verbs (weak verbs)	n-verbs (strong verbs)
(ge) + stem (change) + (e)t	(ge) + stem (change) + en
gekauft	gestanden
geheiratet	
gedacht	
eingekauft	aufgestanden
verkauft	verstanden
informiert	

   • When used as auxiliaries in the present perfect, **haben** and **sein** are in the present tense. In the past perfect, **haben** and **sein** are in the simple past.

   Er **hat** eine Flugkarte gekauft.   Er **ist** nach Kanada geflogen.

   Er **hatte** eine Flugkarte gekauft.   Er **war** nach Kanada geflogen.

   • In conversation, past events are usually reported in the present perfect. (The modals, **haben,** and **sein** may be used in the simple past.) The past perfect is used to refer to events happening BEFORE other past events.

   Nachdem wir den Film **gesehen hatten,** haben wir eine Tasse Kaffee getrunken.

b. The simple past   pp. 289–291

   • Forms

t-verbs (weak verbs)		n-verbs (strong verbs)	
ich	(e)te		–
du	(e)test		st
er	(e)te		–
	stem (change) +	stem (change) +	
wir	(e)ten		en
ihr	(e)tet		t
sie	(e)ten		en
kaufte		stand	
heiratete			
dachte			
kaufte ein		stand auf	
verkaufte		verstand	
informierte			

For extra practice with the simple past, see the story of *Die Trappfamilie (Sound of Music)* in the review exercises for Chapters 8–11 of the Workbook.

   • In writing, the simple past is used to describe past events. In dialogues within narration, however, the present perfect is correct.

5. Sentence structure in the past tenses

Er **brachte** einen Freund.	. . . , weil er einen Freund **brachte.**
Er **brachte** einen Freund **mit.**	. . . , weil er einen Freund **mitbrachte.**
Er **wollte** einen Freund **mitbringen.**	. . . , weil er einen Freund **mitbringen wollte.**
Er **hat** einen Freund **mitgebracht.**	. . . , weil er einen Freund **mitgebracht hat.**
Er <u>**hatte**</u> einen Freund <u>**mitgebracht.**</u>	. . . , weil er einen Freund <u>**mitgebracht hatte.**</u>
V1 V2	V2 V1

II. The conjunctions *als, wann, wenn*

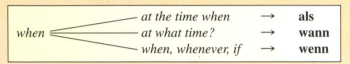

p. 294

III. *Da-* and *wo-*compounds

p. 266

Pronouns following prepositions refer to people; **da-** and **wo-**compounds refer to objects and ideas. Most accusative and dative prepositions, and all two-way prepositions, can be part of such compounds. Prepositions beginning with a vowel are preceded by **dar-** and **wor-.**

> Er wartet **auf einen Brief.**
>
> **Worauf** wartet er? Er wartet **dar**auf.

IV. Cases

pp. 211–213

1. Genitive

   a. Masculine and neuter nouns have endings in the genitive singular.

   -es: for one-syllable nouns and nouns ending in **-s, -ss, -ß, -z, -tz, -zt** (des Kopf**es,** Hals**es,** Fluss**es,** Fuß**es,** Salz**es,** Platz**es,** Arzt**es** *[physician's]*).

   -s: for nouns of more than one syllable and proper nouns (des Bahnhof**s,** Lothar**s,** Lothar Müller**s**).

   b. N-nouns usually end in **(-e)n; der Name** is an exception (des Herr**n,** des Student**en;** BUT des Nam**ens**).

2. Summary of the four cases

   a. Interrogative pronouns

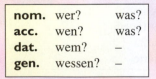

nom.	wer?	was?
acc.	wen?	was?
dat.	wem?	–
gen.	wessen?	–

b. Use of the four cases and forms of **der**- and **ein**-words

	use	follows . . .	masc.	neut.	fem.	pl.
nom.	subject, predicate noun	heißen, sein, werden	der dieser ein mein	das dieses ein mein	die dieses eine meine	die dieses keine meine
acc.	direct object	durch, für, gegen, ohne, um	den diesen einen meinen			
		an, auf, hinter, in, neben, über, unter, vor, zwischen				
dat.	indirect object	aus, außer, bei, mit, nach, seit, von, zu	dem diesem einem meinem	dem diesem einem meinem	der dieser einer meiner	den diesen keinen meinen
		antworten, danken, gefallen, gehören, helfen, zuhören				
gen.	possessive	(an)statt, trotz, während, wegen	des dieses eines meines	des dieses eines meines	der dieser keiner meiner	der dieser keiner meiner

V. Adjective endings

1. Preceded adjectives

pp. 237–239

Predicate adjectives and adverbs have no endings. Adjectives followed by nouns do have endings.

	masculine	neuter	feminine	plural
nom.	der neue Krimi	das neue Stück	die neue Oper	die neuen Filme
acc.	den neuen Krimi	das neue Stück	die neue Oper	die neuen Filme
dat.	dem neuen Krimi	dem neuen Stück	der neuen Oper	den neuen Filmen
gen.	des neuen Krimis	des neuen Stückes	der neuen Oper	der neuen Filme

	masculine	neuter	feminine	plural
nom.	ein neuer Krimi	ein neues Stück	eine neue Oper	keine neuen Filme
acc.	einen neuen Krimi	ein neues Stück	eine neue Oper	keine neuen Filme
dat.	einem neuen Krimi	einem neuen Stück	einer neuen Oper	keinen neuen Filmen
gen.	eines neuen Krimis	eines neuen Stückes	einer neuen Oper	keiner neuen Filme

Comparing the two tables above, you can see:

- Adjectives preceded by the definite article or any **der**-word have either an **-e** or **-en** ending.

- Adjectives preceded by the indefinite article or any **ein**-word have two different adjective endings WHENEVER **ein** HAS NO ENDING: **-er** for masculine nouns and **-es** for neuter nouns. Otherwise the **-en** ending predominates and is used in the masculine accusative singular, all datives and genitives, and in all plurals.

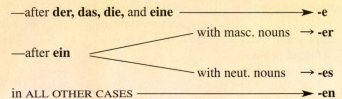

after **der**-words			
	masc.	**neut.**	**fem.**	**pl.**
nom.				
acc.		-e		
dat.				
gen.		-en		

after **ein**-words			
	masc.	**neut.**	**fem.**	**pl.**
nom.	-er	-es	-e	
acc.		-es	-e	
dat.				
gen.		-en		

Or, to put it in another way, the endings are:

- in the NOMINATIVE and ACCUSATIVE SINGULAR

    —after **der, das, die,** and **eine** ——————————→ **-e**

    —after **ein** ⟨ with masc. nouns → **-er** / with neut. nouns → **-es**

- in ALL OTHER CASES ——————————————→ **-en**

    Der alt**e** Fernseher und das alt**e** Radio sind kaputt *(broken)*.

    Mein alt**er** Fernseher und mein alt**es** Radio sind kaputt.

pp. 268–269   2. Unpreceded adjectives

a. Unpreceded adjectives have the endings that the definite article would have, if it were used.

> Heiß**e** Suppe und heiß**er** Tee schmecken bei kalt**em** Wetter prima.

b. The following words are often used as unpreceded adjectives: **andere, einige, mehrere, viele,** and **wenige.**

> Er hat mehrer**e** interessant**e** Theaterstücke geschrieben.

c. **Viel** and **wenig** in the singular, **mehr** and **ein paar,** numerals, some names of colors (**rosa, lila, beige**), and place names used as adjectives (**Frankfurter, Wiener, Schweizer**) have no endings.

> Ich habe wenig Geld, aber viel Zeit.

> Sie hat zwei Romane und ein paar kurze Fernsehfilme geschrieben.

VI. Sentence structure

p. 219   1. Sequence of adverbs

If two or more adverbs or adverbial phrases occur in one sentence, they usually follow the sequence time, manner, place. The negative **nicht** usually comes after the adverbs of time but before adverbs of manner or place.

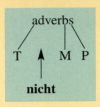

Er fährt morgens gern mit dem Wagen zur Arbeit.

Er fährt morgens **nicht** gern mit dem Wagen zur Arbeit.

2. Summary chart

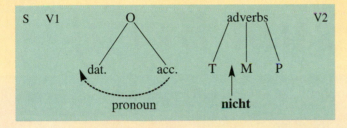

Er kann es ihm heute **nicht** mit Sicherheit *(for sure)* versprechen.

3. Time expressions

   a. Specific time

      To refer to specific time, a definite point in time, or length of time, German uses the ACCUSATIVE: **jeden Tag, nächstes Jahr, eine Woche, einen Monat.**

      Other familiar phrases referring to specific time are:

      - gerade, sofort, am Abend, am 1. Mai, im Mai, in einer Viertelstunde, um zwei Uhr, von Juni bis September, vor einer Woche, Anfang / Ende April, Mitte des Monats

      - vorgestern, gestern, heute, morgen, übermorgen, Montag, Dienstag, Mittwoch usw.

      - früh (Morgen), Vormittag, Mittag, Nachmittag, Abend, Nacht; gestern früh, heute Morgen, morgen Vormittag, Montagnachmittag, Samstagabend usw.

   b. Indefinite and nonspecific time

      - To refer to an indefinite point in time, the GENITIVE is used: **eines Tages.**

      - Familiar time expressions referring to nonspecific times are: montags, dienstags, mittwochs usw.; morgens, mittags, abends, mittwochmorgens, donnerstagabends usw.; bald, damals, danach, manchmal, meistens, monatlich, oft, sofort, stundenlang, täglich, zuerst usw.

NOTE: Review exercises for both vocabulary and structures can be found in the Workbook.

pp. 215–217

Remind students that general time expressions come before specific time expressions: **Er kommt nächstes Jahr im April.**

Note the spelling changes: heute morgen > **heute Morgen;** morgen vormittag > **morgen Vormittag;** Montag abend > **Montagabend;** Dienstag morgens > **dienstagmorgens.**

Kapitel (12)

Wege zum Beruf

Die Wissenschaftlerin Christiane Nüsslein-Vollhard vom Max-Planck-Institut in Tübingen erhielt 1995 für ihre Forschung *(research)* in Embryologie den Nobelpreis für Medizin.

Lernziele

Vorschau
German schools and vocational training

Gespräche + Wortschatz
Professions and education

Fokus
Women in business and industry
Gender bias and language
Foreign workers in Germany
Hard times and social policy
Aysel Özakin

Struktur
12.1 Comparison of adjectives and adverbs
12.2 Future tense
12.3 Predicate and adjectival nouns

Einblicke
Die Berufswahl
Aysel Özakin: *Die dunkelhaarigen Kinder von Berlin*

Video-Ecke
Minidrama: *Anwälte gibt es wie Sand am Meer*
Blickpunkt: *Frauen im Beruf*

Web-Ecke

Vorschau

German Schools and Vocational Training

In Germany, education is under the authority of the individual states. Every child attends the **Grundschule** for the first four years. After that, teachers, parents, and students **(Schüler)** choose the educational track that best suits a child's interests and abilities. About one-third of German students go to a college preparatory school called **(das) Gymnasium, (die) Oberschule**, or **(die) höhere Schule**, which in most of the *Länder* runs from grades 5 through 13. During their final two years, students must pass a series of rigorous exams to earn their diploma **(das Abitur)**, a prerequisite for university admission. All other students attend either a **Hauptschule** or **Realschule**. The **Hauptschule** runs through grade 9 and leads to some form of vocational training. The **Realschule**, a four-year intermediate school covering grades 7 through 10, offers business subjects in addition to a regular academic curriculum, but one less demanding than that of a **Gymnasium**. Its diploma **(die Mittlere Reife)** qualifies students to enter a business or technical college **(Fachschule** or **Fachoberschule)**.

This three-tiered school system has often been criticized for forcing decisions about a child's future too early. Therefore a so-called orientation phase **(Orientierungsstufe)** has been introduced for grades 5 and 6 that gives parents more time to decide what school their child should attend. In another effort to increase flexibility, comprehensive schools **(Gesamtschulen)** have been established that combine the three different types of schools into one and offer a wide range of courses at various degrees of difficulty.

Since school attendance is compulsory from ages six to 18, most of those who end their general schooling at age 15 or 16 must continue in a three-year program of practical, on-the-job training that combines apprenticeships **(Lehrstellen)** with eight to 10 hours per week of theoretical instruction in a vocational school **(Berufsschule)**. Apprentices are called **Lehrlinge** or **Auszubildende** (shortened to **der/die Azubi, -s)**. At the end of their training **(Ausbildung)** and after passing exams at school and at the training site, they become journeymen/journeywomen **(Gesellen/Gesellinnen)**. Five years later, after further practical and theoretical training and after passing another rigorous exam **(Meisterprüfung)**, qualified professionals can obtain the status of masters **(Meister/Meisterinnen)**, a degree that allows them to train the new

To be precise: While the term **Lehrling** is still used strictly for "Handwerker," the term **Azubi** refers to young people being trained for nonacademic professions.

Ask students to have a close look at the chart about the school system. Briefly have them compare it to their own schooling. How long did they attend which school? Ask if their school had something like an apprenticeship program or where one could get such training. What do they think of apprenticeships in general?

(continued on p. 314)

313

generation of **Azubis.** Apprentices are considered invaluable by German business and industry.

Apprenticeships date back to the Middle Ages, when apprentices served for approximately three years under one or several masters in order to learn a trade. This principle extends today to all nonacademic job training. Only few young Germans enter the work force without such preparation for the job market (**Arbeitsmarkt**). Apprenticeship training is carefully regulated in order to ensure a highly skilled workforce.

Gespräche + Wortschatz

CD 5, Track 9

Warm-ups: 1. **Nennen Sie die Verbformen, z.B. sein, war, ist gewesen** (annehmen, arbeiten, bleiben, bringen, denken, erzählen, essen, feiern, finden, geben, geschehen, haben, heißen, hereinkommen, kennen, können, laufen, lesen, müssen, nennen, öffnen, reagieren, sterben, umtauschen, vergessen, verlieren, versprechen, warten, wehtun, werden, wissen)! 2. **Was haben Sie gewöhnlich bei sich?** Was nehmen Sie mit, wenn Sie zur Uni gehen? wenn Sie reisen?

You could ask students why Elke wants to become a carpenter and Trudi a dentist, and what they think of their arguments. What are the advantages and disadvantages (**Vorteile und Nachteile**) of these two professions?

Weißt du, was du einmal werden willst?

TRUDI   Sag mal Elke, weißt du schon, was du einmal werden willst?
ELKE   Ja, ich will Tischlerin werden.
TRUDI   Ist das nicht viel Schwerarbeit?
ELKE   Ach, daran gewöhnt man sich. Ich möchte mich vielleicht mal selbstständig machen.
TRUDI   Das sind aber große Pläne!
ELKE   Warum nicht? Ich habe keine Lust, immer nur im Büro zu sitzen und für andere Leute zu arbeiten.
TRUDI   Und wo willst du dich um eine Lehrstelle bewerben?
ELKE   Überhaupt kein Problem. Meine Tante hat ihre eigene Firma und hat mir schon einen Platz angeboten.
TRUDI   Da hast du aber Glück.
ELKE   Und wie ist es denn mit dir? Weißt du, was du machen willst?
TRUDI   Vielleicht werde ich Zahnärztin. Gute Zahnärzte braucht man immer, und außerdem verdient man sehr gut.
ELKE   Das stimmt, aber das dauert doch so lange.
TRUDI   Ich weiß, aber ich freue mich trotzdem schon darauf.

A. Was stimmt?
1. Elke will _____ werden.
    a. Lehrerin   b. Sekretärin   **c.** Tischlerin
2. Sie möchte später gern _____.
    a. selbstständig sein   b. im Büro sitzen   c. für andere Leute arbeiten
3. Elkes Tante hat _____ für sie.
    a. eine Lehrerstelle   **b.** eine Lehrstelle   c. ein Möbelgeschäft
4. Trudi will _____ werden.
    a. Augenärztin   b. Kinderärztin   **c.** Zahnärztin
5. Zahnärzte sollen gut _____.
    a. dienen   **b.** verdienen   c. bedienen

B. Jetzt sind Sie dran! Sprechen Sie mit Ihrem Partner/Ihrer Partnerin über Ihre Berufspläne. Bereiten Sie ein kleines Gespräch vor; es darf auch länger (*longer*) sein. Präsentieren Sie es dann vor der Klasse!

S1   Weißt du schon, was du mal werden willst?
S2   Ich werde . . .
S1   Und warum?
S2   . . . Und wie ist es denn mit dir? Weißt du, was du machen willst?
S1   . . .
S2   Ist das nicht sehr . . . ?
S1   . . .

Wortschatz 1

Der Beruf, -e *(profession, career)*

der Architekt, -en, -en[1]	*architect*	der Rechtsanwalt, ⁓e[1]	*lawyer*
Arzt, ⁓e[1]	*physician, doctor*	Reiseleiter, -	*travel agent*
Betriebswirt, -e	*graduate in business management*	Sekretär, -e	*secretary*
		Wissenschaftler, -	*scientist*
Geschäftsmann, ⁓er[2]	*businessman*	Zahnarzt, ⁓e	*dentist*
Hausmann, ⁓er[2]	*househusband*	die Geschäftsfrau, -en[2]	*business-woman*
Ingenieur, -e	*engineer*		
Journalist, -en, -en	*journalist*	Hausfrau, -en[2]	*housewife*
Krankenpfleger, -	*(male) nurse*	Krankenschwester, -n	*nurse*
Künstler, -	*artist*		
Lehrer, -	*teacher*		
Polizist, -en, -en	*policeman*		

„Der Kontakt zu den Menschen gefällt mir."

(continued on p. 316)

Fokus — *Women in Business and Industry*

In Germany as in North America, in the past many jobs were considered exclusively "men's work." There has been a considerable shift in attitude, and more professions are now open to both sexes. In 1970, 37 percent of all apprentices were women; in 2000, this figure rose to nearly 50 percent. Likewise, the proportion of professionally trained working women increased from 38 percent in 1970 to 47 percent in 1998. In technical and scientific professions, however, women still make for a rather low showing in the statistics.

At the university level, women account for only 20 percent of those studying technical and engineering subjects—courses leading to fast-growth professions. Instead, they are well represented in the arts and humanities, where career potential is more limited. More recently, an increasing number of female students is pursuing degrees in economics, law, and business administration. As this trend is relatively new, it is not yet reflected by the composition of leadership positions at the top of the professional ladder. Only 8 percent of senior consultants and around 9 percent of all full professors are women; in business and industry, 20 percent of the top positions are occupied by women. However, this situation should improve as more highly trained women enter the workforce.

Der Meister zeigt, wie's geht.

Die Ausbildung *(training, education)*

Die Schule, -n *(school)*[3]

der Kurs, -e[4]	*course*	die Erfahrung, -en	*experience*
Plan, ⸚e	*plan*	Firma, Firmen	*company, business*
		Klasse, -n[4]	*class*
		Sicherheit	*safety, security*
das Büro, -s	*office*	Stelle, -n	*position, job*
Einkommen, -	*income*	Stunde, -n[5]	*hour*
Geschäft, -e	*business*	Verantwortung	*responsibility*
		Zukunft	*future; also: future tense*

Weiteres

anstrengend	*strenuous*
früher	*earlier; once, former(ly)*
gleich	*equal, same*
hoch (hoh-)[6]	*high*
(un)sicher	*(un)safe, (in)secure*
(an·)bieten, bot an, angeboten	*to offer*
sich bewerben (bewirbt), bewarb, beworben (um)	*to apply (for)*
erklären	*to explain*
sich gewöhnen an (+ *acc.*)	*to get used to*
glauben (an + *acc.*)	*to believe (in)*
Recht haben (hat), hatte, gehabt Du hast Recht.	*to be right You're right.*
verdienen	*to earn, make money*
werden (wird), wurde ist geworden	*to become, be*
Was willst du ([ein]mal) werden?	*What do you want to be (one day)?*
Ich will . . . werden.	*I want to be a(n) . . .*
Ach was!	*Oh, come on!*
Das ist doch lächerlich.	*That's ridiculous.*
einerseits / andererseits	*on the one hand / on the other hand*
Genau!	*Exactly! Precisely!*
Im Gegenteil!	*On the contrary!*
Nun / also / na ja / tja, . . .	*Well, . . .*
Unsinn!	*Nonsense!*

---

[1] In most cases, the feminine forms can be derived by adding **-in** (der Architekt/die Architekt**in**; der Ingenieur/die Ingenieur**in**). Some require an umlaut in the feminine form (der Arzt/die **Ä**rztin; der Rechtsanwalt/die Rechtsanw**ä**ltin) and / or other small changes (der Franzose/die Franz**ö**sin). For convenience, we are listing only the masculine forms, unless irregular changes are required for the feminine forms. In ads, both forms are usually listed as: **Journalist/in** or **Journalist(in).**

[2] Note: der Geschäfts**mann**/die Geschäfts**frau** (likewise, der Haus**mann**/die Haus**frau**); when referring to *business people*, the plural **Geschäftsleute** is common.

[3] When talking about elementary or secondary school, German refers to **die Schule.** At the postsecondary level, it becomes **die Hochschule** or **die Universität.** When asking a university student to which school he/she is going, the answer would be, for instance, **Ich studiere an der Universität in Tübingen.**

[4] The word **Kurs** is a rather general term for *class,* e.g., **Sie sind in meinem Deutschkurs.** In schools, but not in higher education, the word **Klasse** is commonly used for a group of students or classmates, but also for a specific grade (level).

[5] When talking about an instructional period in elementary or secondary school, German refers to **die Stunde.** At the university level, that becomes more specified, e.g., **die Vorlesung, das Seminar. Stunde,** of course, also refers to work hours at a job (**Wie viele Stunden arbeitest du?**)

[6] **hoh-** is the attributive adjective; **hoch** is the predicate adjective and adverb: die **hohen** Berge BUT Die Berge sind **hoch.**

Zum Erkennen: der Tischler, - *(cabinet maker)*; die Schwerarbeit *(hard / menial work)*; Überhaupt kein Problem! *(No problem at all!)*; AUCH: das Adverb, -en; die Aussage, -n *(statement)*; die Form, -en; der Komparativ, -e *(comparative)*; das substantivierte Adjektiv -e *(adjectival nouns)*; der Superlativ, -e *(superlative)*; der Vergleich, -e *(comparison)*; besprechen *(to discuss, talk about)*; sowie *(as well as)*

If students ask: **der Angestellte, -n, -n** *employee*; **der Buchhalter, -** *book keeper*; **der Fernfahrer, -** *truck driver*; **der Fonotypist, -en, -en** *audio typist*; **der Friseur, -e** *barber*; **die Friseuse, -n** *hairdresser*; **der Haushälter, -** *house keeper*; **der Kassierer, -** *cashier*; **der Kaufmann, -leute** *trained employee in some branch of business*; **der Koch, ̈-e / die Köchin, -nen** *cook*; **der Krankengymnast, -en, -en** *pysical therapist*; **der Psychiater, -** *psychiatrist*; **der Systemberater, -** *computer consultant*; **der Telefonist, -en, -en** *switchboard operator*; **der Zahntechniker, -** *dental technician*

Zum Thema

A. Kurze Fragen

1. Was ist die weibliche *(fem.)* Form von Ingenieur? Betriebswirt? Reiseleiter? Künstler? Arzt? Rechtsanwalt?
2. Was ist die männliche *(masc.)* Form von Architektin? Lehrerin? Krankenschwester? Geschäftsfrau? Hausfrau?
3. Wo arbeitet die Apothekerin? der Bäcker? der Fleischer? die Sekretärin? die Hausfrau? der Pfarrer *(pastor)*? der Lehrer? die Professorin? der Verkäufer?

B. Was sind das für Berufe? Sagen Sie die Berufe auf Englisch und erklären Sie dann auf Deutsch, was die Leute tun!

C. Zu welchem Arzt/welcher Ärztin geht man?

1. Wenn man Zahnschmerzen hat, geht man zum . . .
2. Wenn man schlechte Augen hat, geht man zum . . .
3. Mit einem kranken Kind geht man zum . . .
4. Wenn man Hals-, Nasen- oder Ohrenprobleme hat, geht man zum . . .
5. Frauen gehen zum . . .

C. 1. Zahnarzt 2. Augenarzt 3. Kinderarzt 4. Hals-Nasen-Ohrenarzt 5. Frauenarzt

Fokus — *Gender Bias and Language*

The collective German plural, in the same way as English, has been reinforcing outmoded notions that certain professions are only for men, for example, **Ärzte, Wissenschaftler,** and so on. Women have been left out of the picture and out of speech. Today, however, many official communications use both masculine and feminine forms to break out of this pattern, e.g., **Ärzte und Ärztinnen, Wissenschaftler und Wissenschaftlerinnen.** Some publications have opted for a more equal new formation, e.g., **ÄrztInnen, WissenschaftlerInnen.**

D. Früher und heute. Was waren früher typische Männer- und Frauenberufe? Machen Sie mit den anderen eine Liste und besprechen Sie dann, wie das heute ist!

E. Ein interessanter Beruf

1. **Das ist mir wichtig.** Fragen Sie Ihren Partner/Ihre Partnerin, was ihm/ihr am Beruf wichtig ist und in welcher Reihenfolge (*sequence*)! Vergleichen Sie dann Ihre Antworten mit den Resultaten der anderen!

☐ Reisen   ☐ wenig Stress
☐ freies Wochenende   ☐ wenig Papierkrieg (*paper work*)
☐ lange Sommerferien   ☐ Arbeit in der freien Natur
☐ saubere Arbeit   ☐ Abenteuer (*adventure*)
☐ interessante Arbeit   ☐ Abwechslung (*variety*)
☐ Kreativität   ☐ Aussichten (*prospects*) für die Zukunft
☐ elegante Kleidung   ☐ eigener Firmenwagen
☐ flexible Arbeitszeit ☐ Verantwortung
☐ Prestige   ☐ Kontakt zu Menschen
☐ Sicherheit   ☐ Selbstständigkeit
☐ Erfahrung   ☐ hohes Einkommen

2. **In welchen Berufen findet man das?** Schauen Sie sich mit Ihrem Partner/Ihrer Partnerin Ihre Listen noch einmal an und sagen Sie dann, wo man diese Kriterien (*criteria*) findet!

Aussprache: b, d, g

CD 5, Track 10

Lesen Sie auch Teil III. 3 in *Zur Aussprache* im *Arbeitsbuch!*

1. [p]   O**b**st, Her**b**st, Er**b**se, hü**b**sch, o**b**, hal**b**, gel**b**
         BUT [p / b] verlie**b**t / verlie**b**en; blei**b**t / blei**b**en; ha**b**t / ha**b**en
2. [t]   un**d**, gesun**d**, anstrengen**d**, Gel**d**, Han**d**, sin**d**
         BUT [t / d] Freun**d** / Freun**d**e; Ba**d** / Bä**d**er; Kin**d** / Kin**d**er; wir**d** / wer**d**en
3. [k]   Ta**g**, Zu**g**, We**g**, Bahnstei**g**, Flugzeu**g**, Ber**g**
         BUT [k / g] fra**g**st / fra**g**en; flie**g**st / flie**g**en; trä**g**st / tra**g**en; le**g**st / le**g**en

---

HÖREN SIE ZU!   TRACK 24

Was bin ich?

Zum Erkennen: unterwegs (*on the go*); die Katastrophe; Politiker (*politicians*); weg (*gone*); Klienten (*clients*); ein Testament machen (*to set up a will*)

Welcher Sprecher ist was auf dieser Liste? Schreiben Sie die Nummer des Sprechers links neben den richtigen Beruf!

_____ Architekt/in	__3__ Journalist/in	__5__ Rechtsanwalt/-anwältin
_____ Reiseleiter/in	_____ Künstler/in	_____ Sekretär/in
__1__ Hausmann/-frau	__2__ Lehrer/in	__4__ Zahnarzt/-ärztin
_____ Ingenieur/in	_____ Polizist/in	_____ Zeitungsverkäufer/in

---

If students ask: *accountant* **der Wirtschaftsprüfer, -;** *banker* **der Bankier, -s;** *conductor* **der Dirigent, -en, -en;** *electrician* **der Elektriker, -;** *insurance agent* **der Versicherungsagent, -en, -en;** *kindergarden teacher* **die Kindergärtnerin, -nen;** *mechanic* **der Mechaniker, -;** *(house) painter* **der Maler, -;** *pilot* **der Pilot, -en, -en;** *plumber* **der Klempner, -;** *real estate broker* **der Grundstücksmakler, -;** *stockbroker* **der Börsenmakler, -;** *tax consultant* **der Steuerberater, -**

Struktur

12.1 Comparison of adjectives and adverbs

In English and German, adjectives have three degrees:

POSITIVE	COMPARATIVE	SUPERLATIVE
cheap	*cheaper*	*cheapest*
expensive	*more expensive*	*most expensive*

Whereas there are two ways to form the comparative and the superlative in English, there is only ONE WAY in German; it corresponds to the forms of *cheap* above.

NOTE: In German there is no equivalent to such forms as *more expensive* **and** *most expensive.*

1. In the COMPARATIVE adjectives add **-er;** in the SUPERLATIVE they add **-(e)st.**

billig	billig**er**	billig**st-**

a. Many one-syllable adjectives with the stem vowel **a, o,** or **u** have an umlaut in the comparative and superlative, which is shown in the end vocabulary as follows: warm **(ä),** groß **(ö),** jung **(ü).**

warm	wärmer	wärmst-
groß	größer	größt-
jung	jünger	jüngst-

Students could learn these as pairs: alt-jung; gesund-krank; kalt-warm; kurz-lang; rot-schwarz.

Other adjectives that take an umlaut include: alt, arm, dumm, gesund, kalt, krank, kurz, lang, nah, rot, schwarz.

b. Most adjectives ending in **-d** or **-t,** in an **s**-sound, or in vowels add **-est** in the superlative.

gesund	gesünder	gesündest-
kalt	kälter	kältest-
heiß	heißer	heißest-
kurz	kürzer	kürzest-
neu	neuer	neuest-

A few adjectives ending in **-el** or **-er** (e.g., **dunkel, teuer**) drop the **-e-** in the comparative: **dunkler, teurer.**

Note that with the spelling reform, the extra **-e-** after words ending in vowels is optional, e.g., **neu(e)st-, frei(e)st-.**

Gesünder leben in Lübeck

Adjectives and adverbs that follow this pattern include: alt (ä), bekannt, beliebt, charmant, ernst, intelligent, interessant, kompliziert, laut, leicht, nett, oft (ö), rot (ö), schlecht, talentiert, verrückt; hübsch, weiß, süß, schwarz (ä), stolz; frei, schlau

c. A few adjectives and adverbs have irregular forms in the comparative and / or superlative.

gern	**lieber**	**liebst-**
groß	**größer**	**größt-**
gut	**besser**	**best-**
hoch (hoh-)	**höher**	**höchst-**
nah	**näher**	**nächst-**
viel	**mehr**	**meist-**

Big Mäc-Esser fahren besser

2. The comparative of PREDICATE ADJECTIVES (after **sein, werden,** and **bleiben**) and of ADVERBS is formed as described above. The superlative, however, is preceded by **am** and ends in **-sten.**

billig	billig**er**	**am** billig**sten**

Die Wurst ist billig.	*The sausage is cheap.*
Der Käse ist billig**er.**	*The cheese is cheaper.*
Das Brot ist **am** billig**sten.**	*The bread is cheapest.*

Ich fahre **gern** mit dem Bus.	*I like to go by bus.*
Ich fahre **lieber** mit dem Fahrrad.	*I prefer to (I'd rather) go by bike.*
Ich gehe **am liebsten** zu Fuß.	*Best of all I like (I like best) to walk.*

Ich laufe **viel.**	*I walk a lot.*
Theo läuft **mehr.**	*Theo walks more.*
Katrin läuft **am meisten.**	*Katrin walks the most (i.e., more than Theo and I).*

CAUTION: **Meisten** in **die meisten Leute** is an adjective; **am meisten** is an adverb of manner; and **meistens** an adverb of time.

Die **meisten** Leute gehen gern spazieren.	*Most people love to walk.*
Mein Vater geht **am meisten** spazieren.	*My father walks the most.*
Mein Vater geht **meistens** in den Park.	*My father goes mostly to the park.*

3. As you know, adjectives preceding nouns are called ATTRIBUTIVE ADJECTIVES. In the comparative and superlative they have not only the appropriate comparative or superlative markers, but also the adjective endings they would have in the positive forms (see Chapters 9 and 10).

der gut**e** Käse	der besser**e** Käse	der best**e** Käse
Ihr gut**er** Käse	Ihr besser**er** Käse	Ihr best**er** Käse
gut**er** Käse	besser**er** Käse	best**er** Käse

Haben Sie keinen besser**en** Käse? Doch, aber besser**er** Käse ist teu(e)r**er.**

4. There are four special phrases frequently used in comparisons:

a. When you want to say that one thing is like another or not quite like another, use

(genau)so . . . wie   or   **nicht so . . . wie**

NOTE: Ich bin **so alt wie** er (nominative). Ich bin **älter als** er (nominative).

Ich bin **(genau)so alt wie** er.	*I'm (just) as old as he is.*
Sie ist **nicht so fit wie** ich.	*She is not as fit as I am.*

b. If you want to bring out a difference, use the

comparative + als

Ich bin **älter als** Helga.	*I'm older than Helga.*
Sie ist **jünger als** er.	*She is younger than he (is).*

c. If you want to express that something is getting continually more so, use

> **immer** + comparative

Die Tage werden **immer länger.**   *The days are getting longer and longer.*
Ich gehe **immer später** ins Bett.   *I'm getting to bed later and later.*
Autos werden **immer teuerer.**   *Cars are getting more and more expensive.*

d. If you are dealing with a pair of comparatives, use

> **je** + comparative . . . **desto** + comparative

Je länger, **desto** besser.   *The longer, the better.*

Je länger ich arbeite, **desto**   *The longer I work, the more tired I am.*
müder bin ich.

Je früher ich ins Bett gehe, **desto**   *The earlier I go to bed, the earlier I get up*
früher stehe ich morgens auf.   *in the morning.*

If you prefer, **je . . . desto = je . . . umso.** Note that after the spelling reform **umso** is now always written together.

Note that **je** introduces a dependent clause. The **desto + comparative** phrase is followed by a main clause in inverted word order.

> **Je exakter die Diagnose,**
> **desto größer die Chance für eine**
> **erfolgreiche Therapie.**

Übungen

A. Komparativ und Superlativ. Nennen Sie den Komparativ und den Superlativ, und dann die Formen des Gegenteils!

BEISPIEL: schnell   **schneller, am schnellsten**
          langsam   **langsamer, am langsamsten**

billig, gesund, groß, gut, hübsch, intelligent, jung, kalt, kurz, laut, nah, sauber, schlau, schrecklich, schwer, süß, viel

A: billiger, am billigsten; gesünder, am gesündesten; größer, am größten; besser, am besten; hübscher, am hübschesten; intelligenter, am intelligentesten; jünger, am jüngsten; kälter, am kältesten; kürzer, am kürzesten; lauter, am lautesten; näher, am nächsten; sauberer, am saubersten; schlauer, am schlau(e)sten; schrecklicher, am schrecklichsten; schwerer, am schwersten; süßer, am süßesten; mehr, am meisten

B. Ersetzen Sie die Adjektive!

BEISPIEL: Diese Zeitung ist so langweilig wie die andere Zeitung. (interessant)
          Diese Zeitung ist so interessant wie die andere Zeitung.

1. Axel ist so groß wie Horst. (alt, nett)
2. Hier ist es kühler als bei euch. (kalt, heiß)
3. Fernsehsendungen werden immer langweiliger. (verrückt, dumm)
4. Je länger das Buch ist, desto besser. (spannend / interessant; komisch / populär)

C. Antworten sie mit NEIN! Benutzen Sie das Adjektiv oder Adverb in Klammern für den Komparativ!

> BEISPIEL: Ist dein Großvater auch so alt? (jung)
> **Nein, er ist jünger.**

1. Waren eure Schuhe auch so schmutzig? (sauber)
2. Verdient Jutta auch so wenig? (viel)
3. Ist seine Wohnung auch so toll? (einfach)
4. Sind die Verkäufer dort auch so unfreundlich? (freundlich)
5. Ist es bei Ihnen auch so laut? (ruhig)
6. Ist die Schule auch so weit weg? (nah)
7. Ist Ihre Arbeit auch so anstrengend? (leicht)

D. Wie geht's weiter? Beenden Sie die Sätze zuerst mit einem Komparativ und dann mit einem Superlativ!

> BEISPIEL: Inge spricht schnell, aber . . .
> **Inge spricht schnell, aber Peter spricht am schnellsten.**

1. Willi hat lange geschlafen, aber . . .
2. Brot zum Frühstück schmeckt gut, aber . . .
3. Ich trinke morgens gern Tee, aber . . .
4. Die Montagszeitung ist dick, aber . . .
5. Ich spreche viel am Telefon, aber . . .
6. Deutsch ist schwer, aber . . .
7. Hier ist es schön, aber . . .

> **American Express Travelers Cheques**
>
> *Das sicherste Geld der Welt für die schönsten Wochen des Jahres.*

E. Ersetzen Sie die Adjektive!

> BEISPIEL: Peter ist der sportlichste Junge. (talentiert)
> **Peter ist der talentierteste Junge.**

1. Da drüben ist ein moderneres Geschäft. (gut)
2. Mein jüngster Bruder ist nicht verheiratet. (alt)
3. Das ist die interessanteste Nachricht. (neu)
4. Zieh dir einen wärmeren Pullover an! (dick)
5. Die besten Autos sind sehr teuer. (viel)

F. Eine bessere Stelle. Was fehlt?

1. Möchtest du nicht <u>lieber</u> Beamtin *(civil servant)* werden? *(rather)*
2. Der Staat *(state)* bezahlt <u>besser als</u> deine Firma. *(better than)*
3. Da hast du <u>die größte</u> Sicherheit. *(the greatest)*
4. Beim Staat hast du <u>genauso viel</u> Freizeit <u>wie</u> bei deiner Firma. *(just as much . . . as)*
5. Vielleicht hast du <u>mehr</u> Zeit <u>als</u> jetzt. *(more . . . than)*
6. Es ist auch nicht <u>so</u> anstrengend <u>wie</u> jetzt. *(as . . . as)*
7. <u>Immer mehr</u> Leute arbeiten für den Staat. *(more and more)*
8. Den <u>meisten</u> Leuten gefällt es. *(most)*
9. Ich finde es beim Staat <u>am interessantesten</u> und <u>am sichersten</u>. *(the most interesting, the most secure)*
10. Eine <u>schönere</u> Stelle gibt es nicht. *(nicer)*
11. <u>Je älter</u> du wirst, <u>desto schwerer</u> ist es zu wechseln. *(the older . . . the harder)*
12. Vielleicht verdienst du etwas <u>weniger</u>, aber dafür hast du <u>meistens</u> keine Probleme. *(less, mostly)*

G. Das ist uns am wichtigsten. Sehen Sie sich mit den anderen die folgende Tabelle an und machen Sie so viele Vergleiche wie möglich! Wie vergleichen sich Ihre Prioritäten mit den Prioritäten der anderen? Fehlt etwas auf der Liste, was Ihnen vielleicht auch sehr wichtig ist?

Gesundheit	54%	Geld	22%
Liebe	52%	Spaß	16%
Freundschaft	45%	Freizeit	12%
Familie	43%	Sex	10%
Gerechtigkeit *(justice)*	25%	Karriere	9%

BEISPIEL: Gesundheit ist am wichtigsten. Sie ist wichtiger als . . . Aber Liebe ist fast genauso wichtig wie . . .

H. Interview. Fragen Sie einen Nachbarn/eine Nachbarin, . . . !

1. ob er/sie jüngere Geschwister hat; wer am jüngsten und am ältesten ist

2. was er/sie am liebsten isst und trinkt; ob er/sie abends meistens warm oder kalt isst

3. wo er/sie am liebsten essen geht; wo es am billigsten und am teuersten ist

4. welche Fernsehsendung ihm/ihr am besten gefällt; was er/sie am meisten sieht

5. was er/sie am liebsten in der Freizeit macht; was er/sie am nächsten Wochenende tut

6. welche amerikanische / kanadische Stadt er/sie am schönsten und am hässlichsten findet und warum

7. welche Eigenschaften ihm/ihr bei einem Freund/einer Freundin oder Partner/Partnerin am wichtigsten sind

8. wo er/sie jetzt am liebsten sein möchte und warum

Die größten Ereignisse, das sind nicht unsere lautesten, sondern unsere stillsten Stunden.

Friedrich Wilhelm Nietzsche

Friedrich Nietzsche (1844 – 1900)

If students ask: **Ereignisse** *events;* **stillsten** *quietest.*

12.2 Future tense

As you know, future events are often referred to in the present tense in both English and German, particularly when a time expression points to the future.

Wir **gehen** heute Abend ins Kino.
{ *We're going to the movies tonight.*
We will go to the movies tonight
We shall go to the movies tonight. }

In German conversation, this construction is the preferred form. German does have a future tense, however. It is used when there is no time expression and the circumstances are somewhat more formal.

werden . . . + infinitive			
ich **werde** . . . gehen		wir **werden** . . . gehen	
du **wirst** . . . gehen		ihr **werdet** . . . gehen	
er **wird** . . . gehen		sie **werden** . . . gehen	

It is more important for students to RECOGNIZE the future tense than be able to USE it actively. Understanding the future tense is an important foundation for learning the subjunctive.

1. The FUTURE consists of **werden** as the auxiliary plus the infinitive of the main verb.

   Ich **werde** ins Büro **gehen.** *I'll go to the office.*
   Wirst du mich **anrufen?** *Will you call me?*

2. If the future sentence also contains a modal, the modal appears as an infinitive at the very end.

werden . . . + verb infinitive + modal infinitive

Please note that we are not using the DOUBLE INFINITIVE in dependent clauses in this text.

Ich **werde** ins Büro **gehen müssen.**	*I'll have to go to the office.*
Wirst du mich **anrufen können?**	*Will you be able to call me?*

3. Sentences in the future follow familiar word order rules.

Er **wird** auch **kommen.**
Er **wird** auch **mitkommen.**
Er <u>**wird**</u> auch <u>**mitkommen wollen.**</u>
   V1   V2

Ich weiß, dass er auch **kommen wird.**
Ich weiß, dass er auch <u>**mitkommen wird.**</u>
                          V2   V1

4. The future form can also express PRESENT PROBABILITY, especially when used with the word **wohl.**

| Er wird **wohl** auf dem Weg sein. | *He is probably on the way (now).* |
| Sie wird **wohl** krank sein. | *She is probably sick (now).* |

5. Don't confuse the modal **wollen** with the future auxiliary **werden!**

| Er **will** auch mitkommen. | *He wants to (intends to) come along, too.* |
| Er **wird** auch mitkommen. | *He will come along, too.* |

Remember that **werden** is also a full verb in itself, meaning *to get, to become.*

| Es **wird** kalt. | *It's getting cold.* |

Übungen

I. Sagen Sie die Sätze in der Zukunft!

BEISPIEL: Gute Zahnärzte braucht man immer.
            Gute Zahnärzte wird man immer brauchen.

1. Dabei verdiene ich auch gut. 2. Aber du studierst einige Jahre auf der Universität. 3. Ich gehe nicht zur Uni. 4. Meine Tischlerarbeit ist anstrengend. 5. Aber daran gewöhnst du dich. 6. Dieser Beruf hat bestimmt Zukunft. 7. Ihr seht das schon. 8. Eines Tages mache ich mich selbstständig. 9. Als Chefin *(boss)* in einem Männerberuf muss ich besonders gut sein. 10. Das darfst du nicht vergessen.

J. Beginnen Sie jeden Satz mit „Wissen Sie, ob . . . ?"!

BEISPIEL: Er wird bald zurückkommen.
            Wissen Sie, ob er bald zurückkommen wird?

1. Wir werden in Frankfurt umsteigen.
2. Sie wird sich die Sendung ansehen.
3. Zimmermanns werden die Wohnung mieten.
4. Willi und Eva werden bald heiraten.
5. Müllers werden in Zürich bleiben.
6. Er wird fahren oder fliegen.

K. Was bedeutet das auf Englisch?

BEISPIEL: Martina wird Journalistin.
            Martina is going to be a journalist.

1. Walter will Polizist werden. 2. Die Kinder werden zu laut. 3. Ich werde am Bahnhof auf Sie warten. 4. Petra wird wohl nicht kommen. 5. Wir werden Sie gern mitnehmen. 6. Sie wird Informatik *(computer science)* studieren wollen. 7. Oskar wird wohl noch im Büro sein. 8. Wirst du wirklich Lehrer?

L. Was hältst du davon?

1. **Verschiedene Aussagen.** Reagieren Sie ganz kurz darauf wie im Beispiel! Wechseln Sie sich ab!

   BEISPIEL: Eltern sind verantwortlich für alles, was ihre Kinder tun.
   Das stimmt. / Quatsch! / Unmöglich! . . .

   a. Die Schweiz ist keine Reise wert.
   b. Wir haben heute viel zu viel Freizeit.
   c. Wir leben heute gesünder als unsere Eltern und Großeltern.
   d. Es ist heute noch wichtiger als früher, Fremdsprachen zu lernen.
   e. Wir sitzen alle zu viel vor dem Fernseher.
   f. Fernsehen macht dumm.
   g. Kinder interessieren sich heute nicht mehr für Märchen.
   h. Die meisten Menschen verdienen lieber weniger Geld und haben mehr Freizeit.
   i. Wenn mehr Menschen weniger arbeiten, können mehr Menschen arbeiten.
   j. Je länger man im Ausland arbeitet, desto besser sind die Berufschancen.
   k. Weil Deutschland eines der größten Industrie- und Handelsländer der Welt ist, wird es für Amerikaner und Kanadier immer interessanter, Deutsch zu lernen.
   l. Ich stelle mir vor, dass es in den nächsten Jahren in der Wirtschaft viel besser aussehen wird.
   m. Kriminalität in den Schulen hat mit Langeweile *(boredom)* zu tun.

2. **Na ja.** Bilden Sie verschiedene Aussagen in der Zukunft! Die anderen reagieren darauf.

   BEISPIEL: Morgen haben wir eine Prüfung.
   Wirklich? / Ach was! / Schrecklich!

   Je billiger das Benzin *(gasoline),* desto größer werden die Autos.
   Ja, das ist verrückt.

Optional English-to-German practice:
1. Children, I want to tell you something.
2. Your mother is going to be a lawyer. 3. I'll have to stay home. 4. I'll (do the) cook(ing). 5. *Helga,* you will do the laundry **(die Wäsche waschen).** 6. Karl and Maria, you will (do the) clean(ing). 7. We'll (do the) shop(ping) together. 8. We'll have to work hard. 9. But we'll get used to it. 10. When we get tired, we'll take a break **(eine Pause machen).** 11. Your mother will make a lot of money (earn well). 12. And we will help her. (See answer key in the Appendix.)

Fokus — *Foreign Workers in Germany*

In the 1950s, the West German and Turkish governments signed a contract that allowed Turkish workers to be recruited to work in Germany as guest workers **(Gastarbeiter).** In 1961, 2,500 Turks were living in Germany; today there are 2.3 million, many of them second- and third-generation residents. In the 1960s and 1970s, Turks were mainly employed in mining and in the steel and auto industries; today more and more are working in the service sector. Turks are by far the biggest ethnic group in Germany, and they are becoming more involved in domestic politics and service organizations. In addition to foreign guest workers from around the Mediterranean and asylum-seekers from all over the world, Germany also has received many ethnic immigrants **(Aussiedler),** most of them from the successor states to the Soviet Union. Although discrimination against immigrants still exists, education and fluency in the language help to facilitate integration into German society.

Deutschunterricht in der Grundschule

12.3 Nouns with special features

1. Certain predicate nouns

   As you already know, German—unlike English—does NOT use the indefinite article before predicate nouns denoting professions, nationalities, religious preference, or political adherence (see Chapter 1, *Zum Thema*).

Er ist **Amerikaner.**	*He is an American.*
Sie ist **Ingenieurin.**	*She's an engineer.*

   However, when a predicate noun is used in the singular and preceded by an adjective, the definite article **ein** is used. In the plural, that does not apply.

Er ist **ein** typischer Amerikaner.	*He's a typical American.*
Sie ist **eine** gute Ingenieurin.	*She's a good engineer.*
Das sind interessante Leute.	*They are interesting people.*

2. Adjectival nouns

   ADJECTIVAL NOUNS are nouns derived from adjectives, that is, the original noun is dropped and the adjective itself becomes the noun. Adjectival nouns are used in English, but not very often. Plural forms usually refer to people, singular nouns to abstract concepts.

   > Give me your **tired** *(people),* your **poor.**
   >
   > *The movie:* The **Good,** the **Bad,** and **the Ugly.**
   >
   > *The **best** is yet to come.*

   German uses adjectival nouns quite frequently. They are capitalized to show that they are nouns, and they have the endings they would have had as attributive adjectives, depending on the preceding article, case, number, and gender. Use the same system you have already learned to put the correct endings on adjectival nouns (see below and Chapters 9 and 10). Masculine forms refer to males, feminine forms to females, and neuter forms to abstract concepts.

der Alte	*the old man*	mein Alter	*my old man, my husband*
die Alte	*the old woman*	meine Alte	*my old woman, my wife*
die Alten	*the old people*	meine Alten	*my old people, my parents*

das Alte	*the old, that which is old, old things*
das Beste	*the best thing(s)*
das Wichtigste	*the most important thing*

   After **etwas** and **nichts, viel** and **wenig,** the adjectival noun will always be NEUTER.

etwas Interessantes	*something interesting*
nichts Neues	*nothing new*
viel Hässliches	*a lot of ugly things*
wenig Schönes	*not much that's beautiful*

   Examples of common adjectival nouns are:

der/die Angestellte	*employee*
der/die Bekannte[1]	*acquaintance*
der/die Deutsche	*German person*
der/die Kranke	*sick person*
der/die Verlobte	*fiancé / fiancée*
Also: **der Beamte**[2]	*civil servant*

---

[1] These adjectival nouns are commonly listed as **der Bekannte (ein Bekannter) / der Deutsche (ein Deutscher),** assuming that the rest of the forms can be deduced.

[2] der Beamte BUT die Beam**tin!**

	SINGULAR		PLURAL
	masc.	**fem.**	
nom.	der Deutsche ein Deutscher	die Deutsche eine Deutsche	die Deutschen keine Deutschen
acc.	den Deutschen einen Deutschen		
dat.	dem Deutschen einem Deutschen	der Deutschen einer Deutschen	den Deutschen keinen Deutschen
gen.	des Deutschen eines Deutschen	der Deutschen einer Deutschen	der Deutschen keiner Deutschen

Also: **der/die Verwandte** *relative*

Students could practice converting adjectives like **verliebt, verheiratet, verrückt,** etc. into nouns (**Verliebte, Verheiratete, Verrückte);** in addition, also superlatives like billigst-, teuerst-, liebst-, größt-, höchst-, nächst-, etc. (**das Billigste, Teuerste, Liebste,** etc.).

Karl ist Beamt**er** und seine Frau Beamt**in.**

Ein Beamt**er** hat das gesagt. Wie heißt der Beamt**e?**

Hast du den Beamt**en** da drüben gefragt? Ich sehe keinen Beamt**en.**

Have students express these examples in English.

Übungen

M. Artikel oder nicht? Entscheiden Sie in den folgenden Sätzen, ob man da einen Artikel braucht oder nicht! Wenn ja, welchen Artikel? Wiederholen Sie dann den Satz auf Englisch!

ZUM BEISPIEL: er / sein / Komponist.
Er ist Komponist.
He is a composer.

1. sie / sein / Wissenschaftlerin 2. sie / sein / sehr gut / Biologin 3. er / werden / Hausmann 4. er / sein *(simple past)* / schlecht / Lehrer / aber / er / sein *(future)* gut / Hausmann 5. sie / sein / lustig / Österreicherin 6. er / sein / gemütlich / Schweizer 7. wir / sein / gut / Nachbarn

M: 1. Sie ist Wissenschaftlerin. *She is a scientist.* 2. Sie ist eine sehr gute Biologin. *She's a very good biologist.* 3. Er wird Hausmann. *He's going to be a houseman.* 4. Er war ein schlechter Lehrer, aber er wird ein guter Hausmann sein. *He was a poor teacher, but he'll be a good houseman.* 5. Sie ist eine lustige Österreicherin. *She is a jovial Austrian.* 6. Er ist ein gemütlicher Schweizer. *He's an easy-going / sociable Swiss.* 7. Wir sind gute Nachbarn. *We're good neighbors.*

N. Substantivierte Adjektive. Welches substantivierte Adjektiv passt dazu?

BEISPIEL: Bist du mit diesem Herrn **verwandt** *(related to)?*
Nein, das ist kein **Verwandter** *(relative)* von mir.

1. Herr Jürgens war lange bei uns **angestellt.** Geben Sie dem __Angestellten__ die Papiere!
2. Er ist uns allen gut **bekannt.** Er ist ein guter __Bekannter__ von uns allen.
3. Jetzt hat er seine Arbeit verloren und sucht, wie viele **deutsche** Kollegen, eine andere Stelle. Wie ihm geht es vielen __Deutschen__ .
4. Er ist mit einer Schweizerin **verlobt.** Seine __Verlobte__ ist Krankenpflegerin.
5. Sie pflegt *(takes care of)* **kranke** Menschen. Alle ihre __Kranken__ lieben sie.
6. Herr Jürgens träumt von einer **Beamten**stelle. Als __Beamter__ verdient man ganz gut.
7. Wenn er damit kein Glück hat, will er sich **selbstständig** machen. __Selbstständige__ müssen schwer arbeiten.
8. Das wird für ihn kein Problem sein, denn er ist sehr **fleißig.** Er ist wirklich ein __Fleißiger__ .
9. Er ist auch **unternehmungslustig.** __Unternehmungslustige__ finden immer einen Weg.
10. Seine Verlobte weiß, dass er nicht **faul** ist. Mit __Faulen__ hat sie nichts zu tun.

O. Das ist nichts Neues. Lesen Sie durch die folgende Adjektivliste und reagieren Sie dann auf die Aussagen Ihres Partners/Ihrer Partnerin mit einem substantivierten Adjektiv!

BEISPIEL: Er hat wieder mal kein Geld.
Das ist nichts Neues!

besonder-, besser, billig, dumm, furchtbar, interessant, schön, toll, traurig, verrückt . . .

S1   Ist diesem Geschäft ist nichts, was mir gefällt.
S2   Ich finde auch nichts . . .
S1   Gehen wir zu dem Laden da drüben!
S2   Wenn du meinst. Vielleicht gibt's da etwas . . .
S1   Carlos sagt, dass sein Vater ihm einen Porsche kaufen wird.
S2   Und so etwas . . . soll ich glauben?
S1   Hast du von der Katastrophe in Spanien gehört?
S2   Ja, es gibt doch viel . . . auf dieser Welt.
S1   Und doch gibt es auch viel . . . , worüber man sich freuen kann.
S2   . . .

Fokus — *Hard Times and Social Policy*

The worldwide trend toward industrial efficiency, high productivity, and low labor costs, coupled with the enormous expenses of reunification, has led to high unemployment **(Arbeitslosigkeit),** uncommon in Germany before 1990. Rebuilding and privatizing the uncompetitive, formerly state-run industries in the new federal states during an era of increased international competition and recession turned out to be much more difficult than anticipated; the extensive modernization necessitated costly federally financed training and retraining programs, as well as large-scale early retirements **(Frührente).**

The increased unemployment is mitigated by generous unemployment benefits. Indeed, despite some cutbacks in social benefits, the fundamental principles of a social policy aimed at achieving a high degree of social justice have not changed. All sorts of assistance is provided to those in need, including social security **(Rentenversicherung),** public welfare **(Sozialhilfe),** and health insurance **(Krankenversicherung).** With people living ever longer, an important addition to this tightly knit net is long-term care insurance **(Pflegeversicherung),** which was put into law in the early 1990s.

Labor unions **(Gewerkschaften)** have always been very important in Germany. However, with the onset of recessionary times since reunification, they have been forced to compromise on their long-standing goals of

Besuch bei der Ärztin

job security with ever higher pay and more benefits. Nevertheless, labor unions remain strong and were instrumental in reducing the 40-hour work week in some industries to 36 hours, or even less in some large industrial companies, in order to save jobs. As unions participate in the decision-making process **(Mitbestimmungsrecht),** their relationship with management has, with few exceptions, been a flexible, cooperative, nonconfrontational partnership—which has contributed to industrial peace and to one of the highest standards of living in the world.

Zusammenfassung

P. Die zehn beliebtesten Lehrberufe *(professions based on apprenticeship programs).* Besprechen Sie *(discuss)* mit den anderen, wie sich das zwischen Ost und West vergleicht.

DIE BELIEBTESTEN LEHRBERUFE
Lehrlinge zur Zeit in Ausbildung

NEUE BUNDESLÄNDER

Bankkaufmann/-frau	6 980
Gas- und Wasserinstallateur/-in	7 040
Maler/Lackierer/-in	7 372
Koch/Köchin	7 557
Elektroinstallateur/-in	7 829
Bürokaufmann/-frau	10 116
Kfz-Mechaniker/-in	10 162
Industriemechaniker/-in	10 626
Einzelhandelskaufmann/-frau	15 240
Maurer/-in	19 864

ALTE BUNDESLÄNDER

Zahnarzthelfer/-in	34 695
Friseur/-in	39 119
Elektroinstallateur/-in	42 251
Arzthelfer/-in	47 716
Groß- und Außenhandelskaufmann/-frau	47 994
Bankkaufmann/-frau	58 105
Bürokaufmann/-frau	58 847
Industriekaufmann/-frau	59 693
Einzelhandelskaufmann/-frau	61 304
Kfz-Mechaniker/-in	74 846

Graphik: Christoph Blumrich

Quelle: Statistisches Bundesamt

1. Welche Berufe sind in beiden Bundesländern besonders beliebt? Nennen Sie fünf!
2. Was ist in den neuen Bundesländern beliebt, aber gehört nicht zu den beliebtesten Lehrberufen in den alten Bundesländern?
3. Was ist in den alten Bundesländern beliebt, aber gehört nicht zu den beliebtesten Lehrberufen in den neuen Bundesländern?
4. In den neuen Bundesländern ist die Lehre für . . .
   a. . . . beliebter als . . .
   b. . . . fast genauso beliebt wie . . .
   c. . . . weniger beliebt als . . .
5. In den alten Bundesländern ist die Lehre für . . .
   a. . . . beliebter als . . .
   b. . . . fast genauso beliebt wie . . .
   c. . . . weniger beliebt als . . .
6. In beiden Ländern stehen . . . und . . . an 8. und 9. Stelle der 10 beliebtesten Lehrberufe.

Q. Kurzgespräch mit den Eltern. Bereiten Sie ein Gespräch mit dem Vater oder der Mutter (Ihrem Partner/Ihrer Partnerin) vor und präsentieren Sie den Dialog danach vor der Klasse!

You are discussing your job choice (**Autoverkäufer, Beamter, Krankenpfleger/in,** etc.) with your parents. They are not happy with your decision and express their disagreement. You agree or disagree with their objections.

After students have glanced at the professions in *Wortschatz I* and the illustration in *Zum Thema,* play the **Vokabelspiel:** One student goes silently through the alphabet until somebody says STOP. At that point, he/she tells the others a certain letter (such as **M**), and they then write down certain German professions starting with that letter, e.g., **Maler** or **Makler.** Limit that time, and then see who produces the most professions.

Note that the *Zum Schreiben* section of the Workbook has additional practice on job comparisons. In it, Ingeborg writes to her uncle Alfred asking him for advice concerning job options and where to live and work in Germany.

Q: As preparation for that talk with the parents, you might ask students to have a look at the chart in the *Zum Schreiben*-section of the Workbook

Mobil telefonieren, wo Deutschland am schönsten ist. Zu Hause.

R. Zukunftspläne. Auf Deutsch bitte!

1. Did you *(pl. fam.)* know that Volker wants to become a journalist? 2. He doesn't want to be a teacher. 3. There are only a few positions. 4. I've gotten used to it. 5. Trudi is as enterprising as he is. 6. She was my most talented student. 7. If she wants to become a dentist, she will become a dentist. 8. She's smarter, more independent, and nicer than her brother. 9. She says that she will work hard. 10. I know that she'll be self-employed one day. 11. I'll go to her rather than to another dentist (I'll go rather to her than . . .). 12. The more I think of it, the better I like the idea.

Einblicke

Lesestrategie: Guter Rat

Manchmal ist der letzte Satz besonders informativ. Finden Sie die Sätze, wo die Sprecher das Wichtigste zusammenfassen *(summarize)*!

Wortschatz 2

der Arbeiter, -	*(blue-collar) worker*
Bereich, -e	*area, field*
Handel	*trade*
Ort, -e	*place, location; town*
Rat	*advice, counsel*
das Praktikum, Praktiken	*internship*
Unternehmen, -	*large company*
die Arbeitslosigkeit	*unemployment*
Berufswahl	*choice of profession*
Entscheidung, -en	*decision*
(Fach)kenntnis, -se	*(special) knowledge, skill*
darum	*therefore*
(gut) ausgebildet	*well-trained*
ins / im Ausland	*abroad*
jedoch	*however*
unbedingt	*definitely*
unter (+ *dat.*)	*among*
aus·sehen (sieht aus), sah aus, ausgesehen (wie + *nom.*)	*to look (like)*
bitten, bat, gebeten (um)	*to ask (for), request*
erwarten	*to expect*
genießen, genoss, genossen	*to enjoy*
hoffen	*to hope*
sich Sorgen machen (um)	*to be concerned, worry (about)*
sich *(dat.)* vor·stellen	*to imagine*
ich stelle mir vor, dass . . .	*I imagine that . . .*

Vor dem Lesen

A. Was denken Sie?

1. Ist es schwer, in den USA, in Kanada oder in Ihrem Land Arbeit zu finden?
2. Was für Stellen findet man leicht? 3. Welche Jobs sind schwerer zu finden?
4. Wie ist es für Leute mit einer Universitätsausbildung, für so genannte Akademiker?
5. Welche Berufe haben eine gute Zukunft? 6. Welche Probleme gibt es mit vielen Stellen?

B. Gehen wir angeln! Lesen Sie Sich mit Ihrem Partner/Ihrer Partnerin den Text gemeinsam durch. Welche Berufe sowie *(as well as)* Komparative und Superlative finden Sie darin?

C. Was ist das?

der Akademiker, Auslandsaufenthalt, Briefsortierer, Computerkünstler, Experte, Job, Telekommunikationsspezialist, Tourismus; das Filmstudio, Industrieunternehmen, Risiko, Studium, Team; die Arbeitszeit, Berufsmöglichkeit, Flexibilität, Lebenskrise, Mobilität, Perspektive, Suche (nach); Handelsbeziehungen, Informatikkenntnisse; in der Zwischenzeit; absolut, beruflich, intensiv, kreativ, optimal, qualifiziert; jobben, organisieren, reduzieren

C: As pointed out earlier, it might be helpful to quickly read these words aloud in class — possibly as a chain reaction — since their pronunciation is often quite different from the English. Reading them aloud also helps students to recognize relatively easy, but still unfamiliar vocabulary.

Die Berufswahl

(Eine öffentliche Diskussion an der Universität Göttingen)

CD 5, Track 12

Wie viele andere Studenten und Studentinnen, macht Lore Weber sich Sorgen um ihre berufliche Zukunft. Sie hat darum eine Diskussionsgruppe organisiert und eine Professorin und andere Studenten gebeten, Ideen beizutragen°.

to contribute

LORE WEBER: Eine der wichtigsten Entscheidungen heute ist die Frage der Berufswahl. Obwohl es besser wird, ist die Arbeitslosigkeit immer noch° hoch, nicht nur unter den Arbeitern, sondern auch unter uns Akademikern. Viele Industrieunternehmen werden in den nächsten Jahren weitere° Arbeitsplätze abbauen° und im öffentlichen Dienst° wird es nicht nicht besser aussehen. Einige meiner Freunde mit fertiger Ausbildung suchen seit Monaten Arbeit und jobben in der Zwischenzeit als Bedienung oder als Verkäufer, Taxifahrer oder Briefsortierer bei der Post. Wir fragen uns alle, wie unsere Zukunft aussehen wird, und hoffen, dass wir durch unsere Diskussion eine bessere Vorstellung° davon bekommen. Ich möchte jetzt Frau Professor Weigel bitten, ihre Perspektive über das Problem zusammenzufassen. Frau Professor Weigel!

still

additional / cut back / civil service

idea

PROFESSOR WEIGEL: Vielen Dank, Frau Weber! Auf die Frage nach sicheren Berufen kann man nur schwer eine Antwort geben. Ich stelle mir vor, dass die Berufswahl immer komplizierter wird. Zu den Berufen mit Zukunft zählen aber bestimmt Umweltexperten° und Biochemiker, Telekommunikations- und Computerspezialisten, Betriebswirte und Mathematiker. Selbstständige in den verschiedenen Bereichen, vor allem auch im Tourismus, werden sicher genug Arbeit finden. Auch für Lehrer wird es eine größere Nachfrage° geben. Jedoch sinkt der Bedarf° für Rechtsanwälte und Architekten. Den Geisteswissenschaftlern° unter Ihnen empfehle ich, flexibel zu bleiben und auch außerhalb° Ihres Studiums praktische Erfahrungen zu sammeln, zum Beispiel bei Verlagen° und anderen Firmen oder durch Auslandsaufenthalte. Was Sie unbedingt brauchen, sind Informatikkenntnisse. Neben guten Sprach- und Fachkenntnissen wird man Zusatzqualifikationen° suchen, zum Beispiel Flexibilität, Mobilität und die Fähigkeit°, immer wieder Neues zu lernen und kreativ zu denken, im Team zu arbeiten und Umbrüche° als Chance statt als Risiko zu sehen. Es ist heute keine Lebenskrise mehr, wenn man den Job wechselt. Eins ist jedoch klar°: Eine gute und breite° Ausbildung ist und bleibt die beste Sicherheit.

environmental . . .

demand / need
humanities scholars
outside of / publishing houses

additional . . . / ability
radical changes

One thing is for sure / broad

CHRISTL MEININGER: Ich leite° seit drei Jahren ein Wellness-Hotel. Ich liebe meine Arbeit, aber die Suche nach qualifizierten Arbeitskräften° habe ich mir leichter vorgestellt. Ich glaube, dass Bereiche wie Wellness, Freizeit und Beratung° immer beliebter werden. Wir leben heute unter größerem Stress als früher und sind viel gesundheitsbewusster° geworden. Man wird also mehr und mehr Geld für sein eigenes Wohlbefinden° ausgeben. Mein Rat: Lernen Sie das, was Ihnen Spaß macht, und lernen Sie viel! Fit machen für den Job muss sich jeder selbst°. Je mehr man in seinem Fach° weiß, desto besser.

REINHOLD HOLTKAMP: Ich bin Grafik-Designer und arbeite freiberuflich°, oft natürlich auch nachts. Als Familienvater genieße ich es, jeden Tag mit meiner Frau und den Kindern zusammenzusein. Das finde ich optimal. Kreativität ist für mich nicht an Ort oder Arbeitszeit gebunden°; darum kann ich genauso gut° zu Hause arbeiten. Mein Rat: Arbeiten Sie intensiv, bleiben Sie flexibel und erwarten Sie keine absolute Sicherheit!

Margin glosses:
- direct
- workers
- counseling
- more health-conscious
- well-being
- himself / special field
- freelance
- not tied to / just as well

Dieser Grafik-Designer arbeitet lieber freiberuflich zu Hause als irgendwo (*somewhere*) in einem Büro.

BRIGITTE SCHINDLER: Ich studiere Kunst und Informatik. Ich hoffe, dass ich eines Tages als Computerkünstlerin für ein Filmstudio oder beim Fernsehen arbeiten werde. Wichtig finde ich es, dass die Arbeit Spaß macht. Nur wenn man etwas gern tut, wird man wirklich gut sein. Und weil die Arbeitslosigkeit unter uns Frauen größer ist als unter Männern, müssen wir einfach besser sein. Ich versuche gerade, einen Platz für ein Praktikum in Amerika zu finden. Je mehr man gemacht hat, desto besser die Chancen. Auslandserfahrung ist wichtig. Mit der wachsenden Bedeutung° der EU, wo wir mit unserer Ausbildung überall arbeiten können, und Deutschlands Handelsbeziehungen mit der ganzen Welt werden unsere Berufsmöglichkeiten immer interessanter. Die Konkurrenz° wird natürlich auch größer. Ich stelle mir vor, dass jedes bisschen Erfahrung hilft. Die besten Jobs werden immer die Besten bekommen.

Margin glosses:
- growing importance
- competition

Es ist nicht gut genug, klug zu sein. Es ist besser, gut zu sein.

Nach dem Lesen

A. Was stimmt? Aussagen zum Text.

1. Viele Industrieunternehmen werden in den nächsten Jahren ___.
   - **a.** Arbeitsplätze reduzieren
   - b. die billigsten Arbeiter haben
   - c. ihre Probleme zusammenfassen

2. Frau Professor Weigel glaubt, dass Studenten vor allem ___ brauchen.
   - a. Auslandsaufenthalte
   - b. Rechtsanwälte
   - **c.** Flexibilität, Mobilität und Kreativität

3. Christl Meininger ___.
   - a. möchte am liebsten in einem Wellness-Zentrum arbeiten
   - **b.** hatte es sich leichter vorgestellt, qualifizierte Arbeitskräfte für ihr Hotel zu finden
   - c. meint, dass die Menschen heute weniger gesundheitsbewusst sind als früher

4. Reinhold Holtkamp ___.
   - a. ist Angestellter bei einer Grafik-Design-Firma
   - b. hasst seine Arbeit, weil er wenig Zeit für seine Familie hat
   - **c.** genießt es, zu Hause arbeiten zu können

5. Brigitte Schindler stellt sich vor, dass ___.
   - a. Informatik für sie sehr schwer sein wird
   - **b.** Frauen beruflich besser sein müssen als Männer
   - c. praktische Erfahrungen in der Berufswelt nicht immer helfen

B. Blick auf die Arbeitsmarktsituation. Wiederholen Sie die Sätze in der Zukunft!

1. Die Berufswahl bleibt eine der wichtigsten Entscheidungen. 2. So fragen wir uns alle, wie unsere Zukunft aussieht. 3. Habe ich mit meiner Ausbildung gute Berufsmöglichkeiten oder sitze ich eines Tages auf der Straße? 4. Absolute Sicherheit gibt es in keinem Beruf. 5. Man muss flexibel bleiben. 6. Praktische Erfahrung im Ausland und Sprachkenntnisse helfen auch. 7. Die Konkurrenz wird immer größer. 8. Mit einer guten Ausbildung können die Deutschen in Zukunft überall in der EU arbeiten.

C. Wunschprofil von Arbeitgebern *(employers)*. Sehen Sie sich mit den anderen die folgende Tabelle an! Wie viele Aussagen mit Komparativen und Superlativen können Sie darüber machen?

BEISPIEL: Flexibilität ist den Arbeitgebern am wichtigsten.

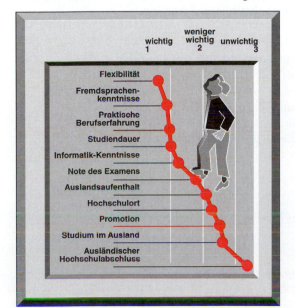

Optional activity: **Wie geht's weiter?**
1. Lore Weber macht sich Sorgen um . . .
2. Darum hat sie eine . . . organisiert
3. Frau Weigel ist . . . 4. Christl Meininger denkt, dass . . . 5. Reinhold Holtkamp freut sich, dass . . . 6. Für Akademiker sieht der Arbeitsmarkt . . . aus. 7. Für Rechtsanwälte und Architekten sieht die Zukunft . . .
8. Viele Studenten jobben als . . . , während sie auf eine Stelle warten.
9. Die beste Sicherheit ist immer noch . . .
10. Außerdem muss man . . . sein.

You could also have students make comparative statements about the weather map on p. 18, the menu on p. 79, the train schedule on p. 210, and the TV program on p. 276.

B: 1. wird . . . bleiben 2. werden . . . fragen, aussehen . . . wird 3. werde . . . haben, werde . . . sitzen 4. wird . . . geben 5. wird . . . bleiben müssen 6. werden . . . helfen 7. wird . . . werden 8. werden . . . arbeiten können

Optional tongue twister: Zahnarzt zieht Zähne mit Zahnarztzange *(pliers)* im Zahnarztzimmer.

D. So wird's werden. Was fehlt?

1. <u>Die meisten</u> Leute müssen in der Zukunft wenigstens einmal ihren Beruf wechseln. *(most)*
2. Gute theoretische Kenntnisse werden <u>genauso</u> wichtig sein <u>wie</u> praktische Erfahrungen. *(just as . . . as)*
3. <u>Je mehr</u> praktische Erfahrung man hat, <u>desto besser</u> sind die Berufschancen. *(the more . . . the better)*
4. Man wird auch <u>immer mehr</u> Zusatzqualifikationen suchen. *(more and more)*
5. <u>Sobald</u> man seine Prüfungen hinter sich hat, muss man bereit sein *(willing)*, dorthin zu ziehen, wo es Arbeit gibt. *(as soon as)*
6. Wer nicht flexibel ist, wird <u>weniger</u> Chancen auf dem Arbeitsmarkt haben und vielleicht auch <u>weniger</u> verdienen. *(fewer; less)*

E. Was bin ich? Nehmen Sie die *Hören-Sie-zu*-Übung auf Seite 318 als Muster und schreiben Sie ein paar Sätze! Lesen Sie laut, was Sie geschrieben haben! Die anderen sagen dann, was Sie sind.

F. An wen denke ich? Jemand in Ihrer Gruppe von vier oder fünf Studenten denkt an eine bekannte Person. Die andern dürfen bis zu 20 Fragen stellen, um herauszufinden, woran dieser Jemand denkt.

HÖREN SIE ZU! TRACK 25

Drei Lebensläufe *(résumés)*. Hören Sie sich an, was die drei jungen Deutschen über sich zu erzählen haben! Bevor Sie aber die folgenden Fragen beantworten, lesen Sie noch einmal kurz durch die *Vorschau* am Anfang des Kapitels!

Zum Erkennen: halbtags *(part-time)*; verlassen *(to leave)*; Schwerpunktfächer *(majors)*; der Vorarbeiter *(foreman)*; zum Militär *(to the army)*; der Autounfall *(accident)*

Richtig oder falsch?

<u>f</u> 1. Die Schmidts haben zwei Kinder, eine Tochter und einen Sohn.
<u>r</u> 2. Claudias Vater ist Ingenieur, ihre Mutter Sekretärin.
<u>f</u> 3. In ihrer Freizeit ist Claudia stinkfaul.
<u>r</u> 4. Wolf Wicke ist am 23.11.1987 geboren.
<u>f</u> 5. Wolf macht eine Lehre und geht zur Hauptschule.
<u>f</u> 6. Wolf war schon beim Militär.
<u>f</u> 7. Christinas Mutter lebt nicht mehr.
<u>r</u> 8. Christinas Bruder ist fünf Jahre älter als sie.
<u>f</u> 9. Nach dem Abitur hat sie zuerst ein Jahr gearbeitet.
<u>r</u> 10. Jetzt ist sie Medizinstudentin in Heidelberg.

G. Ein kleiner Aufsatz *(composition)*. Schreiben Sie 8–10 Sätze über eins der folgenden Themen!

1. Mein Lebenslauf
2. Was ich einmal werden möchte / wollte und warum
3. Mein Leben in . . . Jahren. So stelle ich mir mein Leben in in 10, 20 oder 30 Jahren vor.

Fokus — Aysel Özakin

Aysel Özakin (born in Turkey in 1942) came to Germany in 1981, studied French, and won several German literary prizes, including the award of city writer in Hamburg and a fellowship at the Günter Grass House. Today she lives in England, where she was married to a British painter, the late Bryan Ingham, and continues to write poetry, short prose, and novels, mostly in English. Part of her work belongs to Germany's **Ausländerliteratur,** a literature addressed to foreigners and Germans alike that describes her experiences in Germany. This story, taken from a larger collection called *Soll ich hier alt werden? Türkin in Deutschland,* takes place in Kreuzberg during the 1980s, a district in Berlin that was and still is home to many foreigners, especially Turkish people. It has also become associated with young Germans from the counterculture scene who, in their protest against materialism, occupied old houses slated to be torn down or modernized. They opposed the city's renovation program largely because it would force them out of their low-cost housing and prevent them from continuing the alternative lifestyle they preferred.

These literary pieces are extra readings rather than substitutes for the Einblicke readings. The latter are closely tied to the chapter grammar and also introduce new active vocabulary.

Die dunkelhaarigen Kinder von Berlin

Ich bemühe mich°, sie nicht aus den Augen zu verlieren. Auf dem Platz hinter der Kirche spielt ein junger Deutscher Gitarre und singt dazu. Leute stehen dabei, die° trinken Bier und essen Kuchen. Man hört laute Stimmen°, es wird geküsst°, gespielt. Die Gesichter sind rot, grün, blau oder gelb angemalt. Alle bewegen sich° im Rhythmus der Musik. Ich bemühe mich, sie nicht aus den Augen zu verlieren: dieses kleine Mädchen, diesen kleinen Körper mit dem Kopftuch°.—Der Sänger mit den dreckigen Jeans . . . brüllt° in das Mikrofon. Er protestiert gegen die Kleinbürgerlichkeit°, gegen die Polizei, gegen den Konservatismus.

Das kleine Mädchen ist angezogen wie eine arme, ältere Frau . . . Ich möchte wissen, wie sie sich Jahre später sehen wird.—Die Fete° der jungen Hausbesetzer° geht weiter. Das Mädchen läuft mit anderen dunklen Kindern zu dem Stand, der° für Kinder aufgebaut wurde° . . . Die blonden Kinder sitzen auf den Schultern der Erwachsenen°. Deren° Gesichter sind genauso bunt wie die° ihrer Kinder . . . Das kleine Mädchen mit dem Kopftuch nimmt einen Pinsel° . . . und tupft sich° einen roten Punkt auf die Nase. Sie schaut in den Spiegel und lächelt . . . Ein verkrampftes° Lächeln. Ein altes, ein einsames° Kind.

Ich stehe unmittelbar° hinter ihr . . . Wie sie, bin ich kein Teil dieser blonden Welt und werde es nie sein. Ich komme daher, wo° sie auch hergekommen. Ich hatte Gelegenheit°, mich zu entwickeln°, frei zu werden. Ich könnte hier tanzen, singen. Aber etwas in mir hält mich gefangen° . . .—Das Licht der Straßenlaterne° erhellt die Gesichter der fröhlichen jungen Leute. Das sind Menschen, die° ihre Jugend°, ihre Freiheit in ganzer Fülle° erleben wollen. Sie machen sich lustig über° allen Besitz° und über alle, die auch das Leben wie einen Besitz behandeln°. Sie sind mir sympathisch°, aber ich weiß, dass ich nie eine von ihnen sein kann.

Jetzt halte ich die Hand des kleinen Mädchens. Sie wird rot°, geniert sich° vielleicht, weil ich Türkisch spreche; vielleicht auch, weil sie sich angemalt hat . . . Was wird sie denken, wenn sie an ihre Kindheit hier zurückdenkt? . . . Ich frage sie, was ihr Vater macht.

„Er arbeitet in einer Schokoladenfabrik°."

„Und deine Mutter?"

„Spült°" . . .

„Würdest du lieber in der Türkei leben?"

„Ja."

„Warum?"

„Wir besuchen da meinen Opa." . . .

„Was möchtest du später werden?"

„Weiß nicht."

try / they / voices / they're kissing / move / head scarf / screams / narrow-mindedness / party / squatters / that / was put up / adults / their / those / paintbrush / dots / tense / lonely / right / from where / opportunity / develop / keeps me prisoner / lantern / who / youth / to the fullest / make fun of / possession / treat like / I like them. / blushes / is embarrassed / . . . factory / washes dishes

„Möchtet du so werden wie deine Mutter?"

„Nein."

„Wovon träumst du am meisten?"

„Von unseren Hühnern°."

chickens

Die anderen Kinder rufen°. Sie geht.

are calling

Der Sänger trägt jetzt ein Lied über seine Festnahme° vor° . . . Der Schmerz der Un-

arrest / sings

terdrückung° einigt° uns . . . Die Leute auf dem Platz tanzen—jeder so, wie er will. Nur

oppression / unites

mir gelingt es nicht°, meinen Körper vom Druck der Gedanken zu lösen°. Mein Land hat

I can't free myself from my oppressive thoughts.

. . . andere Sorgen. Es hat eine Art der Unterdrückung. Das hält mich zurück . . . Das

kleine Mädchen mit dem Kopftuch tanzt auch . . . Plötzlich erfriert° ihre ganze Freude,

freezes

die Freiheit. Sie schämt sich° der Bewegungen° ihres kleinen Körpers und verlässt° die

is embarrassed / movement / leaves

Menge°. Ich schaue ihr nach, bis ich sie aus den Augen° verliere. Der Himmel fängt an,

crowd / out of sight

Schnee zu streuen°. Das diesige° Grau des Abends senkt sich° auf den Platz.

It starts to snow / misty / descends

Aysel Özakin

Fragen

1. Wer feiert hier und was tun sie?
2. Was für Leute sind zu diesem Straßenfest gekommen?
3. Woran kann man die Hausbesetzer erkennen und woran die ausländischen Kinder?
4. Was hält die Autorin von den Hausbesetzern? Was hat sie mit ihnen gemeinsam?
5. Wen findet sie besonders interessant und warum?
6. Woher kommen beide, das kleine Mädchen und die Autorin?
7. Welchen Vorteil (*advantage*) hat Deutschland der Autorin gebracht?
8. Warum fühlt sie sich trotzdem nicht ganz wohl dort und kann sich nicht so richtig freuen? Was hält sie zurück?
9. Warum ist das kleine Mädchen so schüchtern (*shy*)? Was meinen Sie?
10. Wo arbeiten die Eltern der Kleinen?
11. Wovon träumt sie?
12. Möchte sie wie ihre Mutter werden? Warum (nicht)? Was denken Sie?
13. Warum fühlt sie sich bei den anderen, den „Blonden", nicht wohl?
14. Welche Bedeutung haben der Schnee und das „Grau des Abends"? Was denken Sie?
15. Wie finden Sie die Geschichte und warum?

You could expand questions to problems of all kinds of foreigners living in Germany, not just Turkish people. How do foreigners fare in Austria and Switzerland? Why are people homesick **(Heimweh haben)**? What do they miss? What must they do to improve their lot? Why is there xenophobia **(Ausländerhass)** among some people? Does that exist here in this country, too? How? Also, it might be useful to consult once more the chart in the pre-reading section of Kapitel 1 and make comparisons.

Video-Ecke

- The Minidrama *Anwälte gibt's wie Sand am Meer* shows two students who have taken a job as movers during their vacation. The work is physically demanding, and one of them especially seems to mind it. The other one, by contrast, is in good shape and enjoys some aspects of the job. As they are taking a break, they start projecting their life after school. They have quite different expectations.

- The Blickpunkt *Frauen im Beruf* introduces us to a woman who was born in Turkey, but raised in Berlin. She tells us about her childhood, why she preferred going to school over being at home, why she chose to become a lawyer specializing in women's issues, and about her hopes for the future. She also points out that being a woman in some professions is still not easy in Germany, and especially not if you are an immigrant. She feels that women have to know their rights and fight harder to get good jobs.

Web-Ecke

- For updates, self-assessment quizzes, and
online activities related to this chapter,
visit the **Wie geht's?** Web site at
http://wiegehts.heinle.com. You will visit a
Realschule in Langeoog and meet some of its
students. In addition, you'll compare statistics
dealing with national income and employment
figures, and have a glance at the life of Turkish
people in Germany.

Kapitel (13)

Das Studium

Blick in einen Hörsaal an der Universität

Lernziele

Vorschau
German universities

Gespräche + Wortschatz
University study and student life

Fokus
German bureaucracy
Studying in Germany
Christine Nöstlinger

Struktur
13.1 Subjunctive mood
13.2 Present-time general subjunctive (Subjunctive II)
13.3 Past-time general subjunctive

Einblicke
Ein Jahr drüben wäre super!
Christine Nöstlinger: *Vorurteile*

Video-Ecke
Minidrama: *Amerika ist anders*

Web-Ecke

Vorschau

German Universities

The first German universities were founded in the Middle Ages: Heidelberg in 1386, Cologne in 1388, Erfurt in 1392, Leipzig in 1409, and Rostock in 1419. In the beginning of the 19th century, Wilhelm von Humboldt redefined the purpose and mission of universities, viewing them as institutions for pure research and independent studies by the nation's preeminent minds. In time, however, it became obvious that this ideal conflicted with modern academic requirements.

In an effort to open opportunities to more students **(Studenten),** many practice-oriented universities of applied sciences **(Fachhochschulen)** have been founded.

There is no tradition of private universities in Germany. Practically all universities are state supported and require no tuition fees **(Studiengebühren);** students pay only minimal fees that include public transportation and health insurance. Under the Federal Education Promotion Act (**B**undes**a**usbildungs**f**örderungsgesetz = BAföG), students can obtain financial assistance, part of the amount as grant and the other part as an interest-free loan to be repaid in relatively small portions over several years after the student has finished his or her education (see www.das-neue-bafoeg.de). Principally, most courses of studies are accessible for everyone having gained the general German diploma for higher education **(Abitur).** Openings **(Studienplätze)** are filled on the basis of the average grade received in the **Abitur** and are allocated by a central office in Dortmund, with a certain percentage of places reserved for foreign applicants. In the past, Germans took it for granted that they could study at minimal cost for as long as they wanted. In recent years, however, as record numbers of young people have chosen the academic track, universities have come under extreme pressure to keep up with the influx of students. Admissions restrictions for certain subjects **(Numerus clausus)** are the norm at German universities, and discussions are underway to limit the number of semesters students may study.

Overall, there is a push for greater competition among universities and their faculties that would make German universities more attractive internationally. Since 1998, German universities are allowed to award internationally recognized bachelor's and master's degrees. These have actually become rather popular as graduates increasingly seek jobs outside of Germany. In addition to these new opportunities, a few private institutions of higher learning have begun competing for students, most of them with a strong business orientation. Although these universities are "private," almost all of them also receive support from public funds. In light of many sweeping changes in higher education, many students at public universities fear that eventually tuition payments will be introduced similar to those at American universities. Only time will tell.

DURCHSCHNITTLICHE STUDIENDAUER (IN JAHREN)

MEDIZIN	6,5
CHEMIE	6,4
INGENIEURWISSENSCHAFTEN	6,4
LEHRAMT	7,1
GEISTESWISSENSCHAFTEN	6,6
BETRIEBSWIRTSCHAFT	5,9
JURA	6,2

You might ask students to compare the average time needed in their own country to finish a degree in the fields mentioned.

339

Gespräche + Wortschatz

CD 6, Track 1

Bei der Immatrikulation

PETRA	Hallo, John! Wie geht's?
JOHN	Ganz gut. Und dir?
PETRA	Ach, ich kann nicht klagen. Was machst du denn da?
JOHN	Ich muss noch Immatrikulationsformulare ausfüllen.
PETRA	Soll ich dir helfen?
JOHN	Wenn du Zeit hast. Ich kämpfe immer mit der Bürokratie.
PETRA	Hast du deinen Pass dabei?
JOHN	Nein, wieso?
PETRA	Darin ist deine Aufenthaltserlaubnis; die brauchst du unbedingt.
JOHN	Ich kann ihn ja schnell holen.
PETRA	Tu das! Ich warte hier so lange auf dich.

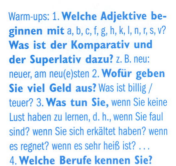

Warm-ups: 1. **Welche Adjektive beginnen mit** a, b, c, f, g, h, k, l, n, r, s, v? **Was ist der Komparativ und der Superlativ dazu?** z. B. neu: neuer, am neu(e)sten 2. **Wofür geben Sie viel Geld aus?** Was ist billig / teuer? 3. **Was tun Sie,** wenn Sie keine Lust haben zu lernen, d. h., wenn Sie faul sind? wenn Sie sich erkältet haben? wenn es regnet? wenn es sehr heiß ist? . . . 4. **Welche Berufe kennen Sie?**

Etwas später

JOHN	Hier ist mein Pass. Ich muss mich jetzt auch bald entscheiden, welche Seminare ich belegen will. Kannst du mir da auch helfen?
PETRA	Na klar. Was studierst du denn?
JOHN	Mein Hauptfach ist moderne Geschichte. Ich möchte Seminare über deutsche Geschichte und Literatur belegen.
PETRA	Hier ist mein Vorlesungsverzeichnis. Mal sehen, was sie dieses Semester anbieten.

Optional activity: Have students spell some of the new words in the dialogue to each other and see how long it takes the partner to recognize the word. While one spells something, the other should not look at the dialogue!

A: 1. Immatrikulationsformular 2. Pass 3. holen 4. Aufenthaltserlaubnis 5. belegen 6. sich interessiert 7. moderne Geschichte 8. Vorlesungsverzeichnis

A. Was fehlt?

1. John füllt gerade ein . . . aus. 2. Leider hat er seinen . . . nicht dabei. 3. Er muss ihn erst . . . 4. Im Pass ist seine . . . 5. John weiß noch nicht, was er . . . soll. 6. Petra fragt ihn, wofür er . . . 7. Sein Hauptfach ist . . . 8. Petra kann ihm helfen, weil sie ihr . . . dabei hat.

B. Jetzt sind Sie dran!
Sie sind bei einem Studienberater *(academic advisor),* weil Sie nicht so richtig wissen, was Sie studieren sollen. Dabei können Sie auch auf die Liste unter Übung B in *Zum Thema* sehen. Wechseln Sie sich ab!

Fokus — *German Bureaucracy*

All residents of Germany must register with the local registration office **(Einwohnermeldeamt)** within seven to 14 days of changing address. Likewise, when moving, residents give notice with an **Abmeldung.** Non-Germans who wish to stay in Germany longer than three months must have a residence permit **(Aufenthaltserlaubnis).** Because of the relatively high unemployment rate, a work permit **(Arbeitserlaubnis)** for non-EU citizens is difficult to obtain and usually is available only if a German or other EU-citizen cannot fill the job. Exceptions are made for students and participants in training programs.

Wortschatz 1

Das Studium *([course of] study)*

der Hörsaal, -säle	*lecture hall*	das Semester, -	*semester*
Mitbewohner, -	*housemate*	Seminar, -e	*seminar*
Professor, -en	*professor*	Stipendium,	*scholarship*
Student, -en, -en[1]	*(college) student*	Stipendien	
Zimmerkollege, -n, -n[2]	*roommate*	System, -e	*system*
das Fach, ⁻er	*subject*	die Fachrichtung, -en	*field of study*
Hauptfach, ⁻er	*major (field)*	(Natur)wissen-	*(natural)*
Nebenfach, ⁻er	*minor (field)*	schaft, -en	*science*
Labor, -s	*lab(oratory)*	Note, -n	*grade*
Quartal, -e	*quarter*	(Seminar)arbeit, -en	*here: term*
Referat, -e	*oral presentation*		*paper*

aus·füllen	*to fill out*
belegen	*to sign up for, take (a course)*
etwas dagegen haben	*to mind sth., lit. to have sth. against sth.*
Hast du etwas dagegen, wenn . . . ?	*Do you mind, if . . . ?*
holen	*to get (fetch)*
lehren	*to teach*
eine Prüfung machen	*to take an exam*
(eine Prüfung) bestehen, bestand, bestanden	*to pass (a test)*
(bei einer Prüfung) durch·fallen (fällt durch), fiel durch, ist durchgefallen	*to flunk, fail (a test)*
ein Referat halten (hält), hielt, gehalten	*to give an oral presentation*
teil·nehmen (nimmt teil), nahm teil, teilgenommen (an + acc.)	*to participate (in)*

Weiteres

Na klar.	*Of course.*
schwierig	*difficult*
wieso?	*why? how come?*

If students ask: *to cram* **pauken;** *to skip class* **schwänzen**

Wir nutzen nur 10% unseres geistigen Potenzials
A. Einstein

[1] The German word **Studenten** generally refers to university students or students at other institutions of higher learning.

[2] BUT: die Zimmerkollegin, -nen.

Zum Erkennen: klagen *(to complain);* das Immatrikulationsformular, -e *(enrollment form);* kämpfen *(to struggle, fight);* die Bürokratie *(here: red tape);* dabei haben *(to bring along);* das Vorlesungsverzeichnis, -se *(course catalog) AUCH:* die Fremdsprache, -n *(foreign language);* der Indikativ; der Konjunktiv, -e *(subjunctive);* analysieren; sich beziehen auf *(+ acc.) (to refer to);* erwähnen *(to mention);* herum·fragen *(to ask around);* hinzu·fügen *(to add);* einander *(each other)*

Aussprache: s, ß, st, sp

Lesen Sie auch Teil III. 6 und 12 in *Zur Aussprache* im *Arbeitsbuch!*

1. [z] sauber, sicher, Semester, Seminar, Pause
2. [s] Ausweis, Kurs, Professor, wissen, lassen, fleißig, Fuß, Grüße
3. [št] Studium, Stipendium, Stelle, studieren, bestehen, anstrengend
4. [st] zuerst, meistens, desto, Komponist, Künstler
5. [šp] Spiel, Sport, Spaß, Sprache, Beispiel, spät

CD 6, Track 2

Zum Thema

A. Deutsch als Fremdsprache *(foreign language).* Stellen Sie Ihrem Partner/Ihrer Partnerin Fragen über diesen Schein *(certificate).* Wechseln Sie sich dabei ab! Erzählen Sie dann den anderen in etwa fünf Sätzen, was Sie über Theresa Rumery herausgefunden haben!

Universität Regensburg
Lehrgebiet
Deutsch als Fremdsprache

Frau/Herrn **Theresa R u m e r y**

Aus   U S A

wird hiermit bescheinigt, dass sie/er an dem DEUTSCHKURS
Konversation - studienbegleitende Oberstufe I (2 SWS)
mit Referat zum Thema:

„Die Frauenbewegung in Deutschland"

im Winter-Semester 2001/02 regelmäßig teilgenommen hat.

Sie/Er hat den Kurs mit „sehr gut" (Note 1) bestanden/nicht bestanden.

Regensburg, den 09.02.2002

(Dr. Armin Wolff)
Akademischer Direktor

Bewertung:
Bestanden: Sehr gut (1); gut (2); befriedigend (3); ausreichend (4); *Nicht bestanden:* mangelhaft (5); ungenügend

Optional practice: Wohnen Sie im Studentenheim? Haben Sie Ihr eigenes Zimmer oder teilen Sie es mit einem Zimmerkollegen oder einer Zimmerkollegin? Wie heißt er/sie? Ist er/sie nett? Haben Sie im Studentenheim einen Kühlschrank? Kann man dort kochen? Wie ist das Essen in der Mensa? Wo essen Sie meistens? Wo essen Sie am liebsten?

NOTE: **Sehr gut (1)** = A; **gut (2)** = B; **befriedigend (3)** = C; **ausreichend (4)** = D; **mangelhaft (5),** = E; **ungenügend (6)** = F

B. Sag mal, was studierst du? Finden Sie Ihr Hauptfach in der Liste; wenn es nicht dabei ist, fügen Sie es hinzu *(add)!* Fragen Sie dann herum *(around),* wer das auch noch studiert!

BEISPIEL: **S1** Sag mal, was studierst du?
S2 Ich studiere Psychologie. Und du?
S1 Ich studiere Volkswirtschaft.

Accounting is part of **Betriebswirtschaft;** *the accountant* = **der Wirtschaftsprüfer, -.**

English
home economics
computer science
law
mining
business administration / nursing / political science
agriculture / Romance languages

teaching
forestry / mechanical engineering
civil engineering
(macro) economics
veterinary science
dentistry

Anglistik°	Gesundheitswissenschaft	Naturwissenschaft
Archäologie	Hauswirtschaft°	Pädagogik
Architektur	Informatik°	Pharmazie
Astronomie	Jura°	Philosophie
Bergbau°	Kommunikationswissenschaft	Physik
Betriebswirtschaft°	Krankenpflege°	Politologie°
Biochemie	Kunst	Psychologie
Biologie	Landwirtschaft°	Romanistik°
Chemie	Lebensmittelchemie	Soziologie
Elektrotechnik	Lehramt°	Sport
Forstwirtschaft°	Maschinenbau°	Theologie
Chemie	Linguistik	Tiefbau°
Geographie	Mathematik	Volkswirtschaft°
Geologie	Medizin	Tiermedizin°
Germanistik	Mineralogie	Zahnmedizin°
Geschichte	Musik	

C. Fragen übers Studium. Fragen Sie einen Nachbarn/eine Nachbarin, . . . !

1. wie viele Kurse er/sie dieses Semester / Quartal belegt hat und welche
2. welche Kurse er/sie besonders gut findet, und worin er/sie die besten Noten hat

3. ob er/sie viele Arbeiten schreiben muss; wenn ja, in welchen Fächern
4. ob er/sie schon Referate gehalten hat; wenn ja, worin und worüber
5. ob er/sie außer Deutsch noch andere Sprachen spricht oder lernt
6. wie lange er/sie noch studieren muss
7. was er/sie danach macht
8. wie die Chancen sind, in seinem/ihrem Beruf eine gute Stelle zu bekommen
9. in welchen Berufen es momentan schwierig ist, Arbeit zu finden
10. wo es noch bessere Möglichkeiten gibt

C. This exercise could also be done in writing.

HÖREN SIE ZU!　　TRACK 26

Ein guter Start

Zum Erkennen: das Privileg; wissenschaftlich *(scientific)*; wirtschaftswis-
senschaftlich *(economic)*; verbessern *(to improve)*; Vollzeitstudenten; die Abschlussarbeit *(thesis)*; Karriere *(career)*

Was stimmt?

1. Den MBA _____.
   a. gibt es nur in Amerika　　b. wird es bald auch in Deutschland geben
   c. gibt es jetzt auch in Deutschland
2. Die Studenten am Europa-Institut kommen vor allem aus _____.
   a. Deutschland　　**b.** dem Ausland　　c. Amerika
3. Dieses Europa-Institut ist in _____.
   a. Saarbrücken　　b. Heidelberg　　c. Worms
4. Terry Furman war in Deutschland auf dem Gymnasium und hat dann in _____ Jura
   studiert.
   a. Frankreich　　b. Spanien　　**c.** England
5. Der Franzose Dominique Laurent ist _____ und verspricht sich vom MBA bessere
   Berufschancen.
   a. Rechtsanwalt　　**b.** Ingenieur　　c. Geschäftsmann
6. Am Ende des MBAs steht _____ mit einer Abschlussarbeit.
   a. ein Praktikum　　b. eine Lehre　　c. eine Auslandsreise
7. Die Wissenschaftliche Hochschule in Koblenz ist _____.
   a. schon alt　　**b.** privat　　c. öffentlich
8. Dort kostet der MBA _____.
   a. nichts　　b. nicht sehr viel　　**c.** viel Geld

Struktur

13.1 Subjunctive mood

Until now, almost all sentences in this book have been in the INDICATIVE MOOD.
Sentences in the indicative mood are assumed to be based on reality. Sometimes, however, we want to speculate on matters that are unreal, uncertain, or unlikely; or we wish
for something that cannot be; or we want to approach other people less directly, more
discretely and politely. For that purpose we use the SUBJUNCTIVE MOOD.

Assure students that there is nothing extra-
ordinary about the subjunctive. It is used
all the time in everyday speech.

1. Polite requests or questions

Would you like a cup of coffee?

Would you pass me the butter?

Could you help me for a moment?

2. Hypothetical statements and questions

He should be here any moment.

What would you do?

You should have been there.

3. Wishes

If only I had more time.

I wish you would hurry up.

I wish I had known that.

4. Unreal conditions

If I had time, I'd go to the movies. (But since I don't have time, I'm not going.)

If the weather were good, we'd go for a walk. (But since it's raining, we won't go.)

If you had told me, I could have helped you. (But since you didn't tell me, I couldn't help you.)

Contrast the sentences above with real conditions:

If I have time, I'll go to the movies.

If the weather is good, we'll go for a walk.

In real conditions, the possibility exists that the events will take place. In unreal conditions, this possibility does not exist or is highly unlikely.

NOTE:

- The forms of the PRESENT-TIME SUBJUNCTIVE are derived from the simple past: *If I told you (now) . . .*

- Those of the PAST-TIME SUBJUNCTIVE are derived from the past perfect: *If you had told me (earlier) . . .*

- Another very common way to express the subjunctive mood is with the form *would: I'd go; I would not stay home.*

Übung

A: This exercise is intended to give students a feeling for the subjunctive vs. the indicative. You might ask them to look for such sentences in conversation or in assignments for other subjects. You also can bring similar sentences to class until the students are confident about the subjunctive. They must become aware of this difference in English before trying to cope with it in German.

A. Indikativ oder Konjunktiv *(subjunctive)?* Analysieren Sie die Sätze und sagen Sie, ob sie im Indikativ oder Konjunktiv sind. Entscheiden Sie auch, ob sie sich auf jetzt, früher oder später beziehen *(refer to)!*

BEISPIEL: If you don't ask, you won't know.   **= indicative: now or later**
How would you know?   **= subjunctive: now**
What would you have done?   **= subjunctive: earlier**

A. 1. indicative, now or later 2. subjunctive, earlier 3. subjunctive, now 4. indicative, later 5. subjunctive, now 6. indicative, earlier 7. subjunctive, now 8. subjunctive, earlier 9. subjunctive, now or later 10. subjunctive, earlier 11. subjunctive, earlier 12. indicative, now or later

1. If she can, she'll write.
2. If only I had known that.
3. They could be here any minute.
4. Will you take the bike along?
5. Would you please hold this?
6. I had known that for a long time.
7. We should really be going.
8. I wish you had told me that.
9. If you could stay over a Saturday, you could fly for a lower fare.
10. What would they have done if you hadn't come along?
11. If we had had the money, we'd have bought it.
12. If she has the money, she'll give it to us.

13.2 Present-time general subjunctive

German has two subjunctives. The one most commonly used is often referred to in grammar books as the GENERAL SUBJUNCTIVE or SUBJUNCTIVE II. (the SPECIAL SUBJUNCTIVE or SUBJUNCTIVE I, primarily found in written German, is explained in Chapter 15.)

1. Forms

The PRESENT-TIME SUBJUNCTIVE refers to the present (now) or the future (later). As in English, its forms are derived from the forms of the simple past. You already know the verb endings from having used the **möchte**-forms of **mögen,** which are actually subjunctive forms. All verbs in the subjunctive have these endings:

Infinitive	Simple Past, Indicative	Present-time Subjunctive
mögen	mochte	möchte
	mochtest	möchtest
	mochte	möchte
	mochten	möchten
	mochtet	möchtet
	mochten	möchten

Point out that in many verbs, the umlaut constitutes the difference between indicative and subjunctive. Omitting the umlaut is not just a misspelling or a minor error. In quizzes and tests, students should lose full points for incorrect use of it.

a. T-verbs (weak verbs)

The present-time subjunctive forms of regular t-verbs are identical to those of the simple past. Their use usually becomes clear from context.

Infinitive	Simple Past, Indicative	Present-time Subjunctive
glauben	glaubte	glaubte
antworten	antwortete	antwortete

Wenn Sie mir nur **glaubten!**   If only you believed me!
Wenn er mir nur **antwortete!**   If only he would answer me!

b. Irregular t-verbs (mixed verbs)

Most of the irregular t-verbs, which include the modals, have an umlaut in the present-time subjunctive. Exceptions are **sollen** and **wollen.**

Infinitive	Simple Past, Indicative	Present-time Subjunctive
haben	hatte	hätte
bringen	brachte	brächte
denken	dachte	dächte
wissen	wusste	wüsste
dürfen	durfte	dürfte
müssen	musste	müsste
können	konnte	könnte
mögen	mochte	möchte
sollen	sollte	sollte
wollen	wollte	wollte

Hättest du Zeit?   Would you have time?
Könntest du kommen?   Could you come?

Modals with an umlaut in the infinitive also have one in the subjunctive (**dürfte, könnte, möchte, müsste**), whereas those without an umlaut do not have one in the subjunctive (**sollte, wollte**).

haben
ich hätte	wir hätten
du hättest	ihr hättet
er hätte	sie hätten

wissen
ich wüsste	wir wüssten
du wüsstest	ihr wüsstet
er wüsste	sie wüssten

Refer students to part 7a or b in the Appendix.

c. N-verbs *(strong verbs)*

The present-time subjunctive forms of n-verbs add the subjunctive endings to the past stem. If the past stem vowel is an **a, o,** or **u,** the subjunctive forms have an umlaut.

Infinitive	Simple Past, Indicative	Present-time Subjunctive
sein	war	**wäre**
werden	wurde	**würde**
bleiben	blieb	**bliebe**
fahren	fuhr	**führe**
finden	fand	**fände**
fliegen	flog	**flöge**
geben	gab	**gäbe**
gehen	ging	**ginge**
laufen	lief	**liefe**
sehen	sah	**sähe**
tun	tat	**täte**

sein		gehen	
ich wäre	wir wär**en**	ich ginge	wir ging**en**
du wär**est**	ihr wär**et**	du ging**est**	ihr ging**et**
er wäre	sie wär**en**	er ginge	sie ging**en**

Wenn ich du **wäre, ginge** ich nicht.	*If I were you, I wouldn't go.*
Wenn er **flöge, könnte** er morgen hier sein.	*If he were to fly, he could be here tomorrow.*

Because of its simplicity, the **würde**-form is very common in everyday speech. It is preferred especially where there are irregular subjunctive forms **(kennte, nennte; begönne, hülfe, stünde,** etc.), which we avoid in this text.

d. **Würde**-form

In conversation, speakers of German commonly use the subjunctive forms of **haben, sein, werden, wissen,** and the modals.

Hättest du Zeit?	*Would you have time?*
Das **wäre** schön.	*That would be nice.*
Was **möchtest** du tun?	*What would you like to do?*
Wenn ich das nur **wüsste!**	*If only I knew that!*

For the subjunctive forms of other verbs, however, German speakers frequently substitute a simpler verb phrase that closely corresponds to the English *would + infinitive*. It is <u>preferred</u> when the subjunctive form is identical to the indicative form, as is the case with t-verbs and with the plural forms of n-verbs whose subjunctive forms don't have an umlaut (e.g., **gingen**). It is also frequently used in the conclusion clause of contrary-to-fact conditions.

Das täte ich nicht.	
Das **würde** ich nicht **tun.**	*I wouldn't do that.*
Wenn er mir nur glaubte!	
Wenn er mir nur **glauben würde!**	*If only he would believe me!*
Wir gingen lieber ins Kino.	
Wir **würden** lieber ins Kino **gehen.**	*We would rather go to the movies.*
Wenn sie Zeit hätte, käme sie mit.	
Wenn sie Zeit hätte, **würde** sie **mitkommen.**	*If she had time, she would come along.*

Wenn ich meinen Eltern alles erzählen würde, na dann gute Nacht!

2. Uses

You are already familiar with the most common uses of the subjunctive in English. Here are examples of these uses in German.

a. Polite requests or questions

Möchtest du eine Tasse Kaffee?	*Would you like a cup of coffee?*
Würdest du mir die Butter geben?	*Would you pass me the butter?*
Dürfte ich etwas Käse haben?	*Could I have some cheese?*
Könntest du mir einen Moment helfen?	*Could you help me for a minute?*

b. Hypothetical statements and questions

Er sollte jeden Moment hier sein.	*He should be here any minute.*
Das wäre schön.	*That would be nice.*
Es wäre mir lieber, wenn er hier wäre.	*I'd prefer it if he would be here.*
Was würdest du tun?	*What would you do?*
Ich würde ihm alles erzählen.	*I'd tell him everything.*

c. Wishes

- Wishes starting with **Wenn . . .** usually add **nur** after the subject or any pronoun object.

Wenn ich nur mehr Zeit hätte!	*If only I had more time!*
Wenn er mir nur glauben würde!	*If only he'd believe me!*

- Wishes starting with **Ich wünschte, . . .** have BOTH CLAUSES in the subjunctive.

Ich wünschte, ich hätte mehr Zeit.	*I wish I had more time.*
Ich wünschte, du würdest dich beeilen.	*I wish you'd hurry.*

d. Unreal conditions

Wenn ich morgen Zeit hätte, würde ich mit dir ins Kino gehen.	*If I had time tomorrow, I'd go to the movies with you.*
Wenn das Wetter schöner wäre, würden wir draußen essen.	*If the weather were nicer, we'd eat outside.*
Wenn wir euch helfen könnten, würden wir das tun.	*If we could help you, we would do it.*

Contrast the preceding sentences with real conditions.

Wenn ich morgen Zeit habe, gehe ich mit dir ins Kino.	*If I have time tomorrow, I'll go to the movies with you.*
Wenn das Wetter schön ist, essen wir draußen.	*If the weather is nice, we'll eat outside.*
Wenn wir euch helfen können, tun wir es.	*If we can help you, we'll do it.*

Wenn ich ein Vöglein° wär'
und auch zwei Flügel° hätt',
flög' ich zu dir.
Weil's aber nicht kann sein,
weil's aber nicht kann sein,
bleib' ich allhier°.

Mein Hut°, der hat drei Ecken.
Drei Ecken hat mein Hut.
Und hätt' er nicht drei Ecken,
dann wär' es nicht mein Hut.

Translating these songs might help clarify the difference between the indicative and the subjunctive. You could sing them, too. **"Mein Hut . . ."** can be a lot of fun as you leave out one word in each round and replace it with a gesture.

little bird

wings

hat

right here

WAS WÄRE ICH NUR OHNE DICH?

Übungen

B. Was tun? Auf Englisch bitte!

1. Wohin möchtest du gehen?
2. Wir könnten uns einen Film ansehen.
3. Wir sollten uns eine Zeitung holen.
4. Ich würde gern ins Kino gehen.
5. Ich wünschte, ich wäre nicht so müde.
6. Ich würde lieber zu Hause bleiben.
7. Hättest du etwas dagegen, wenn ich ein paar Freunde mitbringen würde.
8. Es wäre mir lieber, wenn wir allein gehen würden.
9. Hättest du morgen Abend Zeit?
10. Ich ginge heute lieber früh ins Bett.
11. Morgen könnte ich länger schlafen.
12. Dann wäre ich nicht so müde.
13. Du könntest dann auch deine Freunde mitbringen.
14. Wäre das nicht eine bessere Idee?

C. Geben Sie das Imperfekt und die Konjunktivform!

BEISPIEL:	ich hole	**ich holte**	**ich holte**
	du bringst	**du brachtest**	**du brächtest**
	er kommt	**er kam**	**er käme**

1. ich frage, mache, hoffe, belege, lächele, studiere, versuche
2. du arbeitest, antwortest, beendest, erwartest, öffnest, heiratest
3. er muss, kann, darf, soll, mag
4. wir bringen, denken, wissen, haben
5. ihr bleibt, schlaft, fliegt, seid, gebt, esst, singt, sitzt, tut, seht, versprecht, werdet, fahrt

D. Reisepläne. Was fehlt?

1. **BEISPIEL: Bauers *würden* nach Wien *fahren*.**
   a. Dort _würden_ wir erst eine Stadtrundfahrt machen.
   b. Dann _würde_ Dieter sicher den Stephansdom ansehen. Und du _könntest_ dann durch die Kärtner Straße bummeln. Natürlich _könntet_ ihr auch in die Hofburg gehen.
   c. Ja, und einen Abend _würden_ wir in Grinzing feiern.
   d. Das _würde_ euch gefallen.

2. **BEISPIEL: Ute *führe* in die Schweiz.**
   a. Ich _könnte_ mit ein paar Freunden in die Schweiz fahren. (können)
   b. Erst _führen_ wir an den Bodensee. (fahren)
   c. Von dort _ginge_ es weiter nach Zürich und Bern. (gehen)
   d. In Zürich _sähe_ ich mir gern das Thomas-Mann-Archiv (*archives*) _an_. (ansehen)
   e. Ihr _solltet_ auch nach Genf fahren. (sollen)
   f. Dort _müsstest_ du Französisch sprechen. (müssen)
   g. Das _wäre_ keine schlechte Idee! (sein)

E. Sagen Sie's höflicher (*more politely*)!

1. **BEISPIEL: Können Sie uns die Mensa zeigen?**
   Könnten Sie uns die Mensa zeigen?

   a. Darf ich kurz mit Ihnen sprechen? b. Haben Sie Lust mitzukommen? c. Können wir uns an einen Tisch setzen? d. Haben Sie etwas Zeit?

2. **BEISPIEL:**   Rufen Sie mich morgen an!
Würden / Könnten Sie mich morgen anrufen?

a. Erzählen Sie uns von der Reise! b. Bringen Sie die Fotos mit! c. Machen Sie mir eine Tasse Kaffee! d. Geben Sie mir die Milch!

F. Wünsche

1. **Beginnen Sie mit „Ich wünschte, . . . "!**

BEISPIEL: Das Seminar ist schwer.
Ich wünschte, das Seminar wäre nicht so schwer.

a. Ich muss viel lesen. b. Das nimmt viel Zeit. c. Ich bin müde. d. Ihr seid faul.

2. **Beginnen Sie mit „Wenn . . . nur . . . "!**

BEISPIEL: Ich wünschte, ich könnte schlafen.
Wenn ich nur schlafen könnte!

a. Ich wünschte, wir hätten keine Referate.
b. Ich wünschte, ich wüsste mehr über das Thema Wirtschaft.
c. Ich wünschte, du könntest mir helfen.
d. Ich wünschte, diese Woche wäre schon vorbei.

G. Wiederholen Sie die Sätze im Konjunktiv!

BEISPIEL: Wenn das Wetter schön ist, kann man die Berge sehen.
Wenn das Wetter schön wäre, könnte man die Berge sehen.

1. Wenn es möglich ist, zeige ich euch das Schloss.
2. Wenn du das Schloss sehen willst, musst du dich beeilen.
3. Wenn ihr zu spät kommt, ärgert ihr euch.
4. Wenn das Schloss zu ist, können wir in den Schlosspark gehen.
5. Wenn ihr mehr sehen wollt, müsst ihr länger hier bleiben.

H. Eine besondere Art von Studium. Was fehlt?

Studium mit staatlichen britischen Abschlüssen (auch ohne Abitur ab 25 Jahre).
2 Jahre EURO-AKADEMIE Köln + Praktikum + 1 Jahr Uni in Großbritannien:
B.A. (Hons.) in European Business Management
- Management + Wirtschaft + Sprachen
MBA - Master of Business Administration
- 2 Jahre Köln + 2 Jahre Uni in GB
Beginn: Jährlich August und Februar. Prospekt anfordern! Tel. 02 21/ 73 60 74
EURO AKADEMIE, Elsa-Brändström-Straße 8 · 50668 Köln

1. Günther, ich habe gerade von einer Euro-Akademie gelesen, wo man seinen B.A. in Management, Wirtschaft und Sprachen <u>machen könnte</u>. *(could make)* 2. Dafür <u>müsste</u> man zwei Jahre in an dieser Akademie in Köln und dann ein Jahr in England <u>studieren</u>. *(would have to study)* 3. Dazu <u>käme</u> noch ein Praktikum. *(would come)* 4. Wenn du <u>wolltest</u>, <u>könntest</u> du dort auch deinen Magister (M.A.) <u>machen</u>. *(wanted, could make)* 5. Dazu <u>müsstest</u> du außer in Köln noch zwei Jahre an der Uni in England <u>studieren</u>. *(would have to study)* 6. Weil du über 25 Jahre alt bist, <u>bräuchtest</u> du kein Abitur. *(would need)* 7. Mensch, <u>wäre</u> das nicht was für dich? *(would be)* 8. Das ganze Studium <u>dürfte</u> nicht länger als vier Jahre <u>dauern</u>. *(ought to take)* 9. Dann <u>hättest</u> du deinen Abschluss in der Tasche. *(would have)* 10. Du <u>könntest</u> entweder im August oder im Februar <u>anfangen / beginnen</u>. *(could start)* 11. Ich <u>wünschte</u>, ich <u>wäre</u> noch einmal so jung wie du! *(wish, were)* 12. Ich <u>täte / würde</u> das <u>/tun</u>. *(would do)*

I. Zwei wichtige Fragen für junge Deutsche: Was wäre, wenn . . . ? Schauen Sie sich die folgenden Tabellen an und stellen Sie den anderen in Ihrer Gruppe Fragen darüber! Beschreiben Sie dann, wie das bei ihnen aussähe, was ihnen wichtig und weniger wichtig wäre. Wenn Sie wollen, können Sie auch eigene Aussagen hinzufügen.

BEISPIEL: **Wenn ich so leben könnte, wie ich wollte, zöge ich . . .**
Wenn meine Oma mir so viel Geld hinterlassen würde, brächte ich . . .

. . . Sie so leben könnten, wie Sie wollten?	
als Globetrotter um die Welt ziehen	25%
als Single in einer Penthouse-Wohnung wohnen	16%
als Handwerker/in in einer Kleinstadt leben	14%
als Chirurg/in mit Familie in einer Villa wohnen	13%
als Künstler in einem alten Haus leben	12%
als Playboy / Model immer da sein, wo etwas los ist	8%
Aktivist/in für Greenpeace sein	4%
als Bundespräsident/in im Schloss Bellevue wohnen	4%

. . . Ihre Oma Ihnen 5000 Euro hinterlassen würde?	
Ich bringe das Geld zur Bank.	43%
Ich verreise.	25%
Ich kaufe mir Kleidung.	20%
Ich kaufe etwas Größeres.	19%
Ich frage mich, wo die restlichen 45 000 Euro sind.	10%
Ich feiere mit Freunden und zahle alles.	6%
Ich kaufe Aktien *(stocks)*.	5%
Ich gebe den Armen etwas.	3%

J. Wie geht's weiter?

BEISPIEL: Ich wäre glücklich, wenn . . .
Ich wäre glücklich, wenn ich gut Deutsch sprechen könnte. Und du?

1. Ich wäre froh, wenn . . .
2. Ich fände es prima, wenn . . .
3. Es wäre furchtbar, wenn . . .
4. Ich würde mich ärgern, wenn . . .
5. Ich würde sparen, wenn . . .
6. Ich wüsste, was ich täte, wenn . . .

K. Dürfte ich . . . ? Fragen Sie Ihren Partner/Ihre Partnerin um Erlaubnis *(for permission)* und hören Sie, was er/sie dazu zu sagen hat, ob er/sie es erlaubt oder nicht! Wechseln Sie sich ab!

1. mal kurz dein Buch haben
2. deine Hausaufgaben sehen / abschreiben *(copy)*
3. mein Radio anmachen / eine neue Kassette spielen
4. deinen Kuli / deinen Pullover . . . borgen *(borrow)*
5. für dich zahlen / dir die Rechnung geben
6. deine Kreditkarte / dein Handy / dein Auto . . . borgen

13.3 Past-time general subjunctive

You already know that a simple-past form in English can express the present-time subjunctive (referring to *now* or *later*). The past-perfect form, or *would have* + participle, expresses the same thought in the PAST-TIME SUBJUNCTIVE (referring to *earlier*).

NOW OR LATER:	If I *had* time, I *would go* with you.
EARLIER:	If I *had had* time, I *would have gone* with you.

If students are not comfortable with English sentences in the past-time subjunctive, set aside a few minutes to make up some sample sentences.

1. Forms

   a. In German, the forms of the past-time subjunctive are based on the forms of the <u>past perfect.</u> The past-time subjunctive is very easy to learn because it simply consists of a form of **hätte** or **wäre** plus the past participle:

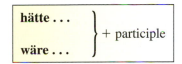

Hättest du das **getan?**	*Would you have done that?*
Das **hätte** ich nicht **getan.**	*I wouldn't have done that.*
Ich **wäre** lieber ins Kino **gegangen.**	*I would have rather gone to the movies.*
Wärest du nicht lieber ins Kino **gegangen?**	*Wouldn't you have rather gone to the movies?*
Ich wünschte, du **hättest** mir das **gesagt!**	*I wish you had told me that!*
Wenn ich das **gewusst hätte, wären** wir ins Kino **gegangen.**	*If I had known that, we would have gone to the movies.*

   b. All modals follow this pattern in the past-time subjunctive:

This double construction of *verb infinitive* + *modal infinitive* is also called the DOUBLE INFINITIVE CONSTRUCTION. You may wish to introduce that term.

> **hätte . . .** + verb infinitive + modal infinitive

Du **hättest** mir das **sagen sollen.**	*You should have told me that.*
Wir **hätten** noch ins Kino **gehen können.**	*We still could have gone to the movies.*

   For now, avoid using these forms in dependent clauses.

2. Uses

   The past-time subjunctive is used for the same purposes as the present-time subjunctive. Note that there are no polite requests in the past.

   a. Hypothetical statements and questions

Ich wäre zu Hause geblieben.	*I would have stayed home.*
Was hättet ihr gemacht?	*What would you have done?*
Hättet ihr mitkommen wollen?	*Would you have wanted to come along?*

   b. Wishes

Wenn ich das nur gewusst hätte!	*If only I had known that!*
Ich wünschte, du wärest da gewesen.	*I wish you had been there.*

   c. Unreal conditions

Wenn du mich gefragt hättest, hätte ich es dir gesagt.	*If you had asked me, I would have told you.*
Wenn du da gewesen wärest, hättest du alles gehört.	*If you had been there, you would have heard everything.*

Übungen

L. Sagen Sie die Sätze in der Vergangenheit!

1. **BEISPIEL:**   Sie würde das tun.
   Sie hätte das getan.

   a. Sie würde euch anrufen. b. Ihr würdet ihr helfen. c. Ihr würdet schnell kommen. d. Du würdest alles für sie tun.

2. **BEISPIEL:**   Hannes sollte nicht so viel Schokolade essen.
   Hannes hätte nicht so viel Schokolade essen sollen.

   a. Wir dürften ihm keine Schokolade geben. b. Das sollten wir wissen. c. Er könnte auch Obst essen. d. Wir müssten besser aufpassen.

M. Was wäre gewesen, wenn . . . ?

1. **Wiederholen Sie die Sätze in der Vergangenheit!**

   BEISPIEL: Wenn ich es wüsste, würde ich nicht fragen.
   Wenn ich es gewusst hätte, hätte ich nicht gefragt.

   a. Wenn wir eine Theatergruppe hätten, würde ich mitmachen.
   b. Wenn der Computer billiger wäre, würden wir ihn kaufen.
   c. Wenn ich Hunger hätte, würde ich mir etwas kochen.
   d. Wenn sie fleißiger arbeitete, würde es ihr besser gehen.

2. **Und dann?** Was würden Sie tun oder hätten Sie getan? Wechseln Sie sich ab!

   BEISPIEL: **S1**   **Ich hatte keinen Hunger. Wenn ich Hunger gehabt hätte, wäre ich in die Küche gegangen.**
   S2   **Und dann?**
   S1   **Dann hätte ich mir ein Wurstbrot gemacht.**

   a. Gestern hat es geregnet. Wenn das Wetter schön gewesen wäre, . . .
   b. Ich bin nicht lange auf der Party geblieben. Wenn ich zu lange gefeiert hätte, . . .
   c. Natürlich hatten wir letzte Woche Vorlesungen. Wenn wir keine Vorlesungen gehabt hätten, . . .

N. Hoppla, hier fehlt was! Wie war das bei deinen Großeltern?

1. **Ein paar imaginäre** *(imaginary)* **Großeltern.** Hören Sie, was Ihnen Ihr Partner/Ihre Partnerin mit Hilfe der Information im Anhang über seinen/ihren imaginären Großvater vorliest *(reads to you)*! Schauen Sie dabei auf die Tabelle unten *(chart below)* und machen Sie ein Kreuz *(check mark)* unter **Ja** oder **Nein,** je nachdem *(depending on)*, was der Großvater getan oder nicht getan hat. Wechseln Sie sich dann ab! Während Sie den unteren Text (S1) über Ihre imaginäre Großmutter vorlesen, macht Ihr Partner/Ihre Partnerin Kreuze in seine/ihre Tabelle im Anhang. Vergleichen Sie am Ende, ob die ausgefüllten Tabellen stimmen!

   Und was sagt Ihnen Ihr Partner/Ihre Partnerin?

	Ja	Nein
Der Opa ist aus Deutschland gekommen.	x	
Die Familie ist mit dem Schiff gefahren.		
Der Opa ist gern nach Amerika gekommen.		
Die Familie hat in New York gewohnt.		
Er ist Polizist geworden.		
Er konnte gut singen.		
Er hat gelernt, Klavier zu spielen.		
Er ist dieses Jahr nach Deutschland gefahren.		

S1: Meine Oma ist gern zur Schule gegangen. Sie war besonders gut in Mathe. Wenn ihre Familie Geld gehabt hätte, hätte sie gern studiert. Sie wäre furchtbar gern Lehrerin geworden. Aber sie musste als Kindermädchen *(nanny)* bei einer reichen Familie arbeiten. Dann hat sie meinen Großvater kennen gelernt und geheiratet. Meine Oma liebt Kinder und sie hätte gern eine große Familie gehabt. Sie hatten aber nur ein Kind. Sie ist immer gern gereist. Wenn mein Großvater länger gelebt hätte, hätten sie zusammen eine große Weltreise gemacht.

Mathe = Mathematik

2. **Meine Großeltern.** Erzählen Sie einander *(each other)* von Ihren wirklichen Großeltern und stellen Sie auch Fragen über sie!

N.2: This could also be a written exercise.

Fokus — *Studying in Germany*

Studying in Germany is considerably different from studying in North America. Students enter the university with a broad general education received during their years at the **Gymnasium** and can therefore immediately focus on a chosen major **(Hauptfach)** without being concerned about subjects unrelated to their respective course of studies.

All academic syllabi are divided into so-called basic and main studies. Depending on the particular major, students have to attend a certain number of required classes but are still free to choose their own emphasis of studies by selecting from a variety of optional classes. Lecture courses **(Vorlesungen)** have little discussion and a written exam at the end of the term; seminars **(Seminare),** require research papers and class presentations; **Übungen** have discussions, daily assignments, and a test **(Klausur)** at the end. A few years ago, students still had to collect certificates **(Scheine)** for each attended course; today, the partial introduction of the international credit-point system at many institutions has changed that.

Ultimately, students are responsible for their own progress and for acquiring the necessary knowledge to pass the qualifying intermediate exam **(Zwischenprüfung)** and eventually the comprehensive final exam **(Abschlussprüfung).** The basic degree in the arts and humanities is equivalent to the American M.A. **(Magister);** in the natural sciences and in engineering, students acquire an M.Sc. or M.Eng. degree **(Diplom).** Some graduates choose to continue their studies to obtain a doctorate. Those who wish to become teachers, medical doctors, or lawyers must pass a comprehensive state exam **(1. Staatsexamen)** in their field, followed by a second exam **(2. Staatsexamen)** after an internship of several years. The academic calendar is officially divided into a winter semester (from mid-October to mid-February) and a summer semester (from about mid-April to mid-July, varying somewhat from state to

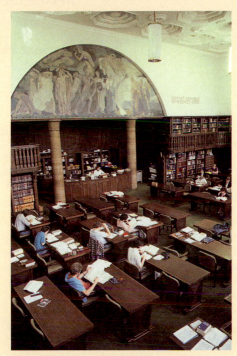

In der Bibliothek in Tübingen

state. The vacation period **(vorlesungsfreie Zeit;** literally: a period without classes)—a two-month term in spring and three months in late summer—is intended for students to catch up on work, to take a job, or to go on vacation. German universities are academically self-governing and are headed by a president **(Rektor)** elected for several years. Purely administrative matters are handled by a permanent staff of civil servants under the direction of a chancellor **(Kanzler).**

Foreigners can study one or two semesters in Germany through one of the many partnerships with other universities abroad. In addition to this, there are more than 150 European study programs that stipulate that at least two semesters must be completed abroad (see www.studieren-in-deutschland.de).

Zusammenfassung

O. Indikativ oder Konjunktiv? Was bedeutet das auf Englisch?

1. Wenn er uns besuchte, brachte er immer Blumen mit.
2. Können Sie mir Horsts Telefonnummer geben?
3. Wenn du früher ins Bett gegangen wärest, wärest du jetzt nicht so müde.
4. Gestern konnten sie nicht kommen, aber sie könnten uns morgen besuchen.
5. Er sollte gestern anrufen.
6. Ich möchte Architektur studieren.
7. Sie waren schon um 6 Uhr aufgestanden.
8. Ich wünschte, er ließe nicht immer alles auf dem Sofa liegen.

P. Guter Rat ist teuer *(hard to come by)*

1. **Was soll ich tun?** Jemand in Ihrer Gruppe erwähnt *(mentions)* ein Problem, echt *(real)* oder nicht echt (zum Beispiel: er/sie hat kein Geld oder keine Energie / Hunger oder Durst / etwas verloren . . .), und die anderen geben Rat.

   BEISPIEL: Ich bin immer so müde.
   Wenn ich du wäre, würde ich früher ins Bett gehen.

2. **Was hätte ich tun sollen?** Geben Sie Rat, was man tun oder nicht hätte tun sollen!

   BEISPIEL: Ich habe meine Schlüssel verloren.
   Du hättest besser aufpassen sollen.

Q. Kommst du mit? Auf Deutsch bitte!

1. Would you *(sg. fam.)* like to go **(fahren)** with us to Salzburg? 2. We could go by train and stay in the youth hostel. 3. It ought to be quieter now than in the summer. 4. That would be nice. 5. I'd come along, if I could find my youth hostel ID, **(Jugendherbergsausweis).** 6. I wish you *(pl. fam.)* had thought of it earlier. 7. Then I could have looked for it. 8. If I only knew where it is. 9. I'd like to see the Mirabell Garden, the Mozart house, and the castle **(die Burg).** 10. The city is supposed to be wonderful. 11. Without my ID card **(Ausweis)** I'd have to stay home.—Here it is! 12. If you *(sg. fam.)* hadn't talked **(reden)** so much, you'd have found it more quickly.

Blick auf Salzburg mit seiner Burg

Einblicke

Lesestrategie: Wer sagt was?

Tina, Margaret und Bernd besprechen die Idee eines Auslandsstudiums. Wer von den drei Studenten stellt die meisten Fragen? Wer gibt die meisten Antworten?

Wortschatz 2

an deiner/seiner Stelle	*in your/his shoes; if I were you/he*
auf diese Weise	*(in) this way*
ausländisch	*foreign*
bestimmt	*surely, for sure; certain(ly)*
deshalb	*therefore*
jedenfalls	*in any case*
so dass	*so that*
sowieso	*anyhow*
wahrscheinlich	*probably*
wenigstens	*at least*
Angst haben (vor + *dat.*)	*to fear, be afraid (of)*
an·nehmen (nimmt an), nahm an, angenommen	*to suppose; to accept*
auf·hören	*to end; to stop doing something*
teilen	*to share; also: to divide*

Extra practice with *in your shoes*, e.g., **ich: an meiner Stelle** (du, er, sie / *sg.*, wir, ihr, sie / *pl.*, Bernd, Margaret, Margaret und Tina, Frau Meier)

Vor dem Lesen

A. Allerlei Fragen
1. Würden Sie gern in Europa studieren? Wo, wann und wie lange?
2. Worauf würden Sie sich freuen?
3. Denken Sie, es würde mehr oder weniger kosten, drüben zu studieren?
4. Was würden Sie in den Ferien tun?
5. Hat Ihre Uni ein Austauschprogramm? Wenn ja, mit welcher Universität?
6. Haben Sie Freunde, die *(who)* drüben studiert haben? Wenn ja, wo; und wie hat es Ihnen gefallen?

B. Gehen wir angeln! Lesen Sie mit Ihrem Partner/Ihrer Partnerin still durch den folgenden Text! Welche Konjunktive finden Sie darin? Wie würde man das auf Englisch sagen?

C. Was ist das?

der Grammatikkurs, Intensivkurs, Lesesaal; das Archiv, Auslandsprogramm; die Sprachprüfung; teilmöbliert

Ein Jahr drüben wäre super!

(Gespräch an einer amerikanischen Universität)

CD 6, Track 4

TINA	Hallo, Margaret!
MARGARET	Tag, Tina! Kennst du Bernd? Er ist aus Heidelberg und studiert ein Jahr bei uns.
TINA	Guten Tag! Na°, wie gefällt's dir denn hier?
BERND	Sehr gut. Meine Vorlesungen und die Professoren sind ausgezeichnet. Ich wünschte nur, es gäbe nicht so viele Prüfungen!
TINA	Habt ihr keine Prüfungen?
BERND	Doch, aber weniger. Dafür° haben wir nach ungefähr vier Semestern eine große Zwischenprüfung und dann am Ende des Studiums das Examen.

well

instead

TINA	Ich würde gern einmal in Europa studieren.
MARGARET	Ja, das solltest du unbedingt.
TINA	Es ist bestimmt sehr teuer.
MARGARET	Ach was, so teuer ist es gar nicht. Wenigstens hat mein Jahr in München auch nicht mehr gekostet als ein Jahr hier.
TINA	Wirklich?
BERND	Ja, unsre Studentenheime und die Mensa sind billiger als bei euch und wir haben praktisch keine Studiengebühren°. Ohne mein Stipendium könnte ich nicht in Amerika studieren.
TINA	Ist es schwer, dort drüben einen Studienplatz zu bekommen?
BERND	Wenn du Deutsche wärest, wäre es wahrscheinlich nicht so einfach—je nachdem°, was du studieren willst. Aber als Ausländerin in einem Auslandsprogramm hättest du gar kein Problem.
TINA	Ich muss noch mal mit meinen Eltern sprechen. Sie haben bestimmt Angst, dass ich ein Jahr verlieren würde.
MARGARET	Wieso denn? Wenn du mit einem Auslandsprogramm nach Deutschland gingest, würde das doch wie ein Jahr hier zählen.
TINA	Ich weiß nicht, ob ich genug Deutsch kann.
MARGARET	Keine Angst! Viele Studenten können weniger Deutsch als du. Du lernst es ja schon seit vier Jahren. Außerdem bieten die meisten Programme vor Semesteranfang einen Intensivkurs für ausländische Studenten an. Damit würdest du dich auch auf die Sprachprüfung am Anfang des Semesters vorbereiten. Wenn du die Prüfung wirklich nicht bestehen solltest—was ich mir nicht vorstellen kann, denn dein Deutsch ist gut—dann müsstest du eben° einen Grammatikkurs in „Deutsch als Fremdsprache" belegen und sie am Ende des Semesters wiederholen.
TINA	Das geht. Vielleicht kann ich doch im Herbst ein Semester nach Deutschland.
MARGARET	Im Herbst ginge ich nicht, weil das Wintersemester in Deutschland erst Mitte Februar aufhört.
TINA	Mitte Februar? Und wann ist das Frühjahrssemester°?
BERND	Bei uns gibt es ein Wintersemester und ein Sommersemester. Das Wintersemester geht von Mitte Oktober bis Mitte Februar, das Sommersemester von Mitte April bis Mitte Juli. Du müsstest deshalb ein ganzes Jahr bleiben oder nur für das Sommersemester kommen. Ein ganzes Jahr wäre sowieso besser, denn dann hättest du zwischen den Semestern Zeit zu reisen.
MARGARET	Stimmt. In der Zeit bin ich auch viel gereist. Ich war in Frankreich, Spanien, Italien, Griechenland und danach noch in Ungarn.
TINA	Super! Was für Vorlesungen sollte ich belegen?
BERND	Im ersten Semester würde ich nur Vorlesungen belegen, keine Seminare. Da hört man nur zu und schreibt mit°. Im zweiten Semester solltest du dann aber auch ein Seminar belegen. Bis dann ist dein Deutsch jedenfalls gut genug, so dass du auch eine längere Seminararbeit schreiben oder ein Referat halten könntest.
TINA	Seminararbeiten und Referate auf Deutsch?
MARGARET	Am Anfang geht's langsam, aber man lernt's.
BERND	Ich mach's ja auch auf Englisch. Übrigens, bei euch ist das Bibliothekssystem viel besser. Wir müssen Bücher immer zuerst bestellen, was oft Tage dauert. Man kann nicht einfach in die Archive wie hier. Und die Fachbibliotheken° leihen keine Bücher aus°, außer am Wochenende.
TINA	Ich kann mir ja die Bücher kaufen.
BERND	Das wäre viel zu teuer! Dann würde ich schon lieber im Lesesaal sitzen.
TINA	Und wie ist das mit Studentenheimen?
MARGARET	Wenn du an einem Auslandsprogramm teilnimmst, hast du keine Probleme.
BERND	An deiner Stelle würde ich versuchen, ein Zimmer im Studentenheim zu bekommen. Auf diese Weise lernst du leichter andere Studenten kennen. Die Zimmer sind nicht schlecht, teilmöbliert und mit Bad. Die Küche auf einem Flur müsstest du aber mit fünf oder sechs anderen Studenten teilen.

tuition

depending on

just

spring . . .

takes notes

departmental libraries / lend out

TINA	Da habe ich nichts dagegen. Findet ihr, Heidelberg wäre besser als Berlin oder München?
BERND	Ach, das ist schwer zu sagen.
MARGARET	Ich glaube, wenn ich Berlin gekannt hätte, hätte ich bestimmt dort studiert. Mir hat es da sehr gut gefallen. Aber erst musst du wissen, ob du wirklich nach Deutschland willst. Wenn du das weißt, dann kann ich dir weiterhelfen.
TINA	Danke! Macht's gut! Ich muss zur Vorlesung.

Heidelberg am Neckar mit Blick auf die Altstadt und das Schloss

Nach dem Lesen

A. Ein Jahr im Ausland. Was fehlt?

a. Angst haben b. Europa c. ein Jahr d. die Küche e. München f. Prüfungen g. Sommersemester h. Sprachprüfung i. andere Studenten j. Vorlesungen k. Heidelberg l. Wintersemester

1. Bernd ist aus __k__ und studiert __c__ in Amerika.
2. Ihm gefallen nur die vielen __f__ nicht.
3. Tina möchte gern in __b__ studieren.
4. Margarets Jahr in __e__ hat nicht viel mehr gekostet als ein Jahr zu Hause.
5. Tinas Eltern __a__, dass ihre Tochter drüben ein Jahr verliert.
6. Ausländische Studenten müssen vor Semesteranfang eine __h__ machen.
7. Das __l__ geht von Mitte Oktober bis Ende Mitte Februar, das __g__ von Mitte April bis Mitte Juli.
8. Im ersten Semester sollte Tina nur __j__ belegen.
9. In einem Studentenheim kann man leichter __i__ kennen lernen.
10. In einem deutschen Studentenheim muss man __d__ mit anderen Studenten teilen.

B. Das Studium hier und dort. Vergleichen Sie als Gruppe die beiden Systeme! Machen Sie Listen!

1. Prüfungen 2. Studiengebühren 3. Semesterkalender 4. Kurse 5. Bibliotheken

Optional questions: **Richtig oder falsch?** 1. Das amerikanische Prüfungssystem ist genauso wie das deutsche System. (F) 2. Wenn Bernd kein Stipendium bekommen hätte, wäre er nicht nach Amerika gekommen. (R) 3. In Deutschland gibt es hohe Studiengebühren. (F) 4. Wenn Tina an eine deutsche Uni ginge, müsste sie eine Sprachprüfung bestehen. (R) 5. Die Prüfung wäre am Ende des Semesters. (F) 6. Die deutschen Semester sind zu anderen Zeiten als hier. (R) 7. Weil die Fachbibliotheken keine Bücher ausleihen, wäre es besser, wenn Tina sich alle Bücher kaufen würde. (F) 8. Im Studentenheim könnte Tina leichter andere Studenten kennen lernen. (R) 9. Leider gäbe es nur ein Bad auf dem Flur. (F)

C. An der Uni. Was fehlt?

1. Bernd _wünschte_, es _gäbe_ nicht so viele Prüfungen. *(wishes, there were)*
2. Wenn Bernd kein Stipendium _bekommen hätte_, _hätte_ er hier nicht _studierren können_. *(had gotten, could have studied)*
3. Wenn Tina mit einem Austauschprogramm nach Deutschland _ginge / gehen würde_, _würde_ das wie ein Jahr hier _zählen_. *(would go, would count)*
4. Tina _müsste_ ein ganzes Jahr _bleiben_, oder sie _könnte_ nur für das Sommersemester _gehen_. *(would have to stay, could go)*
5. Ein ganzes Jahr drüben _wäre_ besser. *(would be)*
6. Dann _hätte_ Tina Zeit, zwischen den Semestern zu reisen. *(would have)*
7. In einem Studentenheim _würde_ Tina leichter deutsche Studenten _kennen lernen_. *(would get to know)*
8. Wenn Margaret Berlin _gekannt hätte_, _hätte_ sie dort _studiert_. *(had known, would have studied)*
9. Wenn sie nicht an einer deutschen Uni _studiert hätte_, _könnte_ sie nicht so gut Deutsch _sprechen_. *(had studied, could speak)*
10. Tina _hat Angst_, dass ihr Deutsch nicht gut genug _wäre_. Aber das _sollte_ kein Problem _sein_. *(is afraid, would be, shouldn't be)*

D. Das Vorlesungsverzeichnis. Lesen Sie das Verzeichnis und beenden Sie die Sätze mit Ihrem Partner/Ihrer Parnerin!

1. In allen Vorlesungen geht es um *(it's about)* . . .
2. Mich würde besonders die Vorlesung über . . . interessieren. Sie wäre . . . von . . . bis . . .
3. Außerdem dürfte Professor . . . s Vorlesung über . . . interessant sein.
4. . . . würde mich nicht / weniger interessieren, weil . . .

D: Before assigning this exercise, give students the meaning of these words: **die wirtschaftlichen Verhältnisse** *economic conditions;* **die Gesellschaft** *society;* **der Gegensatz** *contrast;* **die Volksherrschaft** *here: domination by the people;* **das Ostjudentum** *East European Jewry;* **der Weltkrieg, -e** *world war*

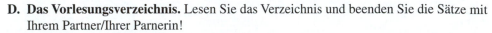

Geschichte der Stadt Rom in der Zeit der römischen Republik 3st., Mo 11 - 13, Mi 12 - 13	Lippold
Die sozialen und wirtschaftlichen Verhältnisse in der griechischen Welt von der Archaischen Zeit bis zum Beginn des Hellenismus 2st., Mo 14 - 15.30	Hennig
Kirche und Gesellschaft im früheren Mittelalter (5.-12. Jahrhundert) 3st., Do 12-13, Fr 11 - 13	Hartmann
Deutschland und Frankreich im 15. und 16. Jahrhundert. Der Beginn eines europäischen Gegensatzes 2st., Di, Mi 9 - 10	Schmid
Politik und Geschichte in Deutschland nach 1945 2st., Do 13 - 15	Haan
Demokratie oder Volksherrschaft? Zur Geschichte der Demokratie seit dem späten 18. Jahrhundert II 2st., Do 16 - 18	Lottes
Deutschland in der Industrialisierung 2st., Di 10 - 11, Mi 11 - 12	Bauer
Bayerische Geschichte zwischen 1800 und 1866 2st., Mi, Do 11 - 12	Volkert
Wirtschaft und Gesellschaft Bayerns im Industriezeitalter 2st., Mo, Di 11 - 12	Götschmann
Das Ostjudentum (19./20. Jahrhundert) 2st., Mi, Fr 8 - 9	Völkl
Europa zwischen den Weltkriegen (1919-1939) 2st., Mo 10 -12	Möller

E. Am liebsten würde ich . . . Beenden Sie die Sätze und vergleichen Sie sie dann mit den Sätzen der anderen!

1. Wenn ich könnte, würde ich einmal in . . . studieren.
2. Am liebsten würde ich in . . . wohnen, weil . . .
3. Am Anfang des Semesters . . .
4. Am Ende des Semesters . . .
5. Während der Semesterferien . . .

F. Ein Kurzgespräch mit Margaret. Bereiten Sie mit Ihrem Partner/Ihrer Partnerin den folgenden Dialog vor und präsentieren Sie ihn danach vor der Klasse!

You call Margaret, who has been to Germany. Introduce yourself and inquire whether you might ask her some questions. She says to go ahead, and you ask whether you should study in Germany. She replies that she would do so if she were you. You ask her for how long you should go. She suggests that you go (for) a year. You would learn more German and see more of Europe. You ask whether you could have lunch together the next day. She says she would prefer it if you could have supper. You agree and say good-bye.

G. Das wäre schön! Schreiben Sie sechs bis acht Sätze im Konjunktiv über eines der Themen!

1. Ein Jahr drüben wäre super!
2. Mein Traumhaus
3. Meine Traumfamilie
4. Das würde mir gefallen.
5. Das hätte mir gefallen.
6. Das wäre schrecklich!

HÖREN SIE ZU!   TRACK 27

Zwei Briefe

Zum Erkennen: das Stellenangebot *(job opening)*; erfüllen *(to fulfill)*; ADAC *(AAA)*; beigelegt *(enclosed)*; sich vorstellen *(to introduce or present oneself)*; absolvieren *(to complete)*; vermitteln *(to help find)*; das Formular *([application] form)*

Richtig oder falsch?

___f___ 1. Dagmar Schröder hat Touristik studiert.
___r___ 2. Sie würde gern als Reiseleiterin arbeiten.
___r___ 3. Sie spricht gut Italienisch.
___f___ 4. Das Reisebüro hätte aber gern jemanden mit Russischkenntnissen.
___r___ 5. Frau Schröder hofft, dass ihre Auslandsaufenthalte für sie sprechen.
___r___ 6. Dem Brief ist ein Lebenslauf beigelegt.
___f___ 7. Joe Jackson studiert Betriebswirtschaft in Seattle, Washington.
___f___ 8. Er würde gern ein Praktikum in Österreich absolvieren.
___r___ 9. Davor würde er aber gern noch etwas mehr Geschäftsdeutsch lernen.
___r___ 10. Er würde sich freuen, wenn ihm die Carl-Duisburg-Gesellschaft in Köln Informationen und Formulare dazu schicken könnte.

Fokus — *Christine Nöstlinger*

Christine Nöstlinger (born in Vienna in 1936) is one of Austria's most eminent authors writing for children and young adults. Since her first success in 1970 (*Die feuerrote Friederike*), she has written more than a 100 books and won numerous prizes. Highly individualistic, humorous, and witty in style, her stories give a realistic description of social backgrounds, often siding with the weak (e.g., *Das Austauschkind*) and criticizing traditional patterns of society. Her humane views are reflected in books dealing with Austria's recent past (e.g., *Rosa Riedl Schutzgespenst,* *Der geheime Großvater*). In addition to writing children's literature, she also writes stories and verse for adults in Viennese dialect, contributes to a variety of magazines and newspapers, and works for Austrian broadcasting. In 1996, Nöstlinger joined SOS Mitmensch, a social organization concentrating on the integration of refugees and foreigners and fighting xenophobia. "Ohne Vorurteile" is taken from her best-seller *Mein Tagebuch* (1989), a collection of short sketches dealing with contemporary family life in a changing society.

Ohne Vorurteile

who / prejudices
were / capable / ambitious
basically
positions / fill
sad

Der Chef von Frau M. ist ein Mann, der° keine Vorurteile° kennt. Und schon gar keine gegen Frauen! Frauen, sagt er immer, seien° genauso tüchtig° und strebsam° im Beruf wie Männer. Im Grunde genommen°, sagt er, hätte er nichts dagegen, alle „höheren" Posten° in seiner Firma mit Frauen zu besetzen°.

Darum war er auch schon vor zwanzig Jahren ehrlich bekümmert°, als er der damals noch sehr jungen Frau M. „den besseren" Posten nicht geben konnte und ihr einen sehr jungen Mann vorziehen musste.

before long / are gone
that I can count on
for a year's leave / temporary help

„Schauen Sie", erklärte er damals der Frau M., „Sie sind jung verheiratet. Sie werden sicher demnächst° ein Kind bekommen. Dann fallen Sie für ein Jahr aus°. Aber auf diesem Posten brauche ich eine Person, mit der ich rechnen kann°. So eine verantwortungsvolle Stellung kann ich nicht ein Karenzjahr lang° mit einer Aushilfskraft° besetzen!"

understood / foreseen
pregnant / twins / at home
quietly / babysat / many

Frau M. sah das ein°, wurde—ganz wie der Chef vorausgesehen° hatte— schwanger°, bekam Zwillinge°, war ein Jahr daheim und arbeitete dann bei ihrem lieben Chef brav° weiter. Die Zwillingen versorgte° die Oma. Als, nach etlichen° Jahren, wieder ein „besserer" Posten frei wurde, bewarb sich Frau M. wieder, denn mit den Zwillingen war ihr Bedarf an Nachwuchs gedeckt° und sie konnte ihrem Chef versichern°, dass kein Karenzjahr mehr drohte°. Aber der arme Chef konnte ihr den Posten wieder nicht geben.

she had enough kids
assure / would be coming

needs total commitment
overtime
trouble / takes care of
half a brain

„Schaun Sie", erklärte er ihr, „diese Stellung bedarf ganzen Einsatzes°! Eine Mutter, das weiß man, hat keine Freude mit Überstunden°. Und wenn die Kinder krank werden, gibt es auch immer Zores°. Ja, ja, die Oma hütet° die Kinder! Aber seien Sie doch ehrlich, eine Mutter ist mit ihrem halben Hirn° immer daheim bei den Kindern und nicht im Büro!"

altogether / child-care leave
is hard to tell / performance / less
that of
grown-up

Also arbeitete Frau M. weiter in ihrer alten Position. In achtzehn Jahren nahm sie insgesamt° vier Tage Pflegeurlaub. Ob sie „mit halbem Hirn" nicht im Büro war, lässt sich schwer entscheiden°, jedenfalls war ihre Arbeitsleistung° nicht geringer° als die° ihrer männlichen Kollegen.

Nun sind Frau M.s Zwillinge erwachsen° und in Frau M.s Firma ist wieder einmal ein „höherer" Posten zu besetzen. Den musste ihre der Chef—leider, leider—wieder verweigern°.

refuse
for sure
bother
I'd welcome
energetic
can't do

Gewiss°, nun muss Frau M. auch nicht mehr mit dem „halben Hirn" bei den Kindern sein, auch Überstunden würden sie nicht mehr stören°, aber nun erklärt ihr der Chef: „Ja doch! Eine Frau wäre mir sehr willkommen° für diesen Posten. Eine vitale°, dynamische Person. Aber in Ihrem Alter, liebe Frau M., schafft man das doch nicht° mehr!"

Christine Nöstlinger

If students ask: *to sue* **jemanden Verklagen;** *to insist on* **bestehen auf (+ dat.),** *to fight for* **kämpfen um;** *right* **das Recht, -e**

Fragen

1. Was verstehen Sie unter Vorurteilen?
2. Welche typischen Vorurteile gibt es gegen Frauen in der Berufswelt?
3. Was hätte Frau M. gern gehabt?
4. Warum bekam sie das erste Mal, als eine bessere Stelle frei wurde, den Job nicht? Wie reagierte sie darauf?
5. Wer spielt heutzutage *(nowadays)* bei Familien mit Kindern oft eine große Rolle? Was tun sie zum Beispiel?
6. Welche Ausrede *(excuse)* hatte der Chef das zweite Mal, als eine bessere Stelle frei wurde? Warum ist das unfair?
7. Welche Ausrede hatte der Chef das dritte Mal? Wie reagierte Frau M. darauf?
8. Was wäre Ihre Reaktion? Was würden Sie tun, wenn Ihnen so etwas passieren würde?
9. Finden Sie, dass Frau M.s Erfahrung typisch für viele Frauen im Berufsleben ist? Können Sie andere Beispiele geben?
10. Glauben Sie, dass das eines Tages besser wird? Warum (nicht)?

Video-Ecke

- In the Minidrama *Amerika ist anders,* Daniela has just received her invitation to an interview with Fulbright for an exchange program in the United States. She is very anxious do do well in her courses and in the interview in order to qualify herself. Her brother is not too impressed. It doesn't make much sense to him to seek a scholarship in the United States, especially because Daniela is a German studies major. He also thinks that student life in America is very different from that in Germany— until their friend arrives to educate him.

Web-Ecke

- For updates, self-assessment quizzes, and online activities related to this chapter, visit the ***Wie geht's?*** Web site at **http://wiegehts.heinle.com**. You will check out various universities and what they have to offer.

Kapitel (14)

Einst und jetzt

Der Kurfürstendamm mit Blick auf die Gedächtniskirche

Lernziele

Vorschau
Chronicle of German history since
  World War II

Gespräche + Wortschatz
Once and now

Fokus
Berliners
Berlin today
Berlin, a multicultural melting pot
Berlin's past
Bertolt Brecht
Erich Kästner

Struktur
14.1 Relative clauses
14.2 Indirect speech

Einblicke
Berlin, ein Tor zur Welt
Bertolt Brecht: *Maßnahmen gegen die Gewalt*
Erich Kästner: *Fantasie von übermorgen*

Video-Ecke
Minidrama: *Eine Stadt mit
  vielen Gesichtern*
Blickpunkt: *Mein Berlin*

Web-Ecke

Vorschau

Chronicle of German History since World War II

EXTRABLATT

Berliner Zeitung

MITTWOCH, 3. OKTOBER 1990 ● EXTRABLATT ● 46. JAHRGANG ● KOSTENLOS ● 90 020 ● ISSN 0323–5793

Adé DDR — Willkommen Deutschland! Nach 45 Jahren sind wir wieder ein Volk in einem geeinten Land

Festakt im Schauspielhaus / Schwarzrotgoldene Fahne vor dem Reichstag / Berlin seit heute wieder deutsche Hauptstadt

Letzte Nachrichten aus der DDR

1945   Unconditional surrender of Germany (May 9). The Allies assume supreme power, dividing Germany into four zones and Berlin (in the middle of the Russian zone) into four sectors. Potsdam Conference determines Germany's new borders.

1947   American Marshall Plan provides comprehensive aid for the rebuilding of Europe, including West Germany. Plan is rejected by the Soviet Union and its Eastern European satellites.

1948   Introduction of D-Mark in the Western Zone leads to the Soviet blockade of West Berlin. Allies respond with Berlin Airlift (June 1948 – May 1949).

1949   Founding of the Federal Republic of Germany in the West (May 23) and the German Democratic Republic (October 7) in the East.

1952   East Germany begins to seal the border with West Germany (May 27).

1953   Workers' uprising in East Berlin (June 17) is crushed by Soviet tanks.

1954   West Germany becomes a NATO member.

1955   East Germany joins the Warsaw Pact. West Germany becomes a sovereign country; the occupation is ended.

1961   East Germany constructs the Berlin Wall and extensive fortifications along the border to West Germany to prevent East Germans from fleeing to the West.

1970   As an important step in his new *Ostpolitik*, West German Chancellor Willy Brandt meets with East German Premier Willi Stoph in Erfurt, East Germany.

1971   Four-Power Agreement on Berlin guarantees unhindered traffic between West Berlin and West Germany. De facto recognition of East Germany.

1973   Bundestag approves treaty of mutual recognition with East Germany. Brandt's opponents accuse him of forsaking the goal of unification.

1989   Opening of Hungarian border to Austria (September 10) brings streams of refugees from East to West Germany, protest rallies take place all across East Germany. Berlin Wall opens on November 9.

1990   Economic union of both German states (July 2) is followed by German re-unification (October 3). First all-German elections are held (December 2).

1994   Last Allied troops withdraw from Berlin.

You might ask students how old they were when the Berlin Wall was opened and what he / she remembers about that day? Have they been to the new *Bundesländer* or met anybody from there? Any interesting stories to share?

(continued on p. 364)

1999   Reopening of the renovated Reichstag building.

2000   Relocation of the federal government to Berlin complete.

2002   After 54 years, Germans say good-bye to the deutsche mark with the introduction of the euro.

Gespräche + Wortschatz

Hier ist immer etwas los.

CD 6, Track 5

Warm-ups: 1. **Was könnte man an der Uni studieren?** Nennen Sie so viele Fächer oder Fachbereiche wie möglich! Sie haben eine Minute. 2. **Was möchten Sie einmal werden?** Warum? Was wäre dabei weniger schön? 3. **Wie geht's weiter?** Wenn das Wetter heute besser wäre, . . . Wenn ich könnte, . . . Wenn ich Geld bräuchte, . . . Wenn ich heute nicht hier sein müsste, . . .

HEIKE	Und das hier ist die Gedächtniskirche mit ihren drei Gebäuden. Wir nennen sie den „Hohlen Zahn," den „Lippenstift" und die „Puderdose".
MARTIN	Berliner haben doch für alles einen Spitznamen.
HEIKE	Der alte Turm der Gedächtniskirche soll als Mahnmal so bleiben, wie er ist. Die neue Gedächtniskirche mit dem neuen Turm ist aber modern.
MARTIN	Und sie sehen wirklich ein bisschen aus wie ein Lippenstift und eine Puderdose. Sag mal, wohnst du gern hier in Berlin?
HEIKE	Na klar! Berlin ist unheimlich lebendig und hat so viel zu bieten, nicht nur historisch, sondern auch kulturell. Hier ist immer was los. Außerdem ist die Umgebung wunderschön.
MARTIN	Ich hab' irgendwo gelesen, dass 24 Prozent der Stadtfläche Wälder und Seen sind, mit 800 Kilometern Fahrradwegen.
HEIKE	Ist doch toll, oder?
MARTIN	Wahnsinn! Sag mal, warst du dabei, als sie die Mauer durchbrochen haben?
HEIKE	Und ob! Das werde ich nie vergessen.
MARTIN	Ich auch nicht, obwohl ich's nur im Fernsehen gesehen habe.
HEIKE	Wir haben die ganze Nacht gewartet, obwohl es ganz schön kalt war. Als das erste Stück Mauer kippte, haben wir alle laut gesungen: „So ein Tag, so wunderschön wie heute, so ein Tag, der dürfte nie vergeh'n."
MARTIN	Ich sehe immer noch die Leute oben auf der Mauer tanzen und feiern.
HEIKE	Ja, das war schon ein einmaliges Erlebnis. Damit hatte niemand gerechnet.
MARTIN	Ein völlig unerwarteter Augenblick.
HEIKE	Wer hätte gedacht, dass das alles so schnell gehen würde und so friedlich?
MARTIN	Seitdem hat sich hier vieles verändert. Die Spuren der Mauer sind fast verschwunden. Bist du froh, dass Berlin wieder Hauptstadt ist?
HEIKE	Und ob!
MARTIN	Du lebst also gern hier?
HEIKE	Ja natürlich. Wir Berliner klagen und machen uns lustig über unsere Stadt, aber wir lieben sie.

A. Richtig oder falsch?

  f   1. Martin ist Berliner.

  r   2. Der „Hohle Zahn" ist ein Teil der Gedächtniskirche.

  f   3. Er soll die Berliner an den Zahnarzt erinnern.

  f   4. Martin hat verschiedene Spitznamen für die Berliner.

  r   5. Heike gefällt's unheimlich gut in Berlin.

  r   6. Heike war dabei, als sie die Mauer durchbrochen haben.

  f   7. Martin hat dort auch mitgefeiert.

  f   8. Das Ganze geschah an einem schönen, warmen Nachmittag.

These stamps are no longer valid as they show DM prices, but they are of interest historically.

___f___ 9. Als das erste Stück Mauer kippte, haben die Leute die Polizei gerufen.

___r___ 10. Manche haben auf der Mauer getanzt.

___f___ 11. Seitdem hat sich in Berlin nicht viel verändert.

___f___ 12. Die Touristen klagen über die Berliner, weil die Berliner sich immer über sie lustig machen.

B. Jetzt sind Sie dran! Was würden sie einem ausländischen Besucher (Ihrem Partner/Ihrer Partnerin) sagen, dem *(to whom)* Sie Ihre eigene Stadt zeigen? Machen Sie es so interessant, wie möglich!

S1 Und das ist . . .
S2 . . .
S1 Ja, wir finden das auch . . .
S2 Wie ist das Leben . . . ?
S1 . . .
S2 Ist hier kulturell viel los?
S1 . . .
S2 Die Umgebung ist . . .
S1 Wie findest du/finden Sie . . . ?
S2 . . .

Wortschatz 1

Einst und jetzt *(once and now)*

der Augenblick, -e	*moment*	die Grenze, -n	*border*
Frieden	*peace*	Mauer, -n	*wall*
Krieg, -e	*war*	Umgebung	*surrounding(s)*
Spitzname, -ns, -n	*nickname*		
Turm, ⸚e	*tower*		
das Erlebnis, -se	*experience*		
Gebäude, -	*building*		
Volk, ⸚er	*people (as a whole or nation)*		

NOTE the difference between **Wand** and **Mauer:** A **Wand** is usually thinner and part of the inside of a house. A **Mauer** is much thicker—like an outside wall of a castle—and usually freestanding.

Weiteres

einmalig	*unique, incredible*
historisch	*historical(ly)*
unerwartet	*unexpected(ly)*
unheimlich[1]	*tremendous(ly), extreme(ly)*
wunderschön	*very beautiful*
berichten	*to report*
erinnern (an + *acc.*)[2]	*to remind (of)*
sich erinnern (an + *acc.*)[2]	*to remember*
führen	*to lead*
klagen (über + *acc.*)	*to complain (about)*
sich lustig machen (über + *acc.*)	*to make fun of*
(sich) verändern	*to change*
verschwinden, verschwand, ist verschwunden	*to disappear*
vorbei·führen (an + *dat.*)	*to pass by, guide along*
kaum	*hardly, barely, scarcely*
oder?	*isn't it? don't you think so?*
Und ob!	*You bet. / You better believe it.*

Give students other examples with **unheimlich,** e.g., very very beautiful (exciting, fast, tired, etc.).

Examples with **erinnern:** Peter, please remind me of the exam. Why do I always have to remind you? Can't you remember anything? I remember the vacation very well!

[1] A very common phrase: **unheimlich schön, unheimlich interessant,** etc.

[2] **Ich werde dich an die Karten erinnern.** *(I'll remind you of the tickets.)* BUT **Ich kann mich nicht daran erinnern.** *(I can't remember it.)*

Zum Erkennen: hohl *(hollow);* der Lippenstift, -e *(lipstick);* die Puderdose, -n *(compact);* als Mahnmal *(as a memorial of admonishment);* lebendig *(lively);* bieten *(to offer);* die Stadtfläche *(. . . area);* durchbrochen *(broken through);* (um)kippen *(to tip over);* vergehen *(to pass);* friedlich *(peacefully);* die Spur, -en *(trace);* AUCH: die Funktion, -en *(function);* das Relativpronomen, - *(relative pronoun);* der Relativsatz, ̈e *(relative clause);* das vorhergehende Wort, ̈er *(antecedent);* die indirekte Rede *(indirect speech);* bestätigen *(to confirm);* definieren; unterstreichen *(to underline);* Damit hat niemand gerechnet. *(Nobody expected / was counting on that.)*

Mauerdurchbruch am 9.11.1989

Zum Thema

A. Wie geht's weiter? Benutzen Sie Ihre Fantasie!

BEISPIEL: . . . sieht gut aus.
             Mein Bruder sieht gut aus.

If you have pictures of the **Schwangere Auster, Hungerkralle,** or **Telespargel,** bring them to class to illustrate the reason for these nicknames.

Fokus — *Berliners*

Berliners are known for their self-assured manner, their humor, and their "big mouth" **(Berliner Großschnauze).** They always manage to find the right words at the right time, especially when it comes to choosing amusing names for places around their city. Besides the nicknames mentioned in the dialogue, there are the **Schwangere Auster** *(pregnant oyster),* a cultural center; the **Hungerkralle** *(hunger claw),* the monument to the Berlin Airlift; the **Telespargel** *(television-asparagus),* the television tower; the old **Palazzo Prozzo** *(Braggarts' Palace)* or **Honeckers Lampen-laden** *([East German leader Erich] Honecker's lampstore),* the former parliament building of East Germany; and the **Mauerspechte** *(wall woodpeckers),* the souvenir hunters who chipped away at the Berlin Wall after it was opened.

1. . . . sieht aus wie ein(e) . . .
2. . . . hat viel zu bieten.
3. Ich erinnere mich gern an . . .
4. . . . war immer etwas los.
5. . . . machten uns lustig über . . .
6. Ich kann mich noch gut an die Zeit erinnern, als . . .
7. Bitte erinnere mich nicht an . . . !
8. . . . hat sich . . . verändert.
9. . . . sollte(n) nicht so viel über . . . klagen.
10. Eigentlich geht es . . . unheimlich . . .

B. Stadtplan von Berlin. Sehen Sie auf den Stadtplan und beenden Sie dann die Sätze mit einem Wort aus der Liste!

a. Brandenburger
b. Dom
c. Fernsehturm
d. Gedächtniskirche
e. Juni
f. Kulturen der Welt
g. Philharmonie
h. Reichstagsgebäude
i. Spree
j. Stadtplan
k. Unter den Linden
l. Zoo(logische Garten)

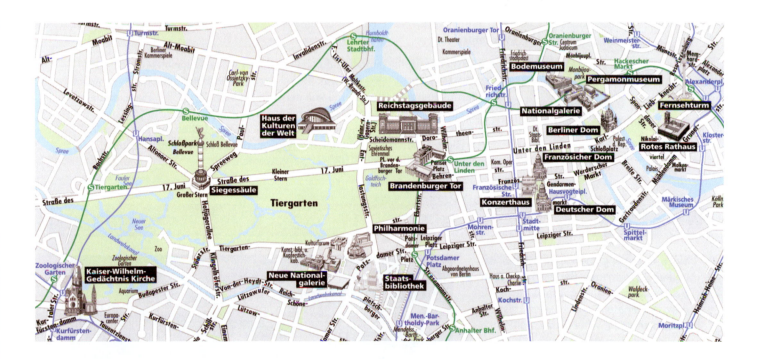

1. Dieser __j__ von Berlin zeigt Ihnen, wo die verschiedenen Straßen und wichtigsten Gebäude sind. 2. Im Südwesten ist der Kurfürstendamm oder Ku'damm. Er führt zur __d__ 3. In der Nähe ist auch der __l__. 4. Quer durch den großen Park läuft eine lange Straße. Sie erinnert an den 17. __e__ 1953, als die Ostberliner und die Deutschen in Ostdeutschland gegen die Sowjetunion rebellierten. 5. Sie führt vorbei am Großen Stern mit der Siegessäule (*Victory Column*) und weiter bis zum __a__ Tor (*gate*). 6. Die Straße hat verschiedene Namen. Östlich vom Brandenburger Tor heißt sie __k__. 7. Südlich vom Brandenburger Tor ist der Potsdamer Platz und an der Potsdamer Straße die Staats bibliothek und die __g__. 8. Ganz in der Nähe vom Brandenburger Tor ist auch das für den Bundestag (*federal parliament*) renovierte __h__ mit der neuen Glaskuppel, die (*which*) nachts den Himmel von Berlin erhellt (*brightens up*). 9. Nicht weit davon ist das Haus der __f__, die frühere Kongresshalle mit dem Spitznamen „Schwangere Auster". 10. Unter den Linden führt ins alte Zentrum von Berlin und auf eine Insel mit dem Pergamonmuseum und dem Berliner __b__. 11. Auf beiden Seiten der Insel fließt (*flows*) die __i__. 12. Beim Dom bekommt die Straße wieder einen neuen Namen und geht weiter bis zum Alexanderplatz mit dem modernen __c__, „dem Telespargel".

You may want to point out how easy it is to form adjectives from the names of cities (e.g., Berlin**er**, Brandenburg**er**, Potsdam**er**) and to mention that these adjectives don't have the usual endings: das alt**e** Tor BUT das Brandenburger Tor.

CD 6, Track 6

Aussprache: pf, ps, qu

Lesen Sie auch Teil III. 19, 21 und 22 in *Zur Aussprache* im *Arbeitsbuch!*

1. [pf]   **Pf**arrer, **Pf**effer, **Pf**lanze, **Pf**und, A**pf**el, Ko**pf,** em**pf**ehlen
2. [ps]   **Ps**ychologe, **Ps**ychologie, **ps**ychologisch, **Ps**alm, **Ps**eudonym, Ka**ps**el
3. [kv]   **Qu**atsch, **Qu**alität, **Qu**antität, **Qu**artal, be**qu**em

---

HÖREN SIE ZU!   TRACK 28

Die Info-Box

Zum Erkennen: das Niemandsland *(no man's land);* schwärmen von *(to rave about);* die Baustelle *(construction site);* Kräne *(cranes);* mittendrin *(right in the middle of it);* Tiefbauingenieur *(civil engineer)*

Was fehlt?

1. Martin und Heike bummeln durch Geschäfte, wo in den achtziger Jahren *(in the 1980s)* noch __Niemandsland__ war. 2. Von der __Mauer__ ist kaum noch was zu sehen. 3. Martins Freunde schwärmten von der Info-Box am __Potsdamer__ Platz, damals eine ganz große Baustelle. 4. Von dort konnte man __alles__ übersehen. 5. Die Computeranimationen __in__ der Info-Box, sagt Martin, hätten ihn besonders interessiert. 6. Sie hätten ihm einen __Einblick__ in den Städtebau der Zukunft gegeben. 7. Martin möchte __(Tiefbau)ingenieur__ werden.

Fokus — *Berlin Today*

Since becoming the capital of the re-unified Germany, Berlin has seen tremendous changes, especially as a new government and business district is constructed where the wall once stood. The historic Reichstag building has been transformed by the British architect Sir Norman Foster into a modern seat of parliament, with a glass dome atop the roof to represent a link between past and present. Numerous embassies and organizations are located in Berlin, and numerous prominent German and foreign firms have chosen Berlin as their headquarters.

Berlin now boasts some 30 art museums, two important symphony orchestras, three opera houses, numerous theaters and cabarets, and three major universities. Young people from all over Europe have come to appreciate Berlin's ground-breaking music scene, the highlight of which, the annual "Love Parade," draws up to a million ravers.

More than any other city in Europe, Berlin has embodied both the confrontation of the Cold War and the growing together of the continent ever since. Its proximity to Poland, only 65 miles away, symbolizes Germany's reaching out toward the countries of the former Soviet Union and its role as mediator between East and West.

Der Sitz des Bundestages im Berliner Reichstagsgebäude

Struktur

14.1 Relative clauses

RELATIVE CLAUSES supply additional information about a noun in a sentence.

> There's the professor **who** teaches the course.
> He taught the course **(that)** I enjoyed so much.
> He teaches a subject **in which** I'm very interested (I'm very interested in).
> He's the professor **whose** course I took last semester.

English relative clauses may be introduced by the relative pronouns *who, whom, whose, which,* or *that.* The noun to which the relative pronoun "relates" is called the ANTECEDENT. The choice of the relative pronoun depends on the antecedent (is it a person or a thing?) <u>and</u> on its function in the relative clause. The relative pronoun may be the subject *(who, which, that),* an object or an object of a preposition *(whom, which, that),* or it may indicate possession *(whose).* German relative clauses work essentially the same way. However, whereas in English the relative pronouns are frequently omitted (especially in conversation), IN GERMAN THEY MUST ALWAYS BE USED.

Point out that relative clauses in German work the same way as in formal English.

To be more precise, relative pronouns in English are omitted only if they are objects or objects of prepositions.

> Ist das der Roman, **den** ihr gelesen habt? *Is that the novel you read?*

1. Forms and use

    The German relative pronouns have the same forms as the definite article, EXCEPT FOR THE GENITIVE FORMS AND THE DATIVE PLURAL.

	masc.	neut.	fem.	pl.
nom.	der	das	die	die
acc.	den	das	die	die
dat.	dem	dem	der	denen
gen.	dessen	dessen	deren	deren

> **erdgas**
> ENERGIE, MIT DER WIR LEBEN KÖNNEN

The form of the relative pronoun is determined by two factors:

- Its ANTECEDENT: is the antecedent masculine, neuter, feminine, or in the plural?

    > Das ist **der Fluss, der** auf der Karte ist.
    > Das ist **das Gebäude, das** auf der Karte ist.
    > Das ist **die Kirche, die** auf der Karte ist.
    > Das sind **die Plätze, die** auf der Karte sind.

- Its FUNCTION in the relative clause: is the relative pronoun the subject, an accusative or dative object, an object of a preposition, or does it indicate possession?

    > Ist das der Mann, **der** in Berlin wohnt? = SUBJECT
    > Ist das der Mann, **den** du meinst? = ACCUSATIVE OBJECT
    > Ist das der Mann, **dem** du geschrieben hast? = DATIVE OBJECT
    > Ist das der Mann, **mit dem** du gesprochen hast? = OBJECT OF A PREPOSITION
    > Ist das der Mann, **dessen** Tochter hier studiert? = GENITIVE

The following examples indicate the antecedent and state the function of the relative pronoun (RP) in each relative clause.

> ... ANTECEDENT, (preposition +) RP _____ V1.

Da ist der Professor. Er lehrt an meiner Universität.

Da ist **der Professor, der** an meiner Universität lehrt.

*That's **the professor who** teaches at my university.*

ANTECEDENT: der Professor = sg. / masc.

PRONOUN FUNCTION: subject > nom.

Wie heißt der Kurs? Du findest ihn so interessant.

Wie heißt **der Kurs, den** du so interessant findest?

*What's the name of **the course (that)** you find so interesting?*

ANTECEDENT: der Kurs = sg. / masc.

PRONOUN FUNCTION: object of **finden** > acc.

Da ist der Student. Ich habe ihm mein Buch gegeben.

Da ist **der Student, dem** ich mein Buch gegeben habe.

*There's **the student to whom** I gave my book (I gave my book to).*

ANTECEDENT: der Student = sg. / masc.

PRONOUN FUNCTION: object of **geben** > dat.

Kennst du die Professorin? Erik hat ihr Seminar belegt.

Kennst du **die Professorin, deren Seminar** Erik belegt hat?

*Do you know **the professor whose seminar** Erik took?*

ANTECEDENT: die Professorin = sg. / fem.

PRONOUN FUNCTION: related possessively to **Seminar** > gen.

Das Buch ist von einem Autor. Ich interessiere mich sehr für ihn.

Das Buch ist von **einem Autor, für den** ich mich sehr interessiere.

*The book is by **an author in whom** I'm very interested.*

ANTECEDENT: der Autor = sg. / masc.

PRONOUN FUNCTION: object of **für** > acc.

Die Autoren sind aus Leipzig. Der Professor hat von ihnen gesprochen.

Die Autoren, von denen der Professor gesprochen hat, sind aus Leipzig.

*The authors **of whom** the professor spoke are from Leipzig.*

ANTECEDENT: die Autoren = pl.

PRONOUN FUNCTION: object of **von** > dat.

CAUTION: Don't use the interrogative pronoun in place of the relative pronoun!

Wer hat das Seminar gegeben?

Das ist der Professor, **der** das Seminar gegeben hat.

Who gave the seminar?

*That's the professor **who** gave the seminar.*

2. Word order

a. Relative pronouns can be the objects of prepositions. If that is the case, the preposition will always precede the relative pronoun.

Das Buch ist von einem Autor, **für den** ich mich sehr interessiere.

*The book is by an author **in whom** I'm very interested.*

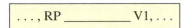

b. The word order in THE RELATIVE CLAUSE is like that of all subordinate clauses: the inflected part of the verb (V1) comes last. Always separate the relative clause from the main clause by a comma.

$$\ldots, \text{RP} \underline{\hspace{3cm}} \text{V1}, \ldots$$

Der Professor, <u>der</u> den Prosakurs <u>lehrt,</u> ist sehr nett.
RP   V1

c. Relative clauses immediately follow the antecedent unless the antecedent is followed by a prepositional phrase that modifies it, by a genitive, or by a verb complement (V2).

Das Buch von Dürrenmatt, **das wir lesen sollen,** ist leider ausverkauft.

Das Buch des Autors, **das wir lesen sollen,** ist teuer.

Ich kann **das Buch** nicht bekommen, **das wir lesen sollen.**

EUROCARD. Für Leute, die auch sonst gute Karten haben.

Übungen

A. Analysieren Sie die Sätze! Finden Sie das vorhergehende Wort (*antecedent*), beschreiben Sie es und nennen Sie die Funktion des Relativpronomens im Relativsatz!

> **BEISPIEL:** Renate Berger ist eine Frau, die für gleiche Arbeit gleiches Einkommen möchte.
> ANTECEDENT: **eine Frau = sg. / fem.**
> PRONOUN FUNCTION: **subject > nom.**

1. Der Mann, der neben ihr arbeitet, verdient pro Stunde € 1,– mehr.
2. Es gibt leider noch viele Frauen, deren Kollegen ein höheres Gehalt (*salary*) bekommen.
3. Und es gibt Frauen, denen schlecht bezahlte Arbeit lieber ist als keine Arbeit.
4. Was denken die Männer, deren Frauen weniger Geld bekommen als ihre Kollegen?
5. Der Mann, mit dem Renate Berger verheiratet ist, findet das nicht so schlecht.
6. Aber die Frauen, die bei der gleichen Firma arbeiten, ärgern sich sehr darüber.
7. Frau M. in Christine Nöstlingers Geschichte war so eine Frau, die sich ärgerte aber sich nicht beklagte.
8. Sie war eine Frau, die bei der Arbeit fleißig und zuverlässig war.
9. Den besseren Job, von dem sie träumte, bekamen aber immer andere.
10. Der Chef, den sie hatte, war ein Mensch mit großen Vorurteilen gegen Frauen.
11. Chefs, die so denken wie Frau M.s Chef, gibt es überall.
12. Das ist ein Problem, das andere Firmen auch haben.
13. Die Berufe, in denen fast nur Frauen arbeiten, sind am schlechtesten bezahlt.
14. Wir leben in einer Welt, in der Gleichberechtigung noch nicht überall Realität ist.

B. Rundfahrt durch Berlin. Während Sepp ein paar Bilder von seinem Besuch in Berlin zeigt, stellen seine österreichischen Freunde Fragen darüber. Antworten Sie wie im Beispiel und benutzen Sie dabei Relativpronomen!

1. **BEISPIEL:** Ist das der Alexanderplatz?
   Ja, das ist der Alexanderplatz, der so bekannt ist.

   a. Ist das der Fernsehturm? b. Ist das das Rote Rathaus? c. Ist das der Berliner Dom? d. Ist das das Hotel Adlon? e. Sind das die Museen?

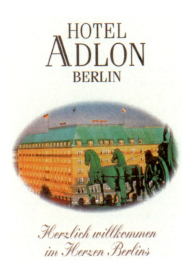

HOTEL
ADLON
BERLIN

*Herzlich willkommen
im Herzen Berlins*

2. **BEISPIEL:** Ist das der Potsdamer Platz?
   Ja, das ist der Potsdamer Platz, den du da siehst.

   a. Ist das die Leipziger Straße? b. Ist das das Konzerthaus? c. Ist das der Französische Dom? d. Ist das die Spree? e. Ist das das Nikolaiviertel?

3. **BEISPIEL:** Ist das die Hochschule für Musik?
   Ja, das ist die Hochschule für Musik, zu der wir jetzt kommen.

   a. Ist das der Zoo? b. Ist das die Siegessäule? c. Ist das die alte Kongresshalle? d. Ist das das Reichstagsgebäude? e. Sind das die Universitätsgebäude?

4. **BEISPIEL:** Wo ist der Student? Sein Vater lehrt an der Universität.
   Da ist der Student, dessen Vater an der Universität lehrt.

   a. Wo ist die Studentin? Ihre Eltern wohnten früher *(formerly)* in Berlin. b. Wo ist das Mädchen? Ihr Bruder war so lustig. c. Wo ist der Herr? Seine Frau sprach so gut Englisch. d. Wo sind die alten Leute? Ihr Sohn ist jetzt in Amerika.

C. **Was gefällt Ihnen?** Lesen Sie sich mit den anderen die folgende Liste durch und nennen Sie Beispiele mit Relativpronomen!

   1. Buch 2. Film 3. Fernsehsendung 4. Zeitschrift 5. Schlagersänger(in) *(pop singer)* 6. Komponist(in) 7. Restaurant 8. Auto 9. Stadt

D. **Kein Wiedersehen.** Ergänzen Sie die fehlenden Relativpronomen!

   1. Der junge Mann, _der_ da steht, heißt David.
   2. Das Mädchen, mit _dem_ er spricht, heißt Tina.
   3. Das andere Mädchen, _das_ daneben steht, heißt Margaret.
   4. Sie sprechen über einen Film, _der_ früher einmal im Kino gelaufen ist.
   5. Der Film, über _den_ sie sprechen, spielte in Berlin.
   6. Die Geschichte spielte kurz vor dem Bau der Mauer, _die_ Berlin von 1961 bis 1989 geteilt hat.
   7. In den fünfziger Jahren sind viele mit der S-Bahn, _die_ ja quer durch *(right through)* die Stadt fuhr, geflohen.
   8. Ein junger Mann, _dessen_ Freundin nicht wusste, ob sie in den Westen wollte, fuhr mit der S-Bahn nach West-Berlin und blieb dort.
   9. Die Freundin, _deren_ Arbeit in Halle war, ging in den Osten zurück.
   10. Das war kurz vor dem Tag, an _dem_ man die Mauer baute.
   11. Es war ein völlig unerwarteter Augenblick, _der_ ihr Leben total verändern sollte.
   12. Den Freund, _den,_ sie in West-Berlin zurückgelassen hatte und _der_ dort auf sie wartete, würde sie nie wiedersehen.
   13. Am Ende des Filmes, _der_ in der DDR gedreht wurde *(was filmed)*, blieb nur die Erinnerung an den Freund.
   14. So wie ihnen ging es vielen Menschen, durch _deren_ Privatleben plötzlich diese schreckliche Mauer ging.
   15. Heute ist von der Mauer, _die_ so viel Leid brachte, kaum mehr etwas zu sehen.

E. **Verbinden Sie die Sätze!** Verbinden Sie die Sätze mit Hilfe von Relativpronomen! Wenn nötig, übersetzen Sie *(translate)* den Satz zuerst!

   BEISPIEL: Der Ku'damm ist eine bekannte Berliner Straße. Jeder kennt sie.
   (The Ku'damm is a famous Berlin street [that] everyone knows.)
   Der Ku'damm ist eine bekannte Berliner Straße, die jeder kennt.

   1. Die Gedächtniskirche gefällt mir. Ihr habt schon von der Gedächtniskirche gehört.
   2. Der alte Turm soll kaputt bleiben. Die Berliner nennen ihn „Hohlen Zahn".
   3. Der Ku'damm beginnt bei der Gedächtniskirche. Am Ku'damm gibt es viele schöne Geschäfte.
   4. Mittags gingen wir ins Nikolaiviertel. Es hat schöne alte Gebäude und die älteste Kirche Berlins.

5. Da gibt's auch kleine Restaurants. Man kann in den Restaurants gemütlich sitzen.
6. Wir waren ins „Wirtshaus *(n.)* zum Nußbaum" gegangen. Seine Alt-Berliner Küche ist bekannt.
7. Mein Freund hat mir wirklich alles gezeigt. Seine Familie wohnt in Berlin.
8. Seine Schwester war auch sehr nett. Ich bin mit ihr am Abend in eine Disko in den Hackeschen Höfen gegangen.
9. Diese Disko war in der Nähe der Neuen Synagoge. Die Atmosphäre der Disko war einmalig.
10. Die Synagoge ist im maurischen Stil *(Moorish style)* gebaut. In dieser Synagoge hatte Albert Einstein am 29.1.1930 ein Violinenkonzert gegeben.

F. Woran denke ich? Definieren Sie Ihrem Partner/Ihrer Partnerin verschiedene Wörter mit Relativsätzen, die er oder sie dann versucht zu erkennen. Wechseln Sie sich ab!

BEISPIEL: Ich denke an ein Tier mit zwei Beinen, das klein ist und fliegen kann.
Ist es ein Vogel? . . .
Ich denke an jemanden in der Klasse, der immer zu spät kommt.
Ist es . . . ?

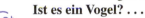
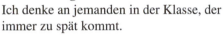

Fokus — *Berlin, a Multicultural Melting Pot*

Berlin is one of Europe's most cosmopolitan urban centers, with more than 400,000 foreign nationals of more than 180 countries living within the city limits. In addition to an influx of Jews from the former Soviet Union since the fall of the Berlin Wall in 1989, the country's liberal asylum laws, and the need for manual laborers have drawn people to Berlin from around the globe. Relations with the German majority, however, have shown signs of strain. Because some residents claim their neighborhoods are being "taken over" by foreigners, local politicians have discussed placing limits on the number of foreign residents in some areas to avoid "ghettoization." Although many leaders of ethnic communities in Berlin agree that more integration is needed, they have dismissed such calls for "quotas on foreigners" as outrageous. Despite such problems, the presence and continuing influx of foreigners adds to the cosmopolitan flair of Berlin, and the traditional homogeneous German society is thus changing rapidly in the capital of the reunited Germany.

Diese Synagoge ist heute ein jüdisches Museum.

14.2 Indirect speech

When reporting what someone else has said, you can use DIRECT SPEECH with quotation marks, or INDIRECT SPEECH without quotation marks.

Heike said, "Berlin has a lot to offer."

Heike said (that) Berlin has a lot to offer.

Often, corresponding direct and indirect speech will require different personal pronouns and possessive adjectives, depending on who reports the conversation.

- If Heike says to Martin "I'll bring my map," and she reports the conversation, she will say: *I told him I would bring my map.*
- If Martin reported the conversation, he would say: *She told me she would bring her map.*
- If a third person reported, he or she would say: *She told him she would bring her map.*

In spoken German such indirect reports are generally in THE INDICATIVE when the opening verb is in the <u>present</u> (**Sie sagt, . . .).** However, when the opening verb is in the <u>past</u> (**Sie sagte, . . .),** the subjunctive usually follows. This section focuses on the latter.

If you feel that indirect speech is not necessary in the first year, or that your students can't handle it at this time, omit this section. Skip exercises G–I and K–L in the *Zusammenfassung,* and E in *Nach dem Lesen.*

Direct speech:	„Ich **bringe** meinen Stadtplan mit."
Indirect speech: Indicative Subjunctive	 Sie sagt, sie **bringt** ihren Stadtplan mit. Sie sagte, sie **würde** ihren Stadtplan **mitbringen.**

NOTE: In German, opening quotation marks are placed at the bottom of the line, especially in handwriting. Many publishers now use an alternative form of quotation marks: »Ich bringe meinen Stadtplan mit.«

1. Statements

    The tense of the indirect statement is determined by the tense of the direct statement.

    a. Direct statements in the present or future are reported indirectly in the present-time subjunctive or the **würde**-form.

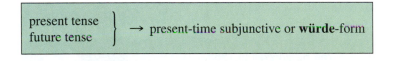

    „Ich komme später."   Sie sagte, sie käme später.

    „Ich werde später kommen."   Sie sagte, sie würde später kommen.

    b. Direct statements IN ANY PAST TENSE are reported indirectly in the past-time subjunctive.

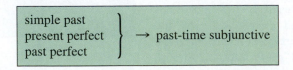

    „Sie hatte keine Zeit."

    „Sie hat keine Zeit gehabt."   Sie sagte, sie hätte keine Zeit gehabt.

    „Sie hatte keine Zeit gehabt."

c. The conjunction **dass** may or may not be used. If it is not used, the clause retains the original word order. If **dass** is used, the inflected part of the verb comes last.

Sie sagte, sie käme morgen.

Sie sagte, **dass** sie morgen **käme.**

Sie sagte, sie hätte andere Pläne gehabt.

Sie sagte, **dass** sie andere Pläne gehabt **hätte.**

2. Questions

The tense of the indirect question is also determined by the tense of the direct question. Indirect YES / NO QUESTIONS are introduced by **ob,** and indirect INFORMATION QUESTIONS by the question word.

Er fragte: „Hast du jetzt Zeit?"	*He asked, "Do you have time now?"*
Er fragte, **ob** sie jetzt Zeit hätte.	*He asked whether she had time now.*
Er fragte: „Wo warst du?"	*He asked, "Where were you?".*
Er fragte, **wo** sie gewesen wäre.	*He asked where she had been.*

3. Imperatives

Direct requests in the imperative are expressed indirectly with the auxiliary **sollen.**

Sie sagte: „Frag(e) nicht so viel!"	*She said, "Don't ask so many questions."*
Sie sagte, er **sollte** nicht so viel **fragen.**	*She said he shouldn't ask so many questions.*

For extra practice with indirect speech, see the anecdote about Frederick the Great and Moses Mendelssohn in the *Zum Schreiben* section of Chapter 14 in the Workbook.

Übungen

G. Von Bonn nach Berlin. Bestätigen Sie *(confirm),* dass die Leute in Phillips Familie das wirklich gesagt haben! Beginnen Sie die indirekte Rede mit **dass!**

BEISPIEL: Hat Phillip Sanders gesagt, er hätte vorher in Bonn gewohnt?
Ja, er hat gesagt, dass er vorher in Bonn gewohnt hätte.

1. Hat Phillip gesagt, seine Familie wäre nicht gern nach Berlin gezogen *(moved)?*
2. Hat seine Mutter gesagt, sie wäre lieber in Bonn geblieben?
3. Hat seine Mutter gesagt, sie hätten dort ein wunderschönes Haus mit Garten gehabt?
4. Hat sein Bruder gesagt, er wollte nicht die Schule wechseln?
5. Hat sein Bruder gesagt, er würde lieber in Bonn sein Abitur machen?
6. Hat Phillip gesagt, er könnte auch hier Freunde finden?
7. Hat Phillip gesagt, er würde Berlin eine Chance geben?

H. Verschiedene Leute im Gespräch. Auf Englisch bitte!
1. **Elke erzählt über Trudi**

Trudi sagte, . . .

a. sie wollte Zahnärztin werden. b. gute Zahnärzte würde man immer brauchen. c. sie könnte leicht weniger arbeiten, wenn sie mal Kinder hätte. d. als Zahnarzt würde man gut verdienen. e. man müsste natürlich lange studieren, aber darauf würde sie sich schon freuen.

2. **Bernd erzählt über Carolyn**

Carolyn sagte, . . .

a. sie hätte letztes Jahr in Deutschland studiert: b. es hätte ihr unheimlich gut gefallen. c. sie hätte die Sprachprüfung leicht bestanden. d. während der Semesterferien wäre sie in die Schweiz gefahren. e. sie wäre erst vor drei Wochen zurückgekommen.

G: 1. Ja, er hat gesagt, dass seine Familie nicht gern nach Berlin gezogen wäre. 2. Ja, sie hat gesagt, dass sie lieber in Bonn geblieben wäre. 3. Ja, sie hat gesagt, dass sie dort ein wunderschönes Haus mit Garten gehabt hätten. 4. Ja, er hat gesagt, dass er nicht die Schule wechseln wollte. 5. Ja, er hat gesagt, dass er lieber in Bonn sein Abitur machen würde. 6. Ja, er hat gesagt, dass er auch hier Freunde finden könnte. 7. Ja, er hat gesagt, dass er Berlin eine Chance geben würde.

H: As additional practice, have students repeat parts 1–2 with the conjunction **dass.** You could also have them convert these sentences into direct speech. H.1 = present-time subjunctive: a. Trudi said (that) . . . a. she wanted to become a dentist. b. they would always need good dentists. c. she could easily work less, if she had children one day. d. as a dentist you would earn well. e. you would, of course have to study for a long time, but she'd look forward to that. (Note that translations may vary.)

H.2 = past-time subjunctive: Carolyn said (that) . . . a. last year she studied in Germany. b. she really liked it a lot. c. she passed the language exam easily. d. during the summer vacation she went / drove to Switzerland. e. she came back only three weeks ago.

H.3 = He asked her . . . a. whether she liked / would like Berlin better now. b. whether she was / had been there at the opening of the Wall c. how long she had been (living) in Berlin d. where the Brandenburg Gate was e. how one would get there f. what else there still was to see here. She told him . . . g. he should / ought to look at the museums h. he should go to a concert i. he should visit the film festivals

H.4 = a. Leonie told (us) that she was in / had been to Berlin last summer. b. She did an internship at a hospital there. c. She worked a lot, but also saw an awful lot. d. She met many nice people. e. Of course, she also was in / went to Potsdam. f. She liked it especially well. g. She also visited the film studios in Babelsberg, where Marlene Dietrich had played / starred in the main role in *The Blue Angel*. h. When Leonie said that she'd probably go back to Berlin this summer, her sister Simone wanted to know whether she could come along. i. Leonie thought that that wasn't / wouldn't be a bad idea. j. The apartment would be big enough for both.

3. **Martin und Heike**

Er hat sie gefragt, . . .

a. ob ihr Berlin jetzt besser gefallen würde. b. ob sie beim Mauerdurchbruch *(opening of the Wall)* dabei gewesen wäre. c. wie lange sie schon in Berlin wäre. d. wo das Brandenburger Tor wäre. e. wie man dorthin käme. f. was es hier noch zu sehen gäbe.

Sie hat ihm gesagt, . . .

g. er sollte sich die Museen ansehen. h. er sollte in ein Konzert gehen. i. er sollte die Filmfestspiele besuchen.

4. **Leonie und Simone**

a. Leonie erzählte, dass sie letzten Sommer in Berlin gewesen wäre. b. Sie hätte dort ein Praktikum an einem Krankenhaus gemacht. c. Sie hätte viel gearbeitet aber auch unheimlich viel gesehen. d. Sie hätte viele nette Leute kennen gelernt. e. Natürlich wäre sie auch in Potsdam gewesen. f. Das hätte ihr besonders gut gefallen. g. Auch hätte sie die Filmstudios in Babelsberg besucht, wo Marlene Dietrich die Hauptrolle in dem Film *Der blaue Engel* gespielt hatte. h. Als Leonie sagte, dass sie diesen Sommer wahrscheinlich wieder nach Berlin gehen würde, wollte ihre Schwester Simone wissen, ob sie mitkommen könnte. i. Leonie meinte, dass das keine schlechte Idee wäre. j. Die Wohnung wäre groß genug für beide.

I. **Was hat er/sie gesagt?** Stellen Sie Ihrem Nachbarn/Ihrer Nachbarin ein paar persönliche Fragen. Berichten Sie dann den anderen in indirekter Rede!

BEISPIEL: Er/sie hat mir erzählt, er/sie wäre aus Chicago, er/sie hätte zwei Brüder . . .

Zusammenfassung

J. **Ein toller Tag.** Ergänzen Sie das fehlende Relativpronomen!

1. Christa Grauer ist eine junge Frau, __die__ mit einem Computer die Anzeigetafeln *(scoreboards)* in einem Kölner Fußballstadion bedient *(operates)*. 2. Sie erzählt von einem Tag, __den__ sie nie vergessen wird. 3. Eine Woche nach dem 9. November 1989, einem Tag, __der__ Geschichte gemacht hat, spielte die deutsche Fußballnationalmannschaft (. . . *team*) gegen Wales. 4. Vor dem Spiel, zu- __dem__ 60 000 Menschen gekommen waren, schrieb Christa wie immer die dritte Strophe *(stanza)* des Deutschlandliedes auf die Anzeigetafeln. 5. Das hatte sie schon 14 Jahre lang getan. Aber es gab wenige Spiele, bei __denen__ die Leute wirklich mitsangen. 6. Aber diesmal sangen Tausende mit, denn die Strophe, __deren__ Text ihnen bisher nicht viel bedeutet hatte, bewegte sie *(moved them)* plötzlich sehr.

This is the third stanza of the original national hymn composed by Fallersleben in 1841.

> Einigkeit und Recht und Freiheit für das deutsche Vaterland.
> Danach lasst uns alle streben, brüderlich mit Herz und Hand.
> Einigkeit und Recht und Freiheit sind des Glückes Unterpfand.
> Blüh im Glanze dieses Glückes, blühe deutsches Vaterland.
>
> *Hoffmann von Fallersleben (1798–1874)*

K. **Stimmen der Zeit.** Berichten Sie in direkter Rede, was die zwei Sprecher gesagt haben!

1. **Hiroko Hashimoto, Journalistin**

   a. Hiroko sagte, sie wäre Journalistin und arbeitete freiberuflich *(freelance)* für eine japanische Firma. b. Ihr Mann wäre Deutscher und Wissenschaftler an der Technischen Universität. c. Ihr hätte Berlin schon immer gefallen, aber jetzt wäre es noch viel interessanter geworden. d. Hier gäbe es alles und auch Leute aus der ganzen Welt. e. Am Wochenende nähmen sie oft ihre Fahrräder und führen in die Umgebung. f. Kaum eine andere Stadt hätte so viel zu bieten. g. Sie hätte nie gedacht, dass sie so lange hier bleiben würde. h. Aber sie fühlten sich hier unheimlich wohl.

2. **Moha Rezaian, Schüler**

   a. Moha sagte, er wäre Schüler an einem Gymnasium. b. Seine Eltern wären vor Jahren aus dem Iran gekommen, weil sein Onkel in Kreuzberg einen Teppichladen gehabt hätte. c. Seine Schwester und er wären aber in Berlin geboren und hier groß geworden. d. Sie wären noch nie im Iran gewesen und würden den Rest der Familie nur von Besuchen kennen. e. Sein Vater hätte jetzt ein Autogeschäft und verdiente gut. f. Das würde ihn aber nicht interessieren. g. Er wollte Arzt werden. h. So könnte er vielen Menschen helfen.

K.1: Hiroko sagte: a. „Ich bin . . . und arbeite . . . b. Mein Mann ist . . . c. Mir hat Berlin . . . gefallen, aber jetzt ist es . . . geworden d. Hier gibt es . . . e. Am Wochenende nehmen wir . . . und fahren . . . f. hat . . . zu bieten g. Ich habe nie gedacht, dass ich . . . hier bleibe h. Aber wir fühlen uns . . ."

K.2: Moha sagte: a. „Ich bin . . . b. Meine Eltern sind . . . gekommen, weil mein Onkel . . . gehabt hat c. Meine Schwester und ich sind . . . geboren . . . groß geworden d. Wir sind . . . gewesen und kennen . . . e. Mein Vater hat . . . verdient . . . f. Das interessiert mich . . . g. Ich will . . . werden h. So kann ich . . . helfen."

Fokus — *Berlin's Past*

Today it is nearly impossible to pass through Berlin without uncovering reminders of the city's long history. Founded more than 750 years ago, Berlin became the seat of the Prussian kings in 1701. The Brandenburg Gate, constructed at the end of the 18th century, was intended as a "Gate of Peace." Instead, it would witness two centuries of war and revolution.

Unter den Linden, the city's most prominent boulevard, led up to the famous gate. Here Napoleon's victorious army paraded through Berlin; revolutionaries erected barricades in 1848 and 1918; and the Nazis staged their book burnings in 1933. After World War II, the devastated capital was divided into Allied and Soviet sectors. At first it was relatively easy to cross from one zone to the other. But Berlin soon became the first battlefield in the Cold War. The Soviet blockade of the Allied zones in 1948–1949 triggered the Berlin airlift, a humanitarian effort that won over the hearts of West Berliners. Later, as increasing numbers of East Berliners fled to the West, the East German regime constructed the Berlin Wall in 1961. The wall, which cut through the heart of the city, was reinforced with minefields, self-firing machine guns, and steel fences to prevent East Germans from escaping. The Brandenburg Gate stood right next to the wall, just inside East Berlin.

Blick aufs Brandenburger Tor

For almost 30 years, West Berlin remained an island of capitalism in Communist East Germany—until Mikhail Gorbachev's spirit of reform in the Soviet Union swept across Eastern Europe. Again, thousands of East Germans tried to flee to West Germany, and in the confusion that ensued, a Communist Party official mistakenly announced an easing of travel restrictions. Almost by accident, the wall was opened on November 9, 1989. Reunification followed a year later, and the Brandenburg Gate once more took its central location in the city. (For a chronicle of the Wall, see www.chronik-der-mauer.de/chronik/index-html)

L. Hoppla, hier fehlt was! Reaktionen auf den Mauerdurchbruch. Hier sind 13 Aussagen, die verschiedene Leute damals darüber gemacht haben. Manche Aussagen zeigen, von wem sie sind und andere nicht. Lesen Sie sich die Liste von Leuten durch und fragen Sie dann Ihren Partner/Ihre Partnerin, wer die verschiedenen Aussagen gemacht haben könnte! Ihr Partner/Ihre Partnerin benutzt die Tabelle und Liste im Anhang. Wechseln Sie sich ab!

Liste von Leuten:

ein Major der DDR-Grenztruppe	ein afrikanischer Diplomat	Michail Gorbatschow
Richard Nixon	die Autorin Christa Wolf	der Autor Stephan Heym
ein Ostberliner Taxifahrer	Sophia Loren	Ronald Reagan
ein kanadischer Fußballspieler	der Autor Günter Grass	der Cellist Rostropowitsch

BEISPIEL: S1 Wer hat gesagt, es wäre eine verrückte Zeit? War das Richard Nixon?

S2 Nein, das war nicht Richard Nixon, sondern ein Major der DDR-Grenztruppe. Und wer hat gesagt, vor seinen Augen hätte die Freiheit getanzt? War das . . .?

S1:

WER?	AUSSAGEN
Major der DDR-Grenztruppe	„Es ist eine verrückte Zeit."
NBC-Korrespondent:	„Vor meinen Augen tanzte die Freiheit."
Ostberliner Taxifahrer	„So viel Fernsehen habe ich noch nie gesehen."
Westberliner Polizist über seinen Kollegen in Ost-Berlin:	„Wir haben uns jeden Tag gesehen. Jetzt will ich ihm mal die Hand schütteln *(shake)*."
Afrikanischer Diplomat	„Ich dachte, die Deutschen können nur Fußball spielen oder im Stechschritt *(goose-step)* marschieren, aber jetzt können sie sogar Revolutionen machen."
Autor Wolf Biermann:	„Ich muss weinen vor Freude, dass es so schnell und einfach ging. Und ich muss weinen vor Zorn *(anger)*, dass es so elend *(terribly)* lange dauerte."
Autor Günter Grass	„Jetzt wird sich zeigen, ob der jahrzehntelangen Rhetorik von den ,Brüdern und Schwestern' auch entsprechendes *(corresponding)* politisches Handeln *(action)* folgen wird."
Autor Günter Kunert:	„Das Volk, von dem man nun wieder glaubhaft *(convincingly)* sprechen darf, ist über die unerwartete Erfüllung *(fulfillment)* eines Traumes selber dermaßen perplex *(so baffled)*, dass ihm die Worte des Triumphes fehlen."
Autor Stephan Heym	„Die einzige Chance, die wir haben, den Sozialismus zu retten *(save)*, ist richtiger Sozialismus."
Ex-Bundeskanzler Willy Brandt:	„Ich bin Gott dankbar, dass ich das noch erleben darf."
Amerikanischer Präsident Ronald Reagan:	„Auf beiden Seiten sind Deutsche. Der Kommunismus hat seine Chance gehabt. Er funktioniert nicht."
Tschechischer Reformpräsident Alexander Dubček:	„Wir haben zu lange im Dunkeln gelebt. Treten wir *(let's step)* ins Licht!"
Cellist Mstislaw Rostropowitsch	„Mauern sind nicht für ewig *(forever)* gebaut . . . In Berlin habe ich für mein Herz gespielt."

M. Kurzgespräch über zwei Freunde

You tell a fellow student, Gunther, that two mutual friends, Karin and Thomas, didn't return from a car trip to Italy yesterday, as they had said they would. You are worried that they might have had an accident (**einen Autounfall haben**) or bad weather as they crossed the mountains (**schlechtes Wetter / Schnee in den Bergen**), or that their car broke down (**eine Panne haben**). Gunther tries to reassure you. He comes up with various ideas as to why they might have been delayed: they wanted to stay a little longer, stopped to see another museum or town, are probably arriving any minute, etc.

N. Eine bekannte Berlinerin: Käthe Kollwitz. Auf Deutsch bitte!

1. Käthe Kollwitz was an artist who was at home in Berlin. 2. Her pictures and sculptures (**Skulpturen**) were full of compassion (**voller Mitgefühl**) for poor people, whose suffering (**Leid**) she wanted to show. 3. They remind us of hunger and war, which make the life of people terrible. 4. Kaiser Wilhelm II was no friend of her art, which for him was "gutter art" (**Kunst der Gosse**). 5. In 1918 she became professor at the Art Academy (**Kunstakademie**) in Berlin, at which she taught until 1933. 6. Then came the Nazis, who also didn't like / care for her art, and she lost her position. 7. She died (**starb**) in 1945, shortly before the end of the war.

Optional practice: Have students make up relative clauses for each of the nouns below, e.g., **die Universität: die Universität, an der er studiert,** . . . (1. der Kurs 2. die Professorin 3. das Austauschprogramm 4. die Studenten 5. das Stipendium 6. der Hörsaal 7. der Beruf 8. die Leute)

Käthe Kollwitz (1867–1945)

N: 1. Käthe Kollwitz war eine Künstlerin, die in Berlin zu Hause war. 2. Ihre Bilder und Skulpturen waren voller Mitgefühl für arme Leute, deren Leid sie zeigen wollte. 3. Sie erinnern uns an Hunger und Krieg, die das Leben der Menschen furchtbar machen. 4. Kaiser Wilhelm II. war kein Freund ihrer Kunst, die für ihn „Kunst der Gosse" war. 5. (Im Jahre) 1918 wurde sie Professorin an der Kunstakademie in Berlin, an der sie bis 1933 lehrte. 6. Dann kamen die Nazis, denen ihre Kunst auch nicht gefiel (die ihre Kunst auch nicht mochten), und sie verlor ihre Stelle. 7. Sie starb 1945, kurz vor (dem) Ende des Krieges / Kriegsende.

„Mutter und toter Sohn", eine Skulptur von Käthe Kollwitz in der Berliner Neuen Wache

Einblicke

Lesestrategie: Was erwarten Sie?

Sie haben schon viel über die Stadt Berlin gelernt. Was erwarten Sie (*expect*), wenn Sie den Titel „Besuch in Berlin im Jahre 1985" lesen?

Wortschatz 2

der Gedanke, -ns, -n	*thought*
das Tor, -e	*gate*
die Heimat	*homeland, home*
Insel, -n	*island*
Jugend	*youth*
Luft	*air*
Macht, ⸚e	*power*
Mitte	*middle*
(Wieder)vereinigung	*(re)unification*
berühmt	*famous*
leer	*empty*
aus·tauschen	*to exchange*
erkennen, erkannte, erkannt	*to recognize*
verlassen (verlässt), verließ, verlassen	*to leave (a place)*

Vor dem Lesen

A. Allerlei Fragen

1. Wo liegt Berlin? 2. An welchem Fluss liegt es? 3. Was sind die Daten des 2. Weltkrieges? 4. In wie viele Teile war Berlin geteilt? 5. Wann endete die Teilung *(division)* von Berlin? 6. Was war Ost-Berlin bis dahin *(then)?* 7. Seit wann ist Berlin wieder die Hauptstadt / der Regierungssitz *(seat of parliament)* von Deutschland? 8. Was wissen Sie noch über Berlin?

B. Gehen wir angeln! Unterstreichen Sie *(underline)* zusammen mit Ihrem Partner/Ihrer Partnerin alle Relativpronomen und vorhergehenden Wörter im Lesetext! Wie viele Beispiele haben Sie gefunden?

C. Was ist das?

der Bomber, Einmarsch, Ökologe, Sonderstatus, Städteplaner; das Angebot, Turmcafé; die Blockade, Luftbrücke, Metropole, Olympiade, Orientierung, Passkontrolle, Rampe, Rote Armee; *(pl.)* die Medikamente, Westmächte, zwanziger Jahre; grenzenlos, kapitalistisch, sowjetisch, sozialistisch, teils, total blockiert, ummauert, (un)freiwillig

CD 6, Track 8

Berlin, ein Tor zur Welt

Besuch in Berlin im Jahre 1985

Da saßen wir nun, Vater und Tochter, im Flugzeug auf dem Weg zu der Stadt, die er eigentlich nie vergessen konnte: Berlin. „Ich bin schon lange in Amerika, aber Berlin . . . Nun, Berlin ist eben meine Heimat. Da bin ich geboren und aufgewachsen°." Und dann wanderten seine Gedanken zurück zu den zwanziger bis vierziger Jahren, zu der Zeit, als er dort gelebt hatte. Die Viereinhalbmillionenstadt, von deren Charme und Esprit er heute noch schwärmt°, hatte seine Jugend geprägt°. Und er erzählte mir von dem, was er dort so geliebt hatte: von den Wäldern und Seen in der Umgebung und von der berühmten Berliner Luft; von den Museen, der Oper und den Theatern, deren Angebot damals einmalig gewesen wäre; vom Kabarett mit seiner typischen „Berliner Großschnauze" und den Kaffeehäusern, in denen immer etwas los war. „In Berlin liefen eben alle Fäden° zusammen, nicht nur kulturell, sondern auch politisch und wirtschaftlich. Es war einst die größte Industriestadt Europas. Die Zentralverwaltung° fast aller wichtigen Industriefirmen war in Berlin. Und man kannte sich, tauschte Gedanken aus, auch mit Wissenschaftlern an der Universität. Einfach fantastisch!"

have grown up

raves / shaped

threads

headquarters

„Und dann kam 1933. Viele verließen Berlin, teils freiwillig, teils unfreiwillig. Die Nazis beherrschten° das Straßenbild°. Bei der Olympiade 1936 sah die ganze Welt nicht nur Berlins moderne S-Bahn und schöne Straßen, sondern auch Hitler. Und drei Jahre später war Krieg!" Nun sprach er von den schweren Luftangriffen° und den Trümmern°, die diese hinterlassen° hatten, vom Einmarsch der Roten Armee, der Teilung Deutschlands unter den vier Siegermächten° (1945) und auch von der Luftbrücke, mit der die Westmächte auf die sowjetische Blockade reagiert hatten. „Plötzlich waren wir total blockiert, eine Insel. Es gab nichts zu essen, keine Kleidung, kein Heizmaterial°, keine Medikamente, kaum Wasser und Strom°. An guten Tagen landeten in den nächsten 10 Monaten alle paar Minuten britische und amerikanische Transportflugzeuge — wir nannten sie die Rosinenbomber° — und brachten uns, was wir brauchten. Ohne die Westmächte hätten wir es nie geschafft°!" . . .

dominated / ... scene

air raids / rubble
left behind
victorious Allies

fuel
electricity

raisin ...
accomplished

Ein „Rosinenbomber" während der Blockade

Dann kamen wir in West-Berlin an. Erst machten wir eine Stadtrundfahrt. „Es ist wieder schön hier; und doch, die Weite° ist weg. Berlin schien früher grenzenlos, und jetzt . . . überall diese Grenze." Immer wieder stand man vor der Mauer, die seit 1961 mitten durch Berlin lief. Besonders traurig machte ihn der Blick auf das Brandenburger Tor, das auf der anderen Seite der Mauer stand. Und doch gefiel mir diese ummauerte Insel. West-Berlin war wieder eine lebendige Metropole, die unheimlich viel zu bieten hatte.

wide-open space

Der Besuch in Ost-Berlin, der damaligen° Hauptstadt von Ostdeutschland, war wirklich ein Erlebnis, wie eine Reise in eine andere Welt. Allein schon die Gesichter der Vopos° am Checkpoint Charlie und das komische Gefühl, das man bei der Passkontrolle hatte! Berlin-Mitte war für meinen Vater schwer wiederzuerkennen. Der Potsdamer Platz, der früher voller Leben gewesen war, war leer. Leichter zu erkennen waren die historischen Gebäude entlang Unter den Linden: die Staatsbibliothek, die Humboldt-Universität und die Staatsoper. Interessant waren auch das Pergamonmuseum, der Dom und gegenüber davon der Palast der Republik, den die Berliner „Palazzo Prozzo" nannten und in dem die Volkskammer° saß. Dann über allem der Fernsehturm, dessen Turmcafé sich dreht°. Wir sahen auch einen britischen Jeep, der Unter den Linden Streife fuhr°, was uns an den Sonderstatus Berlins erinnerte. Hier trafen die kapitalistische und die sozialistische Welt aufeinander°; und für beide Welten waren Ost- und West-Berlin Schaufenster° zweier gegensätzlicher° Systeme.

then

GDR police (Volkspolizei)

GDR house of representatives
turns / patrolled

came together
display windows / opposing

Heute

Heute ist das alles Geschichte. Die Berliner können wieder reisen, wohin sie wollen. Berlin ist keine Insel mehr. Ich erinnere mich noch gut an die Reaktion meines Vaters, als wir den Mauerdurchbruch im amerikanischen Fernsehen sahen. Immer wieder sagte er

tears

„Wahnsinn! Dass ich das noch erleben durfte!" und ihm standen Tränen° in den Augen. Unsere Gedanken gingen damals zurück zu Präsident Kennedys Worten 1963 an der Mauer: „Alle freien Menschen sind Bürger Berlins . . . Ich bin ein Berliner!"

John F. Kennedy in Berlin am 26.6.1963

achieved

dome

shines / lantern

enlightenment

observation deck / look down

closed

location

Seit der Wiedervereinigung hat sich in Berlin viel verändert. Politiker, Städteplaner, Architekten und Ökologen haben enorme Arbeit geleistet°. Da, wo einst die Mauer stand, stehen jetzt moderne Gebäude und die alte Mitte Berlins ist wieder Stadtmitte geworden. Die moderne Kuppel° des Reichstagsgebäudes hat eine neue, symbolische Funktion. Einerseits strahlt° sie in der Nacht wie eine Laterne°, wie eine Art Erhellung der Vernunft oder Aufklärung°. Andererseits haben die Leute, die auf der Rampe nach oben zur Aussichtsplatform° laufen, die Möglichkeit, auf ihre Politiker herabzuschauen°. Hier diskutiert man nicht mehr hinter verschlossenen° Türen, sondern die Demokratie ist offener geworden. Als Hauptstadt des vereinten Deutschlands in einem neuen Europa hat Berlin neue Aufgaben bekommen und durch seine Lage°—nur rund 100 km zur polnischen Grenze—erlebt es jetzt auch eine größere Orientierung nach Osten. Berlin ist wieder ein Tor zur Welt.

Nach dem Lesen

Optional activity: Was ist das?
1. die vierziger Jahre 2. eine Olympiade
3. eine Metropole 4. die Luftbrücke
5. ein Rosinenbomber 6. die Westmächte
7. Vopos 8. ein Schaufenster 9. ein
Fernsehturmcafé 10. Unter den Linden

A. Richtig oder falsch?

_f_ 1. Der Vater und die Tochter fliegen nach Amerika.

_r_ 2. Der Vater hatte lange in Berlin gelebt.

_r_ 3. Er hatte Berlin sehr geliebt.

_f_ 4. In Berlin war aber damals nicht viel los.

_r_ 5. 1939 hatte der Krieg begonnen.

_r_ 6. 1945 teilten die Siegermächte Deutschland und Berlin.

_f_ 7. Die Luftbrücke brachte den Berlinern nur Rosinen.

_r_ 8. Von 1961 bis 1989 teilte die Mauer Berlin.

_f_ 9. Ein Vopo war ein ostdeutsches Auto.

_f_ 10. Der Potsdamer Platz war der „Palazzo Prozzo" Ost-Berlins.

_r_ 11. Unter den Linden ist eine berühmte alte Straße in Berlin.

_f_ 12. Ost-Berlin war ein Schaufenster des Kapitalismus.

_f_ 13. Der Vater ist beim Öffnen der Mauer in Berlin gewesen.

_f_ 14. Präsident Nixon sagte 1963: „Ich bin ein Berliner."

_f_ 15. Seit dem Jahr 2000 ist Berlin wieder die Hauptstadt Deutschlands.

_f_ 16. Politiker und Städteplaner können sich nicht entscheiden, was sie mit Berlin tun sollen.

_f_ 17. Wo einst die Mauer stand, ist jetzt ein langer Park.
_r_ 18. Von Berlin sind es nur 100 km bis zur polnischen Grenze.

B. Was fehlt?

1. Mir gefällt diese Stadt, in der____ mehr als drei Millionen Menschen wohnen.
2. Es ist ein Kulturzentrum *(n.)*, das____ unheimlich viel zu bieten hat. 3. Die
Filmfestspiele, deren____ Filme meistens sehr gut sind, muss man mal gesehen haben.
4. Der letzte Film, den____ ich mir angesehen habe, war herrlich. 5. Ein anderer Film,
an dessen____ Titel *(m.)* ich mich nicht erinnern kann, war etwas traurig. 6. Es war ein
Film, in dem____ mehrere berühmte Schauspieler mitspielten. 7. Der Hauptdarsteller
(main actor), der____ am Ende seine Heimat verlässt, hieß Humphrey Bogart.
8. Morgen Abend gehe ich mit Heike, deren____ Vater Extrakarten hat, ins Hebbel
Theater. 9. Es ist ein kleines Theater, das____ seit 1998 unter der Leitung
(leadership) der Intendantin *(artistic director)* Neele Härtling steht und kein
eigenes Ensemble hat. 10. Sie machen international zeitgenössisches *(contemporary)* Theater, das____ Künstler aus aller Welt anzieht *(attracts)*. 11. Zu dem
Stammpublikum *(regular clients)* gehören Leute, die____ sich für Neues und Experi-
mentelles interessieren. 12. Oft präsentieren sie auch junge Künstler aus Mittel-
und Osteuropa, die____ dort, wo sie herkommen, renommiert sind *(are well-known)*,
aber hier unbekannt sind. 13. Robert Wilson ist einer der amerikanischen Künstler,
der____ hier immer wieder seine Produktionen gezeigt hat. 14. Richard Forman, Lori
Anderson und Tricia Brown sind andere amerikanische Künstler, mit denen____ sie seit
Jahren zusammen arbeiten. 15. Morgen sehen wir ein Stück von einer Künstlerin
aus Litauen *(Lithuania)*, deren____ Namen ich vergessen habe. Ich freue mich darauf.

> **„Berlin ist mehr
> ein Weltteil als
> eine Stadt."**
>
> *Jean Paul*
> *Deutscher Dichter*
> *(1763–1825)*

C. Gespräch zwischen Vater und Tochter. Lesen Sie das Gespräch und berichten Sie
indirekt zusammen mit einem Partner/einer Partnerin, was die beiden gesagt
haben!

BEISPIEL: **S1** Die Tochter fragte, wie lange er dort gewohnt hätte.
            S2 Er sagte, dass er ungefähr 25 Jahre dort gewohnt hätte.

TOCHTER	Wie lange hast du dort gewohnt?
VATER	Ungefähr 25 Jahre.
TOCHTER	Wohnten deine Eltern damals auch in Berlin?
VATER	Nein, aber sie sind 1938 nachgekommen.
TOCHTER	Hast du dort studiert?
VATER	Ja, an der Humboldt-Universität.
TOCHTER	Hast du dort Mutti kennen gelernt?
VATER	Ja, das waren schöne Jahre.
TOCHTER	Und wann seid ihr von dort weggegangen?
VATER	1949.
TOCHTER	Erzähl mir davon!
VATER	Ach, das ist eine lange Geschichte. Setzen wir uns in ein Café! Dann werde ich dir davon erzählen.

C: Sie fragte, ob seine Eltern damals auch
in Berlin gewohnt hätten. Er sagte, dass sie
erst 1938 nachgekommen wären. — Sie
fragte, ob er dort studiert hätte. Er sagte,
dass er an der Humboldt-Universität
studiert hätte. — Sie fragte, ob er dort ihre
Mutter (Mutti) kennen gelernt hätte. Er
sagte ja, und dass das schöne Jahre gewesen wären. — Sie fragte, wann sie von dort
weggegangen wären. Er sagte, dass sie
1947 weggegangen wären. — Sie bat ihn, er
sollte ihr davon erzählen. Er sagte, dass
das eine lange Geschichte wäre. Sie sollten
sich in ein Café setzen. Dann würde er ihr
davon erzählen.

D. Wie geht's weiter? Beenden Sie die Sätze als Relativsätze. Vergleichen Sie Ihre Sätze
mit denen *(those)* der anderen!
1. Berlin ist eine Stadt, die . . .
2. Berlin ist eine Stadt, in der . . .
3. Berlin ist eine Stadt, deren . . .
4. Berlin ist eine Stadt, von der . . .
5. Berlin ist eine Stadt, um die . . .

Optional tongue twister: Der Mondschein
(moonlight) schien schon schön.

E. Das wäre etwas / nichts für mich. Wenn Sie die Wahl hätten, würden Sie in Berlin
leben oder dort studieren wollen? Warum (nicht)? Schreiben Sie 8–10 Sätze!

Maßnahmen gegen die Gewalt

large room / violence
criticized / noticed / withdrew
looked around

Als Herr Keuner, der Denkende, sich in einem Saale° vor vielen gegen die Gewalt° aussprach°, merkte° er, wie die Leute vor ihm zurückwichen° und weggingen. Er blickte sich um° und sah hinter sich stehen — die Gewalt.

„Was sagtest du?", fragte ihn die Gewalt.

„Ich sprach mich für die Gewalt aus", antwortete Herr Keuner.

backbone / to be broken
I for sure

Als Herr Keuner weggegangen war, fragten ihn seine Schüler nach seinem Rückgrat°. Herr Keuner antwortete: „Ich habe kein Rückgrat zum Zerschlagen°. Gerade ich° muss länger leben als die Gewalt."

Und Herr Keuner erzählte folgende Geschichte:

here: dictatorship / issued
of those / controlled
just the same
demanded / serve
washed himself / lay down
before going to sleep
covered him with a blanket /
    chased away the flies / watched
    over / obeyed / he avoided carefully
over
dictating / wrapped / rotten / dragged
bed / white-washed / breathed a sigh
    of relief

In die Wohnung des Herrn Egge, der gelernt hatte, nein zu sagen, kam eines Tages in der Zeit der Illegalität° ein Agent, der zeigte einen Schein vor, welcher ausgestellt° war im Namen derer°, die die Stadt beherrschten°, und auf dem stand, dass ihm gehören sollte jede Wohnung, in die er seinen Fuß setzte; ebenso° sollte ihm auch jedes Essen gehören, das er verlangte°, ebenso sollte ihm auch jeder Mann dienen°, den er sähe.

Der Agent setzte sich in einen Stuhl, verlangte Essen, wusch sich°, legte sich nieder° und fragte mit dem Gesicht zur Wand vor dem Einschlafen°: „Wirst du mir dienen?"

Herr Egge deckte ihn mit einer Decke zu°, vertrieb die Fliegen°, bewachte° seinen Schlaf, und wie an diesem Tage gehorchte° er ihm sieben Jahre lang. Aber was immer er für ihn tat, eines zu tun hütete er sich wohl°: das war, ein Wort zu sagen. Als nun die sieben Jahre herum° waren und der Agent dick geworden war vom vielen Essen, Schlafen und Befehlen°, starb der Agent. Da wickelte° ihn Herr Egge in die verdorbene° Decke, schleifte° ihn aus dem Haus, wusch das Lager°, tünchte° die Wände, atmete auf° und antwortete: „Nein."

Bertolt Brecht

Fokus — *Bertolt Brecht and Erich Kästner*

- **Bertolt Brecht** (1898–1956) is one of Germany's most celebrated 20th-century playwrights. His theory of the "epic theater" has had a considerable influence on modern theories of drama. By using various visual techniques and artificial acting styles—such as having the actors deliver their lines in a deliberately expressionless way—he tried to minimize the audience's rapport with the action, while increasing its awareness of the play's moral and political message. Brecht fled Berlin in 1933, seeking refuge in Switzerland, Denmark, Finland, and finally the United States (1941–1947). He returned to East Berlin in 1949 and founded the Berlin Ensemble. Brecht's works include *Die Dreigroschenoper* (1928; first film adaptation in 1931), *Mutter Courage und ihre Kinder* (1939), *Der gute Mensch von Sezuan* (1942), *Das Leben des Galilei* (1938/39), and *Der kaukasische Kreidekreis* (1945). Some of his works have been set to music; he worked extensively with composers Kurt Weill, Hanns Eisler, and Paul Dessau.

- **Erich Kästner** (1899–1974) was a German writer known for his sarcastic poems—often directed against narrow-mindedness and militarism—and his witty novels and children's books. In 1933 Kästner's disrespectful books were banned and burned by the Nazis. His works include the poem collection *Bei Durchsicht meiner Bücher* (1946), the stories *Emil und die Detektive* (1929), *Das fliegende Klassenzimmer* (1933), *Konferenz der Tiere* (1949), *Das doppelte Lottchen* (1949), and the comedy *Die Schule der Diktatoren* (1956).

Fantasie von übermorgen

Und als der nächste Krieg begann,
da sagten die Frauen: Nein!

und schlossen Bruder, Sohn und Mann
fest in der Wohnung ein°.   *locked up*

Dann zogen sie, in jedem Land,
wohl vor des Hauptmanns° Haus   *captain*
und hielten Stöcke° in der Hand   *sticks*
und holten die Kerls° heraus.   *guys*

Sie legten jeden übers Knie,
der diesen Krieg befahl°.   *ordered*
die Herren der Bank und Industrie,
den Minister und General.

Da brach so mancher Stock entzwei°.   *broke apart*
Und maches Großmaul° schwieg°.   *big mouth / shut up*
In allen Ländern gab's Geschrei°,   *screaming*
und nirgends gab es Krieg.

Die Frauen gingen dann wieder nach Haus,
zum Bruder und Sohn und Mann,
und sagten ihnen, der Krieg sei aus°!   *was over*
Die Männer starrten° zum Fenster hinaus   *stared*
und sahn die Frauen nicht an . . .

Erich Kästner

Fragen

1. **Bertolt Brechts Geschichte**

   a. Was tat Herr Keuner, als er sich von der Gewalt bedroht sah *(felt threatened)*?
   b. Waren da andere, die genauso handelten wie er?
   c. Was hielten seine Schüler von ihm, als sie ihn so feige *(cowardly)* sahen? Was hatten sie erwartet?
   d. Wie reagierte er auf ihre Frage?
   e. Wie vergleicht sich sein Verhalten gegenüber *(behavior toward)* der Gewalt mit dem von Herrn Egge?
   f. Was ist typisch für Agenten der Gewalt? Wie reagieren die Leute normalerweise auf sie?
   h. Was passiert mit vielen Agenten der Gewalt, wenn sie zu lange an der Macht sind?
   i. Wie reagiert Herr Egge auf den Tod *(death)* des Agenten und warum?
   j. Was halten Sie von seinem Verhalten und von Brechts Kurzgeschichte?

2. **Erich Kästners Gedicht**

   a. Was taten die Frauen in Kästners Gedicht, als es wieder Krieg geben sollte?
   b. Wen hielten sie dafür verantwortlich?
   c. Wie reagierten die Männer, als sie hörten, dass es keinen Krieg mehr geben sollte? Warum?
   d. Sagt das etwas über die Männer? Ist das fair?
   e. Führen die Frauen anders als die Männer? Wenn ja, wie?
   f. Sind die meisten Frauen gegen den Krieg? Wenn ja, warum vielleicht?

g. Glauben Sie, dass die Welt anders aussähe, wenn mehr Frauen an der Macht wären? Warum (nicht)?

h. Spricht dieses Gedicht nur von den Deutschen?

i. Warum der Titel „Fantasie von übermorgen"?

j. Was halten Sie von Kästners Gedicht?

B. Ein kleiner Unterschied. Schreiben Sie einen Aufsatz von 8–10 Sätzen, in dem Sie Brechts Geschichte und Kästners Gedicht vergleichen! Wo gibt es Parallelen und Unterschiede? Welches der beiden ist effektiver? Was denken Sie?

HÖREN SIE ZU!   TRACK 29

Ein paar Gedanken von so genannten Ossis *(eastern Germans)*

Zum Erkennen: das Textilgeschäft, -e *(clothing store);* viel geschafft *(accomplished a lot);* profitieren; garantieren; das Gefängnis, -se *(prison);* existieren; die Direktorin, -nen *(principal)*

Richtig oder falsch?

__r__   1. Die Wiedervereinigung Deutschlands war nicht so leicht, wie man sich das vorgestellt hatte.

__r__   2. Nach drei Jahren waren die Menschen im Westen nicht so optimistisch über die Zukunft wie die Menschen im Osten.

__r__   3. Nach drei Jahren hatten mehr als 75 Prozent der Ostdeutschen ein Auto und fast alle hatten Farbfernseher.

__r__   4. Ein Arbeiter in Ostdeutschland verdiente damals so viel wie 30 Arbeiter in Russland.

__r__   5. In Altdöbeln hatte man in drei Jahren 164 neue Geschäfte und Firmen eröffnet.

__r__   6. Jutta Laubach ist eine Altdöbelner Geschäftsfrau, die ein Textilgeschäft aufgemacht hat.

__f__   7. Sie fand das alte System besser, weil früher alles garantiert war.

__r__   8. Helga Müller weinte, als sie hörte, dass die Berliner Mauer plötzlich offen war.

__r__   9. Sie glaubte, dass der Kommunismus ein gutes System war.

__r__ 10. Monika Bernhart findet ihr neues Leben schwerer, aber schöner.

__r__ 11. Franziska Bungart war 13, als die Mauer fiel.

__r__ 12. Für ihren Mann Sebastian und sie ist das alles schon längst Geschichte.

__r__ 13. Der Computer, ohne den sie fast nicht mehr leben können, ist Teil ihres Alltags geworden

__f__ 14. Sie träumen davon, eines Tages mal nach Amerika zu reisen.

Video-Ecke

- In the Minidrama *Eine Stadt mit vielen Gesichtern,* we see Martin playing host to his aunt from Weimar whom he has not seen for a long time. His aunt, a passionate photographer, remembers the hard times in East Germany very well. She has also brought photos to show. Martin is very interested in his aunt's pictures because he can relate to some of the locations. Then in comes his sister and everything is fine *(Alles ist Sahne),* as she helps entertain her aunt.

- In the Blickpunkt *Mein Berlin,* we meet an architect who has lived in Berlin all his life. We listen as he remembers the war, the blockade, the construction of the Wall and its demise. We also get a sense of his excitement over reunification and the changes that have taken place since then. According to him, the Potsdamer Platz has become a meeting place for Berliners and people from all over the world and the Reichstagsgebäude with its modern dome a symbol of enlightenment and hope for a more open democracy.

Web-Ecke

- For updates, self-assessment quizzes, and online activities related to this chapter, visit the *Wie geht's?* Web site at **http://wiegehts.heinle.com**. You will go sightseeing in Berlin and Potsdam, check out what's going on in Berlin right now and during the Love Parade, and be introduced to several famous Berliners.

Kapitel (15)

Deutschland, Europa und die Zukunft

Das Goethe-Schiller-Denkmal vor dem Nationaltheater in Weimar

Lernziele

Vorschau
The path to a united Europe

Gespräche + Wortschatz
Nature and environmental protection

Fokus
Cultural capital Weimar
The German spelling reform
In search of an identity
Lessing, Goethe, Schiller

Struktur
15.1 Passive voice
15.2 Review of the uses of **werden**
15.3 Special subjunctive (Subjunctive I)

Einblicke
Der Wind kennt keine Grenzen
Lessing: *Der Esel in Begleitung*
Lessing: *Nur anders, nicht besser*
Goethe: *Erinnerung*
Schiller: *An die Freude*

Video-Ecke
Minidrama: *Der Wind, der Wind, das himmlische Kind*

Web-Ecke

Vorschau

The Path to a United Europe

1945 World War II leaves Europe devastated and hungry.

1949 The North Atlantic Treaty Organization (NATO) and the Council of Europe are established.

1950 France launches Schuman Plan, which proposes putting French and West German coal and steel production under a single authority.

1951 Italy, Belgium, the Netherlands, and Luxembourg found the European Coal and Steel Community (ECSC), known as Montanunion.

1957 France, Germany, Italy, Belgium, the Netherlands, and Luxembourg establish the European Economic Community (EEC) and the European Atomic Energy Commission (EURATOM), known collectively as the Treaties of Rome. The EEC, EURATOM, and ECSC are called the "European Communities," or EC.

1960 Great Britain, Austria, Switzerland, Portugal, and the Scandinavian countries form the European Free Trade Association (EFTA), an alternative to the EEC.

1973 Denmark, Ireland, and Great Britain join the EC.

1979 First direct elections to the European Parliament are held.

1981 Greece joins the EC.

1986 Spain and Portugal become members of the EC.

1989 With the fall of the Berlin Wall, Europe's division is ended.

1990 German unification extends EC membership to the former East Germany.

1993 Signed in 1991, the Maastricht Treaty now goes into effect, paving the way to economic and monetary union and increasing political unity. The "European Communities" are now called the European Union (EU).

1995 The entry of Austria, Finland, and Sweden into the EU brings the number of member states to 15. The Schengen Agreement, an EU treaty that makes passport-free travel possible between signatory states, goes into effect.

1997 The heads of the member states draw up the Amsterdam Treaty, which lays out internal reform and expansion eastward.

1999 The euro is introduced as common currency for financial transactions in 11 member states, marking the beginning of the end of the deutsche mark and the various national EU currencies.

2002 The euro replaces national currencies such as the deutsche mark and schilling in all daily transactions.

Point out that originally the European Community's goals were more of an economic nature, therefore its earlier abbreviations EEC (European Economic Community).

Again, bringing along some euro coins and banknotes might be of interest. Ask students to find out about the current exchange rate to the dollar. You could also ask them to research online to find a recent article about the EU, its present members and those that have applied for membership.

Diese Geldscheine kann man in allen Ländern der EU benutzen.

Gespräche + Wortschatz

CD 6, Track 9

Besuch in Weimar

TOM Komisch, dieses Denkmal von Goethe und Schiller kenne ich doch! Ich glaube, ich habe es schon irgendwo gesehen.

DANIELA Warst du eigentlich schon mal in San Francisko?

TOM Na klar!

DANIELA Warst du auch im Golden Gate Park?

TOM Ach ja, da steht genau das gleiche Denkmal! Das haben, glaub' ich, die Deutsch-Amerikaner in Kalifornien einmal bauen lassen.

DANIELA Richtig! Übrigens, weißt du, dass Weimar 1999 Kulturhauptstadt Europas war?

TOM Nein, das ist mir neu. Wieso denn?

DANIELA Im 18. Jahrhundert haben hier doch viele berühmte Leute gelebt und die Weimarer Republik ist auch danach benannt.

TOM Ja ja. Aber heute früh, als ich am Mahnmal vom Konzentrationslager Buchenwald auf die Stadt herabblickte, hatte ich sehr gemischte Gefühle.

DANIELA Ja, da hast du natürlich Recht.

In der Altstadt

DANIELA Schau mal, die alten Häuser hier sind doch echt schön.

TOM Ja, sie sind gut restauriert worden. Ich finde es vor allem schön, dass hier keine Autos fahren dürfen.

DANIELA Gott sei Dank! Die Fassaden hätten die Abgase der Trabbis[1] nicht lange überlebt.

TOM Bei uns gibt es jetzt auch eine Bürgerinitiative, alle Autos in der Altstadt zu verbieten, um die alten Gebäude zu retten.

DANIELA Das finde ich gut.

TOM Sind die Container da drüben für die Mülltrennung?

DANIELA Ja, habt ihr das auch?

TOM Das schon, aber da könnte man ganz bestimmt noch viel mehr tun. Zum Beispiel weiß ich nie, wohin mit alten Batterien oder Medikamenten.

DANIELA Die alten Batterien bringst du zur Tankstelle und die alten Medikamente zur Apotheke.

TOM Das geht bei uns nicht und so landet schließlich vieles in der Mülltonne.

DANIELA Das ist bei uns verboten.

TOM Das sollte es auch sein. Ihr seid da eben weiter als wir.

---

[1] The **Trabant,** or **Trabi** (see drawing above), was an East German car with a two-stroke engine that emitted roughly nine times more hydrocarbons and five times more carbon dioxide than cars with four-stroke engines. Nicknamed **Plastikbomber, Asphaltblase** (Asphalt Bubble), or **Rennpappe** (Racing Cardboard), it was nevertheless expensive by GDR standards. People had to save the equivalent of 10–27 months' salary; credit did not exist. Delivery of the 26 HP car normally took at least 10 years; and its spare parts were one of the underground currencies of the former GDR.

A. Richtig oder falsch?

   r   1. Tom und Daniela sind in Weimar.

   f   2. Sie sehen ein Denkmal von Goethe und Nietzsche.

   f   3. Eine Kopie dieses Denkmals steht in New York.

   r   4. Die Gebäude in der Innenstadt sind schön restauriert.

___r___ 5. Im Zentrum gibt es auch eine Fußgängerzone.

___r___ 6. Tom kommt aus einer Stadt, in deren Altstadt bis jetzt noch Autos fahren
dürfen.

___r___ 7. Für die Mülltrennung gibt es in Weimar besondere Container.

___f___ 8. Tom meint, dass es das bei ihm zu Hause nicht gibt.

___f___ 9. Tom weiß zum Beispiel nie, wohin mit alten Zeitungen und
Kartons *(boxes)*.

___f___ 10. Die landen bei ihm gewöhnlich in der Mülltonne.

B. Jetzt sind Sie dran! Sprechen Sie mit Ihrem Partner/Ihrer Partnerin, was
er/sie davon hält, alle Autos in der Altstadt zu verbieten. Was wäre schön?

They could also make a list of cars that are gas guzzlers **(Benzinschlucker)** and thereby put special demands on the environment. Should those cars be forbidden or people who drive them pay more taxes **(Steuern)**?

Fokus — *Cultural Capital Weimar*

In 1985, the European Community selected for the first time a cultural capital of Europe: Athens. Luxembourg, Thessaloniki, Stockholm, and other cities followed. Weimar had this honor for the year 1999. It is not only the smallest of the European cultural capitals to date; it is also the first city from one of the former communist countries to bear this title.

Weimar boasts a proud cultural history. Johann Sebastian Bach was court organist there in the early-18th century. Goethe, who lived and worked in Weimar from 1775 until his death, drew Schiller, Gottfried Herder, and many others to the town, which, nourished by genius, gave birth to "Weimar Classicism." Franz Liszt was musical director in Weimar in the mid-19th century, and the philosopher and author Friedrich Nietzsche lived there during his last years as well. In 1919, following World War I, the National Assembly met in Weimar to draft a constitution for the new republic—henceforth known as the Weimar Republic. The assembly chose this site because of its popular associations with Germany's classical tradition. The new republic lasted only 14 years, dissolved by Hitler soon after he was appointed chancellor in

Auf dem Marktplatz in Weimar

1933. During the Nazi period, Weimar and its traditions were used selectively to promote Nazi ideology and some of Goethe's works were even banned from schools. On the Ettersberg, a hill above the town, a memorial recalls the nearby Nazi concentration camp of Buchenwald. Since the fall of East Germany, tourists from across Europe are again flocking to Weimar's historical and cultural landmarks.

Wortschatz 1

Die Landschaft *(landscape, scenery)*

Die Umwelt *(environment)*

der Abfall, -̈e	*trash*	das Denkmal, -̈er	*monument*
Bau, -ten	*building; structure*	Gebiet, -e	*area, region*
Müll	*garbage; waste*	Naturschutzgebiet, -e	*nature preserve*
(Umwelt)schutz	*(environmental) protection*		

die Erhaltung	*preservation*	die Rede, -n	*speech*
Küste, -n	*coast*	Sammelstelle, -n	*collection site*
Mülltonne, -n	*garbage can*	Verschmutzung	*pollution*
Natur	*nature*		

Weiteres

allerdings	*however*
echt schön[1]	*really pretty*
schließlich	*after all, in the end*
übrigens	*by the way*
umweltbewusst	*environmentally aware*
ab·reißen, riss ab, abgerissen	*to tear down*
(wieder) auf·bauen	*to (re)build*
finanzieren	*to finance*
garantieren	*to guarantee*
planen	*to plan*
reden (mit + *dat.* / über + *acc.*)	*to talk (to / about)*
renovieren	*to renovate*
restaurieren	*to restore*
retten	*to save, rescue*
schaden	*to hurt, damage*
schonen	*to go easy on, protect*
schützen	*to protect*
trennen	*to separate*
verbieten, verbot, verboten	*to forbid*
verwenden	*to use, utilize*
weg·werfen (wirft weg), warf weg, weggeworfen	*to throw away, discard*
zerstören	*to destroy*

JEDER TAG IST TAG DER UMWELT

Wirf Altglas nicht fort, Container stehn an jedem Ort!

Altglas

[1] Similarly: **echt interessant, echt billig, echt komisch** usw.

Zum Erkennen: bauen lassen *(to have built);* benennen nach *(to name after);* das Konzentrationslager, - *(concentration camp);* herab·blicken auf *(to look down on);* gemischte Gefühle *(mixed feelings);* die Fassade, -n; die Abgase *(exhaust fumes);* überleben *(to survive);* die Bürgerinitiative, -n *(citizens' initiative);* der Container, -; das schon *(here: sure);* die Batterie, -n; die Tankstelle, -n *(gas station);* die Medikamente *(pl. medicine);* ihr seid da eben weiter *(in that regard, you are just more progressive);* AUCH: das Aktiv *(active voice);* das Passiv *(passive voice);* die Zeitform, -en *(tense);* auf·schreiben *(to write down);* erfahren *(to find out)*

Zum Thema

A. Im Rathaus. Als Radioreporter hören Sie sich die Rede eines Städteplaners an. Berichten Sie Ihren Zuhörern *(listeners),* was Sie gehört haben!

BEISPIEL: Er hat gesagt, wir sollten nicht auf die Bürger hören, die immer . . .

„Hören Sie nicht auf die Bürger, die immer wieder alles, ja die ganze Altstadt, retten wollen. Viele alte Innenhöfe *(inner courts)* sind dunkel und hässlich. Abreißen ist viel billiger und einfacher als renovieren. Wenn man die alten Gebäude abreißt und die Innenstadt schön modern aufbaut, dann kommt bestimmt wieder Leben in unser

Zentrum. Auf diese Weise kann man auch die Straßen verbreitern *(widen)* und alles besser planen. Fußgängerzonen sind sicher schön und gut, aber nicht im Zentrum, denn alle wollen ihr Auto in der Nähe haben. Das ist doch klar, weil's viel bequemer und sicherer ist! Ich kann Ihnen garantieren, wenn Sie aus dem Zentrum eine Einkaufszone machen, zu deren Geschäften man nur zu Fuß hinkommt *(gets to),* dann verlieren Sie alle, meine Damen und Herren, viel Geld!"

B. Altbau oder Neubau? Wo würden Sie lieber wohnen? Was spricht dafür und was dagegen? Stellen Sie mit Ihrem Partner/Ihrer Partnerin eine Liste auf und machen Sie eine Meinungsumfrage *(opinion poll)!*

C. Schützt unsere Umwelt! Fragen Sie einen Nachbarn/eine Nachbarin, . . . !

1. was er/sie mit Altglas, Altpapier, alten Batterien, alten Farben, altem Öl, alten Medikamenten, alten Dosen *(cans),* Plastikflaschen und Plastiktüten *(. . . bags)* macht
2. was er/sie mit alter Kleidung, alten CDs oder alten Büchern macht
3. ob er/sie eine Waschmaschine oder Spülmaschine *(dishwasher)* benutzt; wenn ja, wie viel Waschmittel oder Spülmittel er/sie dafür benutzt
4. wofür er/sie Chemikalien *(chemicals)* benutzt und wie oft
5. ob er/sie manchmal ein Umweltverschmutzer ist; wieso (nicht)
6. ob er/sie gern Musik hört; wenn ja, ob er/sie sie auf laut oder leise *(quiet)* stellt und ob andere darüber manchmal auch böse sind
7. ob er/sie einen Hund hat; wenn ja, was für einen Hund und ob er/sie beim „Gassi gehen" seine „Geschäfte" aufsammelt
8. was er/sie und seine/ihre Freunde für die Umwelt tun

If you are curious: **s. erbauen an** *to enjoy;* **der Abfall-Wurf** *littering;* **das Waschmittel, -** *laundry detergent;* **in kleinen Gaben** *in small amounts;* **üblich** *customary;* **entgegen·nehmen** *to accept;* **der Verstand** *common sense;* **der Ölwechsel** *oil change;* **sei helle** *be smart;* **Gassi gehen** *to walk the doggie*

Students might enjoy talking about (their) dogs (e.g., **der Schäferhund, -e; Labrador, -e; Dobermann, -̈er; Collie, -s; Pudel, -; Spitz, -e;** *[pomeranian],* **Terrier, -; Dackel, -;** *[dachshund],* **Cockerspaniel, -s; Pekinese, -n).**

Waschmittel brauch in kleinen Gaben, willst Du gesundes Wasser haben.

Aussprache

Glottal Stops. Lesen Sie auch Teil II. 42 in Zur Aussprache im *Arbeitsbuch!*

1. +Erich +arbeitet +am +alten Schloss.
2. Die +Abgase der +Autos machen +einfach +überall +alles kaputt.
3. +Ulf +erinnert sich +an +ein +einmaliges +Abendkonzert +im +Ulmer Dom.
4. +Otto sieht +aus wie +ein +alter +Opa.
5. +Anneliese +ist +attraktiv +und +elegant.

CD 6, Track 10

Mit dem Pferdewagen durchs Wattenmeer oder Watt

Ask students if they know of any such mudflats in their own country. Have they ever have walked there or gone looking for clams?

HÖREN SIE ZU!   TRACK 30

Habitat Wattenmeer

Zum Erkennen: das flache Vorland *(tidal flats)*; grenzen an *(to border on)*; die Ebbe *(low tide)*; die Flut *(high tide)*; die Muschel, -n *(clam)*; das Paradies; die Krabbe, -n *(crab)*; knabbern *(to nibble)*; der Pferdewagen, - *(horse-drawn carriage)*; der Seehund, -e *(seal)*; das empfindliche Ökosystem *(delicate ecosystem)*; das Düngemittel, - *(fertilizer)*; der Kompromiss, -e; das Reservat, -e *(reservation)*; der Fischfang *(fishing)*; begrenzt *(limited)*

Richtig oder falsch?

_f__ 1. Das Wattenmeer liegt vor der Ostseeküste.
_f__ 2. Alle 12 Stunden wechselt es von Ebbe zu Flut.
_r__ 3. Bei Ebbe kann man weit ins Watt hinaus laufen.
_r__ 4. Dabei kann man alle möglichen *(alls sorts of)* Tiere beobachten.
_r__ 5. Gehfaule können auch mit dem Pferdewagen ins Watt fahren.
_r__ 6. Wegen seines empfindlichen Ökosystems haben die Deutschen dieses Gebiet zum Naturschutzgebiet erklärt.
_r__ 7. Auch die Dänen und Niederländer sind am Schutz dieser Landschaft interessiert.
_f__ 8. Die Dänen dürfen noch im Wattenmeer fischen, aber nicht die Deutschen.

Struktur

15.1 Passive voice

English and German sentences are in one of two voices: the active or the passive. In the AC-TIVE VOICE the subject of the sentence is doing something; it's "active."

The students ask the professor.

In the PASSIVE VOICE, the subject is not doing anything, rather, something is being done to it; it's "passive."

The professor is asked by the students.

Note what happens when a sentence in the active voice is changed into the passive voice: The direct object of the active becomes the subject of the passive.

The passive voice is treated only briefly because by now many students will be saturated with verb forms. If you want your students to use the passive, elaborate on the explanations; there are plenty of exercises for active mastery of the passive. Otherwise, teach the passive for recognition only. In that case, use exercises C and D for translation into English and omit exercises F and H.

subj.   obj.
*The students ask **the professor.***

***The professor** is asked by the students.*
subj.   obj. of prep.

In both languages, the active voice is used much more frequently than the passive voice, especially in everyday speech. The passive voice is used when the focus is on the person or thing at whom the action is directed, rather than on the agent who is acting.

Active Voice	**Die Studenten** fragen den Professor.
Passive Voice	**Der Professor** wird von den Studenten gefragt.

1. Forms

   a. In English the passive voice is formed with the auxiliary *to be* and the past participle of the verb. In German, it is formed with the auxiliary **werden** and the past participle of the verb.

werden . . . + past participle			
ich	**werde**	*I am (being)*	
du	**wirst**	*you are (being)*	
er	**wird**	*he is (being)*	
		gefragt	*asked*
wir	**werden**	*we are (being)*	
ihr	**werdet**	*you are (being)*	
sie	**werden**	*they are (being)*	

Der Professor **wird** von den Studenten **gefragt.**

Die Professoren **werden** von den Studenten **gefragt.**

Wissen, was gespielt wird

Der neue Kalender der Semperoper ist da!

www.semperoper.de

   b. The passive voice has the <u>same tenses</u> as the active voice. They are formed with the various tenses of **werden + the past participle of the verb.** Note, however, that in the perfect tenses of the passive voice, the past participle of **werden** is **worden!** When you see or hear **worden,** you know immediately that you are dealing with a sentence in the passive voice.

PRESENT	Er **wird** . . . gefragt.	*He is being asked . . .*
SIMPLE PAST	Er **wurde** . . . gefragt.	*He was asked . . .*
FUTURE	Er **wird** . . . gefragt **werden.**	*He will be asked . . .*
PRES. PERF.	Er **ist** . . . gefragt **worden.**	*He has been asked . . .*
PAST PERF.	Er **war** . . . gefragt **worden.**	*He had been asked . . .*

Die Altstadt wird renoviert.	*The old part of town is being renovated.*
Die Pläne wurden letztes Jahr gemacht.	*The plans were made last year.*
Alles wird finanziert werden.	*Everything will be financed.*
Das ist entschieden worden.	*That has been decided.*
Manche Gebäude waren im Krieg zerstört worden.	*Some buildings had been destroyed during the war.*

In subordinate clauses, the pattern is:

Ich weiß, dass die Altstadt renoviert wird.

, dass die Pläne letztes Jahr gemacht wurden.

, dass alles finanziert werden wird.

, dass alles schon entschieden worden ist.

, dass manche Gebäude im Krieg zerstört worden waren.

c. Modals themselves are not put into the passive voice. Rather, they follow this pattern:

> modal . . . + past participle + **werden**

In this book only the present and simple past tense of the modals will be used.

PRESENT	Er **muss** . . . gefragt **werden.**	*He must (has to) be asked.*
SIMPLE PAST	Er **musste** . . . gefragt **werden.**	*He had to be asked*

Das Gebäude muss renoviert werden.	*The building must be renovated.*
Das Gebäude sollte letztes Jahr renoviert werden.	*The building was supposed to be renovated last year.*

In subordinate clauses the inflected verb stands at the end.

Ich weiß, dass das Gebäude renoviert werden **muss.**

, dass das Gebäude letztes Jahr renoviert werden **sollte.**

2. Expression of the agent

If the agent who performs the act is expressed, the preposition **von** is used.

Der Professor wird **von den Studenten** gefragt.	*The professor is asked by the students.*
Alles ist **vom Staat** finanziert worden.	*Everything was financed by the state.*

3. Impersonal use

In German, the passive voice is frequently used without a subject or with **es** functioning as the subject.

Hier darf nicht gebaut werden.	*You can't build here.*
Es darf hier nicht gebaut werden.	*Building is not permitted here.*

4. Alternative to the passive voice

One common substitute for the passive voice is a sentence in the active voice with **man** as the subject.

Hier darf nicht gebaut werden.

Es darf hier nicht gebaut werden.

Man darf hier nicht bauen.

Übungen

A. Trier. Aktiv oder Passiv?

A: 1P, 2A, 3P, 4P, 5P, 6P, 7P, 8A

1. Trier was founded by the Romans in 15 B.C.
2. Its original name was *Augusta Treverorum.*
3. Under Roman occupation, Germania along the Rhine and Danube had been transformed into a series of Roman provinces.
4. The names of many towns are derived from Latin.
5. Remnants from Roman times can still be seen today.
6. New discoveries are made from time to time.
7. Beautiful Roman museums have been built.
8. One of them is located in the former *Colonia Agrippina* (Köln).

> „Je weniger die Leute darüber wissen,
> wie Würste und Gesetze gemacht werden,
> desto besser schlafen sie nachts."
>
> Otto von Bismarck

B. Köln. Was bedeutet das auf Englisch?

1. a. Köln wurde während des Krieges schwer zerbombt.
   b. Achtzig Prozent der Häuser in der Innenstadt waren zerbombt *(destroyed by bombs)* worden.
   c. Inzwischen *(in the meantime)* ist Köln wieder schön aufgebaut und restauriert worden.
   d. Zur Karnevalszeit wird hier schwer gefeiert.
   e. Es ist eine Stadt, in der jedes Jahr verschiedene Messen *(fairs)* gehalten werden.
   f. Die Popkomm, Kölns Messe für Popmusik und Unterhaltung, wird von einem großen Musikfestival begleitet *(accompanied),* das in der ganzen Stadt gefeiert wird.
2. a. Erst mussten natürlich neue Wohnungen gebaut werden.
   b. Manche alten Gebäude konnten gerettet werden.
   c. Der Dom musste restauriert werden.
   d. Die alten Kirchen aus dem 12. Jahrhundert dürfen auch nicht vergessen werden.
   e. Das kann natürlich nicht ohne Geld gemacht werden.
   f. Durch Bürgerinitiativen wurde genug Geld für die Restaurierung gesammelt.
3. a. In der Altstadt wird in Parkgaragen geparkt.
   b. Es wird viel mit dem Bus gefahren.
   c. In der „Hohen Straße" wird nicht Auto gefahren.
   d. Dort wird zu Fuß gegangen.
   e. Dort wird gern eingekauft.
   f. In der Vorweihnachtszeit wird die Fußgängerzone mit vielen Lichtern dekoriert.

B.1: a. Cologne was heavily bombed during the war. b. Eighty percent of the houses in the inner city had been destroyed by bombs. c. In the meantime, Cologne has been nicely rebuilt and restored. d. During the carnival season, there is lots of celebrating going on / they celebrate a lot. e. It is a city in which different fairs are held every year. f. The Popkomm, Cologne's fair for pop music and entertainment, is accompanied by a big music festival that's celebrated all over town

B.2: a. First of all, of course, new apartments had to be built. b. Some old buildings could be saved. c. The cathedral had to be restored. d. The old churches from the 12th century should / must also not be forgotten. e. That can't be done, of course, without money. f. Through some citizens' initiatives, enough money for the restoration was collected.

B.3: a. In the old part of town, there are parking garages / people park in parking garages. b. Many take the bus. c. You can't drive / there's no driving in the "Hohe Straße." d. There you walk. e. There's lots of shopping / people like to shop there. f. In the pre-Christmas season, the pedestrian area is decorated with many lights.

C. Ein schönes Haus. Sagen Sie die Sätze im Aktiv!

1. **BEISPIEL:**   Nicht alle Gebäude waren vom Krieg zerstört worden.
   Der Krieg hatte nicht alle Gebäude zerstört.

   a. Viele Gebäude sind von Planierraupen *(bulldozers)* zerstört worden.
   b. Dieses Haus wurde von den Bürgern gerettet.
   c. Viele Unterschriften *(signatures)* wurden von Studenten gesammelt.
   d. Das Haus ist von der Uni gekauft worden.
   e. Die Fassade wird von Spezialisten renoviert werden.
   f. Die Hauspläne werden von Architekten gemacht.

2. **BEISPIEL:**   Der Hausplan darf von den Architekten nicht sehr verändert werden.
   Die Architekten dürfen den Hausplan nicht sehr verändern.

   a. Ein Teil soll von der Stadt finanziert werden.
   b. Der Rest muss von der Uni bezahlt werden.

C.1: a. Planierraupen haben . . . zerstört. b. Die Bürger retteten . . . (haben . . . gerettet). c. Die Studenten sammelten . . . (haben . . . gesammelt). d. Die Uni hat . . . gekauft. e. Spezialisten werden . . . renovieren. f. Architekten machen . . .

C.2: a. Die Stadt soll . . . finanzieren. b. Die Uni muss . . . bezahlen. c. Die Universität konnte . . . ausbauen. d. Die Studenten dürfen . . . benutzen.

c. Das Haus konnte von der Universität als Gästehaus ausgebaut werden.
d. Der große Raum im Parterre darf von den Studenten als Treffpunkt (*meeting place*) benutzt werden.

C.3: a. Dort tauscht man . . . aus. b. Man spricht . . . c. Heute Abend gibt man . . . d. Letzte Woche hat man . . . gezeigt (zeigte man . . .). e. Hier wird man . . . halten.

3. **BEISPIEL:**   Das Gästehaus wird viel besucht.
   Man besucht das Gästehaus viel.

a. Dort werden Gedanken ausgetauscht.
b. Es wird auch Englisch und Italienisch gesprochen.
c. Heute Abend wird ein Jazzkonzert gegeben.
d. Letzte Woche wurde ein Film gezeigt.
e. Hier werden auch Seminare gehalten werden.

D: 1. ist . . . empfohlen worden 2. wurde . . . gezeigt 3. war verboten worden 4. wird . . . geredet werden 5. konnte . . . gelernt werden 6. sollte . . . wiederholt werden

D. Ein alter Film. Wiederholen Sie die Sätze im Passiv, aber in einer anderen Zeitform!

BEISPIEL: Ein alter Film wird gespielt. (*simple past*)
   Ein alter Film wurde gespielt.

1. Er wird von den Studenten sehr empfohlen. (*present perfect*)
2. Zu DDR-Zeiten wird er nicht gezeigt. (*simple past*)
3. Er wird verboten. (*past perfect*)
4. Es wird viel darüber geredet. (*future*)
5. Daraus kann viel gelernt werden. (*simple past*)
6. Er soll übrigens wiederholt werden. (*simple past*)

E: 1. Ein Formular muss noch ausgefüllt werden. *A form still has to be filled out.* 2. Dann kann es am ersten Schalter abgegeben werden. *Then it can be turned in at the first counter.* 3. Auf der Post dürfen auch Telefongespräche gemacht werden. *You are also allowed to make telephone calls at the post office.* 4. Dollar sollen auf der Bank umgetauscht werden. *Dollars should / ought to be exchanged at the bank.* 5. Nicht überall kann mit Reiseschecks bezahlt werden. *Not everywhere can you pay with travelers' checks.* 6. Taxifahrer wollen mit Bargeld bezahlt werden. *Taxi drivers want to be paid in cash.*

F: Remind students not to express the agent! 1. Am anderen Tisch wird Französisch gesprochen. 2. Mittags wird warm gegessen. 3. Dabei wird gemütlich geredet. 4. Natürlich wird nicht mit vollem Mund geredet. 5. Übrigens wird die Gabel in der linken Hand gehalten. 6. Und vor dem Essen wird „Guten Appetit!" gesagt.

E. Post und Geld. Wiederholen Sie die Sätze im Passiv, aber mit einem Modalverb! Wie heißt das auf Englisch?

BEISPIEL: Das Paket wird zur Post gebracht. (sollen)
   Das Paket soll zur Post gebracht werden.
   The package is supposed to be taken to the post office.

1. Ein Formular (*form*) wird noch ausgefüllt. (müssen)
2. Dann wird es am ersten Schalter abgegeben. (können)
3. Auf der Post werden auch Telefongespräche gemacht. (dürfen)
4. Dollar werden auf der Bank umgetauscht. (sollen)
5. Nicht überall wird mit Reiseschecks bezahlt. (können)
6. Taxifahrer werden mit Bargeld bezahlt. (wollen)

F. Im Restaurant. Sagen Sie die Sätze im Passiv!

BEISPIEL: Hier spricht man Deutsch.
   Hier wird Deutsch gesprochen.

1. Am anderen Tisch spricht man Französisch.
2. Mittags isst man warm.
3. Dabei redet man gemütlich.
4. Natürlich redet man nicht mit vollem Mund.
5. Übrigens hält man die Gabel in der linken Hand.
6. Und vor dem Essen sagt man „Guten Appetit!"

G. Schont die Parkanlagen! Sie und ein Freund (Ihr Partner/Ihre Partnerin) sind in einem deutschen Park und sehen dieses Schild. Sie lesen es, sind aber nicht ganz sicher, ob Sie es richtig verstanden haben. Sagen Sie, was Sie darunter verstehen! Wechseln Sie sich nach jedem Satz ab!

You might ask students about their own city. Do their parks have such restrictions? Which parks do they enjoy in particular and why?

BEISPIEL: S1 Es wird gebeten, auf den Wegen zu bleiben.
   S2 Ich glaube, das bedeutet, dass man auf den Wegen bleiben soll.

SCHONT DIE PARKANLAGEN!

Es wird gebeten°:

Auf den Wegen zu bleiben

Blumen nicht abzupflücken°

Hunde an der Leine° zu führen

Denkmäler sauber zu halten

Im Park nicht Fußball zu spielen

Fahrräder nicht in den Park mitzunehmen

you're requested

pick

leash

H. Die Party: Was muss noch gemacht werden? Sagen Sie im Passiv, dass alles schon gemacht (worden) ist!

> **BEISPIEL:**   Fritz und Lisa müssen noch angerufen werden.
> **Fritz und Lisa sind schon angerufen worden.**

1. Die Wohnung muss noch geputzt werden. 2. Der Tisch muss noch in die Ecke gestellt werden. 3. Die Gläser müssen noch gewaschen werden. 4. Das Bier muss noch kalt gestellt werden. 5. Die Kartoffelchips müssen noch in die Schüssel *(bowl)* getan werden.

I. Wohin damit? Fragen Sie Ihren Partner/Ihre Partnerin, was bei Ihnen zu Hause mit Dingen wie alten Blumen, alten Telefons, Haushaltsmaschinen usw. gemacht wird! Benutzen Sie dabei das Passiv!

> **BEISPIEL:**   Was macht ihr mit alten Blumen?
> **Alte Blumen werden bei uns auf den Kompost geworfen.**
> Bei uns auch. / Bei uns nicht. Bei uns . . .

H: 1. Die Wohnung ist schon geputzt worden. 2. Der Tisch ist schon in die Ecke gestellt worden. 3. Die Gläser sind schon gewaschen worden. 4. Das Bier ist schon kalt gestellt worden. 5. Die Kartoffelchips sind schon in die Schüssel getan worden.

Fokus — *The German Spelling Reform*

As you are completing your first year of German, you should be aware of the German spelling reform that was adopted in 1998. The spelling that you were introduced to in *Wie geht's?* follows the new guidelines, but older texts, especially literary ones, might not. So don't be concerned when words are occasionally spelled differently than you have learned.

The most visible change was the partial abolition of the ß, which the Swiss dropped long ago. Under the new rules, the ß is now used only after a long vowel or dipthong, e.g., **Größe, heiß;** after a short vowel it is replaced with an *ss*, e.g., **daß > dass** and **er/sie ißt > isst.** The guidelines also allow now the triplication of consonants in compound nouns, e.g., **Schiffahrt >**

Schifffahrt; Balletheater > Balletttheater. Many of the changes dealt with imported words. For instance, the diphthong *ai* in foreign words became *eingedeutscht* with an umlauted *ä* (e.g., **Affaire > Affäre**); *ph* and *ch* can be replaced with *f* and *sch* (e.g., **Asphalt > Asfalt; Sketch > Sketsch**). Also affected were the capitalization of certain phrases (e.g., **auf deutsch > auf Deutsch; gestern abend > gestern Abend**), certain word combinations (e.g., **wieviel > wie viel; kennenlernen > kennen lernen; radfahren > Rad fahren**), some hyphenation (e.g., **bakken > ba-cken; mei-stens > meis-tens**), and punctuation. Since German is a living language and still evolving, do not be surprised by certain variations.

15.2 Review of the uses of *werden*

Distinguish carefully among the various uses of **werden**.

1. **werden** + predicate noun / adjective = a FULL VERB

Er wird Arzt.	*He's going to be a doctor.*
Es wird dunkel.	*It's getting dark.*

2. **werden** + infinitive = auxiliary of the FUTURE TENSE

Ich werde ihn fragen.	*I'll ask him.*

3. **würde** + infinitive = auxiliary in the PRESENT-TIME SUBJUNCTIVE

Ich würde ihn fragen.	*I would ask him.*

4. **werden** + past participle = auxiliary in the PASSIVE VOICE

Er wird von uns gefragt.	*He's (being) asked by us.*
Goethe wurde 1749 geboren.	*Goethe was born in 1749.*

NOTE: To express *I was born . . .*, either **ich bin . . . geboren** or **ich wurde . . . geboren** are used. The simple past of the passive form must be used for people who are no longer living.

Übungen

J. Was ist was? Lesen Sie die folgenden Sätze und analysieren Sie sie mit Ihrem Partner/Ihrer Partnerin! Sagen Sie, wie **werden** benutzt wird und wie Sie das auf Englisch sagen würden! Wechseln Sie sich ab!

BEISPIEL: Leonie ist nach Amerika eingeladen worden.
   werden + past participle = PASSIVE VOICE
   Leonie was invited (to go) to America.

J: 1. full verb *(wants to become)* 2. passive *(had to be paid)* 3. full verb *(became)* 4. passive *(was explained)* 5. subjunctive *(would do)* 6. subjunctive *(would work)* 7. passive + future *(won't be allowed)* 8. full verb *(is getting)* 9. future *(will help)*.

1. Leonie möchte Englischlehrerin werden.
2. Das Studium dort musste von ihr bezahlt werden.
3. Es ist allerdings teurer geworden, als sie dachte.
4. Das wurde ihr nie erklärt.
5. Was würdest du an ihrer Stelle tun?
6. Ich würde ein Semester arbeiten.
7. Das wird nicht erlaubt werden.
8. Übrigens wird ihr Englisch schon viel besser.
9. Der Amerikaaufenthalt wird ihr später helfen.

May be omitted if desired.

15.3 Special subjunctive

German has another subjunctive, often called the SPECIAL SUBJUNCTIVE or SUBJUNCTIVE I. English only has a few remnants of this subjunctive.

   Thanks be to God! Long live Freedom! Be that as it may.

In German, the special subjunctive is used in similar expressions.

   Gott sei Dank!

   Es lebe die Freiheit!

   Wie dem auch sei.

Other than in such phrases, Subjunctive I is rarely heard in conversation. It is primarily used in formal writing and indirect speech, often to summarize another person's findings or opinion. It is most frequently encountered in critical literary or scientific essays, in literature, and in news articles, where it distances the author from his or her report and preserves a sense of objectivity.

In general, the forms of the third person singular are the ones used most often because they clearly differ from those of the indicative. When the forms of the special subjunctive are identical with those of the indicative, the general subjunctive is used. At this point, you need only to be able to recognize the forms of the special subjunctive and know why they are used.

1. PRESENT-TIME forms

The PRESENT-TIME forms of the special subjunctive have the same endings as the general subjunctive and are added to the stem of the infinitive:

glauben	
ich glaube	wir glauben
du glaubest	ihr glaubet
er glaube	sie glauben

Verbs that have a vowel change in the second and third person singular of the indicative don't have that vowel change in the special subjunctive. Note that the first and third person singular forms of **sein** are irregular in that they do not have an **-e** ending.

Infinitive	Special Subj. er / es / sie	Indicative er / es / sie
haben	**habe**	hat
sein	**sei**	ist
tun	**tue**	tut
denken	**denke**	denkt
fahren	**fahre**	fährt
sehen	**sehe**	sieht
werden	**werde**	wird
wissen	**wisse**	weiß
dürfen	**dürfe**	darf
können	**könne**	kann
mögen	**möge**	mag
müssen	**müsse**	muss
wollen	**wolle**	will

ich habe	wir haben
du habest	ihr habet
er habe	sie haben

ich müsse	wir müssen
du müssest	ihr müsset
er müsse	sie müssen

ich sei	wir seien
du seiest	ihr seiet
er sei	sie seien

Er sagte, er **habe** keine Zeit.	*He said he had no time.*
Er sagte, sie **sei** nicht zu Hause.	*He said she wasn't home.*

Möge diese Welt mit Gottes Hilfe eine Wiedergeburt der Freiheit erleben!

This is the text of the Liberty Bell in Berlin's Schöneberger Rathaus, a present of the Americans after the Berlin Blockade.

2. To refer to the FUTURE *(to later),* combine the special subjunctive of **werden** with an infinitive.

> **werde . . .** + infinitive

Er sagte, er **werde** bald fertig **sein.**	*He said he'd be finished soon.*

3. To form the PAST-TIME special subjunctive, use the special subjunctive of **haben** or **sein** with a past participle.

> **habe . . .**
> **sei . . .** } + past participle

Er sagt, er **habe** keine Zeit **gehabt.**	*He says he didn't have time.*
Er sagte, **sie sei** nicht zu Hause **gewesen.**	*He said she hadn't been home.*

Übungen

K. Finden Sie den Konjunktiv und unterstreichen Sie ihn!

1. **Städte deutscher Kultur**

Mein Onkel schrieb, dass Weimar, Leipzig, Halle, Wittenberg und Eisenach wichtige deutsche Kulturstädte seien. In Weimar sei Johann Wolfgang von Goethe Theaterdirektor und Staatsminister gewesen und dort habe Friedrich von Schiller seine wichtigsten Dramen geschrieben. In Leipzig habe Johann Sebastian Bach 27 Jahre lang Kantaten und Oratorien für den Thomanerchor komponiert. Dieser Knabenchor *(boys choir)* sei heute noch sehr berühmt. Nicht weit von Leipzig liege Halle, wo Georg Friedrich Händel geboren worden sei. In Wittenberg, das man heute die Lutherstadt nenne, habe Martin Luther mit seinen 95 Thesen die Reformation begonnen. Sein Zimmer auf der Wartburg bei Eisenach, wo er die Bibel ins Deutsche übersetzt hat, sei heute noch zu besichtigen. Man könne auch heute noch sehen, wo er dem Teufel ein Tintenfass nachgeworfen habe *(had thrown an inkwell at the devil).* Er wisse allerdings nicht, woher diese Geschichte komme. Er glaube sie nicht.

Die Wartburg bei Eisenach

2. **Gedanken zur Umwelt**

Die Wissenschaftler sagten, dass man mit mehr Wohlstand *(affluence)* mehr Energie brauchen werde. Mehr Energie bedeute aber mehr Kohlendioxid-Emissionen *(carbon dioxide . . .).* Kohlendioxid sei mitverantwortlich für den so genannten Treibhauseffekt *(greenhouse effect).* Damit man die Umwelt nicht noch mehr verschmutze und ihr auf diese Weise noch mehr schade, müsse man alles tun, um sie zu schützen. Es müsse mehr in die Umwelttechnologie investiert werden. Die Nordamerikaner und Europäer tragen dabei eine besondere Verantwortung, denn sie, mit nur 10 Prozent der Weltbevölkerung, verbrauchen *(consume)* fast die Hälfte der Energie. In Asien liege der Verbrauch bei etwa einem Viertel der Weltenergie, obwohl allein in China 20 Prozent der Menschheit *(mankind)* lebe. Darüber solle man sich echt einmal Gedanken machen. Die Begrenzung *(restriction)* des Klimawechsels und seiner Konsequenzen sei für viele Wissenschaftler die wichtigste Herausforderung *(challenge)* des 21. Jahrhunderts.

KLIMA UND UMWELT

Fokus — *In Search of an Identity*

The unification of Germany and the progressive rise of an ever more integrated Europe have been contributing toward a new assessment of what it means to be German. This search for a national identity goes back to a time well before Bismarck united the country in 1871. For centuries, Germany had been divided into numerous small, autocratically ruled principalities. This fragmentation contributed to the significant diversity among various parts of Germany, yet also inhibited the development of a broadly based democratic consciousness. While most Germans continue to reject nationalism and embrace the idea of a united Europe enthusiastically, a new pride in their own localities is noticeable at the same time. A new interest in local dialects, history, and the restoration and rebuilding of destroyed historical sites is symptomatic of this trend.

Zusammenfassung

L. Der Leipziger Hauptbahnhof. Übersetzen Sie die verschiedenen, unterstrichenen Verbformen!

1. Der Leipziger Hauptbahnhof <u>ist</u> zu einem modernen Einkaufszentrum <u>umgebaut worden.</u> 2. Auf den drei neuen Ebenen *(levels),* die durch große Freitreppen verbunden sind *(are connected),* gibt es viele schöne Geschäfte und es <u>wird</u> viel <u>gebummelt.</u> 3. Wer auf der Durchreise ist und etwas Zeit hat, <u>wird</u> es hier interessant <u>finden.</u> 4. Eberhard Roll hat in der Nähe von Bahnsteig 13 / 14 seinen Juwelierladen *(jewelry store).* Er hat als Schüler erlebt, wie am 7. Juli 1944 der Bahnhof <u>zerbombt wurde.</u> 5. Er sagt, dass er den Tag nie <u>vergessen werde.</u> 6. Heute ist er stolz, einer der ersten Mieter des neuen Hauptbahnhofs <u>gewesen zu sein.</u> 7. In den ersten sieben Tagen nach der Eröffnung <u>wurden</u> fast 1,2 Millionen Besucher täglich <u>gezählt.</u> 8. Die Innenstadt <u>ist</u> mit dem neuen Bahnhof um eine Attraktion reicher <u>geworden.</u> 9. Übrigens <u>werden</u> die meisten Geschäfte im Bahnhof auch sonntags nicht <u>geschlossen.</u> 10. Andere Städte <u>werden</u> dem Beispiel <u>folgen.</u>

L: 1. was / has been converted 2. there's / people do a lot of strolling around 3. will find 4. was destroyed by bombs 5. would forget 6. to have been 7. were counted 8. has become 9. are (being) closed 10. will follow

Im Leipziger Hauptbahnhof

M. Wo ist mein Pass? Auf Deutsch bitte!

1. Yesterday was a bad day. 2. First I lost my passport. 3. Then my handbag and my money were stolen **(gestohlen).** 4. I tried to pay with traveler's checks.

M: 1. Gestern war ein schlechter Tag. 2. Erst habe ich meinen Pass verloren. 3. Dann wurden meine Tasche und mein Geld gestohlen. 4. Ich versuchte, mit Reiseschecks zu bezahlen. 5. Aber ohne meinen Pass wurden meine Schecks nicht angenommen. 6. Es war gut, dass Anne da war. 7. Die Rechnung wurde von Anne bezahlt. 8. Heute Morgen / früh wurde ich von der Polizei angerufen. 9. Man hatte / sie hatten meine Tasche gefunden. 10. Aber mein Pass ist noch nicht gefunden worden. 11. Ich wünschte, ich wüsste, was ich damit gemacht habe. 12. Ich hoffe, er wird bald gefunden (werden) / dass er bald gefunden (werden) wird.

5. But without my passport, my checks weren't accepted. 6. It was good that Anne was there. 7. The bill was paid by Anne. 8. This morning, I was called by the police (**die Polizei**). 9. They had found my handbag. 10. But my passport hasn't been found yet. 11. I wish I knew what I did with it. 12. I hope it will be found soon.

Einblicke

Lesestrategie: Europäisierung, was ist das?

Was verstehen Sie unter Europäisierung? Was haben die Europäer gemeinsam? Was wollen die einzelnen Staaten nicht aufgeben? Suchen Sie nach Stichwörtern *(keywords)* im Text und machen Sie eine Liste!

Wortschatz 2

der (Geld)schein, -e	*banknote*
Staat, -en	*state*
das Jahrtausend, -e	*millennium*
die Bevölkerung	*population*
Münze, -n	*coin*
einzeln	*individual(ly)*
endlich	*finally*
gefährlich	*dangerous*
inzwischen	*in the meantime*
stolz (auf + *acc.*)	*proud (of)*
typisch	*typical(ly)*
vereint	*united*
verbinden, verband, verbunden	*to connect, tie together, link*
wachsen (wächst), wuchs, ist gewachsen	*to grow*

Vor dem Lesen

A. **Fragen über das eigene Land**
1. Wie lange ist dieses Land schon ein Bundesstaat?
2. Wird Ihre Ausbildung im ganzen Land anerkannt *(recognized)* oder müssen Prüfungen wiederholt werden? Können Sie überall arbeiten?
3. Was finden Sie typisch für Ihr Land (Amerika, Kanada usw.)?
4. Gibt es etwas, was typisch ist für die Bewohner *(residents)* mancher Staaten? Gibt es Spitznamen für sie?
5. Gibt es regionale Dialekte? Wenn ja, wo?
6. Glauben Sie, dass Amerikaner (Kanadier usw.) einen besonders hohen Lebensstandard haben? Wieso (nicht)?

B. **Diagnose Identitätsschwund** *(loss of identity).* Fragen Sie die anderen, . . . !
1. was Sie unter dieser Zeichnung *(drawing)* auf Seite 405 verstehen
2. wer die Diagnose macht und wer auch zuschaut
3. wer diese Leute im Bett sind
4. was das Bett symbolisiert
5. welche Leute sie an ihrem Hut / ihrer Mütze *(cap)* erkennen können
6. was sie von der Zeichnung halten

C. Was ist das?

die Kooperation, Luftverschmutzung, Schwierigkeit, Souveränität; aufwachsen, zusammenwachsen, formulieren; arrogant, europaweit, geteilt, kritisch, offiziell, regional, weltoffen; im Prinzip, teilweise, zu Beginn

Der Wind kennt keine Grenzen.

CD 6, Track 12

Inzwischen hat ein neues Jahrtausend begonnen und Europa verbindet eine neue, gemeinsame Währung°, der Euro. Wer heute nach Deutschland kommt, zahlt nicht mehr mit der Deutschen Mark, sondern mit Euromünzen und Euroscheinen. Europa soll enger° zusammenwachsen. Jeder Europäer soll zum Beispiel in jedem europäischen Land arbeiten dürfen; und auch seine Ausbildung soll europaweit anerkannt° werden. Das heißt aber nicht, dass Europa ein einziger Bundesstaat wird, sondern es soll ein loser Staatenbund° sein, in dem die einzelnen Staaten ihre Souveränität, ihre eigene Sprache und Kultur behalten wollen. Auf eine europäische Hauptsprache hat man sich nicht einigen° können.

　Natürlich fühlen sich die Deutschen als Europäer, aber sie wollen auch Deutsche bleiben. Vor allem aber muss Deutschland selbst erst einmal° zusammenwachsen, denn es war ja bis 1990 offiziell ein geteiltes Land. Als die Mauer dann endlich fiel, existierte sie weiter in den Köpfen: Plötzlich gab es „Ossis" und „Wessis"°. Viele Westdeutsche meinten, dass die „Ossis" unselbstständige und ehrgeizlose arme Teufel° seien. Andererseits meinten viele Ostdeutsche, dass die „Wessis" arrogant seien und dächten, ihnen gehöre die Welt. Sie würden immer alles besser wissen—daher° der Spitzname „Besserwessis".

　Was verbindet nun eigentlich alle Deutschen? Natürlich die Sprache, Kultur und Geschichte, aber im Prinzip gibt es eigentlich wenig, was typisch für alle Deutschen wäre. Vielleicht sind es die kleineren Dinge im Leben. So könnte man zum Beispiel sagen, dass die meisten gesellig° sind und gern in Straßencafés oder Gartenrestaurants sitzen, dass sie Fußball lieben und sich in Vereinen organisieren. Die Familie und die Freizeit bedeutet ihnen oft mehr als der Staat. Sie sind ein reiselustiges° Volk, aber sie lieben auch ihre Heimat: die Landschaft, in der sie aufgewachsen sind, die Stadt oder das Dorf. Viele sind wieder stolz auf ihre Herkunft°; regionale Dialekte werden wieder mehr gesprochen und auch im Radio und im Theater gepflegt°. Das mag teilweise historische Gründe° haben, denn die Bevölkerung bestand schon immer aus° verschiedenen Volksstämmen° und sie waren nur kurze Zeit EIN Staat, nämlich von Bismarcks Reichsgründung° 1871 bis zum Ende des 2 Weltkrieges 1945. Mit der zunehmenden° Europäisierung möchten viele gerade heute ihre regionale Identität nicht verlieren.

---

currency

closer

recognized

loose confederation

agree on

first of all

East and West Germans

poor devils without ambition

hence

social

travel-hungry

origin

cultivated

reasons / consisted of

ethnic groups

founding of the Second German Empire / increasing

share
believing in authority

leather pants

gets involved / struggle for

...consumption

taken seriously
overcome

Wenn es schon schwer zu sagen ist, wie die Deutschen sind, so kann man doch sehen, dass sie europäischer geworden sind, das heißt weltoffener und informierter. Auch ist die Bevölkerung mit einem größeren Anteil° von Ausländern multi-kultureller geworden. Die Deutschen sind heute kritischer und nicht mehr so autoritätsgläubig° wie zu Beginn des 20. Jahrhunderts. Das so genannte typisch Deutsche ist nicht mehr so wichtig; das Ausländische ist interessanter geworden. Es werden Jeans statt Lederhosen° getragen. Die Musik in Deutschland ist international. Man isst besonders gern italienisch, und französischer Wein wird genauso gern getrunken wie deutsches Bier. Ja, und man engagiert sich° wieder. Der Kampf um° Umweltschutz und um eine bessere Lebensqualität ist auch sehr wichtig geworden und man weiß, wie wichtig die Kooperation der Nachbarländer dabei ist. Natürlich wollen die Deutschen ihren hohen Lebensstandard erhalten, aber sie glauben, das dürfte auch mit weniger Energieverbrauch° und weniger Chemie möglich sein. Mülltrennung wird zum Beispiel in weiten Kreisen der Bevölkerung sehr ernst genommen°. Auch wissen sie, dass zum Beispiel die Luftverschmutzung nur europaweit bewältigt° werden kann, denn der Wind kennt keine Grenzen.

Nach dem Lesen

Optional activity: Fragen: 1. Wo gibt es normalerweise Grenzen? 2. Wo spielen Grenzen heutzutage keine Rolle mehr? Was für Probleme müssen die Europäer gemeinsam bekämpfen? 3. Was verbindet die Europäer? Warum haben viele oft noch „Grenzen" in den Köpfen? 4. Was halten Sie von der „Diagnose Identitätsschwund"? Glauben Sie, dass mit der Europäisierung die einzelnen Staaten ihre Identität verlieren? Warum (nicht)? 5. Wie ist das in Ihrem Land? Was für Nationalitäten gibt es da? Ist es dabei zu einem Identitätsschwund gekommen? Warum (nicht)?

A. Was passt?

1. Die Ausbildung der verschiedenen europäischen Staaten soll in Zukunft in ganz _____ anerkannt werden.
   a. Amerika   b. Deutschland   **c.** Europa
2. Damit können die Deutschen _____ überall in Europa studieren oder arbeiten.
   a. fast   b. kaum   c. vielleicht
3. Als die Mauer 1989 fiel, existierte sie weiter in manchen _____.
   a. Bäuchen   b. Gesichtern   **c.** Köpfen
4. Manche Westdeutschen dachten, dass „Ossis" _____ seien.
   a. unselbstständig   b. arrogant   c. gefährlich
5. Manche Ostdeutschen dachten, dass „Wessis" _____.
   a. arme Teufel seien   b. alle arm wären   **c.** immer alles besser wüssten
6. Vielleicht kann man allgemein (in general) von den Deutschen sagen, dass sie _____.
   a. keine Fragen stellen   **b.** reiselustig sind   c. alle Dialekt sprechen
7. Sie lieben ihre _____.
   a. Heimat   b. Spitznamen   c. Ausländer
8. Die Deutschen sollen _____ geworden sein.
   a. autoritätsgläubiger   b. weltfremder   **c.** weltoffener
9. Auch sind sie umweltbewusster geworden und nehmen _____ ernst.
   a. alle Schwierigkeiten   b. alles Ausländische   **c.** den Umweltschutz
10. Sie wissen, dass zum Beispiel die Luftverschmutzung nur _____ mit den Nachbarn bewältigt werden kann.
    a. allein   b. einzeln   **c.** gemeinsam

B. Noch einmal in indirekter Rede! Wiederholen Sie den Lesetext (Paragraphen 3–4) in indirekter Rede! Benutzen Sie dabei den Konjunktiv I!

BEISPIEL: Der Autor fragte sich, was alle Deutschen **verbinde.** Natürlich die Sprache, Kultur und Geschichte, aber im Prinzip **gebe** es eigentlich wenig, was typisch für alle Deutschen **sei.**

C. Typisch Deutsch! Machen Sie mit den anderen eine Liste mit all den Eigenschaften, die der Autor im Text über die Deutschen erwähnt! Wie sehen diese (these) im Vergleich zu dem Bild aus, das Sie von den Deutschen haben?

D. Meinungsumfrage unter Deutschen. Was erfahren Sie (learn) durch die Meinungsumfrage unter deutschen Jugendlichen im Alter von 18–25 Jahren? Wie hätten Sie darauf reagiert? Machen Sie eine Meinungsumfrage in Ihrer Klasse!

Wovor haben Sie am meisten Angst?	
Umweltkatastrophen	24%
Krieg	21%
Arbeitslosigkeit	17%
Einsamkeit *(loneliness)*	15%
Kriminalität	12%
Scheidung *(divorce)* der Eltern	5%
Prüfungen	4%
Ausländer	2%

Beim Wort „Europa" denke ich an . . .	
Kultur	29%
Zukunft	28%
Frieden	26%
Bürokratie	23%
Zahlmeister *(paymaster)* Deutschland	22%
Heimat	16%
Nichts Besonderes	16%

Ich fühle mich vor allem als . . .	
Deutscher	31%
Kölner, Leipziger, Münchner . . .	16%
Europäer	14%
Weltbürger	13%
Hesse, Sachse, Thüringer . . .	10%
Ostdeutscher oder Westdeutscher	6%

E. Hoppla, hier fehlt was! Hallo, Herr Nachbar! Schauen Sie sich die folgende Collage mit den verschiedenen nationalen Eigenschaften an! Eine zweite Collage ist im Anhang. Finden Sie mit Ihrem Nachbarn/Ihrer Nachbarin heraus, was die Leute aus diesen 12 Ländern charakterisiert. Sie brauchen nicht alles über sie aufzuschreiben, nur ein paar Wörter.

Die Iren: <u>sehr sportlich,</u> . . .	Die Italiener: . . .
Die Luxemburger: . . .	Die Holländer: . . .
Die Portugiesen: . . .	Die Spanier: . . .

S1:

BEISPIEL: **S1** Wie sind die Iren?
S2 Die Iren lieben den Sport. Jeder zweite . . . Und wie sind die Belgier?
S1 Sie haben . . .

Versorgte Belgier

Belgien ist mit Medikamenten super versorgt, hat die meisten Apotheken je Einwohner.

Patente Deutsche

Die Deutschen sind in Europa die größten Erfinder – sie melden jährlich über 260 000 Patente an.

Gesunde Griechen

Die Griechen essen die meisten Vitamine. Je Einwohner und Jahr 195 Kilo Gemüse und 76 Kilo Obst.

Gesellige Dänen

Die Dänen sind die geselligsten Europäer. 83 Prozent der Bevölkerung sind Mitglieder in Vereinen.

Lebensfrohe Franzosen

In Frankreich leben die Europäer am längsten, besonders Frauen. Sie werden im Schnitt älter als 80.

Belesene Briten

Die Briten sind zeitungsgierig. Auf jeden kommen 3 Zeitungen – Europa-Rekord im Zeitungslesen.

F. Was wäre, wenn . . . ? Stellen Sie sich vor, Sie hätten in ein anderes Land geheiratet! Was würde Ihnen als typisch amerikanisch (kanadisch usw.) dort fehlen? Oder meinen Sie, dass Sie überall gleich *(equally)* zu Hause sein könnten? Schreiben Sie 8–10 Sätze!

Zwei kurze Fabeln

Der Esel in Begleitung

lion / donkey / accompany /
  encountered
walked proudly / up high / trumpeted
  reluctantly / impertinent / shouted
  at / related
accompaniment

Ein Löwe° erlaubte einst einem Esel°, ihn zu begleiten°. Eines Tages begegnete° ihnen ein Esel. „Guten Tag, Bruder!", sagte dieser Esel freundlich. Der Esel, der neben dem Löwen einherstolzierte°, warf den Kopf in die Höhe° und trompetete unwillig°. „Unverschämt°!", fuhr er seinen Verwandten an°. „Warum soll ich unverschämt sein, wenn ich dich grüße?", fragte der andere Esel. „Sind wir nicht verwandt°?" „Bist du etwa, weil du mit einem Löwen gehst, besser als ich? Du bleibst auch in Begleitung° eines Löwen das, was du bist, ein Esel wie ich!"

Nur anders, nicht besser

red dear / kind
inexperienced
thundering rifle
invented
sighed / you are drawing conclusions
  too fast / continued
arrows / bows / just as bad off

Zwei Hirsche° trafen sich. Den einen hatte die gütige° Natur schon Jahrhunderte leben lassen, der andere war jung und unerfahren°. Der alte Hirsch sagte zu seinem Enkel: „Ich kann mich noch an jene Zeiten erinnern, als der Mensch das donnernde Feuerrohr° noch nicht erfunden° hatte." „Welch glückliche Zeit muss das für uns Hirsche gewesen sein!", seufzte° der Enkel. „Du schließt zu voreilig°", sagte der alte Hirsch. „Die Zeit war anders, aber nicht besser!" Und er fuhr fort°. „Der Mensch hatte anstatt des Feuerrohrs Pfeile° und Bogen°, und wir waren ebenso schlimm dran° wie jetzt."

Gotthold Ephraim Lessing

Erinnerung

continue wandering

grab

Willst du immer weiter schweifen°?
Sieh, das Gute liegt so nah.
Lerne nur das Glück ergreifen°,
Denn das Glück ist immer da.

Johann Wolfgang von Goethe

Fokus — *Lessing, Goethe, and Schiller*

- **Gotthold Ephraim Lessing** (1729–1781) was one of the most influential figures of the German Enlightenment. After studying theology and medicine, he began his writing career in Leipzig, where two of his early comedies, *Der Freigeist* and *Die Juden* (both written in 1740), were performed. The first exposes a free-thinker's intolerance; the second is a plea for racial and religious tolerance. Representing a break with the French style of his day, Lessing's domestic tragedy *Miß Sara Sampson* (1755) exemplifies English literary concepts. His comedy *Minna von Barnhelm* (1767) was published after the Seven Years' War (1756–1763). As an art and theater critic, Lessing made his mark with *Laokoon* (1766) and the *Hamburgische Dramaturgie* (1767–1768). *Emilia Galotti* (1722) exerted a strong influence on the **Sturm und Drang** movement, whose chief exponents were Goethe and Schiller. Lessings final years were dominated by polemics against the influential clergyman Johann Melchior Goeze. Silenced by a ban on publishing futher articles, he wrote his parable about religious tolerance, *Nathan der Weise* (1799), and his moral testament, *Die Erziehung des Menschengeschlechts* (1780).

- **Johann Wolfgang von Goethe** (1749–1832) was one of Germany's greatest poets, novelists, and playwrights. He was also a leading thinker and scientist. His works include *Faust, Wilhelm Meister,* and *Die Leiden des jungen Werther,* a sensationally successful novel about a sensitive young man alienated from the world around him, which Napoleon is said to have read seven times. Because of his vast scope of knowledge and his comprehensive interest in the world of human experience, Goethe is often referred to as "the last universal man."

- **Friedrich von Schiller** (1759–1805) ranks second only to Goethe among the leading figures of classical German literature. His dramas, often pleas for human freedom and dignity, inspired liberals in their fight for liberty during the early 1800s and during the Revolution of 1848. His works include *Don Carlos, Die Jungfrau von Orleans, Maria Stuart,* and *Wilhelm Tell.* The last stanza of his well-known poem "Ode an die Freude," set to music by Beethoven, has been selected as anthem for a unified Europe—to be played instrumentally rather than sung at special occasions, thus avoiding the use of any particular language.

An die Freude

Freude, schöner Götterfunken°, Tochter aus Elysium,
Wir betreten feuertrunken°, Himmlische°, dein Heiligtum°!
Deine Zauber° binden wieder°, was die Mode° streng geteilt;
Alle Menschen werden Brüder, wo dein sanfter Flügel weilt°.

Friedrich von Schiller

bright spark of divinity

fire-inspired we enter / Heavenly one /
sanctuary / magic powers / reunite /
custom / under the sway of thy
gentle wing[s]

Fragen

A. Lessings Fabeln

1. Warum ist der Esel in der ersten Fabel so unheimlich stolz?
2. Mit wem will er plötzlich nichts mehr zu tun haben? Warum?
3. Was symbolisiert der Löwe? der Esel?
4. Worüber sprechen die beiden Hirsche in der zweiten Fabel von Lessing?
5. Was hat sich über die Jahrhunderte geändert, was aber nicht?
6. Was halten Sie von den beiden Fabeln?
7. Kennen Sie andere Fabeln? Wenn ja, können Sie eine erzählen?
8. Was ist so besonders an Fabeln? Warum werden sie immer wieder gelesen?

B. Die beiden Gedichte und mehr

1. Woran denkt Goethe, wenn er von „weiter schweifen" redet? Was meinen Sie?
2. Was sollte man mehr erkennen?
3. Glauben Sie, dass Goethe dieses Gedicht als junger oder als älterer Mensch geschrieben hat? Warum?
4. Was ist die Hauptidee in Schillers Gedicht?
5. Was halten Sie von der Idee dieser Strophe *(stanza)* als Europahymne?
6. Warum wird die Hymne oft nicht gesungen, sondern nur instrumental gespielt?
7. Haben Sie schon mal etwas anderes von diesen drei Autoren gelesen? Wenn ja, was?
8. Was würden Sie gern einmal von ihnen lesen oder im Theater sehen?

In order to avoid great length and difficulty,
we chose these brief selections. You could
also have students read other pieces by
these authors, if necessary, even in English,
e.g., *Nathan der Weise* with Lessing's famous ring parable. When asked by the sul-
tan about which of the three great religions
he thinks is the true one, the wise Jew re-
sponds with the story about three rings
that are so alike that one cannot
distinguish one from another. Goethe's
poem "Der Erlkönig" or Schiller's poem
"Der Ring des Polykrates" might also be of
interest to students.

HÖREN SIE ZU!   TRACK 31

Europa-Schulen

Zum Erkennen: erziehen *(to educate, raise);* die Klassenkameradin *(classmate);* das Lehrbuch, ¨-er *(textbook);* chauvinistisch; die Flotte *(fleet);* sich konzentrieren auf *(to concentrate on);* der Rektor, -en *(vice chancellor)*

Was stimmt?

1. Europa-Schulen gibt es in _____.
   a. jedem Land der EU
   b. mehreren europäischen Ländern
   c. auf der ganzen Welt
2. Die Schüler lernen _____.
   a. keine Fächer in ihrer Muttersprache
   b. manche Fächer in ihrer Muttersprache
   c. nicht mehr als zwei Sprachen
3. Sie lernen Geschichte _____.
   a. immer in ihrer Muttersprache
   b. aus internationalen Lehrbüchern
   c. nie in ihrer Muttersprache
4. In französischen Lehrbüchern liest man _____.
   a. nicht viel über solche Länder wie Belgien oder Luxemburg
   b. interessante Information über englische Kultur
   c. stolz, wie Nelson die spanische Flotte bei Trafalgar zerstört hat
5. Die Schüler lernen im Geschichtsunterricht, _____.
   a. chauvinistischer zu werden
   b. die Geschichte ihres eigenen Landes objektiver zu sehen
   c. gutes Deutsch

Video-Ecke

- In the Minidrama *Der Wind, der Wind, das himmlische Kind,* Jean Paul visits with his friends. For the first time, he becomes consciously aware of their lifestyle. He is impressed with the history connected to the house and admires the paintings and furniture. This old house, however, also talks. Jean Paul keeps hearing noises, his friends are amused. Is there a ghost sneaking around somewhere?

Web-Ecke

- For updates, self-assessment quizzes, and online activities related to this chapter, visit the *Wie geht's?* Web site at **http://wiegehts.heinle.com**. You will learn more about the EU and the euro, visit Weimar and other cities in the new *Länder,* and become acquainted with environmental concerns of people in German-speaking countries.

Rückblick: Kapitel 12–15

I. Comparison

pp. 319–321

1. The comparative is formed by adding **-er** to an adjective, the superlative by adding **-(e)st**. Many one-syllable adjectives and adverbs with the stem vowel **a, o,** or **u** have an umlaut.

Exercises in the *Rückblick* sections of the Workbook correspond to this review.

Positive	Comparative	Superlative
schnell	schneller	schnellst-
lang	länger	längst-
kurz	kürzer	kürzest-

A few adjectives and adverbs have irregular forms in the comparative and superlative.

Positive	Comparative	Superlative
gern	lieber	liebst-
groß	größer	größt-
gut	besser	best-
hoch	höher	höchst-
nah	näher	nächst-
viel	mehr	meist-

2. The comparative of predicate adjectives and of adverbs ends in **-er;** the superlative is preceded by **am** and ends in **-sten.**

> Ich esse schnell.
> Du isst schneller.
> Er isst am schnellsten.

3. In the comparative and superlative, adjectives preceding nouns have the same endings under the same conditions as adjectives in the positive form.

> der gut**e** Wein   der besser**e** Wein   der best**e** Wein
> Ihr gut**er** Wein   Ihr besser**er** Wein   Ihr best**er** Wein
> gut**er** Wein   besser**er** Wein   best**er** Wein

4. Here are four important phrases used in comparisons:

Gestern war es nicht **so heiß wie** heute.	*. . . as hot as . . .*
Heute ist es **heißer als** gestern.	*. . . hotter than . . .*
Es wird **immer heißer.**	*. . . hotter and hotter.*
Je länger du wartest, **desto heißer** wird es.	*The longer . . . , the hotter . . .*
Je heißer, desto besser.	*The hotter, the better.*

II. Relative clauses

pp. 369–371

1. Relative clauses are introduced by relative pronouns.

	masc.	neut.	fem.	plural
nom.	der	das	die	die
acc.	den	das	die	die
dat.	dem	dem	der	**denen**
gen.	**dessen**	**dessen**	**deren**	**deren**

The form of the relative pronoun depends ON THE NUMBER AND GENDER OF THE ANTECEDENT and on the FUNCTION of the relative pronoun WITHIN THE RELATIVE CLAUSE.

> . . . ANTECEDENT, (preposition) RP _____ V1, . . .
> gender? number?   function?

2. The word order in the relative clause is like that of all subordinate clauses: the inflected part of the verb (V1) comes last.

> . . . , RP _____ V1, . . .

Der junge Mann, **der** gerade hier **war,** studiert Theologie.

Die Universität, **an der** er **studiert,** ist schon sehr alt.

III. Future tense
pp. 323–324

1. The future consists of a present tense form of **werden** plus an infinitive.

werden . . . + infinitive	
ich werde . . . gehen	wir werden . . . gehen
du wirst . . . gehen	ihr werdet . . . gehen
er wird . . . gehen	sie werden . . . gehen

Er **wird** es dir **erklären.**

2. The future of a sentence with a modal follows this pattern:

> **werden . . .** + verb infinitive + modal infinitive

Er **wird** es dir **erklären können.**

IV. Subjunctive
p. 343

English and German follow very similar patterns in the subjunctive:

If he came . . .	Wenn er käme, . . .
If he had come . . .	Wenn er gekommen wäre, . . .

German, however, has two subjunctives, the GENERAL SUBJUNCTIVE (SUBJUNCTIVE II) and the SPECIAL SUBJUNCTIVE (SUBJUNCTIVE I); the latter is primarily used in writing. The endings of both subjunctives are the same.

ich **-e**	wir **-en**
du **-est**	ihr **-et**
er **-e**	sie **-en**

1. Forms

   a. GENERAL SUBJUNCTIVE (II) pp. 345–347, 351–352

present time or future time		past time
Based on the forms of the simple past; refers to *now / later*	Based on the forms of **werden** + infinitive; refers to *now / later*	Based on the forms of the past perfect; refers to *earlier*
er **lernte**	er **würde lernen**	er **hätte gelernt**
brächte	würde bringen	hätte gebracht
hätte	(würde haben)	hätte gehabt
wäre	(würde sein)	wäre gewesen
nähme	würde nehmen	hätte genommen
käme	würde kommen	wäre gekommen

- In conversation, the **würde**-form is commonly used when referring to <u>present time.</u> However, avoid using the **würde**-form with **haben, sein, wissen,** and the modals.

Er würde es dir erklären.
Du wärest stolz darauf.

- Modals in the past-time subjunctive follow this pattern:

hätte . . . + verb infinitive + modal infinitive

Er hätte es dir erklären können.

   b. SPECIAL SUBJUNCTIVE (I) pp. 400–401

present time	future time	past time
Based on the forms of the infinitive; refers to *now / later*	Based on the forms of the future; refers to *later*	Based on the forms of the present perfect; refers to *earlier*
er **lerne**	er **werde lernen**	er **habe gelernt**
bringe	werde bringen	habe gebracht
habe	werde haben	habe gehabt
sei	werde sein	sei gewesen
nehme	werde nehmen	habe genommen
komme	werde kommen	sei gekommen

2. Use

   a. The GENERAL SUBJUNCTIVE is quite common in everyday speech and is used in:

- Polite requests or questions

    Könnten Sie mir sagen, wo die Uni ist?   *Could you tell me where the university is?*

- Hypothetical statements or questions

Er sollte bald hier sein.	*He should be here soon.*
Was würdest du tun?	*What would you do?*
Was hättest du getan?	*What would you have done?*

- Wishes

Wenn ich das nur wüsste!	*If only I knew that!*
Wenn ich das nur gewusst hätte!	*If only I had known that!*
Ich wünschte, ich hätte das gewusst!	*I wish I had known that!*

- Unreal conditions

| Wenn wir Geld hätten, würden wir fliegen. | *If we had the money, we'd fly.* |
| Wenn wir Geld gehabt hätten, wären wir geflogen. | *If we had had the money, we would have flown.* |

- Indirect speech (see Section V)

b. The SPECIAL SUBJUNCTIVE is used primarily for indirect speech in news reports and in formal writing, unless the form of the indicative is the same as the subjunctive, in which case the general subjunctive is used.

$$\text{ich komme} = \text{ich } \mathbf{komme} \rightarrow \text{ich } \mathbf{käme}$$

$$\text{ich frage} \;\; = \text{ich } \mathbf{frage} \;\;\; \rightarrow \text{ich } \mathbf{würde\ fragen}$$

pp. 374–375 ## V. Indirect speech

The tense of the indirect statement is determined by the tense of the direct statement.

direct statement	indirect statement
present tense	→ present-time subjunctive or **würde**-form
future tense	→ **würde**-form or **werde**-form
simple past present perfect past perfect	→ past-time subjunctive

The forms in parentheses refer to the special subjunctive; they can be omitted.

„Ich komme nicht."	Sie sagte, sie käme (komme) nicht.
	Sie sagte, sie würde nicht kommen.
„Ich werde nicht kommen."	Sie sagte, sie würde (werde) nicht kommen.
„Ich hatte keine Lust."	Sie sagte, sie hätte (habe) keine Lust gehabt.
„Ich bin nicht gegangen."	Sie sagte, sie wäre (sei) nicht gegangen.
„Ich hatte nichts davon gewusst."	Sie sagte, sie hätte (habe) nichts davon gewusst.

This is also true of questions. Remember to use **ob** when the question begins with the verb.

„Kommt sie mit?"	Er fragte, ob sie mitkäme (mitkomme).
	Er fragte, ob sie mitkommen würde.
„Wird sie mitkommen?"	Er fragte, ob sie mitkommen würde (werde).
„Wo war sie?"	Er fragte, wo sie gewesen wäre (sei).
„Warum hat sie mir nichts davon gesagt?"	Er fragte, warum sie ihm nichts davon gesagt hätte (habe).

Indirect requests require the use of sollen.

| „Frag nicht so viel!" | Er sagte, sie sollte (solle) nicht so viel fragen. |

VI. Passive voice

pp. 395–396

In the active voice, the subject of the sentence is doing something. In the passive voice, the subject is not doing anything; rather, something is being done to it.

1. Forms

werden . . . + past participle	
ich werde . . . gefragt	wir werden . . . gefragt
du wirst . . . gefragt	ihr werdet . . . gefragt
er wird . . . gefragt	sie werden . . . gefragt

2. The tenses in the passive are formed with the various tenses of **werden** + past participle.

er **wird** . . . gefragt	er **ist** . . . gefragt **worden**
er **wurde** . . . gefragt	er **war** . . . gefragt **worden**
er **wird** . . . gefragt **werden**	

Das ist uns nicht erklärt worden.

3. Modals follow this pattern:

modal . . . + past participle + infinitive of **werden**

Das muss noch einmal erklärt werden.

4. In German the passive is often used without a subject or with **es** functioning as the subject.

Hier wird viel renoviert.

Es wird hier viel renoviert.

5. Instead of using the passive voice, the same idea may be expressed in the active voice with the subject **man.**

Man hat alles noch einmal erklärt.

VII. Review of the uses of *werden*

p. 400

1.	FULL VERB:	Er **wird** Arzt.	*He's going to be a doctor.*
2.	FUTURE:	Ich **werde** danach **fragen.**	*I'll ask about it.*
3.	SUBJUNCTIVE:	Ich **würde** danach **fragen.**	*I'd ask about it.*
4.	PASSIVE:	Er **wird** danach **gefragt.**	*He's (being) asked about it.*

REMEMBER: Review exercises for vocabulary and structures can be found in the Workbook.

Appendix

1. Predicting the gender of certain nouns

As a rule, nouns must be learned with their articles, because their genders are not readily predictable. However, here are a few hints to help you determine the gender of some nouns in order to eliminate unnecessary memorizing.

a. Most nouns referring to males are MASCULINE.

> der Vater, der Bruder, der Junge

- Days, months, and seasons are masculine.

> der Montag, der Juni, der Winter

b. Most nouns referring to females are FEMININE; BUT **das Mädchen, das Fräulein** (see c. below).

> die Mutter, die Schwester, die Frau

- Many feminine nouns can be derived from masculine nouns. Their plurals always end in **-nen**.

> sg.: der Schweizer/die Schweizerin; der Österreicher/die Österreicherin
>
> pl.: die Schweizerinnen, Österreicherinnen

- All nouns ending in **-heit, -keit, -ie, -ik, -ion, -schaft, -tät,** and **-ung** are feminine. Their plurals end in **-en.**

> sg.: die Schönheit, Richtigkeit, Geographie, Musik, Religion, Nachbarschaft, Qualität, Rechnung
>
> pl.: die Qualitäten, Rechnungen usw.

There are exceptions, e.g., **der Affe, der Löwe, der Neffe, der Name, das Ende,** etc.

- Most nouns ending in **-e** are feminine. Their plurals end in **-n.**

> sg.: die Sprache, Woche, Hose, Kreide, Farbe, Seite
>
> pl.: die Sprachen, Wochen usw.

c. All nouns ending in **-chen** or **-lein** are NEUTER. These two suffixes make diminutives of nouns, i.e., they denote them as being small. In the case of people, the diminutive may indicate affection, or also belittling. Such nouns often have an umlaut, but there is no plural ending.

> sg.: der Bruder/das Brüderchen; die Schwester/das Schwesterlein
>
> pl.: die Brüderchen, Schwesterlein

- Because of these suffixes, two nouns referring to females are neuter.

> das Mädchen, das Fräulein (seldom used today)

- Most cities and countries are neuter.

> (das) Berlin, (das) Deutschland BUT die Schweiz, die Türkei

2. Summary chart of the four cases

	use	follows . . .	masc.	neut.	fem.	pl.
nom.	Subject, predicate noun **wer? was?**	**heißen, sein, werden**	der dieser[1] ein mein[2]	das dieses ein mein	die diese eine meine	die diese keine meine
acc.	Direct object **wen? was?**	**durch, für, gegen, ohne, um**	den diesen einen meinen			
		an, auf, hinter, in, neben, über, unter, vor, zwischen				
dat.	Indirect object **wem?**	**aus, außer, bei, mit, nach, seit, von, zu** **antworten, danken, gefallen, gehören, glauben,[3] helfen, zuhören** usw.	dem diesem einem meinem	dem diesem einem meinem	der dieser einer meiner	den diesen keinen meinen
gen.	Possessive **wessen?**	**(an)statt, trotz, während, wegen**	des dieses eines meines	des dieses eines meines		der dieser keiner meiner

NOTE: [1] The **der**-words are **dieser, jeder, welcher, alle, manche, solche.**

[2] The **ein**-words are **kein, mein, dein, sein, ihr, unser, euer, ihr, Ihr.**

[3] Ich glaube **ihm.** BUT Ich glaube **es.**

3. Adjective endings

a. **Preceded adjectives**

	masculine	neuter	feminine	plural
nom.	der neue Krimi	das neue Stück	die neue Oper	die neuen Filme
acc.	den neuen Krimi	das neue Stück	die neue Oper	die neuen Filme
dat.	dem neuen Krimi	dem neuen Stück	der neuen Oper	den neuen Filmen
gen.	des neuen Krimis	des neuen Stückes	der neuen Oper	der neuen Filme

	masculine	neuter	feminine	plural
nom.	ein neuer Krimi	ein neues Stück	eine neue Oper	keine neuen Filme
acc.	einen neuen Krimi	ein neues Stück	eine neue Oper	keine neuen Filme
dat.	einem neuen Krimi	einem neuen Stück	einer neuen Oper	keinen neuen Filmen
gen.	eines neuen Krimis	eines neuen Stückes	einer neuen Oper	keiner neuen Filme

Comparing the two tables above, you can see:

- Adjectives preceded by the definite article or any **der**-word have either an **-e** or **-en** ending.
- Adjectives preceded by the indefinite article or any **ein**-word have two different adjective endings WHENEVER **ein** HAS NO ENDING: **-er** for masculine nouns and **-es** for neuter nouns. Otherwise the **-en** ending predominates and is used in the masculine accusative singular, all datives and genitives, and in all plurals.

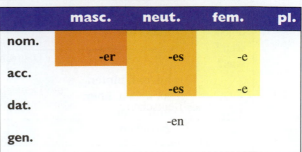

after **der**-words

	masc.	neut.	fem.	pl.
nom.			-e	
acc.				
dat.			-en	
gen.				

after **ein**-words

	masc.	neut.	fem.	pl.
nom.	-er	-es	-e	
acc.		-es	-e	
dat.			-en	
gen.				

Or, to put it in another way, the endings are:

- in the NOMINATIVE AND ACCUSATIVE SINGULAR

  – after **der, das, die,** and **eine** → **-e**

  – after **ein** with masc. nouns → **-er**

  with neut. nouns → **-es**

- in ALL OTHER CASES → **-en**

b. **Unpreceded adjectives**

Unpreceded adjectives take the endings that the definite article would have, if it were used.

der frische	Fisch	das frische	Obst	die frische	Wurst	die frischen	Eier
frischer	Fisch		frisches	Obst	frische	Wurst	frische	Eier

	masculine		neuter		feminine		plural	
nom.	frischer	Fisch	frisches	Obst	frische	Wurst	frische	Eier
acc.	frischen	Fisch	frisches	Obst	frische	Wurst	frische	Eier
dat.	frischem	Fisch	frischem	Obst	frischer	Wurst	frischen	Eiern
gen.	(frischen	Fisches)	(frischen	Obstes)	(frischer	Wurst)	frischer	Eier

Several important words are often used as unpreceded adjectives in the plural: **andere, einige, mehrere, viele, wenige.**

4. Endings of nouns

a. **N-nouns**

	singular	plural
nom.	der Student	die Studenten
acc.	den Studenten	die Studenten
dat.	dem Studenten	den Studenten
gen.	des Studenten	der Studenten

Other n-nouns are: **Herr (-n, -en), Franzose, Gedanke (-ns, -n), Journalist, Junge, Komponist, Mensch, Nachbar, Name (-ns, -n), Polizist, Tourist, Zimmerkollege.**

b. **Adjectival nouns**

	SINGULAR masc.	SINGULAR fem.	PLURAL
nom.	der Deutsche ein Deutscher	die Deutsche eine Deutsche	die Deutschen keine Deutschen
acc.	den Deutschen einen Deutschen		
dat.	dem Deutschen einem Deutschen	der Deutschen einer Deutschen	den Deutschen keinen Deutschen
gen.	des Deutschen eines Deutschen	der Deutschen einer Deutschen	der Deutschen keiner Deutschen

Other adjectival nouns are: **der/die Angestellte, Bekannte, Kranke, Verlobte, der Beamte** (BUT **die Beamtin**).

5. Pronouns

a. **Personal pronouns**

nom.	ich	du	er	es	sie	wir	ihr	sie	Sie
acc.	mich	dich	ihn	es	sie	uns	euch	sie	Sie
dat.	mir	dir	ihm	ihm	ihr	uns	euch	ihnen	Ihnen

b. **Reflexive pronouns**

nom.	ich	du	er / es / sie	wir	ihr	sie	Sie
acc.	mich	dich					
			sich	uns	euch	sich	sich
dat.	mir	dir					

c. **Relative pronouns**

	masc.	neut.	fem.	pl.
nom.	der	das	die	die
acc.	den	das	die	die
dat.	dem	dem	der	denen
gen.	dessen	dessen	deren	deren

6. Comparison of irregular adjectives and adverbs

	gern	groß	gut	hoch	nah	viel
comparative	lieber	größer	besser	höher	näher	mehr
superlative	liebst-	größt-	best-	höchst-	nächst-	meist-

7. N-verbs ("strong verbs") and irregular t-verbs ("weak verbs")

a. Principal parts listed alphabetically

This list is limited to the active n-verbs and irregular t-verbs used in this text. Compound verbs like **ankommen** or **abfliegen** are not included, since their principal parts are the same as those of the basic verbs **kommen** and **fliegen.**

infinitive	present	simple past	past participle	meaning
anfangen	fängt an	fing an	angefangen	*to begin*
backen	bäckt	buk (backte)	gebacken	*to bake*
beginnen		begann	begonnen	*to begin*
bekommen		bekam	bekommen	*to receive, get*
bewerben	bewirbt	bewarb	beworben	*to apply*
bieten		bot	geboten	*to offer*
binden		band	gebunden	*to bind, tie*
bitten		bat	gebeten	*to ask, request*
bleiben		blieb	ist geblieben	*to remain*
bringen		brachte	gebracht	*to bring*
denken		dachte	gedacht	*to think*
einladen	lädt ein	lud ein	eingeladen	*to invite*
empfehlen	empfiehlt	empfahl	empfohlen	*to recommend*
entscheiden		entschied	entschieden	*to decide*
essen	isst	aß	gegessen	*to eat*
fahren	fährt	fuhr	istgefahren	*to drive, go*
fallen	fällt	fiel	gefallen	*to fall*
finden		fand	gefunden	*to find*
fliegen		flog	istgeflogen	*to fly*
geben	gibt	gab	gegeben	*to give*
gefallen	gefällt	gefiel	gefallen	*to please*
gehen		ging	istgegangen	*to go*
genießen	genießt	genoss	genossen	*to enjoy*
geschehen	geschieht	geschah	istgeschehen	*to happen*
haben	hat	hatte	gehabt	*to have*
halten	hält	hielt	gehalten	*to hold; stop*
hängen		hing	gehangen	*to be hanging*
heißen	heißt	hieß	geheißen	*to be called / named*
helfen	hilft	half	geholfen	*to help*
kennen		kannte	gekannt	*to know*
klingen		klang	geklungen	*to sound*
kommen		kam	istgekommen	*to come*
lassen	lässt	ließ	gelassen	*to let; leave (behind)*
laufen	läuft	lief	istgelaufen	*to run; walk*
lesen	liest	las	gelesen	*to read*
liegen		lag	gelegen	*to lie*
nehmen	nimmt	nahm	genommen	*to take*
nennen		nannte	genannt	*to name, call*
reißen	reißt	riss	gerissen	*to tear*
rufen		rief	gerufen	*to call*
scheinen		schien	geschienen	*to shine; seem*
schlafen	schläft	schlief	geschlafen	*to sleep*
schreiben		schrieb	geschrieben	*to write*
schwimmen		schwamm	istgeschwommen	*to swim*
sehen	sieht	sah	gesehen	*to see*
sein	ist	war	istgewesen	*to be*

infinitive	present	simple past	past participle	meaning
singen		sang	gesungen	to sing
sitzen		saß	gesessen	to sit
spinnen		spann	gesponnen	to spin
sprechen	spricht	sprach	gesprochen	to speak
springen		sprang	ist gesprungen	to jump
stehen		stand	gestanden	to stand
steigen		stieg	ist gestiegen	to climb
sterben	stirbt	starb	ist gestorben	to die
tragen	trägt	trug	getragen	to carry; wear
treffen	trifft	traf	getroffen	to meet
treiben		trieb	getrieben	to engage in (sports)
trinken		trank	getrunken	to drink
tun	tut	tat	getan	to do
vergessen	vergisst	vergaß	vergessen	to forget
vergleichen		verglich	verglichen	to compare
verlieren		verlor	verloren	to lose
verschwinden		verschwand	ist verschwunden	to disappear
wachsen	wächst	wuchs	ist gewachsen	to grow
waschen	wäscht	wusch	gewaschen	to wash
werden	wird	wurde	ist geworden	to become; get
werfen	wirft	warf	geworfen	to throw
wissen	weiß	wusste	gewusst	to know
ziehen		zog	(ist) gezogen	to pull; (move)

b. **Principal parts listed by stem-changing groups**

This is the same list as the previous one, but this time it is divided into groups with the same stem changes.

I.	essen	(isst)	aß	gegessen
	vergessen	(vergisst)	vergaß	vergessen
	geben	(gibt)	gab	gegeben
	geschehen	(geschieht)	geschah	ist geschehen
	sehen	(sieht)	sah	gesehen
	lesen	(liest)	las	gelesen
	bitten		bat	gebeten
	liegen		lag	gelegen
	sitzen		saß	gesessen
II.	bewerben	(bewirbt)	bewarb	beworben
	empfehlen	(empfiehlt)	empfahl	empfohlen
	helfen	(hilft)	half	geholfen
	nehmen	(nimmt)	nahm	genommen
	sprechen	(spricht)	sprach	gesprochen
	sterben	(stirbt)	starb	ist gestorben
	treffen	(trifft)	traf	getroffen
	werfen	(wirft)	warf	geworfen
	beginnen		begann	begonnen
	schwimmen		schwamm	ist geschwommen
	spinnen		spann	gesponnen
	bekommen		bekam	bekommen
	kommen		kam	ist gekommen
III.	binden		band	gebunden
	finden		fand	gefunden
	klingen		klang	geklungen
	singen		sang	gesungen

springen		sprang	ist gesprungen
trinken		trank	getrunken
verschwinden		verschwand	ist verschwunden
IV. bleiben		blieb	ist geblieben
entscheiden		entschied	entschieden
scheinen		schien	geschienen
schreiben		schrieb	geschrieben
steigen		stieg	ist gestiegen
treiben		trieb	getrieben
reißen	(reißt)	riss	gerissen
V. bieten		bot	geboten
fliegen		flog	ist geflogen
genießen	(genießt)	genoss	genossen
verlieren		verlor	verloren
ziehen		zog	ist gezogen
VI. einladen	(lädt ein)	lud ein	eingeladen
fahren	(fährt)	fuhr	ist gefahren
tragen	(trägt)	trug	getragen
wachsen	(wächst)	wuchs	ist gewachsen
waschen	(wäscht)	wusch	gewaschen
VII. fallen	(fällt)	fiel	ist gefallen
gefallen	(gefällt)	gefiel	gefallen
halten	(hält)	hielt	gehalten
lassen	(lässt)	ließ	gelassen
schlafen	(schläft)	schlief	geschlafen
laufen	(läuft)	lief	ist gelaufen
heißen	(heißt)	hieß	geheißen
rufen		rief	gerufen

VIII. N-verbs that do not belong to any of the groups above:

anfangen	(fängt an)	fing an	angefangen
backen	(bäckt)	buk (backte)	gebacken
gehen		ging	ist gegangen
hängen		hing	gehangen
sein	(ist)	war	ist gewesen
stehen		stand	gestanden
tun	(tut)	tat	getan
werden	(wird)	wurde	ist geworden

IX. Irregular t-verbs:

bringen		brachte	gebracht
denken		dachte	gedacht
haben	(hat)	hatte	gehabt
kennen		kannte	gekannt
nennen		nannte	genannt
wissen	(weiß)	wusste	gewusst

8. Sample forms of the subjunctive

a. General subjunctive (Subjunctive II)

	können	haben	sein	werden	lernen	bringen	gehen
ich	könnte	hätte	wäre	würde	lernte	brächte	ginge
du	könntest	hättest	wärest	würdest	lerntest	brächtest	gingest
er	könnte	hätte	wäre	würde	lernte	brächte	ginge
wir	könnten	hätten	wären	würden	lernten	brächten	gingen
ihr	könntet	hättet	wäret	würdet	lerntet	brächtet	ginget
sie	könnten	hätten	wären	würden	lernten	brächten	gingen

b. **Special subjunctive (Subjunctive I)**

	können	haben	sein	werden	lernen	bringen	gehen
ich	könne	habe	sei	werde	lerne	bringe	gehe
du	könnest	habest	seiest	werdest	lernest	bringest	gehest
er	könne	habe	seie	werde	lerne	bringe	gehe
wir	können	haben	seien	werden	lernen	bringen	gehen
ihr	könnet	habet	seiet	werdet	lernet	bringet	gehet
sie	können	haben	seien	werden	lernen	bringen	gehen

9. Verb forms in different tenses

a. **Indicative**

	present		simple past		future	
ich	frage	fahre	fragte	fuhr	werde	
du	fragst	fährst	fragtest	fuhrst	wirst	
er	fragt	fährt	fragte	fuhr	wird	fragen / fahren
wir	fragen	fahren	fragten	fuhren	werden	
ihr	fragt	fahrt	fragtet	fuhrt	werdet	
sie	fragen	fahren	fragten	fuhren	werden	

	pres. perf.				past perf.			
ich	habe		bin		hatte		war	
du	hast		bist		hattest		warst	
er	hat	gefragt	ist	gefahren	hatte	gefragt	war	gefahren
wir	haben		sind		hatten		waren	
ihr	habt		seid		hattet		wart	
sie	haben		sind		hatten		waren	

b. **Subjunctive**

PRESENT-TIME

	general subj.				special subj.	
ich	fragte	führe	würde		frage	fahre
du	fragtest	führest	würdest		fragest	fahrest
er	fragte	führe	würde	fragen / fahren	frage	fahre
wir	fragten	führen	würden		fragen	fahren
ihr	fragtet	führet	würdet		fraget	fahret
sie	fragten	führen	würden		fragen	fahren

PAST-TIME

	general subj.				special subj.			
ich	hätte		wäre		habe		sei	
du	hättest		wärest		habest		seiest	
er	hätte	gefragt	wäre	gefahren	habe	gefragt	sei	gefahren
wir	hätten		wären		haben		seien	
ihr	hättet		wäret		habet		seiet	
sie	hätten		wären		haben		seien	

c. **Passive voice**

	present		simple past		future	
ich	werde		wurde		werde	
du	wirst		wurdest		wirst	
er	wird	gefragt	wurde	gefragt	wird	gefragt werden
wir	werden		wurden		werden	
ihr	werdet		wurdet		werdet	
sie	werden		wurden		werden	

	pres. perf.		past perf.	
ich	bin		war	
du	bist		warst	
er	ist	gefragt worden	war	gefragt worden
wir	sind		waren	
ihr	seid		wart	
sie	sind		waren	

10. Translation of the *Gespräche*

p. 2 ## Schritt 1

How are you?   MR. SANDERS: Hello. MS. LEHMANN: Hello. MR. SANDERS: My name is Sanders, Willi Sanders. And what's your name? MS. LEHMANN: My name is Erika Lehmann. MR. SANDERS: Pleased to meet you.

MR. MEIER: Good morning, Mrs. Fiedler. How are you? MRS. FIEDLER: Fine, thank you. And you? MR. MEIER: I'm fine, too. Thank you.

HEIDI: Hi, Ute! How are you? UTE: Hi, Heidi! Oh, I'm tired. HEIDI: So am I. Too much stress. See you later! UTE: Bye! Take care!

p. 5 ## Schritt 2

What's that?   GERMAN PROFESSOR: Listen carefully and answer in German. What is that? JIM MILLER: That's the pencil. GERMAN PROFESSOR: What color is the pencil? SUSAN SMITH: Yellow. GERMAN PROFESSOR: Make a sentence, please. SUSAN SMITH: The pencil is yellow. GERMAN PROFESSOR: Is the notebook yellow, too? DAVID JENKINS: No, the notebook isn't yellow. The notebook is light blue. GERMAN PROFESSOR: Good. SUSAN SMITH: What does *hellblau* mean? GERMAN PROFESSOR: *Hellblau* means *light blue* in English. SUSAN SMITH: And how does one say *dark blue?* GERMAN PROFESSOR: *Dunkelblau*. SUSAN SMITH: Oh, the pen is dark blue. GERMAN PROFESSOR: Correct. That's all for today. For tomorrow please read the dialogue again and learn the vocabulary, too.

p. 9 ## Schritt 3

In the department store   SALESCLERK: Well, how are the pants? CHRISTIAN: Too big and too long. SALESCLERK: And the sweater? MAIKE: Too expensive. CHRISTIAN: But the colors are great. Too bad!

SALESCLERK: Hello. May I help you? SILVIA: I need some pencils and paper. How much are the pencils? SALESCLERK: 55 cents. SILVIA: And the paper? SALESCLERK: 2 euros 40 cents. SILVIA: Fine. I'll take six pencils and the paper. SALESCLERK: Is that all? SILVIA: Yes, thank you. SALESCLERK: 5 euros 70 cents, please.

Schritt 4

p. 14

The weather in April NORBERT: It's nice today, isn't it? JULIA: Yes, that's for sure. The sun is shining again. RUDI: Only the wind is cool. JULIA: Oh, that doesn't matter. NORBERT: I think it's great.

HANNES: Man, what lousy weather! It's already snowing again. MARTIN: So what? HANNES: In Mallorca it's nice and beautiful. MARTIN: But we're here, and not in Mallorca. HANNES: Too bad.

DOROTHEA: The weather is awful, isn't it? MATTHIAS: I think so, too. It's raining and raining. SONJA: And it's so cold again. Only 7 degrees! MATTHIAS: Yes, typical April.

Schritt 5

p. 19

What time is it? RITA: Hi, Axel! What time is it? AXEL: Hi, Rita! It's ten to eight. RITA: Oh no, in ten minutes I have philosophy. AXEL: Take care, then. Bye! RITA: Yes, bye!

PHILLIP: Hi, Steffi! What time is it? STEFFI: Hi, Phillip! It's eleven thirty. PHILLIP: Shall we eat now? STEFFI: OK, the lecture doesn't start till a quarter past one.

MR. RICHTER: When are you finished today? MR. HEROLD: At two o'clock. Why? MR. RICHTER: Are we going to play tennis today? MR. HEROLD: Yes, great! It's now twelve thirty. How about a quarter to three? MR. RICHTER: Fine! See you later!

Kapitel 1

p. 30

At the Goethe Institute SHARON: Roberto, where are you from? ROBERTO: I'm from Rome. And you? SHARON: I'm from Sacramento, but now my family lives in Seattle. ROBERTO: Do you have (any) brothers or sisters? SHARON: Yes, I have two sisters and two brothers. How about you? ROBERTO: I have only one sister. She lives in Montreal, in Canada. SHARON: Really? What a coincidence! My uncle lives there, too.

Later ROBERTO: Sharon, when is the test? SHARON: In ten minutes. Say, what are the names of some rivers in Germany? ROBERTO: In the north is the Elbe, in the east the Oder, in the south . . . SHARON: . . . the Danube? ROBERTO: Right! And in the west the Rhine. Where is Düsseldorf? SHARON: Düsseldorf? Hm. Where's a map? ROBERTO: Oh, here. In the west of Germany, north of Bonn, on the Rhine. SHARON: Oh yes, right! Well, good luck!

Kapitel 2

p. 52

At the grocery store CLERK: Hello. May I help you? OLIVER: I'd like some fruit. Don't you have any bananas? CLERK: Yes, over there. OLIVER: How much are they? CLERK: 90 cents a pound. OLIVER: And the oranges? CLERK: 45 cents each. OLIVER: Fine, two pounds of bananas and six oranges, please. CLERK: Anything else? OLIVER: Yes, two kilos of apples, please. CLERK: 8 euros 10 cents, please. Thank you. Good-bye.

In the bakery CLERK: Good morning. May I help you? SIMONE: Good morning. One rye bread and six rolls, please. CLERK: Anything else? SIMONE: Yes, I need some cake. Is the apple strudel fresh? CLERK: Of course, very fresh. SIMONE: Fine, then I'll take four pieces. CLERK: Is that all? SIMONE: I'd also like some cookies. What kind of cookies do you have today? CLERK: Lemon cookies, chocolate cookies, butter cookies . . . SIMONE: Hm . . . I'll take 300 grams of chocolate cookies. CLERK: Anything else? SIMONE: No, thank you. That's all. CLERK: Then that comes to 9 euros 55 cents, please.

Kapitel 3

p. 76

In the restaurant AXEL: Waiter, the menu, please. WAITER: Here you are. AXEL: What do you recommend today? WAITER: All of today's specials are very good. AXEL: Gabi, what are you having? GABI: I don't know. What are you going to have? AXEL: I think I'll take menu number one: veal cutlet and potato salad. GABI: And I would like menu number two: stuffed beef rolls with potato dumplings. WAITER: Would you like something to drink? GABI: A glass of apple juice. And what about you? AXEL: Mineral water. *(The waiter comes with the food.)* Enjoy your meal! GABI: Thanks, you too . . . Mm, that tastes good. AXEL: The veal cutlet, too.

Later GABI: We'd like to pay, please. WAITER: All right. All together? GABI: Yes. Please give me the bill. AXEL: No, no, no. GABI: Yes, Axel. Today I'm paying. WAITER: Well, one menu number one, one menu number two, one apple juice, one mineral water, two cups of coffee. Anything else? AXEL: Yes, one roll. WAITER: That comes to 30 euros 30 cents, please. GABI: *(She gives the waiter 40 euros)* Make it 32 euros, please. WAITER: And eight euros change (back). Thank you very much.

p. 104 ## Kapitel 4

On the telephone CHRISTA: Hi, Michael! MICHAEL: Hi, Christa! How are you? CHRISTA: Not bad, thanks. What are you doing on the weekend? MICHAEL: Nothing special. Why? CHRISTA: It's Klaus's birthday the day after tomorrow, and we're giving a party. MICHAEL: Great! But are you sure that Klaus's birthday is the day after tomorrow? I think his birthday is on May 7. CHRISTA: Nonsense. Klaus's birthday is on May 3. And Saturday is the third. MICHAEL: OK. When and where is the party? CHRISTA: Saturday at seven at my place. But don't say anything. It's a surprise. MICHAEL: OK. Well, see you then. CHRISTA: Bye. Take care!

Klaus rings Christa's doorbell CHRISTA: Hi, Klaus! Happy birthday! KLAUS: What? MICHAEL: All the best on your birthday! KLAUS: Hi, Michael! . . . Hello, Gerda! Kurt and Sabine, you too? ALL: We're wishing you a happy birthday! KLAUS: Thanks! What a surprise! But my birthday isn't today. My birthday is on the seventh. CHRISTA: Really?—Well, it doesn't matter. We're celebrating today.

p. 130 ## Kapitel 5

Excuse me! Where is . . . ? TOURIST: Excuse me! Can you tell me where the Hotel Sacher is? VIENNESE PASSERBY: First street on the left behind the opera. TOURIST: And how do I get from there to St. Stephen's Cathedral? VIENNESE PASSERBY: Straight ahead along Kärtner Straße. TOURIST: How far is it to the cathedral? VIENNESE PASSERBY: Not far. You can walk (there). TOURIST: Thank you. VIENNESE PASSERBY: You're welcome.

Over there TOURIST: Excuse me. Where is the Burgtheater? GENTLEMAN: I'm sorry. I'm not from Vienna. TOURIST: Pardon me. Is that the Burgtheater? LADY: No, that's not the Burgtheater, but the opera house. Take the streetcar to city hall. The Burgtheater is across from city hall. TOURIST: And where does the streetcar stop? LADY: Over there on your left. TOURIST: Thank you very much. LADY: You're most welcome.

p. 154 ## Kapitel 6

Apartment for rent INGE: Hello, my name is Inge Moser. I've heard that you have a two-room apartment for rent. Is that right? LANDLORD: Yes, near the cathedral. INGE: How old is the apartment? LANDLORD: Fairly old, but it's been renovated and is quite big and light. It even has a balcony. INGE: What floor is it on? LANDLORD: On the fourth floor. INGE: Is it furnished or unfurnished? LANDLORD: Unfurnished. INGE: And how much is the rent? LANDLORD: 550 euros. INGE: Is that with or without heat? LANDLORD: Without heat. INGE: Oh, that's a little too expensive. Thank you very much. Good-bye! LANDLORD: Good-bye!

Living in a co-op INGE: I like your house. HORST: We still have room for you. Come, I'll show you everything . . . Here on the left is our kitchen. It's small but practical. INGE: Who does the cooking? HORST: We all (do): Jens, Gisela, Renate, and I. INGE: And that's the living room? HORST: Yes. It's a bit dark, but that's all right. INGE: I like your chairs. HORST: They're old, but really comfortable. Upstairs there are four bedrooms and the bathroom. INGE: Only one bathroom? HORST: Yes, unfortunately. But down here there is another toilet. INGE: How much do you pay per month? HORST: 200 euros each. INGE: Not bad. And how do you get to the university? HORST: No problem. I walk. It's not far. INGE: (That) sounds good!

Kapitel 7   p. 178

At the bank TOURIST: Hello. Can you tell me where I can exchange money? TELLER: At counter 1. TOURIST: Thank you very much. *(She goes to counter 1.)* Hello. I'd like to exchange (some) dollars into euros. Here are my traveler's checks. TELLER: May I please see your passport? TOURIST: Here you are. TELLER: Sign here, please, then go to the cashier over there. There you'll get your money. TOURIST: Thank you. *(She goes to the cashier.)* CASHIER: 324 euros 63 cents: one hundred, two hundred, three hundred, ten, twenty, twenty-four euros and sixty-three cents. TOURIST: Thank you. Good-bye.

At the hotel reception desk RECEPTIONIST: Good evening. GUEST: Good evening. Do you have a single room available? RECEPTIONIST: For how long? GUEST: For two or three nights; if possible, quiet and with a bath. RECEPTIONIST: Unfortunately today we have only one double room, and that for only one night. But tomorrow there will be a single room available. Would you like to see the double room? GUEST: Yes, I would. RECEPTIONIST: Room number 12, on the second floor to the right. Here's the key. GUEST: Say, can I leave my suitcase here for a minute? RECEPTIONIST: Yes, of course. Put it over there in the corner. GUEST: Thank you. One more thing, when do you close at night? RECEPTIONIST: At midnight. If you come later, you'll have to ring the bell.

Kapitel 8   p. 206

At the post office in the train station UTA: I'd like to send this package to the United States. CLERK: By surface mail or by airmail? UTA: By airmail. How long will it take? CLERK: About one week. Please fill out this parcel form! . . . Just a minute. Your return address is missing. UTA: Oh yes . . . One more thing. I need a telephone card. CLERK: For 5, 10, or 20 francs? UTA: For 20 francs. Thank you very much.

At the ticket counter ANNE: When does the next train for Interlaken leave? CLERK: In ten minutes. Departure at 11:28 A.M., track 2. ANNE: Good grief! And when will it arrive there? CLERK: Arrival in Interlaken at 2:16 P.M. ANNE: Do I have to change trains? CLERK: Yes, in Bern, but you have a connection to the InterCity Express with only a 24-minute stopover. ANNE: Fine. Give me a round-trip ticket to Interlaken, please. CLERK: First or second class? ANNE: Second class.

Kapitel 9   p. 232

On the telephone MRS. SCHMIDT: This is Mrs. Schmidt. ANNEMARIE: Hello, Mrs. Schmidt. It's me, Annemarie. MRS. SCHMIDT: Hi, Annemarie! ANNEMARIE: Is Thomas there? MRS. SCHMIDT: No, I'm sorry. He just went to the post office. ANNEMARIE: I see. Can you tell him that I can't go out with him tonight? MRS. SCHMIDT: Of course. What's the matter? ANNEMARIE: I'm sick. My throat hurts and I have a headache. MRS. SCHMIDT: I'm sorry. I hope you get better soon. ANNEMARIE: Thank you. Good-bye. MRS. SCHMIDT: Good-bye.

See you in a few minutes YVONNE: Mayer residence. DANIELA: Hi, Yvonne! It's me, Daniela. YVONNE: Hi, Daniela! What's up? DANIELA: Nothing special. Do you feel like playing squash or going swimming? YVONNE: Squash? No thanks. I'm still sore from the day before yesterday. I can hardly move. I am hurting all over. DANIELA: Poor baby *(lit.* lame duck)! How about chess? YVONNE: OK, that sounds fine. Are you coming to my place? DANIELA: Yes, see you in a few minutes.

Kapitel 10   p. 256

A glance at the newspaper SONJA: Say, what's on TV tonight? THEO: I have no idea. Nothing special for sure. SONJA: Let me see. *Good Times, Bad Times,* a documentary, and a detective story. THEO: I don't feel like (watching) that. SONJA: Maybe there's something at the movies? THEO: Yes, *Planet of the Apes, Animal,* and *Shrek.* SONJA: I've already seen them all. THEO: *The Caucasian Chalk Circle,* by Brecht, is playing at the theater. SONJA: Not bad. Do you feel like going? THEO: Yes, that sounds good. Let's go.

At the ticket window THEO: Do you still have tickets for tonight? LADY: Yes, in the first row of the first balcony on the left, and on the right in the orchestra. THEO: Two seats in the orchestra. Here are our student ID's. LADY: 10 euros, please. SONJA: When does the performance start? LADY: At 8:15 P.M.

During the intermission THEO: Would you like a cola (drink)? SONJA: Yes, I'd love one. But let me pay. You've already bought the programs. THEO: OK. How did you like the first act? SONJA: Great. I once read the piece in school, but I've never seen it on stage. THEO: I haven't either.

p. 282   ## Kapitel 11

To each his own SONJA: Hey, Nicole, listen! "Wanted: pretty, dynamic, affectionate EVA. Reward: good-looking ADAM with a big heart, end 20s, likes antiques, old houses, fast cars, animals, (and) kids. NICOLE: Hmm, not bad, but not for me. I don't like children and I'm allergic to animals. SONJA: Then have a look at this! "What I'm looking for exists. But how to find it? Artist, beginning 30s, charming, enterprising, musical is looking for a congenial, well-educated, reliable woman with a sense of humor." Does that sound interesting? NICOLE: Yes, perhaps. SONJA: He's looking for someone with a sense of humor. I like that, and I also like music. But whether he likes jazz? SONJA: Perhaps we could meet them both. NICOLE: I don't know. I think it's sort of stupid to meet people through ads in the newspaper. SONJA: Nonsense! Let's try it! What do we have to lose? NICOLE: What do you think, Frank? FRANK: I think you're crazy. But so what, to each his own! . . . Take a look at this! Somebody wants to give away a dog, a cat, and a bird, all together. NICOLE: That's all we need: a whole zoo! No thanks! FRANK: How about a little puppy or a little cat? SONJA: I love animals, but right now I don't have the space and also not enough time for that. FRANK: But such a little kitty doesn't need much. SONJA: Perhaps later. Right now I love my freedom. FRANK: And you want to meet with someone from the newspaper? NICOLE: Oh, you wouldn't understand.

p. 314   ## Kapitel 12

Do you know what you want to be? TRUDI: Say, Elke, do you already know what you want to be? ELKE: Yes, I'd like to become a cabinet-maker. TRUDI: Isn't that very strenuous? ELKE: Oh, you get used to it. Perhaps someday I'll open my own business. TRUDI: Those are big plans. ELKE: Why not? I don't feel like always sitting in an office and working for other people. TRUDI: And where do you want to apply for an apprenticeship? ELKE: No problem at all. My aunt has her own business and has already offered me a position. TRUDI: You're lucky. ELKE: And how about you? Do you know what you want to do? TRUDI: Perhaps I'll be a dentist. Good dentists are always needed and besides, it pays very well. ELKE: That's true, but that takes so long. TRUDI: I know, but I'm looking forward to it anyway.

p. 340   ## Kapitel 13

During registration PETRA: Hi, John. How are you? JOHN: Pretty good, and you? PETRA: Well, I can't complain. What are you doing there? JOHN: I've still got to fill out these registration forms. PETRA: Shall I help you? JOHN: If you have time. I'm always struggling with red tape. PETRA: Do you have your passport with you? JOHN: No, why? PETRA: Your residence permit is in it; you really need it. JOHN: I can get it quickly. PETRA: Do that. I'll wait for you here.

A little later JOHN: Here's my passport. I'll also have to decide soon what seminars I want to take. Can you help me with that, too? PETRA: Sure. What's your major? JOHN: My major is modern history. I'd like to take some seminars in German history and literature. PETRA: Here's my course catalog. Let's see what they're offering this semester.

Kapitel 14 p. 364

There's always something going on here HEIKE: And that's the Memorial Church with its three buildings. We call them the "Hollow Tooth," the "Lipstick," and the "Compact." MARTIN: Berliners have nicknames for everything, you know. HEIKE: The old tower of the Memorial Church is to stay the way it is, as a memorial (to the war). The new Memorial Church with the new tower is modern. MARTIN: And they really look a little like a lipstick and a compact. Tell me, do you like living here in Berlin? HEIKE: Of course! Berlin is really lively and has so much to offer, not only historically but also culturally. There's always something going on here. Besides, the surroundings are beautiful. MARTIN: Somewhere I read that 24 percent of Berlin's total area consists of forests and lakes, with 800 kilometers of biking trails. HEIKE: That's great, isn't it? MARTIN: Awesome! Say, were you there when they broke through the Wall? HEIKE: You bet! I'll never forget that. MARTIN: I won't either, although I only saw it on TV. HEIKE: We waited all night, even though it was really cold. When the first piece of wall tipped over, we all sang loudly: "A beautiful day like today, a day like this should never end." MARTIN: I (can) still see the people dancing and celebrating on top of the Wall. HEIKE: Yes, that was really incredible (*lit.* a unique experience). Nobody anticipated that. MARTIN: A total surprise (*lit.* a completely unexpected moment). HEIKE: Who would have thought that it all would happen so fast and so peacefully? MARTIN: Since then, a lot of things have changed here. The traces of the Wall are almost gone. Are you glad that Berlin is again the capital (of Germany)? HEIKE: You bet! MARTIN: You really like to live here? HEIKE: Yes, of course. We Berliners complain and make fun of our city, but we love it.

Kapitel 15 p. 390

A visit to Weimar TOM: It's funny, but this monument of Goethe and Schiller seems so familiar to me. I think I've seen it somewhere before. DANIELA: Have you (ever) been to San Francisco? TOM: Of course! DANIELA: Were you in Golden Gate Park, too? TOM: I see, there's exactly the same monument! I think the German-Americans in California had it built. DANIELA: Right! By the way, did you know that Weimar was the cultural capital of Europe for the year 1999? TOM: No, that's new to me. How come? DANIELA: In the 18th century, a lot of famous people lived here, and the Weimar Republic is also named for it. TOM: Yes, that's true. But this morning, when I looked down at the town from the memorial of the Buchenwald concentration camp, I had very mixed feelings. DANIELA: Yes, there you have a point (*lit.* you're right).

In the old part of town DANIELA: Look, the old houses here are really pretty, aren't they? TOM: Yes, they've been wonderfully restored. I find it especially nice that no cars are allowed here. DANIELA: Thank God. The façades wouldn't have survived the exhaust fumes of the Trabbis for long. TOM: In our city, there's now also a citizens' initiative to ban all cars from the old part of town in order to save the old buildings. DANIELA: I think that's good. TOM: Are the containers over there for recycling (*lit.* waste separation)? DANIELA: Yes, do you have that too? TOM: We do, but certainly much more could be done in that respect. For example, I never know how to get rid of my old batteries or medicine. DANIELA: The old batteries you bring to the gas station, and the old medicine to the pharmacy. TOM: You can't do that here, and therefore a lot of things finally end up in the garbage can. DANIELA: With us [in Germany], that's forbidden. TOM: And that's the way it should be. In that regard, you're just more progressive than we are.

11. Supplementary charts for *Hoppla, hier fehlt was!*

p. 43 **Kapitel 1**

S2:

Name	Nationalität	Wohnort	Alter
Toni	Schweizer		32
Katja	Deutsche	Ulm	
	Österreicherin		61
Nicole	Französin	Lyon	
Pierre	Franzose		
	Italiener		25
Maria	Spanierin	Madrid	
Tom	Kanadier		28
Amy	Amerikanerin	Miami	

p. 87 **Kapitel 3**

S2:

	Bruder	Schwester	Mutter	Vater	Großeltern
Bild					
Bücher					x
Tennishose					
Hausschuhe				x	
Pulli					
Ringe *(pl.)*					
T-Shirts		x			
Mantel			x		
Messer *(sg.)*	x				
Gläser					

p. 115 **Kapitel 4**

S2:

	Ute	Eva	Max	Toni	ich	Partner/in
an alles denken						
mit dem Essen helfen	x					
Getränke bringen			x		x	
den Sekt öffnen						
viel essen			x		x	
viel trinken			x			
schön singen						
etwas tanzen	x					
mit allen sprechen						
nichts tun						
nicht lange bleiben					x	

S2:

Wer?	Was?	Warum?	Wann?	Information?
Dieter	bei den Wiener Festwochen in Wien sein	Er sieht nicht genug Opern und Theaterstücke. (können)		
	Silvester in Wien feiern		31. 12 – 1. 1.	www.wien-event.at
Sonja	das Museum moderner Kunst besichtigen	Es hat alles, von Pablo Picasso bis Andy Warhol. (sollen)		
	zum Christkindlmarkt am Rathausplatz		17. 11 – 24. 12.	www.christkindlmarkt.at
Karen + Charlie	zum Wiener Eistraum gehen	Da tanzen die Leute auf dem Eis vor dem Rathaus. (dürfen)		

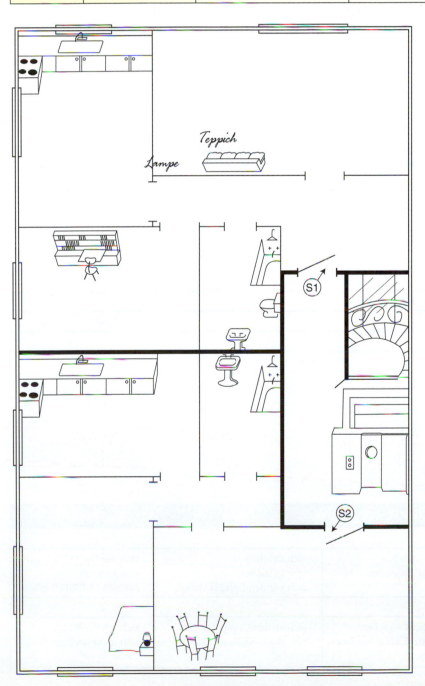

p. 188 **Kapitel 7**

S2:

Vater	bei der Bank vorbeigehen	Ja, gestern.
Vater	Geld umtauschen	Ja.
Mutter	Kamera mitnehmen	
Mutter	die Nachbarn anrufen	
Thomas	die Telefonnummer aufschreiben	
Thomas	die Garagentür zumachen	Nein, noch nicht.
Carla	bei der Post vorbeigehen	Ja, gestern.
Carla	die Fenster zumachen	
Kinder	den Fernseher ausmachen (*turn off*)	
Kinder	die Lichter (*lights*) ausmachen	Nein, noch nicht.
Du	ein paar Bücher mitnehmen	

p. 221 **Kapitel 8**

S2:

Wer	Wann/Wie lange	Wie/Obj. + Präposition	Wo und was
Lucian	ein paar Wochen		
Christl		bei ein- Gastfamilie	in Amerika sein
Steffi		wegen ihr-Prüfung	
Nina + Kim	während d- Ferien		von Passau bis Wien fahren
Ben + Michi			in ein- Pizzeria arbeiten
Günther		trotz d- Wetter	auf der Insel Rügen campen
Jutta	vom 1. bis 31. Juli		
Nicole		wieder	von Griechenland zurückkommen
Yvonne	morgens		
Jochen	mittags	gewöhnlich	

p. 244 **Kapitel 9**

S2:

	Zuerst	Dann	Danach
Elke			
Horst	sich schnell anziehen joggen gehen	sich duschen sich umziehen sich vor den Spiegel stellen	sich die Haare kämmen sich rasieren Joghurt und Müsli essen
Susi			
Ingo	sich das Gesicht waschen sich eine Tasse Kaffee machen sich anziehen	sich an den Computer setzen sich die E-Mails ansehen	sich wieder hinlegen sich nicht beeilen

Kapitel 10

p. 259

S2:

Wo?	Was?	Wann?
Volksbühne	**Macbeth,** Schauspiel von William Shakespeare	19.30
Urania-Theater		
Metropol-Theater	**West Side Story,** Musical von Leonard Bernstein	19.00
Im Dom		
Philharmonie		
Konzerthaus	**Flamenco-Festival,** mit Montse Salazar	20.00
Komodie		
Kammerspiele		
Filmbühne 1	**Das Versprechen,** von Margarethe von Trotta	
Filmbühne 2	**Das Boot,** von Wolfgang Petersen	

Kapitel 11

p. 297

S2:

	Nachdem . . .	Dann . . .
Thomas	die Anzeige lesen	den Besitzer *(owner)* anrufen
Besitzer	über die Katze erzählen	
Thomas	dorthin fahren und s. die Katze ansehen	sich in die Katze verlieben
Thomas	die Katze mit nach Hause nehmen	
die Beiden	ihr etwas Milch geben	mit ihr spielen wollen
die Katze	sich einleben *(get used to the place)*	
die Beiden	die Katze eine Woche haben	wässrige *(watery)* Augen und eine verstopfte *(stuffed-up)* Nase bekommen
Ingo	die Katze zwei Wochen auf seinem Bett haben	
die Beiden	eine lange Diskussion haben	eine Anzeige in die Zeitung setzen
Besitzer	zwei Wochen ohne die Katze sein	
Besitzer	auf die Anzeige antworten	die Katze zurücknehmen

Kapitel 13

p. 353

Und was sagt Ihnen Ihr Partner/Ihre Partnerin?

	Ja	Nein
Die Oma ist gern zur Schule gegangen.	x	
Sie war gut in Mathe.		
Sie hat an der Uni studiert.		
Sie ist Lehrerin geworden.		
Sie hat bei einer reichen Familie gearbeitet.		
Sie hat geheiratet.		
Sie hatte viele Kinder.		
Sie hat mit ihrem Mann eine große Weltreise gemacht.		

p. 352   ## Kapitel 13

S2:

Erzählen Sie Ihrem Partner/Ihrer Partnerin:

Mein Opa ist aus Deutschland gekommen. Seine Familie ist mit dem Schiff nach Amerika gefahren. Opa konnte kein Englisch und er wäre lieber in Deutschland geblieben. Seine Familie hat in New York gewohnt. Er ist Polizist geworden. Er hat sich immer für Musik interessiert. Er konnte gut singen, und ich habe viele deutsche Lieder von ihm gelernt. Wenn er Zeit gehabt hätte, hätte er gelernt, Klavier zu spielen. Er hat seine Verwandten in Deutschland oft besucht. Dieses Jahr wäre er auch nach Deutschland gefahren, wenn er nicht krank geworden wäre.

p. 378   ## Kapitel 14

Liste von Leuten:		
ein NBC-Korrespondent	ein 16-Jähriger aus Ost-Berlin	der Autor Günter Kunert
Lyndon Johnson	der Sänger Wolf Biermann	Willy Brandt
ein Westberliner Polizist	eine amerikanische Studentin	Alexander Dubček
Ronald Reagan	die Cellistin Sophie-Marie Mutter	Leonard Bernstein

S2:

WER?	AUSSAGEN
Major der DDR-Grenztruppe:	„Es ist eine verrückte Zeit."
	„Vor meinen Augen tanzte die Freiheit."
Ostberliner Taxifahrer:	„So viel Fernsehen habe ich noch nie gesehen."
	„Wir haben uns jeden Tag gesehen. Jetzt will ich ihm mal die Hand schütteln (shake)."
Afrikanischer Diplomat:	„Ich dachte, die Deutschen können nur Fußball spielen oder im Stechschritt (goose-step) marschieren, aber jetzt können sie sogar Revolutionen machen."
	„Ich muss weinen vor Freude, dass es so schnell und einfach ging. Und ich muss weinen vor Zorn (anger), dass es so elend (terribly) lange dauerte."
Autor Günter Grass:	„Jetzt wird sich zeigen, ob der jahrzehntelangen Rhetorik von den ,Brüdern und Schwestern' auch entsprechendes (corresponding) politisches Handeln (action) folgen wird."
	„Das Volk, von dem man nun wieder glaubhaft (convincingly) sprechen darf, ist über die unerwartete Erfüllung (fulfillment) eines Traumes selber dermaßen perplex (so baffled), dass ihm die Worte des Triumphes fehlen."
Autor Stephan Heym:	„Die einzige Chance, die wir haben, den Sozialismus zu retten (save), ist richtiger Sozialismus."
	„Ich bin Gott dankbar, dass ich das noch erleben (experience) darf."
Amerikanischer Präsident Ronald Reagan:	„Auf beiden Seiten sind Deutsche. Der Kommunismus hat seine Chance gehabt. Er funktioniert nicht."
	„Wir haben zu lange im Dunkeln gelebt. Treten wir (let's step) ins Licht!"
Cellist Mstislaw Rostropowitsch:	„Mauern sind nicht für ewig (forever) gebaut . . . In Berlin habe ich für mein Herz gespielt."

Kapitel 15

p. 407

Die Belgier: . . . Die Dänen: . . .
Die Deutschen: . . . Die Franzosen: . . .
Die Griechen: . . . Die Briten: . . .

S2:

Sportliche Iren

Die Iren lieben den Sport mehr als alle anderen Europäer. Jeder zweite ist verrückt danach.

Offene Luxemburger

Luxemburg hat europaweit die meisten Ausländer—29%. Die meisten Beamte der EU.

Fleißige Portugiesen

Die Portugiesen sind das fleißigste Völkchen Europas, höchste Jahresarbeitszeit—2025 Stunden.

Schnelle Italiener

Jedes Jahr kommen die Hälfte aller europäischen Telegramme allein aus ihrem Land.

Maritime Holländer

Die Holländer sind die größten Seefahrer Europas. Das Land besitzt fast 4000 Schiffe.

Sehfreudige Spanier

Die Spanier sitzen am häufigsten unter den Europäern vor dem Fernseher—vier Stunden am Tag.

12. Answers for the optional English-to-German practice in the annos

Kapitel 1

p. 38

1. Wir lernen Deutsch. 2. Ich zähle langsam. 3. Woher kommt ihr? 4. Sie kommen aus Kanada. 5. Ich komme / bin aus Amerika. 6. Antwortest du auf Englisch? 7. Nein, ich spreche Deutsch. 8. Sie öffnet das Buch. 9. Ich brauche das Buch. 10. Was sagt sie? 11. Verstehst du das? 12. Wiederholt sie das? 13. Sie heißt Sabrina. 14. Sie wohnen in Wittenberg.

Kapitel 4

p. 113

1. Sie hat noch geschlafen. 2. Sie haben auch geholfen. 3. Hast du (habt ihr, haben Sie) schon gegessen? 4. Haben Sie es gefunden? 5. Ich habe das nicht verstanden. 6. Hast du das gelesen? 7. Ich habe die Frage wiederholt. 8. Wer hat es genommen? 9. Sie haben Wintermäntel gekauft. 10. Meine Tante hat das Geschäft empfohlen. 11. Habt ihr die Bücher verkauft? 12. Ich habe die Rechnungen bezahlt.

Kapitel 5

p. 137

1. Hast du (habt ihr, haben Sie) ihm gedankt? 2. Wir haben ihr gratuliert. 3. Ich habe sie überrascht. 4. Wir zeigen dir (euch, Ihnen) das Schloss. 5. Haben sie euch geantwortet? 6. Ich habe dir geschrieben. 7. Gibst du ihm das Geschenk? 8. Sie glaubt mir nicht.

1. Er will den Dom sehen. 2. Sie müssen zur Post (gehen). 3. Ich kann das nicht lesen. 4. Ihr sollt Deutsch sprechen. 5. Du darfst ein Stück Kuchen bestellen. 6. Sie soll lernen. 7. Wir müssen den Weg finden. 8. Kannst du (könnt ihr, können Sie) mir nicht helfen? 9. Wir möchten nach Wien (fahren). 10. Dürfen wir das Schloss sehen?

Kapitel 7

p. 189

1. Du hast dein Buch nicht zugemacht. 2. Hören Sie zu! 3. Sie sind am Wochenende zurückgekommen. 4. Geht ihr bald aus (weg)? 5. Ich weiß nicht, ob sie mitkommt. 6. Weißt du, wann sie ausgegangen (weggegangen) ist? 7. Ich habe unser Geld umgetauscht. 8. Wen haben Sie mitgebracht?

p. 214   ## Kapitel 8

1. Ist das Evas Zug? 2. Weißt du die Bahnsteignummer / die Nummer des Bahnsteigs? 3. Nein, wo ist der Abfahrtsplan (der Züge)? 4. Ihr Zug fährt in ein paar Minuten ab. 5. Nimm Kurts Paket mit! 6. Kurt ist Student und ein Freund einer Freundin. 7. Eva, hast du die Adresse des Studenten? 8. Nein, aber ich weiß den Namen des Studentenheims. 9. Ich bringe es ihm während der Feiertage / Ferien. 10. Wegen der Prüfungen / Examen habe ich jetzt keine Zeit. 11. Ich schicke dir eine Ansichtskarte / Postkarte statt eines Briefes. 12. Und ich schicke dir eine E-Mail statt einer Ansichtskarte / Postkarte.

p. 244   ## Kapitel 9

1. Otto, zieh dich an! 2. Christian, beeil dich! 3. Anne und Sabrina, zieht ihr euch einen Pullover an? 4. Wir müssen uns noch die Zähne putzen. 5. Peter, kämm dir die Haare! 6. Ich fühle mich nicht wohl. 7. Heute gehen wir alle joggen. 8. Ja, aber ich habe mich erkältet. 9. Dann leg dich hin!

p. 264   ## Kapitel 10

1. Ich freue mich auf die Kunstausstellung. 2. Hast du dich über die Karten informiert / Hast du etwas über die Karten herausgefunden? 3. Wir haben über die / von der Ausstellung gesprochen, aber dann habe ich nicht ans Datum gedacht. 4. Bitte wartet nicht auf mich, sondern geht ohne mich! 5. Ihr wisst, ich interessiere mich nicht für Kunst. 6. Warum ärgerst du dich so über diesen Maler? 7. Ich ärgere mich nicht, aber ich kenne diesen Maler und ich halte nicht viel von seinen Gemälden. 8. Die ganze Stadt spricht von ihm / über ihn.

1. a. Sie sitzt neben ihnen. b. Sie haben zwei Geschenke, eins für sie und eins für ihn. c. Siehst du den Stuhl? Die Geschenke liegen darauf. d. Was ist d(a)rin? e. Ist das für mich? f. Was tut / macht man damit? g. Was hältst du davon? h. Setz dich nicht d(a)rauf! 2. a. Mit wem kommt er? b. Wovon / worüber sprechen sie? c. Woran denkst du? d. Auf wen wartet er? e. Worüber ärgert ihr euch? f. Wofür interessiert sie sich? g. Wem / an wen schreibst du? h. Für wen ist dieses Geschenk?

p. 296   ## Kapitel 11

1. Wir kamen zum Flughafen, nachdem das Flugzeug gelandet war. 2. Als ich ankam, hatten sie schon ihr Gepäck geholt. 3. Nachdem wir sie gefunden hatten, fuhren wir nach Hause. 4. Meine Mutter hatte sich auf diesen Tag gefreut. 5. Nachdem sie ihnen das Haus gezeigt hatte, setzten wir uns ins Wohnzimmer und sprachen von der / über die Familie.

p. 325   ## Kapitel 12

1. Kinder, ich möchte / will euch (et)was sagen. 2. Eure Mutter wird Rechtsanwältin. 3. Ich werde zu Hause bleiben müssen. 4. Ich werde kochen. 5. Helga, du wirst die Wäsche waschen. 6. Karl und Maria, ihr werdet putzen. 7. Wir werden zusammen einkaufen (gehen). 8. Wir werden schwer arbeiten müssen. 9. Aber wir werden uns daran gewöhnen. 10. Wenn wir müde werden, machen wir eine Pause (werden . . . machen). 11. Eure Mutter wird viel Geld / gut verdienen. 12. Und wir werden ihr helfen.

p. 350   ## Kapitel 13

1. Könnt ihr bleiben? 2. Wir könnten spazieren gehen (einen Spaziergang machen). 3. Ich sollte meinen Großvater letzte Woche besuchen. 4. Jetzt müssen wir es (am) Samstag tun. 5. Ich wünschte, ich wüsste, warum er nicht angerufen hat. 6. Ich weiß, er würde mich anrufen, wenn er etwas bräuchte (brauchen würde). 7. Hättet ihr Lust, in ein Restaurant zu gehen? 8. Das wäre schön. 9. Wir wünschten, wir hätten Zeit. 10. Wenn Walter nicht arbeiten müsste, könnten wir bleiben.

1. Schade, wir hätten zu Hause bleiben sollen. 2. Wenn das Wetter besser gewesen wäre, hätten wir im See baden / schwimmen (gehen) können. 3. Aber es hat den ganzen Tag geregnet. 4. Ich wünschte, sie hätten uns nicht eingeladen. 5. Wenn wir zu Hause geblieben wären, hätten wir den Krimi sehen können. 6. Du hättest mit ihr ausgehen sollen. 7. Wenn ich Zeit gehabt hätte, hätte ich sie angerufen. 8. Wenn ich Zeit habe, rufe ich sie morgen an. 9. Ich hatte (gestern) keine Zeit, sie (gestern) anzurufen. 10. Ich hätte vorgestern anrufen sollen, aber ich habe es vergessen.

Kapitel 14   p. 373

1. Wo ist der Hörsaal, in dem Professor Kunert liest? 2. Der Kurs, den er lehrt, ist moderne deutsche Geschichte. 3. Die Studenten, die seine Kurse belegen, müssen schwer / fleißig arbeiten. 4. Geschichte ist ein Fach, das ich sehr interessant finde. 5. Aber ich habe einen Zimmerkollegen, der nichts interessant findet / den nichts interessiert. 6. Er ist ein Mensch, den ich nicht verstehe. 7. Er studiert Fächer, die ihm nicht gefallen / die er nicht mag. 8. Die Freunde, mit denen er ausgeht, sind langweilig. 9. Er lacht / macht sich lustig über seinen Vater, dessen Geld er jeden Monat bekommt. 10. Aber die Frau, mit der er verlobt ist, ist sehr nett.

Vocabularies

German-English

The vocabulary includes all the ACTIVE AND PASSIVE vocabulary used in *Wie geht's?* The English definitions of the words are limited to their use in the text. Each active vocabulary item is followed by a number and a letter indicating the chapter and section where it first occurs.

NOUNS Nouns are followed by their plural endings unless the plural is rare or nonexistent. In the case of n-nouns, the singular genitive ending is also given: **der Herr, -n, -en.** Nouns that require adjective endings appear with two endings: **der Angestellte (ein Angestellter).** Female forms of masculine nouns are usually not listed if only **-in** needs to be added: **der Apotheker.**

VERBS For regular t-verbs ("weak verbs"), only the infinitive is listed. All irregular t-verbs ("irregular weak verbs") and basic n-verbs ("strong verbs") are given with their principal parts: **bringen, brachte, gebracht; schreiben, schrieb, geschrieben.** Separable-prefix verbs are identified by a dot between the prefix and the verb: **mit·bringen.** Compound mixed and n-verbs are printed with an asterisk to indicate that the principal parts can be found under the listing of the basic verb: **mit·bringen*, beschreiben*.** When **sein** is used as the auxiliary of the perfect tenses, the form **ist** is given: **wandern (ist); kommen, kam, ist gekommen.**

ADJECTIVES and ADVERBS Adjectives and adverbs that have an umlaut in the comparative and superlative are identified by an umlauted vowel in parentheses: **arm (ä) = arm, ärmer, am ärmsten.**

ACCENTUATION Stress marks are provided for all words that do not follow the typical stress pattern. The accent follows the stressed syllable: **Balkon', Amerika'ner, wiederho'len.** The stress is not indicated when the word begins with an unstressed prefix, such as **be-, er-, ge-.**

Abbreviations

~	repetition of the key word	*nom.*	nominative
abbrev.	abbreviation	*o.s.*	oneself
acc.	accusative	*pl.*	plural
adj.	adjective	*refl. pron.*	reflexive pronoun
adv.	adverb	*rel. pron.*	relative pronoun
comp.	comparative	*sb.*	somebody
conj.	subordinate conjunction	*sg.*	singular
dat.	dative	*s.th.*	something
fam.	familiar	*S*	Schritt
gen.	genitive	*W*	Wortschatz 1
inf.	infinitive	*G*	Grammatik, Struktur
lit.	literally	*E*	Einblicke (Wortschatz 2)

A

der **Aal, -e** eel

ab- away, off (7G)

ab starting, as of

ab·bauen to reduce, cut back

ab·brechen* to break off

ab·brennen* to burn down

der **Abend, -e** evening; **(Guten) ~!** (Good) evening. (S1); **am ~** in the evening (6E); **gestern ~** yesterday evening (8G); **heute ~** this evening (8G)

das **Abendbrot** evening meal

das **Abendessen, -** supper, evening meal (3W); **zum ~** for supper (3W)

abends in the evening, every evening (S5); **donnerstag ~** Thursday evenings (8G)

das **Abenteuer, -** adventure

aber but, however (S3,2G, 5G); *flavoring particle expressing admiration* (7G)

ab·fahren* (von) to depart, leave (from) (8W)

die **Abfahrt, -en** departure (8W); descent

der **Abfall, ̈e** waste, garbage (15W)

ab·fliegen* (von) to take off, fly (from) (8W)

die **Abgase** (*pl.*) exhaust fumes

ab·geben* to give away, hand in

abhängig (von) dependent (on)

die **Abhängigkeit** dependence

ab·holen to pick up

das **Abitur, -e = Abi** (*coll.*) final comprehensive exam at the end of the *Gymnasium*

die **Abmeldung** report that one is leaving or moving

ab·nehmen* to take s.th. from, take away

abonnie'ren to subscribe

ab·pflücken to pick, break off

ab·reißen* to tear down (15W)

der **Abschluss, ̈e** diploma, degree

die **Abschlussparty, -s** graduation party

die **Abschlussprüfung, -en** final exam

der **Absender, -** return address (8W)

absolut' absolute(ly)

absolvie'ren to complete

sich **ab·wechseln** to take turns

die **Abwechslung, -en** distraction, variety

ach oh; **~ so!** Oh, I see! (9W); **~ was!** Oh, come on! (12W)

die **Achtung** respect; **~!** Watch out! Be careful!

der **ADAC = Allgemeiner Deutscher Automobil-Club** German version of the AAA

ade (*or* **adé**) good-bye, farewell

addie'ren to add

das **Adjektiv, -e** adjective; **substantivierte ~** adjectival noun

der **Adler, -** eagle

die **Adres'se, -n** address (8W)

der **Advents'kranz, ̈e** Advent wreath

die **Advents'zeit** Advent season

das **Adverb', -ien** adverb

die **Aero'bik** aerobics

der **Affe, -n, -n** monkey; **Du ~!** You nut!

(das) **Ägy'pten** Egypt

der **Ägy'pter, -** the Egyptian

ägy'ptisch Egyptian

Aha'! There, you see. Oh, I see.

ähnlich similar; **Das sieht dir ~.** That's typical of you. (8W)

die **Ahnung: Keine ~!** (I have) no idea. (10W)

die **Akademie', -n** academy

der **Akade'miker, -** (university) graduate

akade'misch academic

der **Akkusativ, -e** accusative

der **Akt, -e** act (play)

das **Aktiv** active voice

akti'v active

die **Aktivität', -en** activity

aktuell' up-to-date, current

der **Akzent', -e** accent

akzeptie'ren to accept

all- all (7G); **vor ~em** above all, mainly (10E); **~e drei Jahre** every three years

allein' alone (11E)

allerdings however (15W)

die **Allergie', -n** allergy

aller'gisch gegen allergic to

allerlei all sorts of (2W)

alles everything, all (2W); **Das ist ~.** That's all. (2W)

allgemein' (in) general; **im ~en** in general

der **Alltag** everyday life

die **Alpen** (*pl.*) Alps

die **Alpenblume, -n** Alpine flower

das **Alphabet'** alphabet

als as; (*conj.*) (at the time) when (11G); (*after comp.*) than (12G)

also therefore, thus, so; in other words (10E); well (12W)

alt (ä) old (S3); **stein~** very old; **ur~** ancient

der **Alte (ein Alter)** old man (12G); **die ~, -n, -n** old lady (12G); **das ~** old things (12G)

das **Alter** age

die **Altstadt, ̈e** old part of town

der **Amateur', -e** amateur

ambitiös' ambitious

die **Ameise, -n** ant

(das) **Ame'rika** America (1W)

der **Amerika'ner, -** the American (1W)

amerika'nisch American (1W)

die **Ampel, -n** traffic light

an- to, up to (7G)

an (+ *acc. / dat.*) to, at (the side of), on (vertical surface) (6G)

analysie'ren to analyze

die **Ananas, -** pineapple

an·bieten* to offer (12W)

ander- other (9E; **~e** others (9W); **der / die ~e** the other one; **die ~en** the others (9W); **etwas (ganz) ~es** s.th. (quite) different (9E)

andererseits on the other hand

anders different(ly), in other ways (9E); **Sagen Sie es ~!** Say it differently!

anerkannt recognized, credited

an·erkennen* to recognize; acknowledge

die **Anerkennung, -en** recognition

der **Anfang, ⸚e**   beginning, start
(10W); ~ **der Woche**   at
the beginning of the week
(8G); **am ~** in the beginning (10W)
an·fangen*   to begin, start
(10W)
der **Anfänger, -**   beginner
die **Angabe, -n**   information
das **Angebot, -e**   offering, offer
angeln   to fish (9W);
~ **gehen*** to go fishing (9W)
angepasst   geared / adjusted
to
angeschlagen   posted
der **Angestellte (ein Angestellter) / die Angestellte, -n,
-n** employee, clerk (12G)
die **Anglis′tik**   study of English
der **Angriff, -e**   attack; raid
die **Angst, ⸚e**   fear, anxiety; ~
haben*   (**vor** + *dat.*) to
fear, be afraid (of) (13E); ~
bekommen* to become
afraid, get scared
an·halten*   to continue
der **Anhang**   appendix
anhänglich   devoted,
attached (11W)
sich **an·hören**   to listen to (9G);
Hör dir das an! Listen to
that.
an·kommen*   (**in** + *dat.*)
to arrive (in) (7E); **Das
kommt darauf an.** That
depends. (7E)
an·kreuzen   to mark with an x
die **Ankunft**   arrival (8W)
an·machen   to turn on (a
radio, etc.) (10W)
die **Anmeldung**   reception desk;
registration
die **Annahme, -n**   hypothetical
statement or question
an·nehmen*   to accept (7E);
to suppose (13E)
der **Anorak, -s**   parka
anpassungsfähig   adaptable
an·reden   to address
an·richten   to do (damage)
der **Anruf, -e**   (phone) call
der **Anrufbeantworter, -**   answering machine
an·rufen*   to call up, phone
(7G)
sich **an·schauen**   to look at; to
watch
an·schlagen*   to post

der **Anschluss, ⸚e**   connection
die **Anschrift, -en**   address
(sich) **an·sehen***   to look at (9G); to
watch
die **Ansicht, -en**   opinion, attitude; view
die **Ansichtskarte, -n**   (picture)
postcard (8W)
an·sprechen*   to address,
speak to
(an)statt (+ *gen.*)   instead of
(8G)
anstrengend   strenuous
(12W)
der **Anteil, -e**   share; proportion
die **Antiquität′, -en**   antique
der **Antrag, ⸚e**   application
die **Antwort, -en**   answer
antworten   to answer (S2)
an·wachsen*   to increase
die **Anwaltsfirma, -firmen**   law
firm
die **Anzahl**   number, amount
die **Anzeige, -n**   ad (11W)
die **Anzeigetafel, -n**   scoreboard
(sich) **an·ziehen***   to put on (clothing), get dressed (9G)
der **Anzug, ⸚e**   men′s suit
an·zünden   to light
der **Apfel, ⸚**   apple (2W)
der **Apfelstrudel, -**   apple strudel
die **Apothe′ke, -n**   pharmacy
(2E)
der **Apothe′ker, -**   pharmacist
der **Appetit′**   appetite; **Guten ~!**
Enjoy your meal. (3W)
die **Apriko′se, -n**   apricot
der **April′**   April (S4); **im ~** in
April (S4)
der **Äqua′tor**   equator
das **Äquivalent′**   equivalent
der **Araber, -**   Arab
ara′bisch   Arabic
die **Arbeit, -en**   work (6E); (term)
paper (13W); **bei der ~** at
work; **Tag der ~** Labor Day
arbeiten   to work (1E)
der **Arbeiter, -**   (blue-collar)
worker (12W); **Vor~**
foreman
der **Arbeitgeber, -**   employer
der **Arbeitnehmer, -**   employee
arbeitsam   hard-working;
~ **wie ein Pferd** really
working hard
das **Arbeitsbuch, ⸚er**   workbook
die **Arbeitserlaubnis**   work
permit

das **Arbeitsheft, -e**   workbook
das **Arbeitsklima**   work climate
die **Arbeitskraft, ⸚e**   worker
die **Arbeitsleistung**   output;
performance
der **Arbeitsplatz, ⸚e**   job; job
location
arbeitslos   unemployed
der **Arbeitslose (ein Arbeitsloser) /
die Arbeitslose, -n, -n**
unemployed person
die **Arbeitslosigkeit**   unemployment (12E)
der **Arbeitsmarkt, ⸚e**   job market
der **Arbeitsplatz, ⸚e**   job; place
of employment
das **Arbeitszimmer, -**   study
(6W)
archa′isch   archaic
die **Archäologie′**   archeology
der **Architekt′, -en, -en**   architect (12W)
die **Architektur′**   architecture
das **Archiv′, -e**   archive
ärgerlich   annoying
sich **ärgern über** (+ *acc.*)   to get
annoyed/upset about (10G);
Das ärgert mich. That
makes me mad. (10W)
die **Arka′de, -n**   arcade
arm (ä)   poor (11W)
der **Arm, -e**   arm (9W)
die **Armbanduhr, -en**   wrist-
watch
die **Armee′, -n**   army
die **Armut**   poverty
arrogant′   arrogant
das **Arsenal′, -e**   arsenal
die **Art, -en** (**von**)   kind, type (of)
(10E)
der **Arti′kel, -** (**von**)   article (of)
der **Arzt, ⸚e / die Ärztin, -nen**
physician, doctor (12W)
die **Asche**   ashes
assoziie′ren   to associate
ästhe′tisch   aesthetic
die **Astronomie′**   astronomy
atmen   to breathe
die **Atmosphä′re**   atmosphere
die **Attraktion′, -en**   attraction
attraktiv′   attractive (11W)
auch   also, too (S1); **ich ~** =
me too
auf (+ *acc. / dat.*)   on (top
of) (6G); open (7W)
auf-   up, open (7G)
auf·atmen   to breathe a sigh
of relief

auf·bauen to build, put up (15W); **wieder ~** to rebuild (15W)

aufeinan'der treffen* (ist) to come together

der **Aufenthalt, -e** stay, stopover (8W); **Auslands~** stay abroad

die **Aufenthaltserlaubnis** residence permit

auf·essen* to eat up

auf·fassen to consider (to be)

die **Aufgabe, -n** assignment; task, challenge

auf·geben* to give up

auf·halten* to hold open; to stay

auf·hören (zu + inf.) to stop (doing s.th.) (13E)

die **Aufklärung** enlightenment

der **Aufkleber, -** sticker

auf·machen to open (7G)

die **Aufnahme** acceptance, reception

auf·nehmen* to take (a picture)

auf·passen to pay attention, watch out (7G); **Passen Sie auf!** Pay attention! Watch out! (7W)

der **Aufsatz, ̈-e** essay, composition, paper

der **Aufschnitt (sg.)** assorted meats / cheeses, cold cuts

auf·schreiben* to write down (7G)

auf·stehen* to get up (7G)

auf·stellen to put up, set up

auf·wachsen* to grow up

der **Aufzug, ̈-e** elevator

das **Auge, -n** eye (9W)

der **Augenblick, -e** moment (14W); **(Einen) ~!** Just a minute!

die **Augenbraue, -n** eyebrow

der **August'** August (S4); **im ~** in August (S4)

aus (+ dat.) out of, from (a place of origin) (3G); **Ich bin ~ . . .** I'm from (a native of) . . . (1W)

aus- out, out of (7G)

aus sein* to be over

aus·arbeiten to work out

aus·(be)zahlen to pay out

aus·bilden to train, educate

die **Ausbildung** training, education (12W)

der **Ausdruck, ̈-e** expression

sich **auseinan'der entwickeln** to develop apart

die **Ausfuhr** export

aus·füllen to fill out (13W)

der **Ausgang, ̈-e** exit (7W)

aus·geben* to spend (money) (9E)

aus·bilden to train, educate

ausgebildet (als) trained (as); **gut ~** well-trained (12E)

aus·gehen* to go out (7G)

ausgezeichnet excellent (6E)

aus·helfen* to help out

die **Aushilfskraft, ̈-e** temporary help

das **Ausland** foreign country; **im/ins ~** abroad (12E)

der **Ausländer, -** foreigner (1E)

ausländisch foreign (13E)

der **Auslandsaufenthalt, -e** stay abroad

das **Auslandsprogramm, -e** foreign-study program

aus·leihen* to loan, lend out

aus·lesen* to pick out

aus·machen turn off (a radio etc.) (10W)

aus·packen to unpack

ausreichend sufficient; approx. grade D

aus·richten to tell; **Kann ich etwas ~?** Can I take a message?

die **Aussage, -n** statement

aus·sehen* (wie + nom.) to look (like) (12E)

außer (+ dat.) besides, except for (3G)

äußer- outer

außerdem (adv.) besides (6E)

außerhalb (+ gen.) outside (of)

die **Aussicht, -en (auf + acc.)** prospect (for); view (of)

die **Aussichtsplattform, -en** observation deck

der **Aussiedler, -** emigrant; resettled person

die **Aussprache** pronunciation

aus·steigen* to get off (8W)

aus·stellen to issue; to exhibit

die **Ausstellung, -en** exhibition, show

aus·sterben* to become extinct

der **Austausch** exchange; **das ~programm, -e** exchange program

aus·tauschen to exchange (14E)

die **Auster, -n** oyster

ausverkauft sold out

die **Auswahl (an + dat.)** choice, selection (of) (10E)

der **Ausweis, -e** ID, identification (7W)

aus·werten to evaluate, assess

sich **aus·wirken auf (+ acc.)** to affect

aus·zahlen to pay out

die **Auszeit, -en** time-out

(sich) **aus·ziehen*** to take off (clothing), get undressed (9G)

der **Auszubildende (ein Auszubildender) / die Auszubildende, -n, -n = Azubi, -s (coll.)** trainee

authen'tisch authentic

das **Auto, -s** car (5W)

die **Autobahn, -en** freeway

autofrei free of cars

der **Automat', -en, -en** machine

automatisiert' automated

die **Automobil'branche** car industry

der **Autor', -en** author (10W)

autoritäts'gläubig believing in authority

B

die **Backe, -n** cheek

backen (bäckt), buk (backte), gebacken to bake (9W)

das **Backblech, -e** cookie sheet

der **Bäcker, -** baker

die **Bäckerei', -en** bakery (2W)

das **Bad, ̈-er** bath(room) (6W)

der **Badeanzug, ̈-e** swimsuit

die **Badehose, -n** swimming trunks

baden to bathe, swim (6W); **sich ~** to take a bath (9G)

die **Badewanne, -n** bathtub

das **Badezimmer, -** bathroom

die **Bahn, -en** railway, train (8W); **~übergang, ̈-e** railroad crossing

der **Bahnhof, ̈-e** train station (5W)

der **Bahnsteig, -e** platform (8W)

bald soon (7W); **Bis ~!** See you soon! (9W); **so ~'** as soon as (12E)

baldig soon-to-come

der **Balkon', -s / -e** balcony (6W)

der **Ball, ̈e** ball

das **Ballett'** ballet (10W)

der **Ballett'tänzer, -** ballet dancer

die **Bana'ne, -n** banana (2W); **Alles ~?** Everything all right?

bange worried

die **Bank, -en** bank (7W)

die **Bank, ̈e** bench

der **Bankier', -s** banker

der **Bann** ban

die **Bar, -s** bar, pub

der **Bär, -en** bear; **Du bist ein Brumm~.** You're a grouch.

barfuß barefoot

das **Bargeld** cash (7W)

der **Bart, ̈e** beard

basteln to do crafts

die **Batterie', -n** battery

der **Bau, -ten** building construction (15W)

der **Bauch, ̈e** stomach, belly (9W)

bauen to build (6E); **~ lassen*** to have built

der **Bauer, -n, -n** farmer

der **Bauernhof, ̈e** farm

das **Baugesetz, -e** building code

der **Bauingenieur, -e** structural engineer

das **Bauland** building lots

der **Baum, ̈e** tree (6W)

die **Baumwolle** cotton

die **Baustelle, -n** construction site

der **Baustoff, -e** building material

der **Bayer, -n, -n** the Bavarian

(das) **Bayern** Bavaria (in southeast Germany)

bay(e)risch Bavarian

der **Beamte (ein Beamter) / die Beamtin, -nen** civil servant (12G)

beantworten to answer

der **Bedarf (für)** need (for)

bedeuten to mean, signify (S2)

die **Bedeutung, -en** meaning; significance, importance

bedienen to take care of, serve

die **Bedienung** server, service (3W); service charge

bedroht threatened

sich **beeilen** to hurry (9G)

beeindrucken to impress

beeinflussen to influence

beenden to finish, complete

der **Befehl, -e** instruction, request, command

das **Befehlen** dictating

befehlen (befiehlt), befahl, befohlen to order

befriedigend satisfactory; approx. grade C

befürchten to fear

begegnen (ist) to encounter

begehrt desired

der **Beginn** beginning; **zu ~** in the beginning

beginnen, begann, begonnen to begin (S5)

begleiten to accompany

die **Begleitung** accompaniment

begrenzt limited

die **Begrenzung, -en** limit(ation), restriction

begrüßen to greet, welcome

die **Begrüßung, -en** greeting; **zur ~** as greeting

behalten* to keep

behandeln (wie) to treat like

die **Behandlung, -en** treatment

beherrschen to dominate, rule

bei (+ *dat.*) at, near, at the home of (3G); **Hier ~.** This is __'s office / residence.

beide both (11W)

beige beige

bei·legen to enclose

das **Bein, -e** leg (9W); **auf den ~en** on the go

das **Beispiel, -e** example; **zum ~ (z. B.)** for example (e.g.)

bei·tragen* (zu) to contribute (to)

bekannt well-known (5E); **Das kommt mir ~ vor.** That seems / sounds familiar to me.

der **Bekannte (ein Bekannter) / die Bekannte, -n, -n** acquaintance (12G)

bekommen* (hat) to get, receive (4W)

bekümmert sad

belasten to burden; pollute

belegen to sign up for, take (a course) (13W)

belgisch Belgian

beliebt popular (9E)

die **Belohnung, -en** reward

sich **bemühen** to try (hard)

benennen* nach to name after

benutzen to use

das **Benzin'** gas(oline)

der **Benzin'schlucker, -** gas guzzler

beo'bachten to watch, observe

die **Beo'bachtung, -en** observation

bequem' comfortable, convenient (6W)

der **Berater, -** counselor, adviser, consultant

die **Beratung** counseling

berauben to rob

der **Bereich, -e** area, field (12E)

der **Berg, -e** mountain (1W)

bergab' downhill

bergauf' uphill

die **Bergbahn, -en** mountain train

der **Bergbau** mining

berghoch' uphill

bergsteigen gehen* to go mountain climbing

der **Bericht, -e** report

berichten to report (14W)

berieseln *here:* to shower with

der **Beruf, -e** profession (12W)

beruflich professional(ly); **~ engagiert'** professionally active

die **Berufsschule, -n** vocational school

der **Berufstätige (ein Berufstätiger) / die Berufstätige, -n, -n** someone working in a profession

die **Berufswahl** choice of profession (12E)

berühmt famous (14E)

die **Beschäftigung** activity; occupation

bescheinigen to verify, document

beschreiben* to describe

die **Beschreibung, -en** description

beschriftet labeled

besetzen to fill, occupy

besichtigen   to visit (an attraction), tour (5W)

der **Besitz**   property, possession

besitzen*   to own

der **Besitzer, -**   owner

besonders   especially (3E); **nichts Besonderes** nothing special (9W)

besprechen*   to discuss, talk about

besser   better (12G)

die **Besserung**   improvement; **Gute ~!** Get well soon. I hope you get better. (4W)

best-   best (12G); **am ~en** it's best (12G)

bestätigen   to confirm

bestehen*   to pass (an exam) (13W); **~ aus** (+ *dat.*) to consist of; **es besteht** there is

bestellen   to order (3W)

die **Bestellung, -en**   order

bestimmt   surely, for sure, certain(ly) (13E)

der **Besuch, -e**   visit; visitor(s)

besuchen   to visit (8W); attend

der **Besucher, -**   visitor

beten   to pray

der **Beton'**   concrete

betonen   to stress, emphasize

Betr(eff)   concerning

betreffen*   to concern

betreten*   to enter, step on

der **Betriebswirt, -e**   graduate in business management (12W)

die **Betriebswirtschaft**   business administration

das **Bett, -en**   bed (6W); **ins ~** to bed

die **Bevölkerung**   population (15E)

bevor (*conj.*)   before (4G)

bewachen   to guard, watch over

bewältigen   to overcome, cope with; finish

sich **bewegen**   to move

die **Bewegung, -en**   movement

sich **bewerben (um)**   to apply (for) (12W)

bewerten   to rate

die **Bewertung, -en**   evaluation, grading

der **Bewohner, -**   inhabitant; resi-dent

bewölkt   cloudy

bewusst   conscious(ly)

bezahlen   to pay (for) (3W)

sich **beziehen* auf**   (+ *acc.*) to refer to

die **Beziehung, -en**   relationship (11W)

der **Bezirk, -e**   district

die **Bibel, -n**   Bible

die **Bibliothek', -en = Bib** (*coll.*) library (5W)

die **Biene, -n**   bee

das **Bier, -e**   beer (2W); **~ vom Fass** draught beer

der **Biergarten, ⁝**   beer garden

der **Bierkrug, ⁝e**   stein

bieten, bot, geboten   to offer

der **Biki'ni, -s**   bikini

die **Bilanz', -en: eine ~ auf·stellen**   to make an evaluation

das **Bild, -er**   picture (S2)

bilden   to form; **~ Sie einen Satz!** Make / form a sentence. (8W)

die **Bildung**   education

das **Billard**   billiards

billig   cheap, inexpensive (S3)

binden, band, gebunden   to bind

die **Biochemie'**   biochemistry

der **Bioche'miker, -**   biochemist

der **Bio-Laden, ⁝**   health-food store

der **Biolo'ge, -n, -n / die Biolo'-gin, -nen**   biologist

die **Biologie'**   biology

die **Birne, -n**   pear

bis   to, until; **~ später!** See you later! So long! (S1); **~ bald!** See you soon! (9W); **~ gleich!** See you in a few minutes (9W)

bisher'   until now

bisschen: ein ~   some, a little bit (4E); **Ach du liebes ~!** Good grief!, My goodness!, Oh dear! (2E)

bitte   please (S1); **~! / ~ bitte!** You're welcome. (S5, 2E); **~ schön!** You're welcome. (4W); **Hier ~!** Here you are.; **~ schön?** May I help you?; **Wie ~?** What did you say? Could you say that again? (S5)

die **Bitte, -n**   request

bitten, bat, gebeten (um)   to ask (for), request (12E)

das **Blatt, ⁝er**   leaf; sheet

blau   blue (S2)

der **Blazer, -**   blazer

das **Blei**   lead

bleiben, blieb, ist geblie-ben   to stay, remain (3W)

der **Bleistift, -e**   pencil (S2)

der **Blick (in / auf** + *acc.*)   view (of), glance at (10W)

der **Blickpunkt, -e**   focus

blind   blind

der **Blitz, -e**   flash of lightning

blitzen   to sparkle; **es blitzt** there's lightning

die **Blitzreaktion', -en**   quick reaction

der **Block, ⁝e**   block

die **Blocka'de, -n**   blockade

die **Blockflöte, -n**   recorder (musical instrument)

blockie'ren   to block

der **Blödsinn**   nonsense; **So ein ~!** What nonsense!

blond   blond

bloß   only; **was . . . ~ ?** what on earth . . . ?; **wie . . . ~?** how on earth . . . ?

blühen   to flourish; to bloom

die **Blume, -n**   flower (2E)

der **Blumenkohl**   cauliflower

die **Bluse, -n**   blouse (S3)

der **Boden**   ground, floor

der **Bogen, ⁝**   bow

die **Bohne, -n**   bean (2W)

der **Bomber, -**   bomber

das **Bonbon, -s**   (piece of) candy

der **Bonus, -se**   bonus

das **Boot, -e**   boat

borgen   to borrow

die **Börse, -n**   stockmarket

der **Börsenmakler, -**   stockbroker

böse   angry, mad, upset

der **Bote, -n, -n**   messenger

die **Bouti'que, -n**   boutique

die **Bowle, -n**   alcoholic punch

boxen   to box

die **Branche, -n**   branch

der **Brasilia'ner, -**   Brasilian

brasilia'nisch   Brasilian

der **Braten, -**   roast; **Schweine~** pork roast; **Rinder~** beef roast; **Sauer~** marinated pot roast

die **Bratkartoffeln** (*pl.*)   fried potatoes

die **Bratwurst, ⸚e** fried sausage
der **Brauch, ⸚e** custom
brauchen to need (S3)
brauen to brew
die **Brauerei, -en** brewery
braun brown (S2); **~ ge-brannt** tanned
die **Braut, ⸚e** bride
der **Bräutigam, -e** bridegroom
das **Brautkleid, -er** wedding dress
die **BRD (Bundesrepublik Deutschland)** FRG (Federal Republic of Germany)
brechen (bricht), brach, ge-brochen to break
der **Brei, -e** porridge; **Kartoffel~** (*sg.*) mashed potatoes
breit broad, wide
das **Brett, -er** board; **Schwarze ~** bulletin board
die **Brezel, -n** pretzel
der **Brief, -e** letter (8W)
der **Briefkasten, ⸚** mailbox (8W)
brieflich by letter
die **Briefmarke, -n** stamp (8W)
der **Briefsortierer, -** mail sorter
der **Briefträger, -** mailman
die **Brille, -n** glasses
bringen, brachte, gebracht to bring (3W); **mit sich ~** to bring with it
die **Brokkoli** (*pl.*) broccoli
die **Broschǘre, -n** brochure
das **Brot, -e** bread (2W); **Toast~** piece of toast
das **Brötchen, -** roll (2W); **belegte ~** sandwich
der **Brotwürfel, -** small piece of bread, cube
die **Brücke, -n** bridge (5W)
der **Bruder, ⸚** brother (1W)
das **Brüderchen, -** little brother
brüllen to scream
brummig grouchy
der **Brunnen, -** fountain
die **Brust, ⸚e** chest, breast
das **Buch, ⸚er** book (S2); **Arbeits~** workbook
der **Bücherwurm, ⸚er** bookworm
die **Buchführung** bookkeeping
der **Buchhalter, -** bookkeeper
die **Buchhandlung, -en** bookstore (2W)
das **Büchlein, -** booklet, little book

der **Buchstabe, -n, -n** letter (of the alphabet)
buchstabie´ren to spell; **~ Sie auf Deutsch!** Spell in German!
die **Bude, -n** booth, stand; **Schieß~** shooting gallery
das **Büfett´, -s** dining room cabinet; buffet
das **Bügeleisen, -** (clothing) iron
die **Bühne, -n** stage; **auf der ~** on stage
bummeln (ist) to stroll (5E)
der **Bund, ⸚e** confederation; federal government
die **Bundesbank** central bank
der **Bundesbürger, -** citizen of the Federal Republic
die **Bundesfeier, -n** Swiss national holiday
das **Bundesland, ⸚er** state, province
die **Bundespost** federal postal service
die **Bundesrepublik (BRD)** Federal Republic of Germany (FRG)
der **Bundesstaat, -en** federal state
der **Bundestag** German federal parliament
bunt colorful; multicolored
die **Burg, -en** castle
der **Bürger, -** citizen (10E); **Mit~** fellow citizen
bürgerlich bourgeois, middle-class
der **Bürgersteig, -e** sidewalk
das **Bürgertum** citizenry
das **Büro´, -s** office (12W)
die **Bürokratie´** bureaucracy, red tape
die **Bürste, -n** brush
der **Bus, -se** bus (5W); **mit dem ~ fahren*** to take the bus (5W)
der **Busbahnhof, ⸚e** bus depot
der **Busch, ⸚e** bush
der **Busen, -** bosom
die **Butter** butter (2W); **(Es ist) alles in ~** Everything is all right.

C

das **Café´, -s** café (3W)
die **Cafeteri´a, -s = Cafe´te** (*coll.*) cafeteria

campen to camp; **~ gehen*** to go camping
der **Campingplatz, ⸚e** campground
der **Cappucci´no, -s** cappuccino
die **CD, -s** CD, compact disc (9W)
der **Cellist´, -en, -en** cello player
das **Cello, -s** cello
der **Cent, -s** cent (S3)
das **Chaos** chaos
chao´tisch chaotic
die **Charakterisie´rung, -en** characterization
charakteris´tisch characteristic
charmant´ charming (11W)
der **Charme** charm
der **Chauffeur´, -e** chauffeur
chauvinis´tisch chauvinist
der **Chef, -s** boss
die **Chemie´** chemistry
die **Chemika´lie, -n** chemical
chemisch chemical(ly)
der **Chine´se, -n, -n / die Chine´sin, -nen** Chinese
chine´sisch Chinese
der **Chor, ⸚e** choir (10W)
der **Christbaum, ⸚e** Christmas tree
der **Christkindlmarkt, ⸚e** Christmas fair
der **Clown, -s** clown
der **Cockerspaniel, -** Cocker spaniel
die **Cola** cola drink, soft drink (2W)
das **College, -s** college
der **Collie, -s** Collie; Sheltie
die **Combo, -s** (musical) band
der **Compu´ter, -** computer; **~künstler, -** graphic designer
computerisiert´ computerized
der **Contai´ner, -** container
die **Cornflakes** (*pl.*) Cornflakes, cereal
der **Cousin´, -s** cousin
die **Cousi´ne, -n** cousin
cremig creamy, smooth

D

da there (S2); **~ drüben** over there (5W)
dabei´ along; there; yet; **~ haben*** to have with you
das **Dach, ⸚er** roof

der **Dachboden, ¨** attic
der **Dachdecker, -** roofer
das **Dachgeschoss** attic floor; **im ~** on the attic floor
der **Dackel, -** dachshund
dafür for it; instead
dagegen against it; **Hast du etwas ~, wenn . . . ?** Do you mind, if . . . ? (13W)
daheim' at home
daher therefore; from there
dahin: bis ~ until then
die **Dahlie, -n** dahlia
das **Da-Kompositum, -Komposita** da-compound
damalig (*adj.*) then
damals then, in those days (11W)
die **Dame, -n** lady (5W); **Sehr geehrte ~n und Herren!** Ladies and gentlemen!; **~ spielen** to play checkers (9W)
danach' later, after that (9W)
der **Däne, -n, -n / die Dänin, -nen** the Dane
(das) **Dänemark** Denmark
dänisch Danish
der **Dank: Vielen / herzlichen ~!** Thank you very much. (4W); **Gott sei ~!** Thank God! (8W)
dankbar grateful, thankful
danke thank you (S1); **~ schön!** Thank you very much (4W); **~ gleichfalls!** Thanks, the same to you. (3W)
danken (+ *dat.*) to thank (3G); **Nichts zu ~!** You're welcome. My pleasure. (4W)
dann then (2W)
dar·stellen to portray
der **Darsteller, -** actor
darum therefore (12E); **eben ~** that's why
das that (S2)
dass (*conj.*) that (4G); **so ~** (*conj.*) so that (13E)
der **Dativ, -e** dative
das **Datum, Daten** (*calendar*) date (4W); **Welches ~ ist heute?** What date is today? (4W)
die **Dauer** length, duration
dauern to last (duration) (4W); **Wie lange dauert**

das? How long does that take? (4W)
der **Daumen, -** thumb
die **DDR (Deutsche Demokratische Republik)** German Democratic Republic (GDR)
die **Decke, -n** blanket
definie'ren to define
dein (*sg. fam.*) your (1W)
die **Dekoration', -en** decoration
dekorie'ren to decorate
demnächst' before long
der **Demokrat', -en, -en** democrat
die **Demokratie'** democracy
demokra'tisch democratic
der **Demonstrant', -en, -en** demonstrator
die **Demonstration', -en** demonstration
demonstrie'ren to demonstrate
denken, dachte, gedacht to think (4W); **~ an** (+ *acc.*) to think of / about (10G)
der **Denker, -** thinker
das **Denkmal, ¨er** monument (15W)
denn because, for (2G); *flavoring particle expressing curiosity, interest* (7G)
der **Deo-Stift, -e** deodorant stick
die **Depression', -en** (mental) depression
deshalb therefore (13E)
deswegen therefore
deutsch German
(das) **Deutsch: auf ~** in German (S2); **Sprechen Sie ~?** Do you speak German? (1W); **Hoch~** (standard) High German; **Platt~** Low German (dialect)
der **Deutsche (ein Deutscher) / die Deutsche, -n, -n** the German (1W,12G)
die **Deutsche Demokratische Republik (DDR)** German Democratic Republic (GDR)
(das) **Deutschland** Germany (1W)
deutschsprachig German-speaking
der **Dezem'ber** December (S4); **im ~** in December (S4)
sich **drehen** to turn
d. h. (das heißt) that is (i.e.)

das **Dia, -s** slide (photograph)
der **Dialekt', -e** dialect
der **Dialog', -e** dialogue
dick thick, fat (S3); **~ machen** to be fattening (3E)
dickköpfig stubborn
dienen to serve
der **Dienst, -e** service; **öffentliche ~** civil service
der **Dienstag** Tuesday (S4); **am ~** on Tuesday (S4)
dienstags on Tuesdays (2E)
dies- this, these (7G)
diesig misty
diesmal this time (10W)
das **Diktat', -e** dictation
die **Dimension', -en** dimension
das **Ding, -e** thing
der **Dinosau'rier, -** dinosaur
das **Diplom', -e** diploma (e.g., in natural and social sciences, engineering), M.A.; **der ~ingenieur', -e** academically trained engineer
der **Diplomat', -en, -en** diplomat
direkt' direct(ly)
die **Direkto'rin, -nen** (school), principal, manager
der **Dirigent', -en, -en** (music) conductor
die **Diskothek', -en = Disko, -s** discotheque
die **Diskussion', -en** discussion
diskutie'ren to discuss
sich **distanzie'ren** to keep apart
die **Disziplin'** discipline
die **DM (Deutsche Mark)** German mark
der **Dobermann, ¨er** Doberman
doch yes (I do), indeed, sure (2W); yet, however, but; on the contrary; *flavoring particle expressing concern, impatience, assurance* (7G)
der **Dokumentar'film, -e** documentary
der **Dollar, -(s)** dollar (7W)
der **Dolmetscher, -** interpreter
der **Dom, -e** cathedral (5W)
dominie'ren to dominate
donnern to thunder; **es donnert** it's thundering
donnernd rumbling
der **Donnerstag** Thursday (S4); **am ~** on Thursday (S4)
donnerstags on Thursdays (2E)
doppelt double

das **Doppelzimmer, -**   double room (7W)

das **Dorf, ¨er**   village (8E)

dort   (over) there (4E)

dorthin   to there (5W)

die **Dose, -n**   can

der **Drachenflieger, -**   hangglider

dran   at it; **Jetzt sind Sie ~!** Now it's your turn.

draußen   outside, outdoors; **hier ~** out here; **weit ~** far out

die **Dreißigerin, -nen**   woman in her 30s

die **Droge, -n**   drug

die **Drogerie', -n**   drugstore (2E)

der **Drogist', -en, -en**   druggist

drohen   to threaten

duften   to smell good

dumm (ü)   stupid, silly (10W, 11W); **Das ist (wirklich) zu ~.** That's (really) too bad.

die **Dummheit, -en**   stupidity

der **Dummkopf, ¨e**   dummy

das **Düngemittel, -**   fertilizer

dunkel   dark (6W); **~haarig** dark-haired; **im Dunkeln** in the dark(ness)

dünn   thin, skinny (S3)

durch (+ acc.)   through (2G); **mitten ~** right through; by (agent)

durchbre'chen*   to break through, penetrate

der **Durchbruch**   breaching

durcheinander   mixed up, confused

durch·fallen*   to flunk (an exam) (13W)

der **Durchschnitt**   average; **im ~** on the average

dürfen (darf), durfte, gedurft   to be allowed to, may (5W); **Was darf's sein?** May I help you?

der **Durst**   thirst (2E); **Ich habe ~.** I'm thirsty. (2E)

die **Dusche, -n**   shower

(sich) **duschen**   to take a shower (6W;9G)

der **Duschvorhang, ¨e**   shower curtain

das **Dutzend, -e**   dozen

sich **duzen**   to call each other "*du*"

die **Dyna'mik**   dynamics

dyna'misch   dynamic

E

die **Ebbe**   low tide

eben   after all, just (*flavoring particle*); **mal ~** just for a minute

die **Ebene, -n**   plain

ebenfalls   also, likewise

ebenso   just as, just the same

der **EC, -s**   EuroCity (train)

echt   authentic; **~ schön** really pretty(15W)

die **Ecke, -n**   corner (6W)

egal'   the same; **Das ist doch ~.** That doesn't matter. (8W); **Es ist mir ~.** It's all the same to me. I don't care.; **~ wie/wo** no matter how/where

die **Ehe, -n**   marriage (11W)

ehemalig   former

das **Ehepaar, -e**   married couple

eher   rather

die **Ehre, -n**   honor

ehrgeizig   ambitious

ehrgeizlos   without ambition

ehrlich   honest (11W)

die **Ehrlichkeit**   honesty

das **Ei, -er**   egg (2W); **ein gekochtes ~** boiled egg; **Rühr~** scrambled egg; **Spiegel~** fried egg; **verlorene~er** poached eggs

die **Eidgenossenschaft**   Swiss Confederation

das **Eigelb**   egg yolk

eigen-   own (11W)

die **Eigenschaft, -en**   characteristic (11W)

eigentlich   actual(ly) (4E); **~ schon** actually, yes

die **Eigentumswohnung, -en**   condo (6E)

eilig   hurried; **es ~ haben*** to be in a hurry

ein   a, an (16G,7G); **die ~en** the ones

einan'der   each other

die **Einbahnstraße, -n**   one-way street

der **Einbau**   installation

der **Einblick, -e**   insight

der **Eindruck, ¨e**   impression

eine(r) von Ihnen   one of you

einerseits . . . andererseits   on the one hand . . . on the other hand

einfach   simple, simply (7E)

die **Einfahrt, -en**   driveway; **Keine ~!** Do not enter.

einfarbig   all one color

der **Einfluss, ¨e**   influence (10E)

die **Einfuhr**   import

ein·führen   to introduce

die **Einführung, -en**   introduction

sich **engagie'ren**   to engage, commit o.s.

der **Eingang, ¨e**   entrance (7W)

einig- (*pl. only*)   some, a few (10G); **so ~es** all sorts of things

einigen   to unite; **sich ~ (+ acc.)** to agree (on)

die **Einigkeit**   unity

ein·kaufen   to shop; **~ gehen*** to go shopping (2E, 7G)

die **Einkaufsliste, -n**   shopping list

die **Einkaufstasche, -n**   shopping bag

das **Einkaufszentrum, -zentren**   shopping center

das **Einkommen, -**   income (12W)

ein·laden (lädt ein), lud ein, eingeladen (zu)   to invite (to) (11W)

die **Einladung, -en**   invitation

sich **ein·leben**   to settle down

ein·lösen   to cash (in) (7G); **einen Scheck ~** to cash a check (7W)

(ein)mal   once, (at) one time; **noch ~** once more, again (S3); one order of; (5E); **auch ~** for once; **erst ~** first of all; **nicht ~** not even; **es war ~** once upon a time

einmalig   unique, incredible (14W)

der **Einmarsch, ¨e**   entry, invasion

ein·packen   to pack (in a suitcase)

ein·richten   to furnish

die **Einrichtung, -en**   furnishings and appliances

einsam   lonely

ein·schlafen*   to fall asleep

ein·schließen*   to lock up

sich **ein·schreiben***   to register

das **Einschreibungsformular', -e**   application for university registration sich **ein·setzen (für)**   to support actively

einst   once (14W)

ein·steigen*   to get on / in (8W)

der **Eintritt**   entrance fee

der **Einwohner, -**   inhabitant

das **Einwohnermeldeamt, ¨er**   resident registration office

einzeln   individual(ly) (15E)

das **Einzelzimmer, -**   single room (7W)

einzig-   only

das **Eis**   ice, ice cream (3W)

eisern   (made of) iron

eisig   icy

eiskalt   ice-cold

eitel   vain

ekelhaft   disgusting

sich **ekeln**   to be digusted

der **Elefant', -en, -en**   elephant

elegant'   elegant

der **Elek'triker, -**   electrician

elek'trisch   electric

die **Elektrizität'**   electricity

der **Elek'tromecha'niker, -**   electrical mechanic / technician

elektro'nisch   electronic

die **Elek'trotech'nik**   electrical engineering

das **Element', -e**   element

der **Ell(en)bogen, -**   elbow

die **Eltern** (*pl.*)   parents (1W); **Groß~** grandparents (1 W); **Schwieger~** parents-in-law; **Stief~** step-parents; **Urgroß~** great-grandparents

die **E-Mail, -, -s**   e-mail (8W)

die **Emanzipation'**   emancipation

emanzipiert'   emancipated

emotional'   emotional(ly)

empfangen*   to receive

die **Empfangsdame, -n**   receptionist

empfehlen (empfiehlt), empfahl, empfohlen   to recommend (3W)

die **Empfehlung, -en**   recommendation

empfindlich   delicate; sensitive

das **Ende**   end (10W); **~ der Woche** at the end of the week (8G); **am ~** in the end (10W); **zu ~ sein*** to be finished

enden   to end

endlich   finally (15E)

die **Endung, -en**   ending

die **Energie'**   energy

eng   narrow

sich **engagie'ren (in + *dat.*)**   to get involved (in)

der **Engel, -**   angel

(das) **England**   England (1W)

der **Engländer, -**   the Englishman (1W)

englisch   English

(das) **Englisch: auf ~**   in English (S2); **Sprechen Sie ~?** Do you speak English? (1W)

der **Enkel, -**   grandchild

das **Enkelkind, -er**   grandchild

die **Enkeltochter, ¨**   granddaughter

der **Enkelsohn, ¨e**   grandson

enorm'   enormous; **~ viel** an awful lot

die **Ente, -n**   duck; **Lahme ~!** Poor baby! Lame duck!

entfernt'   away

entgegen·nehmen*   to accept

enthalten*   to contain

der **Enthusias'mus**   enthusiasm

entlang'   along (5W)

sich **entscheiden, entschied, entschieden**   to decide (10W); **~ über (+ *acc.*)** to decide on/about (10G)

die **Entscheidung, -en**   decision (12E); **eine ~ treffen*** to make a decision

entschuldigen   to excuse; **~Sie bitte!** Excuse me, please. (5W)

die **Entschuldigung, -en**   excuse; **~ !** Excuse me! Pardon me! (5W)

sich **entspannen**   to relax (9E)

entsprechen*   to correspond to; **~d** corresponding

entstehen* (ist)   to develop, be built

entwerten   to cancel (ticket); devalue (currency)

(sich) **entwickeln**   to develop; **sich auseinan'der ~** to develop apart

die **Entwicklung, -en**   development

entzwei'·brechen*   to break apart

(sich) **entzwei'·reißen***   to tear (o.s.) apart

sich **erbauen an (+ *dat.*)**   to be delighted about, enjoy

die **Erbse, -n**   pea (2W)

das **Erdbeben, -**   earthquake

die **Erdbeere, -n**   strawberry (2W)

die **Erde**   earth (12E); **unter der ~** underground; **zur ~ fallen*** to fall down

das **Erdgeschoss, -e**   ground level; **im ~** on the ground level

die **Erdnuss, ¨e**   peanut

die **Erdnussbutter**   peanut butter

das **Ereignis, -se**   event

erfahren*   to find out, learn

die **Erfahrung, -en**   experience (12W)

erfinden, erfand, erfunden   to invent

der **Erfolg, -e**   success

erfolgreich   successful

erfrieren* (ist)   to freeze to death

erfüllen   to fulfill; **sich ~** to be fulfilled, come true

die **Erfüllung**   fulfillment

ergänzen   to supply, add to

ergreifen, ergriff, ergriffen   to grab

erhalten*   to keep up, preserve, maintain

die **Erhaltung**   preservation (15W)

die **Erhellung**   illumination

sich **erholen**   to recuperate (9E)

die **Erholung**   recuperation, relaxation

erinnern (an + *acc.*)   to remind (of) (14W); **sich ~ (an + *acc.*)** to remember (14W)

die **Erinnerung, -en (an + *acc.*)**   reminder, memory of

erkalten (ist)   to grow cold; (*poetic*) to become insensitive

sich **erkälten**   to catch a cold (9G)

die **Erkältung, -en**   cold

erkennen*   to recognize (14E); **Zum ~** for recognition (only)

erklären   to explain (12W)

die **Erklärung, -en**   explanation

erlauben   to permit, allow

die **Erlaubnis**   permit, permission

erleben   to experience (9E)

das **Erlebnis, -se**   experience (14W)

erlesen   exquisite, high-quality

die **Ermäßigung, -en**   discount

die **Ernährung**   nutrition

ernst   serious(ly)

die **Ernte, -n**   harvest

das **Erntedank'fest**   (Harvest) Thanksgiving

eröffnen   to open up, establish

erreichen   to reach

erscheinen* (ist)   to appear, seem (4G)

erschrecken (erschrickt), erschrak, ist erschrocken   to be frightened

ersetzen   to replace

erst-   first

erst   only, not until

erwachsen   grown-up, adult

der **Erwachsene (ein Erwachsener) / die Erwachsene, -n, -n**   adult

erwähnen   to mention

erwärmen   to heat (up)

erwarten   to expect (12E)

erzählen   to tell (8W); ~ (**von** + *dat.*) to tell (about) (10G); **nach·~** to retell

erziehen*   to educate, raise

die **Erziehung**   education

das **Erziehungsgeld**   monthly child-raising benefit

der **Esel, -**   donkey, ass; **Du ~!** You dummy!

der **Espres'so, -s**   espresso

der **Esprit'**   esprit

essbar   edible

essen (isst), aß, gegessen   to eat (S5)

das **Essen, -**   food, meal (2W); **beim ~** while eating

der **Essig**   vinegar

das **Esszimmer, -**   dining room (5W)

die **Eta'ge, -n**   floor

ethnisch   ethnic

etliche   many

etwa   about, approximately (10E)

etwas   some, a little (2W); something (3W); **so ~ wie** s.th. like; **noch ~** one more thing, s.th. else; **Sonst noch ~?** Anything else?

euer (*pl. fam.*)   your (7G)

der **Euro, -s**   euro (S3)

(das) **Euro'pa**   Europe

der **Europä'er, -**   the European

europä'isch   European

die **Europäisie'rung**   Europeanization

euro'paweit   all over Europe

der **Evangelist', -en, -en**   evangelist

ewig   eternal(ly); **für ~** forever

exakt'   exact(ly)

das **Exa'men, -**   exam

das **Exemplar', -e**   sample, copy

das **Exil', -e**   exile

existie'ren   to exist

experimentell'   experimental

der **Exper'te, -n, n / die Expertin, -nen**   expert

extra   extra

das **Extrablatt, ⸚er**   special publication

exzen'trisch   excentric

F

fabelhaft   fabulous

die **Fabrik', -en**   factory

das **Fach, ⸚er**   subject (13W); **Haupt~** major (field) (13W); **Neben~** minor (field) (13W); **Schwerpunkt~** major (field)

das **Fach, ⸚er**   special field

der **Fachbereich, -e**   field (of study)

die **Fachkenntnis, -se**   special skill

die **Fach(ober)schule, -n**   business or technical school

die **Fachhochschule, -n**   university of applied sciences

die **Fachrichtung, -en**   field of study, specialization (13W)

das **Fachwerkhaus, ⸚er**   half-timbered house

der **Faden, ⸚**   thread

die **Fähigkeit, -en**   ability

die **Fähre, -n**   ferry

fahren (fährt), fuhr, ist gefahren   to drive, go (by car, etc.) (3G)

die **Fahrerei'**   (incessant) driving

die **Fahrkarte, -n**   ticket (8W)

der **Fahrplan, ⸚e**   schedule (of trains, etc.) (8W)

das **(Fahr)rad, ⸚er**   bicycle (5W); **mit dem ~ fahren*** to bicycle

der **(Fahr)radweg, -e**   bike path

die **Fahrt, -en**   trip, drive (8W)

fair   fair

der **Fall, ⸚e**   case; **auf jeden ~** in any case

fallen (fällt), fiel, ist gefallen   to fall (4E); **~ lassen*** to drop

falsch   wrong, false (S2)

die **Fami'lie, -n**   family (1W)

der **Fami'lienstand**   marital status

fangen (fängt), fing, gefangen   to catch

die **Fantasie', -n**   fantasy, imagination

fantas'tisch   fantastic (9W)

die **Farbe, -n**   color (S2); **Welche ~ hat . . . ?** What color is . . . ? (S2)

der **Farbstoff, -e**   dye, (artificial) color

der **Fasching**   carnival; **zum ~** for carnival (Mardi Gras)

die **Fassa'de, -n**   façade

fast   almost (6E)

die **Fastenzeit**   Lent

die **Faszination'**   fascination

faszinie'ren   to fascinate

faul   lazy (11W)

faulenzen   to be lazy (9W)

die **Faulheit**   laziness

das **Fax, -e**   fax (8W)

das **Faxgerät, ⸚e**   fax machine

der **Februar**   February (S4); **im ~** in February (S4)

fechten (ficht), focht, gefochten   to fence

der **Federball, ⸚e**   badminton (ball)

fehlen   to be missing, lacking (8W); **hier fehlt was** s.th. is missing (here); **was fehlt?** what's missing?

fehlend   missing

der **Fehler, -**   mistake

die **Feier, -n**   celebration, party (4W)

feierlich   festive

feiern   to celebrate (4W)

der **Feiertag, -e**   holiday (4W)

feige   cowardly; **er ist ~** he's a coward

fein   fine

die **Feind, -e**   enemy

feindlich   hostile

das **Feld, -er**   field

das **Fenster, -**   window (S2)

die **Ferien** (*pl.*) vacation (4W)
der **Ferienplatz, ̈e** vacation spot
fern far, distant
die **Ferne** distance
der **Fernfahrer, -** truck driver
das **Ferngespräch, -e** long-distance call
fern·sehen* to watch TV (9W)
das **Fernsehen** TV (the medium) (10E); **im ~** on TV (10W)
der **Fernseher, -** TV set (6W)
fertig finished, done (S5); **~ machen** to finish
das **Fest, -e** celebration (4W)
festgesetzt fixed
festlich festive
die **Festnahme, -n** arrest
das **Festspiel, -e** festival
die **Fete, -n** (*coll.*) party
das **Feuer, -** fire
feuertrunken (*poetic*) fire-inspired; **wir betreten ~** fire-inspired we enter
das **Feuerwerk, -e** firework(s)
die **Figur', -en** figure
der **Film, -e** film (10W)
filmen to shoot a film
die **Finan'zen** (*pl.*) finances
finanziell' financial(ly)
finanzie'ren to finance (15W)
die **Finanzie'rung** financing
finden, fand, gefunden to find (S4); **Ich finde es . . .** I think it's . . . (S4); **Das finde ich auch.** I think so, too. (S4)
der **Finger, -** finger (9W); **Zeige~** index finger
der **Fingernagel, ̈** fingernail
der **Finne, -n, -n / die Finnin, -nen** the Finn
finnisch Finnish
die **Firma, Firmen** company, business (12W)
der **Fisch, -e** fish (2W); Pisces; **ein kalter ~** a cold-hearted person
der **Fischfang** fishing
fit: sich ~ halten* to keep in shape (9E)
flach flat
die **Fläche, -n** area
der **Flachs** flax
die **Flamme, -n** flame
die **Flasche, -n** bottle (3E); **eine ~ Wein** a bottle of wine (3E)

das **Fleisch** (*sg.*) meat (2W)
der **Fleischer, -** butcher
die **Fleischerei', -en** butcher shop
fleißig industrious(ly), hard-working (11W)
flexi'bel flexible
die **Flexibilität'** flexibility
flieder lavender
die **Fliege, -n** fly
fliegen, flog, ist geflogen to fly (8W); **mit dem Flugzeug ~** to go by plane (8W)
fliehen, floh, ist geflohen to flee, escape
fließen, floss, ist geflossen to flow
fließend fluent(ly)
die **Flitterwochen** (*pl.*) honeymoon
flitzen (ist) to dash
das **Floß, ̈e** raft
die **Flöte, -n** flute; **(Block)~** recorder
die **Flotte, -n** fleet
die **Flucht** escape
der **Flüchtling, -e** refugee
der **Flug, ̈e** flight (8W)
der **Flügel, -** wing
der **Flughafen, ̈** airport (8W)
die **Flugkarte, -n** plane ticket
der **Flugsteig, -e** gate
das **Flugzeug, -e** airplane (8W)
der **Flur** hallway, entrance foyer (6W)
der **Fluss, ̈e** river (1W)
die **Flut** high tide
folgen (ist) (+ *dat.*) to follow
folgend following (10E)
der **Fokus** focus
der **Fön, -e** hair dryer
das **Fondue', -s** fondue
die **Fonotypist', -en, -en** audio/dictaphone-typist
fördern to encourage
die **Forel'le, -n** trout
die **Form, -en** form, shape
das **Formular', -e** form
formulie'ren to formulate
der **Forschungszweig, -e** field of research
der **Förster,-** forest ranger
die **Forstwirtschaft** forestry
fort- away
fort·fahren* to drive away; to continue

die **Fotografie'** photography
fotografie'ren to take pictures (9W)
die **Frage, -n** question (1W); **Ich habe eine ~.** I have a question. (S5); **jemandem eine ~ stellen** to ask s.b. a question
fragen to ask (S2); **sich ~** to wonder (9G)
fraglich questionable
der **(Schweizer) Franken, -** (Swiss) franc
(der) **Frankfurter Kranz** rich cake ring with whipped cream and nuts
fränkisch Franconian
(das) **Frankreich** France (1W)
der **Franzo'se, -n, -n / die Franzö'sin, -nen** French person (1W, 2G)
franzö'sisch French (1W)
(das) **Franzö'sisch; auf ~** in French (1W); **Ich spreche ~.** I speak French. (1W)
die **Frau, -en** Mrs., Ms. (S1); woman; wife (1W)
das **Frauchen, -** (*coll.*) owner of a pet
die **Frauenbewegung** women's movement
das **Fräulein, -** Miss, Ms.; young lady
frech impudent, sassy, fresh
die **Frechheit** impertinence
frei free, available (7W)
freiberuf'lich self-employed, freelance
freigiebig generous
die **Freiheit** freedom
das **Freilichtspiel, -e** outdoor performance
frei·nehmen* to take time off
der **Freitag** Friday (S4); **am ~** on Friday (S4); **Kar~** Good Friday
freitags on Fridays (2E)
freiwillig voluntary; voluntarily
die **Freizeit** leisure time (9W)
fremd foreign
das **Fremdenzimmer, -** guest-room
die **Fremdsprache, -n** foreign language
der **Fremdsprachenkorrespon-dent', -en, -en** bilingual secretary

fressen (frisst), fraß, gefressen to eat (like a glutton or an animal); **auf.~** to devour

die **Freude, -n** joy

sich **freuen auf** (+ *acc.*) to look forward to (10G); **Freut mich.** I'm pleased to meet you. (S1); **(Es) freut mich auch.** Likewise, pleased to meet you, too; **Das freut mich für dich.** I'm happy for you. (8W)

der **Freund, -e** (boy)friend (3E)

die **Freundin, -nen** (girl)friend (3E)

freundlich friendly (11W)

die **Freundlichkeit** friendliness

die **Freundschaft, -en** friendship (11W)

der **Frieden** peace (14W)

friedlich peaceful(ly)

frieren, fror, gefroren to freeze

frisch fresh (2W)

der **Friseur', -e** barber, hairdresser

die **Friseu'se, -n** beautician, hairdresser

friesisch Frisian

froh glad, happy (11E); **~e Weihnachten!** Merry Christmas (4W)

fröhlich cheerful, merry; **~e Weihnachten!** Merry Christmas! (4W)

der **Fronleich'nam(stag)** Corpus Christi (holiday)

der **Frosch, ¨e** frog

früh early, morning (8G)

früher earlier, once, former(ly) (12E)

der **Frühling, -e** spring (S4)

das **Frühjahrssemester, -** spring semester

das **Frühstück** breakfast (3W); **Was gibt's zum ~?** What's for breakfast? (3W)

frühstücken to eat breakfast (3W)

frustriert' frustrated

die **Frustrie'rung** frustration

der **Fuchs, ¨e** fox; **schlau wie ein ~** really clever; **ein alter ~** a sly person

sich **fühlen** to feel (a certain way) (9W)

führen to lead (14W)

der **Führerschein, -e** driver's license

die **Führung, -en** guided tour

die **Fülle** abundance; **in ganzer ~** to the fullest

füllen to fill

die **Funktion', -en** function

für (+ *acc.*) for (S2,2G); **was ~ ein . . .?** what kind of a . . . ? (2W)

die **Furcht** fear, awe

furchtbar terrible, awful (S4)

sich **fürchten** (**vor** + *dat.*) to be afraid (of)

der **Fürst, -en, -en** sovereign, prince

der **Fuß, ¨e** foot (9W); **zu ~ gehen*** to walk (5W)

der **Fußball, ¨e** soccer (ball) (9W)

der **Fußgänger, -** pedestrian; **~weg, -e** pedestrian sidewalk; **~überweg, -e** pedestrian crossing; **~zone, -n** pedestrian area

der **Fußnagel, ¨** toenail

G

die **Gabe, -n** gift; **in kleinen ~n** in small doses

die **Gabel, -n** fork (3W)

die **Galerie', -n** gallery

die **Gans, ¨e** goose; **eine dumme ~** a silly person (*fem.*)

ganz whole, entire(ly), all (9E); very; **~ meinerseits.** The pleasure is all mine; **~ schön** quite (nice); **~tags** full-time

das **Ganze** the whole thing; **im Großen und ~n** on the whole

die **Gara'ge, -n** garage (6W)

garantie'ren to guarantee (15W)

die **Gardi'ne, -n** curtain

gar nicht not at all (13E)

der **Garten, ¨** garden (6W); **Bier~** beer garden

das **Gartenstück, -e** garden plot

die **Gasse, -n** narrow street

Gassi gehen* to take a dog on a walk

der **Gast, ¨e** guest (7W)

der **Gastarbeiter, -** foreign (guest) worker

das **Gästezimmer, -** guest room

das **Gasthaus, ¨er** restaurant, inn

der **Gasthof, ¨e** small hotel (7E)

die **Gaststätte, -n** restaurant, inn

die **Gastwirtschaft, -en** restaurant, inn

das **Gebäck** pastry

das **Gebäude, -** building (14W)

geben (gibt), gab, gegeben to give (3G); **es gibt** there is, there are (2W); **Was gibt's?** What's up?; **Was gibt's Neues?** What's new? (9W); **Was gibt's im . . . ?** What's (playing) on . . . ? (10W); **Das gibt's doch nicht!** I don't believe it! That's impossible! (4W)

das **Gebiet, -e** area, region (15W)

gebildet well educated (11W)

geboren: Ich bin . . . ~ I was born . . . (S4); **Wann sind Sie ~?** When were you born? (S4); **Wann wurde . . . geboren?** When was . . . born?

gebrauchen to use, utilize

der **Gebrauchtwagen, -** used car

die **Gebühr, -en** fee

gebunden tied down; **orts~** tied to a certain town or place

der **Geburtstag, -e** birthday (4W); **Wann haben Sie ~?** When is your birthday? (4W); **Ich habe am . . . (s)ten ~.** My birthday is on the . . . (date) (4W); **Ich habe im . . . ~.** My birthday is in . . . (month). (4W); **Alles Gute / Herzlichen Glückwunsch zum ~!** Happy birthday! (4W); **zum ~** at the / for the birthday (4W)

der **Geburtsort, -e** place of birth

das **Gedächtnis** memory

der **Gedanke, -ns, -n** thought (14E)

das **Gedeck, -e** complete dinner

die **Geduld** patience

geduldig patient (11W); **~ wie ein Lamm** really patient

die **Gefahr, -en** danger (12E)

gefährlich dangerous (15E)

das **Gefälle,** - decline

gefallen (gefällt), gefiel, gefallen (+ *dat.*) to like, be pleasing to (3G); **Es gefällt mir.** I like it. (3G); **Das gefällt mir aber!** I really like it. (11W)

gefangen halten* to keep prisoner

das **Gefängnis, -se** prison

gefettet greased

der **Gefrierschrank, ⸚e** freezer

das **Gefühl, -e** feeling; **Mit~** compassion

gegen (+ *acc.*) against (2G); toward (time), around

die **Gegend, -en** area, region (8E)

der **Gegensatz, ⸚e** contrast, opposite

gegensätzlich opposing

das **Gegenteil, -e** opposite (S3); **im ~** on the contrary (12W)

gegenüber (**von** + *dat.*) across (from) (5W)

die **Gegenwart** present (tense)

das **Gehalt, ⸚er** salary

gehen, ging, ist gegangen to go, walk (S5); **Es geht mir ...** I am (feeling) ... (S1); **Wie geht's? Wie geht es Ihnen?** How are you? (S1); **zu Fuß ~** to walk (5W); **Das geht.** That's OK (13E); **Das geht (heute) nicht.** That won't work (today). (9W); **So geht's.** That's the way it goes.

gehorchen to obey

gehören (+ *dat.*) to belong to (3G)

die **Geige, -n** violin

der **Geisteswissenschaftler,** - humanities scholar

geistig mentally, intellectual(ly)

geizig stingy

das **Geländer,** - railing, banister

gelaunt: gut / schlecht ~ in a good / bad mood

gelb yellow (S2)

das **Geld** money (7W); **Bar~** cash (7W); **Klein~** change (7W); **Erziehungs~** government stipend for child care; **~ aus·geben*** to spend money (9E)

der **Geldautomat', -en, -en** ATM machine

der **Geldschein, -e** banknote (15E)

die **Gelegenheit, -en** opportunity, chance

gelingen, gelang, ist gelungen to succeed; **es gelingt mir nicht** I can't.

gelten (gilt), galt, gegolten to apply to, be valid for, be true

das **Gemälde,** - painting (10W)

die **Gemeinde, -n** community

gemeinsam together, shared, joint(ly) (11W); (in) common (15E)

die **Gemeinschaft, -en** community

gemischt mixed

die **Gemse, -n** mountain goat

das **Gemüse,** - vegetable(s) (2W)

gemütlich cozy, pleasant, comfortable, convivial (5E)

die **Gemütlichkeit** nice atmosphere, coziness

genau exact(ly); **~!** Exactly! Precisely! (12W); **~so** the same; **~ wie** (+ *nom.*) just like (9E)

die **Generation', -en** generation

generös' generous

sich **genieren** to be embarrassed

genießen, genoss, genossen to enjoy (12E)

der **Genitiv, -e** genitive

genug enough (5E); **Jetzt habe ich aber ~.** That's enough. I've had it. (10W)

geöffnet open (7W)

die **Geographie'** geography

die **Geologie'** geology

das **Gepäck** baggage, luggage (7W)

die **Gepäckaufgabe, -n** checked luggage room

gepunktet dotted

gerade just, right now (4W); **~ als** just when; **(immer) ~aus'** (keep) straight ahead (5W)

die **Gerechtigkeit** justice

das **Gericht, -e** dish; **Haupt~** main dish

gering' little, small; **~er** less

germa'nisch Germanic

die **Germanis'tik** study of German language and literature

gern (lieber, liebst-) gladly (2W); **furchtbar ~** very much; **~ geschehen!** Glad to ...; **Ich hätte ~ ...** I'd like to have ... (2W)

die **Gesamtschule, -n** comprehensive high school

das **Geschäft, -e** store (2W); business (12W)

geschäftlich concerning business

die **Geschäftsfrau, -en** businesswoman (12W)

der **Geschäftsmann, ⸚er** businessman (12W)

die **Geschäftsleute** (*pl.*) business people (12W)

geschehen (geschieht), geschah, ist geschehen to happen (11E); **Das geschieht dir recht.** That serves you right.

das **Geschenk, -e** present (4W)

die **Geschichte, -n** story, history (8E)

geschickt talented, skillful

geschieden divorced (11W)

das **Geschlecht, -er** gender, sex

geschlossen closed (7W)

der **Geschmack, ⸚er** taste

geschmacklos tacky

das **Geschrei** screaming

die **Geschwindigkeit, -en** speed; **~sbegrenzung** speed limit; **Richt~** recommended speed

die **Geschwister** (*pl.*) brothers and/or sisters, siblings (1W)

der **Geselle, -n, -n / die Gesellin, -nen** journeyman / woman

gesellig sociable

die **Gesellschaft, -en** society

das **Gesetz, -e** law

gesetzlich legal(ly)

gesichert secure

das **Gesicht, -er** face (9W)

das **Gespräch, -e** conversation, dialogue

gestern yesterday (4W,8G); **vor~** the day before yesterday (4W)

gestreift striped

gesucht wird wanted

gesund (ü) healthy (9W)

die **Gesundheit** health

das **Gesundheitsamt** health department

gesundheitsbewusst health conscious

der **Gesundheitsfana′tiker, -** health nut

geteilt divided; shared

das **Getränk, -e** beverage

getrennt separate(d), separately

die **Gewalt** violence

die **Gewerkschaft, -en** trade / labor union

der **Gewinn, -e** profit, benefit

gewinnen, gewann, gewonnen to win (12E)

gewiss for sure

das **Gewitter, -** thunderstorm

sich **gewöhnen an** (+ *acc.*) to get used to (12W)

gewöhnlich usual(ly) (3E)

gierig greedy

gießen, goss, gegossen to pour; **es gießt** it's pouring

das **Gift, -e** poison

der **Giftstoff, -e** toxic waste (15W)

die **Giraf′fe, -n** giraffe

die **Gitar′re, -n** guitar (9W)

die **Gladio′le, -n** gladiola

der **Glanz** brilliance, splendor

das **Glas, ̈er** glass (2E); **ein ~** a glass of (2E)

glauben to believe, think (2W;3G); **Ich glaube es / ihr.** I believe it / her.; **~ an** (+ *acc.*) to believe (in) (12W)

glaubhaft convincing(ly)

gleich equal, same (12W); right away; **Bis ~!** See you in a few minutes! (9W)

gleichberechtigt with equal rights

die **Gleichberechtigung** equality, equal rights

gleichfalls: Danke ~! Thank you, the same to you. (3W)

das **Gleis, -e** track (8W)

der **Gletscher, -** glacier

die **Glocke, -n** bell

glorreich glorious

das **Glück** luck; **~ haben*** to be lucky (4E); **~ gehabt!** I was (you were, etc.) lucky! (4E); **Viel ~!** Good luck! (4W); **Du ~spilz!** You lucky thing!

glücklich happy (11W)

der **Glückwunsch, ̈e** congratulation; **Herzlichen ~ (zum Geburtstag)!** Congratulations (on your birthday)! (4W); **Herzliche Glückwünsche!** Congratulations! Best wishes! (4W)

der **Glühwein** mulled wine

der **Gnom, -e** gnome, goblin

das **Gold** gold (11E)

golden golden

der **Goldfisch, -e** gold fish

(das) **Golf** golf; **Mini~** miniature-golf

der **Gott** God; **~ sei Dank!** Thank God! (8W); **Um ~es willen!** For Heaven's sake! My goodness!

der **Gott, ̈er** god; **schöner Götterfunken** beautiful bright spark of divinity

der **Grad, -e** degree

die **Gramma′tik** grammar

gramma′tisch grammatical(ly)

die **Grapefruit, -s** grapefruit

gratulie′ren (+ *dat.*) to congratulate (4W); **Wir ~!** Congratulations!

grau gray (S2)

die **Grenze, -n** border (14W)

grenzen (an + *acc.*) to border

grenzenlos unlimited, endless

der **Grieche, -n, -n / die Griechin, -nen** the Greek

(das) **Griechenland** Greece

griechisch Greek

die **Grippe** flu

groß (größer, größt-) large, big, tall (S3); **im Großen und Ganzen** on the whole, by and large

die **Größe, -n** size, height

die **Großeltern** (*pl.*) grandparents (1W); **Ur~** great-grandparents

das **Großmaul, ̈er** big mouth

die **Großmutter, ̈** grandmother (1W); **Ur~** great-grandmother

der **Großteil** major part / portion

der **Großvater, ̈** grandfather (1W); **Ur~** great-grandfather

Grüezi! Hi! (*in Switzerland*)

grün green (S2); **ins Grüne / im Grünen** out in(to) nature

der **Grund, ̈e** reason; **aus diesem ~** for that reason; **im ~e genommen** basically

gründen to found

das **Grundgesetz** Constitution, Basic Law

die **Grundschule, -n** elementary school, grades 1–4

das **Grundstück, -e** building lot

der **Grundstücksmakler, -** real estate broker

die **Gründung, -en** founding

die **Grünfläche, -n** green area

die **Gruppe, -n** group

der **Gruß, ̈e** greeting; **Viele Grüße (an +** *acc.* **. . .)!** Greetings (to . . .)!

grüßen to greet; **Grüß dich!** Hi!; **Grüß Gott!** Hello! Hi! (*in southern Germany*)

der **Gummi** rubber

gurgeln to gargle

die **Gurke, -n** cucumber (2W); **saure ~** pickle

der **Gürtel, -** belt

gut (besser, best-) good, fine (S1); **~ aussehend** good-looking (11W); **Das ist noch mal ~ gegangen.** Things worked out all right (again); **na ~** well, all right; **Mach's ~!** Take care. (S1); **sehr gut** approx. grade A; **gut** approx. grade B

das **Gute: Alles ~!** All the best! (4W); **Alles ~ zum Geburtstag!** Happy birthday! (4W)

die **Güte** goodness; **Ach du meine ~!** My goodness! (8W)

gütig kind

das **Gymna′sium, Gymna′sien** academic high school (grades 5–13)

H

das **Haar, -e** hair (9W)

haben (hat), hatte, gehabt to have (S5,2G); **Ich hätte gern . . .** I'd like (to have) . . . (2W)

das **Habitat, -e** habitat

der **Hafen, ⸚** port
die **Haferflocken** (*pl.*) oatmeal
das **Hähnchen, -** chicken
der **Haken, -** hook
    halb half (to the next hour) (S5); **~tags** part-time; **in einer ~en Stunde** in half an hour (8W)
die **Hälfte, -n** half
die **Halle, -n** large room for work, recreation, or assembly
    Hallo! Hello! Hi!
der **Hals, ⸚e** neck, throat (9W); **Das hängt mir zum ~ heraus.** I'm fed up (with it). (10W)
das **Halsband, ⸚er** collar
    Halt! Stop! (7W)
    halten (hält), hielt, gehalten to hold, stop (a vehicle) (5W); **~ von** to think of, be of an opinion (10G)
die **Haltestelle, -n** (bus, etc.) stop (5W)
das **Halteverbot, -e** no stopping or parking
der **Hamburger Matjestopf** pickled herring with sliced apples and onion rings in a sour-cream sauce
der **Hamster, -** hamster
die **Hand, ⸚e** hand (3E,9W)
die **Handarbeit, -en** needlework
der **Handball, ⸚e** handball
der **Handel** trade (12E)
das **Handeln** action
die **Handelsbeziehung, -en** trade relation(s)
die **Handelsnation', -en** trading nation
der **Handschuh, -e** glove
das **Handtuch, ⸚er** towel
der **Handwerker, -** craftsman
das **Handy, -s** cellular phone (8W)
    hängen to hang (up) (6W)
    hängen, hing, gehangen to hang (be hanging) (6W)
    harmo'nisch harmonious
    hart (ä) hard; tough
    hassen to hate
    hässlich ugly (11W)
das **Hauptfach, ⸚er** major (field of study) (13W)
der **Hauptmann, ⸚er** captain
die **Hauptrolle, -n** leading role

die **Hauptsache, -n** main thing
    hauptsächlich mainly
die **Hauptsaison** (high) season
die **Hauptschule, -n** basic high school (grades 5–9)
die **Hauptstadt, ⸚e** capital (1W)
die **Hauptstraße, -n** main street
das **Hauptwort, ⸚er** noun
das **Haus, ⸚er** house (6W); **nach ~e** (toward) home (3W); **zu ~e** at home (3W)
der **Hausbesetzer, -** squatter
das **Häuschen, -** little house
die **Hausfrau, -en** housewife (12W)
der **Haushalt, -e** household
der **Haushälter, -** housekeeper
    häuslich home-loving, domestic
das **Haustier, -e** pet
die **Hauswirtschaft** home economics
die **Haut** skin
die **Hautpflege** skin care
das **Heft, -e** notebook (S2)
    heilig holy; **Aller ~en** All Saints' Day; **~e Drei Könige** Epiphany
der **Heiligabend** Christmas Eve; **am ~** on Christmas Eve
das **Heiligtum** shrine, sanctuary
die **Heimat** homeland, home (14E)
der **Heimcompu'ter, -** home computer
die **Heimreise, -n** trip home
    Heimweh haben* to be homesick
    heiraten to marry, get married (11W)
    heiratslustig eager to marry
    heiß hot (S4)
    heißen, hieß, geheißen to be called; **Ich heiße . . .** My name is . . . (S1); **Wie ~ Sie?** What's your name? (S1)
die **Heizung** heating (system)
das **Heizmaterial'** heating material, fuel
    helfen (hilft), half, geholfen (+ *dat.*) to help (3G)
    hell light, bright (6W); **Sei ~ e!** Be smart!
das **Hemd, -en** shirt (S3); **Nacht~** nightgown
die **Henne, -n** hen
    her- toward [the speaker (7G)]

    herab'·blicken (auf + *acc.*) to look down (on)
    herab'·schauen (auf + *acc.*) to look down (on)
    heran'- up to
    heraus'·finden* to find out
die **Heraus'forderung, -en** challenge
der **Herbst, -e** fall, autumn (S4)
der **Herd, -e** (kitchen) range
    herein'- in(to)
    herein'·kommen* to come in, enter (11E)
    herein'·lassen* to let in
der **Hering, -e** herring
die **Herkunft** origin
der **Herr, -n, -en** Mr., gentleman (S1,2G); Lord; **Sehr geehrte Damen und ~en!** Ladies and gentlemen!
das **Herrchen, -** (*coll.*) owner of a pet
    herrlich wonderful, great (8E)
    herum'- around
    herum'·fragen to ask around
    herum'·laufen* to run around
    herum'·reisen (ist) to travel around
das **Herz, -ens, -en** heart; **mit ~** with feelings
    herzförmig heart-shaped
der **Heurige, -n** (*sg.*) new wine
die **Heurigenschänke, -n** Viennese wine-tasting inn
    heute today (S4); **für ~** for today (S2)
    heutig- of today
    hier here (S2)
die **Hilfe, -n** help (15E)
    hilfsbereit helpful
das **Hilfsverb, -en** auxiliary verb
der **Himmel** sky; heaven; **~fahrt(stag)** Ascension (Day)
    himmlisch heavenly
der **Himmlische (ein Himmlischer) / die Himmlische, -n, -n** Heavenly one
    hin- toward (the speaker) (7G)
    hin und her back and forth
    hinauf'·fahren* to go or drive up (to) (8E)
    hinein'·gehen* to go in(to), enter

hin·kommen* to get / come to

hin·legen to lay or put down; **sich ~** to lie down (9G)

hin·nehmen* to accept

sich **(hin·)setzen** to sit down (9G)

hinter (+ *acc. / dat.*) behind (6G)

hinterlas'sen* to leave behind

der **Hintern, -** behind

die **(Hin- und) Rückfahrkarte, -n** round-trip ticket (8W)

hinun'ter·fahren* to drive down

hinzu'- added to

hinzu'·fügen to add

das **Hirn** brain

der **Hirsch, -e** red dear

histo'risch historical(ly) (14W)

das **Hobby, -s** hobby (9W)

hoch (hoh-) (höher, höchst-) high(ly) (12W)

das **Hochhaus, ⁻er** high-rise building

hoch·legen to put up (high)

die **Hochschule, -n** university, college; **Fach~** university of applied sciences

die **Hochzeit, -en** wedding (11W)

(das) **Hockey** hockey

der **Hof, ⁻e** court, courtyard

hoffen to hope (12E)

hoffentlich hopefully, I hope (5E)

die **Hoffnung, -en** hope

höflich polite(ly)

die **Höhe, -n** height, altitude; **in die ~** up high; **Das ist doch die ~!** That's the limit!

der **Höhepunkt, -e** climax

hohl hollow

die **Höhle, -n** cave

(sich) **holen** (go and) get, pick up, fetch (13W)

der **Holländer, -** the Dutchman

holländisch Dutch

die **Hölle** hell

das **Holz** wood

hölzern wooden

der **Honig** honey

hoppla hoops, whoops

hörbar audible

hören to hear (S2)

der **Hörer, -** listener; receiver

der **Hörsaal, -säle** lecture hall (13W)

das **Hörspiel, -e** radio play

die **Hose, -n** slacks, pants (S3); **Latz~** overall

der **Hosenanzug, ⁻e** pant suit

das **Hotel', -s** hotel (5W,7W)

hübsch pretty (11W)

der **Hügel, -** hill

das **Huhn, ⁻er** chicken

der **Humor'** (sense of) humor

der **Hund, -e** dog (11W); **Fauler ~!** Lazy bum!

hundert hundred; **Hunderte von** hundreds of

der **Hunger** hunger (2E); **Ich habe ~.** I'm hungry. (2E)

hungrig hungry

hüpfen (ist) to hop

der **Hut, ⁻e** hat

hüten to watch (over)

die **Hütte, -n** hut, cottage

I

der **ICE, -s** InterCityExpress (train)

ideal' ideal

das **Ideal', -e** ideal

der **Idealis'mus** idealism

die **Idee', -n** idea (9W); **Gute ~!** That's a good idea!

sich **identifizie'ren** to identify o.s.

iden'tisch identical

die **Identität', -en** identity

idyl'lisch idyllic

ignorie'ren to ignore

ihr her, its, their (7G)

Ihr (*formal*) your (1W,7G)

imaginär' imaginary

die **Imbissbude, -n** snack bar, fast-food stand

die **Immatrikulation'** enrollment (at university)

immer always (4E); **~ geradeaus** always straight ahead (5W); **~ länger** longer and longer (12G); **~ noch** still; **~ wieder** again and again (12G)

der **Imperativ, -e** imperative

das **Imperfekt** imperfect, simple past

in (+ *acc. / dat.*) in, into, inside of (6G)

inbegriffen (in + *dat.*) included (in)

der **India'ner, -** the Native American

der **In'dikativ** indicative

in'direkt indirect(ly)

die **Individualität'** individuality

individuell' individual(ly)

die **Industrie', -n** industry

der **Industrie'kaufmann, -leute** industrial manager

industriell' industrial

das **Industrie'unternehmen, -** large industrial company

der **Infinitiv, -e** infinitive

die **Informa'tik** computer science

die **Information', -en** information

die **Informations'suche** search for information

informativ' informative

(sich) **informie'ren (über** + *acc.*) to inform, get informed (about) (10G)

der **Ingenieur', -e** engineer (12W)

die **Initiati've, -n** initiative

inlineskaten to rollerblade; **~ gehen*** to go rollerblading

innen (*adv.*) inside

der **Innenhof, ⁻e** inner court

die **Innenstadt, ⁻e** center (of town), downtown

inner- inner

innerhalb within

die **Insel, -n** island (14E)

insgesamt' altogether

das **Institut', -e** institute

das **Instrument', -e** instrument; **Musik'~** musical instrument

die **Inszenie'rung, -en** production

intellektuell' intellectual(ly)

intelligent' intelligent (11W)

die **Intelligenz'** intelligence

der **Intendant', -en, -en** artistic director

intensiv' intensive

interessant' interesting (5E); **etwas Interessantes** s.th. interesting

das **Interes'se, -n (an** + *dat.*) interest (in)

sich **interessie'ren für** to be interested in (10G)

international' international

das **Internet** Internet
interpretie′ren to interpret
das **Interview, -s** interview
interviewen to interview
in′tolerant intolerant
das **Inventar′, -e** inventory
inzwi′schen in the meantime
irden (*poet.*) earthen
irgendwie somehow
irgendwo somewhere
(das) **Ita′lien** Italy (1W)
der **Italie′ner, -** the Italian (1W)
italie′nisch Italian (1W)
Iwrith the official Hebrew
language in Israel

J

ja yes (S1); *flavoring particle
expressing emphasis* (7G)
die **Jacke, -n** jacket (S3);
Strick~ cardigan
der **Jäger, -** hunter
das **Jahr, -e** year (S4); **Ein gutes
Neues ~!** Have a good New
Year! (4W)
jahrelang for years
die **Jahreszeit, -en** season
das **Jahrhun′dert, -e** century
-jährig years old; years long
jährlich yearly
das **Jahrtau′send, -e** millennium (15E)
jammern to complain, grieve
der **Januar** January (S4); **im ~**
in January (S4)
der **Japa′ner, -** Japanese
japa′nisch Japanese
je (+ *comp.*) **. . . desto** (+
comp.) **. . .** the . . . the . . .
(12G); **~ nachdem′** de-
pending on
die **Jeans** (*pl.*) jeans (S3)
jed- (*sg.*) each, every (7G)
jedenfalls in any case (13E)
jeder each one, everyone,
everybody
jederzeit any time
jedoch′ however (12E)
der **Jeep, -s** jeep
jemand someone, somebody
(11W)
jetzt now (S5)
der **Job, -s** job
jobben to have a job that is
not one's career
joggen to jog; **~ gehen*** to
go jogging

der **Jogurt** yogurt (frequently
also used with *das*)
der **Journalist′, -en, -en** journalist (12W)
das **Jubilä′um, Jubilä′en** anniversary
der **Jude, -n, -n / die Jüdin, -nen**
Jew
das **Judentum** Jewry
jüdisch Jewish
(das) **Judo: ~ kämpfen** to do
judo
die **Jugend** youth (14E)
die **Jugendherberge, -n** youth
hostel (7E)
der **Juli** July (S4); **im ~** in July
(S4)
jung (ü) young (11W)
der **Junge, -n, -n** boy (1W,2G)
die **Jungfrau, -en** virgin; Virgo
der **Junggeselle, -n, -n** bachelor
der **Juni** June (S4); **im ~** in June
(S4)
Jura: Er studiert ~. He's
studying law.

K

das **Kabarett′, -e** (*or* **-s**) cabaret
das **Kabelfernsehen** cable TV
der **Kaffee** coffee (2W); **~ mit
Schlag** coffee with whipped
cream
der **Kaffeeklatsch** coffeeklatsch,
chatting over a cup of cof-
fee (and cake)
der **Kaiser, -** emperor
der **Kaiserschmarren** pancake
pulled to pieces and sprinkled with powdered sugar
and raisins
der **Kaka′o** hot chocolate
das **Kalb, ̈er** calf; **die ~sleber**
calves' liver
der **Kalen′der, -** calendar
kalt (ä) cold (S4); **~ oder
warm?** with or without
heat?
die **Kälte** cold(ness)
die **Kamera, -s** camera
der **Kamin′, -e** fireplace
der **Kamm, ̈e** comb
(sich) **kämmen** to comb (o.s.) (9G)
die **Kammer, -n** chamber
der **Kampf, ̈e (um)** fight, struggle (for)
kämpfen to fight, struggle
(das) **Kanada** Canada (1W)

der **Kana′dier, -** the Canadian
(1W)
kana′disch Canadian (1W)
der **Kanal′, ̈e** channel
das **Känguru, -s** kangaroo
die **Kanti′ne, -n** cafeteria (at a
workplace)
der **Kanton′, -e** canton
das **Kanu, -s** canoe
der **Kanzler, -** chancellor
kapitalis′tisch capitalist
das **Kapi′tel, -** chapter
das **Käppi, -s** (*coll.*) cap
kaputt′ broken
kaputt·gehen* to get broken, break
das **Karenz′jahr, -e** year's leave
der **Karfreitag** Good Friday
kariert′ checkered
der **Karneval** carnival
die **Karot′te, -n** carrot (2W)
die **Karrie′re, -n** career
die **Karte, -n** ticket (8W); card
(9W); **~n spielen** to play
cards (9W)
die **Kartof′fel, -n** potato (3W);
der ~brei (*sg.*) mashed
potatoes; **die ~chips** (*pl.*)
potato chips; **das ~mehl**
potato flour, starch; **der
~salat** potato salad
der **Käse** cheese (2W); **Das ist
(doch) ~!** That's nonsense.
die **Kasse, -n** cash register,
cashier's window (7W)
das **Kasseler Rippchen, -**
smoked loin of pork
die **Kasset′te, -n** cassette (9W)
die **Kassie′rer, -** cashier; clerk,
teller
die **Katastro′phe, -n** catastrophe
die **Katze, -n** cat (11W); **(Das
ist) alles für die Katz′!**
(That's) all for nothing!; **So
ein süßes Kätzchen!** Such
a cute kitty. (11W)
kaufen to buy (2W)
das **Kaufhaus, ̈er** department
store (2W)
der **Kaufmann, -leute** trained
employee in some branch
of business
kaum hardly, barely,
scarcely (14W)
kein no, not a, not any
(1G)
der **Keller, -** basement
der **Kellner, -** waiter (3W)

die **Kellnerin, -nen** waitress (3W)

kennen, kannte, gekannt to know, be acquainted with (6G)

kennen lernen to get to know, meet (7E)

der **Kenner, -** connoisseur

die **Kenntnis, -se** knowledge, skill (12E)

der **Kerl, -e** guy

der **Kern, -e** core

kernlos seedless

die **Kerze, -n** candle (4E)

die **Kette, -n** chain, necklace

die **Ket'tenreaktion', -en** chain reaction

khaki khaki

das **Kilo, -s (kg)** kilogram

der **Kilome'ter, - (km)** kilometer

das **Kind, -er** child (1W)

der **Kindergarten, ¨** kindergarden

der **Kindergärtner, -** kindergarden teacher

kinderlieb loves children

das **Kinn, -e** chin

das **Kino, -s** movie theater (5W)

die **Kirche, -n** church (5W)

die **Kirsche, -n** cherry

kitschig cheesy

die **Kiwi, -s** kiwi

klagen (über + acc.) to complain (about) (14W)

die **Klammer, -n** parenthesis

klappen to work out

klar clear; **(na) ~!** Sure! Of course! (13W); **eins ist ~** one thing is for sure

die **Klasse, -n** class (12W); **granz große ~** super

die **Klas'senkamerad', -en, -en** classmate

das **Klassentreffen, -** class reunion

das **Klassenzimmer, -** classroom

klassisch classical

die **Klausur, -en** big test

klatschen to clap (10W); to gossip

das **Klavier', -e** piano (9W)

das **Kleid, -er** dress (S3)

der **(Kleider)bügel, -** clothes hanger

der **Kleiderschrank, -̈e** closet

die **Kleidung** clothing (S3)

der **Kleidungsarti'kel, -** article of clothing

klein small, little, short (S3)

die **Kleinbürgerlichkeit** narrow-mindedness

das **Kleingeld** change (7W)

der **Klempner, -** plumber

der **Klient', -en, -en [Kli:ent']** client

das **Klima, -s** climate

die **Klimaanlage, -n** air conditioning

klingeln to ring a (door) bell

klingen, klang, geklungen to sound; **(Das) klingt gut.** (That) sounds good. (6W)

das **Klo, -s** *(coll.)* toilet

klopfen to knock

der **Klops, -e** meat ball

der **Kloß, -̈e** dumpling

das **Kloster, ¨** monastery; convent

der **Klub, -s** club

klug (ü) smart, clever

knabbern to nibble

der **Knabe, -n, -n** boy

die **Knappheit** shortage

die **Kneipe, -n** pub

das **Knie, -** knee (9W)

der **Knirps, -e** little fellow, dwarf

der **Knoblauch** garlic

der **Knöd(e)l, -** dumpling (in southern Germany)

der **Knopf, -̈e** button

der **Knoten, -** knot

knuspern to nibble

k.o. knocked-out; **ich bin ~** I am exhausted

der **Koch, -̈e / die Köchin, -nen** cook

kochen to cook (6W)

der **Koffer, -** suitcase (7W)

das **Kohlendioxid', -e** carbon dioxide

der **Kolle'ge, -n, -n / die Kolle'gin, -nen** colleague; **Zimmer~** roommate (13W)

die **Kolonialisie'rung** colonization

kombinie'ren to combine

der **Komfort'** comfort

komisch funny (strange, comical) (10W)

das **Komitee, -s** committee

kommen, kam, ist gekommen to come (1W); **Komm rüber!** Come on over!

der **Kommentar', -e** commentary

kommentie'ren to comment

kommerziell' commercial

die **Kommo'de, -n** dresser (6W)

kommunis'tisch communist

der **Kom'parativ, -e** comparative

die **Komplikation', -en** complication

kompliziert' complicated (11W)

komponie'ren to compose

der **Komponist', -en, -en** composer (10W)

das **Kompott', -e** stewed fruit

der **Kompromiss', -e** compromise

die **Konditorei', -en** pastry shop

die **Konferenz', -en** conference

der **Konflikt', -e** conflict

der **Kongress', -e** conference

der **König, -e** king (11E); **Heilige Drei ~e** Epiphany (Jan. 6)

die **Königin, -nen** queen (11E)

das **Königreich, -e** kingdom

die **Konjunktion', -en** conjunction

der **Kon'junktiv** subjunctive

die **Konkurrenz'** competition

können (kann), konnte, gekonnt to be able to, can (5G)

die **Konsequenz', -en** consequence

konservativ conservative

das **Konservie'rungsmittel, -** preservative

das **Konsulat', -e** consulate

die **Kontakt'linse, -n** contact lense

das **Konto, -s (or Konten)** account

der **Kontrast', -e** contrast

die **Kontrol'le, -n** control

kontrollie'ren to control, check

die **Konversation', -en** conversation; **~sstunde, -n** conversation lesson

das **Konzentrations'lager, -** concentration camp

sich **konzentrie'ren (auf + acc.)** to concentrate (on)

das **Konzert', -e** concert (10W)

die **Kooperation'** cooperation

der **Kopf, -̈e** head (9W)

kopf·stehen* to stand on one's head

das **Kopftuch, -̈er** head scarf

die **Kopie', -n** copy

der **Kopie′rer, -** copy machine
der **Korb, ⁼e** basket
der **Korbball, ⁼e** basketball
der **Körper, -** body (9W)
  körperlich physical(ly)
der **Korrespondent′, -en, -en**
  correspondent
  korrigie′ren to correct
  kosten to cost; **Was ~ . . . ?**
  How much are . . . ? (S3);
  Das kostet (zusammen)
  . . . That comes to . . . (S3)
die **Kosten** (*pl.*) cost
  kostenlos free (of charge)
das **Kostüm′, -e** costume; lady's
  suit
die **Krabbe, -n** crab
der **Kracher, -** firecracker
die **Kraft, ⁼e** strength, power
die **Kralle, -n** claw
der **Kran, ⁼e** crane
  krank (ä) sick, ill (9W)
der **Kranke (ein Kranker) / die**
  Kranke, -n, -n sick person (12G)
der **Krankenbesuch, -e** sick visit
die **Krankengymnast′, -en, -en**
  physical therapist
das **Krankenhaus, ⁼er** hospital
die **Krankenkasse, -n** health insurance agency
die **Krankenpflege** nursing
der **Krankenpfleger, -** male
  nurse (12W)
die **Krankenschwester, -n** nurse
  (12W)
die **Krankenversicherung, -en**
  health insurance
die **Krankheit, -en** sickness, ill-
  ness, disease
der **Kranz, ⁼e** wreath;
  Advents′~ Advent wreath
der **Krapfen, -** doughnut
der **Kratzer, -** scratch
das **Kraut** cabbage
die **Krawat′te, -n** tie
  kreativ′ creative
die **Kreativität′** creativity
der **Krebs, -e** crab; cancer; Cancer
die **Kredit′karte, -n** credit card
die **Kreide** chalk (S2)
der **Kreis, -e** circle; county
das **Kreuz, -e** cross, mark
die **Kreuzung, -en** intersection
das **Kreuzworträtsel, -** cross-
  word puzzle
der **Krieg, -e** war (14W)

der **Krimi, -s** detective story
  (10W)
der **Krimskrams** old junk
der **Kritiker, -** critic
  kritisch critical(ly)
  kritisie′ren to criticize
die **Krone, -n** crown
  krönen to crown
die **Küche, -n** kitchen (6W);
  cuisine
der **Kuchen, -** cake (2W)
der **Küchenschrank, ⁼e** kitchen
  cabinet
die **Kugel, -n** ball
  kühl cool (S4)
der **Kühlschrank, ⁼e** refrigerator
  (6W)
der **Kuli, -s** pen (S2)
die **Kultur′, -en** culture
  kulturell′ cultural(ly)
  (14W)
sich **kümmern (um)** to take care
  (of)
die **Kunst, ⁼e** art (10W)
der **Künstler, -** artist (12W);
  Compu′ter~ graphic
  designer
die **Kuppel, -n** cupola, dome
der **Kurfürst, -en, -en** elector
der **Kurort, -e** health resort, spa
der **Kurs, -e** course (S5)
  kurz (ü) short (S3); **~ vor**
  shortly before; **vor ~em**
  recently (10W)
die **Kürze** shortness, brevity
das **Kurzgespräch, -e** brief
  conversation
die **Kusi′ne, -n** (*fem.*) cousin
  (1W)
  küssen to kiss
die **Küste, -n** coast (15W)

L

das **Labor′, -s** (*or* -e) lab(oratory) (13W)
der **Laboran′t, -en, -en** lab
  assistant
der **Labrador, -s** Labrador (dog)
  lachen to laugh (10W)
  lächeln to smile (10W)
  lächerlich ridiculous (12W);
  Das ist doch ~. That's
  ridiculous.
  laden (lädt), lud, geladen to
  load
der **Laden, ⁼** store; **Bio-~ /**
  grüne ~ environmental

  store; **Tante-Emma-~**
  small grocery store
die **Lage, -n** location
  lahm lame, lacking enthusiasm; **~e Ente!** Poor baby!
das **Lamm, ⁼er** lamb; **geduldig**
  wie ein ~ really patient
die **Lampe, -n** lamp (6W);
  Hänge~ hanging lamp;
  Steh~ floor lamp
das **Land, ⁼er** country, state
  (1W); **auf dem ~(e)** in the
  country (6E); **aufs ~** in(to)
  the country(side) (6E)
  landen (ist) to land (8W)
die **Landeskunde** cultural and
  geographical study of a
  country
die **Landkarte, -n** map (1W)
die **Landschaft, -en** landscape,
  scenery (15W)
die **Landung, -en** landing
der **Landwirt, -e** farmer
die **Landwirtschaft** agriculture
  landwirtschaftlich agricultural
  lang (ä) (*adj.*) long (S3)
  lange long, for a long time;
  noch ~ nicht not by far;
  schon ~ (nicht mehr) (not)
  for a long time; **wie ~?**
  how long? (4W)
  langsam slow(ly) (S3)
sich **langweilen** to get / be bored
  (9E)
  langweilig boring, dull
  (10W)
  lassen (lässt), ließ, gelassen
  to leave (behind) (7W)
  lässig casual
die **Last, -en** burden
(das) **Latein′** Latin
die **Later′ne, -n** lantern
die **Latzhose, -n** overall
  laufen (läuft), lief, ist
  gelaufen to run, walk
  (3G)
  laut loud(ly), noisy
  (4E;7W); **Lesen Sie ~!**
  Read aloud.; **Sprechen Sie**
  ~er! Speak up. (S3)
  läuten to ring
der **Lautsprecher, -** loudspeaker
  leben to live (6E)
das **Leben** life (9E)
  lebend living; **etwas Leben-**
  des s.th. living
  leben′dig alive; lively

die **Lebensfreude**   joy of living

lebensfroh   cheerful, full of life

der **Lebenslauf, ⁻e**   résumé

die **Lebensmittel** (*pl.*)   groceries (2W)

der **Lebensstandard**   standard of living

die **Leber, -n**   liver; **Kalbs~** calves' liver

der **Leberkäs(e)**   (Bavarian) meatloaf made from minced pork

die **Leberwurst**   liver sausage

der **Lebkuchen, -**   gingerbread

das **Leder**   leather

die **Lederhose, -n**   leather pants

ledig   single (11W)

leer   empty (14E)

legen   to lay, put (flat) (6W); **sich (hin·)~** to lie down (9G)

das **Lehrbuch, ⁻er**   textbook

die **Lehre, -n**   apprenticeship

lehren   to teach (13W)

der **Lehrer, -**   teacher (12W)

der **Lehrling, -e**   apprentice

die **Lehrstelle, -n**   apprentice-ship (position)

leicht   light, easy, easily (6E)

das **Leid**   misery; **Es tut mir ~.** I'm sorry. (5W)

die **Leidenschaft, -en**   passion

leider   unfortunately (5E)

leihen, lieh, geliehen   to lend

die **Leine, -n**   leash

leise   quiet(ly), soft(ly)

leisten   to achieve

leiten   to direct

die **Leiter, -n**   ladder; director

die **Leitung**   leadership

das **Leitungswasser**   tap water

lernen   to learn, study (S2)

der **Lerntipp, -s**   study suggestion

das **Lernziel, -e**   learning objective

lesbar   legible

lesen (liest), las, gelesen   to read (S2); **~ Sie laut!** Read aloud.

der **Leser, -**   reader

die **Leseratte, -n**   bookworm

der **Lesesaal, -säle**   reading room

letzt-   last (10W)

(das) **Letzeburgisch**   Luxembourg dialect

die **Leute** (*pl.*)   people (1W)

licht (*poetic*)   light

das **Licht, -er**   light; **ins ~ treten*** to step out into the light

die **Lichterkette, -n**   candlelight march

lieb-   dear (5E); **~(evoll)** loving (11W)

die **Liebe**   love (11W)

lieben   to love (6E)

lieber   rather (12G); **Es wäre mir ~, wenn . . .** I would prefer it, if . . .

der **Liebling, -e**   darling, favorite; **~sdichter** favorite poet; **~sfach** favorite subject; **~splatz** favorite place

liebst-: am ~en   best of all (12G)

das **Lied, -er**   song (4E); **Volks~** folk song

liegen, lag, gelegen   to lie, be (located) (1W); be lying (flat) (6W)

der **Liegestuhl, ⁻e**   lounge chair

lila   purple

die **Lilie, -n**   lily, iris

die **Limona'de, -n**   soft drink (2W); **die Zitro'nen~** carbonated lemonade

die **Linguis'tik**   linguistics

die **Linie, -n**   line

link-   left; **auf der ~en Seite** on the left

links   left (5W); **erste Straße ~** first street to the left (5W)

die **Linse, -n**   lentil; lense

die **Lippe, -n**   lip

der **Lippenstift, -e**   lipstick

die **Liste, -n**   list

der **Liter, -**   liter

das **Loch, ⁻er**   hole

locken   to lure, attract

der **Löffel, -**   spoon (3W); **Ess~** tablespoon (of); **Tee~** teaspoon

logisch   logical

lokal'   local(ly)

los: ~·werden* to get rid of; **etwas ~ sein*** to be happening, going on; **Was ist ~?** What's the matter? (9W)

lose   loose

lösen   to solve; **sich ~ von** to free o.s. of

die **Lösung, -en**   solution

der **Löwe, -n, -n / die Löwin, -nen**   lion; Leo

die **Luft**   air (14E)

der **Luftangriff, -e**   air raid

die **Luftbrücke**   airlift

die **Luftpost**   airmail; **der ~leichtbrief, -e** aerogram; **per ~** by airmail

die **Luftverschmutzung**   air pollution

die **Lüge, -n**   lie

die **Lust**   inclination, desire, fun; **Ich habe (keine) ~ (zu) . . .** I (don't) feel like (doing s.th.) . . . (9W)

lustig   funny (4E); **reise~** eager to travel; **sich ~ machen (über** + *acc.*) to make fun of (14W)

luxemburgisch   Luxembour-gish

luxuriös'   luxurious

der **Luxus**   luxury

M

machen   to make, do (2W); **Spaß ~** to be fun (4E); **Mach's gut!** Take care! (S1); **Was machst du Schönes?** What are you doing?; **(Das) macht nichts.** (That) doesn't matter. That's okay. (5E); **Das macht zusammen . . .** That comes to . . .

die **Macht, ⁻e**   power (14E); **die Westmächte** (*pl.*) western Allies

das **Mädchen, -**   girl (1W)

das **Magazin', -e**   magazine; feature (e.g., on TV)

die **Magd, ⁻e**   maid

der **Magen, ⁻ / -**   stomach

der **Magis'ter, -**   M.A.

die **Mahlzeit, -en**   meal; **~!** Enjoy your meal (food)!

das **Mahnmal, -e**   memorial (of admonishment)

der **Mai**   May (S4); **im ~** in May (S4)

der **Mais**   corn

mal   times, multiplied by

das **Mal, -e: das erste ~**   the first time (11E); **zum ersten ~** for the first time (11E); **~ sehen!** Let's see.

malen   to paint (9W)

der **Maler, -**   painter(-artist) (10W); house painter

man   one (they, people, you) (3E)

das **Management** management
manch- many a, several, some (7G)
manchmal sometimes (3E)
mangelhaft poor, approx. grade E
die **Mango, -s** mango
manipuliert' manipulated
der **Mann, ̈er** man, husband (1W)
das **Männchen, -** little guy
männlich masculine, male
die **Mannschaft, -en** team
der **Mantel, ̈** coat (S3)
das **Manuskript', -e** manuscript
das **Märchen, -** fairy tale
die **Margari'ne, -n** margarine
die **Mari'ne, -n** navy
der **Markt, ̈e** market (2W)
die **Marmela'de, -n** marmalade, jam (2W)
der **März** March (S4); **im ~** in March (S4)
die **Maschi'ne, -n** machine
der **Maschi'nenbau** mechanical engineering
die **Maske, -n** mask
die **Massa'ge, -n** massage
die **Masse, -n** mass
die **Massenmedien** (*pl.*) mass media
die **Maßnahme, -n** step, measure
das **Material'** material
die **Mathematik'** mathematics
die **Mauer, -n** (thick) wall (14W)
das **Maul, ̈er** big mouth (of animal)
der **Maurer, -** bricklayer
maurisch Moorish
die **Maus, ̈e** mouse; **~efalle, -n** mousetrap
das **Mecha'niker, -** mechanic
die **Medien** (*pl.*) media
das **Medikament', -e** medicine, medication
die **Medizin'** (the field of) medicine
das **Mehl** flour
mehr more (12G); **immer ~** more and more (12G)
mehrer- (*pl.*) several (10G)
die **Mehrwertsteuer, -n** value-added tax
meiden, mied, gemieden to avoid
mein my (1W,7G)

meinen to mean, think (be of an opinion) (11W); **Wenn du meinst.** If you think so. (11W)
die **Meinung, -en** opinion; **meiner ~ nach** in my opinion
die **Meinungsumfrage, -n** opinion poll
meist-: am ~en most (12G)
meistens mostly, usually (7E)
der **Meister, -** master
die **Melo'ne, -n** melon
die **Menge, -n** crowd
die **Mensa** student cafeteria (3W)
der **Mensch, -en, -en** human being, person; people (*pl.*) (1E,2G); **~!** Man! Boy! Hey!; **Mit~** fellow man
die **Menschheit** mankind
das **Menü', -s** complete meal (usually including soup and dessert); **Tages~** daily special
merken to notice, find out
die **Messe, -n** (trade) fair
das **Messegelände, -** fairgrounds
das **Messer, -** knife (3E); **Taschen~** pocket knife
das **Metall', -e** metal
der **Meter, -** meter
die **Metropo'le, -n** metropolis
der **Metzger, -** butcher
die **Metzgerei', -en** butcher shop
mies miserable
die **Miete, -n** rent
mieten to rent (6W)
der **Mieter, -** renter, tenant
die **Mietwohnung, -en** apartment
der **Mikrowellenherd, -e = die Mikrowelle, -n** microwave oven
die **Milch** milk (2W)
das **Militär'** military, army
militä'risch military
der **Million', -en** million
der **Millionär', -e** millionaire
mindestens at least
der **Mindestbestellwert** minimum order
die **Mineralogie'** mineralogy
das **Mineral'wasser** mineral water
der **Minimumbestellwert** minimal order
minus minus

die **Minu'te, -n** minute (S5)
mischen to mix; **darun'ter ~** to blend in
der **Mischmasch** mishmash, hodgepodge
die **Mischung, -en** (**aus** + *dat.*) mixture (of)
misera'bel miserable
die **Mission', -en** mission
mit- together, with, along (7G)
mit (+ *dat.*) with (3G); along
das **Mitbestimmungsrecht** right to participate in the decision-making process
der **Mitbewoh'ner, -** housemate (13W)
mit·bringen* to bring along (7G)
mit·fahren* to drive along
mit·feiern to join in the celebration
das **Mitgefühl** compassion
mit·gehen* to go along (7G)
mit·kommen* to come along (7G)
das **Mitleid** pity
mit·machen to participate
mit·nehmen* to take along (7G)
mit·schicken to send along
mit·singen* to sing along
der **Mittag, -e** noon; **heute ~** today at noon (8G)
das **Mittagessen, -** lunch, midday meal (3W); **beim ~** at lunch; **zum ~** for lunch (3W)
mittags at noon (S5); **dienstag~** Tuesdays at noon (8G)
die **Mitte** middle, center (14E); **~ des Monats** in the middle of the month (8G); mid
das **Mittel, -** means (of)
das **Mittelalter** Middle Ages; **im ~** in the Middle Ages (14W)
mittelalterlich medieval
(das) **Mitteleuro'pa** Central Europe
mittelgroß average size
mitten: ~ durch right middle of (6E); **~drin** right in the middle of it
die **Mitternacht: um ~** at midnight

der **Mittwoch** Wednesday (S4);
  am ~ on Wednesday (S4);
  Ascher~ Ash Wednesday
  mittwochs on Wednesdays
  (2E)

die **Möbel** (*pl.*) furniture (6W)

die **Mobilität'** mobility
  möbliert' furnished
  möchten, mochte, gemocht
  to like (2W;5G); **Ich**
  möchte . . . I would like (to
  have) . . . (2W)

das **Modal'verb, -en** modal auxiliary

die **Mode** fashion; custom;
  ~puppe, -n fashion doll
  modern' modern
  mögen (mag), mochte,
  gemocht to like (5G)
  möglich possible (7W); **Das**
  ist doch nicht ~! That's
  impossible. (7W); **alle ~en**
  all sorts of

die **Möglichkeit, -en** possibility

der **Mohnkuchen** poppy-seed
  cake

der **Moment', -e** moment;
  (Einen) ~! One moment.
  Just a minute. (2W,7W)
  momentan' at the moment,
  right now

der **Monat, -e** month (S4); **im ~**
  a month, per month (6W);
  einen ~ for one month (8G)
  monatelang for months
  monatlich monthly (8G)

der **Mond, -e** moon

der **Mondschein** moonlight

der **Montag** Monday (S4); **am ~**
  on Monday (S4)
  montags on Mondays (2E)

die **Moral'** moral

der **Mörder, -** murderer
  morgen tomorrow (S4,4W);
  Bis ~! See you tomorrow;
  für ~ for tomorrow (S2);
  über~ the day after tomorrow (4W)

der **Morgen** morning: **Guten ~!**
  Good morning. (S1); **heute**
  ~ this morning (8G)
  morgens in the morning
  (S5), every morning;
  montag~ Monday
  mornings (8G)

das **Mosaik', -e** mosaic
  müde tired (S1); **tod~** dead
  tired

die **Müdigkeit** fatigue

der **Müll** garbage (15W)

der **Müller, -** miller

der **Müllschlucker, -** garbage
  disposal

die **Mülltonne, -n** garbage can
  (15W)

die **Mülltrennung** waste separation (15W)

der **Mund, ÷er** mouth (9W)

die **Mundharmonika, -s** harmo-
  nica
  mündlich oral(ly)

die **Münze, -n** coin (15E)

die **Muschel, -n** clam; shell

das **Muse'um, Muse'en** museum (5W)

die **Musik'** music (9E)
  musika'lisch musical (11W)

der **Musiker, -** musician

die **Musik'wissenschaft** musi-
  cology

(der) **Muskat'** nutmeg

der **Muskelkater** charley horse;
  Ich habe ~. My muscles
  are sore. I have a charley
  horse.

das **Müsli** whole-grain granola
  müssen (muss), musste,
  gemusst to have to, must
  (5G)

das **Muster, -** example, model;
  pattern

der **Mustersatz, ÷e** sample sentence

die **Mutter, ÷** mother (1W);
  Groß~ grandmother (1W);
  Schwieger~ mother-in-law;
  Urgroß~ great-grandmother
  mütterlich motherly

der **Mutterschaftsurlaub** maternity leave

die **Muttersprache** mother
  tongue

die **Mutti, -s** Mom

N

na well; **~ also** well; **~ gut**
  well, all right; **~ ja** well
  (12W); **~ klar** of course
  (13W) **~ und?** So what?
  (8W)

nach- after, behind (7G)

nach (+ *dat.*) after (time), to
  (cities, countries, continents) (3G); **je ~** depending
  on

der **Nachbar, -n, -n** neighbor
  (1E,2G)

die **Nachbarschaft, -en** neighborhood; neighborly relations
  nachdem' (*conj.*) after
  (11G); **je ~** depending on
  nacherzählt retold, adapted

die **Nachfrage** demand
  nachher afterwards
  nach·kommen* to follow
  nach·laufen* to run after
  nach·machen to imitate

der **Nachmittag, -e** afternoon;
  am ~ in the afternoon;
  heute ~ this afternoon
  (8G)
  nachmittags in the afternoon (S5), every afternoon

der **Nachname, -ns, -n** last name

die **Nachricht, -en** news (10E)
  nächst- next (11E)

die **Nacht, ÷e** night (7W); **Gute**
  ~! Good night!; **heute ~**
  tonight (8G)

der **Nachteil, -e** disadvantage

die **Nachteule, -n** night owl

das **Nachthemd, -en** nightgown

der **Nachtisch** dessert (3W);
  zum ~ for dessert (3W)

der **Nachtmensch, -en, -en** night
  person
  nachts during the night,
  every night (8G); **sonntag~**
  Sunday nights (8G)

der **Nachttisch, -e** nightstand

der **Nachtwächter, -** night
  watchman
  nach·werfen* to throw after
  nackt naked

die **Nadel, -n** needle
  nah (näher, nächst-) near
  (5W,12G)

die **Nähe** nearness, vicinity; **in**
  der ~ nearby; **in der ~ von**
  (+ *dat.*) near (5W)
  nähen to sew

der **Name, -ns, -n** name (8G);
  Mein ~ ist . . . My name is
  . . . (S1); **Mädchen~**
  maiden name; **Vor~** first
  name; **Nach~** last name;
  Spitz~ nickname (14W)
  nämlich namely, you know

die **Nase, -n** nose (9W); **Ich**
  habe die ~ voll. I'm fed up
  (with it). (10W)
  nass wet

die **Nation′, -en** nation, state
national′ national
der **Nationalis′mus** nationalism
die **Nationalität′, -en** nationality
die **Natur′** nature (15W)
das **Natur′kind, -er** child of nature
natür′lich natural(ly), of
course (2W)
das **Natur′schutzgebiet, -e** nature preserve (15W)
die **Natur′wissenschaft, -en**
natural science (13W)
natur′wissenschaftlich scientific
der **Nebel** fog
neben (+ *acc. / dat.*) beside,
next to (6G)
nebeneinander next to each
other
das **Nebenfach, ̈er** minor (field
of study) (14W)
der **Nebensatz, ̈e** subordinate
clause
neblig foggy
der **Neffe, -n, -n** nephew
negativ negative(ly)
**nehmen (nimmt), nahm,
genommen** to take (S3);
to have (food) (3G)
nein no (S1)
die **Nelke, -n** carnation
nennen, nannte, genannt to
name, call (11E); **Ich
nenne das . . .** That's what I
call . . .
nett nice (11W)
neu new (S3); **Was gibt′s
Neues . . . ?** What's new?
(9W)
die **Neuauflage, -n** new edition
neugierig curious
der **Neujahrstag** New Year's
Day
nicht not (S1); **~ wahr?** is-
n't it? (S4); **gar ~** not at all
(13E); **~ nur . . . sondern
auch** not only . . . but also
(3E)
die **Nichte, -n** niece
nichts nothing (3W);
~ Besonderes / Neues
nothing special / new
(9W)
nicken to nod
nie never (4E); **noch ~** never
before, not ever (4E)

sich **nieder·legen** to lie down
niedrig low
niemand nobody, no one
(11E)
das **Niemandsland** no man's
land
nimmermehr never again;
no longer
nirgends nowhere; **ins
Nirgends** into nowhere
nobel noble
noch still (4W); **~ (ein)mal**
once more, again (S2); **~
ein** another (3W); **~ etwas** s.th. else; **~ lange
nicht** not by far; **~ nie**
never (before), not ever
(4E); **~ nicht** not yet (6E);
Sonst ~ etwas? Anything
else?; **was ~?** what else?;
weder . . . ~ neither . . . nor
(10E); **immer ~** still
der **Nominativ, -e** nominative
die **Nonne, -n** nun
der **Norden: im ~** in the north
(1W)
nördlich (von) to the north,
north (of) (1W)
normal′ normal; by regular
(surface) mail
(das) **Nor′wegen** Norway
der **Nor′weger, -** the Norwegian
nor′wegisch Norwegian
die **Note, -n** grade (13W)
nötig necessary, needed
die **Notiz′, -en** note; **~en
machen** to take notes
der **Novem′ber** November (S4);
im ~ in November (S4)
nüchtern sober
die **Nudel, -n** noodle (3W)
null zero (S3)
der **Numerus clausus** admissions restriction at a university
die **Nummer, -n** number (7W)
nun now (11E); **~, . . .**
well, . . . (12W)
nur only (S4)
die **Nuss, ̈e** nut
der **Nussknacker, -** nutcracker
nutzen to use

O

ob (*conj.*) if, whether (4G);
Und ~! You bet. You better
believe it. (14W)

oben upstairs (6W); up; **~
genannt** above mentioned
der **Ober, -** waiter (3W); **Herr
~!** Waiter! (3W)
die **Oberin, -nen** mother superior
die **Oberschule, -n** college
preparatory school (see
Gymnasium)
die **Oberstufe, -n** upper level
das **Objekt′, -e** object
objektiv′ objective(ly)
das **Obst** (*sg.*) fruit (2W)
obwohl (*conj.*) although
(4G)
oder or (S3,2G); **~?** Isn't it?
Don't you think so? (14W)
der **Ofen, ̈** oven
offen open (2E)
offiziell′ official
öffnen to open; **~ Sie das
Buch auf Seite . . .!** (S5)
Open the book on / to
page . . . !
öffentlich public (10E)
oft often (2E)
ohne (+ *acc.*) without (2G)
das **Ohr, -en** ear (9W)
Oje′! Oops! Oh no!
der **Ökolo′ge, -n, -n / die
Ökolo′gin, -nen** ecologist
die **Ökologie′** ecology
ökolo′gisch ecologic(ally)
das **Ökosystem′, -e** ecological
system
der **Okto′ber** October (S4);
im ~ in October (S4)
das **Öl, -e** oil; lotion
oliv′ olive-colored
der **Ölwechsel** oil change
die **Olympia′de, -n** Olympics
die **Oma, -s** grandma
das **Omelett′, -s** omelet
der **Onkel, -** uncle (1W)
der **Opa, -s** grandpa
die **Oper, -n** opera (10W);
Seifen~ soap opera
die **Operet′te, -n** operetta
das **Opfer, -** victim
optimal′ optimal
optimis′tisch optimistic
oran′ge (color) orange (S2)
die **Oran′ge, -n** orange (2W)
das **Orches′ter, -** orchestra
(10W)
ordentlich orderly; regular
die **Ordinal′zahl, -en** ordinal
number (4W)

die **Ordnungszahl, -en** ordinal number

die **Organisation', -en** organization

(sich) **organisie'ren** to organize

die **Orgel, -n** organ

die **Orientie'rung** orientation

das **Original', -e** original

der **Ort, -e** place, location; town (12E)

der **Ossi, -s** *(nickname)* East German

der **Osten: im ~** in the east (1W)

(das) **Ostern: zu ~** at/for Easter (4W); **Frohe ~!** Happy Easter.

(das) **Österreich** Austria (1W)

der **Österreicher, -** the Austrian (1W)

österreichisch Austrian

östlich (von) east (of), to the east (of) (1W)

der **Ozean, -e** ocean

P

paar: ein ~ a couple of, some (2E)

das **Paar, -e** couple, pair

pachten to lease

packen to pack (7E); to grab

die **Pädago'gik** education

das **Paddelboot, -e** canoe

paddeln to paddle

das **Paket', -e** package, parcel (8W)

die **Paket'karte, -n** parcel form

die **Palatschinken** *(pl.)* crêpes

das **Panora'ma** panorama

die **Panne, -n** mishap

der **Panzer, -** tank

das **Papier', -e** paper (S2)

der **Papier'krieg** paper work, red tape

das **Papier'warengeschäft, -e** office supply store

die **Pappe** cardboard

das **Paradies'** paradise

der **Paragraph', -en, -en** paragraph

das **Parfüm', -s** perfume

der **Park, -s** park (5W)

die **Parkanlage, -n** park

parken to park (15W)

das **Parkett': im ~** (seating) in the orchestra

der **Parkplatz, -̈e** parking lot

parlamenta'risch parliamentary

die **Partei', -en** (political) party

das **Parter're: im ~** on the first / ground floor (6W)

das **Partizip', -ien** participle

der **Partner, -** partner (11W)

die **Party, -s** party (4W)

der **Pass, -̈e** passport (7W)

passen to fit; **Was passt?** What fits?; **Das passt mir nicht.** That doesn't suit me.

passend appropriate, suitable

passie'ren (ist) to happen (11W)

passiv passive

das **Passiv** passive voice

pauken to cram

die **Pause, -n** intermission, break (10W); **eine ~ machen** to take a break

das **Pech** tough luck; **~ haben*** to be unlucky (4E); **~ gehabt!** Tough luck!; **Du ~ vogel!** You unlucky thing!

der **Pekine'se, -n, -n** Pekinese

pendeln (ist) to commute; **hin- und her·~** to commute back and forth

die **Pension', -en** boarding house; hotel (7E)

die **Pensionie'rung** retirement

das **Perfekt** present perfect

permanent' permanent

perplex' baffled

die **Person', -en** person; **pro ~** per person

persön'lich personal(ly)

die **Persön'lichkeit, -en** personality

die **Perspekti've, -n** perspective

pessimis'tisch pessimistic

der **Pfannkuchen, -** pancake

der **Pfarrer, -** (Protestant) minister; cleric

der **Pfeffer** pepper (3W)

die **Pfeffermin'ze** peppermint

die **Pfeife, -n** pipe

pfeifen, pfiff, gepfiffen to whistle, boo

der **Pfeil, -e** arrow

das **Pferd, -e** horse (11W); **arbeitsam wie ein ~** really working hard

der **Pferdewagen, -** horse-drawn buggy

(das) **Pfingsten** Pentecost

der **Pfirsich, -e** peach

die **Pflanze, -n** plant

das **Pflaster, -** bandaid

pflaume plum-colored

die **Pflaume, -n** plum

die **Pflegemutter, -̈** foster mother

pflegen to take care of; **er pflegt zu tun** he usually does

die **Pflegeversicherung, -en** long-term care insurance

die **Pflicht, -en** duty, obligation

das **Pflichtfach, -̈er** required subject

das **Pfund, -e** pound (2W); **zwei ~** two pounds (of) (2W)

die **Pharmazie'** pharmaceutics, pharmacy

die **Philologie'** philology

der **Philosoph', -en, -en** philosopher

die **Philosophie'** philosophy

die **Physik'** physics

der **Physiker, -** physicist

physisch physical(ly)

das **Picknick, -s** picnic

picknicken to (have a) picnic; **~ gehen*** to go picnicing

piepen to peep, chirp; **Bei dir piept's!** You're cuckoo. You must be kidding.

der **Pilot', -en, -en** pilot

der **Pinsel, -** paintbrush

die **Pizza, -s** pizza (3W)

der **Plan, -̈e** plan (12W); **Spiel~** schedule of performances

planen to plan (15W)

die **Planier'raupe, -n** bulldozer

das **Plastik** plastic

die **Plastiktüte, -n** plastic bag

die **Platte, -n** record; platter

der **Plattenspieler, -** record player

der **Platz, -̈e** (town) square, place (5W); seat

die **Platzanweiser, -** usher

das **Plätzchen, -** cookie (2W)

plötzlich suddenly (11E)

der **Plural, -e (von)** plural of

plus plus

das **Plusquamperfekt** past perfect

der **Pole, -n, -n / die Polin, -nen** native of Poland

(das) **Polen** Poland

polnisch Polish

die **Politik'** politics

der **Poli'tiker, -** politician
die **Politik'(wissenschaft)** political science, politics
poli'tisch political(ly)
die **Polizei'** (*sg.*) police
der **Polizist', -en, -en** policeman (12W)
die **Pommes frites** (*pl.*) French fries (3W)
der **Po(po), -s** behind
populär' popular
die **Popularität'** popularity
das **Portemonnaie, -s** wallet
der **Portier', -s** desk clerk
das **Porto** postage
das **Porträt, -s** portrait
(das) **Portugal** Portugal
der **Portugie'se, -n, -n / die Portugiesin, -nen** the Portuguese
portugie'sisch Portuguese
das **Porzellan'** porcelain
die **Post** post office (5W); mail (8W)
der **Postbote, -n, -n / die Postbotin, -nen** mail carrier
der **Postdienst** postal service
der **Posten, -** position
das **Postfach, ̈er** PO box (8W)
das **Posthorn, ̈er** bugle
die **Postkarte, -n** plain postcard
die **Postleitzahl, -en** zip code (8W)
die **Postwertzeichen** (*pl.*) postage
prägen to shape, influence
das **Praktikum, Praktika** practical training, internship (12E)
praktisch practical(ly) (6W)
die **Präposition', -en** preposition
das **Präsens** present time
präsentie'ren to present
der **Präsident', -en, -en** president
die **Praxis** practical experience; practice
der **Preis, -e** price; prize
die **Preiselbeeren** (*pl.*) type of cranberries
die **Presse** press; **Tages~** daily press
das **Presti'ge** prestige
prima great, wonderful (S4)
primitiv' primitive
der **Prinz, -en, -en** prince

die **Prinzes'sin, -nen** princess
das **Prinzip', -ien** principle; **im ~** in principle
privat' private (10E)
das **Privat'gefühl, -e** feeling for privacy
das **Privileg', Privile'gien** privilege
pro per
die **Probe, -n** test; **auf die ~ stellen** to test
probie'ren to try
das **Problem', -e** problem (6W); **(Das ist) kein ~.** (That's) no problem. (6W)
problema'tisch problematic
das **Produkt', -e** product
die **Produktion'** production; **Buch~** book publishing
der **Produzent', -en, -en** producer
produzie'ren to produce
der **Profes'sor, -en** professor (13W)
das **Profil', -e** profile
profitie'ren to profit
das **Programm', -e** program, channel (10W)
der **Programmie'rer, -** programmer
das **Projekt', -e** project
das **Prono'men, -** pronoun
proportional' proportional(ly)
die **Prosa** prose
Prost! Cheers!; **~ Neujahr!** Happy New Year!
der **Protest', -e** protest
protestie'ren to protest
protzen to brag
das **Proviso'rium** provisional state
das **Prozent', -e** percent
die **Prüfung, -en** test, exam (1W); **eine ~ bestehen*** to pass an exam (13W); **bei einer ~ durch·fallen*** to flunk an exam (13W); **eine ~ machen** to take an exam (13W)
der **Psalm, -e** psalm
das **Pseudonym', -e** pseudonym
der **Psychia'ter, -** psychiatrist
die **Psychoanaly'se** psychoanalysis
der **Psycholo'ge, -n, -n / die Psycholo'gin, -nen** psychologist

die **Psychologie'** psychology
psycholo'gisch psychological(ly)
das **Publikum** audience; **Stamm~** regular clients
der **Pudel, -** Poodle
die **Puderdose, -n** compact
der **Pudding, -s** pudding (3W)
der **Pulli, -s** sweater (S3)
der **Pullo'ver, -** pullover, sweater (S3); **Rollkragen~** turtleneck sweater
der **Punkt, -e** point
pünktlich on time
die **Puppe, -n** doll
die **Pute, -n** turkey hen
putzen to clean; **sich die Zähne ~** to brush one's teeth (9G)
die **Putzfrau, -en** cleaning lady
die **Pyrami'de, -n** pyramid

Q

der **Quadrat'meter, -** square meter
die **Qual, -en** torment, agony
die **Qualifikation', -en** qualification; **Zusatz~** additional qualification
qualifiziert' qualified
die **Qualität', -en** quality
die **Quan'tität** quantity
der **Quark** (sour skim milk) curd cheese
das **Quartal', -e** quarter (university) (13W)
das **Quartett', -e** quartet
das **Quartier', -s** (*or* **-e**) lodging
der **Quatsch** nonsense (7W)
die **Quelle, -n** source
quer durch all across
die **Querflöte, -n** flute
das **Quintett', -s** quintet
das **Quiz** quiz
die **Quote, -n** quota

R

das **Rad, ̈er** bicyle, bike (9W); **~ fahren*** to bicycle (9W)
das **Radies'chen, -** radish
das **Radio, -s** radio (6W)
der **Rand, ̈er** edge
der **Rang, ̈e** theater balcony; **im ersten ~** in the first balcony
der **Rasen, -** lawn
sich **rasie'ren** to shave o.s. (9G)

der **Rat** advice, counsel (12E)
raten (rät), riet, geraten to advise, guess
das **Rathaus, ̈er** city hall (5W)
(das) **Rätoromanisch** Romansh
die **Ratte, -n** rat
rauchen to smoke
der **Raum** space
räumen to clear
das **Raumschiff, -e** spaceship
reagie′ren (auf + *acc.*) to react (to)
die **Reaktion′, -en** reaction
die **Real′schule, -n** high school, grades 5–10
rebellie′ren to rebel
rechnen to calculate; **~ mit** to count on; **Damit hat niemand gerechnet.** Nobody expected / was counting on that.
die **Rechnung, -en** check, bill (3W)
das **Recht, -e** right; **Du hast ~.** You're right. (12W)
recht: Das geschieht dir ~. That serves you right.
recht-: auf der ~en Seite on the right side
rechts right (5W); **erste Straße ~** first street to the right (5W)
der **Rechtsanwalt, ̈e** die **Rechtsanwältin, -nen** lawyer (12W)
der **Rechtsradikalis′mus** right-wing radicalism
die **Rechtswissenschaft** study of law
die **Rede, -n** speech (15W); **indirekte ~** indirect speech
reden (mit/über) to talk (to/about) (15W)
die **Redewendung, -en** idiom, saying
reduzie′ren to reduce
das **Referat′, -e** oral presentation (13W); **ein ~ halten*** to give an oral presentation (13W)
reflexiv′ reflexive
das **Reform′haus, ̈er** health-food store
das **Regal′, -e** shelf (6E)
regeln to regulate
der **Regen** rain
der **Regenschirm, -e** umbrella

die **Regie′rung, -en** government
das **Regi′me, -s** regime
die **Region′, -en** region
regional′ regional(ly)
der **Regisseur′, -e** director (film)
registrie′ren to register
regnen to rain; **Es regnet.** It's raining. (S4).
regulie′ren to regulate
reiben, rieb, gerieben to rub
reich rich (11W)
das **Reich, -e** empire, kingdom
reichen to suffice; **~ bis an** (+ *acc.*) to go up to
der **Reichtum, ̈er** wealth
reif ripe; mature
die **Reife** maturity; **Mittlere ~** diploma of a *Realschule*
die **Reihe, -n** row
das **Reihenhaus, ̈er** townhouse (6E)
der **Reis** rice (3W)
die **Reise, -n** trip (7E); **eine ~ machen** to take a trip, travel
das **Reisebüro, -s** travel agency
der **Reiseführer, -** travel guide; guide book
der **Reiseleiter, -** tour guide (12W)
reiselustig fond of traveling
reisen (ist) to travel (7E)
der **Reisescheck, -s** traveler's check
reißen, riss, ist gerissen to tear
reiten, ritt, ist geritten to ride (on horseback)
die **Reitschule, -n** riding academy
der **Rektor, -en** university president
relativ′ relative(ly)
das **Relativ′pronomen, -** relative pronoun
der **Relativ′satz, ̈e** relative clause
die **Religion′, -en** religion
das **Rendezvous, -** date
rennen, rannte, ist gerannt to run
renommiert′ renowned, well-known
renovie′ren to renovate (15W)
die **Rente, -n** pension
die **Rentenversicherung** social security

das **Rentier, -e** reindeer
reparie′ren to repair
der **Repräsentant′, -en, -en** representative
repräsentativ′ representative
der **Reservat′, -e** reservation, preserve
reservie′ren to reserve (7E)
die **Reservie′rung, -en** reservation
die **Residenz′, -en** residence
resignie′ren to resign, give up
der **Rest, -e** rest
das **Restaurant′, -s** restaurant (3E)
restaurie′ren to restore (15W)
die **Restaurie′rung** restoration
das **Resultat′, -e** result
retten to save, rescue (15W)
das **Rezept′, -e** recipe
die **Rezeption′, -en** reception (desk)
die **Richtgeschwindigkeit, -en** recommended speed
richtig right, correct (S2); **Das ist genau das Richtige.** That's exactly the right thing.
die **Richtigkeit** correctness
die **Richtung, -en** direction; **in ~** in the direction of
riechen, roch, gerochen to smell
das **Riesenrad, ̈er** ferris wheel
riesig huge, enormous
die **Rindsroulade, -n** stuffed beef roll
der **Ring, -e** ring
rings um (+ *acc.*) all around
das **Risiko, Risiken** risk
der **Ritter, -** knight
der **Rock, ̈e** skirt (S3)
der **Rolladen, ̈** (roller) shudder
die **Rolle, -n** role; **Haupt~** leading role
das **Rollo′, -s** (roller) shudder
der **Rollschuh, -e** roller skate; **~ laufen*** to rollerskate; **~ laufen gehen*** to go roller skating
der **Roman′, -e** novel (10W)
die **Romanis′tik** study of Romance languages
die **Roman′tik** romanticism
roman′tisch romantic

römisch Roman
rosa pink (S2)
die Rös(ch)ti (*pl.*) fried potatoes
   with bacon cubes
die Rose, -n rose
der Rosenkohl Brussel sprouts
die Rosi′ne, -n raisin
rost rost-colored
rot (ö) red (S2); bei Rot at a
   red light
die Rote Grütze berry sauce
   thickened with cornstarch
(das) Rotkäppchen Little Red
   Riding Hood
das Rotkraut red cabbage
rötlich reddish
rot werden* to blush
die Roula′de, -n stuffed beef
   roll
die Routi′ne, -n routine
der Rückblick, -e review
der Rücken, - back
die (Hin- und) Rückfahrkarte,
   -n round-trip ticket
   (8W)
die Rückreise, -n return trip
der Rückgang, ¨e decline
das Rückgrat spine, backbone;
   kein ~ haben to have no
   guts
der Rucksack, ¨e backpack
der Rückweg, -e return trip, way
   back
ruck, zuck quickly, in a jiffy
das Ruderboot, -e rowboat
rudern to row
rufen, rief, gerufen to call
die Ruhe peace and quiet
der Ruhetag, -e holiday, day off
ruhig quiet (7W)
der Ruhm fame
der Rumä′ne, -n, -n / die
   Rumä′nin, -nen Ruman-
   ian
rumä′nisch Rumanian
rühren to stir; sich ~ to
   move; Ich kann mich
   kaum ~. I can hardly move.
der Rum rum
rund round
die Rundfahrt, -en sightseeing
   trip
der Rundfunk radio,
   broadcasting
der Russe, -n, -n / die Russin,
   -nen the Russian
russisch Russian
(das) Russland Russia

S

der Saal, Säle large room, hall
die Sache, -n thing, matter;
   Haupt~ main thing
sächsisch Saxonian
der Saft, ¨e juice (2W)
sagen to say, tell (S2); Wie
   sagt man . . .? How does
   one say. . . ? (S2); Sag mal!
   Say. Tell me (us, etc.).; wie
   gesagt as I (you, etc.) said
die Sahne cream; Alles ist ~.
   Everything is fine.
die Saison′, -s season
der Salat′, -e salad, lettuce (2W)
die Salbe, -n ointment
das Salz salt (3W)
salzig salty
die Salzstange, -n pretzel stick
sammeln to collect (9W)
die Sammelstelle, -n collection
   site (15W)
der Sammler, - collector
der Samstag Saturday (S4);
   am ~ on Saturday (S4)
samstags on Saturdays
   (2E)
der Samt velvet
der Sand sand
die Sanda′le, -n sandal
sanft gentle
der Sängerknabe, -n, -n choir
   boy
der Satellit′, -en satellite
der Satz, ¨e sentence (1W);
   Bilden Sie einen ~! Make
   a sentence.
die Sau, ¨e dirty pig, *lit.* sow;
   Mensch, so ein ~wetter!
   Man, what lousy weather!
sauber clean, neat (S3)
der Sauerbraten marinated pot
   roast
die Sauberkeit cleanliness
sauber·machen to clean
sauer sour; acid
der Sauerbraten marinated pot
   roast
das Sauerkraut sauerkraut
die Säule, -n column
die S-Bahn, -en = Schnellbahn
   commuter train
das Schach: ~ spielen to play
   chess (9W)
schade too bad (S4)
schaden to hurt, damage
   (15W)

der Schaden, ¨ damage; Total′~
   total loss
das Schaf, -e sheep
der Schäferhund, -e German
   shepherd
schaffen to work hard, ac-
   complish; das kann ich
   nicht ~ I can't do it
schaffen, schuf, geschaffen
   to create
der Schaffner, - conductor
die Schale, -n shell, peel
die (Schall)platte, -n record
der Schalter, - ticket window,
   counter (7W)
sich schämen to be embarrassed
der Schaschlik, -s shish kebab
schätzen to appreciate
schauen to look; Schau
   mal! Look!
das Schaufenster, - display window; in die ~ sehen* to go
   window-shopping
das Schaumbad, ¨er bubble bath
der Schauspieler, - actor (10W)
der Scheck, -s check (7W)
sich scheiden lassen* to get
   divorced
die Scheidung, -en divorce
   (11W)
der Schein, -e certificate; Geld~
   banknote (15E)
scheinen, schien, geschienen
   to shine (S4); to seem
   (like), appear (to be) (14E)
schenken to give (as a present) (4W)
die Schere, -n scissors
die Schicht, -en level; die obere
   ~ upper level (of society)
schick chic, neat (11W)
schicken to send (8W)
schief crooked, not straight;
   ~ gehen* to go wrong
die Schießbude, -n shooting
   gallery
das Schiff, -e ship, boat; mit
   dem ~ fahren* to go by
   boat
das Schild, -er sign
die Schildkröte, -n turtle
der Schinken, - ham
der Schirm, -e umbrella
der Schlachter, - butcher
der Schlafanzug, ¨e pyjama
schlafen (schläft), schlief,
   geschlafen to sleep (3E)
schlaflos sleepless

der **Schlafsack, ̈e** sleeping bag

die **Schlafstadt, ̈e** bedroom community

das **Schlafzimmer, -** bedroom (6W)

schlagen (schlägt), schlug, geschlagen to hit

der **Schlager, -** popular song, hit

der **Schlagersänger, -** pop singer

die **Schlagsahne** whipped / whipping cream

das **Schlagzeug** the drums

die **Schlange, -n** snake

schlank slim, slender (11W)

schlau clever, sly; **~ wie ein Fuchs** pretty clever

das **Schlauchboot, -e** rubber boat

schlecht bad(ly) (S1)

schleifen, schliff, geschliffen to drag

der **Schlemmer, -** gourmet

schließen, schloss, geschlossen to lock, close

das **Schließfach, ̈er** locker

schließlich after all, in the end (15W)

schlimm bad, awful

der **Schlips, -e** tie

der **Schlitten, -** sled

das **Schloss, ̈er** palace (5W)

der **Schlüssel, -** key (7W)

der **Schlüsseldienst** locksmith service

das **Schlüsselkind, -er** latchkey child

schmecken to taste (good); **Das schmeckt (gut).** That tastes good. (3W)

schmelzen (schmilzt), schmolz, ist geschmolzen to melt

der **Schmerz, -en** pain, ache; **~en haben** to have pain (9W); **Ich habe (Kopf)-schmerzen.** I have a (head)ache. (9W)

der **Schmetterling, -e** butterfly

der **Schmied, -e** blacksmith

der **Schmutz** dirt

der **Schmutzfink, -en** (dirty) pig

schmutzig dirty (S3)

das **Schnäppchen, -** bargain (8E)

der **Schnee** snow

schneiden, schnitt, geschnitten to cut

schneien to snow; **es schneit** it's snowing (S4)

schnell quick(ly), fast (S3)

der **Schnellweg, -e** express route

das **Schnitzel, -** veal cutlet

der **Schock, -s** shock

die **Schokola'de** chocolate

schon already (1E); **das ~** that's true, sure

schön fine, nice, beautiful (S4)

schonen to protect (15W)

die **Schönheit** beauty

der **Schrank, ̈e** closet, cupboard (6W); **Gefrier~** freezer; **Kleider~** closet; **Küchen~** kitchen cabinet; **Kühl~** refrigerator

der **Schrebergarten, ̈** leased garden

der **Schreck** shock; **Auch du ~!** My goodness!

schrecklich terrible (11W)

schreiben, schrieb, geschrieben to write (S3); **~ Sie bitte!** Please, write! (S5); **Wie schreibt man das?** How do you write that?; **~ an** (+ acc.) to write to (10G)

die **Schreibmaschine, -n** typewriter

der **Schreibtisch, -e** desk (6W)

schreien, schrie, geschrien to scream

die **Schrift, -en** script; (hand)-writing

schriftlich written; in writing

der **Schriftsteller, -** writer, author

der **Schritt, -e** step; pre-unit

schubsen to shove

schüchtern shy

der **Schuh, -e** shoe (S3); **Sport~** gym shoe, sneaker

die **Schule, -n** school (5W)

der **Schüler, -** pupil, student

die **Schulter, -n** shoulder

die **Schüssel, -n** bowl

schütteln to shake

schütten (in + acc.) to dump, pour (into), spill

der **Schutz** protection (15W)

der **Schütze, -n, -n** rifleman, marksman; Sagittarius

schützen to protect (15W)

der **Schwabe, -n, -n / die Schwäbin, -nen** the Swabian

(das) **Schwaben(land)** Swabia

schwäbisch Swabian

die **Schwäche, -n** weakness

der **Schwager, -** brother-in-law

die **Schwägerin, -nen** sister-in-law

schwanger pregnant

schwänzen to skip class

schwärmen (von + dat.) to rave (about)

schwarz (ä) black (S2); **~·fahren*** to ride [on a bus or subway] without paying

das **Schwarzbrot, -e** rye bread

der **Schwede, -n, -n / die Schwedin, -nen** the Swede

(das) **Schweden** Sweden

schwedisch Swedish

schweifen (ist) to wander, roam; **immer weiter·~** to continue wandering

schweigen, schwieg, geschwiegen to remain silent, shut up

das **Schwein, -e** pig, pork; scoundrel; **~ haben*** to be lucky; **~ gehabt!** I was (you were, etc.) lucky!

der **Schweinebraten** pork roast

die **Schweinshaxe, -n** pigs' knuckles

der **Schweiß** sweat

die **Schweiz** Switzerland (1W)

der **Schweizer, -** the Swiss (1W)

Schweizer / schweizerisch Swiss

schwer heavy, hard, difficult (6E)

die **Schwerarbeit** hard / menial work

die **Schwester, -n** sister (1W)

das **Schwesterchen, -** little sister

Schwieger- in-law; **der ~vater** father-in-law; **die ~mutter** mother-in-law; **die Schwiegereltern** parents-in-law

schwierig difficult (13W)

die **Schwierigkeit, -en** difficulty

das **Schwimmbad, ̈er** (large) swimming pool

schwimmen, schwamm, geschwommen to swim (9W); **~ gehen*** to go swimming (9W)

der **Schwimmer, -** swimmer

schwühl humid

der **Schwund** loss

(das) **Schwyzerdütsch** Swiss-German

ein **Sechstel** one sixth

der **See, -n** lake (1W)

die **See** sea, ocean

der **Seehund, -e** seal

das **Segelboot, -e** sailboat

segelfliegen gehen* to go gliding

segeln to sail; **~ gehen*** to go sailing

sehen (sieht), sah, gesehen to see, look (3G); **Mal ~!** Let's see! (13W)

die **Sehenswürdigkeit, -en** sight (worth seeing), attraction

sehr very (S4)

die **Seide, -n** silk

die **Seife, -n** soap

die **Seifenoper, -n** soap opera

die **Seilbahn, -en** cable car

sein his, its (7G)

sein (ist), war, ist gewesen to be (S1, S2, 2G); **Ich bin's.** It's me.; **So bin ich.** That's the way I am.; **Wie wär's mit . . . ?** How about . . . ?

seit (+ *dat.*) since, for (time) (3G)

die **Seite, -n** page; **auf ~** on page, to page (S5); **auf der einen / anderen ~** on the one / other hand

die **Sekretär', -e** secretary (12W)

der **Sekt** champagne (4W)

die **Sekun'de, -n** second (S5)

selbst -self; **~ wenn** even if

selbstbewusst self-confident (11W)

das **Selbstbewusstsein** self-confidence

selbstständig self-employed, independent (11W)

die **Selbstständigkeit** independence

selten seldom

seltsam strange, weird (11W)

das **Semes'ter, -** semester (13W)

das **Seminar', -e** seminar paper (13W)

die **(Seminar')arbeit, -en** term paper

der **Sender, -** (radio or TV) station

die **Sendung, -en** (part of) TV or radio program (10E)

das **Sendungsbewusstsein** sense of mission

der **Senf** mustard

der **Septem'ber** September (S4); **im ~** in September (S4)

die **Serie, -n** series

servie'ren to serve (food)

die **Serviet'te, -n** napkin (3W)

Servus! Hi! *(Bavaria, Austria)*

die **Sesamstraße** Sesame Street

der **Sessel, -** armchair (6W)

der **Sessellift, -e** chairlift

setzen to set (down), put (6W); **sich ~** to sit down (9G); **sich dazu ~** to join sb. at a table

seufzen to sigh

das **Shampoo', -s** shampoo

die **Show, -s** show

sicher sure, certain (4W); safe, secure (12W); **Ja, ~** Yes, sure. (9W); **Es geht ~.** It's probably all right.

die **Sicherheit** safety, security (12W)

sicherlich surely, certainly, undoubtedly (15W)

sichern to secure

sichtbar visible

die **Siedlung, -en** settlement, subdivision

der **Sieg, -e** victory

der **Sieger, -** victor

die **Siegermächte** (*pl.*) victorious Allies

siezen to call each other *"Sie"*

das **Silber** silver

silbern (*adj.*) silver

(das) **Silves'ter: zu ~** at / for New Year's Eve (4W)

singen, sang, gesungen to sing (4W)

sinken, sank, ist gesunken to sink

der **Sinn, -e** mind, sense, meaning; **in den ~ kommen*** to come to mind

die **Situation', -en** situation

die **Sitzecke, -n** corner bench (seating arrangement)

sitzen, saß, gesessen to sit (be sitting) (6W)

der **Ski, -er** ski; **~ laufen*** to ski (9W); **~ laufen gehen*** to go skiing (9W)

der **Skilanglauf** cross-country skiing

der **Skiläufer, -** skier

der **Skilift, -e** skilift

der **Skorpion', -e** scorpion; Scorpio

skrupellos unscrupulous

die **Skulptur', -en** sculpture

die **Slawis'tik** study of Slavic language and literature

die **Slowa'kische Republik'** Slovac Republic

so so, like that; in this way; **~ lala** so so; **~ dass** (*conj.*) so that (13E); **~ ein** such a (7G); **~ so** fair; **~ . . . wie** as . . . as (12G)

sobald' as soon as

die **Socke, -n** sock

das **Sofa, -s** sofa, couch (6W)

sofort' immediately, right away (11E)

sogar' even (6W)

sogenannt so-called

der **Sohn, ¨e** son (1W)

solch- such (7G)

der **Soldat', -en, -en** soldier

sollen (soll), sollte, gesollt to be supposed to (5G)

der **Sommer, -** summer (S4); **im ~** in the summer (S4)

das **Sonderangebot, -e: im ~** on sale, special

sondern but (on the contrary) (5W,5G); **nicht nur . . . ~ auch** not only . . . but also (3E)

der **Sonderstatus** special status

die **Sonne** sun; **Die ~ scheint.** The sun is shining. (S4)

der **Sonnenaufgang, ¨e** sunrise

die **Sonnenblume, -n** sunflower

die **Sonnenbrille, -n** sunglasses

die **Sonnencreme, -s** suntan lotion

das **Sonnenöl** suntan lotion

der **Sonnenuntergang, ¨e** sunset

sonnig sunny

der **Sonntag** Sunday (S4); **am ~** on Sunday (S4); **Toten~** Memorial Day

sonntags on Sundays (2E)

sonst otherwise; **~ noch etwas?** Anything else?

die **Sorge, -n** worry, concern; **sich ~en machen (um)** to be concerned, worry (about) (12E)

die **Sorte, -n** type, variety

sortie'ren to sort

die **Soße, -n** sauce, gravy

die **Souveränität'** sovereignty

soviel' as much as; **~ ich weiß** as much as I know

sowie' as well as

sowieso' anyway, anyhow (13E)

sowje'tisch Soviet

sowohl . . . als auch as well as

die **Sozial'hilfe** social welfare

der **Sozialis'mus** socialism

sozialis'tisch socialist

die **Sozial'kunde** social studies

der **Sozial'pädagoge, -n, - n / die Sozial'pädago'gin, -nen** social worker

die **Soziologie'** social studies, sociology

das **Spanferkel, -** suckling pig

(das) **Spanien** Spain (1W)

der **Spanier, -** the Spaniard (1W)

spanisch Spanish (1W)

spannend exciting, suspenseful (10W)

sparen to save (money or time) (6E)

der **Spargel** asparagus

die **Sparkasse, -n** savings bank

sparsam thrifty

sparta'nisch Spartan, frugal

der **Spaß, ¨e** fun; **~ machen** to be fun (4E); **Das macht (mir) ~.** That's fun. I love it.

spät late; **Wie ~ ist es?** How late is it? What time is it? (S5)

später later; **Bis ~!** See you later! (S1)

der **Spatz, -en** sparrow

die **Spätzle** (*pl.*) tiny Swabian dumplings

spazie'ren gehen* to go for a walk (9W)

der **Spazier'gang, ¨e** walk

der **Speck** bacon

die **Speise, -n** food, dish; **Vor~** appetizer

die **Speisekarte, -n** menu (3W)

der **Speisewagen, -** dining car

die **Spekulation', -en** speculation

das **Spezial'geschäft, -e** specialty shop

die **Spezialisie'rung** specialization

der **Spezialist', -en, -en** specialist

die **Spezialität', -en** specialty

der **Spiegel, -** mirror

das **Spiel, -e** game, play (9W)

spielen to play; **Tennis ~** to play tennis (S5); **Ball ~** to play ball; **Basketball ~** to play basketball; **Dame ~** to play checkers (9W); **Feder-ball ~** to play badminton; **Fußball ~** to play soccer; **Schach ~** to play chess (9W); **Volleyball ~** to play volleyball

der **Spielplan, ¨e** program, performance schedule

der **Spielplatz, ¨e** playground

das **Spielzeug** toys

der **Spieß, -e** spit; spear

der **Spinat'** spinach

die **Spindel, -n** spindle

spinnen, spann, gesponnen to spin (yarn) (11E); **Du spinnst wohl!** You're crazy!

das **Spinnrad, ¨er** spinning-wheel

der **Spitz, -e** pomeranian

die **Spitze, -n** top; **(Das ist) ~!** (That's) super.

der **Spitzname, -ns, -n** nick-name (14W)

spontan' spontaneous

der **Sport** sport(s) (9W); **~ treiben*** to engage in sports (9W)

der **Sportler, -** athlete

sportlich athletic, sporty (11W)

der **Sportverein, -e** sports club

die **Sprache, -n** language (1W)

-sprachig -speaking

sprechen (spricht), sprach, gesprochen to speak (S3); **~ Sie langsam bitte!** Speak slowly, please.; **~ Sie lauter!** Speak louder. (S3); **Man spricht . . .** They (people) speak . . . ; **~ von** (+ *dat.*) / **über** (+ *acc.*) to speak of / about (10G); **Ist . . . zu ~?** May I speak to . . . ?

der **Sprecher, -** speaker

die **Sprechsituation', -en** (situation for) communication

das **Sprichwort, ¨er** saying, proverb

springen, sprang, ist gesprungen to jump (11E)

das **Spritzgebäck** cookies shaped with a cookie press

der **Spruch, ¨e** saying

der **Sprung, ¨e** jump

spülen to wash dishes

die **Spülmaschine, -n** dish-washer

das **Spülmittel, -** dishwashing liquid; detergent

die **Spur, -en** trace

der **Staat, -en** state (15E)

der **Staatenbund** confederation

staatlich public; **~ kontrol-liert** state-controlled

die **Staatsangehörigkeit** citizen-ship

der **Staatsbürger, -** citizen

der **Staatssicherheitsdienst = die Stasi** GDR secret police

das **Stadion, -s** stadium

die **Stadt, ¨e** city, town (1W)

das **Stadtbild, -er** overall ap-pearance of a city

das **Städtchen, -** small town

der **Stadtplan, ¨e** city map (5W)

der **Stadtrand** outskirts (of town)

der **Stamm, ¨e** tribe

der **Stammbaum, ¨e** family tree

stammen (aus + *dat.***)** to stem (from), originate

stampfen to stomp

der **Standard, -s** standard

das **Standesamt, ¨er** marriage registrar

stark (ä) strong; **echt ~** (*coll.*) really super

starren to stare

die **Station', -en** (bus) stop

die **Statis'tik, -en** statistic

statt (+ *gen.*) instead of (8G)

der **Stau, -s** traffic jam

der **Staub** dust

der **Staubsauger, -** vacuum

staunen to be amazed

stechen (sticht), stach, gestochen to prick

der **Stechschritt** goosestep

stecken to stick

stehen, stand, gestanden to stand (or be standing) (6W)

stehen bleiben* to come to a stop, remain standing

stehlen (stiehlt), stahl, gestohlen to steal

steif stiff

steigen, stieg, ist gestiegen to go up, rise, climb

steigern to increase

steil steep

der **Stein, -e** stone

der **Steinbock, ⸚e** ibex; Capricorn

die **Stelle, -n** job, position, place (12W); **an deiner ~** in your shoes, if I were you (13E)

stellen to stand (upright), put (6W); **eine Frage ~** to ask a question

das **Stellenangebot, -e** job opening / offer

sterben (stirbt), starb, ist gestorben to die (11E)

die **Stereoanlage, -n** stereo set

das **Sternzeichen, -** sign of the zodiac

die **Steuer, -n** tax; **Mehrwert~** value-added tax

der **Steuerberater, -** tax consultant

das **Stichwort, ⸚er** key word

Stief-: die ~eltern stepparents; **die ~mutter** stepmother; **der ~vater** step-father

der **Stiefel, -** boot

der **Stier, -e** bull; Taurus

der **Stil, -e** style

still quiet

die **Stimme, -n** voice

stimmen to be right / true; **(Das) stimmt.** (That's) true. (That's) right. (6W)

die **Stimmung, -en** mood

das **Stipen'dium, Stipen'dien** scholarship (13W)

die **Stirn** forehead

der **Stock, ⸚e** stick

der **Stock, -werke: im ersten ~** on the second floor (6W)

stöhnen to complain, moan

der **Stollen, -** Christmas cake / bread with almonds, raisins, and candied peel

stolz (auf + acc.) proud (of) (15E)

der **Stopp, -s** stop

das **Stoppschild, -er** stop sign

der **Storch, ⸚e** stork

stören to bother, disturb

der **Strafzettel, -** (traffic violation) ticket

strahlen to shine

der **Strand, ⸚e** beach

die **Straße, -n** street (5W)

die **Straßenbahn, -en** streetcar (5W)

das **Straßenbild** scene

die **Strategie', -n** strategy

strate'gisch strategic

der **Strauch, ⸚er** bush

streben (nach) to strive (for)

der **Streber, -** one who studies excessively, grind

strebsam ambitious

die **Streife, -n** patrol; **~ fahren** to patrol

der **Streifen, -** strip of land

streng strict(ly)

der **Stress** stress; **zu viel ~** too much stress

das **Stroh** straw

der **Strom** electricity

die **Strophe, -n** stanza

die **Struktur', -en** structure; *here:* grammar

der **Strumpf, ⸚e** stocking

das **Stück, -e** piece; **ein ~** a piece of (2W); **zwei ~** two pieces of (2W); (theater) play (10W)

der **Student', -en, -en** student (S5, 13W)

das **Studen'tenheim, -e** dorm (6W)

die **Studiengebühr, -en** tuition

der **Studienplatz, ⸚e** opening to study at the university

studie'ren to study a particular field, be a student at a university (4E); **~ (an +** *dat.*) to be a student at a university (4E)

der **Studie'rende (ein Studierender) / die Studierende, -n, -n** student

das **Studio, -s** studio

das **Studium, Studien** course of study (13W)

der **Stuhl, ⸚e** chair (S2,5W)

die **Stunde, -n** hour, class lesson (S5, 12W); **in einer halben ~** in half an hour (8W); **in einer Viertel~** in 15 minutes (8W); **in einer Dreiviertel~** in 45 minutes (8W)

stundenlang for hours (5E)

der **Stundenplan, ⸚e** schedule (of classes)

stur stubborn

stürmisch stormy

das **Subjekt', -e** subject

die **Suche** search; **auf der ~ nach** in search for

suchen to look for (2W); **gesucht wird** wanted

der **Süden: im ~** in the south (1W)

südlich (von) south (of), to the south (of) (1W)

super superb, terrific (S4)

der **Superlativ, -e** superlative

der **Supermarkt, ⸚e** supermarket (2W)

su'permodern' very modern

die **Suppe, -n** soup (3W)

surfen to surf; **wind~ gehen** to go windsurfing

süß sweet, cute (11W); **Ach, wie ~!** Oh, how cute! (11W)

das **Sweatshirt, -s** sweatshirt (S3)

der **Swimmingpool, -s** pool

das **Symbol', -e** symbol

die **Sympathie'** congeniality

sympa'thisch congenial, likable (11W); **sie sind mir ~** I like them

die **Symphonie', -n** symphony

die **Synago'ge, -n** synagogue

synchronisiert' dubbed

die **Synthe'tik** synthetics

das **System', -e** system (13W)

der **System'berater, -** computer consultant

die **Szene, -n** scene

T

die **Tabel'le, -n** chart

die **Tablet'te, -n** pill

die **Tafel, -n** (black)board (S2); **Gehen Sie an die ~!** Go to the (black)board.

der **Tag, -e** day (S4); **(Guten) ~!** Hello! Hi! (informal)! (S1); **am ~** during the day (6E); **eines Tages** one day (8G); **jeden ~** every day (8G); **~ der Arbeit** Labor Day

tagelang for days

-tägig days long

täglich daily (8G)

das **Tal, ⸚er** valley

das **Talent', -e** talent

talentiert' talented (11W)

die **Tankstelle, -n** gas station

die **Tante, -n** aunt (1W)

der **Tanz, ⸚e** dance

tanzen to dance (4W)

die **Tasche, -n** bag, pocket (7W); **Hand~** handbag

die **Taschenlampe, -n** flashlight

das **Taschenmesser, -** pocket knife

die **Tasse, -n** cup (2E); **eine ~** a cup of (2E)

die **Tatsache, -n** fact

taub deaf

die **Taube, -n** dove; pigeon

tauchen (in + *acc.*) to dip (into)

tauschen to trade

das **Taxi, -s** taxi (5W)

die **Technik** technic

der **Techniker, -** technician

das **Technikum, -s** technical college

technisch technical

die **Technologie', -n** technology

der **Tee, -s** tea (2W)

der **Teenager, -** teenager

der **Teil, -e** part (1E)

teilen to share, divide (13E)

teilmöbliert partly furnished

die **Teilnahme** participation

teil·nehmen* (an + *dat.*) to participate, take part (in) (13E)

teils partly

die **Teilung, -en** division

teilweise partly

das **Telefon', -e** telephone (6W)

telefonie'ren to call up, phone (8W)

der **Telefonist', -en, -en** switchboard operator

die **Telefon'karte, -n** telephone card (8W)

die **Telefon'nummer, -n** telephone number (8W)

die **Telefon'zelle, -n** telephone-booth

die **Telekommunikation'** telecommunications

der **Teller, -** plate (3W)

das **Temperament', -e** temperament

temperament'voll dynamic (11W)

die **Temperatur', -en** temperature

das **Tempo, -s** speed;

das **Tempolimit, -s** speed limit

das **Tennis: ~ spielen** to play tennis (S5)

der **Teppich, -e** carpet (6W)

die **Terras'se, -n** terrace

der **Terrier, -** Terrier

das **Testament', -e** last will and testament

testen to test

teuer expensive (S3)

der **Teufel, -** devil

der **Text, -e** text

das **Textil'geschäft, -e** clothing store

das **Thea'ter, -** theater (5W)

das **Thema, Themen** topic

der **Theolo'ge, -n, -n / die Theolo'gin, -nen** theologian

die **Theologie'** theology

die **Theorie', -n** theory

die **Therapie', -n** therapy

das **Thermal'bad, ̈er** thermal bath / spa

das **Thermome'ter, -** thermometer

thüringisch Thuringian

der **Tiefbau** civil engineering

der **Tiefbauingenieur', -e** civil engineer

tiefgefroren frozen

die **Tiefkühlkost** frozen foods

das **Tier, -e** animal (11W); **Jedem ~chen sein Pläsierchen.** To each his own.

die **Tierart, -en** animal species

tierlieb fond of animals

das **Tierkreiszeichen, -** sign of the zodiac

die **Tiermedizin'** veterinary science

der **Tiger, -** tiger

die **Tinte** ink

das **Tintenfass, ̈er** inkwell

der **Tipp, -s** hint

der **Tisch, -e** table (S2,5W); **Nacht~** nightstand

die **Tischdecke, -n** tablecloth

der **Tischler, -** cabinet maker

das **Tischtennis: ~ spielen** to play ping-pong

das **Tischtuch, ̈er** tablecloth

der **Titel, -** title

tja well (12W)

der **Toast, -s** (piece of) toast

das **Toastbrot, -e** (piece of) toast

der **Toaster, -** toaster

die **Tochter, ̈** daughter (1W)

der **Tod** death

todmüde dead-tired

Toi, toi, toi! Good luck!

die **Toilet'te, -n** toilet (6W)

tolerant' tolerant

toll great, terrific (S4)

die **Toma'te, -n** tomato (2W)

der **Ton, ̈e** tone, note, pitch

der **Topf, ̈e** pot

das **Tor, -e** gate (14E)

die **Torte, -n** (fancy) cake

tot dead

total' total(ly)

der **Total'schaden, ̈** total wreck

töten to kill

die **Tour, -en** tour

der **Touris'mus** tourism

der **Tourist', -en, -en** tourist (5W)

der **Touris'tikumsatz** spending on travel

das **Tournier', -e** tournament

die **Tracht, -en** (folk) dress / garb

der **Trachtenzug, ̈e** parade with people dressed in traditional dress / garb

traditionell' traditional(ly)

tragen (trägt), trug, getragen to carry (3G); to wear (3G)

die **Tragetasche, -n** tote bag

der **Trainer, -** coach

das **Training** training

die **Träne, -n** tear

das **Transport'flugzeug, -e** transport plane

transportie'ren to transport

die **Traube, -n** grape

trauen to trust

der **Traum, ̈e** dream

träumen (von) to dream (of) (11W)

der **Träumer, -** dreamer

traurig sad (10W)

die **Traurigkeit** sadness

die **Trauung, -en** wedding ceremony

(sich) **treffen (trifft), traf, getroffen** to meet (with) (9W); **Freunde ~** to meet / get together with friends (9W)

das **Treffen, -** meeting, reunion

der **Treffpunkt, -e** meeting place

treiben, trieb, getrieben to push; **Sport ~** to engage in sports (9W)

der **Treibhauseffekt** greenhouse effect

(sich) **trennen** to separate (15W)

die **Treppe, -n** stairs, stairway

das **Treppenhaus, ̈er** stairwell

treten (tritt), trat, ist getreten to step

treu faithful, true, loyal

sich **trimmen** to keep fit

trinken, trank, getrunken
to drink (2W)

das **Trinkgeld, -er** tip

der **Trockner, -** dryer

die **Trommel, -n** drum

die **Trompe'te, -n** trumpet

trotz (+ *gen.* / [+ *dat.*]) in
spite of (8G)

trotzdem nevertheless, in
spite of that (6E)

trüb(e) dim

die **Trümmer** (*pl.*) rubble; ruins

der **Trümmerhaufen, -** pile of
rubble

der **Tscheche, -n, -n / die**
Tschechin, -nen the
Czech

tschechisch Czech

die **Tschechische Republik'** =
(das) Tschechien Czech
Republic

die **Tschechoslowakei'** (former)
Czechoslovakia

Tschüss! So long; (Good-)
bye! (S1)

das **T-Shirt, -s** T-shirt (S3)

tüchtig (very) capable

tun (tut), tat, getan to do
(4W)

tünchen to whitewash

die **Tür, -en** door (S2)

der **Türke, -n, -n / die Türkin,**
-nen the Turk

die **Türkei'** Turkey

türkis' turquoise

türkisch Turkish

der **Turm, ⸚e** tower (14W);
steeple

turnen to do sports or gym-
nastics

die **Turnhalle, -n** gym;

der **Turnverein, -e** athletic club

die **Tüte, -n** bag

typisch typical(ly) (15E)

U

die **U-Bahn, -en = Untergrund-**
bahn subway (5W)

über (+ *acc.* / *dat.*) over,
above (6G); about (10G)

überall everywhere (3E)

überein'·stimmen to agree

überfüllt' (over)crowded

überhaupt' at all; ~ **nicht**
not at all; ~ **kein Problem**
no problem at all

das **Überhol'verbot, -e** no passing

überle'ben to survive

überneh'men* to take over

übermorgen the day after
tomorrow (4W)

übernach'ten to spend the
night (7E)

die **Übernach'tung, -en**
(overnight) accommoda-
tions

überprü'fen to check

überra'schen to surprise
(4W)

die **Überra'schung, -en** surprise
(4W); **So eine ~!** What a
surprise! (4W)

überset'zen to translate

die **Überset'zung, -en** translation

die **Überstunde, -n** overtime

üblich usual, customary

übrig bleiben* to be left, remain

übrigens by the way (15W)

die **Übrigen** the rest

die **Übung, -en** exercise, practice

das **Ufer, -** riverbank

die **Uhr, -en** watch, clock;
o'clock (S5); **Wie viel ~ ist**
es? What time is it? (S5);
~zeit time of the day (7W)

der **Uhrmacher, -** watchmaker

der **Ukrai'ner, -** Ukrainian

ukrai'nisch Ukrainian

um- around, over, from one
to the other (7G)

um (+ *acc.*) around (the cir-
cumference) (2G); at . . .
o'clock (S5); **~ . . . zu** in
order to (9G); **fast ~** almost
over

um sein* to be over / up;
deine Zeit ist ~ your time is
up

sich **um·blicken** to look around

der **Umbruch, ⸚e** radial change

die **Umfrage, -n** survey; **Mei-**
nungs~ opinion poll

die **Umgangsform, -en** manners

umge'ben (von) surrounded
by

die **Umge'bung** (*sg.*) surroundings (14W)

umgekehrt vice versa

(um-)kippen (ist) to tip over

um·leiten to detour

umliegend surrounding

ummau'ern to surround by
a wall

der **Umsatz** sales, spending

sich **um·sehen*** to look around

der **Umstand, ⸚e** circumstance

um·steigen* (**ist**) to change
(trains etc.) (8W)

der **Umtausch** exchange

um·tauschen to exchange

die **Umwelt** environment, surroundings (15W)

umweltbewusst environmentally aware (15W)

sich **um·ziehen*** to change
(clothing), get changed
(9G)

der **Umzug, ⸚e** parade; move,
moving

unabhängig (von) independent (of)

un'attraktiv' unattractive

unbebaut vacant, empty

unbedingt definitely (12E)

unbegehrt undesired

unbegrenzt unlimited

unbequem uncomfortable,
inconvenient (6W)

und and (S1,2G)

und so weiter (usw.) and so
on (etc.) (5E)

unehrlich dishonest (11W)

unentrinnbar inescapable

unerfahren inexperienced

unerwartet unexpected(ly)
(14W)

der **Unfall, ⸚e** accident

unflexibel inflexible

unfreiwillig involuntary

unfreundlich unfriendly
(11W)

der **Ungar, -n, -n** the Hungarian

ungarisch Hungarian

(das) **Ungarn** Hungary

ungebildet uneducated
(11W)

ungeduldig impatient (11W)

ungefähr about, approximately (1E)

ungemütlich unpleasant, uncomfortable

ungenügend insufficient, approx. grade F

ungestört unhindered

unglaublich unbelievable,
incredible; **(Das ist doch)**
~! That's unbelievable /
hard to believe! (10W)

das **Unglück** bad luck
unglücklich unhappy (11W)
unheimlich tremendous(ly), extreme(ly) (14W)
die **Universität', -en = Uni, -s** *(coll.)* university (5W)
unkompliziert' uncomplicated (11W)
unmittelbar right, directly
unmöbliert unfurnished
unmög'lich impossible
unmusikalisch unmusical (11W)
Unrecht haben* to be wrong (11W)
uns us, to us (5G); **bei ~** at our place (3G); in our city / country
unselbstständig dependent (11W)
unser our (7G)
unsicher insecure, unsafe (12W)
der **Unsinn** nonsense (12W)
unsportlich unathletic (11W)
unsympathisch uncongenial, unlikable (11W)
untalentiert untalented (11W)
unten downstairs (6W)
unter (+ *acc. / dat.*) under, below (6G); among (12E); **~einander** among each other
die **Unterdrü'ckung** oppression
der **Untergang** fall, downfall
unterhal'tend entertaining
die **Unterhal'tung** entertainment (10W)
das **Unterneh'men, -** large company (12E)
unterneh'mungslustig enterprising
das **Unterpfand** pledge (for)
der **Unterricht** instruction, lesson, class
der **Unterschied, -e** difference
unterschrei'ben* to sign (7W)
die **Unterschrift, -en** signature
unterstrei'chen, unterstrich, unterstrichen to underline
unterstüt'zen to support
unterwegs' on the go, on the road
untreu unfaithful

unverheiratet unmarried, single (11W)
unverschämt impertinent
die **Unwahrscheinlichkeit** *here:* unreal condition
unwillig reluctant(ly)
unzerstört intact
unzufrieden discontent
unzuverlässig unreliable (11W)
Urgroß-: die ~eltern great-grandparents; **die ~mutter** great-grandmother; **der ~vater** great-grandfather
der **Urlaub** paid vacation (9E); **der Mutterschafts~** maternity leave
ursprünglich original(ly)
der **Urlaubstag, -e** (paid) vacation day
die **USA = Vereinigten Staaten von Amerika** *(pl.)* USA
usw. (und so weiter) etc. (and so on)

V

der **Vampir', -e** vampire
die **Vanil'le** vanilla
die **Variation', -en** variation
variie'ren to vary
die **Vase, -n** vase
der **Vater, ⸚** father (1W); **Groß~** grandfather (1W); **Urgroß~** great-grandfather; **Stief~** step-father
der **Vati, -s** Dad
der **Vegeta'rier, -** vegetarian
verallgemei'nern to generalize
die **Verallgemei'nerung, -en** genralization
(sich) **verändern** to change (14W)
verantwortlich responsible
die **Verantwortung, -en** responsibility (12W)
verantwortungsvoll responsible
das **Verb, -en** verb; **Hilfs~** auxiliary verb; **Modal~** modal auxiliary; **reflexive ~** reflexive verb;
verbannen to ban
verbessern to improve
verbieten, verbot, verboten to forbid, prohibit (15W)
verbinden, verband, verbunden to connect, tie together, link (15E)

verbittert bitter
das **Verbot, -e** restriction
verboten forbidden (15W)
der **Verbrauch** consumption
verbrauchen to consume
der **Verbraucher, -** consumer
verbreiten to distribute, spread
verbreitern to widen
die **Verbreitung, -en** distribution
verbrennen, verbrannte, verbrannt to burn
verbringen* to spend (time)
verbunden in touch, close
die **Verbundenheit** closeness
verdammen to curse; **Verdammt noch mal!** Darn it!
verderben (verdirbt), verdarb, verdorben to spoil
verdienen to earn, make money (12W); to deserve
verdorben rotten
der **Verein, -e** club, association; **Turn~** athletic club
vereinigen to unite; **wieder~** to reunite
die **Vereinigten Staaten (U.S.A.)** *(pl.)* = **die Staaten** *(coll.)* United States (U.S.)
die **Vereinigung** unification (15E)
vereint united (15E)
das **Verfassungsgericht** Constitutional Court
Verflixt! Darn it!
die **Vergangenheit** past (tense); simple past
vergehen* (ist) to pass (time), end
vergessen (vergisst), vergaß, vergessen to forget (10W)
der **Vergleich, -e** comparison
vergleichen, verglich, verglichen to compare (11W)
das **Verhalten** behavior
das **Verhältnis, -se** relationship, condition
verheiratet married (11W)
verhindern to prevent
die **Verkabelung** connecting by cable
verkaufen to sell (2W)
der **Verkäufer, -** salesman, sales clerk (2W)
der **Verkehr** traffic

das **Verkehrsmittel, -** means of transportation

verkrampft tense

der **Verlag, -e** publishing house

verlangen to demand

verlassen (verlässt), verließ, verlassen to leave (14E)

sich **verlaufen*** to get lost

verlegen to transfer, relocate

sich **verlieben (in + acc.)** to fall in love (with) (11W)

verliebt (in + acc.) in love (with) (11W)

verlieren, verlor, verloren to lose (11W)

sich **verloben (mit)** to get engaged (to)

verlobt (mit) engaged (to) (11W)

der **Verlobte (ein Verlobter) / die Verlobte, -n, -n** fiancé(e) (12G)

die **Verlobung, -en** engagement

verlockend tempting

vermieten to rent out (6W)

der **Vermieter, -** landlord

vermissen to miss

vermitteln to help find

verneinen to negate

die **Vernichtung** destruction

die **Vernunft** reason; common sense

verrückt crazy (4E)

verschenken to give away

verschieden various, different (kinds of) (10E)

verschlechtern to deteriorate

verschlingen, verschlang, verschlungen to gulp down, devour

verschlossen locked-up

die **Verschmutzung** pollution (15W)

verschönern to beautify

verschwiegen discreet

verschwinden, verschwand, ist verschwunden to disappear

versichern to insure; **jemandem etwas ~** to assure sb. sth.

die **Versicherung, -en** insurance

der **Versicherungsagent', -en, -en** insurance agent

versinken* to sink (in)

die **Version', -en** version

versorgen to take care of

die **Verspätung** delay; **Der Zug hat ~.** The train is late.

versprechen* to promise (11E)

der **Verstand** reasoning, logic; common sense

verständlich understandable

verständnislos lacking empathy

verständnisvoll understanding

verstecken to hide

verstehen* to understand (S3); **Das verstehe ich nicht.** I don't understand (that). (S5)

versuchen to try (11W)

die **Verteidigung** defense

der **Vertrag, -̈e** contract

das **Vertrauen** trust

vertreiben, vertrieb, vertrieben to chase away

die **Verwaltung, -en** administration

verwandt related

der **Verwandte (ein Verwandter) / die Verwandte, -n, -n** relative

verweigern to refuse

verwenden to use, utilize (15W)

verwitwet widowed

verwöhnen to indulge, spoil; **sich ~ lassen*** to let o.s. be spoiled

das **Verzeichnis, -se** index, catalog

verzeihen, verzieh, verziehen to forgive; **~ Sie (mir)!** Forgive me. Pardon (me)!

die **Verzeihung** pardon; **~!** Excuse me! Pardon me! (5W)

der **Vetter, -** alternate form for *Cousin'*

das **Video, -s** video

der **Videorecorder, -** VCR

die **Videothek, -en** video store

viel- (mehr, meist-) much, many (3W,10G,12G); **ganz schön ~** quite at bit; **so~' ich weiß** as much as I know

vielleicht' perhaps (3E)

vielseitig versatile (11W)

vielsprachig multilingual

viereckig square

die **Viersprachigkeit** speaking four languages

das **Viertel, -: (um) ~ nach** (at) a quarter past (S5); **(um) ~ vor** (at) a quarter to (S5); **in einer ~stunde** in a quarter of an hour (8W); **in einer Drei~stunde** in three quarters of an hour (45 minutes) (8W)

die **Vision', -en** vision

vital' energetic, vital

das **Vitamin', -e** vitamine

der **Vogel, -̈** bird (11W); **Du hast einen ~.** You're crazy.

die **Voka'bel, -n** (vocabulary) word

das **Vokabular'** vocabulary

das **Volk, -̈er** folk; people, nation (14W)

die **Völkerkunde** ethnology

die **Volksherrschaft** *here:* rule by the people

die **Volkskammer (GDR)** house of representatives

das **Volkslied, -er** folk song

der **Volksmarsch, -̈e** group-hiking event

die **Volkspolizei (GDR)** People's Police

der **Volkspolizist, -en, -en = Vopo, -s** member of the GDR People's Police

der **Volksstamm, -̈e** ethnic group

der **Volkswagen, -** VW

die **Volkswirtschaft** (macro)economics

voll full (11E); **Ich habe die Nase ~.** I'm fed up (with it). (10W)

der **Volleyball, -̈e** volleyball

völlig totally

der **Vollzeitstudent, -en, -en** full-time student

von (+ dat.) of, from, by (3G); **~ ... bis** from ... until; **vom ... bis zum** from the ... to the (4W)

vor- ahead, before (7G)

vor (+ acc. / dat.) in front of, before (6G); **~ einer Woche** a week ago (4W); **~ allem** above all, mainly (10E)

voran'·kommen* to advance

der **Vorarbeiter, -** foreman

voraus'gehend preceding

voraus'·sehen* to foresee

vorbei'- past, by (7G)

vorbei'·bringen* to bring over

vorbei'·fahren* to drive by, pass

vorbei'·führen (an + *dat.*) to pass (by), guide along (14W)

vorbei'·gehen* (bei + *dat.*) to pass by (7G)

vorbei'·kommen* to come by, pass by

vorbei' sein* to be over, finished

(sich) **vor·bereiten (auf** + *acc.*) to prepare (for) (13E)

die **Vorbereitung, -en** preparation

die **Vorbeugung, -en** prevention

die **Vorfahrt** right of way

vor·gehen* to proceed; **der Reihe nach ~** to proceed one after the other

vorgestern the day before yesterday (4W)

vor·haben* to plan (to), intend (to)

der **Vorhang, ⸚e** curtain (6W)

vorher ahead (of time), in advance; before, previously

vorher'gehend preceding; **das ~e Wort** antecedent

vor·kommen* (in + *dat.*) to appear (in); **Das kommt mir . . . vor.** That seems . . . to me.

das **(flache) Vorland** *here:* tidal flats

die **Vorlesung, -en** lecture, class (university) (S5); **~sverzeichnis** course catalog

der **Vormittag, -e** (mid-)morning; **heute ~** this (mid-)morning (8G)

der **Vorname, -ns, -n** first name

die **Vorschau** preview

die **Vorsicht: ~!** Careful! (7W)

die **Vorspeise, -n** appetizer, hors d'oeuvre

vor·stellen to introduce; **Darf ich ~?** May I introduce?

sich **vor·stellen** to imagine (12E); **ich stelle mir vor, dass . . .** I imagine that . . . (12E)

die **Vorstellung, -en** performance (10W); idea

der **Vorteil, -e** advantage

der **Vortrag, ⸚e** talk, speech, lecture

vor·tragen* to recite

vorü'bergehend temporary

das **Vorurteil, -e** prejudice

die **Vorwahl, -en** area code (8W)

vor·wärmen to preheat

vor·ziehen* to prefer (9E)

W

die **Waage, -n** scale, Libra

das **Wachs** wax

wachsen (wächst), wuchs, ist gewachsen to grow (15E)

die **Waffe, -n** weapon

die **Waffel, -n** waffel

wagen to dare

der **Wagen, -** car (8W); railroad car (8W)

die **Wahl** choice, selection

wählen to choose; elect; select

das **Wahlfach, ⸚er** elective (subject)

der **Wahnsinn** insanity; **(Das ist ja) ~ !** (That's) That's crazy/awesome / unbelievable! (10W)

wahnsinnig crazy

während (+ *gen.*) during (8G); while (*conj.*)

wahr true; **nicht ~?** isn't it? (S4); **Das kann doch nicht ~ sein!** That can't be true! (7W)

wahrlich (*poetic*) truly

wahrschein'lich probably (13E)

die **Währung, -en** currency

der **Wald, ⸚er** forest, woods (7E)

der **Walzer, -** waltz

die **Wand, ⸚e** wall (S2)

der **Wanderer, -** hiker

wandern (ist) to hike (9W)

der **Wanderweg, -e** (hiking) trail

wann? when?, at what time? (S4,11G)

wäre: Wie wär's mit . . . ? How about . . . ?

die **Ware, -n** goods, wares, merchandise

warm (ä) warm (S4)

die **Wärme** warmth

warnen (vor + *dat.*) to warn (against)

warten to wait; **~ auf (**+ *acc.*) to wait for (10G); **Warten Sie!** Wait! (7W)

warum? why? (2E)

was? what? (S2,2G); **~ für (ein)?** what kind of (a)? (2W); **~ für ein(e) . . . !** What a . . . ! (11W)

das **Waschbecken, -** sink

die **Wäsche** laundry; **~ waschen*** to do the laundry

die **Waschecke, -n** corner reserved for washing

(sich) **waschen (wäscht), wusch, gewaschen** to wash (o.s.) (6W,9G)

der **Waschlappen, -** washcloth (*fig.* wimp)

die **Waschmaschi'ne, -n** washing machine

das **Waschmittel, -** (washing) detergent

das **Wasser** water (2W)

der **Wassermann, ⸚er** Aquarius

der **Wasserski, -er** water ski; **~ laufen*** to water ski; **~ laufen gehen*** to go waterskiing

das **Watt(enmeer)** tidal flats

die **Web-Ecke, -n** *here:* name of updates and online activities

die **Web-Seite, -n** Web page

der **Wechsel** change

der **Wechselkurs, -e** exchange rate

wechseln to (ex)change (7W)

die **Wechselstube, -n** exchange office

weder . . . noch neither . . . nor (10E)

weg away, gone

der **Weg, -e** way, path, trail (5W); route; **nach dem ~ fragen** to ask for directions

wegen (+ *gen.* / [+ *dat.*]) because of (8G)

weg·werfen* to throw away (15W)

weh·tun* to hurt (9W); **Mir tut (der Hals) weh.** My (throat) hurts. I have a sore throat. (9W)

weich soft

weichen, wich, ist gewichen to give way to

die **Weide, -n** willow

(das) **Weihnachten: zu ~** at / for Christmas (4W); **Frohe / Fröhliche ~ !** Merry Christmas!

der **Weihnachtsbaum, ¨e** Christmas tree

das **Weihnachtsessen** Christmas dinner

das **Weihnachtslied, -er** Christmas carol

der **Weihnachtsmann, ¨er** Santa Claus

weil (*conj.*) because (4G)

die **Weile: eine ~** for a while

weilen (*poetic*) to stay, be

der **Wein, -e** wine (2W); **Tafel~** table wine; **Qualitäts~** quality wine; **Qualitäts~ mit Prädikat** superior wine

der **Weinberg, -e** vineyard

weinen to cry (10W)

weinrot wine-red

die **Weinstube, -n** wine cellar, tavern

die **Weintraube, -n** grape

weise wise

die **Weise: auf diese ~** (in) this way (13E)

weiß white (S2)

weit far (5W)

die **Weite** distance; wide-open space(s)

weiter: und so ~ (usw.) and so on (etc.): **~ draußen** farther out; **Wie geht's ~?** How does it go on? What comes next?

weiter- additional

Weiteres *here:* additional words and phrases

weiter·fahren* (*ist*) to drive on, keep on driving (8E); to continue the trip

weiter·geben* to pass on

weiter·gehen* (*ist*) to continue, go on

weiterhin still

welch- which (7G); **Welche Farbe hat . . . ?** What color is . . . ? (S2)

die **Welle, -n** wave

die **Welt, -en** world (11E); **aus aller ~** from all over the world

weltoffen cosmopolitan

wem? (to) whom? (3G)

wen? whom? (2G)

wenig- little (not much), few (10G); **immer ~er** fewer and fewer

wenigstens at least (13E)

wenn (*conj.*) if, (when)ever (4G,11G); **selbst ~** even if

wer? who? (1G); who(so)-ever

die **Werbung** advertisement (10W)

werden (wird), wurde, ist geworden to become, get (3G); **es wird dunkel** it's getting dark; **Was willst du (einmal) ~?** What do you want to be (one day)? (12W); **Ich will . . . ~.** I want to be a . . . (12W)

werfen, (wirft), warf, geworfen to throw (15W)

der **Wert, -e** value; worth

wertvoll valuable

wessen? (+ *gen.*) whose? (8G)

der **Wessi, -s** (*nickname*) West German

die **Weste, -n** vest

der **Westen: im ~** in the west (1W)

westlich von west of

die **Westmächte** (*pl.*) western Allies

der **Wettbewerb, -e** contest

das **Wetter** weather (S4)

wichtig important (1E)

wickeln (in + *acc.*) to wrap (into)

der **Widder, -** ram, Aries

widersteh'en* (+ *dat.*) to withstand

wie? how? (S1); like, as; **~ sagt man . . . ?** How does one say . . . ? (S2); **~ bitte?** What did you say, please? (S5); **so . . . ~** as . . . as (1E); **~ lange?** how long? (4W); **~ gesagt** as I (you, etc.) said

wieder again (S4); **schon ~** already again (S4); **immer ~** again and again, time and again (12G); **Da sieht man's mal ~ !** That just goes to show you. (15W)

der **Wiederaufbau** rebuilding

wieder auf·bauen to rebuild

die **Wiedergeburt** rebirth

wiederho'len to repeat (S2)

die **Wiederho'lung, -en** repetition, review

wieder·hören to hear again; **Auf Wiederhören!** Goodbye. (on the phone) (6W)

wieder·sehen* to see again; **Auf Wiedersehen!** Goodbye (S1)

(wieder)·vereinigen to (re)-unite

die **(Wieder)vereinigung** (re)-unification (14E)

wiegen, wog, gewogen to weigh; **Lass es ~ !** Have it weighed.

der **Wiener, -** the Viennese

die **Wiese, -n** meadow

Wieso' (denn)? How come? Why? (13W)

wie viel? how much? (S3, 3W)

wie viele? how many? (S3, 3W)

wild wild

der **Wille, -ns, -n** will; **Wo ein ~ ist, ist auch ein Weg.** Where there's a will, there's a way.

willkom'men sein* to be welcome

die **Wimper, -n** eyelash

der **Wind, -e** wind

windig windy (S4)

windsurfen gehen* to go wind surfing

der **Winter, -** winter (S4); **im ~** in (the) winter (S4)

das **Winzerfest, -e** vintage festival

wirken to appear

wirklich really, indeed (S4)

die **Wirklichkeit** reality

die **Wirtschaft** economy

wirtschaftlich economical (ly)

der **Wirtschaftsprüfer, -** accountant

das **Wirtschaftswunder** economic boom (*lit.* miracle)

wissen (weiß), wusste, gewusst to know (a fact) (6G); **Ich weiß (nicht).** I (don't) know. (S5); **soviel' ich weiß** as far as I know

die **Wissenschaft, -en** science, academic discipline (13W); **Natur~** natural science(s) (13W) der **Wissenschaftler, -** scientist (12W)

wissenschaftlich scientific

der **Witz, -e** joke; **Mach (doch) keine ~e!** Stop joking!

witzig witty, funny

wo? where? (S2,6G)

die **Woche, -n** week (S4); **diese ~** this week (8G); **zwei ~n** for two weeks (8G)

das **Wochenende, -n** weekend; **am ~** on the weekend (4W); **(Ein) schönes ~!** Have a nice weekend! (4W)

wochenlang for weeks

wöchentlich weekly (8G)

-wöchig weeks long

woher'? from where? (1W)

wohin'? where to? (6G)

das **Wo-Kompositum, -Komposita** wo-compound

wohl *flavoring particle expressing probability*

das **Wohlbefinden** well-being

wohlriechend fragrant

der **Wohlstand** affluence

die **Wohngemeinschaft, -en = WG, -s** group sharing a place to live

wohnen to live, reside (1E)

das **Wohnsilo, -s** (high-rise) apartment (cluster)

der **Wohnsitz, -e** residence

die **Wohnung, -en** apartment (6W)

der **Wohnwagen, -** camper

das **Wohnzimmer, -** living room (6W)

der **Wolf, -e** wolf

die **Wolke, -n** cloud

die **Wolle** wool

wollen (will), wollte, gewollt to want to (5G)

das **Wort, -e** (connected) word; **mit anderen ~en** in other words

das **Wort, -er** (individual) word; **vorher'gehende Wort** antecedent

das **Wörtchen, -** little word

das **Wörterbuch, -er** dictionary

der **Wortschatz** vocabulary

das **Wunder, -** wonder, miracle

wunderbar wonderful(ly) (S1)

sich **wundern: ~ Sie sich nicht!** Don't be surprised.

wunderschön very beautiful (14W)

der **Wunsch, -e** wish (11W); **~traum, -e** ideal dream

(sich) **wünschen** to wish (4W)

die **Wunschwelt** ideal world

die **Wurst, -e** sausage (2W); **Das ist (mir) doch ~!** I don't care.

das **Würstchen, -** wiener, hot dog (2E)

würzen to season

Z

die **Zahl, -en** number (S3); **Ordinal'~** ordinal number (4W)

zählen to count (S3)

der **Zahn, -e** tooth (9W); **sich die Zähne putzen** to brush one's teeth (9G)

der **Zahnarzt, -e / die Zahnärztin, -nen** dentist (12W)

die **Zahnbürste, -n** toothbrush

die **Zahnmedizin'** dentistry

die **Zahnpasta, -pasten** tooth paste

die **Zahnradbahn, -en** cog railway

der **Zahntechniker, -** dental technician

die **Zange, -n** pliers

zart tender

zärtlich affectionate (11W)

die **Zärtlichkeit** affection

der **Zauber** magic (power)

der **Zauberspruch, -e** magic spell

z. B. (zum Beispiel) e.g. (for example)

die **Zehe, -n** toe

das **Zeichen, -** signal, sign

der **Zeichentrickfilm, -e** cartoon, animated film

die **Zeichnung, -en** drawing

der **Zeigefinger, -** index finger

zeigen to show (5W); **Zeig mal!** Show me (us, etc.)!

die **Zeit, -en** time (S5); tense; **die gute alte ~** the good old days

die **Zeitform, -en** tense

zeitgenössisch contemporary

die **Zeitschrift, -en** magazine (10W)

die **Zeitung, -en** newspaper (10W); **Wochen~** weekly newspaper

die **Zelle, -n** cell, booth

das **Zelt, -e** tent

zentral' central(ly)

das **Zentrum, Zentren** center; **im ~** downtown

zerbomben to destroy by bombs

zerbrechen* to break

zerschlagen* to break, smash

zerstören to destroy (15W)

die **Zerstörung** destruction

ziehen, zog, gezogen to pull (11E); to raise (vegetables, etc.)

ziehen, zog, ist gezogen to move (relocate)

das **Ziel, -e** goal, objective; destination

ziemlich quite, fairly (6W)

die **Zigeu'nerin, -nen** gypsy

das **Zimmer, -** room (S2)

der **Zimmerkolle'ge, -n, -n / die Zimmerkolle'gin, -nen** roommate (13W)

der **Zimmernachweis, -e** room-referral service

die **Zimmervermittlung** room-referral agency

das **Zitat', -e** quote

die **Zitro'ne, -n** lemon (2W

die **Zitro'nenlimonade** carbonated lemonade

der **Zitro'nensaft, -e** lemonade

zittern to tremble, shake

zittrig shaky

der **Zoll** customs; toll

die **Zone, -n** zone, area

der **Zoo, -s** zoo

der **Zorn** anger

zu- closed (7G)

zu (+ *dat.*) to, in the direction of, at, for (purpose) (3G); too (S3); closed (2); (+ *inf.*) to (9G); **~ mir** to my place

zu·bleiben* *(ist)* to stay closed

der **Zucker** sugar (3W)

zu·decken to cover

zuerst' (at) first (9W)

der **Zufall, -e** coincidence; **So ein ~!** What a coincidence!

zufrie'den satisfied, content

der **Zug, ̈e**   train (8W); **mit dem
~ fahren*** to go by train
(8W)
zu·halten* to hold closed
das **Zuhau′se** home
zu·hören   to listen (7G);
Hören Sie gut zu! Listen
well/carefully.
der **Zuhörer, -**   listener
die **Zukunft**   future (12W)
zukunftsorientiert′   future-
oriented
zuletzt′   last (of all); finally
zu·machen   to close (7G)
die **Zunge, -n**   tongue
der **Zungenbrecher, -**   tongue
twister
zurück′-   back (7G)
zurück′·bleiben* *(ist)*   to
stay behind
zurück′·bringen*   to bring
back
zurück′·fliegen* *(ist)*   to fly
back

zurück′·geben*   to give
back, return
zurück′·halten*   to hold
back
zurück′·kommen*   to come
back, return (7G)
zurück′·nehmen*   to take
back
zurück′·sehen*   to look back
zurück′·weichen*   to withdraw
sich **zurück′·ziehen***   to withdraw
zusam′men   together (2W);
alle ~ all together; **~ ge-
würfelt** thrown together
zusam′men·fassen   to summarize
die **Zusam′menfassung, -en**
summary
die **Zusam′mengehörigkeit**   af-
filiation; solidarity
zusam′men·wachsen*   to
grow together

der **Zusatz, ̈e**   addition
der **Zuschauer, -**   spectator (10E)
zu·schließen*   to lock
zu·sehen*   to watch; see to it
der **Zustand, ̈e**   conditions
zu·stimmen   to agree
zuverlässig   reliable (11W)
die **Zuverlässigkeit**   reliability
zuvor′   previously; **wie nie ~**
as never before
die **Zwiebel, -n**   onion
der **Zwilling, -e**   twin; Gemini
zwischen (+ *acc. / dat.*)   between (6G); **in~** in the
meantime; **~ durch** in between
die **Zwischenlandung, -en**   stop
over
die **Zwischenzeit**   time in between; **in der ~** in the
meantime, meanwhile

Vocabularies

English-German

Except for numbers, pronouns, **da-** and **wo-**compounds, this vocabulary includes all active words used in this book. If you are looking for certain idioms, feminine equivalents, or other closely related words, use the key word given and look it up in the German-English vocabulary. Irregular t-verbs ("irregular weak verbs") and n-verbs ("strong verbs") are indicated by an asterisk (*); check their forms and auxiliaries in the list of principal parts in the Appendix.

A

able; to be ~   können*
about (approximately)   ungefähr, etwa
above   über (+ *dat.* / *acc.*);
   ~ all   vor allem
abroad   im/ins Ausland
academic discipline   die Wissenschaft, -en
to **accept**   an·nehmen*
ache: I have a (head)~.   Ich habe (Kopf)schmerzen.
acquaintance   der Bekannte (ein Bekannter) / die Bekannte, -n, -n
across (from)   gegenüber (von + *dat.*)
actor   der Schauspieler, -
actual(ly)   eigentlich
ad   die Anzeige, -n
address   die Adresse, -n;
   return ~   der Absender, -
advertising   die Werbung
advice   der Rat
affectionate   zärtlich
afraid: to be ~ (of)   Angst haben* (vor + *dat.*)
after (time)   nach (+ *dat.*);
   (*conj. + past perf.*) nachdem
afternoon   der Nachmittag, -e;
   this ~   heute Nachmittag;
   tomorrow ~   morgen Nachmittag; **yesterday ~**   gestern Nachmittag; **in the ~**   nachmittags, am Nachmittag;
   every ~   nachmittags
afterwards   danach
again   wieder, noch einmal;
   Could you say that ~?
   Wie bitte?; **~ and ~**   immer wieder
against   gegen (+ *acc.*)
ago   vor (+ *dat.*); **a week ~**   vor einer Woche

ahead: straight ~   geradeaus
aid   die Hilfe
air   die Luft
airplane   das Flugzeug, -e
airport   der Flughafen, ¨
all   all-, alles (*sg.*); **That's ~.**   Das ist alles.; **above ~**   vor allem; **after ~**   schließlich;
   ~ sorts of   allerlei
to **allow**   erlauben
allowed: to be ~ to   dürfen*
almost   fast
alone   allein
along (*prefix*)   mit-; (*adv.*) entlang
already   schon
also   auch, ebenfalls
although (*conj.*)   obwohl
always   immer
America   (das) Amerika
American (*adj.*)   amerikanisch; (**person**) der Amerikaner, -
among   unter (+ *acc.* / *dat.*)
and   und
angry: to get ~ about   sich ärgern über (+ *acc.*)
animal   das Tier, -e
annoyed: to get ~ about   sich ärgern über (+ *acc.*)
another   noch ein
to **answer**   antworten
answer   die Antwort, -en
anyhow   sowieso
anyway   sowieso
apart   auseinander
apartment   die Wohnung, -en
to **appear (to be)**   scheinen*, aus·sehen*
to **applaud**   klatschen
apple   der Apfel, ¨
to **apply   (for)**   sich bewerben (um)

approximately   ungefähr, etwa
April   der April; **in ~**   im April
architect   der Architekt, -en, -en
area   das Gebiet, -e, die Gegend, -en
area code   die Vorwahl, -en
arm   der Arm, -e
armchair   der Sessel, -
around (*prefix*)   um-;
   (*prep.*) um (+ *acc.*)
arrival   die Ankunft
to **arrive (in)**   an·kommen* (in + *dat.*)
art   die Kunst, ¨e
artist   der Künstler, -
as   wie; **~ . . . ~**   so . . . wie
to **ask**   fragen, bitten* (um); **to ~ a question**   eine Frage stellen
at (the side of)   an (+ *dat.*);
   (**o'clock**) um . . . (Uhr);
   (**the place of**) bei (+ *dat.*);
   (**a store, etc.**) bei
athletic   sportlich; **un~**   unsportlich
at least   wenigstens
attached   anhänglich
attention: to pay ~   auf·passen
attractive   attraktiv, hübsch
attribute   die Eigenschaft, -en
August   der August; **in ~**   im August
aunt   die Tante, -n
Austria   (das) Österreich
Austrian   (language)   österreichisch; (**person**) der Österreicher, -
author   der Autor, -en
available   frei
away (*prefix*)   ab
awesome: (That's) ~!   Wahnsinn!

B

back *(prefix)* zurück-

bad(ly)   schlecht; schlimm; too ~ schade

bag   die Tasche, -n

baggage   das Gepäck

to bake   backen*

bakery   die Bäckerei, -en

balcony   der Balkon, -s / -e

ballet   das Ballett

banana   die Banane, -n

bank   die Bank, -en

banknote   der (Geld)-schein, -e

barely   kaum

bargain   das Schnäppchen, -

to bathe   baden

bath(room)   das Bad, ̈er; to take a ~ sich baden

to be   sein*; (become) werden*; Be . . .! Sei (Seid, Seien Sie) . . .!

bean   die Bohne, -n

beautiful   (wunder)schön

because *(conj.)* weil, denn; ~ of wegen (+ *gen.* / [*dat.*])

to become   werden*

bed   das Bett, -en; ~room das Schlafzimmer, -

beer   das Bier, -e

before   vor (+ *acc.* / *dat.*); *(conj.)* bevor; not ~ (time) erst; *(adv.)* vorher

to begin   beginnen*, an·fangen*

beginning   der Anfang, ̈e; in the ~ am Anfang; at the ~ of the week Anfang der Woche

behind   hinter (+ *acc.* / *dat.*)

to believe (in)   glauben (*an* + *acc.*); (things) Ich glaube es.; (persons) Ich glaube ihm/ihr; You better ~ it! Und ob!; That's hard to ~! (Das ist doch) unglaublich!; I don't ~ it! Das gibt's doch nicht!

belly   der Bauch, ̈e

to belong to   gehören (+ *dat.*)

below   unter (+ *acc.* / *dat.*)

beside   neben (+ *acc.* / *dat.*)

besides   außer (+ *dat.*); *(adv.)* außerdem

best   best-; it's ~ am besten; All the ~! Alles Gute!

bet: you ~! Und ob!

better   besser; You ~ believe it! Und ob!

between   zwischen (+ *acc.* / *dat.*)

bicycle   das Fahrrad, ̈er

to bicycle   mit dem Fahrrad fahren*

big   groß (ö)

to bike   mit dem Fahrrad fahren*

bill   die Rechnung, -en

billion *(American)* die Milliarde, -n

bird   der Vogel, ̈

birthday   der Geburtstag, -e; on/for the ~ zum Geburtstag; When is your ~? Wann haben Sie Geburtstag?; My ~ is on the . . . Ich habe am . . .(s)ten Geburtstag.; My ~ is in . . . Ich habe im . . . Geburtstag.; Happy ~! Alles Gute/ Herzlichen Glückwunsch zum Geburtstag!

bit: a little ~   ein bisschen

black   schwarz (ä)

blackboard   die Tafel, -n

blouse   die Bluse, -n

blue   blau

boarding house   die Pension, -en

body   der Körper, -

book   das Buch, ̈er

bookstore   die Buchhandlung, -en

border   die Grenze, -n

bored: to get (or be) ~   sich langweilen

boring   langweilig

born   geboren (ist); I was ~ May 3, 1968, in Ulm. Ich bin am 3. 5. 68 in Ulm geboren.

both (things, *sg.*)   beides; *(pl.)* beide

bottle   die Flasche, -n; a ~ of . . . eine Flasche . . .

boy   der Junge, -n, -n

bread   das Brot, -e

break (intermission)   die Pause, -n

breakfast   das Frühstück; (What's) for ~? (Was gibt's) zum Frühstück?; to eat ~ frühstücken

bridge   die Brücke, -n

bright (light)   hell; intelligent

to bring   bringen*; to ~ along mit·bringen*

brother   der Bruder, ̈; ~s and sisters die Geschwister *(pl.)*

brown   braun

to brush (one's teeth)   sich (die Zähne) putzen

to build   bauen, auf·bauen; to re~ wieder auf·bauen; to be built entstehen*; building das Gebäude, -; der Bau, -ten

bus   der Bus, -se

business   das Geschäft, -e

businessman   der Geschäftsmann, ̈er

business management: graduate in ~   Betriebswirt, -e

businesspeople   Geschäftsleute

businesswoman   die Geschäftsfrau, -en

but   aber; doch; not only . . . ~ also nicht nur . . . sondern auch

butter   die Butter

to buy   kaufen

by *(prefix)* vorbei-; *(prep.)* von (+ *dat.*)

C

café   das Café, -s

cafeteria (student)   die Mensa

cake   der Kuchen, -

to call   rufen*; to ~ (up) an·rufen*, telefonieren; to ~ (name) nennen*; to be ~ed heißen*

campground   der Campingplatz, ̈e

can   können*

Canada   (das) Kanada

Canadian *(adj.)* kanadisch; (person) der Kanadier, -

candle   die Kerze, -n

capital   die Hauptstadt, ̈e

car   das Auto, -s, der Wagen, -; railroad ~ der Wagen, -

card   die Karte, -n; post~ die Postkarte, -n; telephone ~ die Telefonkarte, -n

cardigan   die Jacke, -n

to care: Take ~! Mach's gut!

Careful!   Vorsicht!

carpet   der Teppich, -e

carrot   die Karotte, -n

to **carry**   tragen*
case: in any ~   jedenfalls
cash   das Bargeld; **~ register** die Kasse, -n
to **cash (in) (a check)**   ein·lösen
cashier's window   die Kasse, -n
cassette   die Kassette, -n
cat   die Katze, -n
cathedral   der Dom, -e
to **celebrate**   feiern
celebration   das Fest, -e, die Feier, -n
cellular phone   das Handy, -s
cent   der Cent, -s
center   die Mitte
certain(ly)   bestimmt, sicher-(lich)
certificate   der Schein, -e
chair   der Stuhl, ⸚e; **arm~** der Sessel, -
chalk   die Kreide
champagne   der Sekt
change   das Kleingeld
to **change**   (sich) ändern, (sich) verändern; **(clothing)** sich um·ziehen*; **(money, etc.)** wechseln, um·tauschen; **(trains)** um·steigen*
channel   das Programm, -e
characteristic   die Eigen-schaft, -en
charming   charmant
cheap   billig
check   der Scheck, -s; die Rechnung, -en; **traveler's ~** der Reisescheck, -s
cheese   der Käse, -
chic   schick
child   das Kind, -er
choice (of)   die Auswahl (an + *dat.*)
choir   der Chor, ⸚e
Christmas   (das) Weihnach-ten; **at/for ~** zu Weih-nachten
church   die Kirche, -n
citizen   der Bürger, -
city   die Stadt ⸚e; **~ hall** das Rathaus, ⸚er; **~ map** der Stadtplan, ⸚e
civil servant   der Beamte (ein Beamter) / die Beamtin, -nen
to **clap**   klatschen
class (group)   die Klasse, -n; **(time)** die Stunde, -n; **(in-struction, school)** der Un-terricht; **(instruction, uni-versity)** die Vorlesung, -en
clean   sauber
to **clean**   putzen
clerk   der Angestellte (ein Angestellter) / die Angestellte, -n, -n; **(civil servant)** der Beamte (ein Beamter) / die Beamtin, -nen; **(salesman)** der Verkäufer, -
clock   die Uhr, -en; **o'clock** Uhr
to **close**   zu·machen
closed   *(prefix)* zu-; *(prep.)* zu, geschlossen
closet   der Schrank, ⸚e
clothing   die Kleidung
coat   der Mantel, ⸚
coast   die Küste, -n
coffee   der Kaffee
coin   die Münze, -n
cola drink   die Cola
cold   kalt (ä)
cold: to catch a ~   sich erkäl-ten
to **collect**   sammeln
color   die Farbe, -n; **What ~ is . . . ?** Welche Farbe hat . . . ?
colorful   bunt
to **comb**   (sich) kämmen
to **come**   kommen*; **to ~ along** mit·kommen*; **to ~ back** zurück·kommen*; **to ~ in** herein·kommen*; **That comes to . . . (altogether).** Das kostet (zusammen) . . . ; **Oh, ~ on!** Ach was!
comfortable   bequem, gemütlich; **un~** ungemütlich, unbequem
comical   komisch
common   gemeinsam
compact disc, CD   die CD, -s
company   die Firma, Firmen; **large ~** das Unternehmen, -
to **compare**   vergleichen, ver-glich, verglichen
to **complain (about)**   (sich) beschweren (über + *acc.*)
complicated   kompliziert; **un~** unkompliziert
composer   der Komponist, -en, -en
concern   die Sorge, -n
to **be concerned (about)**   sich Sorgen machen (um)

concert   das Konzert, -e
condo   die Eigentumswoh-nung, -en
congenial   sympathisch; **un~** unsympathisch
to **congratulate**   gratulieren
congratulation   der Glück-wunsch, ⸚e; **~s!** Herzli-che Glückwünsche!; **~s on your birthday!** Herzlichen Glückwunsch zum Geburts-tag!
to **connect**   verbinden*
construction   der Bau
to **continue**   weiter·gehen*, weiter·machen
contrary: on the ~   im Gegenteil
convenient   bequem
convivial   gemütlich
to **cook**   kochen
cookie   das Plätzchen, -
cool   kühl
corner   die Ecke, -n
correct   richtig
to **cost**   kosten
council   der Rat
to **count**   zählen
counter   der Schalter, -
country   das Land, ⸚er; **in(to) the ~(side)** auf dem / aufs Land
couple: a ~ of   ein paar
course   der Kurs, -e; **(~ of study)** das Studium; **of ~** natürlich; **(na) klar**
cousin   der Cousin, -s / die Kusine, -n
cozy   gemütlich
crazy   verrückt; **(That's) ~!** Wahnsinn!
to **cry**   weinen
cucumber   die Gurke, -n
cup   die Tasse, -n; **a ~ of . . .** eine Tasse . . .
cupboard   der Schrank, ⸚e
cultural(ly)   kulturell
curtain   der Vorhang, ⸚e

D

daily   täglich
to **damage**   schaden
to **dance**   tanzen
danger   die Gefahr, -en
dangerous   gefährlich
dark   dunkel
date (calendar)   das Datum,

Daten; **What ~ is today?**
Welches Datum ist heute?

daughter die Tochter, ¨

day der Tag, -e; **during the
~** am Tag; **one ~** eines
Tages; **all ~ long, the
whole ~** den ganzen Tag;
each ~ jeden Tag; **in those
~s** damals

dear lieb-; **Oh ~!** Ach du
liebes bisschen!

December der Dezember; **in
~** im Dezember

to **decide (on / about)** sich
entscheiden* (über + acc.)

decision die Entscheidung, -en

definitely unbedingt

dentist der Zahnarzt, ¨e / die
Zahnärztin, -nen

to **depart** (from) ab·fahren*

departure die Abfahrt, -en

to **depend: That ~s.** Das
kommt darauf an.

dependent unselbstständig

desk der Schreibtisch, -e

dessert der Nachtisch

to **destroy** zerstören

to **develop** (sich) entwickeln;
~ apart sich auseinander
entwickeln

devoted anhänglich

to **die** sterben (stirbt), starb, ist
gestorben

difference der Unterschied, -e

different(ly) verschieden,
anders; **Say it ~!** Sagen Sie
es anders!; **s.th. ~** etwas anderes

difficult schwer, schwierig

dining room das Esszimmer, -

dinner das Mittagessen, das
Abendessen

dirty schmutzig

to **discard** weg·werfen*

dishonest unehrlich

to **divide** teilen

divorce die Scheidung, -en

divorced geschieden

to **do** tun*, machen

doctor der Arzt, ¨e / die
Ärztin, -nen

dog der Hund, -e

dollar der Dollar, -(s)

done fertig

door die Tür, -en

dorm das Studenten-
(wohn)heim, -e

downstairs unten

to **dream (of)** träumen (von)

dress das Kleid, -er

dressed: to get ~ (sich)
an·ziehen*; **to get un~**
(sich) aus·ziehen*

dresser die Kommode, -n

to **drink** trinken*

to **drive** fahren*; **to ~ on (keep
on driving)** weiterfahren*;
to ~ up hinauf·fahren*

drugstore die Drogerie, -n

dull langweilig

during während (+ *gen.*)

dynamic temperamentvoll

E

each jed-

ear das Ohr, -en

earlier früher

early früh

to **earn** verdienen

earth die Erde

east der Osten; **~ of** östlich
von

Easter Ostern; **at/for ~** zu
Ostern

East German (*nickname*)
der Wessi, -s

easy leicht

to **eat** essen*

economy die Wirtschaft

educated gebildet; **un~**
ungebildet

education die Ausbildung

egg das Ei, -er

e-mail die E-Mail, -s

employee der Angestellte
(ein Angestellter) / die
Angestellte, -n, -n

empty leer

end das Ende; **in the ~** am
Ende, schließlich; **at the ~
of the week** am Ende der
Woche

to **end** auf·hören

engaged verlobt; **to get ~
(to)** sich verloben (mit)

engineer der Ingenieur, -e

England (das) England

English (*adj.*) englisch; **in ~**
auf Englisch; **(language)**
Englisch; **Do you speak ~ ?**

Sprechen Sie Englisch?;
(person) der Engländer, -

to **enjoy** genießen, genoss,
genossen; **~ your meal.**
Guten Appetit!

enough genug; **That's ~!**
Jetzt habe ich aber genug!

to **enter** herein·kommen*

enterprising unternehmungslustig

entertainment die Unterhaltung

entire(ly) ganz

entrance der Eingang, ¨e

environment die Umwelt

environmentally aware
umweltbewusst

equal gleich

especially besonders, vor
allem

etc. usw., und so weiter

euro der Euro, -s

even sogar

evening der Abend, -e;
this ~ heute Abend;
tomorrow ~ morgen
Abend; **yesterday ~** gestern
Abend; **in the ~** abends, am
Abend; **every ~** jeden
Abend; **Good ~!** Guten
Abend!

evening meal das Abendessen

every jed-; **~ three years**
alle drei Jahre

everything alles

everywhere überall

exact(ly) genau

exam die Prüfung, -en; **to
pass an ~** eine Prüfung
bestehen*; **to flunk an ~**
bei einer Prüfung
durch·fallen*; **take an ~**
eine Prüfung machen

excellent ausgezeichnet

except for außer (+ *dat.*)

exchange der Umtausch

to **exchange** um·tauschen,
aus·tauschen, wechseln

exciting spannend

to **excuse** sich entschuldigen;
~ me! Entschuldigen Sie
bitte! Entschuldigung!
Verzeihung!

exit der Ausgang, ¨e

to **expect** erwarten

expensive teuer

to **experience**   erleben
experience   das Erlebnis, -se;
  die Erfahrung, -en
to **explain**   erklären
extremely (loud)   unheimlich (laut)
eye   das Auge, -n

F

face   das Gesicht, -er
fairly   ziemlich
to **fall**   fallen*; **to ~ in love
  (with)** sich verlieben (in +
  acc.)
fall   der Herbst, -e; **in (the) ~**
  im Herbst
false   falsch
family   die Familie, -n
famous   berühmt
fantastic   fantastisch, toll
far   weit
fast   schnell
fat   dick; **to be ~tening** dick
  machen
father   der Vater, ¨
fax   das Fax, -e
fear   die Angst, ¨e
to **fear**   Angst haben* (vor +
  dat.)
February   der Februar; **in ~**
  im Februar
fed: I'm ~ up (with it).   Ich
  habe die Nase voll.
to **feel (a certain way)**   sich
  fühlen; **How are you (feeling)?** Wie geht es Ihnen?
  Wie geht's?; **I'm (feeling).
  . . .** Es geht mir . . . ; **to ~
  like (doing s.th.)** Lust
  haben* (zu + *inf.*)
to **fetch**   (sich) holen
few   einig- *(pl.);* wenig-; ein
  paar
fiancé(e)   der Verlobte (ein
  Verlobter) / die Verlobte,
  -n, -n
field   das Feld, -er; **(~ of
  study)** das Fach, ¨er; **(of
  specialization)** die
  Fachrichtung, -en; **(major)**
  das Hauptfach, ¨er; **(minor)**
  das Nebenfach, ¨er, das
  Schwerpunktfach, ¨er
to **fill out**   aus·füllen
film   der Film, -e
finally   endlich

to **finance**   finanzieren
to **find**   finden*
fine   gut (besser, best-), schön
finger   der Finger, -
finished   fertig
firm   die Firma, Firmen
first   erst-; **~ of all, at ~**
  (zu)erst
to **fish**   angeln; **to go ~ing** angeln gehen
fish   der Fisch, -e
**flavoring particle for: admi-
  ration** aber; **(curiosity /
  interest)** denn; **(concern,
  impatience, assurance)**
  doch; **(emphasis)** ja
flight (plane)   der Flug, ¨e
to **fly**   fliegen*
floor: on the first / ground ~
  im Parterre; **on the second
  ~** im ersten Stock
flower   die Blume, -n
to **follow**   folgen (ist) (+ *dat.*);
  ~ing folgend
food   das Essen; **Enjoy your
  ~!.** Guten Appetit!
foot   der Fuß, ¨e
for   für (+ *acc.*); **(since)** seit
  (+ *dat.*); *(conj.)* denn
to **forbid**   verbieten*
forbidden   verboten
foreign   ausländisch
foreigner   der Ausländer, -
forest   der Wald, ¨er
to **forget**   vergessen*
fork   die Gabel, -n
formerly   früher
foyer   der Flur
France   (das) Frankreich
free   frei
French *(adj.)*   französisch; **in
  ~** auf Französisch; **(language)** Französisch; **Do
  you speak ~?** Sprechen Sie
  Französisch?; **(person)** der
  Franzose, -n, -n / die
  Französin, -nen
(French) fries   die Pommes
  (frites)*(pl.)*
fresh   frisch
Friday   (der) Freitag; **on Fridays** freitags; **~ night** Freitag Abend; **~ nights**
  freitagnachts
friend   der Freund, -e
friendly   freundlich; **un~** unfreundlich

friendship   die Freundschaft, -en
from   von (+ *dat.*); **(a native
  of)** aus (+ *dat.*); **I'm ~ . . .**
  Ich bin aus . . . , Ich komme
  aus . . .; **(numbers) ~ . . . to**
  von . . . bis; **(place) ~ . . . to**
  von . . . zu/nach
front: in ~ of   vor (+ *acc. /
  dat.*)
fruit   das Obst
full   voll
fun   der Spaß; **to be ~** Spaß
  machen; **to make ~ of** sich
  lustig machen (über +
  acc.)
funny   lustig, witzig;
  komisch
furniture   die Möbel *(pl.)*
future   die Zukunft

G

game   das Spiel, -e
garage   die Garage, -n
garbage   der Abfall, ¨e
garden   der Garten, ¨
gate   das Tor, -e
gentleman   der Herr, -n, -en
genuine(ly)   echt
German *(adj.)*   deutsch; **in ~**
  auf Deutsch; **(language)**
  Deutsch; **Do you speak ~?**
  Sprechen Sie Deutsch?;
  (person) der Deutsche (ein
  Deutscher) / die Deutsche,
  -n, -n
Germany   (das) Deutschland
to **get (become)**   werden*;
  (fetch) holen; **(receive)**
  bekommen*; **to ~ off**
  aus·steigen*; **to ~ on** *or* **in**
  ein·steigen*; **to ~ up**
  auf·stehen*; **to ~ to know**
  kennen lernen; **to go and ~**
  (sich) holen; **to ~ used to**
  sich gewöhnen an (+ *acc.*);
  ~ well soon! Gute
  Besserung; **to ~ together**
  sich treffen*
girl   das Mädchen, -
to **give**   geben*; **(as a present)**
  schenken
glad   froh
gladly   gern (lieber, liebst-)
Glad to meet you.   Freut
  mich.

glance (at)   der Blick (auf + *acc.*)

glass   das Glas, ¨-er; **a ~ of . . .** ein Glas . . .

to **go**   gehen*; **to ~ by (bus, etc.)** fahren* mit; **to ~ by plane** fliegen*; **to ~ out** aus·gehen*; **to ~ up** hin·auf·fahren*

going: What's ~ on?   Was ist los?

good   gut (besser, best-); **~-looking** gut aussehend

Good-bye!   Auf Wiederse-hen! Tschüss!; **(on the phone)** Auf Wiederhören!

goodness: My ~!   Ach du liebes bisschen!, Ach du meine Güte!

grade   die Note, -n

grandfather   der Großvater ¨

grandmother   die Großmut-ter, ¨

grandparents   die Großel-tern *(pl.)*

gray   grau

great (size)   groß; **(terrific)** prima, toll, herrlich

green   grün

greeting   der Gruß, ¨-e

grief: Good ~!   Ach du lie-bes bisschen!

groceries   die Lebensmittel *(pl.)*

to **grow**   wachsen*; **to ~ to-gether** zusammen·wachsen*

to **guarantee**   garantieren

guest   der Gast, ¨-e

to **guide along**   vorbei·führen (an + *dat.*)

guitar   die Gitarre, -n

H

hair   das Haar, -e

half   halb; **in ~ an hour** in einer halben Stunde

hallway   der Flur

hand   die Hand, ¨-e

to **hang (up)**   hängen

to **hang (be hanging)**   hängen*

to **happen**   geschehen*, passieren (ist)

happy   glücklich, froh; **I'm ~ for you.** Ich freue mich für dich.

hard (difficult)   schwer; **~-working** fleißig

hardly   kaum

to **have**   haben*; **to ~ to** müssen*

head   der Kopf, ¨-e

healthy   gesund (ü)

to **hear**   hören

heavy   schwer

Hello!   Guten Tag!

help   die Hilfe

to **help**   helfen* (+ *dat.*)

her   ihr

here   hier

Hi!   Guten Tag! Hallo!

high   hoch (hoh-) (höher, höchst)

to **hike**   wandern (ist)

his   sein

historical(ly)   historisch

history   die Geschichte

hobby   das Hobby, -s

to **hold**   halten*

holiday   der Feiertag, -e

home: at ~ zu Hause; **(toward) ~** nach Hause; **at the ~ of** bei (+ *dat.*); **(homeland)** die Heimat

honest   ehrlich

to **hope**   hoffen; **I ~** hoffentlich

hoffentlich   hopefully

horse   das Pferd, -e

hot   heiß

hotel   das Hotel, -s, der Gasthof, ¨-e, die Pension, -en

hour   die Stunde, -n; **for ~s** stundenlang

house   das Haus, ¨-er

household   der Haushalt

househusband   der Haus-mann, ¨-er

housemate   der Mitbewoh-ner, -

housewife   die Hausfrau, -en

how   wie; **~ much?** wie viel?; **~ many?** wie viele?; **~ much is / are . . . ?** Was kostet / kosten. . . . ?; **~ come?** wieso?; **~ are you?** Wie geht's?, Wie geht es Ihnen?

however   aber, allerdings, doch, jedoch

human being   der Mensch, -en, -en

hunger   der Hunger

hungry: I'm ~ .   Ich habe Hunger.

to **hurry**   sich beeilen

to **hurt**   weh·tun*; **My (throat) hurts.** Mir tut (der Hals) weh; **(to damage)** schaden

husband   der Mann, ¨-er

I

ice, ice cream   das Eis

ID   der Ausweis, -e

idea   die Idee, -n; **(I have) no ~!** Keine Ahnung!

identification   der Ausweis, -e

if *(conj.)*   wenn; ob

ill   krank (ä)

to **imagine**   sich vor·stellen; **I ~ that . . .** Ich stelle mir vor, dass . . .

immediately   sofort

impatient   ungeduldig

important   wichtig

impossible   unmöglich; **That's ~!** Das gibt's doch nicht!

in   in (+ *dat. / acc.*)

income   das Einkommen, -

inconvenient   unbequem

incredible   einmalig, unglaublich

independent   selbstständig

individual(ly)   einzeln

inexpensive   billig

indeed   wirklich, doch

industrious(ly)   fleißig

influence   der Einfluss, ¨-e

inn   der Gasthof, ¨-e

insecure   unsicher

inside   in (+ *dat. / acc.*)

in spite of   trotz (+ *gen.* / [*dat.*]); **~ that** trotzdem

instead of   (an)statt (+ *gen.*)

intelligent   intelligent

interest (in)   das Interesse (an + *dat.*)

interested: to be ~ in   sich interessieren für

interesting   interessant

intermission   die Pause, -n

internship   das Praktikum, Praktiken

to **invite (to)**   ein·laden (lädt ein), lud ein, eingeladen (zu)

island   die Insel, -n

isn't it? nicht wahr?
Italian (*adj.*) italienisch; **in ~** auf Italienisch; **(language)** Italienisch; **Do you speak ~?** Sprechen Sie Italienisch?; **(person)** der Italiener, -
Italy (das) Italien
its sein, ihr

J

jacket die Jacke, -n
jam die Marmelade, -n
January der Januar; **in ~** im Januar
jeans die Jeans (*pl.*)
job die Arbeit; **(position)** die Stelle, -n
joint(ly) gemeinsam
juice der Saft, ⸚e
July der Juli; **in ~** im Juli
to **jump** springen*
June der Juni; **in ~** im Juni
just gerade; **~ like** genau(so) wie; **~ when** gerade als

K

to **keep** behalten*; **to ~ in shape** sich fit halten*
key der Schlüssel, -
kind nett; **what ~ of (a)?** was für (ein)?
kind (of) die Art, -en (von)
king der König, -e
kitchen die Küche, -n
knee das Knie, -
knife das Messer, -
to **know (be acquainted with)** kennen*; **(a fact)** wissen*; **(a skill)** können*
knowledge die Kenntnis, -se
known: well-~ bekannt

L

lab(oratory) das Labor, -s (*or* -e)
lacking: to be ~ fehlen
lady die Dame, -n; **old ~** die Alte, -n, -n
lake der See, -n
lamp die Lampe, -n
to **land** landen (ist)
landscape die Landschaft
language die Sprache, -n

large groß (ö)
last letzt-
to **last (duration)** dauern
late spät; **How ~ is it?** Wie spät ist es?, Wie viel Uhr ist es?
later später; **See you ~.** Bis später!
to **laugh** lachen
lawyer der Rechtsanwalt, ⸚e / die Rechtsanwältin, -nen
to **lay (down)** legen
lazy faul; **to be ~** faulenzen
to **lead** führen
to **learn** lernen
to **leave (behind)** lassen*; **~ from** ab·fahren*; **(a place)** verlassen*
lecture die Vorlesung, -en; **~ hall** der Hörsaal, -säle
left links; **link-**
leg das Bein, -e
leisure time die Freizeit
lemonade die Limonade, -n
to **let** lassen*
letter der Brief, -e
lettuce der Salat
library die Bibliothek, -en
to **lie (to be located)** liegen*; **to ~ down** sich (hin·)legen
life das Leben
light (weight) leicht; **(bright)** hell
likable sympathisch; **un~** unsympathisch
like wie; **just ~** genau(so) wie; **s.th. ~** so etwas wie
to **like** gefallen*; **I ~ it.** Es gefällt mir.; **I really ~it!** Das gefällt mir aber!; **I would ~ (to have)** ich möchte, ich hätte gern
likewise ebenfalls
to **link** verbinden*
to **listen** zu·hören (+ *dat.*); **to ~ to** sich an·hören
little klein; **(amount)** wenig, ein bisschen; **(some)** etwas
to **live** leben; **(reside)** wohnen
living room das Wohnzimmer, -
location der Ort, -e
long (*adj.*) lang (ä); (*adv.*) lange; **how ~?** wie lange?; **So ~!** Tschüss! Bis später!

to **look** sehen*; **to ~ (like)** aus·sehen* (wie + *nom.*); **to ~ at** sich an·sehen*; **to ~ for** suchen; **to ~ forward to** sich freuen auf (+ *acc.*); **~!** Schau mal!
to **lose** verlieren*
loud(ly) laut
love die Liebe; **to be in ~ (with)** verliebt sein* (in + *acc.*); **to fall in ~ (with)** sich verlieben (in + *acc.*)
to **love** lieben
loving liebevoll
luck das Glück; **tough ~** das Pech; **Tough ~!** Pech gehabt!
lucky: to be ~ Glück haben*; **I was (you were, etc.) ~.** Glück gehabt!
luggage das Gepäck
lunch das Mittagessen, -; **for ~** zum Mittagessen

M

mad: That makes me ~. Das ärgert mich.
magazine die Zeitschrift, -en
mail die Post
mailbox der Briefkasten, ⸚
mainly vor allem
major (field of study) das Hauptfach, ⸚er
to **make** machen
man der Mann, ⸚er; **(human being)** der Mensch, -en, -en; **gentle~** der Herr, -n, -en; **old ~** der Alte (ein Alter)
many viele; **how ~?** wie viele?; **~ a** manch-
map die Landkarte, -n; **(city ~)** der Stadtplan, ⸚e
March der März; **in ~** im März)
market der Markt, ⸚e
marmalade die Marmelade, -n
marriage die Ehe, -n
married verheiratet; **un~** unverheiratet
to **marry, get married** heiraten
matter: (That) doesn't ~. Das ist doch egal. (Das) macht nichts.; **What's the ~?** Was ist los?

may dürfen*

May der Mai; **in ~** im Mai

meal das Essen, -; **Enjoy your ~.** Guten Appetit!

to **mean (signify)** bedeuten; **(think)** meinen

meanwhile inzwischen

meat das Fleisch

to **meet (get to know)** kennen lernen; **Glad to ~ you.** Freut mich (sehr, Sie kennen zu lernen); **to ~ with friends** sich mit Freunden treffen*

menu die Speisekarte, -n

merry: ~ Christmas! Frohe/fröhliche Weihnachten!

middle die Mitte; **in the ~ of** mitten in/auf (+ *dat.*); **in the ~ of the month** Mitte des Monats

milk die Milch

millennium das Jahrtausend, -e

minor (field of study) das Nebenfach, -̈er

minute die Minute, -n; **See you in a few ~s!** Bis gleich!

missing: to be ~ fehlen

moment der Augenblick, -e

Monday (der) Montag; **~ morning** Montagmorgen; **on ~s** montags; **~ mornings** montagmorgens

money das Geld; **to make ~** Geld verdienen; **to spend ~** Geld aus·geben*

month der Monat, -e; **per ~** im Monat, pro Monat; **for one ~** einen Monat

monthly monatlich

monument das Denkmal, -̈er

more mehr; **once ~** noch einmal; **~ and ~** immer mehr

morning der Morgen; **early ~** früh (morgen); **mid-~** der Vormittag; **this ~** heute Morgen; **tomorrow ~** morgen früh; **yesterday ~** gestern früh; **in the ~** morgens, am Morgen; **every ~** jeden Morgen; **Good ~!** Guten Morgen!

most meist-; **am meisten**

mostly meistens

mother die Mutter, -̈

mountain der Berg, -e

mouth der Mund, -̈er

movie (film) der Film, -e; **(theater)** das Kino, -s

Mr. Herr

Mrs. Frau

Ms. Frau

much viel (mehr, meist-); **how ~?** wie viel?

museum das Museum, Museen

music die Musik

musical musikalisch; **un~** unmusikalisch

must müssen*

my mein

N

name der Name, -ns, -n; **What's your ~?** Wie heißen Sie?; **My ~ is . . .** Ich heiße . . . , Mein Name ist . . .

to **name** nennen*

napkin die Serviette, -n

nation das Volk, -̈er

natural science die Naturwissenschaft, -en

nature die Natur

nature preserve das Naturschutzgebiet, -e

near (distance) nah (näher, nächst-); **(vicinity)** bei (+ *dat.*), in der Nähe von (+ *dat.*)

neat prima; schick

neck der Hals, -̈e

to **need** brauchen

neighbor der Nachbar, -n, -n

neither . . . nor weder . . . noch

never nie; **~ before** noch nie

nevertheless trotzdem

new neu; **s.th. ~** etwas Neues; **nothing ~** nichts Neues; **What's ~?** Was gibt's Neues?

New Year's Eve Silvester; **at/on ~** zu Silvester

news die Nachricht, -en

newspaper die Zeitung, -en

next nächst-; **~ to** neben (+ *dat. / acc.*); **What comes ~?** Wie geht's weiter?

nice schön, nett

nickname der Spitzname, -ns, -n

night die Nacht, -̈e; **to~** heute Nacht; **last ~** gestern Nacht; **Good ~!** Gute Nacht!; **at / during the ~** nachts, in der Nacht; **every ~** jede Nacht; **to spend the ~** übernachten

no nein

nobody niemand

noisy laut

nonsense der Quatsch, der Unsinn

no one niemand

noodle die Nudel, -n

noon der Mittag, -e; **today at ~** heute Mittag; **tomorrow at ~** morgen Mittag; **at ~** mittags; **after~** der Nachmittag, -e

north der Norden; **in the ~** im Norden; **~ of** nördlich von

nose die Nase, -n

not nicht; **~ any** kein; **~ only . . . but also** nicht nur . . . sondern auch; **~ yet** noch nicht; **~ ever** noch nie; **~ at all** gar nicht

notebook das Heft, -e

nothing (to) nichts (zu); **~ special** nichts Besonderes

novel der Roman, -e

November der November; **in ~** im November

now jetzt, nun; **just ~** gerade

number die Nummern -n, die (Ordinal)zahl, -en

nurse die Krankenschwester, -n; **(male)** der Krankenpfleger, -

O

o'clock Uhr

October der Oktober; **in ~** im Oktober

of course natürlich; doch

off ab-

to **offer** an·bieten*

office das Büro, -s

often oft

oh ach; **~, I see!** Ach so!; **~, come on!** Ach was!; **~ dear!** Ach du liebes bisschen!; **~, how cute!** Ach, wie süß!

okay: That's ~. Das geht.

Das macht nichts.; **That's not ~.** Das geht nicht.

old alt (ä); **~ man** der Alte (ein Alter); **~ lady** die Alte, -n, -n; **~ people** die Alten; **~ things** das Alte

on (top of) auf (+ *acc. / dat.*); **(vertical surface)** an; **~ the first of July** am ersten Juli

once einmal; **~ more** noch einmal; **~ in a while** manchmal; **(formerly)** einst, früher

one (people, they) man

only nur; **(not before)** erst; **not ~ . . . but also** nicht nur . . . sondern auch

open (prefix) auf-; **~** auf, offen, geöffnet

to **open** öffnen, auf·machen

opera die Oper, -n

opinion: to be of an ~ halten von

opposite das Gegenteil, -e

or oder

oral presentation das Referat, -e; **to give an ~** ein Referat halten*

orange die Orange, -n; **(color)** orange

orchestra das Orchester, -

order: in ~ to um . . . zu (+ *inf.*)

to **order** bestellen

other ander-; **~s** andere; **the ~s** die anderen; **s.th. ~ (quite different)** etwas (ganz) anderes; **in ~ ways** anders; **in ~ words** also

our unser

out of aus (+ *dat.*)

over (location) über (+ *acc. / dat.*); **(finished)** vorbei; **~ there** da drüben

own (adj.) eigen-

P

to **pack** packen

package das Paket, -e

page die Seite, -n; **on/to ~ . . .** auf Seite . . .

pain der Schmerz, -en; **to have ~** Schmerzen haben*

to **paint** malen

painting das Gemälde, -

palace das Schloss, ̈er

pants die Hose, -n

paper das Papier, -e; **(term ~)** die (Semester)arbeit, -en

parcel das Paket, -e

parents die Eltern (*pl.*)

to **pardon: ~ me!** Entschuldigung! Entschuldigen Sie! Verzeihung!

park der Park, -s

to **park** parken

part der Teil, -e; **to take ~ (in)** teil·nehmen* (an + *dat.*)

to **participate (in)** teil·nehmen* (an + *dat.*)

partner der Partner, -

party die Party, -s; die Feier, -n

to **pass (an exam)** bestehen*; **to ~ by** vorbei·gehen* (bei + *dat.*), vorbei·kommen*, vorbei·fahren*, vorbei·führen (an + *dat.*)

passport der Pass, ̈e

past (prefix) vorbei-; **in the ~** früher

patient geduldig

to **pay (for)** (be)zahlen

pea die Erbse, -n

peace der Frieden

pen der Kuli, -s

pencil der Bleistift, -e

people die Leute (*pl.*); **(human being)** der Mensch, -en, -en; **(as a whole or nation)** das Volk, ̈er

pepper der Pfeffer

per pro

performance die Vorstellung, -en

perhaps vielleicht

person der Mensch, -en, -en

pharmacy die Apotheke, -n

to **phone** an·rufen*, telefonieren

physician der Arzt, ̈e / die Ärztin, -nen

piano das Klavier, -e; **to play the ~** Klavier spielen

to **pick up** (sich) holen

picture das Bild, -er; **to take ~s** fotografieren

piece das Stück, -e; **(of music or ballet)** das Stück, -e

pink rosa

pizza die Pizza, -s

place (location) der Platz, ̈e, der Ort, -e; **at our ~** bei uns; **in your ~** an deiner Stelle

plan der Plan, ̈e

to **plan** planen, vor·haben*

plane das Flugzeug, -e

plate der Teller, -

platform der Bahnsteig, -e

play das Stück, ̈e

to **play** spielen; **(checkers)** Dame spielen; **(chess)** Schach spielen; **(tennis)** Tennis spielen

pleasant gemütlich; **un~** ungemütlich

to **please** gefallen*

please bitte

pleased: ~ to meet you. Freut mich.

pleasure: My ~. Nichts zu danken!

P.O. box das Postfach, ̈er

pocket die Tasche, -n

police (force) die Polizei; **~man** der Polizist, -en, -en; **~woman** die Polizistin, -nen

pollution die Verschmutzung

poor arm (ä)

population die Bevölkerung

position die Stelle, -n

possible möglich; **That's im~.** Das ist doch nicht möglich!

postcard (w. picture) Ansichtskarte, -n

post office die Post

potato die Kartoffel, -n

pound das Pfund, -e; **a ~ of . . .** ein Pfund . . . ; **two ~s of . . .** zwei Pfund . . .

power die Macht, ̈e

practical(ly) praktisch

precise genau; **~ly!** Genau!

to **prefer** lieber tun*; vor·ziehen*

to **prepare** vor·bereiten; **~ o.s. (~ for)** sich vor·bereiten (auf + *acc.*)

present (gift) das Geschenk, -e

preservation die Erhaltung

pretty hübsch

private privat

probably wahrscheinlich

problem das Problem, -e; **(That's) no ~.** (Das ist) kein Problem.

profession der Beruf, -e; **choice of ~** die Berufs-wahl

professor der Professor, -en

program das Programm, -e; die Sendung, -en

prohibited verboten

to **promise** versprechen*

to **protect** schützen, schonen

protection der Schutz

proud (of) stolz (auf + *acc.*)

public öffentlich

pudding der Pudding, -s

to **pull** ziehen*

pullover der Pullover, -, Pulli, -s

purple lila

to **put (set down)** setzen; **(stand upright)** (hin·)-stellen; **(lay down)** (hin·)-legen; **(hang up)** (hin·)hän-gen; **to ~ on (clothing)** (sich) an·ziehen*; **~ up** (auf·)bauen

Q

quarter das Viertel; **a ~ to** Viertel vor; **a ~ past** Viertel nach; **in a ~ of an hour** in einer Viertelstunde; **(uni-versity quarter)** das Quar-tal, -e

queen die Königin, -nen

question die Frage, -n; **to ask a ~** eine Frage stellen

quick(ly) schnell

quiet(ly) ruhig, leise

quite ziemlich

R

radio das Radio, -s

railway die Bahn, -en

to **rain** regnen; **It's raining.** Es regnet.

rather lieber; ziemlich

to **read** lesen*

ready fertig

really wirklich; echt

to **rebuild** wieder auf·bauen

to **receive** bekommen*

to **recognize** erkennen*

to **recommend** empfehlen*

to **recuperate** sich erholen

red rot (ö)

refrigerator der Kühl-schrank, ̈-e

region die Gegend, -en; das Gebiet, -e

regular normal

relationship die Bezie-hung, -en

to **relax** sich entspannen

reliable zuverlässig; **un~** unzuverlässig

to **remain** bleiben*

to **remember** sich erinnern (an + *acc.*)

to **remind (of)** erinnern (an + *acc.*)

to **renovate** renovieren

to **rent** mieten; **to ~ out** ver-mieten

to **repeat** wiederholen

to **report** berichten

reporter der Journalist, -en, -en

to **request** bitten* (um)

to **rescue** retten

to **reserve** reservieren

to **reside** wohnen

responsibility die Verant-wortung, -en

responsible verantwor-tungsvoll

to **rest** sich aus·ruhen

restaurant das Restau-rant, -s

to **restore** restaurieren

to **return** zurück·kommen*

return address der Absen-der, -

(re)unification die (Wieder-)vereinigung

rice der Reis

rich reich

ridiculous lächerlich

right rechts, recht-; **(cor-rect)** richtig; **You're ~.** Du hast Recht.; **isn't it (~)?** nicht wahr?; **(That's) ~.** (Das) stimmt.; **~ away** sofort

river der Fluss, ̈-e

roll das Brötchen, -

room das Zimmer, -; **bed~** das Schlafzimmer, -; **bath~** das Bad, ̈-er (Badezimmer, -); **dining~** das Esszimmer, -; **living~** das Wohnzim-mer, -; **guest~** das Gäste-zimmer, -; **single ~** das Einzelzimmer, -; **double ~** das Doppelzimmer, -

roommate der Zimmerkol-lege, -n, -n / die Zimmer-kollegin, -nen

round-trip ticket die Hin- und Rückfahrkarte, -n

to **run** laufen*

S

sad traurig

safe sicher; **un~** unsicher

safety die Sicherheit

salad der Salat, -e

salt das Salz

same gleich; **the ~ to you** gleichfalls; **It's all the ~ to me.** Es ist mir egal.

Saturday (der) Samstag; **on ~s** samstags

sausage die Wurst, ̈-e

to **save (money or time)** sparen; **(rescue)** retten

to **say** sagen; **Could you ~ that again? What did you ~?** Wie bitte?; **How does one ~ ...?** Wie sagt man ... ?

scared: to be ~ (of) Angst haben* (vor + *dat.*)

scarcely kaum

scenery die Landschaft

schedule (transportation) der Fahrplan, ̈-e

scholarship das Stipendium, Stipendien

school die Schule, -n

science die Wissenschaft, -en; **natural ~** die Natur-wissenschaft, -en

scientist der Wissenschaft-ler, -

second die Sekunde, -n

secretary der Sekretär, -e

secure sicher

security die Sicherheit

to **see** sehen*; **Oh, I ~.** Ach so!

to **seem** scheinen*

selection (of) die Auswahl (an + *dat.*)

self-confident selbstbewusst

self-employed selbstständig

to **sell** verkaufen

semester das Semester, -

seminar das Seminar, -e

to **send** schicken

sentence der Satz, ̈-e; **to make / form a ~** einen Satz bilden

to **separate** trennen

September der September;
in ~ im September
server die Bedienung
**service (in store or restau-
rant)** die Bedienung
to **set (down)** setzen
several mehrer- *(pl.)*
to **share** teilen
shared gemeinsam
to **shave o.s.** sich rasieren
shelf das Regal, -e
to **shine** scheinen*
shirt das Hemd, -en
shoe der Schuh, -e; **in your/
his ~s** an deiner / seiner
Stelle
shop das Geschäft, -e
to **shop** ein·kaufen; **to go
~ping** einkaufen gehen*
short klein; kurz (ü)
to **show** zeigen; **That goes to ~
you.** Da sieht man's mal.
shower die Dusche, -n; **to
take a ~** (sich) duschen
siblings die Geschwister
(pl.)
sick *(adj.)* krank (ä); **~ person** der Kranke (ein
Kranker) / die Kranke,
-n, -n
to **sign** unterschreiben*
to **sign up** for belegen
to **signify** bedeuten
silly dumm (ü)
simple, simply einfach
since (time) seit (+ *dat.*)
to **sing** singen*
single (unmarried) unverheiratet, ledig
sister die Schwester, -n; **~s
and brothers** die
Geschwister *(pl.)*
to **sit (be sitting)** sitzen*; **to ~
down** sich (hin·)setzen
to **ski** Ski laufen*; **to go ~ing**
Ski laufen gehen*
skill die Kenntnis, -se
skinny dünn
skirt der Rock, ¨e
slacks die Hose, -n
slender schlank
to **sleep** schlafen*
slim schlank
slow(ly) langsam
small klein
to **snow** schneien
soccer: to play ~ Fußball
spielen

sofa das Sofa, -s
soft drink die Limonade, -n
some etwas *(sg.)*; einig- *(pl.
only)*; **(many a)** manch-; **(a
couple of)** ein paar; **(a little
bit)** ein bisschen
somebody jemand
someone jemand
something (to) etwas (zu)
sometimes manchmal
son der Sohn, ¨e
song das Lied, -er
soon bald; **See you ~!** Bis
bald!; **as ~ as** sobald
sore: I have a ~ throat. Mir
tut der Hals weh.
sorry: I'm ~. Es tut mir
Leid.
sort: all ~s of allerlei
so that *(conj.)* so dass
soup die Suppe, -n
south der Süden; **in the ~**
im Süden; **~ of** südlich
von
Spain (das) Spanien
Spanish *(adj.)* spanisch; **in ~**
auf Spanisch; **(language)**
Spanisch; **Do you speak ~?**
Sprechen Sie Spanisch?;
(person) der Spanier, -
to **speak** sprechen*; **~ up
(louder)!** Sprechen Sie
lauter!
special: s.th. ~ etwas Besonderes; **nothing ~** nichts
Besonderes
spectator der Zuschauer, -
speech die Rede, -n
to **spend (money)** aus·geben*
to **spin** spinnen, spann, gesponnen
spoon der Löffel, -
sport(s) der Sport; **to engage in ~** Sport treiben*
sporty sportlich
spring der Frühling, -e; **in
(the) ~** im Frühling
square der Platz, ¨e
stamp die Briefmarke, -n
to **stand (upright), be standing**
stehen*
to **start** an·fangen*
start der Anfang, ¨e
state der Staat, -en
to **stay** bleiben*
stay der Aufenthalt, -e
still noch
stomach der Bauch, ¨e

stop (for buses etc.) die Haltestelle, -n
to **stop (doing s.th.)** auf·hören
(zu + *inf.*)
to **stop (in a vehicle)** halten*;
~! Halt!
stopover der Aufenthalt, -e
store das Geschäft, -e; **department ~** das Kauf-
haus, ¨er
story die Geschichte, -n; **detective ~** der Krimi, -s
straight gerade; **~ ahead**
geradeaus
strange komisch, seltsam
strawberry die Erdbeere, -n
street die Straße, -n; **main ~**
die Hauptstraße, -n
streetcar die Straßenbahn, -en
strenuous anstrengend
strict(ly) streng
to **stroll** bummeln (ist)
student der Student, -en,
-en / die Studentin, -nen
study das Studium, Studien;
(course of ~) das Studium;
(room) das Arbeitszimmer, -
to **study** lernen; **(a particular
field, be a student at a
university)** studieren (an +
dat.)
stupid dumm (ü)
subject das Fach, ¨er
subway die U-Bahn
such so ein *(sg.)*; solch *(pl.)*
sudden(ly) plötzlich
sugar der Zucker
suitcase der Koffer, -
summer der Sommer, -; **in
(the) ~** im Sommer
sun die Sonne; **The ~ is
shining.** Die Sonne scheint.
Sunday (der) Sonntag; **~
early in the morning**
Sonntag früh; **on ~s**
sonntags
superb super
supermarket der Supermarkt, ¨e
supper das Abendessen; **for
~** zum Abendessen
to **suppose** an·nehmen*
sure sicher; doch; (na) klar;
for ~ bestimmt
surely bestimmt, sicher(lich)
surprise die Überraschung,
-en; **What a ~!** Was für
eine Überraschung!

to **surprise** überraschen
surroundings die Umgebung (*sg.*); (**ecology**) die Umwelt
suspenseful spannend
system das System, -e
sweater der Pullover, -; der Pulli, -s
sweatshirt das Sweatshirt, -s
to **swim** schwimmen*, baden
Swiss (person) der Schweizer, -; (*adj.*) Schweizer, schweizerisch
Switzerland die Schweiz

T

table der Tisch, -e
to **take** nehmen*; **to ~ along** mit·nehmen*; **to ~ off (clothing)** (sich) aus·ziehen*; **to ~ off (plane)** ab·fliegen*; (**last**) dauern; **to ~ (a course)** belegen; **to ~ an exam** eine Prüfung machen; **~ care!** Mach's gut!
talented talentiert; **un~** untalentiert
to **talk (to)** reden, sprechen* (mit); **to ~ about / of** reden über (+ *acc.*) / von
to **taste** schmecken; **That tastes good.** Das schmeckt (gut).
taxi das Taxi, -s
tea der Tee, -s
to **teach** lehren
teacher der Lehrer, -
to **tear** down ab·reißen*
telephone das Telefon, -e
tell sagen, erzählen (von + *dat.*)
tennis Tennis
term paper die Arbeit, -en
terrible, terribly furchtbar, schrecklich
terrific toll, super
test die Prüfung, -en; **to take a ~** eine Prüfung machen
than (*after comp.*) als
to **thank** danken (+ *dat.*); **~ you!** Danke!; **~ you very much.** Danke schön! Vielen Dank!; **~ God!** Gott sei Dank!; **~s, the same to you!** Danke, gleichfalls!
that das; (*conj.*) dass; **so ~** (*conj.*) so dass

the . . . the je (+ *comp.*) . . . desto (+ *comp.*)
theater das Theater, -; **movie ~** das Kino, -s
their ihr
then dann; (**in those days**) damals
there da, dort; **over ~** da drüben; **to ~** dorthin; **~ is/ are** es gibt
therefore deshalb, darum
thick dick
thin dünn
thing das Ding, -e
things: all sorts of ~ so einiges; **old ~** das Alte
to **think (of)** denken* (an + *acc.*); (**be of an opinion**) glauben, meinen, halten* von; **I ~ it's . . .** Ich finde es . . .; **I ~ so, too.** Das finde ich auch.; **If you ~ so.** Wenn du meinst.; **Don't you ~ so?** Oder?
thinker der Denker, -
thirst der Durst
thirsty: I'm ~. Ich habe Durst.
this dies-
thought der Gedanke, -ns, -n
throat der Hals, ̈e
through durch (+ *acc.*)
to **throw away** weg·werfen*
Thursday (der) Donnerstag; **~ evening** Donnerstag Abend; **on ~s** donnerstags; **~ evenings** donnerstagabends
ticket die Karte, -n; (**bus, etc.**) die Fahrkarte, -n; (**round-trip ~**) die (Hin- und) Rückfahrkarte, -n; **~ window** der Schalter, -
to **tie together** verbinden*
time die Zeit, -en; **What ~ is it?** Wie spät ist es? Wie viel Uhr ist es?; **at what ~?** wann?; **in the mean~** inzwischen; **one ~** einmal; **the first ~** das erste Mal; **for the first ~** zum ersten Mal
tired müde
to (*prefix*) an-; (*prep.*) zu (+ *dat.*); an (+ *acc.*); (**a country, etc.**) nach
today heute

together (*prefix*) mit-; (*adv.*) gemeinsam, zusammen; **~ with** mit (+ *dat.*)
toilet die Toilette, -n
tomato die Tomate, -n
tomorrow morgen; **the day after ~** übermorgen
too (also) auch; **~ much** zu viel; **me ~** ich auch
tooth der Zahn, ̈e
to **tour** besichtigen
tour guide der Reiseleiter, -
tourist der Tourist, -en, -en
toward the speaker (*prefix*) her-
tower der Turm, ̈e
town die Stadt, ̈e; der Ort, -e
townhouse das Reihenhaus, ̈er
toxic waste der Giftstoff, -e
track das Gleis, -e
trade der Handel
traffic der Verkehr
trail der Weg, -e
train der Zug, ̈e, die Bahn, -en; **~ station** der Bahnhof, ̈e
trained: well-~ gut ausgebildet
training die Ausbildung; **practical ~** das Praktikum, Praktiken
trash der Abfall, ̈e
to **travel** reisen (ist)
travel agent der Reiseleiter, -
tree der Baum, ̈e
tremendously unheimlich
trillion (*American*) die Billion, -en
trip die Reise, -n, die Fahrt, -en; **to take a ~** eine Reise machen
true richtig, wahr; (**That's**) **~.** (Das) stimmt.; **isn't that ~?** nicht wahr?; **That can't be ~!** Das kann doch nicht wahr sein!
to **try** versuchen
T-shirt das T-Shirt, -s
Tuesday (der) Dienstag; **~ at noon** Dienstagmittag; **on ~s** dienstags; **on ~s at noon** dienstagmittags
to **turn: to ~ off (radio, etc.)** aus·machen; **to ~ on (radio, etc.)** an·machen

TV (medium) das Fernsehen; **(set)** der Fernseher, -; **to watch ~** fern·sehen*

type (of) die Art, -en (von)

typical(ly) typisch; **That's ~ of you.** Das sieht dir ähnlich.

U

ugly hässlich

unathletic unsportlich

unbelievable unglaublich; **That's ~!** (Das ist doch) unglaublich!, Wahnsinn!

uncle der Onkel, -

under unter (+ acc. / dat.)

to **understand** verstehen*

undoubtedly sicherlich

unemployment die Arbeitslosigkeit

unexpected(ly) unerwartet

unfortunately leider

unification die Vereinigung

united vereint, vereinigt

United States (U.S.) die Vereinigten Staaten (U.S.A.) (pl.)

university die Universität, -en; die Uni, -s

unlucky: to be ~ Pech haben*; **I was (you were, etc.) ~.** Pech gehabt!

unique einmalig

until bis; **not ~** erst

up (prefix) auf-

upset: to get ~ about sich ärgern über (+ acc.)

upstairs oben

usual(ly) gewöhnlich, meistens

to **use** gebrauchen, benutzen, verwenden

used: to get ~ to sich gewöhnen an (+ acc.)

to **utilize** gebrauchen, verwenden

V

vacation die Ferien (pl.)

various verschieden-

vegetable(s) das Gemüse, -

versatile vielseitig

very sehr; ganz

view (of) der Blick (auf / in + acc.)

viewer der Zuschauer, -

village das Dorf, ¨er

to **visit** besuchen; **(sightseeing)** besichtigen

W

to **wait (for)** warten (auf + acc.)

waiter der Kellner, -; der Ober, -; **~!** Herr Ober!

waitress die Kellnerin, -nen

to **walk** zu Fuß gehen*, laufen*; **to go for a ~** spazieren gehen*

wall die Wand, ¨e; **(thick)** die Mauer, -n

to **want to** wollen*, möchten*

war der Krieg, -e

warm warm (ä)

to **wash (o.s.)** (sich) waschen*

waste der Abfall, der Müll; **toxic ~** der Giftstoff, -e

waste separation die Mülltrennung

watch (clock) die Uhr, -en

to **watch: (TV)** fern·sehen*; **(pay attention)** auf·passen; **~ out!** Passen Sie auf!

water das Wasser

way der Weg, -e; **by the ~** übrigens; **this ~** auf diese Weise

to **wear** tragen*

weather das Wetter

wedding die Hochzeit, -en

Wednesday (der) Mittwoch; **~ afternoon** Mittwochnachmittag; **on ~s** mittwochs; **~ afternoons** mittwochnachmittags

week die Woche, -n; **all ~ long** die ganze Woche; **this ~** diese Woche; **Have a nice ~end!** (Ein) schönes Wochenende!

weekly wöchentlich

weird seltsam

welcome: You're ~. Bitte (bitte)!, Bitte schön!, Nichts zu danken!

well (adv.) gut; **~ also,** na, ja, nun; **Get ~ soon!** Gute Besserung!

west der Westen; **in the ~** im Westen; **~ of** westlich von

what? was?; **~ did you say?** Wie bitte?; **~'s new?** Was gibt's (Neues)?; **~'s on . . . ?**

Was gibt's im . . . ?; **So ~?** Na und?; **~ kind of (a)?** was für (ein)?

when (at what time?) wann?; **(at the time ~)** als (conj.); **~(ever)** (conj.) wenn; **just ~** (conj.) gerade als

where? wo?; **from ~?** woher?; **~ to?** wohin?

whether (conj.) ob

which? welch-?

while (conj.) während

white weiß

who? wer?

whole ganz

whom? wen?, wem?

whose? wessen?

why? warum?, wieso?

wife die Frau, -en

wild wild

to **win** gewinnen*

window das Fenster, -; **ticket ~** der Schalter, -

windy windig

wine der Wein, -e

winter der Winter, - **in (the) ~** im Winter

to **wish** (sich) wünschen

wish der Wunsch, ¨e; **Best ~es!** Herzliche Glückwünsche!

with (prefix) mit-; (prep.) mit (+ dat.); **(at the home of)** bei (+ dat.); **~ me (us . . .)** bei mir (uns . . .)

without ohne (+ acc.)

woman (Mrs., Ms.) die Frau, -en

to **wonder** sich fragen

wonderful(ly) wunderbar, prima, herrlich

woods der Wald, ¨er

word das Wort, ¨er; **in other ~s** also

work die Arbeit

to **work** arbeiten; **That won't ~.** Das geht nicht.

worker (blue-collar) der Arbeiter, -

world die Welt, -en

worry die Sorge, -n

to **worry (about)** sich Sorgen machen (um)

to **write** schreiben*; **to ~ to** schreiben* an (+ acc.); **to ~ about** schreiben* über (+ acc.); **to ~ down** aufschreiben*; **How do you**

~ **that?** Wie schreibt man das?

wrong falsch; **You are ~.** Du hast Unrecht.

Y

year das Jahr, -e; **all ~ long** das ganze Jahr; **next ~** nächstes Jahr; **Have a good New ~!** Ein gutes Neues Jahr!

yellow gelb

yes ja; doch

yesterday gestern; **the day before ~** vorgestern

yet doch; **not ~** noch nicht

young jung (ü)

your dein, euer, Ihr

youth die Jugend

youth hostel die Jugendherberge, -n

Z

zip code die Postleitzahl, -en

Photo Credits

All photographs not otherwise credited are owned by Heinle. We have made every effort to trace the ownership of all copyrighted material and to secure permissions from the copyright holders. In the event of any question arising regarding the use of any material, we will be pleased to make the necessary corrections in future printings.

p. xiv Diaphor Agency/Index Stock Imagery
p. 18 Inter Nationes
p. 20 Innsbruck Tourismus
p. 28 Ulrike Welsch
p. 34 Paul Gerda/eStock
p. 35 Inter Nationes
p. 41 bpa/Engelbert Reineke
p. 44 Gruppe S.F. & H. Fotostudio GmbH, Bregenz
p. 50 European Central Bank
p. 51 Inter Nationes
p. 56 bpa/Arne Schambeck
p. 62 Ulrike Welsch
p. 66 Fremdenverkehrsverein Regensburg e.V./Meier
p. 71 Ingrid Sevin
p. 74 Fremdenverkehrsverein Regensburg e.V.
p. 83 Fremdenverkehrsamt München/Wilfried Hoesl
p. 90 Wien-Tourismus/Bryan Duffy
p. 94 Ingrid Sevin
p. 95 Wien-Tourismus/Gerhard Weinkirn
p. 96 Inter Nationes
p. 102 Innsbruck Tourismus
p. 103 David Simson/Stock Boston
p. 110 Verkehrsverein Tübingen/Rainer Fieselmann
p. 116 Tourismus-zentrale Nürnberg
p. 119 left: Inter Nationes
p. 119 right: Hameln Marketing & Tourismus GmbH
p. 123 Larry Mulvehill/The Image Works
p. 124 top: bpa
p. 124 bottom: Verkehrsverein Landshut e.V.
p. 128 Wien-Tourismus/Nanja Antonczyk
p. 129 Innsbruck Tourismus
p. 131 FridmarDamm/eStock
p. 134 Siegfried Purschke/Ullstein Bilderdienst
p. 141 Dieter Sevin
p. 142 Erich Lessing/Art Resource
p. 143 Wien-Tourismus
p. 145 bottom: Austrian National Tourist Office
p. 146 Austrian National Tourist Office
p. 151 Wien-Tourismus/Willfried Gredler-Oxenbauer
p. 152 Dresden-Werbung & Tourismus GmbH/Sylvio Dittrich
p. 153 Passau Tourismus e.V.
p. 163 G. Hinterlaitner/The Liaison Agency
p. 168 Dieter Sevin
p. 171 top: Inter Nationes
p. 171 bottom left: Fremdenverkehrszentrale Linz
p. 171 bottom right: Inter Nationes
p. 176 bpa/Julia Faßbender
p. 183 Ingrid Sevin

p. 189 Kevin Galvin
p. 195 DJH Archiv
p. 197 top: B. Roland/The Image Works
p. 204 German National Tourist Office
p. 209 Inter Nationes
p. 219 Keystone/The Image Works
p. 223 Bern Tourismus/Wolfgang Kaehler
p. 225 Zürich Tourismus
p. 230 Passau Tourismus e.V.
p. 231 Bern Tourismus
p. 237 Innsbruck Tourismus
p. 241 Inter Nationes/Detlef Gräfingholt
p. 246 Inter Nationes
p. 247 R. Schwerzel/Stock Boston
p. 250 left: Wien-Tourismus/Bryan Duffy
p. 250 right: Alain Revel/Agency Vandystadt
p. 254 Inter Nationes/Anne Kirchbach
p. 255 Wien-Tourismus/Seefestspiele Mörbisch
p. 257 bottom: The Kobal Collection
p. 261 Inter Nationes
p. 262 Zefa Visual Media-Germany/Index Stock Imagery
p. 262 bottom: Wien-Tourismus/Terry Wien
p. 265 Scala/Art Resource
p. 280 Fremdenverkehrszentrale Linz
p. 302 Keystone/The Image Works
p. 312 Max Planck Gesellschaft Pressestelle
p. 315 Inter Nationes/Detlef Gräfingholt
p. 325 bpa/Bernd Kühler
p. 328 bpa/Venohr
p. 332 Ingrid Sevin
p. 338 Inter Nationes/David Ausserhofer
p. 353 Verkehrsverein Tübingen
p. 354 Keystone/The Image Works
p. 357 bpa
p. 362 Ulrike Welsch
p. 366 Rene Burri/MAGNUM
p. 368 bpa/Fritz Mader, Barsbüttel
p. 373 Ulrike Welsch
p. 377 bpa
p. 379 Ingrid Sevin
p. 381 German Information Center
p. 382 German Information Center
p. 388 Margot Granitsas/The Image Works
p. 389 bpa/Arne Schambeck
p. 391 bpa/Lutz Fenske
p. 394 bpa/Fritz Mader, Barsbüttel
p. 402 bpa
p. 403 Leipzig Tourist Service e.V./LTS — T. Schmidt

Text Credits

p. 29 Walter Hanel / Econ Verlag; p. 44 *Deutschland;* p. 45 top: *Deutschland;* p. 45 bottom: *Deutschland;* p. 109 bottom: *Das Zeitbild;* p. 133 Winterthur Tourismus / Robert Gerber; p. 175 TravelPilot; p. 177 *Ratgeber Euro;* p. 183 Courtesy of Sesame Workshop; p. 192 top: Deutscher Jugendherbergsverband; p. 205 Deutsche Bahn; p. 206 Deutsche Bahn; p. 208 Deutsche Bahn; p. 210 top: Deutsche Bahn; p. 228 Hermann Hesse, "Im Nebel," in *Gesammelte Dichtungen,* V (Frankfurt/Main: Suhrkamp, 1952); p. 253 Rose Ausländer, "Noch bist du da," in *Ich höre das Herz des Oleanders. Gedichte 1977-1979,* ed. H. Braun (Frankfurt/Main: S. Fischer, 1984); p. 278 Wolf Biermann, "Ach, Freund, geht es nicht auch dir so?," in *Wolfgang Biermann: Alle Gedichte* (Köln: Verlag Kiepenheuer & Witsch, 1995); p. 283 *Computer Magazin;* p. 293 Inter Nationes; p. 303 Jacob und Wilhelm Grimm, "Der alte Großvater und sein Enkel," in *Die schönsten Märchen* (München: Südwest, 1975), p. 224.; p. 313 Inter Nationes; p. 320 Inter Nationes; p. 329 *Deutschland;* p. 335-336 Aysel Özakin, "Die dunkelhaarigen Kinder von Berlin," in *Soll ich hier alt werden? Türkin in Deutschland. Erzählungen,* translated by H.A. Schmiede (Hamburg: Buntbuch Verlag, 1982); p. 339 *Deutschland;* p. 342 Universität Regensburg; p. 348 Little Monster Cards; p. 350 Homemade Postcards; p. 358 Universität Regensburg; p. 360 Christine Nöstlinger, "Ohne Vorurteile," in *Mein Tagebuch* (Wien: Dachs-Verlag GmbH, 1989); p. 364 bottom: Deutsche Post; p. 367 StadtINFO Verlag GmbH; 384 Bertolt Brecht, "Maßnahmen gegen die Gewalt," in *Gesammelte Werke* (Frankfurt/Main: Suhrkamp Verlag, 1967); p. 385 Erich Kästner, "Fantasie von übermorgen," in *Erich Kästner: Gesammelte Schriften, Vol. I - Gedichte,* ed. Hermann Kesten (Köln: Verlag Kiepenheuer & Witsch, 1959); p. 404 *Deutschland;* p. 404 *Scala;* p. 407 *Journal für Deutschland;* p. 408 Gotthold Ephraim Lessing, "Der Esel in Begleitung" and "Nur anders, nicht besser," in *Das große Fabelbuch* (Wien-Heidelberg: Verlag Carl Ueberreuter, o.J.), pp. 206 and 154.; p. 408 Johann Wolfgang von Goethe, "Erinnerung," in *Goethes Werke,* I, 5. Auflage (Hamburg: Christian Wegner Verlag, 1963); p. 409 Friedrich von Schiller, "An die Freude," *in Sämtliche Werke,* ed. G. Fricke and H. G. Göpfert, 3. Auflage (München: Carl Hanser, 1962).

Index

This index is limited to grammatical entries. Entries appearing in the *Rückblicke* are indicated by parentheses.

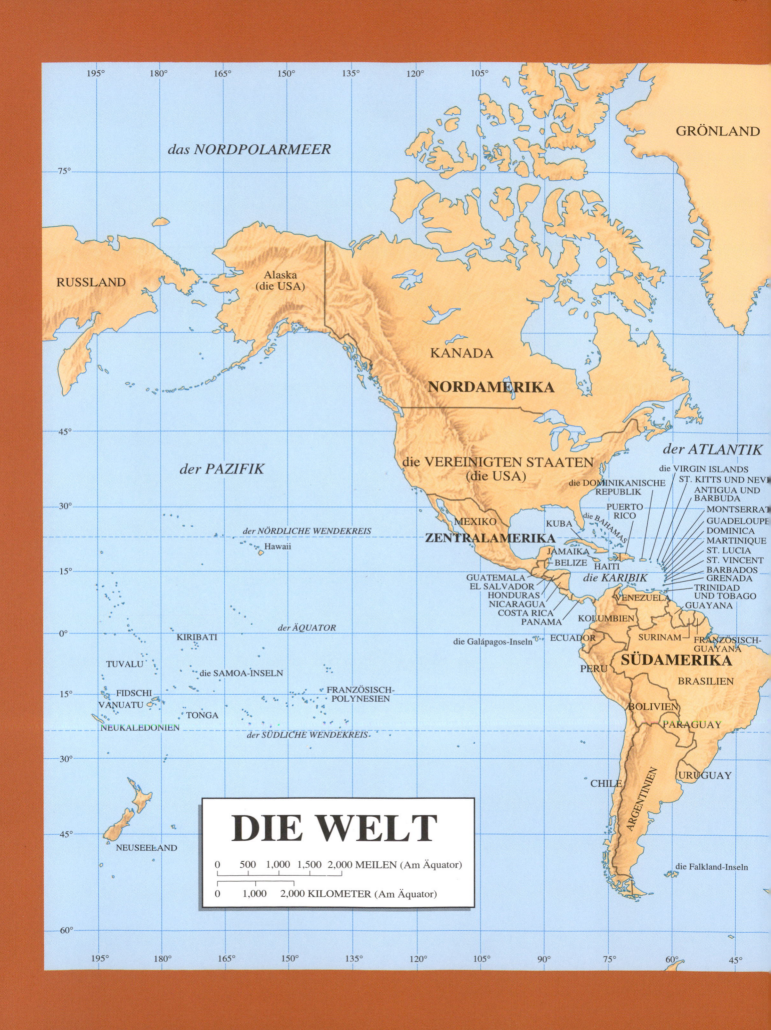